Feminist Genealogies, Colonial Legacies, Democratic Futures

Thinking Gender
Edited by Linda Nicholson

Also published in the series

Feminism/Postmodernism
Linda Nicholson

Gender Trouble
Judith Butler

Words of Power
Andrea Nye

Femininity and Domination
Sandra Bartky

Disciplining Foucault
Jana Sawicki

Beyond Accommodation
Drucilla Cornell

Embattled Eros
Steven Seidman

Erotic Welfare
Linda Singer

Materialist Feminism and the Politics of Discourse
Rosemary Hennessy

An Ethic of Care
Mary Jeanne Larrabee

Feminist Epistemologies
Linda Alcoff and Elizabeth Potter

Gender Politics and Post-Communism
Nanette Funk and Magda Mueller

Engenderings
Naomi Scheman

Feminist Theory and the Classics
Nancy Rabinowitz and Amy Richlin

Postmodern Revisionings of the Political
Anna Yeatman

Moral Dilemmas of Feminism
Laurie Shrage

Subjection and Subjectivity
Diana T. Meyers

Feminist Contentions
Seyla Benhabib, Judith Butler, Drucilla Cornell, and Nancy Fraser

Feminists Read Habermas
Johanna Meehan

Sacrificial Logics
Allison Weir

Feminist Genealogies, Colonial Legacies, Democratic Futures

Edited by
M. Jacqui Alexander
and
Chandra Talpade Mohanty

Routledge
New York and London

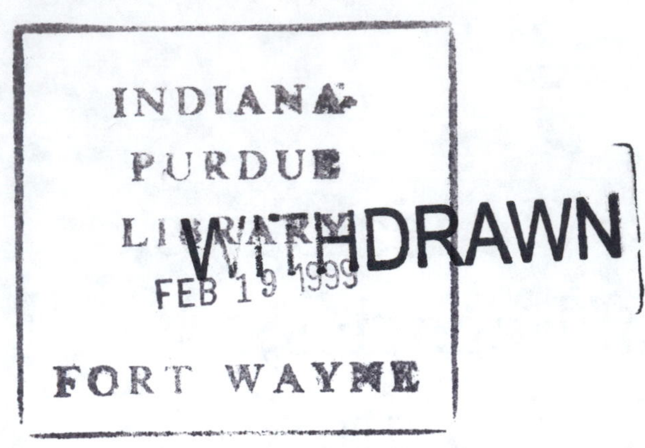

Published in 1997 by
Routledge
29 West 35th Street
New York, NY 10001

Published in Great Britain by
Routledge
11 New Fetter Lane
London EC4P 4EE

Printed in the United States of America on acid-free paper.

Library of Congress Cataloging-in-Publication Data
Feminist genealogies, colonial legacies, democratic futures / edited by M. Jacqui Alexander and Chandra Talpade Mohanty.
p. cm.
Includes bibliographical references and index.
ISBN 0-415-91211-3 (cloth). – ISBN 0-415-91212-1 (pbk.)
1. Feminism–Developing countries. 2. Women–Developing countries–Social conditions. I. Alexander, M. Jacqui. II. Mohanty, Chandra Talpade, 1955– .
HQ1870.9.F45 1995
305.42'09172'4–dc20 95-36341
CIP

Contents

II. Crafting Selves, Reimagining Identities and Cultures

III. Anatomies of Organizing, Building Feminist Futures

This book is dedicated to Audre Lorde
in honor of her life and work

Preface

Bringing this book into the world has been a profoundly collaborative process, both intellectually and politically. In collaborating with the authors, each other, and other sisters and comrades over the years, we have come to know the critical importance of figuring out our communities of belonging, and therefore those communities to which we are accountable. We do not inherit our intellectual neighborhoods (a term we borrow from Toni Morrison); we consciously build them. So our working process has involved actively imagining, crafting, and sustaining these neighborhoods where dissent and struggle have been as important as commitment to a common vision. This challenge has been no less true for our own work together, striving as we have over the last nine years to honor our commitments to intellectual and emotional risk-taking and to clarity, honesty, and friendship.

In dedicating this book to Audre Lorde, we revisit the ways in which her life's work and her presence in the world taught us the necessity of accountability in envisioning, forming, and maintaining community. For us this means becoming attentive to and accountable for the work that we are called upon to do and scrutinizing the very terms and ways in which we gain self- and community definition. We have come to know as well that the task of devising critical analytic tools and taking responsibility for them must also involve taking on the challenge of crafting more nuanced and accurate ways of understanding the world. Our involvement in a transformative and transforming collective project of social justice has taught us about what and how much is at stake in producing liberatory knowledges that enable collective and self-determination for colonized peoples. After all, we develop these tools in order to better understand and engage with the world, and in order to bring about revolutionary change.

Coming to know that we have a stake in producing liberatory knowledge is neither self-evident nor easy. This too requires struggle, risk-taking, and commitment to learning. We continue to learn from our sisters and comrades *how* to have a stake in thinking in this way, and the ethical risks and commitments that accompany this work. For walking this political, intellectual, and spiritual path with us over the years we thank Gloria I. Joseph, Papusa Molina, Andrée Nicola McLaughlin, Linda Carty, Brenda Joyner, Mab Segrest, Sharon Day, Barbara Herbert, Elizabeth Minnich, Leslie Hill, Si Kahn, Zillah Eisenstein, Avtar Brah, Cathie Dunsford, Jinny Chalmers, and Satya Mohanty. We choose to anchor the politics and ethics of our thinking in the knowledge required to understand the stakes that accompany struggles for decolonization in the late twentieth century—stakes that dominant ideologies would reframe and dismiss as moralistic or purely self-interested.

Jacqui has learned much from different people over the years; neighborhoods, as you know, are never, ever uniform. She is humbled to have found a spiritual community which believes in the interconnectedness of all things; in the truth that there are several paths to knowing; and in the indispensability of spiritual moorings. None of this intellectual work would have been possible without the spiritual guidance and support of La Negra Haiti, Teresa Ramirez, Wilma Guzman, Myrna Bain, and the United Cultural Society; the wisdom, courage, and love of Alourdes Kowalski (Mama Lola) and Georgette Champagne (Maggie), who is also a sister. Jacqui deeply appreciates the intellectual guidance and critique of an overlapping community of colleagues, friends, and teachers: Raul Ferrara-Balanquet; colleagues at the New School for Social Research Gary Lemons and Jerma Jackson, whose friendship provided the ground for us to become engaged critics of each other's work; Geeta Patel, who was there to help provide language in those spaces that were difficult to theorize; and Paul Joseph and Rosemary C. R. Taylor, for being early intellectual anchors in the United States. The practice of politics is not easy in these dangerous times, so plenty of respect goes to those whose courage and conviction have not been daunted and who continue to inspire us all: Sharon Day, Mab Segrest, and Lisa Albrecht, whose commitment reflects itself in a combination of collaboration, patience, optimism, and hope; Cathy Cohen, Katherine Acey, Becky Johnson, Angela Bowen, Joan French, and Angela Robertson; the Caribbean Association for Feminist Research and Action; SISTREN; participants in the National Lesbian and Gay Taskforce Progressive People of Color Summit; the recent participants in the United States Urban/Rural Mission network discussions on sexuality and homophobia, initiated by Mab Segrest; and the Black Nation/Queer Nation? conference and ongoing organizing committee. Finally, Jacqui is indebted to Jinny Chalmers and Maya Alexander, both witnesses to the birth of this project. Jinny has been companion and friend, nurturing Jacqui in immeasurable ways, living and teaching the meaning of balance through struggle. Maya, their daughter, has sustained far too many projects for her years. Her curiosity, elegance, and humor are a source of ongoing challenge, inspiration, and joy.

In addition to the folks already acknowledged, Chandra recognizes and honors friends and colleagues whose ideas, affection, and conversations have sustained and challenged her over the years: Ayesha Kagal for her extraordinary capacity for empathy and clarity, and for being a true friend for almost three decades; Lisa Lowe, Gloria Watkins, Biddy Martin, Risa Lieberwitz, Lata Mani, Ruth Frankenberg, Nancy Rabinowitz, and Inderpal Grewal for sharing their lives and their work with her; Norman Rosenberg for being Norman Rosenberg, and for envisioning Pangea Farm; the Grassroots leadership staff—Si Kahn, Alfreda Barringer, Kamau Marcharia, Cathy Howell, Naomi Swinton, James Williams, and Margaret Chambers—for teaching her how to think like an organizer/educator (thanks also to the GL Board). And perhaps most importantly, Chandra thanks Satya Mohanty, her partner, life companion, and philosopher/friend, whose intellectual, emotional, and spiritual generosity over the decades nurtures and challenges her to write and work in the ways that she does. Satya is regularly called upon to give advice on titles for essays and books, and we borrowed our own title for this book from his essay "Colonial Legacies, Multicultural Futures."

Finally, we want to acknowledge people who have been engaged in this project with us at different moments in its evolution: Eileen Kutab, Patricia Fernandez-Kelly, Rabab Abdul-Hadi, Norma Alarcón, María Milagros López, and Yamila Azize Vargas. We thank Sue Hayes for painstaking word-processing work, Caroline Hau, Furaha Worton, and Saradhamanidevi Boopathi for careful proofreading of the manuscript, Lynn Comella for a thoughtful assessment of certain essays and for word-processing, Heather Sibley for her enthusiasm and meticulous attention to different parts of this process, and Heather Lewis for editorial consulting. Much of the final assembling of this collection was done during our two years together at Hamilton College. We thank our colleagues there—Nancy Rabinowitz, Amie McDonald, Susan Sanchez Casal, Shelley Haley, and Margaret Gentry—for sustained intellectual engagement and friendship. Sangeeta Budhiraja's perennial excitement about this project and her steadfast commitment to feminist praxis have, in their own way, kept us going. We offer this book to all of our students, who remind us daily of the reasons for doing this work.

Introduction

Genealogies, Legacies, Movements

M. Jacqui Alexander and Chandra Talpade Mohanty

Feminist Genealogies

We began working on this book in 1988, after being introduced at the first and only meeting of the Women of Color Institute for Radical Research and Action. This meeting was an attempt by about a dozen women of color of various nationalities to collaborate on the transformation of feminist politics and to establish an autonomous institution that would serve women committed to social justice and revolutionary praxis. This book flows out of the collective vision we crafted during that summer. And while the path has been neither linear nor easy, it has shaped our shared political and intellectual commitments; we have changed, grown, and learned how to sustain each other during the last seven years. We have challenged each other to be clear; we have become attuned to the pulse of each other's thinking, and we have developed an analytic language which now truly belongs to both of us. This has required each of us to let go of our inherited beliefs about the ownership of knowledge. And, as a consequence, we now know that our best ideas are produced through working and thinking together.

We both came to feminist studies in the U.S. academy through a series of geographical, political, and intellectual dislocations. Our journeys were marked by an educational process in which anticolonial struggle against the British (in Trinidad and Tobago and India) and the founding of the nation-state infused the fabric of everyday life. Our consciousnesses were thus shaped by the burden of persistent colonialisms and the euphoric promise of nationalism and self-determination. We both inherited the belief that education was a key strategy of decolonization, rather than merely a path toward mainstream credentials and upward mobility. In other words, for us, education was always linked to the political practice of service to community and to nation. However, nationalism at this stage had done little to transform the practices of colonial education, nor had it necessarily imagined us (in Jacqui's case, daughter now lesbian; in Chandra's, woman not mother) as the legitimate heirs of the new nation. Then, as now, nation and citizenship were largely premised within normative parameters of masculinity and heterosexuality.

We both moved to the United States of North America over fifteen years ago. None of the racial, religious, or class/caste fractures we had previously experienced could have prepared us for the painful racial terrain we encountered here. We were not born women of color, but became women of color here. From African American and U.S. women of color, we learned the peculiar brand of U.S North American racism and its constricted boundaries of race. Psychic residues of different colonialisms made it necessary for us to grapple with the nuances of the interconnectedness of struggles for decolonization. Racism against African American people was distinct, although connected to racism against Chicano, Native, or Asian peoples. The challenge of negotiating these politics of racial fragmentation has brought us to this moment. Through a politics of decolonization, we have learned that racial solidarity is necessary, even if that means grappling with the differences between oppositional and relational consciousness. Our own experiences of the multiple sites of racism in the U.S. have also convinced us that we must understand the local as well as the global manifestations of power.

The institutionalization of a particular definition of Women's Studies in the U.S. academy exposed another set of contradictions in our own lives as feminist activists, scholars, and teachers. By "contradictions," we mean the sense of alienation, dislocation, and marginalization that often accompanies a racialized location within white institutions. As "immigrant" women of color, we were neither the "right" color, gender, or nationality in terms of the self-definition of the U.S. academy, or by extension, of the Women's Studies establishment. In Women's Studies contexts, the color of our gender mattered. The citizenship machinery deployed by the state which positioned us as resident aliens ("deviant" non-citizen; "legal" immigrants) operates similarly within Women's Studies: it codifies an outsider status which is different from the outsider status of women of color born in the United States.[1] For instance, our racialization as Caribbean and Indian women was assimilated into a U.S. narrative of racialization, naturalized between African Americans and Euro-Americans. Our experiences could be recognized and acknowledged only to the extent that they resembled those of African American women.

However, the specificities of our national and cultural genealogies—being Black and Brown women—and our statuses as immigrants were constantly being used to position us as foreign, thus muting the legitimacy of our claims to the experiences of different racisms.[2] Working in solidarity with different women of color was at times insufficient to entirely subvert acts of racial fragmentation aimed at separating women of color from each other. We remained (differently) less threatening than African American women to white women, who often preferred to deal with our "foreignness" rather than our racialization in the U.S. This, in turn, sometimes created divisive relations between us and African American feminists. On many occasions we experienced the contradictory ironies of invisibility and hypervisibility which Evelynn Hammonds describes in her essay in this collection. In fact, the experience of these contradictions is partly responsible for our particular reading of injustice and our vision of social transformation. Out of a strong intellectual and political commitment to feminism, we remain committed to the creation of feminist communities, founded on different grounds than those we have experienced in many liberal academic circles.

The feminist genealogies that lie behind this project can be charted on various levels. Besides our own individual and collective genealogies, we want to consider 1) the contours of feminist intellectual and political practice as it is institutionalized within Women's Studies programs in U.S. colleges and universities; 2) the effects of postmodernist theory on the theorization of the experience, consciousness, and social identities of women of color, especially in terms of the formulation of international or global feminisms; and 3) the significance of self-examination and reflection on the genealogies of feminist organizations. In the last case, we want to offer here a comparative, relational way of thinking about feminist praxis that is grounded in the concrete analysis and visionings of the authors/communities in this collection.

The very title of this volume has a history. Over the past seven years, the collection has been renamed twice. Originally titled *Third World Feminism: A Reader*, then *Movements, Histories, Identities: Genealogies of Third World Feminism*, it is now called *Feminist Genealogies, Colonial Legacies, Democratic Futures*. Despite clear continuities in the intellectual and political project of the book, the changes in the title reflect subtle shifts in the discursive and material terrain and in the organizational practices of feminist communities around the world. One of the effects of globalization over the last two decades has been a new visibility of women's issues on the world stage. Witness the large numbers of international conferences on topics like violence against women, women's health, reproductive politics, and "population control." At the same time, feminism has been quantified for consumption within the global marketplace of ideas (we call this "freemarket feminism"). We take issue with this freemarket feminism in crafting our vision of democratic futures. The experiences, histories, and self-reflections of feminists of color and Third-World feminists remain at the center of the anthology, but geopolitical shifts and the particular forms of globalization over the last decade necessitate an active, deliberate focus on questions of genealogies, legacies, and futures in comparative feminist praxis. We have, therefore, deliberately chosen to map these specific paths by which feminist communities, organizations, and movements call up and reflect upon moments in their own collective histories and struggles for autonomy. Thus, our use of words like "genealogies" or "legacies" is not meant to suggest a frozen or embodied inheritance of domination and resistance, but an interested, conscious thinking and rethinking of history and historicity, a rethinking which has women's autonomy and self-determination at its core.

After more than two decades of struggles around questions of racism and heterosexism, a particular characterization of gender—naturalized through the history and experiences of middle class, urban, Euro-American women—continues to be propagated in Women's Studies and gender studies programs in the U.S. academy. By not challenging the hegemony of whiteness (and of capitalism) within academic institutions, for instance, these Women's Studies programs often end up bolstering inherited regimes of race and Eurocentrism. Although in the 1970s, the formulation of the category of gender and its diffusion throughout a variety of disciplines was one of the most important goals of Women's Studies, in the 1990s new and radically different intellectual challenges have emerged. These challenges compel Women's Studies to face head on some of the more crucial questions of class divisions, racialization, and heterosexualization operating within the U.S. polity and within Women's Studies programs themselves. The recent diffusion of Eurocentric consumer culture in the wake of the further consolidation of multinational capital, for example, foregrounds the need to theorize the ways inequality structures values, desires, and needs for different groups and classes of women. Any understanding of women's experiences based on a narrow conception of gender would simply be incapable of fully addressing the homogenizing and hierarchizing effects of economic and cultural processes which are the result of this consumer culture.

This is why *Genealogies* aims to provide a comparative, relational, and historically based conception of feminism, one that differs markedly from the liberal-pluralist understanding of feminism, an inheritance of the predominantly liberal roots of American feminist praxis.[3] Clearly, one of the things being charted here is a convergence between the way gender emerged as a primary category of analysis and the social, demographic, and class composition of those who actually theorized gender in the U.S. academy. In other words, we want to suggest a link between the positions of power held by white women in Women's Studies, the subject of their theorizing, and the kinds of analytic tools they deployed.

In addition, serious intellectual, analytic, and political engagement with the theorizations of women of color has not occurred. Instead, this work has been largely appropriated and often erased, and thus does not figure in the institutional memory or canonical formulations of Women's Studies knowledge. In her detailed analysis of the colonization of the work of women of color within postmodernist feminist theory, Paula Moya demonstrates that the ritual allusion to Chicana women instantiates a postmodernism whose epistemological underpinnings are interrupted by the very lives and analyses of the women of color who are invoked.

The liberal-pluralist multiculturalism that is often evident in women's studies syllabi, with a week or two on "women of color" and "sexuality," testifies to this appropriation of the work of women of color. Token inclusion of our texts without reconceptualizing the whole white, middle-class, gendered knowledge base effectively absorbs and silences us. This says, in effect, that our theories are plausible and carry explanatory weight only in relation to our *specific* experiences, but that they have no use value in relation to the rest of the world. Moreover, postmodernist theory, in its haste to dissociate itself from all forms of essentialism, has generated a series of epistemological confusions regarding the interconnections between location, identity, and the construction of knowledge. Thus, for instance, localized questions of experience, identity, culture, and history, which enable us to understand specific processes of domination and subordination, are often dismissed by postmodern theories as reiterations of cultural "essence" or unified, stable identity.[4]

Postmodernist discourse attempts to move beyond essentialism by pluralizing and dissolving the stability and analytic utility of the categories of race, class, gender, and sexuality. This strategy often forecloses any valid recuperation of these categories or the social relations through which they are constituted. If we dissolve the category of race, for instance, it becomes difficult to claim the experience of racism. Certainly, racism and the processes of racialization are far more complicated now than when W. E. B. Du Bois predicted that the "problem of the color line is the problem of the twentieth century."[5] But the relations of domination and subordination that are named and articulated through the processes of racism and racialization still exist, and they still require analytic and political specification and engagement. Global realignments and fluidity of capital have simply led to further consolidation and exacerbation of capitalist relations of domination and exploitation—what we refer to in this collection as "processes of recolonization." Thus, while the current "color line" may suggest more complicated forms of racialized identities, the hierarchical relationships among racial groups and geographies have not disappeared. Yet, race does not figure in most "first world" considerations of postmodernism.[6] And as Inderpal Grewal and Caren Kaplan persuasively suggest, it is the cultural, political, economic, and social consequences of the historical situations and transformations within (post)modernity that will enable a more sophisticated understanding of transnational, postcolonial, feminist practices.[7]

Understanding the various constructions of self and identity during late capitalism—when transnationalization confounds the postcolonial and women's relationship to it, and when fluid borders permit the mobility of "free" market capital—is a complicated enterprise that cannot be simply invoked by claiming fluid or fractured identities. What kind of racialized, gendered selves get produced at the conjuncture of the transnational and the postcolonial? Are there selves which are formed outside of the hegemonic heterosexual contract that defy dominant (Western) understandings of identity construction? Are they commensurate with the multiple self constructed under (American) postmodernism? What kinds of transformative practices are needed in order to develop nonhegemonic selves? Are these practices commensurate with feminist organizational struggles for decolonization? These are some of the urgent questions we seek to engage, and which the authors in this collection take up. These questions force us to take seriously the authority and validity of consciousness and the experiences of domination and struggle in the formation of identities that are simultaneously social and political.

The rapid institutionalization of a particular brand of postmodernist theorizing in the U.S. academy is signficant for another reason. The knowledge base of a discipline has a profound effect on both pedagogic strategies and the kinds of knowledges that are developed within the classroom. This is one of the central questions that Leslie Roman examines when she argues that "relativist postmodernism" (which rejects "realist epistemologies" that would "weigh a person's or group's subjective claims against and in relation to adequate structural analyses of their objective social locations") has led to a certain kind of racial relativism or white defensiveness in the classroom. By "white defensiveness," Roman means "the relativistic assertion that whites, like 'people of color,' are history's oppressed subjects of racism." It is this sort of defensiveness that prevents teachers from taking critical antiracist pedagogical positions that would adjudicate between "the epistemic standpoints of fundamentally oppressed groups and those in more privileged positions."[8] We cannot overestimate the need for conscious self-reflexivity about the complicity of intellectual frameworks in politics, in the fact that something is at stake, in the very process of reauthorizing and mediating inequalities or regressive politics of different kinds.[9]

Another intellectual and political movement that draws upon earlier formulations of a global sisterhood has taken root in the academy in the 1990s through discussions about international feminism.[10] Beyond the fact that these claims about an international feminism almost always originate in the West, there are some common themes which unite them. Drawing from an often unspecified liberal episteme, they tend to invoke a difference-as-pluralism model in which women in the Third World bear the disproportionate burden of difference. "International" feminism embraces an approach of the articulation of many voices to specify an inclusive feminism—calls for "global sisterhood" are often premised on a center/periphery model where women of color or Third World women constitute the periphery. Race is invariably erased from any conception of the international (based on nation, devoid of race), all the more so because of a strict separation between the international and the domestic, or an understanding of the ways in which they are mutually constituted. To a large extent, underlying the conception of the international is a notion of universal patriarchy operating in a transhistorical way to subordinate all women. The only plausible methodological strategy here, then, is to make visible and intelligible (to the West) the organizational practices and writings of Third-World women through a discrete case-study approach. "International," moreover, has come to be collapsed into the culture and values of capitalism.

Missing from these definitions of "international" (what we refer to as "transnational" from now on) are at least three elements: 1) a way of thinking about women in similar contexts across the world, in *different* geographical spaces, rather than as *all* women across the world; 2) an understanding of a set of unequal relationships among and between peoples, rather than a set of traits embodied in all non-U.S. citizens (particularly because U.S. citizenship continues to be premised within a white, Eurocentric, masculinist, heterosexist regime); and 3) a consideration of the term "international" in relation to an analysis of economic, political, and ideological processes which foreground the operations of race and capitalism (for instance, those which would therefore require taking critical antiracist, anti-capitalist positions that would make feminist solidarity work possible).

To talk about feminist praxis in global contexts would involve shifting the unit of analysis from local, regional, and national culture to relations and processes across cultures. Grounding analyses in particular, local feminist praxis is necessary, but we also need to understand the local in relation to larger, cross-national processes. This would require a corresponding shift in the conception of political organizing and mobilization across borders. The practices of democracy, justice, and equality, for example, would not be subsumed within the white, masculinist definition of the U.S. Ideas about justice would apply across cultural and national borders. The ideologies of "immigrants," "refugees," "guestworkers," and "citizens" would need to be reconceived within new definitions of justice. Our very understanding of democracy and its practices would have to become cross-cultural. In place of relativism, this critical application of feminist praxis in global contexts would substitute responsibility, accountability, engagement, and solidarity. In this collection, therefore, we foreground a paradigm of decolonization which stresses power, history, memory, relational analysis, justice (not just representation), and ethics as the issues central to our analysis of globalization.

Practices of globalization are crucial to the conceptual mapping of genealogies of organizing. The essays in this collection provide sustained analyses of post–Cold War capitalist processes and the contradictory spaces they have opened up for different kinds of feminist mobilization. Thus, the essayists included here challenge the means by which racialization, heterosexualization, class polarization, and the creation of poverty serve to organize capitalism. In contrast to a transhistorical international feminism, they demonstrate that oppositional communities have their own histories of struggles, modes of theorization, and forms of organizing which shape and transform feminist practices. Our framework challenges the still firmly embedded notion of the originary status of Western feminism. It does not simply position Third-World feminism as a reaction to gaps in Western feminism; it does not summon Third-World feminism in the service of (white) Western feminism's intellectual and political projects. Instead, it provides a position from which to argue for a comparative, relational feminist praxis that is transnational in its response to and engagement with global processes of colonization.

Central to our theorization of feminism is a comparative analysis of feminist organizing, criticism, and self-reflection; also crucial is deep contextual knowledge about the nature and contours of the present political economic crisis. Individual analyses are grounded in the contemporary crisis of global capitalism, suggesting that these particular contexts are the ones which throw up very specific analytic and political challenges for organizations. Here, no false dichotomy exists between theory and practice. We literally have to think ourselves out of these crises through collective praxis and particular kinds of theorizing. Crises are what provoke the opportunity for change within organizations. Similarly, certain authors in the text read their own circumstances in relation to processes of globalization in order to consider feminist commitment and organizing within their own contexts. While we would not claim that effects within the academy are necessarily the same as those within other political structures, the critical methodologies used to analyze them are similar.

Over the years, we have worked very closely with each of the authors in this collection, attempting to do so in the spirit of community that we imagined at our initial meeting. Thus, even though this book consists of individually authored essays, the sustained and collective work that has gone into producing it is itself a reflection of a way of doing politics, a mode of organizing that interrupts the more pervasive "professionalized" production of scholarship. The fact that individual authors locate themselves within particular communities of women creates the specific context for each of these analyses. In other words, all the authors connect their work to feminist communities in struggle—their work flows from this connection. Thus, we hope that this volume not only sets in motion certain intellectual projects and dialogues but also establishes the foundation for a much wider discussion among women's communities and organizations throughout the world.

Colonial Legacies: The State, Capitalism, and Processes of Colonization

We use the formulation "colonial legacies" to evoke the imagery of an inheritance and to map continuities and discontinuities between contemporary and inherited practices within state and capital formations. We wish to mark in particular the accelerated processes of recolonization typical of this contemporary moment. At the outset, then, we want to foreground an understanding of the historicity of state and capital in the organization and deployment of sexual politics. Robert Connell defines historicity as "this sense that things 'can never be the same again,' that new possibilities have opened up and old patterns closed off." This, he says, "is exactly what the historicity of gender relations is about."[11] For us, this dialectic relationship between the old and the new provides theoretical and political cues in understanding contemporary relations and hierarchies—what we call an archaeology of state practices—at this juncture in history.

The historicity of the state enables an analysis of contemporary relations and hierarchies and positions the state as a focal point of analysis for feminists. We examine the form and operation of the American state in advanced capitalism (which is different from the advanced capitalist state) as a way to analyze the simultaneous processes that advanced capital has generated in relation to capitalism and to advanced colonialism. M. A. Jaimes Guerrero has argued that the U.S. state manages a set of advanced capitalist relations at the same time that it mediates colonial relations both within its borders (Native peoples and communities of color in the U.S) as well as outside (in Puerto Rico, Hawai'i, and the Pacific these operations are masked by an ideology of statehood and commonwealth status). We focus on the American state because of our own location here and because of its post–Cold War status as the new imperial power in, for example, the Caribbean and India. The intertwining of the global and the local, which is so crucial to our analysis, is also central to Ella Shohat's discussion of post–Third-Worldist aesthetic practices. "In a world of transnational communications," Shohat writes, "the central problem becomes one of tension between cultural homogenization and cultural heterogenization, in which hegemonic tendencies are simultaneously 'indigenized' within a complex disjunctive global cultural economy." Thus, there is an ongoing theoretical challenge to uncover the cultural, political, and economic interplay between the very categories of the global and the local.

One of the central organizing principles of this collection is the imbrication of contemporary practices of postcolonial and advanced colonial states with capitalist processes of recolonization. The theoretical anchor for a number of the essays is precisely the continuities and fractures between the historical and newly emergent forms of colonization. Amina Mama discusses the transformation of forms of violence against women in West Africa, while Honor Ford-Smith shows how aesthetic colonization (the term is Paula Gunn Allen's) by international funding agencies has established a disjuncture between earlier British colonization and contemporary Structural Adjustment Policies (SAP) in Jamaica. Capitalism is analyzed consistently as a set of processes mediated through the simultaneous operation of gendered, sexualized, and racialized hierarchies. Chandra Talpade Mohanty demonstrates, for example, that these hierarchies operate through different gendered ideologies of women's work. The essays understand capitalism in its global, local, and territorial manifestations and in its intersections with feminist analyses and struggles; they recognize that Eurocentrism and territorial colonization are being transformed and refigured across the globe. Clearly the impulse toward recolonization derives from crises within capitalism which then prompt its reconfiguration. Thus, while particular essays in the collection chart the failures of anticolonial nationalisms, the cumulative effect of such movements for self-determination have also helped to provoke the very crises within capitalism that this collection charts.

Since we use specific essays in this collection to ground feminist historical practice and more contemporary modes of organizing, we also mean by "historicity" the use of specific inheritances around counterhegemonic histories that interrupt state and capitalist dominance. The different modes of feminist practice—what Geraldine Heng calls "the varieties of feminism"—assume their particular trajectories from a complicated overlapping of historical matrices of left liberation struggles, contemporary nationalisms (in spite of feminism's contestatory relationship to nationalism), and the very presence and intervention of the state itself. There are no fixed prescriptions by which one might determine in advance the specific counterhegemonic histories which will be most useful. In fact, Heng shows that a feminism under threat might strategically assume "the nationalist mantle" or seek "legitimation and ideological support in local cultural history, by finding feminist or proto-feminist myths, laws, customs, characters, narratives and origins in the national or communal past." What feminism remembers (or can risk remembering), what it records and narrativizes, its resourcefulness in codifying struggle—in terms that are unintelligible to the state (Ford-Smith) or seemingly recognizable and therefore subversive (Panjabi)—and what forms it gives its different political mobilizations are all paradoxically contingent, yet grounded and strategic. The importance of oppositional historical records cannot be mistaken. As Patricia J. Williams has argued, "To be without documentation is too unsustaining, too spontaneously ahistorical, too dangerously malleable in the hands of those who would rewrite not merely the past but [my] future as well."[12] Even memory is not an unmediated category here, for insinuated within counterhegemonic inheritances are the inheritances of violence and trauma, what Elizabeth Alexander has

called "traumatized memory." Such memories must be scrutinized and sifted. For feminism, then, the structuring of new modes of consciousness through praxis is both politically and psychically necessary.

Because no variety of feminism—particularly feminism in the Third World—has escaped state intervention, control, discipline, and surveillance; and because the state (particularly the postcolonial state) facilitates the transnational movement of capital within national borders and is, therefore, instrumental in the reconfiguring of global relationships; and because capitalism and these processes of recolonization structure the contemporary practices of postcolonial and advanced capitalist/colonial states, the state figures centrally in any analytic attempt to grapple with colonial legacies. Thus, a focus on the state seems especially crucial at a time when many of the attempts to manage the global crisis in capitalism are enacted by the state apparatus. Structural Adjustment Policies (SAP), the most recent unequal realignments among multinational capital, the International Monetary Fund, and the World Bank, are a case in point. In her essay, Ayesha Imam points to the specific instance of complicity between the militarized, postcolonial Nigerian state and the institutionalization of SAP. Moreover, unlike other institutions, the state engages in an almost microscopic surveillance of women's bodies and continues to bring more and more areas of daily life under its jurisdiction, even when it lacks the capacity or authority to do so successfully.

We are not suggesting, however, that the imperatives of the postcolonial state and those of advanced capitalist/colonial states are identical. Admittedly, they share these important characteristics: 1) they own the means of organized violence which most often get deployed in the service of "national security"; 2) they are both militarized—in other words, masculinized; 3) they invent and solidify practices of racialization and sexualization of the population; and 4) they discipline and mobilize the bodies of women—in particular Third-World women—in order to consolidate patriarchal and colonizing processes. Women's bodies are disciplined in different ways: within discourses of profit maximization, as global workers and sexual laborers; within religious fundamentalisms, as repositories of sin and transgression; within specifically nationalist discourses, as guardians of culture and respectability or criminalized as prostitutes and lesbians; and within state discourses of the originary nuclear family, as wives and mothers. Both postcolonial and advanced capitalist/colonial states organize and reinforce a cathectic structure based in sexual difference (i.e., heterosexuality), which they enforce through a variety of means, including legislation. In almost all instances, however, these states conflate heterosexuality with citizenship and organize a "citizenship machinery" in order to produce a class of loyal heterosexual citizens and a subordinated class of sexualized, nonprocreative, noncitizens, disloyal to the nation, and, therefore, suspect.[13]

Yet, there are important differences. In the global reconsolidation of capitalism, for instance, postcolonial states are subordinated to advanced capitalist/colonial states, although both mediate capital accumulation. In postcolonial contexts, state managers facilitate the entry and diffusion of international capital within national boundaries and help to produce an exploited feminized workforce in export-processing zones. The U.S. state is similar to a postcolonial state in its ideological approach toward the North American Free Trade Agreement (NAFTA) and the Caribbean Basin Initiative. It utilizes the dictates of the U.S. economy to set the terms by which capital functions across national boundaries. In advanced capitalist/colonial contexts, transnationalization provides the rationale for hypernationalist intervention into the economies of the Third World, undermining power and legitimacy in far more significant ways than in the U.S. state, for example. This raises the charge that the postcolonial state has forfeited its claim to sovereignty (the central nationalist promise) through complicity in its own recolonization. As early as 1972, Hamza Alavi argued that the relative autonomy of the postcolonial state from indigenous and metropolitan class interests seemed to be almost entirely supplanted; in the contemporary period, the more pervasive practice was the postcolonial state as an instrument of global ruling-class interests."[14]

Larger processes of globalization make it both difficult and necessary to talk about the nation-state, to talk specifically about nationalism and, for our purposes, the problematical relationship of Third-World women to it. Anticolonial nationalism has always mobilized women's labor in order to help consolidate popular nationalism, without which state nationalism would never have been able to solidify itself. It is not accidental, therefore, that feminism often emerged within anticolonial movements. But the state mobilization of the feminine is contradictorily inflected. While, as Heng has argued, "women, the feminine, and figures of gender have traditionally anchored the nationalist imaginary," certain women, prostitutes, and lesbians are now being disciplined and written out of the nation's script; they have been invested with the power to corrupt otherwise loyal heterosexual citizens, positioned as hostile to the procreative imperative of nation-building, and, therefore, invested with the ability and desire to destroy it. It is not only around questions of sexuality and gender that nation-states have structured their exclusions, however, but also in relationship to race and class hierarchies. It is these exclusions, as well the state's ambivalent and conflictual relationship to sovereignty, that help to explain the failures of anticolonial nationalism, a central topic for many of the essays in this collection. If, as Ella Shohat has argued, "affiliation with the nation state becomes highly partial and contingent" in the postcolonial context, women's relationship to it is even more so. In very specific ways, the processes of recolonization (which this collection charts) draw material and ideological force from women and women's collectivities in order to reanchor patriarchal and heterosexist imperatives.

The fact that religious fundamentalist movements now occupy center stage in a number of postcolonial and advanced capitalist/colonial states is yet another indication of the contradictory effects of nationalist mobilizations of men and women. Gita Sahgal and Nira Yuval Davis link the global rise of religious fundamentalism to the failure of both capitalism and communism to provide for people's material, spiritual, and emotional needs.[15] They suggest that in postcolonial societies, and among people of color in the West, religious fundamentalism is also linked to the failure of nationalist and socialist movements to bring about liberation from oppression. Fundamentalist movements are deeply heteropatriarchal in suggesting the control and regulation of women's sexuality as the panacea for all these failures.

Analyzing the nexus of state, capital, and patriarchy in the consolidation of religious fundamentalism in India, Amrita Chhachhi shows that state-supported fundamentalism reinforces the shift of control over women from kinsmen to any man of the "religious" community—the public is profoundly patriarchal. Within religious fundamentalist discourses and state practices, women's bodies and minds, as well as the domestic and public spaces they occupy, become the primary ground for the regulation of morality and inscriptions of patriarchal control. This is another crucial arena for mapping the gendered processes of recolonization at the end of the twentieth century.[16]

No understanding of these post–Cold War processes would be complete, however, without an analysis of the strategic function of militarized masculinity in the reproduction of colonization. An official designation of "post–Cold War" does not automatically erase the effects of colonization. In addition to the dislocations and dispersals of Third-World women whose lives were previously tied to militarization, the concept of soldiering (which has historically been linked to masculinity) is also undergoing profound transformation. As the analyses of Alexander and Wekker demonstrate, both state and capitalist processes underscore an existing crisis in hetero-masculinity which must be ideologically veiled in order to mask the processes of normalization which both states undertake. In neocolonial contexts, the crisis becomes evident in the legal (re)production of heterosexuality through state moves to contain desire between women. In "(de)militarized" contexts such as the United States, the figure of the hypermasculinized soldier, previously embodied in the image of whiteness, is diffused globally as the agent of U.S. might, the symbol of white manliness, and the naturalization of Third-World women's sexual labor organized primarily through prostitution. The work of Thanh-dam Truong and Kamala Kempadoo is most useful here in demystifying the extent to which prostitutes' labor contributes to the processes of private capital accumulation and the state's reliance on it as a way to continue the heterosexualization of defense, military productivity, and the like.[17] New kinds of racial and sexual reconfigurations occur in this era of demilitarization and Cold War politics, when white masculinity can no longer figure itself around particular definitions of soldiering. Because of shifts in the U.S economy, for instance, the job of state policing now draws disproportionately on the labor and bodies of people of color, both women and men. The state, no doubt, has to work harder ideologically to resituate white masculinity as its presence, at least in the lower echelons of the military, is being erased.

One of the most dramatic examples of the crisis in heteromasculinity was the recent state-generated discourse in the United States on "gays" in the military. Ostensibly, the purpose of this debate was to determine whether "effeminate" masculinity (practiced, but not spoken) could be relied upon to undertake one of the most important tasks of citizenship: that of loyalty to and defense of one's country. The central preoccupation was whether such feminized masculinity (which was deemed neither masculine nor citizen at all) would jeopardize manly masculinity (heteromasculinity) as it undertook its job: defense of the imperial nation. After months of contestation (including a predictable state lament over its own threatened identity in the context of a reduced military), heteromasculinity reasserted itself, rendered "gay" sexuality present yet silent, and erased lesbian sexuality almost entirely. Further, this conclusion premised homosexuality in whiteness, making it possible for "invisible" lesbian and gay soldiers to intervene in the Third World and within communities of color at home.

At this point, the central analytic formulation about the state and capital's activity in the processes of recolonization poses a fundamental challenge to the ways in which dominant liberal feminism has organized itself. There are many feminist critiques of the failures of liberalism and its epistemic claims around individual rights and liberties, freedom of individual choice, and the mythology of equal access.[18] In spite of these critiques and their very clear understanding of the operations of state power, however, the sanctity of individual right and choice protected by and bolstered through capitalism still constitute its core premises and practices. The writings of Aida Hurtado, Brenda Joyner, Rosalind Petchesky and the experiences of women struggling against U.S. colonization of Puerto Rico and the American state's role in the use of the bodies of Third-World women as instruments of development and "progress" all point to the pitfalls of the ideology about an individual's right to choose.[19] Our analyses have foregrounded questions of colonization, economic imperialism, and territorial sovereignty as central to feminism. In this regard, they part company with liberal formulations of a disinterested state, as well as with the state's representation of itself as national and democratic. We suggest that taking seriously state intervention within and across nations might, at the very least, make it possible to imagine and create solidarity struggles across the artificial borders which both state and capital construct.

Democratic Futures: Feminist Consciousness, Organizing Visions

> Sistren help bring about the awareness of women in me definitely. For the first time even if me go out a street and hear people, whether man or woman, talk tings fi downgrade woman me wouldn't know how to address it. Now me find meself, if me hear anybody say anything to downgrade woman, me can address it. It give me courage to deal wid anybody, no care who you maybe.
>
> Becky (Ford-Smith 1989) [20]

> I start with bodies because political states always have an interest in them; because politics usually derive from such interests; and because, as we move increasingly toward new technologies that redefine female bodies, we must recognize these interests as utterly political. Feminists can insist on using our bodies to push out the boundaries of democratic theory.
>
> Zillah Eisenstein (Eisenstein 1993, 171) [21]

Taken together, the statements of Becky, a member of the Caribbean feminist collective Sistren, and of Zillah Eisenstein, a U.S. feminist political theorist, capture the contradictions and the challenges involved in thinking beyond the various colonizations of our minds and bodies. Becky states that her experience within the Sistren collective was the basis for the transformation of her consciousness, her "awareness as woman," which then enabled her to have the "courage to deal wid anybody." Eisenstein, on the other hand, focuses on the political processes involved in the disciplining of the female body, and on the need for feminists to take these masculinist interests of the state into account in reimagining democracy.

Given the limitations of Western, liberal conceptions of democracy, we want to conceptualize what might be called "feminist democracy" in relation to the project of decolonization—in other words, to think through an anticolonialist, anticapitalist vision of feminist practice. Further, we want to craft a working definition of feminist democracy that is anchored in the analyses and visions provided by the activist-scholars in this collection. Such a vision necessarily involves acknowledging the objectifying, dehumanizing effects of colonization (e.g., imitation of the colonizer, horizontal violence, self-deprecation due to internalized oppression, self-distrust, psychic and material dependency, desire to assimilate)—and building actively anticolonialist relationships and cultures as a crucial part of the project of feminist democracy.[22]

What is our working definition of feminist democracy? First, sexual politics are central to the processes and practices of governance, which means not only the effects of governance on women or "what happens to women" under state rule but also the way the entire apparatus of government treats women.

Secondly, feminist democracy suggests a different order of relationships among people. It suggests understanding socioeconomic, ideological, cultural, and psychic hierarchies of rule (like those of class, gender, race, sexuality, and nation), their interconnectedness, and their effects on disenfranchised peoples *within* the context of transformative collective or organizational practice. Thus, the transformation of relationships, selves, communities, and the practices of daily life leading to self-determination and autonomy for all peoples is crucial in crafting a different order of relationships. Thirdly, in formulations of feminist democracy, agency is theorized differently. Women do not imagine themselves as *victims* or *dependents* of governing structures but as agents of their own lives. Agency is understood here as the conscious and ongoing reproduction of the terms of one's existence while taking responsibility for this process. And agency is anchored in the practice of thinking of oneself as a part of feminist collectivities and organizations. This is not the liberal, pluralist individual self under capitalism. For precisely this reason, decolonization is central to the definition and vision of feminist democracy.

New modes of governance are not possible until the profound effects of hierarchies of colonization are taken into account. What is needed, the essays in this volume suggest, is a *new political culture.* Decolonization involves thinking oneself out of the spaces of domination, but always *within* the context of a collective or communal process (the distinction between identification as a woman and gender consciousness—the former refers to a social designation, the latter to a critical awareness of the implications of this designation). This thinking "out of" colonization happens only through action and reflection, through praxis. After all, social transformation cannot remain at the level of ideas, it must engage practice. In this anthology, it is the concrete analyses of collective and organizational practices within feminist communities that offer provisional strategies for dismantling the psychic and social constellations put in place by colonization. Some essays draw attention to the too-quick transition of Third-World countries from colonized nations, to anticolonial struggles, to nationalist governing bodies which remain stubbornly patriarchal and heterosexist. In other words, these essays chart the failures of anticolonial nationalism and decolonization movements to take seriously the psychic and pedagogical aspects of decolonization, especially in relation to sexual politics. Decolonization has a fundamentally pedagogical dimension—an imperative to understand, to reflect on, and to transform relations of objectification and dehumanization, and to pass this knowledge along to future generations. Our formulation of feminist democratic practice seeks to address the pedagogic failure of inherited nationalism.

Fourthly, our notion of feminist democracy draws on socialist principles to address hierarchies of rule and to craft an alternative vision for change. In spirit, if not always in words, all the contributors to this volume take anticapitalist positions. However, while the contributors provide cartographies of transformational feminist practice, they are very conscious of the limits of these practices. Material forces, relationships, and forms of governance have not changed very much at the end of the twentieth century. In fact, because of the historical resilience of capitalism, we have not had the benefit of socialist practice for any substantial period of time. The truncated script of socialism and the failures of anticolonial nationalism combine to form the backdrop of our working definition of feminist democracy.

Finally, our definition of feminist democracy has specifically transnational dimensions. At this time, global processes clearly require global alliances. Decolonization, in fact, becomes an urgent project precisely because of the homogenization and cross-border domination effected by global capitalist processes. We suggest that feminist democracy needs to include some theorization of transborder participatory democracy which is outside the purview of the imperial. It is transnational feminism, not global sisterhood (defined as a "center/periphery" or "first-world/Third-World" model), that the collection points toward. And since questions of practice are central to this collection, another aspect of our version of feminist democracy involves reimaging the (often artificial) divide between feminist activism and scholarship. The authors here believe that scholarship and analysis are produced through an active dialogic engagement with feminist collectives and movements. This theorization begins from a different space—that of feminist struggle. It is the practice within movements that anchors the theory, the analysis is undertaken to improve the practice.

In what follows, we begin with a brief critique of freemarket/capitalist and procedural notions of democracy, move on to a discussion of some useful feminist theorizations of democracy, and finally arrive at our elaboration of the meaning of feminist democracy, based on the above sketch. In this analysis, we use "Democracy" with a capital *d* (to suggest its congealed, commonsensical usage) when referring to institutionalized, hegemonic (often repressive), freemarket-based uses of the term, and "democracy" (with a small *d* suggesting collective structures, and practices in process) to refer to the feminist rethinking of the idea and promise of this concept. While, on the one hand, a hegemonic rhetoric of Democracy (a disguise for western, liberal capitalist processes) has been constitutive of the very processes of capitalist recolonization, many unjust imperialist practices have, after all, been scantioned in the name of preserving Democracy, a different conception of democracy that guarantees liberation as a permanent condition for all peoples has also provided the material and ideological ground for feminist mobilization.

The term "Democracy" has often been utilized in the service of repressive national and international state practices. However, the analytic and political importance of thinking about the egalitarian and emancipatory aspects of democracy at this time in history cannot be underestimated—after all, democracy does have to be made and remade by each generation.[23] If democracy is to be government by the people, or self-government requiring the people's participation, on the basis of merit not inherited status, then the question of how "the people" is defined becomes fundamental. Thus, one of our major tasks is foregrounding the racialized, gendered, and heterosexualized relations of rule typified under hegemonic Democracy, and analyzing the myth of the "universal citizen." Another task is formulating a working definition of feminist democracy which is anticapitalist and centered on the project of decolonization. In other words, our goal is to elaborate the ways a feminist democracy must interpret the hierarchies of governance, their interconnectedness and effects, while moving from an individual to a collective feminist practice.

We have argued that sexual politics are constitutive of all social relations and that colonizing processes are formulated and practiced through the disciplining of Third-World women's bodies. Ella Shohat's essay on post–Third-Worldist feminist film and video examines the ways in which representations of the racialized female body figure in processes of repression and resistance, while Kavita Panjabi's essay situates the disciplining of the female body (and mind, heart and soul) within the prison narratives of Indian and Argentinian women. This framing of the collection, with analytic centrality given to the experiences, consciousness, and histories of Third-World women, is crucial to our conception of a feminist democratic project. Conceptualizing "the people" and citizenship within the framework of a specifically anticolonialist, feminist understanding of democracy, in this instance, requires theorizing from the epistemological location and experiences of Third-World women. Few Third-World and impoverished women have been the beneficiaries of so-called Democracies around the world, and the key elements of feminist democracy defined above can be usefully clarified within the framework of the histories and experiences of these constituencies.[24]

Hegemonic Democracy, Citizenship, and Capitalist Patriarchies

Our location in the United States, and the dominant position it occupies as *the* Democratic nation par excellence necessitate a clarification of the use of the rhetoric of Democracy by the U.S. state. This section grapples with the hierarchies of rule that we have identified as a crucial aspect of the process of dismantling, decolonizing, and transforming capitalism in order to clear the ground for an anticapitalist, anticolonialist feminist democracy. Earlier discussions of colonialism, capitalism, and state practices suggest that colonial, imperial, sexist, and racist practices of rule by the U.S. state are obfuscated by the rhetoric and ideology of Democracy. The ideology of freedom and Democracy works in such a way that the discourse of human rights is often invoked only when U.S. economic and political interests are at stake. Thus, the U.S. state appears to be Democratic while sanctioning imperialist invasions (e.g., Panama, Grenada, Nicaragua, etc.) in the name of preserving Democracy elsewhere in the world. This imperial aspect of the state is often ignored by U.S. feminists involved in struggles for political change. Liberal feminist demands for equal rights, welfare, and social services, and equal pay for women, while crucial arenas for struggle against the state, address the state as if it were self-evidently Democratic.[25] This theorization of the American state as Democratic by U.S. liberal feminists addressing sexism often obscures relationships of colonial domination and, thus, potentially precludes the formation of alliances between Third-World women within colonizing nations or between women in colonizing and colonized/postcolonial nations.

How do we understand the idea of universal citizenship (for us, citizenship which is defined through and across difference), and the way the state mobilizes a citizenship machinery which excludes and marginalizes particular constituencies on the basis of their "difference"? Iris Marion Young argues that "the ideal of universal citizenship carries at least two meanings in addition to the extension of citizenship to everyone: 1) universality defined as general in opposition to particular; what citizens have in common as opposed to how they differ, and 2) universality in the sense of laws and rules that say the same for all and apply to all the same way; laws and rules that are blind to individual and group differences."[26] However, in the case of capitalist patriarchies which are also so-called Democracies, the construct of the universal citizen has very particular gender-, race-, class-, and sexually-specific contours. Because, during moments of crises under capitalism, citizenship is defined through the figures of the (white) consumer and the taxpayer, and because this racialized, masculinized figure is the basis of a series of exclusions in relation to citizenship (exclusions of the very constituencies from whose locations we theorize), understanding the deployment of these categories is crucial to rethinking democracy. It is this deployment of exclusionary citizenship that leads us to argue for an explicitly anticolonialist feminist democracy. The essays by Jaimes Guerrero, Alexander, Mama, and Bhattacharjee, for instance, present nuanced discussions of citizenship and its exclusions. Law, in particular, functions to adjudicate "differences." The citizenship machinery is not "blind" to differences; in fact, it uses a legal apparatus to transform difference into inequality. In its efforts to remain "blind" to differences in the name of equal treatment, the law often perpetuates the naturalization of heterosexuality and the production of psychic economies that conform to the dictates of the ideological superiority of the heterosexual family. One effect is a foreclosing of the possibilities of same-sex desire. Janet Halley's analysis of U.S. Supreme Court decisions in the late 1980s suggests that legal definitions of the class of homosexuals necessarily involve the less visible constitution of a class of heterosexuals. And Kendall Thomas's interrogation of the effects of Bowers v. Hardwick suggests that on questions of homosexuality the state reneges on its promise to protect *all* citizens from terrorist violence, since it effectively sanctions homophobic violence.[27] Difference, in this context, functions to further consolidate and legislate heterosexual desire and citizenship.

Similarly, David T. Evans suggests that the central ideological mechanisms which shape citizenship in advanced capitalism are the roles of consumer and taxpayer: "The history of citizenship is a history of fundamental, formal, heterosexist patriarchal principles and practices ostensibly, progressively 'liberalized' towards and through the rhetoric of 'equality,' but in practice to effect unequal differentiation."[28] If the (implicitly white) consumer and the taxpayer are now the prototypical modern citizen, the current discourse of welfare dependency of the U.S. state gains great importance for feminist analysis and mobilization. The definition of poor women of color as the paradigmatic welfare recipients (when in fact, white women constitute the largest group on welfare) and the discourses of dependency, cultural deprivation, and psychological personality characteristics that are used to discipline these women indicate that (black) women on welfare are, by definition, neither consumers or taxpayers and, thus, are noncitizens. Tracing the genealogy of "dependency" as a keyword in the U.S. welfare state, Nancy Fraser and Linda Gordon show that the definition that once involved relations of power, domination, and subordination has now been replaced by ones that see "dependency" as a synonym for poverty or personality disorders.[29] Thus, impoverished, black teenage mothers have acquired the status of welfare dependents par excellence in the U.S. citizenship machinery. Evelynn Hammonds' study of the representation of African American women and AIDS in both the mass media and the medical establishment illustrates the contradictory, yet highly visible, location of women of color as dependent (and diseased), while simultaneously denying them access to the resources needed for survival and well-being.

Thus, a crucial question for feminists is whether the failure to address welfare rights on the feminist agenda indicates a valorization of wage-labor in ways that prompt a convergence between state racism and racism within the feminist movement. The state machinery which positions women of color as dependents, and, therefore, morally inferior is a script that feminists in organized movements have yet to challenge. This, then, is one of the most significant ethical, intellectual, and political problems for liberal and socialist feminist movements. It is precisely in theorizing questions of privilege, dependency, and domination from the standpoint of, for instance, women of color as "welfare recipients" or immigrant women as "undocumented workers," that feminist struggles take on explicitly anticolonial and anticapitalist questions.

A number of critics have analyzed the convergence of capitalist values and liberal Democratic understandings of Democracy. Instead of rehearsing these arguments in detail, we draw on Paulo Freire's early work in *Pedagogy of the Oppressed* to sketch the ways in which the "myths" utilized by the ruling class to preserve the capitalist status-quo are simultaneously propositions about "Democracy" within a liberal, capitalist culture. Together, these myths constitute a rhetoric of freedom and equality that consolidates the very oppressive practices and values of capitalist domination. Under these conditions freedom and equality function as guaranteed rights under capitalism, foregrounding questions of economic access and choice, of individual freedom, of economic and social mobility, of equality defined as access, opportunity, and choice, and of private property and ownership as constitutive of self-worth). And these myths beg the question of who is the presumed citizen entitled to these rights. They define freedom as access and the choice to work (rather than the material and psychic conditions that make such access and choices possible on an equitable basis), and equality as the same opportunities and rights under the law, without regard to the fact that the implied legitimate citizen is the white, ruling-class, heterosexual, male consumer and taxpayer. The myth of "private property as fundamental to human development," wherein ownership of land is conflated with the personal value, prestige, and evolution of the owner—in contrast to communal ownership of land or world views which suggest that human beings don't own land but live in relation to it, all suggest a systematic world view whereby capitalist values infuse ideas about citizenship and liberal Democracy. In fact, it is almost as if democracy has been colonized under capitalism, thus making it impossible to raise the question of democracy in relation to socialist practice. Thus, the project of specifying feminist democracy at this point in history involves uncoupling the collapse of capitalism into Democracy and recasting the ethical and substantive understandings of democratic processes in anticapitalist terms.

Questions of freedom, equality, and ownership are taken up variously by a number of authors in this collection. M. A. Jaimes Guerrero's essay exposes the contradiction between discourses of private ownership as linked to progress and development and the use of land-allocation policies to disenfranchise native peoples and sever them from their land. In a different way, Anannya Bhattacharjee's essay on the practices and discourses of immigration, public/private aspects of citizenship, and the sexist, racist, and heterosexist effects of immigration policies on South Asian women in the U.S. exposes the exclusionary definitions of freedom and equality underlying the construct of the U.S. nation-state. Bhattacharjee analyzes the meanings of citizenship from the location of the South Asian immigrant wife/woman, the immigrant domestic worker, and the "undocumented alien." In this context, notions of equality under the law challenge conventional definitions of the presumed legitimate citizen who has actual access and opportunity.

Brazilian political scientist Evelina Dagnino suggests that the rhetoric of the Democratic world order is, in fact, the cement for a truly undemocratic world order. Here, Democracy is an abstract generalization, reduced to a procedural notion, wherein formal mechanisms of representative Democracy are assumed to be identical to a Democratic regime. In this procedural definition of Democracy (what some others have called the "promissary" aspects of Democracy), representation, policies, and effects stand in for democratic practices and culture. Social and cultural practices based on a deeper understanding of democracy—considering the relational, egalitarian aspect of democracy—are erased.[30] This procedural notion of Democracy is challenged by Jaimes Guerrero and Alexander when they raise questions about the meaning of citizenship for women. Writing as outsiders, both take on the state and its exclusions—in relation to native peoples, on the one hand, and lesbians and gay men, on the other. Clearly, representative Democracy, as defined by Dagnino, is an insufficient condition for liberation for both Jaimes Guerrero and Alexander. Taken together with the critique of capitalism and its devastating effects on Third-World, migrant, and immigrant women workers offered by Chandra Talpade Mohanty, these analyses suggest the important challenge for feminists to theorize and practice democracy from an anticapitalist standpoint. Mohanty's essay on the naturalization of capitalist processes through domesticated and heterosexualized definitions of women's work and the hyperexploitation of Third-World women workers in different regions of the globe exposes the exclusionary, masculinist ideology of the "worker" as an important aspect of the social relations of capitalist Democracy and of building solidarities between Third-World women workers across national borders.

The challenge for feminists, then, is to critique and move away from this formulation of the U.S. Democratic state—a formulation that usually leads to the erasure of the centrality of the experiences of colonization in the lives of Third-World women and U.S. women of color. This erasure also allows first-world feminists to polarize "survival" versus "feminist" issues in third- and first-world terms, thus colonizing the experiences of Third-World women and making alliances on materialist terms impossible. Jaimes Guerrero's emphasis on land and territorial rights and political sovereignty as fundamental to liberation for native women contrasts sharply with a liberal feminist notion of liberation, defined, for instance, in terms of demands made on behalf of women to the presumed Democratic U.S. state. In the latter formulation, there is no language or conceptual framework to imagine territorial sovereignty as a feminist demand—or to theorize decolonization as a fundamental aspect of feminist struggle. Thus, the imperial or colonial actions of the presumably Democratic U.S. remain invisible.

Imagining Feminist Democracy: Anatomies of Selves, Communities, Organizing

The preceding discussion foregrounds the hierarchies of governance and rule that produce the liberal individual self under capitalist Democracy. The analysis of the limits of a procedural, free-market understanding of Democracy draws attention to the precise hierarchies against which feminist collectivities and organizations position themselves in crafting practices of decolonization and envisioning transformative feminist democracy. We begin by briefly mapping the arguments about democracy and citizenship under capitalism offered by some feminist political theorists, so as to clarify and sharpen our collective vision of feminist democracy with decolonization at the center.

Feminist political theorists have addressed a number of interrelated questions in thinking through the project of democracy in contemporary first-world nation-states. Critiques of liberal masculinist models of universal citizenship and rights, and the public/private distinctions upon which these rely, are inflected with discussions of race, class, and sexuality in relation to women's bodily rights and integrity. While Jean Bethke Elshtain suggests "the family" and the activities of mothering as the new locus for defining a non-masculinist citizenship, Carole Pateman argues for a sexually differentiated concept of citizenship, one in which a political definition of motherhood would have equal relevance in defining citizenship, as patriotism does for men. Neither of these theorists conceptualize the different meanings of motherhood or mothering that arise from different racial and sexual locations in the polity.[31]

In contrast, Iris Marion Young addresses race when she explores the concept of a "heterogeneous public" and a group differentiated citizenship, whereby various racial, sexual, gendered constituencies could make claims on the state on the basis of their differences, rather than approximating the universal, white male experience.[32] Chantal Mouffe, on the other hand, would like us to imagine a radical democracy where sexual difference eventually becomes irrelevant to the relations of liberty and equality for all.[33] Other feminists, like Nancy Fraser, have argued for rethinking the concept of rights in relation to the interpretation as well as the satisfaction of the needs of different marginalized constituencies of women in the U.S. welfare state.[34] Zillah Eisenstein argues persuasively for rethinking the public/private divide from the point of view of women of color, arguing for the need to continually rethink the concept of democratic rights "to require equality of access via an affirmative and non-interventionist state." She anchors her definition of democracy in reenvisioning a radical discourse of privacy rights which is attentive to the reproductive and bodily politics of U.S. women of color.[35] Patricia J. Williams claims that the problem of rights discourse has been that it critiques rights assertion, rather than rights commitment. Stating that "rights are to law what conscious commitments are to the psyche," Williams underscores the significance of the conferring of rights for all historically disempowered peoples, as symbolic of "all the denied aspects of their humanity."[36]

While we find the work of these theorists useful in defining the limits of citizenship and democratic rights for women under capitalism, we want to refocus these concerns to democratic possibilities in the formulation of citizenship drawing on socialist principles. In what follows, we explore what it might mean to a) address decolonization in relation to democracy, and b) to envision critical consciousness and agency outside free-market, procedural conceptions of individual agency. Thus, the question we ask is, how do women conceive of themselves and their communities in the context of this retheorization? The way to think ourselves out of the limitations of the Western liberal formulations of Democracy analyzed earlier is to imagine political mobilization as the practice of active decolonization. Transformation of consciousness and reconceptualizations of identity are, therefore, necessary aspects of democracy conceptualized as the practice of decolonization.

The centrality of collective practice in transformations of the self and reenvisioning organizational democracy anchors feminist thinking. In fact, feminist thinking, here, draws on and endorses socialist principles of collectivized relations of production and organization. It attempts to reenvision socialism as a part of feminist democracy with decolonization at its center. However, while feminist collectives struggle against hegemonic power structures at various levels, they are also marked by these very structures—it is these traces of the hegemonic which the practice of decolonization addresses. Thus, for instance, Geraldine Heng talks about the ways in which feminism takes on the nationalist mantle in Singapore, and Ayesha Imam examines the contradictions of middle-class sexual politics within the organization WIN in Nigeria. Similarly, Honor Ford-Smith explores the negative effect on Sistren's internal dynamics and collective identity of the ideology of the "Lady Bountiful," the "maternalistic patroness of charity who is either asexual, or whose sexual needs could be met by motherhood within the heterosexual family." These analyses offer a certain clarity of thinking by making visible the contradictions that feminist collectives face at this point in history. These reflections are crucial, coming as they do somewhat early in the life of these organizations. What we learn from them may well point toward new ways of thinking about organizing feminist collectivities—and about crafting decolonizing practices.

The interplay of the hegemonic and the oppositional in thinking about the feminist self is explored in different ways by Gloria Wekker, Paula Moya, and Kavita Panjabi. Wekker's essay on Afro-Surinamese women's critical agency explores what appears to be a different configuration of self, anchored in an "alternative vision of female subjectivity and sexuality, based on West African principles." Her analysis of Mati work in terms of alternative female relationships, ones which have simultaneous affectional, cultural, economic, social, spiritual, and obligational components, suggests a decolonized oppositional script for feminist struggle and for practices of governance. Decolonization involves both engagement with the everyday issues in our own lives so that we can make sense of the world in relation to hegemonic power, and engagement with collectivities which are premised on ideas of autonomy and self-determination, in other words democratic practice. For the Creole working-class women Wekker speaks about, this is precisely the process engaged in. It creates what she calls a "psychic economy of female subjectivity, (which) . . . induces working-class women to act individually and collectively in ways that counteract the assault of the hegemonic knowledge regime, which privileges men, the heterosexual contract, inequality and a generally unjust situation." Here, the investment in the self (what Wekker calls "a multiple self") is not necessarily an investment in upward mobility or in the maintenance of a masculinist, heterosexist, middle-class status quo.

Paula Moya's discussion of Chicana feminism and of the work of Cherríe Moraga operates somewhat differently, though it raises similar questions about consciousness, identity, and collectivity in crafting political selves. Moya's essay illustrates the links between experiences of racial, gender, sexual, and class colonization at institutional and psychic levels, and the trajectory and possibilities of emancipatory feminist praxis along the lines of what Freire calls "conscientization." Analyzing the connections between social location, experience, and cultural identity in U.S. lesbian feminist Cherríe Moraga's work, Moya provides a careful and systematic account of the epistemological and political contributions of women of color in theorizing liberatory practice. By exploring the connections between understandings of the self and the social and by positing a cognitive component in theorizing the self-in-community, Moya articulates the stages involved in the transformation of the consciousness of women of color. This is grounded in the physical realities of their lives—what Moraga calls "theory in the flesh." Both Wekker and Moya theorize agency and subjectivity within the context of collective struggle. But while Wekker suggests a new understanding of the multiple self grounded in an alternative psychic and sexual economy, Moya provides a genealogy of the political self in the context of oppressive, inherited psychic and social structures of governance.

Kavita Panjabi's essay charts a different version of the feminist political self, by asking questions about the meaning of feminist insurgency (of ungovernability) under conditions of extreme deprivation—namely, prison. Claiming that prison testimonios are "narrative reconstructions reflecting upon the prison or concentration camp as a microcosmic embodiment of both the hegemonic or authoritarian and the counterhegemonic or anti-authoritarian relations between the state and the individual," Panjabi explores the creation of the self in Jaya Mitra's and Alicia Partnoy's texts as a form of resistance and survival under physically and mentally repressive conditions. Unlike Wekker and Moya, Panjabi does not foreground an instance of political engagement in women's movements. However, by exploring the construction of oppositional and collective feminist consciousness through the development of strategies of resistance based precisely on the ideologies of family, motherhood, and nurturing used to torture women, it does examine the links between the development of women's selves and larger political struggles against repression. The codification of the experience of repression and resistance—for instance, sharing food as a collective strategy for physical and psychic survival in the prison—provides clues for the construction of counterhegemonic political consciousness as women. This is a form of mobilization through writing. One form of decolonization, of imagining community differently, is thinking oneself out of this space of extreme repression. In exploring women's agency in actively creating counterhegemonic relations, values, and modes of communication to challenge the colonizing dehumanization of the prison, Panjabi's analysis suggests that these genealogies of the political self are different from the narrative of the coming-into-being of the individual female self of liberal feminism.

In the essays by Wekker, Moya, and Panjabi, history, memory, emotion, and affectional ties are all seen as significant, cognitive elements of the construction of critical, self-reflective, feminist selves. While crafting different notions of the self, each of the essays suggests that decolonization coupled with emancipatory collective practice leads to a rethinking of patriarchal, heterosexual, colonial, racial, and capitalist legacies in the project of feminism and, thus, toward envisioning democracy and democratic collective practice. Each suggests that issues of sexual politics in governance are fundamental to thinking through questions of resistance anchored in the daily lives of women, that these issues are an integral aspect of the epistemology of anticolonial feminist struggle.

Similarly, the essays by Honor Ford-Smith, Ayesha Imam, and Vasanth and Kalpana Kannabiran, which focus on the anatomy of feminist organizations, suggest how women define themselves differently by virtue of involvement in political movements. They also point to the limitations of the imagination (often linked to the failures of socialism and anticolonial nationalism) that women's movements often inherit. The analyses illuminate contradictory inheritances, particularly of the practices of domination, encode the organization of collective practices, once again foregrounding the need to address decolonization as a fundamental aspect of feminist struggle. These essays also offer hope in the midst of very debilitating circumstances. As the spaces for progressive transformation shrink in the face of transnational capitalist domination, the essays in this collection point to the interstices, the few collective spaces available for envisioning and enacting alternative futures.

Honor Ford-Smith's analysis of the effects of funding on the Jamaican feminist group Sistren provides an insightful, internal critique of a radical feminist organization which draws upon reactionary and conservative ideologies and colonial constructions of womanhood, voluntarism, etc., while working towards the liberation of women. Questions of power, authority, accountability, responsibility, and leadership in the crafting of democratic practice are all addressed head-on in this essay. Thus, issues related to decolonization, feminist collective practice, subjectivity, and agency as inflected by race and class histories and experiences are all part of Honor Ford-Smith's discussion of the possibilities of democratic organizational practice. This essay explores the relation of culture and pedagogy as a strategy of mobilization and self-determination. Here, questions of popular education are simultaneously questions about the reconstruction of political culture; the analysis of Sistren throws up questions of a radically new political and ethical conscience creating a public culture of dissent.

What is also particular to the various analyses of feminist organizations and movements in this collection, however, is the focus on exploring how certain historical disjunctures enable particular issues to emerge within organizations. In the case of Vasanth and Kalpana Kannabiran's analysis of the Indian women's movement in Hyderabad, Ayesha Imam's analysis of WIN in Nigeria, and Geraldine Heng's exploration of the varieties of Third-World feminism under conditions of extreme state repression in Singapore, the connections between international processes (e.g., SAP and IMF policies) and the collusion of the postcolonial state are fundamental to understanding the genealogy of women's organizing. In all three of these cases, the inherited narratives and practices of feminist organizing and the internal divisions they identify must be framed in the context of larger, global as well as more particular, cultural and historical processes.

Postcolonial state practices, including the critique of a socialist government and democratic state, form the political context for Vasanth and Kalpana Kannabiran's analysis of the emergence of the women's movement in Hyderabad. They trace the paternal and patriarchal genealogy of organizing and the political context in which issues get prioritized within women's groups (SAKHI) as a result of state and religious fundamentalist mobilizations. As in the studies by Honor Ford-Smith and Ayesha Imam, this internal critique of the contradictions of feminist organizing, (particularly the activist/academic divide inherited by SAKHI), is linked to the masculinist politics of left and Communist movements in India. Similarly, Ayesha Imam examines the organizational challenges faced by Women in Nigeria (WIN) given the complicity of the militarized postcolonial Nigerian state with global structural adjustment processes. Reflecting on WIN's internal contradictions, Imam questions its political capacity to intervene in the devastating marginalization of women by SAP and the Nigerian state. Reiterating WIN's ultimate goals, the "democratic transformation of the social relations of gender and class," as the ultimate aim of WIN, Imam maps both the limitations and the successes of feminist organizational practices in the context of profound economic, social, and psychic colonization in Nigeria.

These analyses demonstrate the different demands that must be made on the state, once historical processes—most especially, colonialism—are taken into account. In asking questions about how groups come to formulate the notion of common interests, these essayists agree that women's movements cannot be purely reactive in relation to the state. Certainly, the state is a primary object of organizing, but these essays discourage easy formulations of a linear relationship between repression and resistance whereby critical thinking about experience on the part of oppressed peoples is taken as a given. As Paula Moya puts it, "The simple fact of having been born a person of color [in the United States] or of having suffered the effects of heterosexism or of economic deprivation does not, in and of itself, give someone a better understanding or knowledge of [our] society. The key to claiming epistemic authority for people who have been oppressed in a particular way stems from an acknowledgement that they have experiences—experiences that people who are not oppressed in the same way usually lack—that can provide them with information we all need to understand how hierarchies of race, class, gender and sexuality operate to uphold existing regimes of power in our society." Thus, the experience of repression can be, but is not necessarily, a catalyst for organizing. It is, in fact, the *interpretation* of that experience within a *collective* context that marks the moment of transformation from perceived contradictions and material disenfranchisment to participation in women's movements. Finally, the essays offer collective hope and concrete scripts for rethinking and transforming hierarchies of rule.

The conditions under which feminist movements emerge, the crafting of organizational practices and political agendas, the women who get drawn into the movements, and the visions of new modes of organizational practice are all fundamental issues in thinking about feminist democracy. This thinking includes the question of what it means to imagine oneself as an agent outside repressive state structures. As mentioned earlier, within the essays, feminists imagine themselves as agents (not victims or dependents) in relation to citizenship. This begs the question of what it would mean for Third-World and poor women to envision and demand democratic space where their histories, agency, autonomy, and self-determination would be at the center.

Within the capitalist patriarchal understanding of Democracy, the acquisition of material property and the fulfilling of consumer needs become the marks of self-worth. Thinking differently about feminist democracy, thus, involves decolonization in these very specific anticapitalist terms. In order for solidarity between Third-World women in the geographical Third World and women of color in the first world to take place, imperialist domination and capitalist attitudes towards acquisition and advancement must become part of a feminist project of liberation. Feminist democratic practice in this context, then, cannot be about self-advancement, upward mobility, or maintenance of the first-world status-quo. It has to be premised on the decolonization of the self and on notions of citizenship defined not just within the boundaries of the nation state but across national and regional borders. We would dare to suggest that in the context of feminist democracy defined in the ways we suggest above, capitalist feminism is a contradiction in terms. Conceptually, feminist democracy which is global in scope needs to be based on anticolonialist, socialist principles.

While the notion of transborder participatory democracy (one in which it is not the state but people themselves who emerge as the chief agents in defining the course of the global economic and political processes that structure their lives) has been low on the agenda of women's movements for democracy, perhaps this is an idea whose time has come.[37] Anticolonialist feminist democracy involves thinking transnationally, and, in a world increasingly refigured by global economic and political processes, transnational democracy is as necessary as national democracy. The essays by Shohat, Mohanty, Imam, and Alexander illuminate the effects of international economic and cultural institutions on Third-World women. While it is difficult at this time to conceive of democratic practices of representation, responsibility, and accountability in relation to these institutions (media, tourism, SAP, organization of labor), the need to democratize cannot be ignored. Then, the World Bank, the IMF, and the GATT, organizations that make decisions that affect everyone's lives, can be made more accountable. In fact, decision-making processes in these institutions must be opened up for feminist participation and scrutiny.

In many respects, the central intellectual and political frames of this collection are not coincidental. They have formed the organizing principles of our work and lives over the last decade. Thus, the issues of feminist democracy—decolonization as central to self- and collective transformation; the fundamentally pedagogic character of feminist praxis; the profoundly anticapitalist, socialist imperative in imagining and enacting global feminist struggles—constitute the fabric of our action, reflection, and vision of the future. Over the years of working against the grain in hegemonic, colonizing institutions, and in feminist and other grassroots communities, we have come to learn that the emotional terror produced by attempts to divest oneself of power and privilege and in the struggle for self-determination needs to be scrutinized very seriously. The challenge lies in an ethical commitment to work to transform terror into engagement based on empathy and a vision of justice for everyone. After all, this is at the heart of building solidarity across otherwise debilitating social, economic, and psychic boundaries. The most profound effects of our organizing and envisioning liberation as a permanent condition for all peoples may not be experienced for at least seven generations. As Frantz Fanon has argued, each generation has a responsibility to produce and transform the terms of struggle and liberation so that succeeding generations can assume the ongoing task in different but more advanced ways.[38]

Acknowledgements

We would like to thank Zillah Eisenstein for a careful and provocative response to this essay—we have really benefited from her reading. As always, we are grateful to our families (Jinny Chalmers, Maya Alexander, and Satya Mohanty) for providing immeasurable emotional and intellectual support during the life of this collection.

Section I

Colonial Legacies, Capitalist State Practice, and Feminist Movements

1

Women Workers and Capitalist Scripts: Ideologies of Domination, Common Interests, and the Politics of Solidarity

Chandra Talpade Mohanty

> We dream that when we work hard, we'll be able to clothe our children decently, and still have a little time and money left for ourselves. And we dream that when we do as good as other people, we get treated the same, and that nobody puts us down because we are not like them. . . . Then we ask ourselves, "How could we make these things come true?" And so far we've come up with only two possible answers: win the lottery, or organize. What can I say, except I have never been lucky with numbers. So tell this in your book: tell them it may take time that people think they don't have, but they have to organize! . . . Because the only way to get a little measure of power over your own life is to do it collectively, with the support of other people who share your needs.
>
> Irma, a Filipina worker in the Silicon Valley, California[1]

Irma's dreams of a decent life for her children and herself, her desire for equal treatment and dignity on the basis of the quality and merit of her work, her conviction that collective struggle is the means to "get a little measure of power over your own life," succinctly capture the struggles of poor women workers in the global capitalist arena. In this essay I want to focus on the exploitation of poor Third-World women, on their agency as workers, on the common interests of women workers based on an understanding of shared location and needs, and on the strategies/practices of organizing that are anchored in and lead to the transformation of the daily lives of women workers.

This has been an especially difficult essay to write—perhaps because the almost-total saturation of the processes of capitalist domination makes it hard to envision forms of feminist resistance which would make a real difference in the daily lives of poor women workers. However, as I began to sort through the actions, reflections, and analyses by and about women workers (or wage laborers) in the capitalist economy, I discovered the dignity of women workers' struggles in the face of overwhelming odds. From these struggles we can learn a great deal about processes of exploitation and domination as well as about autonomy and liberation.

A recent study tour to Tijuana, Mexico, organized by Mary Tong of the San Diego–based Support Committee for Maquiladora Workers, confirmed my belief in the radical possibilities of cross-border organizing, especially in the wake of NAFTA. Exchanging ideas, experiences, and strategies with Veronica Vasquez, a twenty-one-year-old Maquila worker fighting for her job, for better working conditions, and against sexual harassment, was as much of an inspiration as any in writing this essay. Veronica Vasquez, along with ninety-nine former employees of the Tijuana factory Exportadora Mano de Obra, S.A. de C.V., has filed an unprecedented lawsuit in Los Angeles, California, against the U.S. owner of Exportadora, National O-Ring of Downey, demanding that it be forced to follow Mexican labor laws and provide workers with three months' back pay after shutting down company operations in Tijuana in November 1994. The courage, determination, and analytical clarity of these young Mexican women workers in launching the first case to test the legality of NAFTA suggest that in spite of the global saturation of processes of capitalist domination, 1995 was a moment of great possibility for building cross-border feminist solidarity.[2]

Over the years, I have been preoccupied with the limits as well as the possibilities of constructing feminist solidarities across national, racial, sexual, and class divides. Women's lives as workers, consumers, and citizens have changed radically with the triumphal rise of capitalism in the global arena. The common interests of capital (e.g., profit, accumulation, exploitation, etc.) are somewhat clear at this point. But how do we talk about poor Third-World women workers' interests, their agency, and their (in)visibility in so-called democratic processes? What are the possibilities for democratic citizenship for Third-World women workers in the contemporary capitalist economy? These are some of the questions driving this essay. I hope to clarify and analyze the location of Third-World women workers and their collective struggles in an attempt to generate ways to think about mobilization, organizing, and conscientization transnationally.

This essay extends the arguments I have made elsewhere regarding the location of Third-World women as workers in a global economy.[3] I write now, as I did then, from my own discontinuous locations: as a South Asian anticapitalist feminist in the U.S. committed to working on a truly liberatory feminist practice which theorizes and enacts the potential for a cross-cultural, international politics of solidarity; as a Third-World feminist teacher and activist for whom the psychic economy of "home" and of "work" has always been the space of contradiction and struggle; and as a woman whose middle-class struggles for self-definition and autonomy outside the definitions of daughter, wife, and mother mark an intellectual and political genealogy that led me to this particular analysis of Third-World women's work.

Here, I want to examine the analytical category of "women's work," and to look at the historically specific *naturalization* of gender and race hierarchies through this category. An international division of labor is central to the establishment, consolidation, and maintenance of the current world order: global assembly lines are as much about the production of people as they are about "providing jobs" or making profit. Thus, naturalized assumptions about *work* and *the worker* are crucial to understanding the sexual politics of global capitalism. I believe that the relation of local to global processes of colonization and exploitation, and the specification of a process of cultural and ideological homogenization across national borders, in part through the creation of the consumer as "the" citizen under advanced capitalism, must be crucial aspects of any comparative feminist project. This definition of the citizen-consumer depends to a large degree on the definition and disciplining of producers/workers on whose backs the citizen-consumer gains legitimacy. It is the worker/producer side of this equation that I will address. Who are the workers that make the citizen-consumer possible? What role do sexual politics play in the ideological creation of this worker? How does global capitalism, in search of ever-increasing profits, utilize gender and racialized ideologies in crafting forms of women's work? And, does the social location of particular women as workers suggest the basis for common interests and potential solidarities across national borders?

As global capitalism develops and wage labor becomes the hegemonic form of organizing production and reproduction, class relations within and across national borders have become more complex and less transparent.[4] Thus, issues of spatial economy—the manner by which capital utilizes particular spaces for differential production and the accumulation of capital and, in the process, transforms these spaces (and peoples)—gain fundamental importance for feminist analysis.[5] In the aftermath of feminist struggles around the right to work and the demand for equal pay, the boundaries between home/family and work are no longer seen as inviolable (of course these boundaries were always fluid for poor and working-class women). Women are (and have always been) in the workforce, and we are here to stay. In this essay, I offer an analysis of certain historical and ideological transformations of gender, capital, and work across the borders of nation-states,[6] and, in the process, develop a way of thinking about the common interests of Third-World women workers, and in particular about questions of agency and the transformation of consciousness.

Drawing specifically on case studies of the incorporation of Third-World women into a global division of labor at different geographical ends of the new world order, I argue for a historically delineated category of "women's work" as an example of a productive and necessary basis for feminist cross-cultural analysis.[7] The idea I am interested in invoking here is not "the work that women do" or even the occupations that they/we happen to be concentrated in, but rather the ideological construction of jobs and tasks in terms of notions of appropriate femininity, domesticity, (hetero)sexuality, and racial and cultural stereotypes. I am interested in mapping these operations of capitalism across different divides, in tracing the naturalization of capitalist processes, ideologies, and values through the way women's work is *constitutively* defined–in this case, in terms of gender and racial parameters. One of the questions I explore pertains to the way gender identity (defined in domestic, heterosexual, familial terms) structures the nature of the work women are allowed to perform or precludes women from being "workers" altogether.

While I base the details of my analysis in geographically anchored case studies, I am suggesting a comparative methodology which moves beyond the case-study approach and illuminates global processes which inflect and draw upon indigenous hierachies, ideologies, and forms of exploitation to consolidate new modes of colonization (what we refer to in the introductory chapter as "recolonization"). The local and the global are indeed connected through parallel, contradictory, and sometimes converging relations of rule which position women in different and similar locations as workers.[8] I agree with feminists who argue that class struggle, narrowly defined, can no longer be the only basis for solidarity among women workers. The fact of being women with particular racial, ethnic, cultural, sexual, and geographical histories has everything to do with our definitions and identities as workers. A number of feminists have analyzed the division between production and reproduction, and the construction of ideologies of womanhood in terms of public/private spheres. Here, I want to highlight a) the persistence of patriarchal definitions of womanhood in the arena of wage labor; b) the versatility and specificity of capitalist exploitative processes providing the basis for thinking about potential common interests and solidarity between Third-World women workers; and c) the challenges for collective organizing in a context where traditional union methods (based on the idea of the class interests of the male worker) are inadequate as strategies for empowerment.

If, as I suggest, the logic of a world order characterized by a transnational economy involves the active construction and dissemination of an image of the "Third World/ racialized, or marginalized woman worker" that draws on indigenous histories of gender and race inequalities, and if this worker's identity is coded in patriarchal terms which define her in relation to men and the heterosexual, conjugal family unit, then the model of class conflict between capitalists and workers needs to be recrafted in terms of the interests (and perhaps identities) of Third-World women workers. Patriarchal ideologies, which sometimes pit women against men within and outside the home, infuse the material realities of the lives of Third-World women workers, making it imperative to reconceptualize the way we think about working-class interests and strategies for organizing. Thus, while this is not an argument for just recognizing the "common experiences" of Third-World women workers, it *is* an argument for recognizing (concrete, not abstract) "common interests" and the potential bases of cross-national solidarity—a common context of struggle. In addition, while I choose to focus on the "Third World" woman worker, my argument holds for white women workers who are also racialized in similar ways. The argument then is about a *process* of gender and race domination, rather than about the *content* of "Third World." Making Third-World women workers visible in this gender, race, class formation involves engaging a capitalist script of subordination and exploitation. But it also leads to thinking about the possibilities of emancipatory action on the basis of the reconceptualization of Third-World women as agents rather than victims.

But why even use "Third World," a somewhat problematic term which many now consider outdated? And why make an argument which privileges the social location, experiences, and identities of Third-World women workers, as opposed to any other group of workers, male or female? Certainly, there are problems with the term "Third World." It is inadequate in comprehensively characterizing the economic, political, racial, and cultural differences *within* the borders of Third-World nations. But in comparison with other similar formulations like "North/South" and "advanced/underdeveloped nations," "Third World" retains a certain heuristic value and explanatory specificity in relation to the inheritance of colonialism and contemporary neocolonial economic and geopolitical processes that the other formulations lack.[9]

In response to the second question, I would argue that at this time in the development and operation of a "new" world order, Third-World women workers (defined in this context as both women from the geographical Third World and immigrant and indigenous women of color in the U.S. and Western Europe) occupy a specific social location in the international division of labor which *illuminates* and *explains* crucial features of the capitalist processes of exploitation and domination. These are features of the social world that are usually obfuscated or mystified in discourses about the "progress" and "development" (e.g., the creation of jobs for poor, Third-World women as the marker of economic and social advancement) that is assumed to "naturally" accompany the triumphal rise of global capitalism. I do not claim to explain *all* the relevant features of the social world or to offer a *comprehensive* analysis of capitalist processes of recolonization. However, I am suggesting that Third-World women workers have a potential identity in common, an identity as *workers* in a particular division of labor at this historical moment. And I believe that exploring and analyzing this potential commonality across geographical and cultural divides provides both a way of reading and understanding the world and an explanation of the consolidation of inequities of gender, race, class, and (hetero)sexuality, which are necessary to envision and enact transnational feminist solidarity.[10]

The argument that multinationals position and exploit women workers in certain ways does not originate with me. I want to suggest, however, that in interconnecting and comparing some of these case studies, a larger theoretical argument can be made about the category of women's work, specifically about the Third-World woman as worker, at this particular historical moment. I think this intersection of gender and work, where the very definition of work draws upon and reconstructs notions of masculinity, femininity, and sexuality, offers a basis of cross-cultural comparison and analysis which is grounded in the concrete realities of women's lives. I am not suggesting that this basis for comparison exhausts the *totality* of women's experience cross-culturally. In other words, because similar ideological constructions of "women's work" make cross-cultural analysis possible, this does not automatically mean women's lives are the *same*, but rather that they are *comparable*. I argue for a notion of political solidarity and common interests, defined as a community or collectivity among women workers across class, race, and national boundaries which is based on shared material interests and identity and common ways of reading the world. This idea of political solidarity in the context of the incorporation of Third-World women into a global economy offers a basis for cross-cultural comparison and analysis which is grounded in history and social location rather than in an ahistorical notion of culture or experience. I am making a choice here to focus on and analyze the *continuities* in the experiences, histories, and strategies of survival of these particular workers. But this does not mean that differences and discontinuities in experience do not exist or that they are insignificant. The focus on continuities is a *strategic* one—it makes possible a way of reading the operation of capital from a location (that of Third-World women workers) which, while forming the bedrock of a certain kind of global exploitation of labor, remains somewhat invisible and undertheorized.

Gender and Work: Historical and Ideological Transformations

"Work makes life sweet," says Lola Weixel, a working-class Jewish woman in Connie Field's film "The Life and Times of Rosie the Riveter." Weixel is reflecting on her experience of working in a welding factory during World War II, at a time when large numbers of U.S. women were incorporated into the labor force to replace men who were fighting the war. In one of the most moving moments in the film, she draws attention to what it meant to her and to other women to work side by side, to learn skills and craft products, and to be paid for the work they did, only to be told at the end of the war that they were no longer needed and should go back to being girlfriends, housewives, and mothers. While the U.S. state propaganda machine was especially explicit on matters of work for men and women, and the corresponding expectations of masculinity/femininity and domesticity in the late 1940s and 1950s, this is no longer the case in the 1990s. Shifting definitions of public and private, and of workers, consumers and citizens no longer define wage-work in visibly masculine terms. However, the dynamics of job competition, loss, and profit-making in the 1990s are still part of the dynamic process that spelled the decline of the mill towns of New England in the early 1900s and that now pits "American" against "immigrant" and "Third-World" workers along the U.S./Mexico border or in the Silicon Valley in California. Similarly, there are continuities between the women-led New York garment-workers strike of 1909, the Bread and Roses (Lawrence textile) strike of 1912, Lola Weixel's role in union organizing during WW II, and the frequent strikes in the 1980s and 1990s of Korean textile and electronic workers, most of whom are young, single women.[11] While the global division of labor in 1995 looks quite different from what it was in the 1950s, ideologies of women's work, the meaning and value of work for women, and women workers' struggles against exploitation remain central issues for feminists around the world. After all, women's labor has always been central to the development, consolidation, and reproduction of capitalism in the U.S.A. and elsewhere.

In the United States, histories of slavery, indentured servitude, contract labor, self-employment, and wage-work are also simultaneously histories of gender, race, and (hetero)sexuality, nested within the context of the development of capitalism. Thus, women of different races, ethnicities, and social classes had profoundly different, though interconnected, experiences of work in the economic development from nineteenth-century economic and social practices (slave agriculture in the South, emergent industrial capitalism in the Northeast, the hacienda system in the Southwest, independent family farms in the rural Midwest, Native American hunting/gathering and agriculture) to wage-labor and self-employment (including family businesses) in the late-twentieth century. In 1995, almost a century after the Lowell girls lost their jobs when textile mills moved South to attract non-unionized labor, feminists are faced with a number of profound analytical and organizational challenges in different regions of the world. The material, cultural, and political effects of the processes of domination and exploitation which sustain what is called the New World Order(NWO)[12] are devasting for the vast majority of people in the world—and most especially for impoverished and Third-World women. Maria Mies argues that the increasing division of the world into consumers and producers has a profound effect on Third-World women workers, who are drawn into the international division of labor as workers in agriculture; in large-scale manufacturing industries like textiles, electronics, garments, and toys; in small-scale manufacturing of consumer goods like handicrafts and food processing (the informal sector); and as workers in the sex and tourist industries.[13]

The values, power, and meanings attached to being either a consumer or a producer/worker vary enormously depending on where and who we happen to be in an unequal global system. In the 1990s, it is, after all, multinational corporations that are the hallmark of global capitalism. In an analysis of the effects of these corporations on the new world order, Richard Barnet and John Cavanagh characterize the global commercial arena in terms of four intersecting webs: the Global Cultural Bazaar (which creates and disseminates images and dreams through films, television, radio, music, and other media), the Global Shopping Mall (a planetary supermarket which sells things to eat, drink, wear, and enjoy through advertising, distribution, and marketing networks), the Global Workplace (a network of factories and workplaces where goods are produced, information processed, and services rendered), and, finally, the Global Financial Network (the international traffic in currency transactions, global securities, etc.).[14] In each of these webs, racialized ideologies of masculinity, femininity, and sexuality play a role in constructing the legitimate consumer, worker, and manager. Meanwhile, the psychic and social disenfranchisement and impoverishment of women continues. Women's bodies and labor are used to consolidate global dreams, desires, and ideologies of success and the good life in unprecedented ways.

Feminists have responded directly to the challenges of globalization and capitalist modes of recolonization by addressing the sexual politics and effects on women of a) religious fundamentalist movements within and across the boundaries of the nation-state; b) structural adjustment policies (SAPs); c) militarism, demilitarization, and violence against women; d) environmental degradation and land/sovereignty struggles of indigenous and native peoples; and e) population control, health, and reproductive policies and practices.[15] In each of these cases, feminists have analyzed the effects on women as workers, sexual partners, mothers and caretakers, consumers, and transmitters and transformers of culture and tradition. Analysis of the ideologies of masculinity and femininity, of motherhood and (hetero)sexuality and the understanding and mapping of agency, access, and choice are central to this analysis and organizing. Thus, while my characterization of capitalist processes of domination and recolonization may appear somewhat overwhelming, I want to draw attention to the numerous forms of resistance and struggle that have also always been constitutive of the script of colonialism/capitalism. Capitalist patriarchies and racialized, class/caste-specific hierarchies are a key part of the long history of domination and exploitation of women, but struggles against these practices and vibrant, creative, collective forms of mobilization and organizing have also always been a part of our histories. In fact, like Jacqui Alexander and a number of other authors in this collection, I attempt to articulate an emancipatory discourse and knowledge, one that furthers the cause of feminist liberatory practice. After all, part of what needs to change within racialized capitalist patriarchies is the very concept of work/labor, as well as the naturalization of heterosexual masculinity in the definition of "the worker."

Teresa Amott and Julie Matthaei, in analyzing the U.S. labor market, argue that the intersection of gender, class, and racial-ethnic hierarchies of power has had two major effects:

> First, disempowered groups have been concentrated in jobs with lower pay, less job security, and more difficult working conditions. Second, workplaces have been places of extreme segregation, in which workers have worked in jobs only with members of their same racial-ethnic, gender, and class group, even though the particular racial-ethnic group and gender assigned to a job may have varied across firms and regions.[16]

While Amott and Matthaei draw attention to the sex-and-race typing of jobs, they do not *theorize* the relationship between this job typing and the social identity of the workers concentrated in these low-paying, segregated, often unsafe sectors of the labor market. While the economic history they chart is crucial to any understanding of the race-and-gender basis of U.S. capitalist processes, their analysis begs the question of whether there is a connection (other than the common history of domination of people of color) between *how* these jobs are defined and *who* is sought after for the jobs.

By examining two instances of the incorporation of women into the global economy (women lacemakers in Narsapur, India, and women in the electronics industry in the Silicon Valley) I want to delineate the interconnections between gender, race, and ethnicity, and the ideologies of work which locate women in particular exploitative contexts. The contradictory positioning of women along class, race, and ethnic lines in these two cases suggests that, in spite of the obvious geographical and sociocultural differences between the two contexts, the organization of the global economy by contemporary capital positions these workers in very similar ways, effectively reproducing and transforming locally specific hierarchies. There are also some significant continuities between homework and factory work in these contexts, in terms of both the inherent ideologies of work as well as the experiences and social identities of women as workers. This tendency can also be seen in the case studies of black women workers (of Afro-Caribbean, Asian, and African origin) in Britain, especially women engaged in homework, factory work, and family businesses.

Housewives and Homework: The Lacemakers of Narsapur

Maria Mies's 1982 study of the lacemakers of Narsapur, India, is a graphic illustration of how women bear the impact of development processes in countries where poor peasant and tribal societies are being "integrated" into an international division of labor under the dictates of capital accumulation. Mies's study illustrates how capitalist production relations are built upon the backs of women workers defined as *housewives*. Ideologies of gender and work and their historical transformation provide the necessary ground for the exploitation of the lacemakers. But the definition of women as housewives also suggests the heterosexualization of women's work—women are always defined in relation to men and conjugal marriage. Mies's account of the development of the lace industry and the corresponding relations of production illustrates fundamental transformations of gender, caste, and ethnic relations. The original caste distinctions between the feudal warrior castes (the landowners) and the Narsapur (poor Christians) and Serepalam (poor Kapus/Hindu agriculturalists) women are totally transformed through the development of the lace industry, and a new caste hierarchy is effected.

At the time of Mies's study, there were sixty lace manufacturers, with some 200,000 women in Narsapur and Serepalam constituting the work force. Lacemaking women worked six to eight hours a day, and ranged in age from six to eighty. Mies argues that the expansion of the lace industry between 1970 and 1978 and its integration into the world market led to class/caste differentation within particular communities, with a masculinization of all nonproduction jobs (trade) and a total feminization of the production process. Thus, men sold women's products and lived on profits from women's labor. The polarization between men and women's work, where men actually defined themselves as exporters and businessmen who invested in women's labor, bolstered the social and ideological definition of women as housewives and their work as "leisure time activity." In other words, work, in this context, was grounded in sexual identity, in concrete definitions of femininity, masculinity, and heterosexuality.

Two particular indigenous hierarchies, those of caste and gender, interacted to produce normative definitions of "women's work." Where, at the onset of the lace industry, Kapu men and women were agricultural laborers and it was the lower-caste Harijan women who were lacemakers, with the development of capitalist relations of production and the possibility of caste/class mobility, it was the Harijan women who were agricultural laborers while the Kapu women undertook the "leisure time" activity of lacemaking. The caste-based ideology of seclusion and purdah was essential to the extraction of surplus value. Since purdah and the seclusion of women is a sign of higher caste status, the domestication of Kapu laborer women—where their (lacemaking) activity was tied to the concept of the "women sitting in the house" was entirely within the logic of capital accumulation and profit. Now, Kapu women, not just the women of feudal, landowning castes, are in purdah as housewives producing for the world market.

Ideologies of seclusion and the domestication of women are clearly sexual, drawing as they do on masculine and feminine notions of protectionism and property. They are also heterosexual ideologies, based on the normative definition of women as wives, sisters, and mothers—always in relation to conjugal marriage and the "family." Thus, the caste transformation and separation of women along lines of domestication and nondomestication (Kapu housewives vs. Harijan laborers) effectively links the work that women do with their sexual and caste/class identities. Domestication works, in this case, because of the persistence and legitimacy of the ideology of the housewife, which defines women in terms of their place within the home, conjugal marriage, and heterosexuality. The opposition between definitions of the "laborer" and of the "housewife" anchors the invisibility (and caste-related status) of work; in effect, it defines women as *non-workers.* By definition, housewives cannot be workers or laborers; housewives make male breadwinners and consumers possible. Clearly, ideologies of "women's place and work" have real material force in this instance, where spatial parameters construct and maintain gendered and caste-specific hierarchies. Thus, Mies's study illustrates the concrete effects of the social definition of women as housewives. Not only are the lacemakers invisible in census figures (after all, their work is leisure), but their definition as housewives makes possible the definition of men as "breadwinners." Here, class and gender proletarianization through the development of capitalist relations of production, and the integration of women into the world market is possible because of the history and transformation of indigenous caste and sexual ideologies.

Reading the operation of capitalist processes from the position of the housewife/worker who produces for the world market makes the specifically gendered and caste/class opposition between laborer and the nonworker (housewife) visible. Moreover, it makes it possible to acknowledge and account for the hidden costs of women's labor. And finally, it illuminates the fundamentally *masculine* definition of laborer/worker in a context where, as Mies says, men live off women who are the producers. Analyzing and transforming this masculine definition of labor, which is the mainstay of capitalist patriarchal cultures, is one of the most significant challenges we face. The effect of this definition of labor is not only that it makes women's labor and its costs invisible, but that it undercuts women's agency by defining them as victims of a process of pauperization or of "tradition" or "patriarchy," rather than as agents capable of making their own choices.

In fact, the contradictions raised by these choices are evident in the lacemakers' responses to characterizations of their own work as "leisure activity." While the fact that they did "work" was clear to them and while they had a sense of the history of their own pauperization (with a rise in prices for goods but no corresponding rise in wages), they were unable to explain how they came to be in the situation they found themselves. Thus, while some of the contradications between their work and their roles as housewives and mothers were evident to them, they did not have access to an analysis of these contradictions which could lead to a) seeing the complete picture in terms of their exploitation; b) strategizing and organizing to transform their material situations; or c) recognizing their common interests as women workers across caste/class lines. As a matter of fact, the Serepelam women defined their lacemaking in terms of "housework" rather than wage-work, and women who had managed to establish themselves as petty commodity producers saw what they did as entrepreneurial: they saw themselves as selling *products* rather than *labor*. Thus, in both cases, women internalized the ideologies that defined them as nonworkers. The isolation of the work context (work done in the house rather than in a public setting) as well as the internalization of caste and patriarchal ideologies thus militated against organizing as *workers*, or as *women*. However, Mies suggests that there were cracks in this ideology: the women expressed some envy toward agricultural laborers, whom the lacemakers saw as enjoying working together in the fields. What seems necessary in such a context, in terms of feminist mobilization, is a recognition of the fact that the identity of the housewife needs to be transformed into the identity of a "woman worker or working woman." Recognition of common interests as housewives is very different from recognition of common interests as women and as workers.

Immigrant Wives, Mothers, and Factory Work: Electronics Workers in the Silicon Valley

My discussion of the U.S. end of the global assembly line is based on studies by Naomi Katz and David Kemnitzer (1983) and Karen Hossfeld (1990) of electronics workers in the so-called Silicon Valley in California. An analysis of production strategies and processes indicates a significant ideological redefinition of normative ideas of factory work in terms of the Third-World, immigrant women who constitute the primary workforce. While the lacemakers of Narsapur were located as *housewives* and their work defined as *leisure time activity* in a very complex international world market, Third-World women in the electronics industry in the Silicon Valley are located as *mothers, wives,* and *supplementary* workers. Unlike the search for the "single" woman assembly worker in Third-World countries, it is in part the ideology of the "married woman" which defines job parameters in the Valley, according to Katz and Kemnitzer's data.

Hossfeld also documents how existing ideologies of femininity cement the exploitation of the immigrant women workers in the Valley, and how the women often use this patriarchal logic against management. Assumptions of "single" and "married" women as the ideal workforce at the two geographical ends of the electronics global assembly line (which includes South Korea, Hong Kong, China, Taiwan, Thailand, Malaysia, Japan, India, Pakistan, the Philippines, and the United States, Scotland, and Italy)[17] are anchored in normative understandings of femininity, womanhood, and sexual identity. The labels are predicated on sexual difference and the institution of heterosexual marriage and carry connotations of a "manageable" (docile?) labor force.[18]

Katz and Kemnitzer's data indicates a definition and transformation of women's work which relies on gender, race, and ethnic hierarchies already historically anchored in the U.S. Further, their data illustrates that the construction of "job labels" pertaining to Third-World women's work is closely allied with their sexual and racial identities. While Hossfeld's more recent study reinforces some of Katz and Kemnitzer's conclusions, she focuses more specifically on how "contradictory ideologies about sex, race, class, and nationality are used as forms of both labor control and labor resistance in the capitalist workplace today."[19] Her contribution lies in charting the operation of gendered ideologies in the structuring of the industry and in analyzing what she calls "refeminization strategies" in the workplace.

Although the primary workforce in the Valley consists of Third-World and newly immigrant women, substantial numbers of Third-World and immigrant men are also employed by the electronics industry. In the early 1980s, 70,000 women held 80 to 90 percent of the operative or laborer jobs on the shop floor. Of these, 45 to 50 percent were Third-World, especially Asian, immigrants. White men held either technican or supervisory jobs. Hossfeld's study was conducted between 1983 and 1986, at which time she estimates that up to 80 percent of the operative jobs were held by people of color, with women constituting up to 90 percent of the assembly workers. Katz and Kemnitzer maintain that the industry actively seeks sources of cheap labor by deskillling production and by using race, gender, and ethnic stereotypes to "attract" groups of workers who are "more suited" to perform tedious, unrewarding, poorly paid work. When interviewed, management personnel described the jobs as a) unskilled (as easy as a recipe); b) requiring tolerance for tedious work (Asian women are therefore more suited); and c) supplementary activity for women whose main tasks were mothering and housework.

It may be instructive to unpack these job labels in relation to the immigrant and Third-World (married) women who perform these jobs. The job labels recorded by Katz and Kemnitzer need to be analyzed as definitions of *women's work,* specifically as definitions of *Third-World/immigrant women's work*. First, the notion of "unskilled" as easy (like following a recipe) and the idea of tolerance for tedious work both have racial and gendered dimensions. Both draw upon stereotypes which infantalize Third-World women and initiate a nativist discourse of "tedium" and "tolerance" as characteristics of non-Western, primarily agricultural, premodern (Asian) cultures. Secondly, defining jobs as supplementary activity for *mothers* and *housewives* adds a further dimension: sexual identity and appropriate notions of heterosexual femininity as marital domesticity. These are not part-time jobs, but they are defined as supplementary. Thus, in this particular context, (Third-World) women's work needs are defined as temporary.

While Hossfeld's analysis of management logic follows similar lines, she offers a much more nuanced understanding of how the gender and racial stereotypes prevalent in the larger culture infuse worker consciousness and resistance. For instance, she draws attention to the ways in which factory jobs are seen by the workers as "unfeminine" or not "ladylike." Management exploits and reinforces these ideologies by encouraging women to view femininity as contradictory to factory work, by defining their jobs as secondary and temporary, and by asking women to choose between defining themselves as women or as workers. Womanhood and femininity are thus defined along a domestic, familial model, with work seen as supplemental to this primary identity. Significantly, although 80 percent of the immigrant women in Hossfeld's study were the largest annual income producers in their families, they still considered men to be the breadwinners.

Thus, as with the exploitation of Indian lacemakers as "housewives," Third-World/immigrant women in the Silicon Valley are located as "mothers and homemakers" and only secondarily as workers. In both cases, men are seen as the real breadwinners. While (women's) work is usually defined as something that takes place in the "public" or production sphere, these ideologies clearly draw on stereotypes of women as home-bound. In addition, the *invisibility* of work in the Indian context can be compared to the *temporary/secondary* nature of work in the Valley. Like the Mies study, the data compiled by Hossfeld and Katz and Kemnitzer indicate the presence of local ideologies and hierarchies of gender and race as the basis for the exploitation of the electronics workers. The question that arises is: How do women understand their own positions and construct meanings in an exploitative job situation?

Interviews with electronics workers indicate that, contrary to the views of management, women do not see their jobs as temporary but as part of a lifetime strategy of upward mobility. Conscious of their racial, class, and gender status, they combat their devaluation as workers by increasing their income: by job-hopping, overtime, and moonlighting as pieceworkers. Note that, in effect, the "homework" that Silicon Valley workers do is performed under conditions very similar to the lacemaking of Narsapur women. Both kinds of work are done in the home, in isolation, with the worker paying her own overhead costs (like electricity and cleaning), with no legally mandated protections (such as a minimum wage, paid leave, health benefits, etc.). However, clearly the meanings attached to the work differ in both contexts, as does the way we understand them.

For Katz and Kemnitzer the commitment of electronics workers to class mobility is an important assertion of self. Thus, unlike in Narsapur, in the Silicon Valley, homework has an entrepreneurial aspect for the women themselves. In fact, in Narsapur, women's work turns the men into entrepreneurs! In the Valley, women take advantage of the contradictions of the situations they face as *individual workers.* While in Narsapur, it is purdah and caste/class mobility which provides the necessary self-definition required to anchor women's work in the home as leisure activity, in the Silicon Valley, it is a specifically *American* notion of individual ambition and entrepreneurship which provides the necessary ideological anchor for Third-World women.

Katz and Kemnitzer maintain that this underground economy produces an *ideological* redefinition of jobs, allowing them to be defined as *other than* the basis of support of the historically stable, "comfortable," white, metropolitan working class. In other words, there is a clear connection between low wages and the definition of the job as supplementary, and the fact that the lifestyles of people of color are defined as different and cheaper. Thus, according to Katz and Kemnitzer, *women* and *people of color* continue to be "defined out" of the old industrial system and become targets and/or instruments of the ideological shift away from class towards national/ethnic/gender lines.[20] In this context, ideology and popular culture emphasize the *individual maximization* of options for personal success. Individual success is thus severed from union activity, political struggle, and collective relations. Similarly, Hossfeld suggests that it is the racist and sexist management logic of the needs of "immigrants" that allows the kind of exploitative labor processes that she documents.[21] However, in spite of Katz and Kemnitzer's complex analysis of the relationship of modes of production, social relations of production, culture, and ideology in the context of the Silicon Valley workers, they do not specify why it is *Third-World women* who constitute the primary labor force. Similarly, while Hossfeld provides a nuanced analysis of the gendering of the workplace and the use of racial and gendered logic to consolidate capitalist accumulation, she also sometimes separates "women" and "minority workers" (Hossfeld, p. 176), and does not specify why it is women of color who constitute the major labor force on the assembly lines in the Valley. In distinguishing between women and people of color, Katz and Kemnitzer tend to reproduce the old conceptual divisions of gender and race, where women are defined primarily in terms of their gender and people of color in terms of race. What is excluded is an *interactive* notion of gender and race, whereby women's gendered identity is grounded in race and people of color's racial identities are gendered.

I would argue that the data compiled by Katz and Kemnitzer and Hossfeld does, in fact, explain why Third-World women are targeted for jobs in electronics factories. The explanation lies in the redefinition of work as temporary, supplementary, and unskilled, in the construction of women as mothers and homemakers, and in the positioning of femininity as contradictory to factory work. In addition, the explanation also lies in the specific definition of Third-World, immigrant women as docile, tolerant, and satisfied with substandard wages. It is the ideological redefinition of women's work that provides the necessary understanding of this phenomenon. Hossfeld describes some strategies of resistance in which the workers utilize against management the very gendered and racialized logic that management uses against them. However, while these tactics may provide some temporary relief on the job, they build on racial and gender stereotypes which, in the long run, can be and are used against Third-World women.

Daughters, Wives, and Mothers: Migrant Women Workers in Britain

> Family businesses have been able to access minority women's labor power through mediations of kinship and an appeal to ideologies which emphasize the role of women in the home as wives and mothers and as keepers of family honor.[22]

In a collection of essays exploring the working lives of black and minority women inside and outside the home, Sallie Westwood and Parminder Bhachu focus on the benefits afforded the British capitalist state by the racial and gendered aspects of migrant women's labor. They point to the fact that what has been called the "ethnic economy" (the way migrants draw on resources to survive in situations where the combined effects of a hostile, racist environment and economic decline serve to oppress them) is also fundamentally a gendered economy. Statistics indicate that Afro-Caribbean and non-Muslim Asian women have a higher full-time labor participation rate than white women in the U.K. Thus, while the perception that black women (defined, in this case, as women of Afro-Caribbean, Asian, and African origin) are mostly concentrated in part-time jobs is untrue, the *forms* and *patterns* of their work lives within the context of homework and family firms, businesses where the entire family is involved in earning a living, either inside or outside the home bears examination. Work by British feminist scholars (Phizacklea 1983, Westwood 1984, 1988, Josephides 1988, and others) suggests that familial ideologies of domesticity and heterosexual marriage cement the economic and social exploitation of black women's labor within family firms. Repressive patriarchal ideologies, which fix the woman's role in the family are grounded in inherited systems of inequality and oppression in Black women's cultures of origin. And these very ideologies are reproduced and consolidated in order to provide the glue for profit-making in the context of the racialized British capitalist state.

For instance, Annie Phizacklea's work on Bangladeshi homeworkers in the clothing industry in the English West Midlands illuminates the extent to which family and community ties, maintained by women, are crucial in allowing this domestic subcontracting in the clothing industry to undercut the competition in terms of wages and long work-days and its cost to women workers. In addition, Sallie Westwood's work on Gujarati women factory workers in the East Midlands hosiery industry suggests that the power and creativity of the shop-floor culture—which draws on cultural norms of femininity, masculinity and domesticity, while simultaneously generating resistance and solidarity among the Indian and white women workers—is, in fact, anchored in Gujarati cultural inheritances. Discussing the contradictions in the lives of Gujarati women within the home and the perception that male family members have of their work as an extension of their family roles (not as a path to financial independence), Westwood elaborates on the continuities between the ideologies of domesticity within the household, which are the result of (often repressive) indigenous cultural values and practices, and the culture of the shopfloor. Celebrating each other as daughers, wives, and mothers is one form of generating solidarity on the shopfloor—but it is also a powerful refeminization strategy, in Hossfeld's terms.

Finally, family businesses, which depend on the cultural and ideological resources and loyalties within the family to transform ethnic "minority" women into workers committed to common familial goals, are also anchored in women's roles as daughters, wives, mothers, and keepers of family honor (Josephides 1988, Bhachu 1998). Women's work in family business is unpaid and produces dependencies that are similar to those of homeworkers whose labor, although paid, is invisible. Both are predicated on ideologies of domesticity and womanhood which infuse the spheres of production and reproduction. In discussing Cypriot women in family firms, Sasha Josephides cites the use of familial ideologies of "honor" and the construction of a "safe" environment outside the public sphere as the bases for a definition of femininity and womanhood (the perfect corollary to a paternal, protective definition of masculinity) that allows Cypriot women to see themselves as workers for their family, rather than as workers for themselves. All conflict around the question of work is thus accomodated within the context of the family. This is an important instance of the privatization of work, and of the redefinition of the identity of women workers in family firms as doing work that is a "natural extension" of their familial duties (not unlike the lacemakers). It is their identity as mothers, wives, and family members that stands in for their identity as workers. Parminder Bhachu's work with Punjabi Sikhs also illustrates this fact. Citing the growth of small-scale entrepreneurship among South Asians as a relatively new trend in the British economy, Bhachu states that women workers in family businesses often end up losing autonomy and reenter more traditional forms of patriarchal dominance where men control all or most of the economic resources within the family: "By giving up work, these women not only lose an independent source of income, and a large network of often female colleagues, but they also find themselves sucked back into the kinship system which emphasizes patrilaterality."[23] Women thus lose a "direct relationship with the productive process," thus raising the issue of the invisibility (even to themselves) of their identity as workers.

This analysis of migrant women's work in Britain illustrates the parallel trajectory of their exploitation as workers within a different metropolitan context than the U.S. To summarize, all these case studies indicate ways in which ideologies of domesticity, femininity, and race form the basis of the construction of the notion of "women's work" for Third-World women in the contemporary economy. In the case of the lacemakers, this is done through the definition of homework as leisure time activity and of the workers themselves as housewives. As discussed earlier, indigenous hierarchies of gender and caste/class make this definition possible. In the case of the electronics workers, women's work is defined as unskilled, tedious, and supplementary activity for mothers and homemakers. It is a specifically American ideology of individual success, as well as local histories of race and ethnicity that constitute this definition. We can thus contrast the *invisibility* of the lacemakers as workers to the *temporary* nature of the work of Third-World women in the Silicon Valley. In the case of migrant women workers in family firms in Britain, work becomes an extension of familial roles and loyalties, and draws upon cultural and ethnic/racial ideologies of womanhood, domesticity, and entrepreneurship to consolidate patriarchal dependencies. In all these cases, ideas of *flexibility*, *temporality*, *invisibility*, and *domesticity* in the naturalization of categories of work are crucial in the construction of Third-World women as an appropriate and cheap labor force. All of the above ideas rest on stereotypes about gender, race, and poverty, which, in turn, characterize Third-World women as workers in the contemporary global arena.

Eileen Boris and Cynthia Daniels claim that "homework belongs to the decentralization of production that seems to be a central strategy of some sectors and firms for coping with the international restructuring of production, consumption, and capital accumulation."[24] Homework assumes a significant role in the contemporary capitalist global economy. The discussion of homework performed by Third-World women in the three geographical spaces discussed above—India, U.S.A., and Britain—suggests something specific about capitalist strategies of recolonization at this historical juncture. Homework emerged at the same time as factory work in the early nineteenth century in the U.S., and, as a system, it has always reinforced the conjoining of capitalism and patriarchy. Analyzing the homeworker as a wage laborer (rather than an entrepreneur who controls both her labor and the market for it) dependent on the employer for work which is carried out usually in the "home" or domestic premises, makes it possible to understand the *systematic* invisibility of this form of work. What allows this work to be so fundamentally exploitative as to be invisible as a form of work are ideologies of domesticity, dependency, and (hetero)sexuality, which designate women—in this case, Third-World women—as primarily housewives/mothers and men as economic supporters/breadwinners. Homework capitalizes on the equation of home, family, and patriarchial and racial/cultural ideologies of femininity/masculinity with work. This is work done at home, in the midst of doing housework, childcare, and other tasks related to "homemaking," often work that never ceases. Characterizations of "housewives," "mothers," and "homemakers" make it impossible to see homeworkers as workers earning regular wages and entitled to the rights of workers. Thus, not just their *production*, but homeworkers' *exploitation* as workers, can, in fact, also remain invisible, contained within domestic, patriarchal relations in the family. This is a form of work that often falls outside accounts of wage labor, as well as accounts of household dynamics.[25]

Family firms in Britain represent a similar ideological pattern, within a different class dynamic. Black women imagine themselves as entrepreneurs (rather than as wage laborers) working for the prosperity of their families in a racist society. However, the work they do is still seen as an extension of their familial roles and often creates economic and social dependencies. This does not mean that women in family firms never attain a sense of autonomy, but that, as a system, the operation of family business exploits Third-World women's labor by drawing on and reinforcing indigenous hierarchies in the search for upward mobility in the (racist) British capitalist economy. What makes this form of work in the contemporary global capitalist arena so profoundly exploitative is that its invisibility (both to the market, and sometimes to the workers themselves) is premised on deeply ingrained sexist and racist relationships within and outside heterosexual kinship systems. This is also the reason why changing the gendered relationships that anchor homework, and organizing homeworkers becomes such a challenge for feminists.

The analysis of factory work and family business in Britain and of homework in all three geographical locations raises the question of whether homework and factory work would be defined in these particular ways if the workers were single women. In this case, the construct of the *worker* is dependant on gender ideologies. In fact, the idea of work or labor as necessary for the psychic, material, and spiritual survival and development of women workers is absent. Instead, it is the identity of women as housewives, wives, and mothers (identities also defined outside the parameters of work) that is assumed to provide the basis for women's survival and growth. These Third-World women are defined out of the labor/capital process as if work in their case isn't necessary for economic, social, psychic autonomy, independence, and self-determination—a nonalienated relation to work is a conceptual and practical impossibility in this situation.

Common Interests/Different Needs: Collective Struggles of Poor Women Workers

Thus far, this essay has charted the ideological commonalities of the exploitation of (mostly) poor Third-World women workers by global capitalist economic processes in different geographical locations. The analysis of the continuities between factory work and homework in objectifying and domesticating Third-World women workers such that their very identity as *workers* is secondary to familial roles and identities, and predicated on patriarchal and racial/ethnic hierarchies anchored in local/indigenous *and* transnational processes of exploitation exposes the profound challenges posed in organizing women workers on the basis of common interests. Clearly, these women are not merely victims of colonizing, exploitative processes—the analysis of the case studies indicates different levels of consciousness of their own exploitation, different modes of resistance, and different understandings of the contradictions they face, and of their own agency as workers. While the essay thus far lays the groundwork for conceptualizing the common interests of women workers based on an understanding of shared location and needs, the analysis foregrounds processes of *repression* rather than forms of *opposition*. How have poor Third-World women organized as workers? How do we conceptualize the question of "common interests" based in a "common context of struggle," such that women are agents who make choices and decisions that lead to the transformation of consciousness and of their daily lives as workers?

As discussed earlier, with the current domination in the global arena of the arbitary interests of the market and of transnational capital, older signposts and definitions of capital/labor or of "the worker" or even of "class struggle" are no longer totally accurate or viable conceptual or organizational categories. It is, in fact, the predicament of poor working women and their experiences of survival and resistance in the creation of new organizational forms to earn a living and improve their daily lives that offers new possibilities for struggle and action.[26] In this instance, then, the experiences of Third-World women workers are relevant for understanding and transforming the work experiences and daily lives of poor women everywhere. The rest of this essay explores these questions by suggesting a working definition of the question of the common interests of Third-World women workers in the contemporary global capitalist economy, drawing on the work of feminist political theorist Anna G. Jonasdottir.

Jonasdottir explores the concept of women's interests in participatory democratic political theory. She emphasizes both the formal and the content aspects of a theory of social and political interests that refers to "different layers of social existence: agency and the needs/desires that give strength and meaning to agency."[27] Adjudicating between political analysts who theorize common interests in formal terms (i.e., the claim to actively "be among," to choose to participate in defining the terms of one's own existence, or acquiring the conditions for choice), and those who reject the concept of interests in favor of the concept of (subjective) individualized, and group-based "needs and desires," (the consequences of choice), Jonasdottir formulates a concept of the common interests of women that emphasizes the former, but is a combination of both perspectives. She argues that the formal aspect of interest (an active "being among") is crucial: "Understood historically, and seen as emerging from people's lived experiences, interests about basic processes of social life are divided systematically between groups of people in so far as their living conditions are systematically different. Thus, historically and socially defined, interests can be characterized as 'objective.'"[28] In other words, there are systematic material and historical bases for claiming Third-World women workers have common interests. However, Jonasdottir suggests that the second aspect of theorizing interest, the satisfaction of needs and desires (she distinguishes between agency and the result of agency) remains a open question. Thus, the *content* of needs and desires from the point of view of interest remains open for subjective interpretation. According to Jonasdottir, feminists can acknowledge and fight on the basis of the (objective) common interests of women in terms of active representation and choices to participate in a democratic polity, while at the same time not reducing women's common interests (based on subjective needs and desires) to this formal "being among" aspect of the question of interest. This theorization allows us to acknowledge common interests and potential agency on the basis of systematic aspects of social location and experience, while keeping open what I see as the deeper, more fundamental question of understanding and organizing around the needs, desires, and choices (the question of critical, transformative consciousness) in order to transform the material and ideological conditions of daily life. The latter has a pedagogical and transformative dimension which the former does not.

How does this theorization relate to conceptualizations of the common interests of Third-World women workers? Jonasdottir's distinction between agency and the result of agency is a very useful one in this instance. The challenges for feminists in this arena are a) understanding Third-World women workers as having objective interests in common as workers (they are thus agents and make choices as workers); and b) recognizing the contradictions and dislocations in women's own consciousness of themselves as workers, and thus of their needs and desires—which sometimes militate *against* organizing on the basis of their common interests (the results of agency). Thus, work has to be done here in analyzing the links between the social location and the historical and current experiences of domination of Third-World women workers on the one hand, and in theorizing and enacting the common *social identity* of Third-World women workers on the other. Reviewing the forms of collective struggle of poor, Third-World women workers in relation to the above theorization of common interests provides a map of where we are in this project.

In the case of women workers in the free-trade zones in a number of countries, trade unions have been the most visible forum for expressing the needs and demands of poor women. The sexism of trade unions, however, has led women to recognize the need for alternative, more democratic organizational structures, and to form women's unions (as in Korea, China, Italy, and Malaysia)[29] or to turn to community groups, church committees, or feminist organizations. In the U.S., Third-World immigrant women in electronics factories have often been hostile to unions which they recognize as clearly modeled in the image of the white, male, working-class American worker. Thus, church involvement in immigrant women workers struggles has been a important form of collective struggle in the U.S.[30]

Women workers have developed innovative strategies of struggle in women's unions. For instance, in 1989, the Korean Women Workers Association staged an occupation of the factory in Masan. They moved into the factory and lived there, cooked meals, guarded the machines and premises, and effectively stopped production.[31] In this form of occupation of the work premises, the processes of daily life become constitutive of resistance (also evident in the welfare rights struggles in the U.S.A.) and opposition is anchored in the systematic realities of the lives of poor women. It expresses not only their common interests as workers, but acknowledges their social circumstance as *women* for whom the artificial separation of work and home has little meaning. This "occupation" is a strategy of collective resistance that draws attention to poor women worker's *building community* as a form of survival.

Kumudhini Rosa makes a similar argument in her analysis of the "habits of resistance" of women workers in Free Trade Zones (FTZ) in Sri Lanka, Malaysia, and the Philippines.[32] The fact that women live and work together in these FTZs is crucial in analyzing the ways in which they build community life, share resources and dreams, provide mutual support and aid on the assembly line and in the street, and develop individual and collective habits of resistance. Rosa claims that these forms of resistance and mutual aid are anchored in a "culture of subversion" in which women living in patriarchal, authoritarian households where they are required to be obedient and disciplined, acquire practice in "concealed forms of rebelling" (86). Thus, women workers engage in "spontaneous" strikes in Sri Lanka, "wildcat" strikes in Malaysia, and "sympathy" strikes in the Philippines. They also support each other by systematically lowering the production target, or helping slow workers to meet the production targets on assembly lines. Rosa's analysis illustrates recognition of the common interests of women workers at a formal "being among" level. While women are conscious of the contradictions of their daily lives as women and as workers, and enact their resistance, they have not organized actively to identify their collective needs and to transform the conditions of their daily lives.

While the earlier section on the ideological construction of work in terms of gender and racial/ethnic hierarchies discussed homework as one of the most acute forms of exploitation of poor Third-World women, it is also the area in which some of the most creative and transformative collective organizing has occurred. The two most visibly successful organizational efforts in this arena are the Working Women's Forum (WWF) and SEWA (Self Employed Women's Association) in India, both registered as independent trade unions, and focusing on incorporating homeworkers, as well as petty traders, hawkers, and laborers in the informal economy into their membership.[33]

There has also been a long history of organizing homeworkers in Britain. Discussing the experience of the West Yorkshire Homeworking Group in the late 1980s, Jane Tate states that "a homework campaign has to work at a number of levels, in which the personal interconnects with the political, the family situation with work, lobbying Parliament with small local meetings.... In practical terms, the homeworking campaigns have adopted a way of organising that reflects the practice of many women's groups, as well as being influenced by the theory and practice of community work. It aims to bring out the strength of women, more often in small groups with a less formal structure and organisation than in a body such as a union."[34] Issues of race, ethnicity, and class are central in this effort since most of the homeworkers are of Asian or Third-World origin. Tate identifies a number of simultaneous strategies used by the West Yorkshire Group to organize homeworkers: pinpointing and making visible the "real" employer (or the real enemy), rather than directing organizational efforts only against local subsidaries; consumer education and pressure, which links the buying of goods to homeworker struggles; fighting for a code of work practice for suppliers by forming alliances between trade unions, women's, and consumer groups; linking campaigns to the development of alternative trade organizations (for instance, SEWA); fighting for visibility in international bodies like the ILO; and, finally, developing transnational links between local grass-roots homeworker organizations—thus, sharing resources, strategies, and working toward empowerment. The common interests of homeworkers are acknowledged in terms of their daily lives as workers and as women—there is no artificial separation of the "worker" and the "homemaker" or the "housewife" in this context. While the West Yorkshire Homeworking Group has achieved some measure of success in organizing homeworkers, and there is a commitment to literacy, consciousness-raising, and empowerment of workers, this is still a feminist group that organizes women workers (rather than the impetus for organization emerging from the workers themselves—women workers organizing). It is in this regard that SEWA and WWF emerge as important models for poor women workers organizations.

Swasti Mitter discusses the success of SEWA and WWF in terms of: a) their representing the potential for organizing powerful women workers' organizations (the membership of WWF is 85,000 and that of SEWA is 46,000 workers) when effective strategies are used; and b) making these "hidden" workers visible as *workers* to national and international policy makers. Both WWF and SEWA address the demands of poor women workers, and both include a development plan for women which includes leadership training, child care, women's banks, and producer's cooperatives which offer alternative trading opportunities. Renana Jhabvala, SEWA's secretary, explains that, while SEWA was born in 1972 in the Indian labor movement and drew inspiration from the women's movement, it always saw itself as a part of the cooperative movement, as well. Thus, struggling for poor women workers' rights always went hand-in-hand with strategies to develop alternative economic systems. Jhabvala states, "SEWA accepts the co-operative principles and sees itself as part of the co-operative movement attempting to extend these principles to the poorest women. . . . SEWA sees the need to bring poor women into workers' co-operatives. The co-operative structure has to be revitalised if they are to become truely workers' organisations, and thereby mobilise the strength of the co-operative movement in the task of organising and strengthening poor women."[35] This emphasis on the extension of cooperative (or democratic) principles to poor women, the focus on political and legal literacy, education for critical and collective consciousness, and developing strategies for collective (and sometimes militant) struggle *and* for economic, social, and psychic development makes SEWA's project a deeply feminist, democratic, and transformative one. Self-employed women are some of the most disenfranchised in Indian society—they are vulnerable economically, in caste terms, physically, sexually, and in terms of their health, and, of course, they are socially and politically invisible. Thus, they are also one of the most difficult constituencies to organize. The simultaneous focus on collective struggle for equal rights and justice (struggle against) coupled with economic development on the basis of cooperative, democratic principles of sharing, education, self-reliance, and autonomy (struggle for) is what is responsible for SEWA's success at organizing poor, home-based, women workers. Jhabvala summarizes this when she says, "The combination of trade union and co-operative power makes it possible not only to defend members but to present an ideological alternative. Poor women's co-operatives are a new phenomenon. SEWA has a vision of the co-operative as a form of society which will bring about more equal relationships and lead to a new type of society."[36]

SEWA appears to come closest to articulating the common interests and needs of Third-World women workers in the terms that Jonasdottir elaborates. SEWA organizes on the basis of the objective interests of poor women workers—both the trade union and cooperative development aspect of the organizational strategies illustrate this. The status of poor women workers as workers and as citizens entitled to rights and justice is primary. But SEWA also approaches the deeper level of the articulation of needs and desires based on recognition of subjective, collective interests. As discussed earlier, it is this level of the recognition and articulation of common interest that is the challenge for women workers globally. While the common interests of women workers as *workers* have been variously articulated in the forms of struggles and organization reviewed above, the transition to identifying common needs and desires (the *content* aspect of interest) of Third-World women workers, which leads potentially to the construction of the *identity* of Third-World women workers, is what remains a challenge—a challenge that perhaps SEWA comes closest to identifying and addressing.

I have argued that the particular location of Third-World women workers at this moment in the development of global capitalism provides a vantage point from which to a) make particular practices of domination and recolonization visible and transparent, thus illuminating the minute and global processes of capitalist recolonization of women workers, and b) understand the commonalities of experiences, histories, and identity as the basis for solidarity and in organizing Third-World women workers transnationally. My claim, here, is that the definition of the social identity of women as workers is not only class-based, but, in fact, in this case, must be grounded in understandings of race, gender, and caste histories and experiences of work. In effect, I suggest that homework is one of the most significant, and repressive forms of "women's work" in contemporary global capitalism. In pointing to the ideology of the "Third-World woman worker" created in the context of a global division of labor, I am articulating differences located in specific histories of inequality, i.e., histories of gender and caste/class in the Narsapur context, and histories of gender, race, and liberal individualism in the Silicon Valley and in Britain.

However, my argument does not suggest that these are *discrete* and *separate* histories. In focusing on women's work as a particular form of Third-World women's exploitation in the contemporary economy, I also want to foreground a particular history that third- and first-world women seem to have in common: the logic and operation of capital in the contemporary global arena. I maintain that the interests of contemporary transnational capital and the strategies employed enable it to draw upon indigenous social hierarchies and to construct, reproduce, and maintain ideologies of masculinity/femininity, technological superiority, appropriate development, skilled/unskilled labor, etc. Here I have argued this in terms of the category of "women's work," which I have shown to be grounded in an ideology of the Third-World women worker. Thus, analysis of the location of Third-World women in the new international division of labor must draw upon the histories of colonialism and race, class and capitalism, gender and patriarchy, and sexual and familial figurations. The analysis of the ideological definition and redefinition of women's work thus indicates a political basis for common struggles and it is this particular forging of the political unity of Third-World women workers that I would like to endorse. This is in opposition to ahistorical notions of the common experience, exploitation, or strength of Third-World women or between third- and first-world women, which serve to naturalize normative Western feminist categories of self and other. If Third-World women are to be seen as the *subjects of theory and of struggle*, we must pay attention to the specificities of their/our common *and* different histories.

In summary, this essay highlights the following analytic and political issues pertaining to Third-World women workers in the global arena: 1) it writes a particular group of women workers into history and into the operation of contemporary capitalist hegemony; 2) it charts the links and potential for solidarity between women workers across the borders of nation-states, based on demystifying the ideology of the masculinized worker; 3) it exposes a domesticated definition of Third-World women's work to be in actuality a strategy of global capitalist recolonization; 4) it suggests that women have common interests as workers, not just in transforming their work lives and environments, but in redefining home spaces so that homework is recognized as work to earn a living rather than as leisure of supplemental activity; 5) it foregrounds the need for feminist liberatory knowledge as the basis of feminist organizing and collective struggles for economic and political justice; 6) it provides a working definition of the common interests of Third-World women workers based on theorizing the common social identity of Third-World women as women/workers; and finally, 7) it reviews the habits of resistance, forms of collective struggle, and strategies of organizing of poor, Third-World women workers. Irma is right when she says that "the only way to get a little measure of power over your own life is to do it collectively, with the support of other people who share your needs." The question of defining common interests and needs such that the identity of Third-World women workers forms a potentially revolutionary basis for struggles against capitalist recolonization, and for feminist self-determination and autonomy, is a complex one. However, as maquiladora worker Veronica Vasquez and the women in SEWA demonstrate, women are already waging such struggles. The end of the twentieth century may be characterized by the exacerbation of the sexual politics of global capitalist domination and exploitation, but it is also suggestive of the dawning of a renewed politics of hope and solidarity.

2

"A Great Way to Fly": Nationalism, the State, and the Varieties of Third-World Feminism

Geraldine Heng

Third-World feminism, by virtue of its vexed historical origins and complicated negotiations with contemporary state apparatuses, is necessarily a chimerical, hydra-headed creature, surviving in a plethora of lives and guises. In some countries, it may manifest itself as an organized national movement, complete with networks and regional chapters. In other countries, it may exist only as a kind of hit-and-run guerilla feminism: a feminism, perhaps, that arises spontaneously around issue-centered activity, that organizes itself in small, temporary neighborhood groupings which may eschew or refuse the name of feminism; or a feminism which piggybacks on that ubiquitous institution of the Third World, the nongovernmental organization (NGO). Third-World feminisms do not have the luxury of predictability; and a feminist theory that would be global in its compass, as in its intentions, must expect to be surprised by the strategies, appearance, and forms of feminism that emerge and are effective in Third-World contexts. As Third-World feminists themselves realize only too well, the difficulty of discussing Third-World feminism arises in the first instance as a difficulty of identifying the concretions and forms of effectivity in the Third World that can be grasped as feminist.

Whatever the particular shape of the local manifestations, however, all Third-World feminisms contend, in differing equations, with three principal factors that condition their emergence and survival. First, Third-World feminism is haunted by its historical origins, which continue to overshadow its character and future prospects. Historically, almost without exception, feminism has arisen in the Third World in tandem with nationalist movements—whether in the form of anticolonial/anti-imperialist struggles, national modernization and reform movements, or religious-nationalist/cultural-nationalist revivalisms. Feminism has coexisted with these movements in a complicated relationship of sympathy and support, mutual use and mutual cooperation, and unacknowledged contestatory tension. As Kumari Jayawardena's (1986) groundbreaking study of early feminisms in the Middle East, South, Southeast, and East Asia repeatedly attests, feminist movements in the Third World have almost always grown out of the same historical soil, and at a similar historical moment, as nationalism. However, because the contestatory nature of the relationship between feminism and nationalism remains underemphasized in scholarship on the subject, both at the historical origin of feminism and nationalism and today, the subtext of many an academic study on women and Third-World anti-imperialist struggle, national reform, or national liberation movements is also inadvertently the record of a triumphant nationalism that makes its gains and wins its accomplishments at the expense of a subordinated feminism.[1]

It is a truism that nationalist movements have historically supported women's issues as part of a process of social inclusion, in order to yoke the mass energy of as many community groups as possible to the nationalist cause (Anderson 1983). I would emphasize, however, that nationalist movements make common cause with women's issues and feminism equally because nationalism requires a certain self-representational vocabulary—a definitional apparatus to imagine and describe itself, to constitute itself ideologically, and to win an essential symbolic momentum. Throughout global history, with few exceptions, women, the feminine, and figures of gender, have traditionally anchored the nationalist imaginary—that undisclosed ideological matrix of nationalist culture. For example, at some point of their historical emergence, nations and nationalisms inevitably posit and naturalize a strategic set of relationships linking land, language, history, and people to produce a crucial nexus of pivotal terms—"motherland," "mother tongue," historical or traditional "mother culture," "founding fathers," etc.—that will hold together the affective conditions, the emotive core, of nationalist ideology and pull a collection of disparate peoples into a self-identified nation.[2] Women's issues do not only offer nationalist movements a vital social platform for the collective mobilization of multiple community groups. Female emancipation—a powerful political symbol describing at once a separation from the past, the aspirations of an activist present, and the utopia of an imagined national future—supplies a mechanism of self-description and self-projection of incalculably more than pragmatic value in the self-fashioning of nations and nationalisms.[3]

The manipulation of women's issues as an ideological and political resource in Third-World nationalist history commonly develops, in contemporary contexts, into the manipulation of women themselves as a socioeconomic resource in Third-World nation-states. While early Third-World feminism negotiated relations of mutual use and mutual contestation with early nationalism, contemporary Third-World feminism is forced to enter into and negotiate a more troubled, complex, and sometimes dangerous oppositional relationship to the contemporary Third-World state. The second factor, then, that impinges upon the character of feminism in the Third World is the presence, intervention, and role of the state itself. In contemporary Southeast Asia, the state, at its most benign, is a fiscal beneficiary of the exploitation of women, and, at its least benign, an active agent structuring the exploitation itself.

In Thailand and the Philippines, for instance, the state's GNP is bolstered substantially by prostitution, a growth industry that fuels the tourist trade, and sustains foreign exchange income. Thai NGOs estimate a growth figure of two million prostitutes by the year 2000, of which (with the intensifying fear of AIDS and the concomitant increased demand for virgins and children) as many as 800,000 would be children under fifteen years of age (Tan 1991). This spectacularly cynical form of female/child exploitation has perhaps been the most extensively studied of feminist issues: the critical nexus of state policy, foreign capital, banks, and the hotel-construction industry, that supports and encourages Thai prostitution, for example, has been cogently documented (Truong 1990). By contrast, the exportation of Filipino, Thai, Indonesian, Sri Lankan, and other female domestic workers to East Asian, Middle Eastern, and First-World destinations is only beginning to be studied. Yet, the Philippines exports 60,000 female domestic workers to Hong Kong alone, and reaps HK $1 billion annually from remittances these workers send back ("Filipino Senator Calls for Ban"); in Singapore, there were 65,000 foreign domestic workers in 1992 (Heyzer and Wee 1992). Host countries, like the countries of origin of the domestic workers, also profit from the expropriation of female domestic labor that is commonly left outside the purview of protective employment legislation. Singapore, for example, extracts a maid "levy" from the employers of domestic workers (since April 1991, S$300 per worker), a sum that is often greater than the wages the workers themselves earn. The Singapore government reaps S$234 million annually from the maid levy (Heyzer and Wee 1992), and a massive S$1.3 billion in 1992 from all foreign-worker levies ("Govt. Replies to MPs"). Malaysia expected to garner M$80 million from levies on foreign workers in 1992 ("Govt. Likely to Collect $48m"). More invisibly, but just as exploitatively, state-owned or state-affiliated airline industries throughout Southeast Asia (and South and East Asian countries) routinely sell the sexualized images and personal charm and services of their female flight attendants, in the highly competitive and highly profitable commercial air-travel market, through aggressive global marketing and media advertising, for the profit of the national coffers.

The forceful divergence of feminist and national interests in the Third World is further complicated by the looming and often interventionist role of the state as a regulatory, juridical, administrative, or military force in Third-World countries. Because governments in contemporary Southeast Asia exercise considerable control over public institutions and organizations within state boundaries, for instance, feminism often adapts by refusing to constitute feminist activity along formal lines. To evade state control, legislative interference, or other governmental regulatory activity, feminism in Southeast Asia has sometimes assumed the character of informal collectivities and local groups, existing humbly but usefully as small-scale feminisms.

A third factor mediating the adaptations and strategies of feminism in the Third World is the ambivalence of Third-World nations—and Third-World nationalism—to the advent of modernity. Perhaps because nationalism is itself of modern provenance or because the nation is a modern construct whose ideological bases must be continually renewed and secured, an attendant anxiety over modernity, particularly in the sociocultural register, is endemic in Third-World contexts. Even where a systemic transformation to modernity, in economic and social organization, is sought and implemented by nations and nationalisms in the Third World as a desideratum of development, a resistance to the totalizing implications of modernization is invariably sedimented at some juncture of the modernization process. Acceptance of modernity's incursions, then, comes to operate selectively: a division in the rhetoric of nationalist discourse appears, distinguishing between the technological and economic machinery of modernization (which can continue to be deemed useful, indeed, essential to the nation), and the cultural apparatus of modernization—the alarming detritus of modernity's social effects—which may be guarded against as contaminating, dangerous, and undesirable.[4] Correlatively, in countries where modernization or reform follows the nation's emergence from Western colonial subjection, or where a resurgent religious traditionalism is the dominant mode of nationalist culture, nationalist antipathy to modernity's social impact may be expressed as antipathy to the West and to Western cultural modalities. The ease with which, historically, the "modern" and the "Western" have been conflated and offered as synonymous, interchangeable counters in both nationalist and Orientalist discourse has meant that a nationalist accusation of modern and/or foreign—that is to say, Western—provenance or influence, when directed at a social movement, has been sufficient for the movement's delegitimization.

Given feminism's uneasy status in the Third World, its problematic relations with nationalism, and (like nationalism) its relatively brief genealogy, Third-World feminism has been especially liable to manipulation by nationalists for its symbolizing potential, as a capsule instance of the encroachment of modernity and/or Westernization. Just as women's issues, female emancipation, and feminism lend themselves to nationalist self-figuration at a given historical moment of nationalist formation, so do they lend themselves to the symptomatic figuration of nationalism's ambivalence to both modernity and the West. Antifeminist nationalists in Egypt and elsewhere in the Middle East, for instance, have historically represented feminism as the subversive figure, at once of a destabilizing modernity and of a presumptuous Western imperialism (Philipp 1978). Indeed, nationalism is so powerful a force in the Third World that to counter the charge of antinationalism—the assertion that feminism is of foreign origin and influence, and therefore implicitly or expressly antinational—the strategic response of a Third-World feminism under threat must be, and has sometimes been, to assume the nationalist mantle itself: seeking legitimation and ideological support in local cultural history, by finding feminist or protofeminist myths, laws, customs, characters, narratives, and origins in the national or communal past or in strategic interpretations of religious history or law. That is to say, through the glass of First-World feminisms, Third-World feminisms may appear to be willfully naïve, nativist, or essentialist in their ideological stakes: the requirement of an unexceptionable genealogy, history, or tradition for feminism must assume decisive priority.

In the section that follows, I track the vicissitudes and adaptations of feminism in one Southeast Asian country, focusing with particular, though not exclusive, emphasis on the postcolonial nation-state of Singapore.

A common denominator in the linked national histories of Singapore, Malaysia, and Indonesia is the appearance of feminism in dramatic concert with nationalism in anticolonial independence movements. Feminist women leaders arose who were also prominent nationalist political organizers; political parties on the left and the right articulated feminist goals in the anti-imperialist struggle, with the twin aims of mobilizing mass support and attaching to themselves a powerfully symbolic instrument of ideological self-description; women's groups were institutionalized that had formal affiliations to, or close informal ties with, national political parties; and, finally, all three countries witnessed the absorption of feminist leaders and feminist issues into political structures that dispersed and disengaged feminist interests in the postcolonial period.

In contrast to the history of feminism in Indonesia,[5] where the first institutional women's movements began as independent partners of nationalist organizations to which they were not initially subordinated, feminism in Singapore and Malaysia arose as a subset of nationalist politics, so that the hierarchical relationship of feminism to nationalism—an asymmetry of tension and use—was plainly visible from the outset. The two principal factions contesting for national political power in the wake of British colonial administration in Singapore—a Communist faction, later grouped as the

Barisan Socialist, and social democrats organized as the People's Action Party, or PAP (which subsequently formed the postcolonial government that rules Singapore today)—both harnessed feminist issues to their national platforms. The first created a Singapore Women's Federation as a front organization for revolutionary activity, and the second sponsored a Women's League and women's subcommittees in 1956 under the direction of central PAP party leadership.[6]

By their own recorded account, the People's Action Party saw women's issues and feminist-activist women as a resource to be mined. A former Cabinet Minister notes in passing that "the Communists had recognized the potential of exploiting [the] injustice [suffered by women]" before the PAP had, "and were first in the field to organise women into their fold" (Ong 1979).[7] Significantly, the theme of female emancipation enabled the essentially reform-minded PAP, whose leadership was dominated by English-educated male elites, to present itself in powerfully revolutionary terms, the ideological resonance of which echoed and approximated the revolutionary discourse of their competitors, the Chinese-educated and China-backed Communists, whose own impetus and direction issued from the revolutionary politics of the People's Republic of China. In a section of the party's 1959 manifesto, *The Tasks Ahead: PAP's Five-Year Plan 1959–1964*, which originally appeared as a pre-election campaign speech by the most prominent woman feminist leader in the party, Chan Choy Siong, the theme of female emancipation is presented ringingly, in a reverberative vision of the imagined nation-to-be as a feminist-socialist utopia within a section entitled "Women in the New Singapore"[8]: "In a full socialist society, for which the P.A.P. will work for [*sic*], all people will have equal rights and opportunities, irrespective of sex, race or religion. There is no place in a socialist society for the exploitation of women."[9] The manifesto announces a feminist agenda in the declarative terms of social revolution:

> We will encourage women to take an active part in politics. We will help them organise a unified women's movement to fight for women's rights. We will encourage women to play their proper part in Government administration. We will open up new avenues of employment for women. We will insist that the welfare of widows and orphans must be the responsibility of Government. We will insist that married women be given an opportunity to live a full life, including the right to work on level terms with others. Under the law maternity leave and allowances will be compulsory. The P.A.P. Government will establish more creches to look after children while mothers are at work. We will encourage factories employing large numbers of women to provide creches on factory sites. The present marriage laws which permit polygamy will be

> amended. The P.A.P. believes that a necessary condition for a stable home and family is monogamous marriage . . . it is essential that women and their families should be protected against unscrupulous husbands who treat their wives as chattels and abandon their children and families without any thought for their future. (*The Tasks Ahead*)[10]

PAP and Communist women worked to advance feminist and party goals without distinguishing between these interests, within the overarching frame and under the orders of their institutional organizations. A PAP-authorized history of the party, published in 1979, baldly chronicles the cooptation of women's energies for party purposes in the simple language of use: "The Women's League was active in rallying women members and supporters to campaign for the PAP. . . . They were especially effective in house to house canvassing, cooking food for Party workers, distributing leaflets, and providing speakers at rallies. The women worked as hard as the men and their contribution to the success of the Party was visible to all" (Ong 1979). After the PAP successfully wrested power and constituted a national government, Chan Choy Siong was sidelined in the Party. Unlike her male compatriots and peers, she was never destined to achieve Cabinet rank. In a parliament of eighty-one elected representatives in Singapore in 1993, among seventy-seven PAP Members of Parliament, two are women.[11] Once the PAP assumed national control, Communist women activists—more difficult to track because of their self-protective anonymity and their subsequent dispersal—were either forcibly deported to China and exiled or politically rehabilitated by the new national government; some went underground, slipping away to join the proscribed Malayan Communist Party (MCP), to wage guerilla warfare against the postcolonial governments of Singapore and Malaysia.[12]

In Malaysia, as in Singapore, the first women's political movement, Angkatan Wanita Sedar (AWAS, or the Movement of Conscious Women), would seem to have been created at the instigation of a nationalist political party. In 1945, Parti Kebangsaan Melayu Malaya (the PKMM, or Malay Nationalist Party) founded AWAS, as much because women were needed by the party as "to arouse in Malay women the consciousness of equal rights they have with men, to free them from old bonds of tradition and to socialize them'" (Dancz 1987). AWAS fell victim in the nationalist cause in 1948, proscribed by the British colonial administration.[13] Typically, AWAS's core leadership of politically active women—Malay women politicized by an early radical Islamic education in Indonesia in the 1930s, under Indonesian teachers active in the nationalist struggle against the Dutch colonial administration—were absorbed into women's sections of national political parties or the Communist underground (Dancz 1987; Karim 1983). Aishah Ghani, the first president of AWAS, became a member of the women's division of the United Malay Nationalist Organization (UMNO), the principal political party of the ruling National Front in postcolonial Malaysia, and eventually served as president of UMNO's second women's wing (Wanita UMNO) and Minister of Social Welfare in the Malaysian Cabinet. Sakinah Junid enlisted in the Pan-Malayan Islamic Party (PMIP)—now Parti Islam Se Malaya (PAS)—and later became president of Parti Islam's women's section, Dewan Muslimat; Samsiah Fakeh, the second president of AWAS, "continued her revolutionary struggles underground, working closely with the Malayan Communist Party" (Karim 1983).[14]

In Singapore, in 1961, the postindependence government formed by the People's Action Party passed legislation addressing the legal rights of women and children, in partial fulfillment of campaign pledges to feminist nationalists and female voters. This legislative document, known as the Women's Charter, synchronously enfranchised women and produced, effectually, a legal definition of feminine identity codified around marriage, divorce, and relationship to children, as much as it also ruled in other matters on women's status as individual citizens. The Charter, in effect, legislated a description of female identity by establishing legal responses to a wide-ranging set of presumptive questions (What is a woman? What does she need? What is the nature/what are the conditions of her sexuality? What is her place? What is the place of her relationships to others?). In thus specifying legal conditions pertaining specially to women and children—awarding, in that process, rights that were unquestionably vital, indeed, essential to women at the time—the Charter also enacted and codified a description of women as specially gendered subjects under the law, a sexualized codification directed specially to the state's female citizens.[15] No comparable legislation exists that describes the configuration or borders of masculine identity under the law.

Historically, the enactment of the Women's Charter was simultaneously an enfranchising and a disenfranchising moment for feminists. After the establishment of the Charter, it was widely felt that there were "no more problems" confronting women,[16] because the most urgent and dramatic inequities had been addressed. Men and women alike felt that Singaporean women, unlike women in other Third-World nations, had no need of feminism or a feminist movement, and until the 1980s, women's groups in Singapore assumed the form of recreational, athletic, or cultural clubs, charity or professional associations, and social work and community service organizations—a voluntary or involuntary playing-out, at the community level, of the authorized identities established for women under the law.

The production and legitimation of particular feminine identities—commonly an implicit, more than an explicit, process—is of enduring importance to contemporary Third-World states. A dramatic example is the (re)donning of the *hijab* or veil by Muslim women in the Middle East, signalling the deployment of a traditional feminine identity as a powerfully symbolic icon of Islamic cultural nationalism.[17] In Singapore, in 1983, the very survival of the nation was presented as hinging on the production of appropriate kinds of feminine identity when Prime Minister Lee Kuan Yew raised the specter of a dystopian national future that would unfold if well-educated women willfully continued to refuse to marry and reproduce children in numbers adequate to the maintenance of class and racial elites (Heng and Devan 1992). States also profit from the manipulation of women and feminine identity as an economic resource: the production of a sexualized femininity as a commodity for negotiation and trading in the profitable, if competitive, air-travel-services market in Asia underscores the necessarily oppositional relationship between feminist interests and state-sponsored descriptions of the national interest in the contemporary Third World.[18]

Singapore, in particular, has exploited a sexualized Asian femininity to sell the services of its national air carrier, Singapore Airlines (SIA), with incomparably spectacular commercial success.[19] So globally familiar is the airline's "Singapore Girl"—never a "woman," and certainly no mere "flight attendant," but "a great way to fly," as every male business traveler around the world knows—that Madame Tussaud's of London, when it "wanted to feature a figure from air travel" among its waxworks, "found the Singapore Girl to be the most recognizable air travel figure in the world today" (Lee 1993). That the image of the Singapore woman which the airline and the state sell on the air services market is a sexual one is readily attested to. Singapore law courts recently tried a rash of sexual-molestation cases, where male air passengers of varied descriptions, races, and national origins had apparently found it impossible to resist fondling or otherwise sexually handling stewardesses on SIA flights. Indeed, so successful at evocation is the soft-focus image of the "Singapore Girl" in her figure-hugging, Pierre Balmain-designed *sarong kebaya*, that a bar-cum-brothel in Thailand was reported to have clad its hostesses in copycat imitations of the SIA flight uniform (Tan 1991).[20]

Singapore is not, however, unique among Third-World states in touting and marketing the serviceability of its women and a fantasmatic Asian femininity. A recent multipart feature in the *Asia Magazine* (16–18 August 1991) admiringly reports how Thailand, Malaysia, the Philippines, and Indonesia all exploit, with varying degrees of success, a calculated image of their female citizens to promote national airline industries. Playing to a fantasy of what Asian women are putatively like, the countries describe the romantic sexuality, exoticism, beauty, youth, and charm of their female flight attendants, and the women's innate, instinctual desire to please and serve. The phenomenon of trading in feminine identity is commonplace in Asia; any cursory survey of the advertising of other Asian carriers will disclose the extent to which

Third-World nations in the East casually sell the sexualized images and personal services of their female national subjects on the world market.[21]

That the legitimation of some feminine identities over others can be a matter of considerable national profit and national interest in the Third-World state is clear from this commercial equation. In Singapore, the proven and continuing success of the national carrier's advertising campaigns is propped upon an exploitation of the discourse of Orientalism, a Western discourse which the Eastern state rides in its flawless manipulation of a projected feminine image. In the course of that manipulation, an exemplary collusion is put in place between postcolonial state corporatism (SIA as a government-affiliated national carrier) and neocolonial Orientalist discourse on the serviceability and exoticism of the Asian woman: a collusion that produces, through the *techne* of transnational global advertising and marketing, a commercial enterprise generating substantial fiscal surpluses, and vindicated at the outset as nationalist. For the nationalist credentials of this particular project of antifeminist exploitation are never in doubt. Corporate and marketing executives of Singapore Airlines and the carrier's advertising agency, the Batey Group, when condescending to defend their marketing strategies to Singapore feminists, have instinctively tricked themselves out in nationalist drag.

More recently, the editor of the *Straits Times*, the country's principal English-language daily newspaper, insinuated a suggestion that attempts by Western nations to spread the values of liberal democracy, human rights, and civil liberties to developing nations may be driven, sinisterly, by a covert desire to weaken the economic competitiveness of the Third World. Festooning himself with the impeccable nationalist credentials of state-sponsored sexism, the editor smirked: "Younger Singaporeans should think hard before they lap up whatever is in vogue. . . . Is the Singapore Girl really a sexist symbol that ought to be replaced or would agitation on this issue erode Singapore Airlines' competitive edge? They would do well to remember that competition between nations can only hot up, and that losers will be left by the wayside."The accompanying cartoon illustrating the editor's contentions featured a set of posters on a barbed-wire fence representing the constitutive barrier of a Western checkpoint on the correctness of the political record of developing nations. One of the posters demands the presentation of a human-rights record; on another poster is emblazoned "Women's Rights Charter." Surreptitiously, the illustration and the newspaper columnist tap a reservoir of Third-World suspicion at the multifariousness of Western imperialisms, and clearly, feminism and human rights are here offered as imperialisms of the economically corrosive, objectionably vogueish kind.[22]

By contrast, Malaysian feminists note the more explicit and direct depiction of feminism by Islamic nationalists in Malaysia as a pernicious species of cultural infiltration—as a foreign, Western, and modern encroachment that symbolizes the many encroachments that have undermined Malay Muslim culture from the beginning of colonization:

> The massive recruitments of Malaysian women into [the *dakwa* Islamic movement] is perceived . . . to be part of a re-education or resocialization process, whereby women can be rescued from the throes of Westernization that have permeated Malay culture from the beginning of colonialism to the present. . . These community movements are a powerful instrumental force in projecting feminism as a component of Western liberalism which has no niche in Eastern cultures. (Karim 727)

One feminist response to the imputation by Malay Islamic nationalists that feminism is Western, antitraditional, or secular in its origins and nature, has been to cite contemporary feminist Islamic exegetes on the Qu'rän who offer rereadings of that sacred text as authorizing the equality of men and women.[23] Another feminist strategy in Southeast Asia has also been to suggest a local genealogy for feminism, by pointing to notable women figures in communal or national history and folklore. In the Philippines, for instance, there were "pre-Spanish priestesses or *katalonans* . . . heroines of the Spanish revolution, the women leaders of the Japanese occupation" (Shahani 1975); in Vietnam, there were the feminist Ho Xuan Huong and folkloric resistance fighters like the Trung sisters and Trieu Thi Trinh, or Doan Thi Diem, and Bui Thi Xuan[24] (Marr 1976); Singapore had the community-founding matriarch Yang Meleking (Wee 1987); and "the traditionally high status of women" in the Southeast Asian region's past, particularly before colonization, is frequently cited. (Shahani 1975).[25]

However partial or interstitial such efforts, the fundamentally oppositional relations between the interests of the state and those of feminism in the contemporary Third World makes dangerous the total abandonment of nationalist discourse, of any variety, to the exclusive monopoly of the state. In Singapore, the state's successful combination of nationalist discourse—in particular, the discourse of national survival and of approved forms of political participation—together with a formidable array of instrumentalities and apparatuses of power at the state's disposal, has determined the very nature and horizon of possibility for feminist activism.

In May 1987, twenty-two persons were arrested by the Singapore government under the powers granted by the Internal Security Act, as part of a putative "Marxist conspiracy" ostensibly threatening the state and national interests. Among the political prisoners were two founder-members of the Association of Women for Action and Research (AWARE), a vigorous feminist organization then practicing critique and activism on a variety of fronts.

A number of other founder-members were convinced that they had themselves either narrowly escaped detention, or were yet vulnerable to arbitrary seizure. The government immediately disseminated propaganda justifying the arrests and proceeded to ban or dismantle community activist groups it identified as Marxist- or left-oriented. Shocked, perhaps, into a sense of immediate vulnerabililty, or possibly convinced of a threat to its legitimacy and survival, AWARE was silent on the arrests, took no stand on the political prisoners, and issued no statements on its imprisoned founder-members. The two women, with the other prisoners, were detained without trial and subjected to physical and psychological abuse. One of them was subsequently rehabilitated, and released after a public confession and renunciation of politics; the other eventually fled to self-exile in the United Kingdom.[26]

The arrest of its founder-members proved to be a watershed in the self-defined role and activism of AWARE. Created in December 1985 by a group of feminist women whose political opinions ranged from ideological left to liberal center, AWARE, unlike other women's groups in Singapore, had a reputation for being confrontational and critical, its politics "vociferous." In recent years, however, AWARE's public profile has quietly altered, and the organization has come to emphasize community and welfare services to women, rather than critique. Its current commitments include a scheme for loans to women "to prevent women from falling into the hands of loan sharks" (Chau 1992), and a telephone "Helpline" that women can call for advice and counseling on a range of problems, including "marital difficulties," "issues such as male-female relationships," "family sexuality, mental health problems, violence against women, work-related issues and medical matters" (AWARE round-up 1993, 39). In 1992, its executive director was quoted as saying that "the association's main emphasis now is research" ("Winning by Persuasion" 1993), and AWARE's president in 1992–93 was quoted in a women's fashion magazine as saying that she preferred the term "woman centredness" to describe her commitment, rather than the term "feminism," because "feminism is a lonely cause. You are always met with disagreement and disfavour."[27]

Whatever the organization's self-definition today, the work that AWARE undertakes is excellent feminist work in the context of Singapore society. Many of the organization's projects are identifiably if quietly feminist: its Helpline is a version of a battered-women's emergency hotline; it organizes reading and discussion sessions for children on gender roles, workshops for women on a variety of subjects, support groups, free legal consultation sessions, and a reading circle and film nights to discuss women's issues. AWARE's research projects and publications target women in the workplace and childcare facilities, information-gathering on women and health, child education and gender socialization issues, and the generation of feminist literary and discursive materials. In reporting on the organization's current projects, AWARE's mailings to members disclose that the organization works for social change by appealing to, negotiating with, and petitioning various government bodies invisibly, behind the scenes.

That is to say: AWARE's varied activities share the common factor of emphasizing service, information, and support, while avoiding analysis and engagement of a directly and stringently political kind. In particular, the organization avoids engagement with subjects that would be deemed sensitive or suspect by the Singapore government. These would include all issues of race, class, ethnicity, and sexual preference; the identification of structural and systemic, rather than contingent, inequities in society; the analysis of state apparatuses of power in the lives of Singapore women; and, indeed, government policies and positions on controversial issues of national importance, including a national population policy thinly premised on a form of social eugenics (Heng and Devan 1992). In the voiding of controversy, then, AWARE in effect requires itself to practice a form of feminism that is ironically evacuated of political content. It is a feminism, moreover, that must of necessity disengage itself from all recognition of difference, all social fronts, beyond the single focal point of gender; a feminism that must look past race, class, ethnicity, and sexuality; ignore the operations of ideology, of transnational collusions, and of technologies and instrumentalities of power; and blind itself to the controlling and manipulative force of state institutions; a feminism that must, in short, bracket off and put aside the varied discursivities, categories of difference, and totalizing institutions that crisscross and intersect with gender in the real world.

Indeed, Article 23 (e) of the constitution of AWARE, in compliance with legislation governing the formation and activities of societies in Singapore, explicitly prohibits the organization from involvement in the political: "The Society shall not indulge in any political activity or allow its funds and/or premises to be used for political purposes."[28] Implicit in this formulation is the understanding that what constitutes "political activity," and what defines a purpose as "political," will, in the context of Singapore—given the history of the Singapore government's use of its powers for political detention—be decided upon contingently, from moment to moment, by the state as it sees fit.[29]

Despite the carefully noncritical face of feminism in Singapore, however, the PAP moved to establish a Women's Wing within its own party in 1989, ostensibly in order to "help raise public awareness about women's issues"—some fourteen years after the PAP's Women's Affairs Bureau had become defunct. The move, in effect, added the Party's presence to the extant women's groups in Singapore, a presence through which the Party apparently hoped to wrest the initiative and ground—as well as public attention—on women's issues. Sensing a potential risk in the divergence of feminist interests from state interests, even in the light of the peaceable activities among women's groups in Singapore, the government moved to co-opt organizational energies nationally, by constituting, as before, a feminist group of sorts under its own party banner.[30] Unlike the fiery manifesto of 1959, however, the PAP's public statement on the Wing details, in no uncertain terms, the subordination of the Wing's semifeminist interests to the party and party-defined national interests. "The Wing," the Party declared, rather than constituting "a women's lobby group" or "pressure group," would instead "help Singaporean women become better informed about national issues." Chief among its charges would be the duty of "familiarizing members with the PAP philosophy, the role of women in politics, the national budget, health and other issues" ("PAP's Women's Wing" 1992). The year after its inception, the Wing was assigned by the PAP leadership "the task of looking into a proposal to set up a family services centre to coordinate welfare programmes for the needy" ("Women's Wing to Study" 1990); in 1993, Prime Minister Goh Chok Tong, responding to a suggestion that a Women's Affairs Bureau be reestablished in the Party, remarked that such a bureau, if formed, "should not confine itself to tackling 'women's problems.' Instead, it would have to address family and social problems as well" ("Worrying Trends" 1993). The Party today continues to assign a ragbag of duties and tasks to its Women's Wing, most of which, true to the received notions established by the Women's Charter, of what constitutes women's concerns and issues, concentrates on the provision of service to others, notably children, families, and the poor.

In June 1993, two books commissioned by the Women's Wing, addressing the status of women in Singapore, were publicly launched. The texts, one academic and the other popular, offer the most feminist of the Wing's articulated positions on women in Singapore, and perhaps express the extent of what might be hoped for from a government-authorized, state-managed, and party-directed "women's movement" in the Third World. A newspaper article, reporting on the books' contents, mistily notes: "Realities of gender differences are implicitly acknowledged, there is pride in past achievements, hope in looking ahead and a gentle prodding for more attention to be paid to the inequalities and challenges that remain" ("Story of the Singapore Woman" 1993). For all the misty hopefulness palpable in the equating of "inequalities" with "challenges," however, the launching of the books was used, with brutal irony, as an occasion for the current Prime Minister of Singapore to reiterate the accusations directed against women by his predecessor ten years before. Highly educated women, Prime Minister Goh noted pointedly, were still not reproducing babies at a rate adequate to the maintenance of class elites. This, he implied, was a women's issue of the utmost urgency.[31] Without any apparent consciousness of insult or irony, or even condescension, the Prime Minister went on to close the issue of gender inequalities in Singapore: "While some differences remained in the way men and women were treated, such as in the country's immigration laws, these were products of the largely patriarchal society here and would have to be accepted, he said" ("Worrying Trends" 1993).[32]

The PAP's attempt to coopt feminism to subserve the party's political purposes, state legislation prohibiting registered organizations from activity that might be construed as "political," even the arrest of individual feminists under the Internal Security Act in Singapore—all these events inscribe relatively dulcet moments in the history and fortunes of Third-World feminism. Saskia Wieringa, charting the history of the Indonesian left-feminist organization Gerakan Wanita Indonesia (or GERWANI), a movement whose membership in 1965 comprised 1.5 millon people, records the starkest possible fate for institutional feminism in the Third World when she details the organization's destruction by the Indonesian military government, and the torture, brutalization, and demonization of GERWANI women. Indeed, the array of hazards confronting feminism in the Third World is instructive. Because of the vast instrumentalities that range from preventive or punitive legislation to military or police intervention—and because an institutionalized feminist movement draws attention to itself and appears to the state to possess a capacity, incipient or actual, for the exertion of pressure on national political culture—successful forms of feminism in the Third World have sometimes been informal, unobtrusive, small-scale feminisms.[33] Feminist scholars observe that some of the most effective feminist groups in Southeast Asia—effective in the constituencies of women they reach, their commitment to critical and transformative work, and their empowerment of women at the grassroots level—are often not even registered organizations as such (Heyzer 1986). Many are simply "small groups of women, made up frequently of trusted friends," though these groups may be "more or less aware of one another" and may "exist within networks" (128). Organizing women in poor communities, rural villages, plantations, or city squatter areas in Malaysia, the Philippines, and Thailand, these feminists work with local women in order ultimately to "phase themselves out of . . . leadership positions as the local women become more confident" (128). In a different locality of the Third World, Peruvian feminists have concluded that, as Saskia Wieringa notes, "it is not necessary to join in a large-scale movement . . . you can work in a much more fruitful way in small autonomous groups" (Wieringa 1988).

The relative safety or success of small-scale feminist activism in the Third World should not, however, be overemphasized. In Singapore, from 1982 to 1987, guerilla feminisms of precisely this nature existed: informal collectivities of women supported and aided domestic workers abused by employers, offered legal services in working-class districts to prostitutes and disenfranchised others, conducted social analysis and critique through community theater and drama, met to discuss, educate, critique and transform on a variety of fronts. In many ways, the organization which became AWARE was forged in that critical matrix of repeated, issue-specific, local interventions. Nevertheless, this feminist network of small groups was inexorably dismantled when the Singapore government banned a number of community networks in 1987, in the name of an alleged plot against the state.

No variety of feminism in the Third World, then, is secure from the intervention of the state, nor from the power of any who are able to wield the discourse of nationalism with unchallenged authority. The history of feminism in Singapore, as elsewhere, has been instructive. Rights historically granted to women by patriarchal authority in order to accomplish nationalist goals and agendas do not necessarily constitute acts of feminism, though as practices of power, the granting of such rights may function, both initially and today, to the very real advantage of women. In contrast, rights seized upon and practices initiated by women in the pursuit of their imagined collective interest, even if—like the work of AWARE and others—such practices and acts seem only uncomfortably or unfamiliarly to fit received descriptions of feminism, are indisputably feminist practices. For in Third-World states, ultimately, all feminisms are at risk; all must write their own scripts and plot their continuing survival from moment to moment. It is a profound tribute to feminist resourcefulness and tenacity that varieties of feminism continue to survive and proliferate in the multiple localities of the Third World today.[34]

3

Sheroes and Villains: Conceptualizing Colonial and Contemporary Violence Against Women in Africa[1]

Amina Mama

Violence against women has been a central concern of the international women's movement over the last two decades. In many countries, violent abuse has been taken up as the most salient and immediate manifestation of women's oppression by men, and in Africa, in particular, widespread violence against women is now probably the most direct and unequivocal manifestation of women's oppressed status. In most societies, rape and domestic violence have on occasion provoked public outrage, but it has been left to women's organizations and movements to take more concerted action. Both the different manifestations of violence that can be considered as gendered and the diverse character of antiviolence praxis can be illustrated with examples from different areas of the developing world. For instance, the most dynamic campaigns in the Caribbean were initially provoked by the common occurrence of rape, the trivialization of which had led feminists to establish the first rape-crisis centers and, thereafter, to initiate campaigns and highly innovative cultural actions. On the Indian subcontinent, sati and dowry deaths have been responded to at least as vehemently as rape, and it has been rape by government officials that has most provoked the wrath of feminists. African women's campaigns, for their part, have been less movement-based, with individuals and welfare and health groups campaigning against genital mutilation, child marriages, and other indigenous practices.[2] Even so, Africans have been surprisingly reticent on wife-beating and sexual harassment, despite their prevalence and the negative effects of both on personal and public life. The widespread harassment and intimidation of women by power-crazed police and the overzealous implementation of antiwomen decrees and edicts by military forces also needs our serious attention.

A few incidents will illustrate both the severity of the situation and the range of forms that woman abuse takes:

- Piah Njoki was blinded in 1983 when her Kenyan husband, aided by two other men, gouged out both her eyes for bearing him daughters and not sons. In court, Mrs. Njoki implored the judge not to send her husband to prison, since she would then be left alone to fend for herself and her daughters in her state of blindness.
- On July 13, 1991, a group of male students attacked the girls' dormitories at St. Kizito secondary school in Kenya, raping seventy-one and killing nineteen.
- In 1987, twelve-year-old Hauwa Abubakar, from Nigeria, died after having both legs amputated. Her husband had attacked her with an axe after she had repeatedly run away from him.
- In 1983, several thousand women were detained by the Zimbabwean authorities, and many of them subjected to beating and other forms of abuse during "Operation Clean Up."

These examples raise a number of important questions about the social and cultural milieux in which abuse occurs, about the social and economic factors which oblige many women to tolerate life-threatening situations, and about the kind of political climate which empowers officials to perpetrate mass abuses against women on the streets of many African cities. All such situations have a history to them, and much of this essay is devoted to excavating this past, to tracing the genealogy of the conditions which foster violence against women, one of the most unpalatable facts of postcolonial life. It is my view that the prevalence of so many pernicious forms of gendered violence demands both historical and contemporary analysis. By deepening our understanding of violence against women during the epoch of imperialism, we will be better able to comprehend and so to counteract the multiple forms of violence meted out against women in postcolonial African states today. Imperialism is the major trope of this analysis because it is the common historical force that makes it possible to consider an area as large and diverse as the African continent as having general features that transcend the boundaries of nation, culture, and geography. This collective African experience—being conquered by the colonizing powers; being culturally and materially subjected to a nineteenth-century European racial hierarchy and its gender politics; being indoctrinated into all-male European administrative systems, and the insidious paternalism of the new religious and educational systems; and facing the continuous flow of material and human resources from Africa to Europe—has persistently affected all aspects of social, cultural, political, and economic life in postcolonial African states.

The conditions of women's lives in Europe and Africa are also linked, since these two regions have been inextricably bound together in a dynamic of growing inequality since the dawn of colonialism. Imperialism, therefore, provides an important lens for studying the dynamics that have led to the present conditions, not to simplify or impose homogeneity on the diversities within either region but to lay out a foundation which may direct our investigation of the specificities of particular contexts.

I begin by examining the historical evidence which indicates that colonial penetration was both a violent and a gendered process, which exploited preexisting social divisions within African culture. Paying particular attention to gender, I argue that the colonial period saw an increased vulnerability of African women to various forms of violence. Since the relationship between Europe and Africa entailed Africa's subjection by Europe, it may be worthwhile to take a look at gender relations and gender violence at the imperial source before addressing the genesis and perpetuation of gender violence in colonial and postcolonial Africa.

The final part of this essay examines the forms of resistance that women have spearheaded, indicating the strategies deployed by women in different parts of the African continent and comparing these to other Third-World and Western feminist antiviolence struggles.

The Colonial Period

Patriarchy at the Imperial Source

When imperialism is traced back to its roots in European history, the violent and male-dominated character of the civilization that set out to "civilize" the African continent emerges quite clearly. The history of gender violence in Europe raises many questions about European masculinity and about the gender ideologies that lay behind the emergence of today's European states. The misogynistic character of that nascent political culture can perhaps be most dramatically illustrated with reference to the witch-hunts and inquisitions of the Middle Ages. It is now common knowledge that over a four-hundred-year period (from the fourteenth to the seventeenth century), several million women were systematically dismembered, disfigured, and tortured before being drowned or burned alive (Chesler 1972, Mies 1986). Mies also cites the example of a lawyer in Leipzig, Germany, who personally sentenced 20,000 women to death in the course of his highly successful career.

More recently, during the last century, the lot of European women was so miserable that in 1853 a certain Mr. Fitzroy put it to the English House of Commons that the nation should treat married women "no worse than domestic animals" (Dobash and Dobash 1980). With the Industrial Revolution and the development of capitalist social relations, the European working classes, particularly women and children, were exploited in evil ways that would subsequently be perfected on African slaves and forced laborers in the colonies. Literature and public records indicate that physical violence characterized relations between men and women as well as between ruling and oppressed classes and between adults and children. Women from the oppressed classes were sexually as well as economically exploited and many of those who moved to the cities found themselves choosing between the brothel and the poorhouse. A great many were rounded up and deported in shiploads to the New World colonies where an even tougher existence awaited those who survived the passage. It is ironic that the Europeans, who came from such a patriarchal civilization, nevertheless had the audacity to pose as heroic protectors and uplifters of women when they arrived in the colonies (Mies 1986).

At the dawn of imperialism, Europe was also giving shape to and developing its racist ideologies and practices. As far back as the sixteenth century, Queen Elizabeth, the "Virgin Queen" who stood for purity, virtue, and whiteness, made several attempts to have black people removed from the kingdom; her 1601 proclamation called for the banishment of "blackamoores." In later centuries, the pedestalization of upper-class white womanhood was counterpoised to an inferiorized construction of blackness. Black people were cast as hypersexual, corrupt, and pathogenic. Black women attracted sexual fascination, and by the nineteenth century, had come to feature in the white male psyche as a metaphor for Africa, the dark and unknown continent, waiting to be penetrated, conquered, and despoiled. In the case of Saartjie Baartman, who, as "The Hottentot Venus," was displayed, catalogued, and had her genitals dissected, this dehumanization was rationalized, first, as harmless "entertainment," then, under the guise of "scientific interest."[3]

The oppression of women within Europe had a direct bearing on the treatment of women in the colonies. McClintock (1991b) argues that Britain's notorious Contagious Diseases Acts of 1864, 1866, and 1869, scapegoated women at a time when several key military defeats inflicted on the imperial armies had provoked a crisis in European masculinity. "Corrupt" women were blamed for weakening the troops, so attempts were made to regulate prostitution, both in Britain and in the colonies.[4] It hardly needs to be pointed out that legislation of this sort primarily affected women from the lower social strata, not upper- and middle-class women.

In eighteenth- and nineteenth-century Europe, class, race, and sexual inequalities acted in concert with one another, generating a repressive imperial ideology that was to be reflected in all aspects of colonial, legal, and administrative treatment of the subject peoples. This was to have particular implications for gender relations, rendering African women more vulnerable to the violence emanating from both European and African sources.

Race and Sex in the Colonies

The development of legislative controls over relations between European men and African women indicates the contradictory sexuality of imperial masculinity, straddled as it was on the twin horns of the dilemma that resulted from simultaneous desire and contempt. It also indexes the steady degradation of African women's ascribed status under colonial regimes. In the early period, trading and other relations between European men and Africans followed the initial contact between their respective civilizations. The nineteenth-century institution of "signareship" and the significant numbers of interracial cohabitations and marriages found along the West Coast of Africa point to the existence of a great many relationships between French merchants and African women, although the racial politics of these liaisons have not been the subject of much discussion.[5]

The British appear to have had a more puritanical attitude toward interracial unions. This is reflected in the 1909 "concubinage circular," which imposed penalties on British men for having sex with African women. In 1914, Lord Lugard, the governor general of Nigeria, tactlessly issued "Secret Circular B," which equated miscegenation with bestiality.[6] Marriage to African women was made taboo in other parts of Africa, too. In 1905, the Germans, confronted with the so-called "bastard problem" in the territory that was to become Namibia, forbade marriage to African women, while, at the same time, encouraging prostitution and concubinage. In 1907, they declared marriages contracted before that date to be null and void, and in 1908, retroactivated this principle to dispossess all the offspring of such unions in order to exclude them from the possibility of claiming their German father's citizenship or inheriting property and land in the Fatherland (Mies 1986).

On the other hand, it was not uncommon for the colonizers to organize prostitution services for their troops, so that their desires for local women could be satiated in ways which did not undermine the racial status-quo (Enloe 1989), with some even going so far as to reserve certain women "for white men only."

It would seem from this discussion that the legal status of African women was steadily degraded as imperialism advanced, consolidating patriarchal and racist gender values which commodified African women by encouraging prostitution but outlawing the contract of legitimate marriages between white men and black women. We shall see that these trends were continued by colonial states which cast all African women in urban areas as "prostitutes" and subjected them to periodic waves of victimization and harassment, while, at the same time, creating conditions that made the numerous services provided by women indispensable to the colonized male workforce.

The Colonial State and Violence toward Women

Rape appears to have been a frequent accompaniment to military conquests, and was a favored means of ensuring the defeat and pacification of entire nations. Unfortunately, the historical record has been very scant on this subject. Even so, the limited evidence that is available suggests that sexual violence was an integral part of colonization.

Fanon (1980) notes the link between conquest of land and peoples and the violation of women, a link which has subsequently been identified as characterizing colonial literature of the Rider Haggard genre (Stott 1989). According to both, the colonized woman becomes associated in the mind of the European with fantasies of rape and despoliation. Such fantasies are fueled by the inaccessibility of local women (in Muslim areas), but more widely function as a metaphor for conquest of African lands and the humiliation of peoples.

The harsh reality of conquest in Africa included widespread violation and degradation of African women. Where there was resistance, rape and sexual abuse were inflicted on women and the same treatment was meted out to the wives, mothers, daughters, and sisters of men who were suspected of being members of the resistance movements simply to humiliate them.

The use of violent techniques in various European attempts to crush the nationalist movements in many parts of Africa also demonstrates the inadequacy of "gender-only" analysis. To simplify the nature of colonization and the violence that it deployed as just another instance of "male violence" is to obscure the full character of imperialism and the internal contradictions it has so successfully exploited.

In many parts of the continent, colonial regimes intent on the forcible introduction of waged- and migrant-labor systems, sought to restrict the movement of African women, who were expected to remain in the rural areas and continue to engage in subsistence production, while their menfolk were lured to the mines and towns. Nonetheless, women also migrated to the towns to earn money by providing support services; other women abandoned homesteads that were then in decline. Still others, as women have done throughout the ages, moved away to escape violent marriages or quite simply migrated in search of new ways of living. Whatever the case, women moved to the towns in large numbers and, as they were excluded from wage-work in the formal sector, found innovative ways of living on the margins of colonial society and its economy.[7]

Lacking any clear policy or any real knowledge, the colonial state demonstrated confused and contradictory attitudes toward African women. For example, Schmidt (1991) notes that in colonial Zimbabwe, official attitudes toward African women were even worse than those toward men, apparently because while men were "remarkably receptive of European ideas," women tended to "cling to old superstitions, the old customs and the old methods." She further notes that African women were said to wield immense power over men, and that women's sexual demands were identified as obstructing the recruitment of men to work for the colonizers. Certainly, the presence of women in the colonial towns was viewed with immense suspicion. Measures taken to remove women from the urban areas included periodic round-ups and forcible deportations, often carried out with the connivance of elderly African men, who felt frustrated by what they saw as a loss of control over their homesteads. For example, in 1915, the British colonial officers attempted to restrict the number of "free women" in the Nigerian city of Katsina, proposing that those within the city walls be given seven days to marry, while those defined as prostitutes be driven away. Similarly, in Kenya, during the 1940s, local councils passed such oddly named measures as the "Lost Women Ordinance," which sought to limit the movement of women to the towns.

Women, for their part, waged intermittent struggles against the losses of power that they experienced. To cite only two examples out of a great many that occurred across the continent, in Eastern Nigeria, women rose up periodically throughout the 1920s to resist the introduction of a range of measures which they saw as undermining their rights (Van Allen 1972, Amadiume 1987). The colonial state responded to the Women's War with military action, killing at least fifty women. In Western Nigeria, women organized against colonially appointed chiefs and ousted some of the rulers who became too autocratic (Mba 1982).

So far, this discussion has mainly addressed the violent treatment meted out to African women by a colonial state which excluded women from all political and administrative structures and from the wage economy that was rapidly superseding precolonial modes of production. But it is also worth noting that overt violence, including widespread abuse of women and the reinforcement of the interests of male despots by the colonial regime, was not the whole picture. There was also the seemingly "benevolent" side of colonial patriarchy, a side which sought to "domesticate" and, so, to incorporate a small but significant number of African women. There is now a substantial literature addressing the ways in which the colonizers introduced a bourgeois Victorian ideology of domesticity into Africa. While the vast majority of African women gained no access to education at all, a minority was invited to acquire the graces of "civilized" femininity, namely, to be schooled in embroidery, cake decoration, and flower arranging. The purpose was to turn these women into suitable wives for those African men who performed administrative roles in the colonial state. Much of this indoctrination was undertaken by well-intentioned European women anthropologists, missionaries, and teachers, who set out for the African interior to educate and "uplift" the natives.[8] Hunt (1990) documents the activities of Le Foyer Sociale, a social institution specifically designed by the Belgians to create a small cadre of elite Congolese housewives. These colonially constructed "new women" were to stay at home and keep house for the small numbers of African men in the employ of the colonial regime.[9] Like other class ideologies, domesticity has affected even those who were not part of the elite that actually became European-style housewives. The dominance of the wife-and-mother ideal, an ideal which negated women's social and economic contribution, facilitated the devaluation of their work within the colonial economy.

In addition to perpetrating crude and overt acts of violence against African women, then, the colonization process also transformed African gender relations in complex, diverse, and contradictory ways that we have yet to fully understand. We now know that these transformations, and the dynamic between the colonial regime and the colonized society, varied across social classes. They must also have varied in part according to the character of gender relations in the preexisting social and political systems, and the cultural, political, and economic powers that women had been able to mobilize in defense of their gender. Prevailing gender ideologies have much bearing on the types of violence that are manifested in a given context. The confinement of women to the economically dependent role of housewife is a condition that has made it difficult for many women to leave otherwise unbearably violent situations. In other words, the domestication of women is a precondition for the crime we define as domestic violence. Similarly, the power to coerce, intimidate, and harass that is wielded by officials and men in uniform in dictatorial societies is a condition for the widespread rape and abuse of women that occur under repressive regimes, since this power is sanctioned by military, religious, or other male-dominated authorities.

African Nationalist Movements and the Gender Question

If, as we have seen, colonialism brutalized, degraded, and domesticated African women, to what extent have the nationalist movements challenged the misogynistic and sexually contradictory legacies of the white masters? Have African women experienced greater liberation since the demise of colonial regimes, or have the nationalists merely continued the trajectories of contempt and disempowerment? What has been the role of women in anti-imperialist struggles, and how has this affected their position in post-colonial states?

Anne McClintock usefully reminds us of the gendered and continuously contested character of nations when she writes:

> All nationalisms are gendered, all are invented, and all are dangerous.... They represent relations to political power and to the

> technologies of violence ... legitimizing, or limiting, people's access to the rights and resources of the nation-state (McClintock 1991a).

The foregoing discussion of rape and conquest indicates that colonialism also humiliated women, not only as colonial subjects but also in gender-specific ways. African nationalist discourses have often proclaimed the need to recover the damaged manhood of the African man. Cynthia Enloe (1989) points to the masculinity of many nationalist discourses and the exploitation of male humiliation by liberation movements; she identifies this as a source of male bias in emergent nations. But to what extent have African men been concerned with restoring the dignity of African women? It is now amply documented that women, who were completely excluded from the colonial administrative and political structures, actively participated in the nationalist movements as fighters and party activists. And on many occasions, they took independent action in defense of their own interests as women.

Still, today, women protest the betrayal of women's interests by the nation-states, citing Algeria and Zimbabwe as instances in which men have reneged on their promise to share the fruits of independence. But is there an empirical basis for this sense of betrayal? An examination of gender relations within nationalist discourses may deepen our understanding of the sources of present-day inequalities and enable more effective responses than angry polemics against the men who have monopolized power for themselves. What, then, were the terms on which women participated in these resistance struggles? Perhaps the poor status of the vast majority of women in postcolonial African countries can be traced to the terms of this participation!

The constructions of women in nationalist ideologies have been contradictory. On the one hand, nationalists have called for their own "new woman," while on the other hand, they have construed women as the bearers and upholders of traditions and customs, as reservoirs of culture.[10] In a great many contexts, the terms on which women participated in nationalist struggles have simply not been commensurate with fundamental changes in gender relations. The appearance of harem women on the streets of Egypt during the 1920s to protest against the British may have been welcomed by all supporters of national liberation, but it did not transform male attitudes towards women. Some time later, when the Wafdist Party disagreed with women on key political issues, Huda Sharaawi and other women broke away to form the Egyptian Feminist Union, which not only took more radical positions on a number of key political issues but also defended women's interests (Sharaawi 1986, Badran 1988).

National liberation movements such as the Nkrumah-led CPP, although radical when it came to establishing hegemony over traditional chiefs, cannot be described as propounding a radical gender politics, even though the movement derived enormous support from women's organizations. For all his revolutionary vision, Kwame Nkrumah was unable to view women beyond their reproductive and nurturing roles. He referred to women as: "Mothers of the nation, the beauty that graced the homes and the gentleness that soothed men's tempers" (Tsikata 1989). Many of the nationalists who inherited power from the colonial masters were overtly conservative when it came to matters of sexual politics. Jomo Kenyatta, for example, perhaps wishing to appear nationalistic in the face of missionary activity, asserted that "No Kikuyu worthy of the name would want to marry a girl who [had] not been excised, as this operation [was] a prerequisite for receiving a complete moral and religious education" (Kenyatta 1953).[11] Similar examples can be found in the writings of Sekou Touré, Julius Nyerere, and many other founding fathers of African nationalism. In 1955, Oliver Tambo made what must have been one of the most radical statements of his generation when he not only declared women's emancipation to be a national priority and a precondition for victory but also went so far as to deplore "outmoded customs" and call upon Congressmen to share in domestic work so that women could also be politically active. At the other extreme, one of the most retrograde examples was the Nigerian nationalist leader Tafawa Balewa, who opposed women being given the vote in the northern part of the country, despite the enfranchisement of women in the south.[12]

The African countries cited as most progressive on "the woman question" have tended to be those that have involved women in military action, and not coincidentially women across the globe have adopted posters of women carrying guns as icons of revolutionary feminism.[13] Urdang's (1989) study of women's place in the Mozambican war for independence reveals that most of the women fighters actually performed inglorious but necessary tasks (catering, porterage, etc). Others were dispatched to rural areas because as women in a sexually unequal society, they were able to shame men into volunteering. The participation of women in Namibia and in the ongoing liberation war in South Africa has also been studied, but this will require ongoing consideration if majority rule is to include more equal participation of women (not least of all because black women in South Africa have been so oppressed and excluded). It is now clear that even progressive statements from the leadership do not suffice to effect change in the gender relations of a society.

And what happened to women in those places where victory has been secured? Regrettably, the treatment of women in several of the independent states proves that participation in military activity does not necessarily translate into progressive gender politics. As revolutionary a hero as the late

Samora Machel is on record reinforcing the sexual division of labor by calling on Mozambican women, but not men, to clean up the streets of Maputo. Reports from Zimbabwe inform us that many of the women who joined men in the bush to fight the white settler regime found themselves rejected in favor of more traditionally feminine women once the fighting was over. But if the gender relations amongst the fighters were as unequal in the field as Urdang's evidence suggests, what basis was there for assuming gender equality would be a necessary fruit of military victory?[14] Even if things were far more progressive on the field of battle, it is quite clear that it is necessary to wage a continuing struggle to deepen women's liberation, even after national independence has been granted or won by military action.

It seems clear that African women entered the postcolonial period at an immense disadvantage and under global conditions which, while increasingly unfavorable to Africa as a whole, nonetheless favored men, who arrogate to themselves the authority of articulating the nation's culture and politics. This background offers some insight into why postcolonial societies have continued to be so oppressive to women.

Gender Ideologies and Violence in Postcolonial Africa

The gender politics of postcolonial African governments vary widely, but women continue to be underrepresented in positions of influence (Parpart and Staudt 1989). It often seems that those nations that opted for a socialist model of development have been more progressive than those that did not. In the nascent socialist states, strong women's organizations ensured women's participation in political life by waging campaigns for women's rights, and taking it upon themselves to challenge practices such as wife-beating and forced marriages. The existence of official women's organizations did much to raise the profile of women in the newly independent states. As a result, the legal and constitutional situation for women in Tanzania, Angola, Mozambique, or even Zimbabwe is ahead of many Western countries. Economic dependence continues to preclude fuller exercise of legal rights, however, and issues such as land ownership and the implementation of progressive marriage laws leave much to be desired.

On the other hand, states pursuing capitalist models of development show a different structure and practice of gender inequality. Wamalwa (1989) describes how male Kenyan Parliamentarians repeatedly opposed the replacement of old colonial laws and resisted the introduction of a Marriage Bill in 1968 which would have made wife-beating a criminal offense punishable by six months imprisonment; the Kenyan politicians claimed that wife-beating was "a normal customary practice." In West African states like Nigeria, bureaucratic, social, and cultural inequality prevail but, in practice, most women exercise a high degree of autonomy, a situation facilitated by their involvement in independent economic activities. The high public profile of the wives of the military elite gives the impression that at least these women are extremely powerful in contemporary Nigeria, but even a cursory examination of the empirical evidence indicates this to be far from the truth (WIN 1985).

Since the economic crisis gripped the continent in the 1970s, African women have faced some of the harshest living conditions and forms of oppression in the modern world. The decline of many African economies has been accompanied by political crises, and it is in this context that sexual and coercive controls over women have often been exercised with a vengeance, just as they were in the colonial period. This is exemplified by the "clean-up campaigns" that have taken place in a number of countries. The evidence from Zimbabwe (Jacobs and Howard 1987), Gabon, Zambia, Tanzania, and other nations reveals that these campaigns are frequently accompanied by widespread abuse of women. The women rounded up in Gabon in 1985, for example, were made available to soldiers for the latter's sexual pleasure (Tabet 1991).

Postcolonial national ideologies continue to call upon women to play a circumscribed role, this time as Mothers of the Nation. Mobutu's official doctrine involves the mass "promotion" of women to mere wives and mothers, in an economic climate that compels women to engage in all forms of work outside the home, and often to support entire households. In the postcolonial context, Mobutu's ideology of domesticity distorts the real production relations of the whole country by devaluing women's economic contributions, and thus facilitating greater exploitation of both women and men by international capitalism. Recent research conducted in Zimbabwe shows that since the end of the liberation war, the proportion of women gaining access to education has actually fallen, and that this is most pronounced in the field of higher education (Gaidzanwa 1991). In addition to the public victimization of women by postcolonial regimes, there is also a high tolerance of domestic violence. A Zimbabwean women's group informs us that between January and December 1990, in Harare alone, there were 576 reports of rape and 17,646 reports of assault, of which approximately 5,000 were defined as domestic assaults (Taylor and Stewart 1991). There is no reason to assume that Harare is different from any other postcolonial African capital.

There are a great many ways in which official ideologies interact with civil institutions to reinforce the subordination of women, both directly and indirectly. In Nigeria, we have seen a close interaction between the military governments' campaigns and rising religious fundamentalism, both of which target women directly but also promote violence against them. One of the most unpopular regimes mounted a "War Against Indiscipline" campaign, which attributed the country's worsening economic and political crisis to "moral decadence and laxity." Consequently, dispossessed beggars, homeless people, street hawkers, and women were subjected to all manner of harassment. At the time, the media diffused negative images of women, blaming them for widespread immorality and corruption. In this context, in 1986, the military governor of Kano State issued an edict which outlawed single women and which included the ultimatum that women had three months to get married or "be dealt with."[15] A year later, an underground Muslim brotherhood known as "yan daukar amariya" was uncovered when several of its members were arrested for the rape and violent abuse of women.[16] The professed purpose of this fraternity was to molest and violate any woman found on the streets alone, on the basis that those women had no right to be there.

Wamalwa (1989) comments on the underreporting of violence, and draws our attention to the fact that 40 percent of all cases of domestic violence identified by a preliminary survey in Kenya involved the murder or manslaughter of the woman. This suggests an extremely high tolerance for violence. More recently, during the public outcry over the massacre at St. Kizito school, the headmaster was reported to have remarked that the boys "meant no harm, they only wanted to rape." In any case, most of the press coverage focused on the killings rather than on the rapes.[17] As in many other contexts, woman abuse exists "beyond the law" since the existing legal provisions are not enforced by male police, magistrates, or courts. No man has ever been given the full sentence for rape in Kenya.

Reports by human-rights organizations reveal disturbing evidence of women being detained, sexually abused, and tortured by repressive regimes in Sudan, Mauritania, and Somalia.[18] In short, it seems that a tolerance for violence against women has continued to characterize African social and political life since independence; violence itself appears to be proliferating under the harsh and desperate economic and political conditions now prevailing in many parts of the continent. The final part of this essay considers what measures have been taken to curb this disturbing situation, and how these initiatives compare with those taken in other parts of the world.

Anti-Violence Struggles and Strategies

From the evidence presented above, it is clear that the coercive control of women, endemic in the colonial period, has gone unchallenged by postcolonial regimes. The evidence from women's studies in the West indicates that there, too, women are far from equal in most areas of social life. While a great many changes in women's positions and ways of living have occured in Africa as well as in Europe, violence against woman has continued to be widespread in both regions. Given the historical continuities and fractures in the structural relationships between black and white women in Europe and in the African colonies, it would be worthwhile to analyze the role violence plays in configuring these processes.

Feminist Praxis on Violence in the West

In the West, women have mobilized and campaigned both inside and outside state structures, with sometimes impressive results. In several European and North American countries, the laws and legal procedures affecting abused women have been changed. Policing practices have come under particularly heavy criticism (Edwards 1986), and this has led some police forces to introduce special training on how to respond better to domestic violence. Improved access to public housing and the provision of refuges for battered women are other concrete results of a long and committed struggle by women's movements. However, a recent study of responses to violence against black women in London indicated that these strategies have been less effective in ameliorating the situation of black and minority women who have been subjected to violence (Mama 1989b).

Mainstream Western feminist theorizations of violence often do not take into account the realities of black women's lives. This is partly because, in the West, it has been radical feminists who have been at the forefront of the organized campaigns aimed at eradicating male violence against women. Within radical feminist discourse, gender is regarded as the most fundamental social division, and men are viewed as being inherently and irredeemably aggressive. In keeping with this view, radical feminists treat women as if they were a single homogeneous group, devoid of class and racial inequalities, reduced to mere instances of male power. Socialist and liberal feminists have been less vocal in this area of feminist praxis, with the result that these particular radical views have dominated the antiviolence movement.

Feminist responses to violence against women in late-capitalist countries have also presumed a certain type of state structure, namely one that provides welfare support, such as housing, and a law-abiding, if recalcitrant, police force. It has been assumed that most women live in nuclear marriages with breadwinning husbands upon whom they are economically dependent. However, these assumptions do not hold for many black and working-class women. For one thing, public services have failed miserably in their attempts to offer appropriate support to black women, and welfare professionals (mostly from parochial middle-class backgrounds) have often demonstrated their class prejudices. For another, because of racism, black women face additional hardships in obtaining public housing, appropriate police protection, or legal support. On account of the increasingly discriminatory immigration laws many black women constantly confront the risk of being deported when and if they seek assistance, or of being racially harassed when and if they seek police or legal intervention.

Even within the so-called liberal democracies of Western Europe, women are subordinated in diverse ways, a fact which feminist theorists of violence have yet to fully address. But the transfer of European feminist theories and strategies to Africa cannot be easy. Not only are there historical biases which have not been purged, but these theories have also been developed in late-capitalist contexts under a specific set of conditions that are very different from those in African countries. Britain, for example, is a welfare state, and there are complex legal and public policy considerations which are preconditions for even the limited success of the women's movements there. Even within such contexts, black feminists have found it necessary to organize autonomously with a view to articulating a different antiviolence politics—drawing attention to acts of violence against both sexes, acts of aggression perpetrated by the state itself, the deaths of black men in police custody, and police assaults on black women. Also, they have had to highlight the vulnerability of black people to racial attacks on the streets and in housing estates. In short, black feminists in the so-called liberal democracies have concluded that it is inadequate to theorize violence as an inherently male characteristic with only women as victims.

To illustrate further the nontransferability of Western feminist strategies to the developing world, consider what happened when the British strategy of establishing refuges for women was adopted by some Indian women's groups. In the absence of long-term housing options for battered women in the Subcontinent, where there is not the same kind of public housing as in Britain, new problems of homelessness and destitution were created for the women survivors, who, having left their homes, had neither a home to return to nor any other alternative accommodation.

African Antiviolence Struggles

Only in very few countries has the state has been the main vehicle for antiviolence activism. In Uganda, women Parliamentarians have been extremely vocal. Perhaps because the rape and abuse of women had become so widespread during the years of dictatorship and war, after much heated debate, the controversial Immorality Act was passed in 1990.[19] This contains provisions for stringent sentences for rape (life imprisonment) and child rape (death sentence).[20] At the time of this writing, no one has yet been convicted or sentenced under these provisions but, at the local level, rape cases are being reported and dealt with by the local Resistance Councils.[21]

In other African countries, women's projects have been able to secure donor funding to conduct research and produce resource material and information packages for use in antiviolence work. The Tanzanian Women's Media Association in Dar Es Salaam and the Women and Law in Southern Africa research network are just two examples. In Nigeria, despite the huge amount of publicity surrounding the First Lady's "Better Life Programme," including the recent launching of a multimillion-dollar center for women's development, there has been no official action on woman abuse. Rather, it was left to an autonomous and relatively low-profile organization like

Women in Nigeria to hold the first ever workshop on the subject as recently as March 1992.

It also needs to be said, on the basis of the ungathered evidence of millions of women all over the continent, that African women have not been passive recipients of abuse, as some authorities would have us believe. The evidence that is available suggests that they have found numerous ways of resisting the humiliations meted out to them, both individually and with the help of sympathetic friends and relatives. In the same way, African communities daily house and support millions of refugees locally, with none of the hostility that affluent nations now direct toward the few thousand who have been driven as far as Europe. Here, where there is no welfare-delivery system, it must be said that for every abused women who makes the headlines by being killed or maimed, or for each of those who suffer in clubbed-down silence, there must be many thousands who receive local support and who engage in a hidden struggle for their survival and dignity—a continuous struggle that neither receives nor demands acknowledgment.

Conclusion

From the historical record, we saw how, during the colonial period, new gender ideologies were introduced, ideologies regarding women's and men's status across the African continent. Colonial gender ideologies were the product of both internal and external factors, and were fed by cultural and material conditions which interacted in complex ways as we entered the postcolonial epoch. There is clearly a need for more detailed study of these developments in particular locales, even as we forge international links. We need to understand and theorize the diversity within different nations and across the African continent, and the ways in which Europe underdeveloped different parts of Africa differently, common legacies at the level of state structures and circumscribed constructions of womanhood notwithstanding.

This essay has sketched a general framework which highlights the ways in which the European chauvinistic constructions of femininity and a marginalizing ideology of domesticity decreased the legal and social status of African women in many spheres of life, in both rural and urban areas. As I have shown, when we consider the history of woman abuse, we must recognize that there have been pernicious continuites between colonial, nationalist, and postcolonial systems.

I have tried to argue that perhaps because of the pervasiveness and extreme character of woman abuse in the region, African women have had to rely on their own indigenous strategies; some have left violent situations while others embark upon completely different lifestyles, often with the covert support of other women or sympathetic members of their communities. No doubt, many of these heroic responses have been invisible because they have usually been individual reactions to horrendous conditions and have remained unsupported by the communities at large. In recent years, women have begun to resist violence in a more collective manner, both within and outside state structures. Women have deployed different strategies in different countries with varying degrees of success. It is high time that these bold initiatives won more definite support at the local, national, and international levels.

4

Erotic Autonomy as a Politics of Decolonization: An Anatomy of Feminist and State Practice in the Bahamas Tourist Economy

M. Jacqui Alexander

And the Trees Still Stand

We are here
because you beat back the bush
because you raked rocks and stones
because you pitched scalding tar
to make that road
You uprooted lignum vitae trees
to turn that unchartered road
into a journey with landmarks
And because you replanted
those trees of life
we are here[1]

Marion Bethel wrote this tribute to the women of DAWN[2] and in memory of the women of the suffrage movement who severed the colonial connection between property ownership, respectability, and citizenship. She uses this poem to establish a deliberate link with a particular history of women's political struggle in the Bahamas. Foregrounded in Bethel's incantation is a conscious political move on the part of women in the contemporary women's movement in the Bahamas to choose from particular feminist genealogies, particular histories of struggle, especially at a moment when the legacy of British gentility and respectability continues to assert itself and threatens to mold and usurp understandings of the self. According to Bethel, the choice of a legacy is fraught with bush, entangled, and unchartered road; a tumultuous journey out of which a path must be cleared. But she also suggests that the political strategic work of movement-building involves danger, pitching scalding tar, simultaneously deploying tools that might entrap, ensnare, or liberate. These symbols of contradiction and liberation deliberately evoke the ideological dialectic in which the women's movement is now positioned.

The history to which the contemporary women's movement lays claim is one that fundamentally contradicts the imperial legacy of nineteenth century and early twentieth century organizations such as the Queen Mary Needlework Guild, Women's Corona Society, and the Imperial Order of Daughters of Empire, which drew their ideological strength from the British imperial state, the fledging infrastructure of which was established in 1718. These were organizations whose ideologies of "gentility" and femininity gave primacy to service—service to the queen and to the British nation, which, in practice, meant servicing white militarized masculinity as "daughters" during the Second World War. In essence, then, femininity was deployed in the service of, and out of allegiance to, British colonial norms.[3] Women in the suffrage movement and the National Council of Women, however,[4] sought to contradict this imperial legacy of Britain as patriarch by attempting to reconcile the imposed epistemic opposition between woman and citizen that was characteristic of colonial relations of rule. This evolution—from daughter to lady to woman to citizen—epitomized political constestation within and among women's organizations in the Bahamas and emerged as a major point of contestation with the state. Should women be perennial daughters raised as ladies and be always already defined by their relationship to men? Or should woman and citizenship signify a certain autonomy—what the state might regard as "erotic autonomy"—and sexual agency?

Women's sexual agency, our sexual and our erotic autonomy have always been troublesome for the state. They pose a challenge to the ideological anchor of an originary nuclear family, a source of legitimation for the state, which perpetuates the fiction that the family is the cornerstone of society. Erotic autonomy signals danger to the heterosexual family and to the nation. And because loyalty to the nation as citizen is perennially colonized within reproduction and heterosexuality, erotic autonomy brings with it the potential of undoing the nation entirely, a possible charge of irresponsible citizenship or no citizenship at all. Particularly for the neocolonial state it signals danger to respectability—not only to respectable Black middle-class families, but, most significantly, to Black middle-class womanhood, given the putative impulse of this eroticism to corrupt, and to corrupt completely. In this matrix, then, particular figures have come to embody this eroticism and have historically functioned as the major symbols of threat. At this contemporary moment in the neocolonial state's activity in the global diffusion of sexualized defintions of morality, sexual and erotic autonomy have been most frequently cathected unto the body of the prostitute and the lesbian. Formerly conflated in the imaginary of the (white) imperial heteropatriarch, the categories lesbian and prostitute now function together within Black heteropatriarchy as outlaw, operating outside the boundaries of law and, therefore, poised to be disciplined and punished within it.[5]

A great deal of analytic work has been done by feminists in different parts of the world on demystifying the state's will to represent itself as disinterested, neutered, and otherwise benign.[6] We now understand how sex and gender lie, for the state, at the juncture of the disciplining of the body and the control of the population and are, therefore, constitutive of those very practices.[7] Feminists have clarified the patriarchal imperatives at work within the state apparatus, making it possible to examine the ways in which masculinized gestures of normalization exert and deploy force, generate new sexual meanings, displace and reinscribe old ones, and discipline and punish women in disproportionate ways for a range of imputed infractions, not the least of which has to do with being woman. Much less work has been done, however, on elaborating the processes of heterosexualization at work within the state apparatus and charting the ways in which they are constitutively paradoxical: that is, how heterosexuality is at once necessary to the state's ability to constitute and imagine itself, while simultaneously marking a site of its own instability.[8]

In this essay, I want to extend my own earlier analysis of the operation of these processes of heterosexualization within the state.[9] Specifically, I want to combine the twin processes of heterosexualization and patriarchy—what Lynda Hart calls "heteropatriarchy"—in order to analyze the significance of a moment of crisis when state-sponsored violence moved to foreclose desire between women. The passage of the 1991 Sexual Offences and Domestic Violence Act, which criminalized lesbian sex and moved to reestablish primogeniture under the guise of protecting women against domestic violence, signals, for me, the mobilization of an unstable heteropatriarchy, reelaborating and reinventing itself as supreme. But why was it necessary for the state to shore up its inherited power? Why this reinvention of heteropatriarachy? What, to use Lynda Hart's terms, are the productive breaks in the "heteropatriarchal symbolic order" that require the state to clothe itself, as it were?[10] I want to argue here that there are certain functions of heteropatriarchy which supercede the sexual or the marking of sexual difference. At this historical moment, for instance, heteropatriarchy is useful in continuing to perpetuate a colonial inheritance (which is why I use the term neocolonial) and in enabling the political and economic processes of recolonization.

In one sense, then, this essay offers a retheorization of the shape and contours of a neocolonial state premised within heteropatriarchy and a more general sexual politics. While the Black nationalist party (The People's Liberal Party) wrested power from an elite group of white owners in 1972, which was formerly influential in the colonial legislature, it seized ownership of some of the more popular symbols of Black working-class political struggle, like the Burma Road rebellion, and claimed the right of women to vote (initiated in 1962) as its own benevolent achievement.[11] This would mark its first attempt to erase the memory of popular struggle. It narrowed its own vision of popular nationalism, turning the mobilization of women, youth, trade unions, and churches on which it relied for support into a Constitutional Convention, organized in Britain, in which the Queen was retained as head of State. The imperial government retained control over foreign affairs and defense, and the Bahamas lost sovereignty over those portions of Bahamian territory that were negotiated away under the United Bahamian Party (UBP). Part of what this essay will narrativize is the extent to which these early politics of compromise and erasure, the state's desire to neutralize political struggle through its control over the instruments of co-optation and coercion, foreshadow the more contemporary politics of recolonization.

By "recolonization," I mean the attempts by the state, and the global economic interests it represents, to achieve a psychic, sexual, and material usurpation of the self-determination of the Bahamian people. In this regard, heteropatriarchal recolonization operates on at least three levels simultaneously. At the discursive level, it operates through law, which is indispensable in the symbolic and material reproduction and consolidation of heteropatriarchy and in the elaboration of a cathectic structure based primarily in sexual difference. I shall demonstrate the ways in which the law forges a continuity between white imperial heteropatriarchy—the white European heterosexual inheritance—and Black heteropatriarchy. This unity is crucial to the creation of a marginal underground of noncitizens, historically figured around the "common" prostitute and the "sodomite" (killed by Balboa to mark the advent of imperialism), and now extended by the neocolonial state to include lesbians and people who are HIV-infected.[12] To the extent that citizenship is colonized within heterosexuality, the state can produce a group of nonprocreative noncitizens who are objects of state surveillance and control and who are subject to its apparent processes of normalization and naturalization that serve to veil the ruses of power.[13]

Also at the discursive-juridicial level, I establish the continuity with white European inheritance (between the heterosexual and patriarchal) by analyzing accounts of domestic violence. State managers recodified the texts in terms of class-based symbols of the matrimonial home in order to continue the somewhat orderly patrilineal transfer of private property under the most disorderly and injurious circumstances of wife-beating, rape, sexual abuse, and incest. This literal resituation of the law of the father and the privileges of primogeniture through state domestication of violence not only distanced parliamentary partriarchy from domestic patriarchy but also narrowed the defintions of violence which feminists had linked to the organizing episteme of heteropatriarchy itself.[14] From the official story, we know almost nothing about women's experiences of violence in the home. These were ideologically fragmented in the legal text. Women were made culpable for not reporting these acts (perpetrated against themselves and their daughters) and the burden of criminality was shifted onto them, drawing them more tightly into the state mechanisms of surveillance, positioning them simultaneously as victim and policer, all under the ideological gaze of the heteropatriarchal state as protector. And finally, discursive recolonization occurs as well in the legal reinvention of normative, dyadic heterosexuality and in the mythic reelaboration of sexual decadence as the basis for the destruction of the nation of Sodom and Gomorrah, and now, by extension, the Bahamas.

Heteropatriarchal recolonization operates through the consolidation of certain psychic economies and racialized hierarachies, and within various material and ideological processes initiated by the state, both inside and beyond the law. These actions can be understood clearly as border policing, in this instance, the unequal incorporation of the Bahamas into an international political economy on the basis of serviceability (e.g., tourism). Attempts to guard against the contamination of the body politic by legislating heterosexuality are contradictorily bolstered by state gestures that make borders permeable for the entry of multinational capital. Making the nation-state safe for multinational corporations is commensurate with making it safe for heterosexuality, for both can be recodified as natural, even supernatural. Tourism and imperialism—through multinational capital production—are now as integral to the natural order as heterosexuality.

Methodologically, I focus upon tourism because it has been the major economic strategy of modernization for the Bahamian state. It has now been transformed from its tentative beginnings as a leisure activity of a white imperial elite, the domain of a primarily British foreign mercantile class, to a mass-based tourism (particularly in the period following WWII) dominated by North Americans and Canadians but with disproportionate representation from the United States. Currently, approximately two-thirds of the gross national product of the Bahamas is derived from tourism. For our purposes, the significance of tourism lies in its ability to draw together powerful processes of (sexual) commodification and (sexual) citizenship.[15] The state institutionalization of economic viability through heterosexual sex for pleasure links important economic and psychic elements for both the imperial tourist (the invisible subject of colonial law) and for a presumably "servile" population whom the state is bent on renativizing. It would seem that at this unstable moment of heteropatriarchy, socializing citizens into heterosexuality through legal mandate and through service in tourism is more urgent for the state than socializing them into self-determination, one of the major promises of anticolonial nationalism.

Psychic recolonization occurs, then, not only through the attempts to produce a servile population in tourism but also through the state's attempts to repress, or at least to co-opt, a mass-based movement led by feminists. In other words, it seems the law (positioned as order) functions both to veil ruptures within heteropatriarchy and to co-opt mobilization of another kind, that is, the sort of popular feminist political mobilization that made the break visible in the first place. It would be necessary for the state to work, and work hard, to recast the official story, to displace popular memory of the people's struggle with the state's own achievements (in this instance, The Sexual Offences and Domestic Violence Act of 1989). But the fact is that Bahamian feminism, however ambiguously or contradictorily positioned, helped to provoke the political rupture by refusing the state conflation of heterosexuality and citizenship and by implicating the state in a range of violences. In this regard, then, and as a prelude, I would like to locate myself within this narrative.

I write as outsider, neither Bahamian national nor citizen, outside the repressive reach of the Bahamian state, recognizing that the consequences of being disloyal to heterosexuality and, therefore, to the Bahamian state fall differently on my body than on the bodies of those criminalized lesbians in the Bahamas for whom the state has foreclosed (if only temporarily) any public expression of community. Against the state's recent moves at reconsolidating heterosexuality, I write as outlaw in my own country of birth; both states confound lesbian identity with criminality. I write, then, against the "myth of lesbian impunity."[16] However, I am not an outsider to the region, for feminist solidarity crosses state-imposed boundaries. And, unlike the Bahamian state, which almost entirely aligns itself with the United States and foreign multinational-capitalist interests, a regional feminist movement, of which Bahamian women are a part, consciously chooses links with the wider Caribbean region and with diasporic women living elsewhere.

I live in the United States of North America as a noncitizen, an alien, as "immigrant" and "foreigner," and perennial suspect, at a time when the American state is still engaged in reinventing and redrawing its own borders.[17] As a "legal" alien, I am subject to being convicted of crimes variously defined as "lewd, unnatural, lascivious conduct; deviate sexual intercourse; gross indecency; buggery or crimes against nature."[18] I am simultaneously writing against hegemonic discourses produced within metropolitan countries, and even within oppositional lesbian, gay, and bisexual communities that position the Third World as barbaric (in contrast to American civilized democracy), even in the midst of the daily escalation of racist and homophobic violences (which the state itself legitimates), the sexualization of citizenship from both secular and religious fundamentalisms, and the consolidation of heterosexism and white supremacy through new population control policies which link the terms of "foreign aid" (read "imperialism") to the presence of nuclear families.[19] I write out of a desire to contradict prevalent metropolitan impulses that explain the absence of visible lesbian and gay movements (in this instance in the Caribbean) as a defect in political consciousness and maturity, using evidence of publicly organized lesbian and gay movements in the U.S. (as opposed to elsewhere) as evidence of their originary status (in the West) and superior political maturity. These imperial tendencies within oppositional movements (witness the imperialist practices within white gay tourism) have occasioned a marked undertheorization of the imbrication of the imperial and the national, of the colonial within the postmodern.[20] Such theorization might enable a more relational and nuanced understanding of the operation of state processes between neocolonial and advanced-capitalist states around their systematic practices of heterosexualization, for, clearly, both states, although differently positioned, are constantly involved in the reconsolidation of borders and in the repressive deployment of heteropatriarchy in domains other than the sexual.[21]

In what follows, I analyze the state mobilization to reinvent heteropatriarchy within the Sexual Offences and Domestic Violence Act of 1991 by elaborating two examples: first, the literal resituation of the law of the father and of primogeniture that preserves intact the transfer of property even in the event of disruptive domestic violence within heterosexual marriage; and second, the minute ways in which the state works to reinvent heterosexuality by, on the one hand, creating a class of loyal (heterosexual) citizens and a subordinate class of lesbians, gay men, prostitutes, and people who are HIV-infected, and, on the other hand, reviving the myth of the apocalyptic destruction of Sodom (and now, by extension, the Bahamas) by an oversexed band of nonprocreative noncitizens. The state actively socializes loyal heterosexual citizens into tourism, its primary strategy of economic modernization by sexualizing them and positioning them as commodities. Bahamian feminism, then, has been maneuvered into a thoroughly contradictory position, and has been forced to rely on a corrupt nationalist state, a state that draws upon imperial constructions of sexuality in order to present itself as the savior of the people.

Domesticating Violence or Feminists Publicize the "Private"

For many women in the Bahamas, the popular feminist mobilization of the mid-1980s recalled the time three decades earlier when the Women's Suffrage Movement agitated for—and won—the right for all adults to vote.

Then, the colonial state had made ownership of property, wealth, whiteness, and masculinity the primary condition of citizenship. In fact, owners of real property could vote more than once if they owned land in more than one constituency.[22] However, universal adult suffrage severed the colonial link between ownership of property, colonial respectability, manliness, and rights of political representation, and conceded the right to vote to the majority of Black Bahamians (both men and women), the bulk of whom were working class. Not only did the contemporary feminist movement reach back and draw upon strategies of political education and mobilization such as public meetings, marches and rallies, petitions and demands for legal protection, but, like its progenitor, it also refused the narrow designation of "the woman question" and formulated its political vision in terms of a mass-based struggle for popular justice. In general, both the movement for universal suffrage of the 1950s and the political platform of violence against women of the 1980s and 1990s were formulated in terms that implicated sexual politics in the very organization of social relations rather than as a peripheral category of significance pertaining only to women.

The recent mobilization based on violence against women functioned as a point of convergence for very many different women's organizations. Among them were: the Women's Desk, contradictorily positioned between the state machinery (as evidence of its international obligations to "women's rights") and the women's movement; Lodges with an active membership anchored within an African-based spiritual cosmology; The Women's Crisis Center; professional women's organizations, such as ZONTA; church-affiliated women's groups; autonomous feminist groups; and individual women parliamentarians. All of these groups had different, often conflicting theories about the origins of violence and the most effective strategies to combat it.[23] Nonetheless, for the majority of them, violence was defined not so much in terms of a social history of violence but as the cumulative coagulation of sexual "offences" (such as rape, incest, woman, or wife battery), and sexual harassment perpetrated by men against women. The combined work of these organizations—particularly the Women's Desk, which, through a series of workshops and seminars, had identified "violent crimes against women" as a major organizational focus—gave collective force to a political agenda that would shape the public conscience for more than a decade.[24]

Prior to 1981, when the Women's Desk was created, the Women's Crisis Center had begun to document an increased incidence of rape and incest. After a major mobilization against rape, it turned its attention to the violence of incestuous familial relations. Most acts of incest were committed against girls under ten years old.[25] Female victims of incest outnumbered male victims by a ratio of almost ten to one. Three- and five-year-old girls were being brought to hospitals where they were diagnosed with spontaneous orgasms and sexually transmitted diseases.[26] Combined cases of physical and sexual abuse were being reported to social services at a rate of three to five daily. All together, these data shattered the myth of the sanctity, safety, and comfort of the matrimonial home. Two "Take Back the Night" marches had underscored the violence of the streets, where "strangers" presumably committed at least 25 percent of all physical and sexual abuse. In addition, a series of radio and television broadcasts sponsored by the Women's Crisis Center challenged the media's self-imposed silence around physical and sexual violence perpetrated against women. When the media did report such cases, they gave the impression that the abuses were idiosyncratically imagined and enforced or simply irrational and, therefore, extreme.[27]

In addition to insisting that incest be removed from the colonial penal code as "unlawful carnal knowledge" and be treated instead as a separate crime, the first petition against incest, which the Center drafted in March 1988, demanded the following: that the proceedings against such crimes occur in chambers; that the names of survivors not be published; that some safe refuge be provided for girls taken out of homes; that reporting to the police of sexual abuse from *professionals* be mandatory; and that court-mandated psychological evaluation and treatment be provided for the offenders. Besides organizational endorsement from the Church (which sidestepped the question of violence against women to define incest as an infraction against the Divine) and some members of the medical profession (who worried that if incest continued at the current rate, family groups would be extinct by the year 2000), civic groups, lawyers, and 10,000 Bahamians who were not organizationally affiliated agreed that evidence needed to be presented to the state about pervasive sexualized violence; that the state ought to do something that neither private organizations nor individual citizens felt empowered to do. Indeed, the mobilization pointed to something far deeper and far more profoundly disturbing than individual criminality or individual concupiscence would suggest, and gave some official recognition to what Bahamians all knew or suspected to be true: that the normalization of violent sex inside and outside of the family had produced a real existential dilemma. Something had gone terribly amiss in the human organization of things. And in "a small place," like the Bahamas, such a public, mass-based move at denaturalizing violence could not help but infuse the fabric of daily life with a new, albeit contentious vocabulary on sexual politics. It would challenge inherited definitions of manliness, which had historically been based on ownership—sometimes as owner of property—but more often as owner and guardian of womanhood.[28]

Not all segments of the movement understood violence solely in terms of the combined expression of physical and sexual abuse. Denaturalizing violence meant that it could also be linked to the imperatives of the political economy and exposed in its imbrication with the organizing logic of heteropatriarchy itself. This is what other segments of the movement effected: in particular, DAWN, an autonomous women's organization (not linked to church, party, or state), refused the inherited legal conflation of wife and mother. The members of DAWN argued that the existing legal mandate requiring wives to cohabit with their husbands and, implicitly, to bear offspring did not necessarily compel motherhood.[29] Women, those with "husbands" and those without, were free to engage in heterosexual sex for pleasure alone, without having to satisfy the patriarchal state's desire for biological paternity or reproduction.[30]

Within the broad framework of reproductive freedom, DAWN politicized the state's recirculation of the modernization discourses of the 1950s, which had marked women's bodies with a recalcitrant, unruly sexuality—as reproducing too much, threatening the "body politic," and threatening "development" and progress. In its public mobilizations against the introduction of Norplant and other pharmaceuticals into the Bahamas, DAWN implicated Black masculinity (in this instance, the state, organized medicine, and Planned Parenthood) in the white, imperial forfeiture of women's agency. The state had acquiesced to the unexamined introduction and diffusion of Norplant, an invasive birth-control procedure, without the knowledge or consent of women, enabling and reinforcing the metropolitan ideology of backward Third-World women as silent, yet willing receptacles of the technologies of development and modernity.[31] Generallly then, DAWN challenged state enforcement of compulsory motherhood and, with it, the overall colonization of citizenship and subjectivity within normative heterosexuality. It expanded the definition of violence against women to include ongoing state economic violence and the "silent" destruction of "citizens" and "noncitizens" alike. In this sense, DAWN aligned itself with the regional feminist movement of the Caribbean, which resisted state attempts at domesticating violence and saw violence against women along a continuum of patriarchal violences expressed in different sites and within different domains. Violence within the domestic sphere, then, did not originate there but drew strength from, and at times was legitimated by, larger organized state and economic violence, which was itself responsible for the increase of sexual violence within the home.[32]

It was this larger feminist vision of the historicized violences of heteropatriarchy, only partially understood as "sexual offences," that the state coopted, narrowed, and brought within its juridicial confines as the Sexual Offences and Domestic Violence Act of 1991.[33] The passage of this legislation became a major symbol of victory for women and for feminists. Incest, sexual harassment, and sexual assault of a spouse (*almost* defined as rape) were introduced as new crimes. Incest of an adult on a minor or dependent carried, upon conviction, the possibility of life imprisonment and a minimum sentence of seven years. However, only the attorney general, not the women who were incested, sexually harassed, or assaulted, could be relied upon to present true testimony to the court. Moreover, these sexual offences were spatially separated in the legal text from domestic violence, contradicting what women had demonstrated: that almost all instances of violent sex were accompanied by violent physical coercion. The popular demand for professionals to report on incest and sexual abuse of minors and dependents was transformed in the legislation to the following:

> Any person who a) is the parent or guardian of a minor; b) has the actual custody, charge or control of a minor; c) has the temporary custody, care, charge or control of a minor for a special purpose, as his attendant, employer or teacher, or in any other capacity; or d) is a medical practitioner, or a person registered under the Nurses and Midwives Act, and has performed a medical examination in respect of a minor, and who has reasonable grounds for believing that a sexual offence has been committed in respect of that minor, shall report the grounds for *his* belief to a police officer as soon as reasonably practicable. (emphasis mine)

The penalty for failure to report is a fine of $5,000 or imprisonment for two years, the same penalty for an employer who has sexually harassed his employee.

But precisely because there are these significant disjunctures between what women demanded and what was conceded, precisely because women (and not just *any* person) are drawn into the state's mechanisms of surveillance in ways they had not anticipated, it becomes clear that, in this instance, the state folded its own interests into a disciplinary narrative that it could later claim, (by virtue of its name at least), as evidence of *its* benevolent paternalism. History was being constantly renarrativized in these terms: Women's Crisis Week was "proclaimed by the (then) Prime Minister Linden Pindling [to be] aimed at increasing public awareness of family violence;"[34] "Only the Bahamas has enacted legislation pertaining to sexual harassment;"[35] "MPs Passed the Sexual Offences Bill to provide greater protection for women on the job.... The bill was an important piece of social legislation, particularly sections outlawing sexual harassment on the job and domestic violence."[36] Parliamentarians invoked a Bahamas residing at the pinnacle of constitutional evolution: "We happen to have, unlike the British, a written constitution which has embodied in it ... certain principles with regard to freedom of conscience which protects your rights of privacy."[37] There is evidence here of the state's desire to usurp the popular narrative of struggle and convert it into a hegemonic narrative of deliverance, seen *only* as initiated by itself as benign patriarch. It is crucial that we understand, therefore, the uses to which "sexual offences" and "domestic violence" were put. How were these social and material practices converted into categories that were deployed by the state to do its own work, the work of the state?

Ensuring the Law of the Father: Domestic Violence as Proxy

The law's new provision relating to domestic violence (and bear in mind that the title of this Act was the Sexual Offences and Domestic Violence Act), made it possible for *any* party in the marriage to apply to the Supreme Court for an injunction that would restrain the other party from molestation and from using violence. Nowhere in the text of the law are there definitions of domestic violence, except in a single vague reference stating that the Supreme Court might consider attaching a power of arrest to the injunction in cases where the Court is satisfied that "the other party has caused actual bodily harm to the applicant." Rather, one finds defintions of the following: "apartment," "child of the family," "dwelling," "matrimonial home," "mortgage," and "mortgager." But why the foregrounding of property and its simultaneous conflation with marriage? How is it that domestic violence came to be narrowly codified as *"actual* bodily harm," in contrast, presumably, to *imagined* or *psychic* harm, or fear of threat? Why is there a spatial, and therefore ideological distancing in the legal narrative between "actual bodily harm" as an element of domestic violence on the one hand, and incest and rape in marriage on the other? Are these not enacted within the same sphere that has been ideologicaly coded as the "domestic"? Are they not undertaken by the same patriarch?

The conflation of property with marriage is not coincidental. The Bahamian legislation borrowed directly from the Domestic Violence and Matrimonial Proceedings Act of 1976 and 1983 and, in this way, inherited the underlying epistemological frame that immediately codifies matrimony and coverture in terms of the obligations of the "wife" and the economic and fiduciary responsibilities of the husband implied in such relations.[38] In almost all instances, any discussion of marriage is accompanied by a discourse on the disposition of proprietary interests in the event of marital rupture.[39] In fact, this is precisely what law intervenes to adjudicate. The legislation states:

> On an application for a [restraining] order under this section, the court may make such order as it thinks just and reasonable having regard to the conduct of the parties to the marriage in relation to each other and otherwise, to their respective needs and financial resources .... [It] may order a party occupying the matrimonial home or any part thereof ... to make periodical payments to the

> other in respect of the occupation . . . ; or may impose on either party obligations as to the repair and maintenance of the matrimonial home or the discharge of any liabilities in respect of the matrimonial home.[40]

Given the disproportionate gendered ownership of property in favor of men, and the frequency with which financial paternity is adjudicated through the courts, the legislation guarantees only a *promise* of financial retribution for women during moments of rupture. One is simply not talking about *any* party in a marriage!

The framework of coverture, which has an explicit operating assumption that the "wife is *sub potestate viri,*"[41] and the historic link between property ownership and maleness work to fix the notion of the propertyless housewife, of woman as nonowner, wage earner, perhaps, but nonowner of wealth.[42] It is difficult to obtain statistics on the accumulation of wealth in the Bahamas, but an analysis of household income gives at least a partial sense of where wealth might reside as well as some sense of whether the legal injunction to "discharge of liabilities" and the promise of financial retribution might be fulfilled. As one moves up the income ladder in the Bahamas, the gap demarcating gendered earning capacity becomes significantly greater. At the highest earning capacities recorded (those most likely to accrue wealth through earnings), women's earnings become almost insignificant: 4 percent of men earn upwards of $60,000, as opposed to just over 0.5 percent of women.[43] Approximately 58 percent of the population earned less than $20,000 in 1988, and 30 percent of those households earned less than $10,000 annually. Women's changing relationship to marriage is indicated by the fact that about 40 percent of the households in the Bahamas are headed by women, the mean household income of which is $12,000, thus making femaleness an index of poverty.[44] The earning capacity of state managers, on the other hand, places them among the highest recorded earners, in class proximity, if not in class affiliation, with the white indigenous owning class from whom they presumably distanced themselves in the anticolonial struggle.[45] This was the very class that disenfranchised the Black Bahamian working-class majority by using property ownership and wealth as rights to political representation.

If one were to invest these statistics with some degree of authority, one would have to conclude that households are not the primary sites for the generation of wealth. One would have to look elsewhere, which, in this instance, means the profit generated by multinational capital. The state's gesture of domesticating violence speaks, then, to the ideological production of primogeniture, which would, in the first instance, continue the system of property inheritance and transfer that rests solidly with men.[46] Not only does the neocolonial state protect the economic interests of its own state managers but it also protects those of the small indigenous owning class whose interests are oftentimes forfeited by multinational interests. If, as the state purports, the law intervenes on behalf of women, it also intervenes on its own behalf to ensure that heterosexual disruption does not shift the fiscal responsibility of the matrimonial patriarch onto that of the public patriarch. And while in the contemporary Bahamas this may be somewhat of an archaic worry since the state is constantly eroding its share of the social wage to favor privatized multinational economic strategies, the state continues to draw on notions of women as nonessential wage earners in order to preserve this ideological disjuncture between the public and the private, even while women are drawn in to compensate for severe state retrenchments. In practice, many women do not earn wages at all.[47] Of those who are unemployed, more than 61 percent are women.[48] Economic violence is enacted both publicly and privately, and domestic violence legislation, ostensibly framed to protect women's interests, now stands in to continue primogeniture and to ensure property transfer within a small, white, upper-class stratum and the more recently constituted Black, upper-middle-class.

The ideological production of primogeniture is even more starkly exposed in examining women's relationship to these legal "protections." For working-class and poor women, the dissolution of property (which emerges as the major trope in the legal discussion) is of no consequence in the face of violent masculinity, for they own neither "dwelling" nor "apartment;" they are neither "mortgagor," nor "mortgagee." On "domestic" day, Friday, which is the day many working-class women appear in magistrate's court seeking maintenance for their "natural and legitimate" children or injunctions against their battering partners, it is not the ownership of property that has brought them there, but its absence. Indeed, their propertylessness ensures that at the day's end their cases would not have been heard nor would the summonses they had demanded been served.[49] For middle-class and upper-middle-class women who may own property, one of the primary questions they confront is how to disentangle themselves from the web of well-established social relationships that protect *their* middle-class and upper-middle-class "husbands" from being defined as, or being accorded the treatment of criminals, a category that nature and abnormal proclivity have presumably reserved only for the working class, for lesbians and gay men, prostitutes, and Haitians.[50] The proximity of these men to—indeed, their location within—the central domains of power that cross party affiliation ensures legal, cultural, and gender immunity from demotion in status and from the immediate popular scourge of working-class resentment over the disjuncture between what upper-middle-class "husbands" profess to do (i.e., the semblance of respectability and the disproportionate rewards they inherit and/or mobilize through it) and what they actually do.[51] For most women who stand outside the legal definitions of "party to a marriage," no such claims can be made for relief from the court. Domestic violence as a legal construct—or, more accurately, women's experience of physical, sexual, and psychic violence together, in a space that has been designated as private—operates as a proxy to ensure the allocation of private property within disruptive heterosexual marriage. The shift in women's relationship to, and dependence upon marriage (70 percent of children in the Bahamas are brought into being outside of heterosexual marriage) might both increase the state's anxiety around questions of heterosexual respectability as well as threaten the ideology of primogeniture. Moreover, the relative inability of indigenous classes to accrue wealth might also interrupt the continued gendered accumulation of private property. Thus, state promulgation of the ideology of primogeniture and of itself as the benign patriarch, and its interest in the property relations of heterosexual marriage become much more urgent and significantly more fragile in the face of such threats.

By offering only minor allusions to the widespread occurence of "domestic" violence in a legislative narrative that is ostensibly dedicated to eradicating it, and by making it possible for "*any* party" in the marriage to be perpetrator and "victim" of that violence, the legal text authorizes and flattens the asymmetrical exercise of violence and power within domestic relations. This apparent gender neutrality or sexual democratization by fiat is only possible, of course, because the state has detached sexual assault from physical violence, the very associations that the feminist movement established.[52] Indeed, the text arbitrarily recodes women's experiences of violence in that sphere, within the confines of a class- and race-specific matrimonial home recast with fictions of harmony, order, and shades of the sacred. In so doing, it works to mask the political terrain of the immediate feminist struggle against violence, attempting now to contain a broad, popular movement within the courts in terms that are antithetical to that popular memory. Now, women who are beaten, incested, or raped are rendered triply suspect: as woman, as "victim," and as possible liar (even extortionist), positioned to retrieve their legitimacy by relying on the authority of the Attorney General who alone must determine the veracity of their complaints, because women carry no legitimacy of their own. The legal mandate for women to report crimes of incest and the sexual abuse of themselves and their daughters reinforces the popular-cultural sentiment that women are culpable for the sexual "lapses" in heteromasculinity. This does not take into consideration the context in which women's lives are situated, especially when telling demands the confessional mode that the law itself appropriates.[53]

To the extent that the state as ideal typical patriarch chides women for wanting more (in light of the entanglements around implementing the law), or dismisses their demands for the transformation of the mechanisms of punishment (even as women's demands are being misnamed in the service of disciplining and criminalizing womanhood while authorizing patriarchal violence), women are forced publicly to remain focused on the court system and its skewed, narrow definitions of violence in order to legitimize their broader claims.[54] The gesture works to place women in the role of perennial supplicant, the permanently grateful, and otherwise, as guardian of the minimal.

"Domestic" violence as a legal construct, in its capacity to be placed within the boundaries of law (albeit nominally, and simultaneously recodified as the disposition of property within the matrimonial home), and to be outside of the law (in the sense of the patriarchal refusal to legislate seriously against it), aims to discipline and even to foreclose an emancipatory praxis that might demystify patriarchal power within the home. This emancipatory praxis might imagine the domestic sphere as a space where one form of patriarchal power coagulates, yet disperses to produce different kinds of violences, which include wife beating, incest, rape, and the sexual abuse of girl children and young women, (because both girls and women are figured as sexual property). Thus, the spatial fragmentation of the physical and the sexual upon which the legal text insists, dissolves almost instantaneously in the face of pervasive practice, for it is the *same* patriarch within the boundaries of the *same* home who disciplines and terrorizes through physical *and* sexual force, turning daughters into women, women into wives, and both into mothers. It seems a travesty, then, that a set of complicated psychosexual practices, so poorly understood and undertheorized, so urgently awaiting historical and cultural specification, conspire, in the instance of the legislation, to further criminalize women for not reporting. It seems a travesty to position women as *the* cultural producers of heteropatriarchy and, subsequently, as complicit in its reproduction, in a way that presumably renders the heteropatriarchal state more progressive than violent domestic patriarchy and more progressive than women.

Configuring the Nation as Heterosexual; Or, The Time When There Were No Lesbians and Gay Men in the Bahamas; Or, The State and the Closet

I want to read the injunctions and stipulations within the Sexual Offences Act, in the first instance, as a strained self-reflection on heterosexualized violences, which include incest, rape, sexual assault and abuse, and sexual harassment. We saw earlier the ideological fragmentation within the legal text that made these violences appear as if they were idiosyncratic, individually imagined and enforced, or otherwise irrational and extreme. But given their pervasiveness, their widespread occurence, the politicization of which originated within the feminist movement, one is inclined to ask whether these violences were not a permanent, or at least a long-standing element of the heteromasculine condition. As the expurgated, these violences must have had an original placement within heterosexual desire. For that violence to thoroughly interrogate itself would actually necessitate going outside the boundaries and limits inscribed by law. Within the legal narrative, however, only *displacement* can occur, for the legal discourse is conducted narrowly, as if incest and rape were only to be understood as sins against God or crimes against "man," as if they primarily took place on the outside, as if there were no ideological and material links between state/parliamentary patriarchy and domestic patriarchy, for instance, and, as if homosexuality could only be imagined as residing at the pinnacle of perverted heterosexualized violence. This narrow content resides within the rhetorical form prescribed within law, and this is why, methodologically, it is crucial to take them apart.

The conflations within the legal narrative are by now familiar: the systematic conflation of perverted heterosexual *violence*, such as rape or incest, with same-sex *desire*, establishing a continuum of criminality in which same-sex desire is the apotheosis of a range of violences including murder, robbery, dishonesty, lying, rape, domestic violence, adultery, fornication, and incest. Thus constructed, the psyche of criminality is the psyche of homosexuality. Moral weight—or, more accurately, "the logic of the narrative's discrimination"—is established through the designation of penalties which are attached to these crimes.[55] Both "unnatural crimes" of "adult male sexual intercourse with another male," and "adult female sexual intercourse with another female" are second only to possible life imprisonment for rape. In fact, if minimum sentencing penalties were to be enforced (seven and fourteen years on first and second convictions, respectively), these "unnatural crimes," which carry a sentence of twenty years upon conviction if committed in a public place, carry *the* most severe penalty of all possible sexual sins and crimes. Unlike other crimes, there are no mitigating circumstances to which one could appeal for mercy from the court, or presumably from God.

There were brief moments when state managers directed the gaze at each other, but became so blinded and hysterical that debate was foreclosed altogether. At these moments they pondered the weightiness of their task and whether their own (im)moral caliber made them best suited to attend to this most crucial national task:

> The real answer [to crime] does not lie with this parliament, except in so far as the example that we as parliamentarians give by the manner in which we live our lives . . . and because the lives we live shout so loudly that nobody listens to what we say . . . it becomes imperative that once we take on the mantle of responsibility and become public servants we recognize that every aspect of our lives is a daily mirror.[56]

"Officials [were] taking money left and right every day from people they [were] having dealings with," and "since most of the complaints about sexual harassment were about ministers," state managers were not quite sure whether a certain criminal element, most often associated with the streets or the home, had crept into parliament's own august halls. They wondered what to do with their own "sodomites" within parliament:

> Buggery as it is called in this law is an absolute offence.... But I can't accuse honorable members of parliament of committing criminal offenses ... the rules prevent me from doing so even if I wanted to.... It is reasonable to assume that this place has its share of gays, even parliament is not excluded.

And what of the police force whose historic mission it was to fulfill the state mandate of surveillance?

> Who [was] going to arrest the police who is *that* way inclined?

Did the homosexual "proclivity" of not telling on each other privilege sexual loyalty above loyalty to state and nation?

> You will not have any homosexual who will consent to have or carry on homosexual activities or sodomy with another homosexual making complaints against the other one. The only way you will be able to catch a homosexual and prosecute him is if you have informants.... Separate from that you will never get them....

Were criminal penalties sufficient to reverse such unnatural proclivity?

> When they go to jail, do they stop being lesbians, stop being homosexuals? Does the urge disappear?

Surely a distinction ought to be made between force and consent:

> Shouldn't the lesbian who has committed this crime by forcing herself upon somebody else be treated more severely than two lesbians who are consenting adults. There should be a distinction between fondling, for instance, and the actual act itself. The actual abominable act.

They pondered aloud over the implicit contradiction of criminalization for homosexual parliamentarians when adulterous heterosexual ones, while immoral, had not yet been treated as criminal. They wondered whether "normal" husbands and wives performed sex acts that resembled buggery:

> These acts which are made offences are not exclusive today of the homosexual or lesbian and they come about in normal sex performance.

The answer was not clear-cut, however. Did God intend heterosexual buggery?

> Let's check it out and see if it is what God intended for that offence to be between husband and wife.

In the end they conceded their authority to medicine and science:

> The doctors and the scientists will be able to tell us whether that causes any physical problems; obviously if it did cause much physical harm it wouldn't be carried on.

Understanding for a brief moment the extent of the power of fiat that resided in the office of the Attorney General on questions of sexual harassment, and assuming that the attorney general would always be male, they puzzled about the conflictual operation of fiat in *his* hands when *he* was, often, the sexual harasser. They noted:

> Many an attorney general has committed the offence of sexual harassment.

In the end, however, these confrontations were reduced to party disagreements, and, as reported in the media, rested on the (then) opposition's objection to the state legislating the private lives of citizens. And because these disagreements were merely cosmetic, they were not sufficient to undo the underlying conflations upon which the heterosexual imaginary insists. So, it seems that the law continued to provide a "civilized," presumably neutral, and objective mode of escape from a major ontological conundrum: how to accord lesbians and gay men the respect of fully embodied human beings, not reduced to a perfunctory mind/body dichotomy in which the dismembered body could be imagined only as a dangerous sexual organ. As one state manager put it,

> Just because he is a sissy does not mean he might not go to heaven.... I don't believe his soul is a sissy.... It's only the body, his sissy body.

And what about protecting the constitutional rights of bodies detached from their souls, which were not human beings, after all? Once homophobia began to govern the disciplinary mechanisms, it seemed to matter little to state managers whether homosexual "sin" and "crime" could be constitutionally sanctioned or whether homosexuality was simply anathema to it.

No other kind of critique or interrogation is necessary because the law has now presumably emptied the society, emptied heterosexuality of the chaotic, the disorderly, the criminal. Both the law and heterosexuality have now been sanitized to function as the repository of order, returning each to an originary moral position. Thus articulated, the law would have presumably satisfied its civilizing mission, functioning silently, as early British mandates had commissioned it to do, while constructing and defending its own hierarchies.[57] Parliamentarians put it well, "The laws we pass are intended to keep us civilized." Law can dispense only what *it* has been destined to do and, simultaneously, it can provide a rationale for state intervention to ensure order and, in this instance, the viability of the nation. It could provide the "moral" ground to expunge anything that threatens that viability.

This state self-reflection on heterosexuality, although strained, is important at another level. It is enacted from a dual gaze: from a recognition of seeing itself, coupled with the pervasive worry about how it is seen—by Bahamians, by church pundits, but more important, by those who bestowed independence and their successors. The worry is buried in the discussion of constitutionality and the prerequisites of mature, civilized governance. This is how the question was posed as the government presented its case for passing the sexual offences bill:

> Does the state have the right to define dimensions of sexual conduct between its citizens? Does the government have the right to enter the bedrooms of the citizens of this country?

It provided its own (un)ambivalent response:

> The government has decided that it thinks, in its wisdom, that the state has the right to define the dimensions of social and moral relationships between men and women, and to define the dimensions which are lawful and thereby . . . the dimensions which are unlawful.

But the moral difficulty resided in the historical dilemma in which both the state and the church found themselves, and in the very question which the Wolfenden Commission of England had debated three decades earlier: the relationship between the sinner and sin, between illegality and immorality, the distinction between sin and crime. State managers urged rhetorically:

> Let us preach against homosexuality and preach against lesbianism as a sin, but should we put someone into jail for what we believe is an unnatural sex act?

This debate on sin and crime was conducted in the Bahamian parliament under the symbolically watchful eyes of British royal pedigree and their designates from 1767 to the present, and within the discursive parameters outlined by them—the very governors who had disciplined the oversexualized, infantilized "native." After all, the racialized psychic impasse of colonization reflected Britain's own fictive construction: "they cannot govern themselves." Nationalism may have contradicted the imperial discourse that used the fictions of science to explain "native" *incapacity* to govern in terms of biology. Yet, the psychic residue of colonization operates to convert double consciousness (the term comes from W. E. B. Du Bois) into a double bind.[58] Acting through this psychic residue, the neocolonial state continues the policing of sexualized bodies, drawing out the colonial fiction of locating subjectivity in the body (as a way of denying it) as if the colonial masters were still looking on, as if to convey legitimate claims to being civilized. Parliamentarians reflected:

> We have to be careful that we do not give the public, who still have to understand the functioning of this independent state of ours, the wrong impression, when we know the situation is entirely otherwise. That is one thing I respect the British for . . . although I didn't want them to dominate my country, the true fact of the matter is that the Englishman would tell you what the facts of the situation are on one side and interpret the facts as his opinion somewhere else. . . . I accept that that is the constitutional position.

Not having dismantled the underlying presuppositions of British law, Black nationalist men, now with some modicum of control over the state apparatus, continue to administer and preside over these same fictions.

Moreover, no nationalism could survive without heterosexuality—criminal, perverse, temporarily imprisoned, incestuous or as abusive as it might be, nationalism needs it. It still remains more conducive to nation-building than same-sex desire, which is downright hostile to it, for women presumably cannot love themselves, love other women, and love the nation simultaneously. In the words of one state manager, "One thing God did was to give man an undying urge to ensure survival of the human race." In this instance, the state feels compelled to honor Divine will. At this point, however, we still need to understand further the processes through which heterosexuality is reified and the kinds of mythologies that the state recirculates to ensure its ideological longevity, to ensure that the moral boundaries that mark the closet will not in any way be contravened.

The State of the Closet; Or, the State and the Closet

The nation has always been conceived in heterosexuality, since biology and reproduction are at the heart of its impulse. The citizenship machinery is also located here, in the sense that the prerequisites of good citizenship and loyalty to the nation are simultaneously sexualized and hierarchized into a class of good, loyal, reproducing, heterosexual citizens, and a subordinated, marginalized class of noncitizens, who, by virtue of choice and perversion, choose not to do so. But there are also ways the state works, through the law to position the nation as heterosexual. There are three primary gestures. The first, which I discussed earlier, is the normalization of violent heterosexuality in relation to same-sex desire.

The second, is the organization of an internal homophobic discourse on homosexual ontology, on the nature and origins of homoeroticism, its passion and desire, which operates through a contradictory quasi-scientific discourse to present itself as truth about character:

> You see the lesbian, the natural lesbian and the natural homosexual, God created them the way they are.... The good Doctor from Garden Hills has said that the homosexual tendencies are not inherited ones.

While intimately aware of its own ignorance ("I don't have any scientific basis for what I am saying ... but I think I am free to project my own views ... I checked with the Speaker of the House and he thought so too"), this homopbobia utilizes classificatory systems that can only be reminiscent of colonial relations of rule, replete with minute details of physiognomy and anatomy, which, much like the colonial period, function to interpret important dimensions of self. The legislative hearings overflow with these convoluted pronouncements:

> Buggery is completed on penetration and we are being very candid so that we can understand. Penetration of the anus by any member I suppose. But if you are talking about the offence of buggery, then penetration of the anus by the penis. That's it.... And in the case of lesbianism, then it is two women who have sexual intercourse. ... You see what I mean.... What I am getting at here is that in the case of buggery, what we call homosexuality, the whole sexual act itself is penetration of the anus with the penis.... In the case of lesbianism there is no penetration necessary. Stimulation of the vulva for anything would amount to sexual intercourse.... They are not the same thing.... If you have a man who stimulates the anus of another man by any means but does not penetrate, he is

> not guilty of buggery. Do you see what I mean? . . . The nature of the lesbian act is different from the male homosexual act. There is no anatomical comparison possible, so [with] the whole question of the homosexual there is no anatomical comparison.

And it is in these spaces of open meaning—open, as well, to confusion and wide interpretation, and arrived at without consensus—where strands of "evidence" are culled idiosyncratically from science, medicine, and common sense, that homophobia comes to reside.

The third strategy involved in the legal resituation of the heterosexual was a gesture that invoked nostalgia for an idyllic Bahamas, free from Western decadent incursions, a Bahamas that was not peopled by lesbians and gay men. The ideological scaffolding for these three moves was assembled through the twin paradoxical strategies of spectacularization and erasure of lesbians and gay men, which served in the end to reposition and naturalize hegemonic heterosexuality.

Erasure is most immediately visible in the nostalgic invocation of sexual "purity," imagined within a geography (and a home) that only heterosexuals inhabit:

> It is true, as the honorable member of St. Michael has said, that as we grew up, as we developed, we knew nothing or very little of these learned responses or these alternative lifestyles. . . . Homosexuality was something that was extremely rare. . . . In our communities, when I was younger we probably knew and could count on one hand those people who engaged openly in homosexuality.

What does it mean to invoke such nostalgia and to suggest that some originary, unambivalent moment for the heterosexual founding of a Bahamian nation were immediately recoupable and collectively intelligible? What is the historical time frame within which this contradictory memory is summoned?

Presumably the time in which there were no lesbians and gay men in the Bahamas was the era of the consolidation of colonization, the period that provided the ideological moorings for anticolonial nationalism. Here, it is important to counter the mythology of (sexual) purity. The nineteenth century witnessed an ongoing struggle among different kinds of white masculinities for power: the wrecker, the rogue, the pirate, and the white gentleman.[59] The white masculine rogue and wrecker would actually lay the groundwork for Ernest Hemingway's twentieth-century discovery of Bimini, and this would become important in the symbolic and material transfer of imperialism from British to American hands, installing tourism, which would commodify Black women's bodies for sexual pleasure. It was in this period of the consolidation of the colonial nation that sodomy laws were introduced, as one of the potential offences against the (white, male British) person. The legal elimination of the sodomite, who at the onset of colonization was the indigenous Indian, would help to fix the notion that white European heterosexual interests were best matched with those of the colonized, and that European *civilization* was necessary to conquer the *savage* sodomite. Whether the contemporary Bahamian state can apprehend the continuities between its own gestures of violence and erasure and those of the colonial state is as significant as the fact that both are engaged in promoting and extending the heterosexual inheritance. "I am just a normal Bahamian male," said one state manager, "and a normal Bahamian male is not homosexual."

The belief in the perils of (American) imperialism and homosexuality, that "the whole concept of the acceptability of homosexual behavior between consenting adults is essentially an American phenomenon" that Bahamians have adopted, means, that at least in the state's view, there is no space for indigenous agency for lesbians and gay men who presumably become homosexual by virtue of Western influence, although the process through which homosexuality becomes foisted unto Bahamians is somewhat unclear. There is no consensus among state managers about origins. Thus, the summoning of memories around heterosexual inheritance marks an attempt to foreclose any counterhegemonic memory of an insurgent sexuality that would have to be housed outside of state structures because of the excessive sexualization, codification, regulation, and disciplining required of those very bodies. Communities of lesbians in the Bahamas, who claim neither Western decadence nor protection of the white European father, in tandem with the work of many Caribbean feminists in Suriname, Curaçao, Jamaica, Grenada, and Carriacou, elaborate such a counterhegemonic memory and subsequently form the basis of community around mati work, *kachapera,* man royals, and *zami,* which interrupt the state's continued adjudication of heterosexual inheritance.[60] The point here is one of the paradoxes of negation: "That which a culture negates is necessarily included within it."[61] State managers are caught in their homage to the West as the harbinger of civilization and progress and the harbinger of sexual destruction. For feminists, a continued challenge lies in constructing a contemporary vocabulary for same-sex desire beyond the point where the hegemonic and oppositional meet.

The violent erasure of insurgent sexualities in the period of flag independence can be linked more directly to the state's activity in re-establishing the nation as heterosexual, in ideological and material terms imagined and practiced through patriarachy and masculinity. It means redrawing a fictive nation as masculine and patriarchal at this historical moment when popular masculinity has generated the belief that men would have to leave the Bahamas to keep their masculinity intact. In the wake of the passage of the

Sexual Offences Act, popular fears surfaced of a nation of women (read: lesbians) who have rendered men home-less, nation-less even by exercising their newly bestowed power to report coercive sex as marital rape, to report the pimps who sexually exploit them, the fathers, cousins, and uncles who incest them, and their bosses who sexually harass or exploit them. These fears dovetail, in this instance, with an overall state impulse to control and criminalize women.[62]

The legislative fiction of the nation as masculine means reasserting the foundation of masculinity in procreation so that same sex-masculinity is positioned as femininity engaged in sex purely for satisfying desire (sissies), presumably not in the interest of the nation. And same-sex femininity is really femininity in drag, woman as manhater who defies biology, medicine, and psychiatry, who anatomically, according to state managers, cannot be compared to homosexual man, heterosexual man, or heterosexual woman; she is a species unto herself, who engages in something *approximating* normal sex. In the absence of a penis, she can only "stimulate the anus or the vagina or vulva of another," purely for satiating pleasure, presumably not in the interest of the nation.

Additionally, the fiction of the nation as masculine masks the mass mobilization of women for the national movement, without which state-generated popular nationalism would not have been able to consolidate itself.[63] The popular, mass-based suffrage movement of the 1950s, which was the vehicle for universal suffrage, provided visibility for an emerging Black nationalist state, anxious to signal to Britain its newly acquired knowledge about citizenship, rights, and loyalties, and, therefore, its capacity for self-rule.[64] In a real sense, this mass movement of the 1950s was disciplined through the accession of the vote, which state managers usurped and claimed as their own accomplishment. The offical narrative would record the Voting Rights Act of 1962 as among the earliest and most significant of its achievements, erasing the memory of that popular struggle and the significance of the women involved: Mother Butler, Mother Donaldson, Doris Johnson, Eugenia Luckhart, Mary Ingraham, Mable Walker, U. J. Mortimer, Gladys Bailey, Georgina Symonette, and Madge Brown—the very women for whom Marion Bethel dedicated the poem with which I began.[65]

And finally, I wish to mention here a point to which I shall return in the final section of the essay: the contradictory representational impulse of the nation as masculine. The fiction of the nation as masculine attempts to cancel out the economic when the state relies upon tourism as its primary economic strategy, and it, in turn, rests on women's bodies, women's sexual labor, and the economic productivity of women's service work in this sector to propel the economic viability of the nation.

The paradoxical counterpart of erasure in the consolidation of hegemonic heterosexuality is spectacularization. State managers relied heavily on biblical testimony in order to fix this specter, using reiteration and almost incessant invocation to God and to Sodom:

> As the legend goes, God destroyed a whole city because of corruption. In the 19th chapter of Genesis, it tells how the cities of Sodom and Gomorrah were destroyed because of homosexuality. This is a very important defense to me. And I am now living in the Bahamas and I would not want the country destroyed because of homosexuality.

But how did same-sex love come to find itself in Sodom and in the Bahamas? How do sexuality and geography collide? Unfortunately, neither the biblical discourse nor the state-generated discourse on the origin of homosexuality is settled on these questions. State managers were not quite clear whether "homosexual tendencies [were] inherited ones," whether "*they* were born like that," or whether "the vast majority of *them* were induced or enticed into *that* condition by succumbing to the temptation of those homosexuals who presently [held] high office in the country." The power of Sodom in providing "the most important defense" for state managers makes it possible for the sexual destruction of Sodom to operate as truth, in spite of contentious ecclesiastical debate about the impetus for destruction. Sodom requires no point of reference other than itself; it can assert authority without comparison, evidence, or parallel.[66] Its power lies in its ability to distort, usurp, or foreclose other interpretative frameworks, other plausible explanations for the destruction of Sodom, or other formulaic and experiential dimensions of homosexuality that oppose and refuse state constructions of the criminal presumably reinforced by biblical authority. Such formulations would take the place of an overdetermined state preoccupation with what lesbians and gay men do in bed, and the power of our sex in destroying the nation. The myth of Sodom sexualizes and eroticizes, and, in so doing, reduces ontology to the body, a contradictory move for Black state nationalism (a "race" people, for whom the justification for slavery presumably carried biblical weight) to premise citizenship in physiognomy, the basis of colonial refusal to admit agency and self-determination.

The conflation of lesbian and gay sexuality with mass destruction, with ominous apocalyptic visions of genocide and omnicide spill outside of the biblical legend into other domains. For state managers, no place was safe:

> I thought the number of them was growing, and I thought they were engaged in various forms of activity.... The atmosphere at her majesty's prison is conducive to homosexual activity.... This

> is where you take it when you can't have it.... Most of them are in influential positions, and they use these positions to intimidate and corrupt young boys and young girls.... Some of them have such influential positions that they control hundreds of people, sometimes thousands.

Sexualization and destruction are complete with the prostitute's body and the "AIDS infested body" spreading contagion and destruction:

> They have one single commodity with which they deal, and that is their body ... with that AIDS infested body they seek to ply their trade to get the cocaine to feed their habit.

The significance of these sexual practices lies also in the fact that they are invested with the power to corrupt otherwise loyal citizens of the nation, even those who are temporarily (out)law. Criminality does not forfeit heterosexuality or heterosexual citizenship. However, homosexuality forfeits citizenship, because within homosexuality inheres the power to dissolve the family, the foundation of the nation (homosexual sodomy is grounds for dissolving a marriage), and the nation itself.[67] Homosexuals occupy relative, rather than absolute citizenship, or, rather, none at all, and would now have to earn rights in order to move outside the closet and regain entry into the moral heterosexual community it has presumably contravened.[68] Because the requirement of citizenship is the requirement to be heterosexual, the state can now create a context for establishing its own secular narrative of salvation and deliverance. According to its understanding, only an act of God—not even that of state managers who can only legislate the unenforceable ("homosexuals will never tell on each other")—might extend a gesture of mercy toward the Bahamas and save it from sexual destruction. In the interim, however, the state can act as savior and deliverer. It can simultaneously claim a biblical pedigree and appropriate the powerful, foundational biblical narrative of deliverance in which Moses, God's chosen deliverer, brings the Hebrews out of bondage. The Progressive Liberal Party appropriated a version of the theme from Exodus—"This land is mine, God gave this land to me"—as a mobilizing symbol.[69] How this symbol was put to use in the service of the economic, to position the state as heterosexual patriarch and economic savior, is the subject I explore in the next section.

"This Land Is Mine": Tourism as Savior and Other Fictions

Earlier, we saw how the state eroticized the dissolution of the nation and produced apocalyptic (mythic) visions of dread disease and mass destruction premised in prostitution and the practice of lesbian and gay sex in ideological terms: the prostitute's body (with potential disease, was imagined as working-class, a perennial threat to middle-class respectability and femininity); the sodomitic body (oftentimes imagined as white European or white Bahamian and financially well-off, was always objectified and hypersexualized); and the immoral lesbian body (deracialized, was simultaneously spectacularized and hidden, lying somewhere outside of the heterosexual imagination, yet a perennial threat to domestic space). All of these bodies are conjoined in the state-constructed imperative to circumscribe boundaries around the body politic (making it safe for imperialism), or establishing quarantine within it (making it safe for loyal heterosexual citizens).

This eroticization of the dissolution of the nation is made visible by the state while it masks its own role in the eroticized production of citizenship, and in the commodification of the nation as broker for multinational capital interests, so much so that even the notion of the nation-state is made unstable. Whose hands hold the power of national extinction when 85 cents of every dollar made by state-supported multinational capital in tourism reverts to those corporations in their countries of origin? Nonetheless, these sexual, "symbolic" consumption practices provide a real base for the social processes of capital accumulation from which the state disproportionately benefits.[70] For whom, one might ask, is it "better in the Bahamas?"

In the discussion that follows, I will examine tourism against the state narrative of its economic importance to citizens (which positions the state as savior), and foreground, instead, the processes of the commodification of sexual pleasure, the production of loyal sexualized citizens to service heterosexuality, tourism, and the nation simultaneously. There are profound, contradictory implications of socializing a population as "natives" 500 years after colonial conquest, instead of socializing them for self-determination.

At the outset, we need to understand the state-managed semiotic system and its generative role in the excessive production of a tourist culture through which the Bahamas is inscribed and managed. Admittedly, the system functions differently for (imperial) tourists and has different implications for Bahamians according to their racial or gender status; different implications for prostitutes whose sexual labor marks them as potential vectors of disease; different implications for women who do "legitimate" grossly underpaid work as chamber maids, cooks, or otherwise service white femininity through more personalized services such as hair-braiding and the like. For the tourist, the state-managed system adheres to the feminization of nature through symbols of unspoiled, virgin territory, waiting to be transformed and possessed by imperial (heterosexual) design; the evocation of a land steeped in pathos and, by extension, mystery; a rewriting of history and renovating the narrative of colonization as a celebratory one of mutual consent, reminiscent only of imperial travel writing and rescue narratives.[71] For Bahamians, it involves the excessive production of a tourist culture and the almost painstaking building of an ideology that premises faithful Bahamian citizenship upon a faithfulness to tourism.

While state managers in the Ministry of Tourism presented Bahamians to the outside as perennially willing, hardworking people, underneath they worried about how to turn a recalcitrant population into a band of "warm and genial Bahamians" who were indeed ready and willing to serve. Every major throne speech delivered in Parliament devoted substantial time and space to the benefits and rewards of tourism. Tourism offered the opportunity to confer civilization, modernity, and progress: "Tourism and resort development will provide the main thrust for the vast programme of economc expansion that will take the Bahamas to First-World status . . . it will make the Bahamas one of the finest world-class tourist and resort destinations. . . ." It promised increased spending, "some $400m . . . between 1988 and 1992 to provide new tourist facilites and upgrade existing ones." It promised jobs, "at least 3,000 permanent jobs in the tourist industry alone," and it extended a special invitation to Bahamians to join the international community in the rehearsing of history: "By 1992, the 500 year anniversary of Columbus' landing in the Bahamas, the infrastructure and accomodations will be in place in San Salvador, thereby enabling us to host the international community at that historic island."[72]

Was the ideology generated in order to veil the economic difficulties in tourism? This was the very period in which the media disinterestedly announced a "Big Slump in Tourism," "sluggishness," "lay offs in the hotel industry," and a "general decline in the volume of tourist days." Besides, what did First-World status mean in the midst of unemployment, particularly when Bahamians identified the transparency of the veil. The state accelerated its pace: "Let a Bahamian introduce you to the Bahamas." Tourists were promised "warm and genial Bahamians," personalized services with a host family whose "leisure, occupational or religious interests [were] similar" to theirs, like "shar[ing] an evening of pleasant conversation over a cool island drink." Advertising brochures displayed photographs of colorfully garbed Black people and Black women with flowers in their hair. It proved difficult in practice, however, for the state to mobilize the "hundreds of volunteers" promised to tourists.

In addition, there were rumors of "poor attitudes," "bad service," and downright "rudeness" on the part of Bahamians. So, in the 1970s, the Ministry initiated a major smile campaign, in which Bahamians were urged to remind themselves of being courteous by wearing smile buttons. It was unsuccessful. So, each year thereafter, the Ministry was forced to devise new strategies. The state could not quite accomplish such a formidable task on its own—this promised conversion of former sullen "slaves" into a contemporary band of smiling obsequious "natives"—so the Rotary Club, linked to the local chamber of commerce (which blamed the government for its own economic plight), took matters into its own hands. The Rotarians wanted Bahamians to see that "tourism affect[ed] them too." It produced a set of bumper stickers rhetorically asking ordinary Bahamians, including the 58 percent working in the tourist industry, "What have you done for tourism today?"[73] The expectation was that Bahamians would come to see that their interests were inextricably linked to the tourist presence and that their daily duty as Bahamians rested in an ongoing consciousness of the tourist. That consciouness had material implications, as well, for, in any given month, the number of tourists was likely to exceed the number in the population.

In 1990, for instance, there were 3.6 million visitors, a monthly average of 302,000 in a population of 259,000.[74] In public television broadcasts, the Rotarians maintained, "in almost all instances the dollar start[ed] with the tourist." They hoped that Bahamians would adopt the Rotary's own motto: "service above self," that they would learn to adapt "even if the tourists annoyed" them, or, at the very least, they would stop to help tourists instead of rudely "speeding past" in their cars. The Prime Minister attended "Hospitality Leadership" forums sponsored by private industry and assured Bahamians that they were not to blame for their own poor attitudes and the bad service they gave to tourists; the blame rested, instead, at the door of "hard-nosed, high pressure, North American management techniques" that were introduced, insensitively, into an island culture.[75]

But what were the symbols upon which the state relied? A major symbol in the state-organized system for the tourist devolves upon the organization and creation of paradise, with all of its comforts and contents. Paradise actually exists, of course, in the form of Paradise Island, the name given to the most unattractively named Hog Island after it was bought by Huntingdon Hartford for $10,000,000 in 1959.[76] It exists, as well, in an obsessive preoccupation with cleanliness and order. A case in point is the set of instructions developed by the Ministry of Tourism for the use of the Straw Market where women are the major owners and sellers. They state: "The stall and its immediate surroundings *must* be kept clean and tidy at *all* times"; "Goods *must* be displayed on or around the said stall only and in *no other unauthorized location*. They may not be hung from ceilings, on louvres or anywhere else except with the expressed permission of the Ministry of Tourism"; "Only the stall owners and two other helpers will be allowed at the stalls"; and "*Loud* and *boisterous* behaviour as well as the use of *obscene language* will not be tolerated." (emphases Ministry of Tourism) As Mr. Pindling, former Prime Minister and Minister of Tourism admonished the nation, "People visit the Bahamas to relax and have a good time and they want to do so in a peaceful and *clean* environment." The labor involved in creating such peace and cleanliness rested squarely upon Bahamians. There are no beggars or homeless people in and around Nassau, for they might contaminate paradise; none of the evidence of the sordid effects of economic decay that would suggest that paradise was not paradise after all.

From the advertisements, it seems that there is something for everyone in paradise. "The law now says you can cruise the Bahamas duty-free; some people have been doing it for years," says the Ministry of Tourism. Cruising grounds; carefree; taxfree. Sex and capital combined. "For those who believe wild life should be preserved." Nature and sex combined. "Come to Bimini . . . only 50 miles away from Hemingway's hideaway–home of the Hemingway championship tournament." And, for everyone, the provision of "world-class" facilities, by which is meant European facilities, for, after all, (underdeveloped) paradise peopled by natives is quite different from (imperial) paradise inhabited by the civilized.[77]

Columbus may have first landed in San Salvador, but it is Hemingway who owns the discovery of Bimini way after nineteenth-century tourism took hold–and, as the irony of imperial history would have it, twenty miles from San Salvador, the site of the origin of "New World" colonization. Hemingway occupies an important psychic space in the American literary imagination, and in the imagination of Bahamian state managers, for it continues to market its attractiveness on the basis of its proximity to North America (particularly the South) and to the legend of Hemingway's discovery of Bimini. It was here that Hemingway fashioned the narratives in which he commanded the presence of Black people and erased them.[78] It was here that he perfected the practice of having Black people anticipate the desires of white people, even before whites gave them voice. It was here, then, that he developed the trope of serviceability of Black people, the serviceability upon which tourism is anchored. Additionally, it was here that Hemingway developed his prowess at shooting sharks and fish (the basis of current championships), and recirculating the tradition of white, predatory, roguish (hetero)masculinity, daring and powerful enough to dominate nature. And, in spite of claims that Hemingway was gay, his refusal to disaffiliate from whiteness bears all the markings of imperialism, and links him to what Toni Morrison identifies as "American Africanism."[79] I am not making an argument here for linking Hemingway's presumed homosexuality with the contemporary homosexual, even if one were to be able to identify such a figure.[80] I am interested, however, in foregrounding the imperial, for, in the contemporary period, the erotic consumptive patterns of white gay tourism follow the same trajectory as those of white heterosexual tourism. In his faithfulness to white masculinity as rogue and pirate, his construction of the availability of Bimini as "a blank, empty space," and his view of the "serviceability of Black people," Hemingway continued the imperial narrative that preceded him. Accordingly, nature figures as raw material for American

(European) creative expansiveness, nature is positioned to collude in phantasmic representations of Black people, the very rhetorical strategies that state and private corporations utilize to market Bahamians and the Bahamas to the rest of the world.

Of course, Hemingway's "discovery" of Bimini also becomes a powerful signifier that inaugurates the escalated transfer of political, economic, and cultural hegemony in the region from British to United States of North American hands.[81] Researchers at the North American Commission on Latin America (NACLA) have found that the Caribbean is perhaps more thoroughly dominated by transnational capital than any other region of the Third World. It hosts the branches, subsidiaries, and affiliates of more than 1,740 U.S. corporations and an additional 560 companies affiliated with other foreign firms. The Resource Center in the United States reports that more than three quarters of all hotel rooms in the Bahamas are owned indirectly or outright by North American interests, including Playboy, Resort International Britannia Beach Hotel, Sheraton, and ITT. Approximately 13 percent of all U.S. finance-related investment abroad is located in the Bahamas. In addition, there are U.S. military installations, missile-tracking stations, U.S. Navy and Coast Guard, and an underwater-test-and-evaluation center there.[82] Given what we know about the link between militarized masculinity and the growth of heterosexual prostitution elsewhere, it would be most plausible to assume that such prostitution exists here as well.

The organization of this psychic syntax (the term is Kobena Mercer's) within the state's semiotic system is grammatically disturbing, both in the production of the tourist and in the (re)production of the "native" whom the state must present as citizen under a consititutionally independent Bahamas as it appropriates claims to civility.[83] The mass production of the imperial tourist psyche rests in the power of an ideology wherein an entire population (particularly women) could be mobilized into service on one's behalf; the belief that the foreign currency one provides is indispensable to the operation of the economy and vital for the very population which services one. This produces psychic occlusions of different kinds. The most significant is that the organization of tourism is presented so as to erase the complicity of the tourist in the production of tourism. Neither the penalties for not conforming to the rules of the Straw Market, nor the exent to which the state disciplines the population to ensure that it works to make things "Better in the Bahamas" for tourists, and not themselves, is made visible. And, as Jamaica Kincaid suggests, "It never occurs to the tourist that the people who inhabit the place cannot stand you . . . that behind the closed doors they laugh at your strangeness."[84] Or, that the well-practiced rituals of dissemblance that characterize friendliness have more to do with the rituals of asymmetry and survival, or the desire to keep a job when there are none, than with the fictions of "native" character.

State reliance on silence and invisibility erase the work that women do to make it better for tourists, and worse for themselves. I am referring here to the level of superexploitation in the workforce, the reductions in household income, and the increase of women-headed households in poverty at a time of the tourist production of the economy. Someone has to work to make it better in the Bahamas; 58 percent of the workforce work to do so, and the largest percentage are women. Simply put, women are not the beneficiaries of tourism. Moreover, erasure of this fact makes it possible for the state to impute a willingness on the part of women in the Bahamas to be complicit in the terms of their own exploitation and erasure, in the same way that the state made women complict in, responsible for, or the originators of the perpetration of (hetero)sexualized violence within the home. Still, there is a contradictory and ironic state reliance on women who work as prostititutes and as a lure to tourists, whom state managers outlaw, and therefore wish to be kept hidden.[85] Everyone knows and talks about prostitution linked to business in hotel casinos and with American soldiers. There is no mistake that sex is what is being sold here. What inheres within this mask of "respectability" is that all self-respecting Black gentlemen know the rules of the game, how to buy and sell sex, and how to maintain a guarded reticence about it; yet, no respectable women sell sex to tourists. It is the "common" whore who prostitutes her labor (in the service of the nation) to make Bahamas better for the tourist. State managers rely almost insidiously, therefore, upon the (tacit) acquiescence of her somewhat fixed location between the boundaries of (im)morality and (il)legality to maintain and consolidate the silence.[86]

Sexual commodification and consumption are evident not only in the earlier trope of the imperial rescue of virgin land but also in other types of commodification of women's bodies. White-owned private capital need not be as discrete as Black masculinity, which must carry the burden of respectability for the world. A set of postcards designed by Charm Kraft Inc., printed in Ireland and distributed by Island Merchants Ltd., which owns sole rights of distributorship, market white femininity and the availability of their sex as part of tourism. An invitation to "Come to the Bahamas where summer never ends" is accompanied by photos of seminude white women with the caption, "Feeling Hot, Hot, Hot ... in the Bahamas." In another, "Ooh, Bahamas: want to do something besides stroll along white sand beaches, swimming in aqua-marine waters? Well there's always biking," is accompanied by white seminude women bikers, presumably exclaiming, "Oooh! Bahamas." It is indeed difficult to ascertain whom these women represent—for the cards assume so much of a surreal quality. Do they erase the women who trade in sex? Are they so homogenized, so hypercommercialized, so generic (they could really be on beaches anywhere) that their objectification becomes cliché?

It would be important to determine the extent to which this sexual commodification pertains as well to the homosexual male body, and whether it enters another underworld, as it were, when the gay body, tourist or indigenous, turns prostitute, either as an extension of gay culture or, exploited transnationally, as another exotic part of the transnational trade in sex.[87]

Black women are also sexualized and exoticized in this tourist drama; in fact, white imperial tourism would not be complete without eroticized blackness. The sinister script also finds expression in commercial advertising and the production of certain fetishes that get signified as "culture." Bahama Mama (Bahama Papa has been recently added to complete the ideology of family nuclearity) is a buxom, caricatured, hypersensualized figure who can be bought in the market in the Bahamas. She can also be consumed as "hot and spicy sausage" at any "Nice and Easy" convenient store in the United States. Upon their return home, tourists can continue to be intoxicated by the Bahamas by ordering Bloody Mary with Bahama Mama-alterity as instruments of pleasure. European fantasies of colonial conquest, the exotic, the erotic, the dark, the primitive, of danger, dread, and desire all converge here on virgin beaches and aquamarine waters, enabled by Black state mangers and their white multinational counterparts. Black masculinity is deeply complicit in managing phantasmic constructions of Black femininity, satisfying white European desire for restless adventure, satisfying white European longing for what is "rare and intangible."[88]

Tourism as a metasystem makes it possible for the state to circumscribe and demarcate boundaries around the nation while servicing imperialism. The evidence is that the state simultaneously reenacts the dissolution of the nation through these political-economic gestures, which it ideologically recodes as natural, as (super) natural, or as the savior. It is able to present itself as savior of the people through tourism, and by legislating against "disease-infested AIDS bodies" at a time when tourism was experiencing one of its worst slumps. The Sexual Offences and Domestic Violence Act has made it possible to have imprisoned (for five years) anyone with HIV infection who has consensual sex without disclosing their HIV status. Thus, tourism as imperial practice, in its elaboration of heteropatriarchy, becomes an important site for the dissolution of the nation and the construction of a national identity fashioned from the proclivities and desires of the imperial masculine subject, the invisible subject of the legal text. It assists in the production of a specific cultural form dutifully chiseled from a mold produced *elsewhere*. Five hundred years after conquest, seven- and ten-year-old girls work in the market, offering songs to tourists in exchange for 25 cents. For whom is it "better in the Bahamas?" What does it mean to resocialize a generation into the benefits of the landfall, to rewrite the history of Bahamians as one with "pirates and princes," and to prepare one's country, one's identity in the service of service, to argue that "as Bahamians we have many, many personalities . . . we can be whatever *you* want your vacation to be"? How, precisely, are citizens to be socialized for self-determination and autonomy through the tropes of the landfall? How is it tenable for Black state managers to insist upon independence and adopt strategies that are diametrically opposed to it: to socialize citizens into heterosexuality and not into self-determination?[89]

In whose interest is heteropatriarachy reinvented? This essay suggests that Black heteropatriarchy takes the bequeathal of white colonial masculinity very seriously, in its allegiance to the Westminster model, an originary nuclear family (which is not the dominant family form in the Bahamas), its conscientious management of law and the reproduction of its false ontologies. The legal subject of colonial law, which Black heteropatriarchy now continues to adjudicate, was neither slave nor woman.[89] Heteropatriarchal nationalist law has not sufficiently dislodged the major epistemic fictions constructed during colonial rule nor has it dismantled its underlying presuppositions; neither has it dislodged any of the received notions of womanhood. The (in)visible subject of imperial law has not been entirely replaced, not in nationalist law, nor in any of the neocolonial state's contemporary gestures to adjudicate the imperial through law and within the political economy. The ideal typical citizen is still premised within heterosexuality and maleness and this, for women, prostitutes, lesbians, gay men, those who are HIV-infected, and all who occupy the marginalized category of noncitizens, poses a profound dilemma. If, however, these groups cease making demands upon the state, they make it more possible for the state to solidify noncitizenship status, to continue to make citizenship masculine, and to continue to make women irrelevant to the project of nation-building.

Central also to the reinvention of heterosexuality is the state's attempt to foreclose lesbian desire, however voyeuristically and therefore inaccurately imagined by state managers, reminiscent in fact of the detailed surreptitious sexual narratives of Britain's nineteenth-century purity society. There was never an organized demand to criminalize lesbianism during the political mobilization for the passage of the Sexual Offences and Domestic Violence Act. The organized feminist demand coalesced around the restraining of violent domestic patriarchy. Behind closed doors, however, state managers sought to keep the erotic within the boundaries of the domestic heterosexual home, disrupted as it was by wife beating, rape, and incest. If husbands now had to rely upon the consent of their wives for sex, if they could no longer resort to physical and psychic violence or coercion in the "matrimonial" home, if, in other words, domestic patriarchy were in perennial need of restraint, then heterosexuality itself was at risk, and therefore needed to be defended. On no account could it be forfeited. In other words, from the state's vantage point erotic autonomy for women could only be negotiated within the narrow confines of a disrupted heterosexual. Autonomous eroticism could only go so far—it could not leave the confines of the matrimonial bed to inhabit a space that could be entirely oppositional to it, entirely unaccountable to it, or even partially imagined outside of it. Much like colonial master narratives in which masters could not imagine or anticipate their absence (for power cannot predict its own destruction), so, too, heterosexuality remains unable to imagine *its* own absence. The state as surrogate patriarch can distance itself from violent domestic patriarchy only temporarily, in order to appear more progressive than it, for ultimately it comes to the defense of the domestic patriarch in legally recouping the matrimonial bed. And while women and feminist groups may make demands on the state, undoing this historical, homosocial, ultimately homophobic bonding is a formidable task indeed.

On the one hand, women and women's groups, in spite of differences in their ideological and material class base, appear to have derivative access, if not direct access, to the state. Small size, in this instance, facilitates fluidity, and one might argue, a certain proximity to the halls of power. This fluidity enables a possible entanglement within the presumably open, yet coercive web of state patronage, especially in a context where the state is the major employer. But there is a certain duplicity attendant with coercive power: there are risks and costs embedded in women's decision to engage, in their decision to craft the very terms of engagement, or in their refusals to engage at all. Shifting political alignments among women's groups, and differences among working-class women's organizations linked to the church, for instance, and middle-class women's and service organizations such as Zonta, reflect superficial shifts in situational power, although clearly the power of discursive definition is not insignificant. But this power is of a different valence than state coagulated power, sometimes permeable, at times coercive, at times securing its own interest on behalf of patriarchal nation. Given the fact that the state is able to contravene almost entirely women's own definitions of domestic violence, of sexual and physical abuse and construct its own narrative of heterosexual deliverance, it has at least partially created a defined space where women struggle over situational power while it continues to exert its inherited power. In this sense, then, the political economic serviceability of working-class women in tourism is matched by women's serviceability in another domain, for the state can draw upon women's political mobilizations as evidence of its own legitimate and advanced political governance, as evidence of its constitutional, even politically mature evolution, as evidence that democracy is working. Establishment of a woman's desk, a place behind which women can only presumably sit, provides international legitimacy for the state which is seen as adhering to civilized international conventions. The links that these groups have established make it possible for the state to allow only certain women in as symbolic representatives of women's struggles, while simultaneously continuing to diffuse certain narrow definitions of femininity. How can feminists rely on a patriarchal state that draws epistemic fodder from sexualized, imperial, regressive symbols, while making emancipatory demands upon it? How can feminists continue to lay claim on a thoroughly corrupt state? What are the responsibilities of feminists within the state apparatus to those on the outside? Even as feminist mobilizations help to provoke ruptures in heteropatriarchy and compel the state to work harder to reconstitute itself, they have not been able to interrupt sexualized practices within tourism, which occupy a sacred place in the Bahamas.

While we have understood the meaning and limits of state repression, we have done little to fully appreciate the nuanced ways in which heteropatriarchy is indispensable to it. As the organizing episteme within the state, heteropatriarchy is avidly mobilized to serve many fictions. Most significantly, it enables a homosocial, homophobic, and in a real sense, a morally bankrupt state to position itself as patriarchal savior to women, to citizens, to the economy, and to the nation.

It would seem that in this moment of the historical evolution of the Bahamian state, emancipatory feminist projects are hard pressed to continue to draw legitimacy from the state. It seems crucial for the feminist movement to reformulate a new vocabulary for an understanding of domestic violence, for instance, in terms that are not located within the state's mechanisms of surveillance. Instead of being premised within the state's misrepresentation of domestic violence and its deployment of the law of the father, feminists would need an emancipatory praxis that would dissolve the carefully programmed dimensions of the survivors' internal psychic landscape that has taught her: "if mih man don't beat me, he don't love me;" "is so man stop;" or that her daughter is "too womanish for she own good and it can't have two woman living in one house;" or that more generalized, internalized shame that begets silence and the conviction that women are women's worst enemies and only men are women's best friends. One would urgently need an emancipatory praxis that deconstructs the power of heterosexual lore that positions women as their own worst erotic enemies and rivals, that might explode mothers' inherited discomfort with the emerging, restless sexuality of their own daughters, a sexuality that is often viewed as threatening and anxious to usurp. We might have to speak the unspeakable and name the competitive heterosexuality, an unnamed homosexual desire between mother and daughter, its complicated, as yet unspecified origins, and its contradictory societal sanctions and approbations. It would be an emancipatory praxis anchored within a desire for decolonization, imagined simultaneously as political, economic, psychic, discursive, *and* sexual.

A major challenge lies, therefore, in crafting interstitial spaces beyond the hegemonic where feminism and popular mobilization can reside. It would mean developing a feminist emancipatory project in which women can love themselves, love women, and transform the nation simultaneously. This would mean building, within these interstices, new landmarks for the transformative power of the erotic, a meetingplace where our deepest yearnings for different kinds of freedom can take shape and find rest.

5

Civil Rights versus Sovereignty: Native American Women in Life and Land Struggles

Marie Anna Jaimes Guerrero

This essay explores conflicts between civil rights and sovereignty in the liberation struggles of American indigenous peoples. Understanding these conflicts is crucial in locating the position of native women in relation to both patriarchal tribal structures and to the United States, which I define here as an advanced colonial/capitalist state. An overview of the historical legal disenfranchisement of native peoples and two contemporary court cases involving women's loss of tribal status demonstrate that it is insufficient to view the U.S. solely as an advanced capitalist state. To fully comprehend the struggles of native peoples, and specifically native women, we must also understand the U.S. as an advanced colonial state, because territorial colonization remains integral to the relationship between the state and native peoples.

I wish to argue in this essay that the mainstream feminist movement has been ineffective and inconsistent when faced with the issues of land rights and sovereignty (feminism versus "indigenism"). The movement's reluctance to grapple with questions of indigenism makes solidarity politics among native women and white women difficult and also makes some native women reluctant to claim feminism. Any feminism that does not address land rights, sovereignty, and the state's systematic erasure of the cultural practices of native peoples, or that defines native women's participation in these struggles as non-feminist, is limited in vision and exclusionary in practice.

For the purposes of this discussion, "land rights" need to be understood in a context of culture and territoriality. This context differs from what we traditionally understand as proprietary rights. Similarly, tribal sovereignty must be understood in its cultural context, one that reflects a self-determination and self-sufficiency traditionally predicated on reciprocity rather than individual ownership. Here, too, this context differs from the Eurocentric construction of sovereignty from which the political concept is derived. These definitions are crucial in theorizing the nature of the U.S. polity and its racially subordinated populations, in this instance, native peoples.

Neither mainstream feminism nor the notion of proprietary rights enables an understanding of native peoples' histories of organizing—histories in which native women have played important roles at local, regional, and even international levels. In addition to clouding and erasing these histories, the contradictory location in which native women find themselves—both inside and outside the tribe—has no place in these inherited paradigms. Yet the successes of Indian women can be seen in our reemergence as visible leaders and activists and through our positions in tribal governance.[1] We have always been inspired by the traditions of matrilineal societies, and matrifocal spheres of female power continue to be handed down to younger generations. But despite a rich tradition of female power bases, and despite some women's contemporary roles as leaders, these are troubled times for native women—times when sexism in Indian politics compounds, and is compounded by, racism and sexism in the U.S. polity. Indian women are sometimes forced to choose between loyalty to their male-controlled tribal groups and loyalty to other "third-world" women in the patriarchal hierarchy, subjected as it were to a "trickle-down patriarchy."[2] Yet it is these colonizing practices which themselves prefigure the kinds of strategies of resistance that native women employ.

Civil Rights versus Sovereignty

In this section, I argue that the legal apparatus of the U.S. government plays a central role in defining critical questions regarding liberation struggles for gender equality, while simultaneously charting an agenda for the rights of tribal peoples and their communities. It is in the context of this advanced stage of American colonialism that issues of "civil rights versus sovereignty" and "feminism versus indigenism" gain critical importance.

As traditionally communal peoples, native women organize their liberation struggles against American colonization from the premise of collective human rights—a practice that some of us refer to as *indigenism*.[3] This practice diverges radically from the priorities and sociopolitical agendas of the white, middle-class women's movement, some of which are individualist rather than communal in orientation. As long as class hierarchy and an elitist leadership prevail, and as long as the ideological schisms and differences surrounding various definitions of "feminism" continue to be grounded in a Eurocentric worldview, the struggles of native women will be subordinated within feminist agendas. In addition, traditional indigenous peoples, both women and men, often resist socialist/communist as well as socialist/feminist resolutions to our subordination by the nation state. This is so in spite of the valuable Marxist-Leninist work on labor theory that has been so important to understanding our contemporary experience of advanced colonization. One reason for the persistent critique by native people of these progressive movements is that the Eurocentric paradigm continues to be perpetuated at the expense of the universal indigenist worldview.

I am suggesting here that the struggle between Indian nations and the American state over questions of sovereignty and incorporation into the U.S. polity are most visible when one examines the contradictions that emerge over the tribal status of native women. Civil rights and sovereignty, moreover, are fundamentally gendered issues and practices because patriarchy operates both inside and outside the tribe to define belonging (the tribal status) of native women. These two patriarchal structures can, in concert, literally determine whether native women's claims to membership within tribes are honored or ignored.

The primary mechanism that has created the precarious position native women now occupy is the forcible incorporation of tribal cosmologies and structures of governance into the federal system and its own Eurocentric epistemology. Unlike other racially subordinated groups whose relationships to the American state have been defined largely by forced exclusion, the relationships of native peoples have been predicated on practices of forced inclusion.

Three legislative acts eloquently demonstrate the American state's continued agenda of forced inclusion with regard to native peoples. Presented chronologically, they are:

- *The Indian Citizenship Act* (ICA 1924): Passed as a "clean-up measure," picking up all those missed or excluded by the General Allotment Act; the law (ch 233,43 Stat. 25) unilaterally conferred U.S. citizenship on "all non citizen Indians born within the territorial limits of the (U.S.)." A number of indigenous nations, notably the Hopi and Onondaga, have refused to acknowledge that the Citizenship Act is in any way binding upon them, and continue to engage in such expressions of sovereignty as issuing their own passports.
- *The Indian Reorganization Act* (IRA 1934): The IRA (ch 576 Sat. 948, now codified as 25 U.S.C. 461-279, also known as the "Wheeler-Howard Act") was imposed by the (U.S.) to supplant traditional forms of indigenous governance in favor of a tribal council structure modeled after corporate boards. In order to put a "democratic face" on the maneuver, it was stipulated that each

reorganized Native Nation agree to the process by referendum. The referenda were then systematically rigged by (then) Commissioner of Indian Affairs John Collier. One result has been a deep division between "traditionals" and "progressives" (who endorse the IRA form of government) on many reservations to this day.

• *The Indian Civil Rights Act* (ICRA 1968): While it negated many of the worst potentialities of its infamous Termination policy, the Act (P.L. 90-248; 82 Stat. 77, codified in part as 25 U.S.C. 1301 et seq.) served to bind the forms assumed by indigenous governments as a functional part of the federal system itself. Such incorporations, however, afforded Indian peoples only constraints upon their sovereignty rather than any of the constitutional protections of basic rights and other benefits supposedly accruing to members of the U.S. polity. The Act was then amended in 1986, under provision of the federal Anti Drug Abuse Act (P.L. 99-570, 100 Stat. 3207) to allow tribal courts greater powers of penalization on certain types of criminal offenses.[4]

These three acts, individually and in combination, serve the U.S. colonialist agenda of undermining tribal sovereignty under the guise of conferring "civil rights." The Indian Citizenship Act, for example, illustrates the untenable choice between legal citizenship according to state criteria versus loyalty to and citizenship in Indian sovereign nations. Clearly, citizenship by legal fiat contests and undercuts tribal sovereignty, potentially marking native peoples as second-class citizens, even "third-world" refugees within U.S. territory.

Deloria and Lytle's theories prove useful to understanding what is epistemologically and politically at stake here. They argue that "civil rights depend first of all upon a social-contract theory of government, which Indian tribes do not possess. But they also depend upon a kind of government that allocates the sovereign powers to branches, and then separates the branches of government to act as a check and balance protection for the citizenry." In their view, the true impact of the Indian Civil Rights Act (ICRA) of 1968 was that it requires only *one* aspect of tribal government—the tribal court—to found a formal institution, one completely modeled on the federal judiciary.

With the implementation of the ICRA, the informality of Indian life, which had served as a repository of cultural traditions and customs, was suddenly abolished. The ICRA distorted reservation life by imposing rules and procedures. Indian society traditionally included a complex set of responsibilities and duties among its members. But under the ICRA, Indian society was transformed into a very different society, one based on rights conferred through government. ICRA, in effect, negated any sense of collective responsibility that Indians had to each other. As a result, people did not have to confront one another within their community to resolve their problems. Instead, they had only to file suit in tribal court.[5]

Within most tribes, the philosophical clash brought about by federal reorganization has resulted in complex problems of jurisdiction that center around conflicts between tribal sovereignty and civil-rights issues. These conflicts most often pit native women (and their children) as individuals against a predominantly male tribal group's authority—one that asserts "sovereignty" over any individual civil-rights grievances as defined by state typologies.

Two legal cases demonstrate these sociopolitical problems. The first of these—Martinez v. Southern Ute Tribe (151 F., Supp. 476, 1957)—was also the first modern civil-rights case. The case concerned the right of a tribe to determine its own membership for tribal governance. Because of the federally imposed Indian Reorganization Act (IRA of 1934), a male-dominated tribal council determined whether a Pueblo woman had the right to continued membership in the tribe. The woman lost her case on the grounds that the district court would not intervene in the tribe's decision not to grant her membership, citing the latter's sovereignty in its internal affairs.[6]

The second case—Martinez v. Santa Clara Pueblo (436 U.S. 49, 1978)—occurred two decades later but also involved a Pueblo woman (also named Martinez, but not related to the woman in the earlier case). As a former member of the Santa Clara Pueblo, she and her children were denied tribal status because she had married an Indian man from outside the tribe. In this case, Ms. Martinez sued the male-dominated Pueblo council, arguing her loss of tribal status and her children's loss of inter-tribal status as a civil-rights grievance. What further complicated this case, and what is still confounding today, is that prior to reorganization by the IRA, Pueblo traditional society, as an ethnologist testified in court, was matrilineal, so it would most likely have automatically reconferred tribal status to Ms. Martinez's children. But under IRA, the Pueblo governance and court system had been reorganized as an extension of the U.S. federal government. And through this reorganization, its matrilineal traditions had been eroded.

This case was further complicated by the fact that Martinez had married a Navajo (Dineh) man who came from a tribe not subject to IRA reorganization. Because her husband's tribe still practiced matrilineal customs while her own tribe had discarded them, Ms. Martinez and her children faced a double bind that denied them membership in either her Santa Clara Pueblo tribe or her husband's Navajo tribe. The case presents a particularly nasty entanglement of sovereignty and jurisdictional claims, clearly illustrating how native women and their children can become caught in a triangle of disenfranchisement. Ms. Martinez was denied not only her IRA "civil rights" but also tribal membership in both her own Santa Clara Pueblo tribe and her husband's Navajo tribe.[7] Her children suffered the same fate.

The two Martinez cases demonstrate the significance gender plays in understanding the legal and material implications of "civil rights versus sovereignty" and the disproportionate burden placed on women as members of native tribes and presumed citizens of the U.S. polity. Sexism and racism in the American state and the sexism within tribal contexts operate more often than not to nullify any demands native women can make as citizens. Citizenship, then, continues to be based on chauvinist and patriarchal terms.

But civil rights are neither understood nor practiced on the same terms in all of North America. A comparison between the U.S. and Canadian government systems illustrates that there can, in fact, be variations in federal Reserve Indian/Aboriginal policy. One example is a Canadian government ruling in favor of tribal reinstatement for a New Brunswick Tobique Reserve woman and her child. Sandra (Sappier) Lovelace used the existing Canadian Indian Act to claim that her civil rights had been violated when the male-dominated Tobique council took away her Reserve status because she married outside the tribe and left the community. She subsequently left her husband and returned to the Tobique Reserve with her young son. Even though she still had relatives on the reserve, the council denied her housing and the other services to which she had been entitled under previous tribal membership.

This move by the council resulted in Lovelace and her son becoming welfare dependents of her relatives. With the support of a native women's group, the Lovelace case went all the way to the United Nations (Dec. 29, 1977) and eventually caught the attention of the Canadian women's movement. This women's alliance made a significant contribution to pressuring the Canadian government to amend the Indian Act of 1985 so that it would include provisions to protect women and their children who found themselves in similar predicaments. Their argument was that Lovelace was in need of the Canadian government's protection from the arbitrariness and capriciousness of a predominantly male tribal leadership that could deny an Indian woman and her child, among others, their Indian status. In this case, the relevant issues were employment opportunities and tribal reinstatement, of which the latter would provide housing and other services on the reserve. The male tribal leadership retaliated, claiming that both the Canadian government and the United Nations had preempted the council's tribal *sovereignty*.[8]

The two Martinez cases (1957, 1978), illustrate the complex issues, contradictions, and problems that emerge when two societal systems are thrown into philosophical and ideological conflict. In the case of native peoples and the U.S. government, the inherent conflicts escalate in proportion to the degree of federal intervention into the internal affairs of a given tribe, which is actually a former nation recognized by nation-to-nation treaties and other international agreements. Tribal leaders in the U.S. are now mandated by the federal government to "spell out" civil-rights codes to be incorporated into the respective tribe's IRA constitutions.[9] This mandate now exists in part because of the 1973 Wounded Knee U.S. military operation and the 1978 Martinez case, both of which raised complex and disconcerting questions about gender and justice.[10]

The contradictory and unwelcome effects of what Indians call dual citizenry—simultaneous Indian and American citizenship—are substantiated by many examples. Perhaps the most explosive of these was the Indian occupation and subsequent siege known as the Wounded Knee Occupation of 1973, which occurred on the Pine Ridge Indian reservation in South Dakota. Deloria and Lytle observed that during this occupation, "the tribal government was consistently used by one group of Indians to harass and oppress another group of Indians. When violence (finally) erupted, there was no role for the tribal court except to echo the sentiments of one side of the intra-tribal dispute." The American Indian Movement was brought in at the request of traditional reservation residents called elders. They protested the "tyrannical" abuses of the IRA-imposed tribal government and accused the tribal council, chaired by the notorious Dickie Wilson, of being an "oppressive creation of the EuroAmericans colonial mentality."[11] But they also asserted that the idea of civil rights provided no guarantees that such rights would be automatically protected.

To summarize, the effect of Indian Citizenship Act, the Indian Reorganization Act, and the Indian Civil Rights Act has been a consistent and systematic whittling away of the legal claims of tribal sovereignty for all native peoples. In addition, the two Martinez cases and the Canadian Lovelace case illustrate that the contradictions and resulting problems of dual citizenry fall disproportionately on native women, denying them legal autonomy within their own tribes as well as within federal contexts.

U.S. State and Advanced Colonization: Land, Race, Blood, and Legitimizing "Indianness"

Any comprehensive understanding of the American state's colonizing processes must begin with the acknowledgment that the terms "American Indian" or "Native American" are federal constructions, predicated on "race" and other criteria generated by federal Indian policy and court decisions. In fact, one of the ongoing strategies of advanced colonization is the continued codification of the category of "Indian" in ways that exacerbate the political, economic, and cultural conditions of Indian people. Another effect of these state processes of homogenization (the creation of a "Pan Indianism") is the aggravation of already-existing divisions among and within native groups. At this point, however, I want to place this dominant/subordinate relationship between the U.S. state and Indians/tribes into an historical context.

In the 1830s, Chief Justice Marshall of the Supreme Court determined that Indian tribes in the U.S. were "domestic dependent nations." In this decision, the original bilateral relationship between tribes as nations and the U.S. government was transformed into a unilateral relationship that kept Indian peoples in perpetual subordination to a "settler state, called the United States of America."[12]

Vine Deloria provides a legal response to this development in comments concerning the court decision in *Native American Church v. Navajo Tribal Council* (272 F. 2nd 131, 1959). The issue at stake was whether the Navajo tribal council had the jurisdiction to prohibit the use of peyote by the Church. The court ruled that "Indian tribes are not states. They have a status higher than states. They are (however) subordinant and dependent nations possessed of all powers as such only to the extent that they have been expressly required to surrender them by the superior sovereign, the United States."[13] This legal discourse couches the relationship as a "trust responsibility" or "guardianship" of Indian populations and as "wards" of the U.S. government. In actuality, it is a paternalistic relationship of great advantage to the U.S. government because it colonizes tribal peoples as "wards," always under the control and domination of their oppressors.[14] If, as this schematic suggests, native peoples are subjected to the state, native women in particular will be positioned as second-class citizens at best. In the worst-case scenario, poor native groups will live as third-class refugees in their homelands.

The federal government has had a long history of legislating the criteria that determine who is Indian. These criteria rely upon a racial/racist policy of "blood quantum" formula that is implemented by the Bureau of Indian Affairs. In contrast to inherited kinship systems and cultural traditions, which did not hold to a "race" construct to determine tribal membership, this contemporary formula relies upon the narrow notion of "blood quantum" to determine who has Indian blood.[15]

There are material effects of these legal codifications within Indian communities in which the Bureau of Indian Affairs becomes a major disciplining agent, determining who has legitimate claim to be Indian. For instance, the 1990 BIA Indian Arts and Crafts Act (P.L. 101644104 Dysy. 4662) denied "non-federally recognized" native artists, many of whom are political activists, freedom of expression in the Indian art market. Today, an "uncertified" native artist who sells his or her work as an Indian can be fined, arrested, and imprisoned for "impersonating an Indian." This act, which codifies political censorship of the arts, also threatens art galleries, shops, and so forth with bankruptcy. To date, this remains a controversial issue that pits "federally recognized" Indians against those who are "uncertified." Similar divisive tactics are currently being used against Native American educators, academics, and writers who are labeled "ethnic frauds."[16]

The federal imposition of "blood quantum" criteria to determine who is Indian has generated complicated gender tribal politics in ways that disproportionately affect women. I am referring here to the complications that arise when a native woman marries a non-Indian man and the marginalized status that she and her "mixed-blood" children occupy as a result. In most instances, the woman must relinquish her Indian identity and lose tribal membership altogether. There are exceptions, however, depending upon which families have control over tribal politics on the reservations and which "federally recognized" tribe has access to the political apparatus of the U.S. governance system in federal partisan politics. But when a native American woman marries a non-Indian man, she and her mixed children always have the most to lose.

This was not the case in precolonial times, when elaborate traditional kinship systems organized relationships within clan structures. These traditional structures determined kinship relations within extended families and the communal society as a whole. In Lakota society, for example, women who were taken in (or raided) from other native nations would be considered Lakota members once they learned the native language and other customs. However, their children, in the tradition of the Great Plains nations as matrilineal societies, would be considered Lakota by birth, regardless of "mixed-blood" biology.[17]

Additionally, native people had been intermarrying with non-Indians long before the onset and establishment of EuroAmerican colonialism. This would not *traditionally* have been a problem in an indigenous society that based its membership on kinship systems (or moities) and cultural criteria, which included *naturalization* of non-Indians through intermarriage and other means.[18] It was not unusual, then, for native societies to practice exogamy as a custom and tradition.[19] It did, however, become a problem when Eurocentric males took native women as their "squaws" (a Euro-sexist term), usually without legal license or sanction, and then often took their land from them under patriarchal law.[20] Native women historically faced and currently face more disadvantages than native men, who, when they marry outside the tribe, continue to benefit from the patriarchal operation of tribal membership. Women lose their tribal/Indian status whether they marry other Indians or not.[21]

Often times many native North American women find themselves marginalized as "third-world" women in "ethnic minority" populations. Often they are single parents with small children, no longer enjoying the traditional support of an extended-family network and kinship structure. This is especially true for those who have left the reservation community and married outside the tribe. These women and their "mixed-blood" children become the ground upon which certain ruthlessly divisive federal government policy gets shaped—policy that is being adopted by some Indian leaders themselves. Some tribal leaderships are calling for a complete prohibition against marriage outside the tribe, with compliance a requirement for holding tribal membership. This proposal, if enacted, could have dire consequences within the clan, not the least among them being the breaking of internal mechanisms that safeguard against incest.

Resistance to Genocide as "National Sacrifice Peoples"

Codification of "Indian" status is just one way in which the U.S. state has mounted its assault on native peoples. No other racialized group in the U.S. has been legislated against through official state policy as has the native population. This state strategy began in the early colonial period, when an underdeveloped American state was threatened by the existence of autonomous nations in the invaded territory. It marked the beginning of struggles over sovereignty.

Before a systematic U.S. campaign for colonization had fully emerged, the Indian-Settler wars had already ended the lives of many native peoples through military massacres and the inhumane treatment of men, women, and children. These inhumane military operations took place from the late 1860s to 1900s, in order to keep native populations corralled in what were essentially concentration camps.[22] One example was the Bosque Renondo roundup, 1864–1868, during which Navajo, Apaches, and Pueblos were taken to Fort Summer, New Mexico. There, many starved to death as a result of government "neglect." Even the cavalry stationed at the Fort to guard the prisoners attempted to appeal to the authorities rather than watch Indians die before their eyes. Another atrocity was the Sand Creek Massacre of Cheyennes and Arapahos by the Colorado militia. This assault was motivated by statehood, even though these nations were under a white flag of peace. These acts of genocide reflect just part of a long and complex history of U.S. government "policy" to effect removal and containment on designated reservations.

The systematic displacement of native peoples from their land base, which was both their economic source of livelihood as well as their spiritual foundation, set up conditions for colonially induced despair. Benchmarks in U.S. state policy provide a clear picture of these processes of colonization. They are: Allotment, in the 1800s; Termination, in the 1950s; and Relocation, which began in the 1940s and continues today. These state policies provide evidence of deliberate duplicity by federal agencies (primarily the Department of Interior) and state authorities to subjugate native peoples through the fraudulent seizure of Indian lands and natural resources. The ideology of "eminent domain" for the "common good," used in mainstream population centers, coupled with the designation of certain sites for "national security," mask a massive displacement of native peoples under the guise of pro-development schemes.[23] "Common good" has meant damage to the environment and the ecosystem and the practice of environmental racism so widespread that native peoples and their cultures are now being classified as endangered species in the U.S.

The social and material effects of advanced colonization are clearly devastating. U.S. Census data from 1980 and 1990 show that the average life expectancy of reservation-based males is approximately forty-seven years, and the life expectancy of their female counterparts is just three years longer. In 1980, nearly one in four American Indian families was maintained by a single woman, over twice the rate for non-Indians. And 47 percent of these single mother families were considered poor by federal guidelines. Native women also act as the sole breadwinner for 23 percent of households, compared with 14 percent within the general population. In addition, the poverty rate for Indian women with children under six stands at a shocking 82 percent—both on and off the reservations. The poverty rates on reservations stand at 27.5 percent, compared with 12.4 percent in the general population. However, almost two thirds of the 1.5. million census-reported American Indians (individuals and families) live off reservations in urban centers such as Los Angeles, Chicago, and Minneapolis.

Census data reveal that during 1990, four out of ten people who identified themselves as American Indians were Cherokee, Navajo (Dineh who have the largest land base), Chippewas, or Sioux (Dakota, Lakota, Nakota). Other groups in the top ten included the Choctaw, Pueblo, Apache, Iroquois, Lumbee, and Creek. The smaller groups included Cayusa (Washington State) with 126 members, the Pequot (Connecticut) with 200, the Croatan (Carolinas) with 111, and the Siuslaw with 44.51 (a figure resulting from the rigid codification standards determining who can be identified as "American Indian").

Those Indians who live on reservations bear a disproportionate risk of disease and illness because of the bureaucracy of federal Indian health services. These health services are overwhelmingly inefficient. Off the reservation, other environmental hazards contribute to poor health and illness. Chicana researcher Elizabeth Martinez reports that children living around military installations and chemical contamination sites and those exposed to farming pesticides and lead poisoning have higher rates of cancer and other illnesses. Navajo teenagers have cancer rates that are cumulative from generation to generation and stand at seventeen times the national average as a the result of uranium spills, primarily in the Southeast.[24] Three out of five of the largest commercial hazardous-waste landfills in the U.S., which have been cited for numerous environmental violations, are located in or near communities of color.

In the discussion that follows, I delineate in greater detail the material effects of targeting native lands and peoples as expendable populations. This targeting is another instance of the consequences of the advanced colonization of native peoples.

Health

There is evidence that the general health of native peoples, both on and off the reservations, is in jeopardy due to the breakdown of their immune systems. This is occurring even in the younger generations. In June 1993 an "influenza plague" reported among Navajo children in Arizona was attributed to poor hygiene and rodent droppings, but this "flu" diagnosis is being challenged as it is discovered that the illness is more likely the result of toxic dumping (i.e., uranium tailings). Alarming data on the incidence of AIDS within Indian country indicate that reservation-based tribal peoples could be decimated by the AIDS epidemic, in addition to other diseases. A recent study among native American peoples showed that native American peoples experience the highest prevalence of HIV/AIDS of any racial group in the U.S. Native peoples also have elevated rates of other STDs (sexually transmitted diseases), such as highly evident gonorrhea and syphilis infection. This history of elevated disease rates stems from a combination of factors, including, but not limited to, alcohol and drug use among AI/AN youth, and the effects of long-term unemployment and poverty. Among the key findings of the Indian Health Service survey was that "HIV is present in Indian Health Service prenatal patients, and was found in four out of five rural settings from which at least 1000 specimens had been received."[25] Interestingly, these health studies almost never weigh radioactive dumping and chemical toxic waste as factors, despite the fact that both are rampant on several Indian reservations, especially in the Southwest, which has the largest land-based Indian populations.

The latest concern in the area of Indian health-care policy and practice in the U.S. is the federal IHS policy of utilizing American Indian children as guinea pigs for "new" experimental drugs. One federal official working with the IHS actually stated that she encourages medical experiments on Indian people because Indians have no other access to health care. Of particular concern in this area is the continued targeting of Indian children for hepatitis vaccine A and B programs, which are suspected of making one susceptible to the HIV virus. The Traditional Dena'ina Tribe (in Sterling, Alaska) have been subjected to hepatitis A vaccination. And in South Dakota, parents in the Lakota community at Pine Ridge have led a protest against the usage of a hepatitis B vaccination not yet licensed by the Federal Food and

Drug Administration (FDA). A class-action complaint was filed in the U.S. District Court of Rapid City (S.D.), but the federal government responded by attempting to have it thrown out of court as "Indian parent hysteria." The Denver-based American Indian Anti-defamation Council (AIADC) has listed the culprits in this court case as the U.S. Department of Health and Human Services, the Bureau of Indian Affairs, the IHS itself, the Aberdeen Area Indian Health Service Area Office, the Centers for Disease Control, and the FDA.

The AIADC has also reported that Smith Kline Beecham Biologicals, an international drug corporation, has been testing vaccine A on Native American children. It recently pleaded guilty to a "thirty-four count federal complaint for failing to report twenty-five deaths during its testing of another drug (not identified) which (also) has not been marketed in the U.S." As a result of this "negligence," the corporation has had to pay a $100,000 fine.[26] Such IHS vaccine programs also operate within large, urban, federally funded Indian programs that target Indian peoples and other ethnic groups for medical experimentation, including sterilization. Women of All Red Nations (WARN), a national women's organization, has consistently documented the ways in which women of color and native women have become targets of birth-control experimentation. This is a deliberate form of genocide of native peoples and their communities.[27]

Foster Care

Charges of physical genocide correspond to charges of cultural genocide. A classic case of cultural genocide involved the government's practice of placing Indian children in "foster" homes. The government justified these placements by citing the dire economic conditions on Indian reservations—conditions created by the implementation of federal Indian policy. The cultural genocide implicit in this foster-care practice finally led to the passage in 1978 of the Indian Child Welfare Act, which was designed to combat the use of foster care as a form of U.S.-government sanctioned abuse. Here too, Native women have been in the forefront of the movement to pass this reform measure.[28]

With the hard-fought passage of the Indian Child Welfare Act of 1978 (PL. 95-608; 92 Stat. 3609, codified as 25 U.S.C. 1901 et seq.) the federal government was finally forced to renounce its century-old policy of forcibly and systematically transferring the care of native children to non-Indians—a policy implemented through mechanisms that ranged from a compulsory boarding-school system to wholesale adoptions. The Act, for the first time in history, established specific procedures for the adoption or foster-care placement of native children. It is likely that a contributing factor to the passage and terms of the Indian Child Welfare Act was the increased discussion of ratifying the 1948 Convention of Punishment and Prevention of the Crime of Genocide. This convention contained an article that would have prohibited such child-transfer policies. While the Indian Child Welfare Act appears to be a positive step, the application and interpretation of the Act remains unclear.[29]

Suicide, Alcohol, and Drugs

Suicide—particularly suicide involving alcohol and drugs—and car accidents are reportedly on the increase among Indian youth. These fatal trends correspond to early deaths within the adult Indian population and cannot be understood unless the intensity of colonially induced despair in some Indian communities is recognized. Patterns of alcohol-related family abuse, diseases, deaths from exposure, and "hit-and-run" accidents exist among the adult populations—male and female—both on and off the reservations.[30] In addition, reports place "the infant mortality rate among American Indians and Native Alaskan tribes as varying from 10.7 to 19.9 per 1000 live births."[31]

Sterilization and Abortion

There are correlations between earlier colonial treatment of native women and the contemporary targeting of Indian women (and other women of color) for sterilization. I am referring specifically to the sterilization of Indian women, which occurred primarily between 1968 and 1970, and the population-control strategies that were carried out on the bodies of Puerto Rican women between the 1930s and the 1960s.

In 1972, Dr. Connie Uri found evidence that the Indian Health Service (IHS), under the federal government's auspices, was sterilizing native women. She also found evidence that in 1973, 132 native women were sterilized in an IHS-operated hospital in Claremore, Oklahoma. One hundred of these cases were nontherapeutic. The sole purpose was to render a woman incapable of reproduction. Most of these procedures were performed by physicians or nurses on women who were unaware of and unprepared for the long-term consequences of sterilization—women who had not consented to these operations.[32] Additionally, the U.S. General Accounting Office (GAO), at the request of Senator James Abourezk (D-S.D.), announced in a 1976 report that more than 3,400 American Indians, mostly women, had been sterilized by the IHS between 1973 and 1976. The report also stated that there had been thirty-six violations of a court-ordered moratorium on sterilizing persons under twenty-one.[33]

Women of All Red Nations (WARN) conducted independent research and found that since 1972 approximately 42 percent of all native women of childbearing age had been sterilized without their consent through IHS programs. These statistics reflect just a few of the documented cases. The full story is not yet known and may never be fully disclosed. Yet, as a result of strong organizing by WARN, IHS was transferred in 1978 from the Bureau of Indian Affairs (BIA) to the Department of Health and Human Services. The intent of this transfer was to increase IHS accountability and thus deter such practices in the future.[34]

The case of Marina Greywind stands out as an example of one harrowing scenario faced by a native woman who sought an abortion. The traditional birth-control practices of native women include the termination of a fetus when the mother's life is in danger. In traditional indigenous societies, such individual decisions were made by the woman with the communal support of other woman and her family, as well as with a strong sense of duty and responsibility to her people. Greywind, a Lakota woman living on the streets of Fargo, North Dakota, had an alcohol addiction at the time she became pregnant after an apparent rape. A militant anti-abortion group found out about her case and offered her $11,000 to carry her baby to term rather than seek the abortion she wanted. Greywind refused the money and went ahead with the abortion. She was taken to court by an anti-abortion group and charged with criminally endangering a fetus. Greywind pleaded guilty to the abortion but later reversed the plea upon her attorney's advice. She was sentenced to a nine-month prison term. Although she had the abortion *after* she was charged, the prosecutors insisted that the terms of the charge be retained.[35] The last information on this case had it in an appeals process, but the whereabouts of the defendant were unknown. No consideration was given to the fact that the woman was oppressed *as* a native American. Actually, this case could set a horrendous precedent that violates a native women's tribal and civil rights while the media and courts continue to "blame the victim."[36]

Native Cosmologies and Women's Leadership

Native American women have a long and life-sustaining legacy of respect and empowerment within traditional indigenous societies. Tradition is defined here within the context of indigenous values and belief systems, not within a Eurocentric context that defines tradition as backward or conservative in relation to European progress. *Traditionally*, then, native women have held important and influential positions within their communal societies, such as the Creek and Cherokee Nations, and the Haudenosaunee's Iroquois Confederacy in New York State. The latter employed the longhouse form of government, wherein clan mothers selected male council leaders. Other such societies have included the Narragansett of Rhode Island, the Delaware, and the Algonquin peoples along the Atlantic coast, who generically referred to themselves as "women," a term considered a supreme compliment.[37]

Similar government traditions in which women played critical roles are found, in various forms, among the Southwest tribal peoples, such as the Navajos (Dineh) and Pueblos, and among the Great Plains nations and the Northwest fishing societies. These indigenous cultures were more often *matrilineal*–the mother determined lines of descendancy and kinship. Bases of power and spheres of influence were both matrifocal and patrifocal, and perhaps most closely approximated *egalitarianism* in human society. Sociocultural communal structures were designed to balance internal conflicts, including gender conflicts, among the membership. Native women were typically accorded a greater social value in indigenous tradition, primarily because of their biological ability to bear children. And native women often tended to be less combatant than men, though there were notable exceptions. The Lakota women of the Great Plains, for example, traditionally maintained at least four warrior societies of their own.[38]

Historically, the native woman's role as childbearer was important to her and to her tribe. Almost all tribal groups believed that the survival of the people as a nation depended on future generations. Yet travelers and colonial authorities generated a colonial discourse that rewrote native practices of sexuality and reproduction as oversexed behaviors. A Eurocentric stereotype labeled native women as less constrained in the expression of sexuality than Europeans. This stereotype prompted Amerigo Vespucci (after whom the Western hemisphere was named) to remark that "New World" women were so "lustful and promiscuous" that they made eunuchs of their male counterparts.[39]

Paradoxically, white American feminism appropriated this symbol of unconstrained sexuality as liberatory. Native peoples' traditions with regard to fertility, birth control, and female sexuality gave native women a great deal of choice and responsibility in private matters. However, native women often solicited the support of their relatives and close clanswomen in making these "private" decisions. It is unlikely, therefore, that one's individual sexuality within these kinship and clan relations was at the core of one's identity or existence.

In indigenous cosmologies, powerful female deities rivaled or complemented male deities. Androgynous entities in the spirit world integrated feminine and masculine principles.[40] This integration was also reflected in transsexual identities among both genders in a number of native cultures (i.e., the *Winkte* among the Lakota, the Navajo, and the Yaquerne–what the French called the *berdache* tradition). Native communities thus sanctioned fluid sexual and gender roles and practices, some of which native and non-native anthropologists have documented.

An example of this fluidity occurs within the Lakota, Najavo (Dineh) and Yaqui tribes, where some native males would assume an exaggerated female expression similar to that of modern-day transvestites. The Lakota called them *winktes*, meaning young men "captured by the moon." These individuals would sometimes become second wives in a polygamous marriage and were highly valued by both their spouses and the community.[41] If not married, they lived with other *berdaches* in a special sphere that included sacred rituals. But this was not necessarily a fixed status throughout their lifetime. These individuals could decide to re-enter the more dominant heterosexual and conventional society at any time without opposition. The traditional *winkte* practice quickly went underground in response to the harsh criticisms and moral judgments that Christian Europeans used against native societies. Most Christian Europeans deemed these individuals abominations.

A female counterpart to this tradition clearly existed, though there is even less information about it. There are, however, stories of "warrior women" who chose to dress like men and hunt with them.[42] These were women who did not want to abide by the more conventional roles of the women in the general society, including motherhood. But there are also some indications that these women never withdrew from the matrifocal spheres among their people, and therefore did not separate from other women in the way the male *berdaches* seemed to separate from other men.

It is well documented that reducing the status of Indian women within their pre-Columbian nations was a top priority for European colonizers eager to weaken and destabilize indigenous societies. Pre-conquest, native women were still valued in their respective societies. Cherokee women, for instance, enjoyed substantial personal freedom and exercised significant economic and political power. As matrilineal authorities in what is now called the "domestic domain," they held the land, raised the crops, and controlled most of the family food supply. Theda Perdue has observed that in the case of the Cherokee, government officials, teachers, and missionaries did the most to upset traditional Cherokee sex roles, and that by the Removal era of the 1830s, (male) tribal leaders had adopted nontribal ideas about the role of women in their society.[43] But the Cherokee were not atypical among other traditional matrilineal Indian societies. The Dineh/Navajo and the Iroquois Confederacy nations, among others, were similarly transformed even though they formally still held to matrilineal traditions in kinship practice.

Yet colonization had different effects on the existing gender regimes of different nations. M. C. Wright has found that while the introduction of the fur trade weakened traditional tribal cultures in the Pacific Northwest, intermarriage, combined with the fur traders' demand for native women's mediation and translation skills as tribal representatives, helped to strengthen women's position within their tribes. Indian women became prominent by occupying those roles within the villages. But these did not solidify their economic position. Ultimately women were pushed further out of public life, and their importance in overall affairs diminished because traditional nationhood continued to be predicated upon kinship and reciprocal relations.[44]

This European-wrought disempowerment has also created mythologies of native women as meek, docile, and subordinated to males—mythologies typically dramatized in Eurocentric books and movies and diffused among anthropologists and other social scientists who tended to foist their own racist and sexist attitudes onto native peoples and particularly onto native women. Native women were also mythologized by the British as "beasts of burden" or "squaws," a myth inherited by later generations of American colonialists.[45] There are numerous other racist-sexist stereotypes, from the licentious seductress to its opposite, the equally denigrating "Cherokee princess."[46] And yet it must be said that throughout this post-conquest disempowerment by Europeans, North American native women have continued to protest their negation and resist oblivion in American history.

Native American Women in Life and Land Struggles

Native peoples have always mounted strong resistance to European encroachment, and native women activists have been in the vanguard of indigenous liberation struggles in North America. Indeed, they have historically been the backbone of indigenous nations in the northern hemisphere.[47] Today, this tradition continues with the re-emergence of native women's leadership as tribal chair*women* of their respective nations.[48] In fact, a constant in the precolonial and colonial history of native peoples has been the consistent political mobilization of women on behalf of their communities. In addition, native women in the U.S. and Canada have held other, less visible leadership positions throughout the twentieth century in areas such as Indian education and community development, and land and resource reclamation and restoration.

However, the remaining problems can be daunting. They are particularly exacerbated by the prevailing racism and sexism that exists within our own communities, within the male-controlled leadership of tribal partisan politics, and within colonial relations in the U.S. Not paradoxically, these colonialisms have given rise to the formation of indigenous women's organizations throughout North America. These organizations reassert native women's rights, reclaim matrilineal and matrifocal traditions, and demand self-determination as a way of regaining lost sociopolitical status. Among these organizations are WARN, the Indigenous Women's Network in the U.S. and Canada, the Native Women's Association of Canada, and the women of the Metis Nations in Alberta.[49] These organizations have called attention to the impact of European colonization, the operation and effects of "trickle-down patriarchy" within Indian nations, and the ways in which these internal patriarchal structures act in concert with racism and classism propagated under advanced colonization.

American Indian women figure prominently in grassroots movements for the reclamation of land and resources as well as in human-rights struggles throughout the U.S. Land struggles, therefore, are as much about self-determination as they are about questions of economic development and the preservation and restoration of "sacred sites" for spiritual practices. Marie Lego, an elder of the Achumawi in Northern California, provided inspirational leadership in the 1970s during the "Pit River Indian Land Claims Settlement," which was actually a federal fraud dispute. Her family and supporters protested the "settlement" of their ancestral lands by Peabody Coal, Inc., until they were starved off the area. In Washington State, women such as Janet McCloud (Tulalip) and Ramona Bennett (Puyallup) had leading roles in the "fish-in" demonstrations of the 1960s, which initially used a framework of civil disobedience and principled nonviolence to dramatize the threats posed to their livelihood.

The same sort of dynamic emerged in the early 1970s, when elder Oglala Lakota women, Ellen Moves Camp and Gladys Bissonette, led the establishment of the Oglala Sioux Civil Rights Organization (OSCR) on the Pine Ridge Reservation in South Dakota. The OSCR was established following the Wounded Knee Siege of 1973, a resistance that ended when federal authorities came in with machine guns. Bissonette later became a primary negotiator for what was called the "independent Oglala Nation."

During the mid-1990s, in what has been ironically called the "Navajo-Hopi Joint Use Area" in Arizona, the federal government was still attempting to forcibly relocate more than ten thousand Dine (Navajos) in order to make way for corporate exploitation of the rich coal reserves under Indian lands. Again, women, including the elders, have stood at the forefront of resistance by refusing to leave their homes at Big Mountain. Pauline Whitesinger was the first to resist relocation. She was joined by the elder leadership, which included Roberta Blackgoat and Katherine Smith, who met the federal authorities with rifles in hand. Such women have constituted a literal physical barrier, blocking the government's relocation/mining efforts for more than a decade.

Other activist Indian women, including Lorelei Means and Madonna Thunderhawk in South Dakota, have organized for self-determination of Indian health and water rights. The efforts of these women include the coordination of international forums on indigenous rights to water, health, and the environment. These same women are co-founders of WARN, which calls for the "decolonization" of Indian peoples by way of an alliance between grassroots struggle and urban activism.[50]

Winona LaDuke (Anishinabe) has been in the forefront of the White Earth Land struggle to restore her people's tribal landbase. She is a well-known activist for environmental native rights who has been involved in the James Bay case, a corporate water diversion project in the Southwest.[51] LaDuke also serves as president of the Indigenous Women's Network, an inter-American organization that is both Canadian- and U.S.-based. Two native women were also among the four original founders of the American Indian Movement (AIM) in 1968: Mary Jane Wilson (Anishinabe), from Minneapolis, and Betty Banks, then wife of Dennis Banks.[52]

In these liberation struggles, the costs of uncompromised activism have often been high. Native men and women, many of them AIM activists, have paid dearly, sometimes with their lives. Indian activist Anna Mae Aquash (a Canadian Micmac and the mother of two children) was found murdered execution-style in South Dakota in the aftermath of the 1973 Wounded Knee Occupation. Aquash is just one example of the many women who have become martyrs for the movement. There are many similar stories from the past quarter century, any one of which demonstrates the extent to which Indian women and men have galvanized to form the center of contemporary Indian resistance.[53]

The epistemological underpinning of my argument is rooted in an indigenous worldview. This worldview posits that all living things found in the natural order—animal, plant, and mineral—are valued by virtue of their potential rather than their actual manifestations of "sacredness." It encompasses humanity, nonhuman species, and the natural environment and honors the interrelatedness and the wholeness of creation. In this worldview, it is proper to take the lives of animals for food, shelter, and general survival needs, but not for commercial profit or material gain, especially if a species is in danger of extinction. This is the meaning of indigenous conservation, which differs from the preservation ideologies espoused by environmental fundamentalists, whose views figure more prominently in the contemporary environmental movement than the indigenous episteme.[54]

This essay has illuminated how native women's resistance—and survival—is grounded in an indigenous heritage of self-determination only partially reflected in our contemporary sociopolitical leadership. Indigenism is thriving as a liberation movement inspired by our Indian cosmologies. It differs markedly from any feminism that limits the scope of our experiences and liberation struggles by defining them solely in terms of sexism. One can understand why the struggle for self-determination is simultaneously a struggle against patriarchy and a struggle for a land base that is ecologically safe and whole. As we enter the twenty-first century, native women continue to organize in multiple ways: as activists struggling against patriarchal tribal leaders; as political organizers against U.S. advanced colonization; and as writers, poets, artists, teachers, and scholars all working for the restoration of traditional indigenous rights. Native American women in North America will likely become even more visible in the fight for our people's rights and for the rights of indigenous women. Our resistance will continue to be transformative and visionary. Our long heritage includes not only the many courageous survivors of colonialist disempowerment, but our ancestors in Spirit as well as in struggle. It is in this Spirit and tradition that native women engage in indigenous liberation movements against colonization. We seek to build alliances and coalitions with other colonized groups, including third-world feminists, ecofeminists, gays and lesbians, and all other disenfranchised and dispossessed peoples, regardless of gender.

Section II

Crafting Selves, Reimagining Identities and Cultures

6

Postmodernism, "Realism," and the Politics of Identity: Cherríe Moraga and Chicana Feminism

Paula M. L. Moya

> If we are interested in building a movement that will not constantly be subverted by internal differences, then we must build from the inside-out, not the other way around. Coming to terms with the suffering of others has never meant looking away from our own.
>
> Cherríe Moraga, *This Bridge Called My Back*

In her foreword to the second edition of *This Bridge Called My Back,* co-editor Cherríe Moraga admits to feeling discouraged about the prospects for a Third-World feminism. The three years intervening between the first and second editions of *Bridge* have confirmed her insight that "Third World feminism does not provide the kind of easy political framework that women of color" run to in droves. Time has strengthened her awareness that women of color are not a "'natural' affinity group" but are people who, across sometimes painful differences, "come together out of political necessity." However, if Moraga has abandoned an easy optimism, she has not forsaken her dream of building a "broad-based U.S. women of color movement capable of spanning borders of nation and ethnicity." Urging us to "look deeply" within ourselves, Moraga encourages us to come to terms with our own suffering in order to challenge and, if necessary, "change ourselves, even sometimes our most cherished block-hard convictions." In calling for us to look within ourselves, Moraga demonstrates her comprehension that coalitions across difference require a thorough understanding of how we are different from others, as well as how they are different from us. Because differences are relational, our ability to understand an "other" depends largely on our willingness to examine our "self." For Moraga, in the service of a larger project, "difference" is something to be deliberately and respectfully engaged.

In another context, we see a quite contrary treatment of the concept of "difference." Within the field of U.S. literary and cultural studies, the institutionalization of a discourse of postmodernism has spawned an approach to difference that ironically erases the distinctiveness and relationality of difference itself. Typically, postmodernist theorists either *internalize* difference so that the individual is herself seen as "fragmented" and "contradictory" (thus disregarding the distinctions that exist between different kinds of people), or they attempt to "subvert" difference by showing that "difference" is merely a discursive illusion (thus leaving no way to contend with the fact that people experience themselves as different from each other). In either case, postmodernists reinscribe, albeit unintentionally, a kind of universalizing sameness (we are all marginal now!) that their celebration of "difference" had tried so hard to avoid.

Under the hegemonic influence of postmodernism within U.S. literary and cultural studies, the feminist scholar concerned with engaging difference in the way Moraga suggests will be bound by certain theoretical and methodological constraints. She will be justifiably wary of using categories of analysis (such as "race" or "gender") or invoking concepts (like "experience" or "identity") that have been displaced or "deconstructed" by postmodernist theorists. If, as Judith Butler and Joan Scott claim in their introduction to *Feminists Theorize the Political*, concepts like "experience" and "identity" enact a "silent violence ... as they have operated not merely to marginalize certain groups, but to erase and exclude them from the notion of 'community' altogether," then any invocation of these "foundational" concepts will be seen as always already tainted with exclusionary and totalizing forms of power (xiv). Given the current theoretical climate within U.S. literary and cultural studies, the feminist scholar who persists in using categories such as "race" or "gender" can be presumptively charged with essentialism, while her appeals to "experience" or "identity" may cause her to be dismissed as either dangerously reactionary or hopelessly naive. If, on the contrary, she accepts the strictures placed on her by postmodernism, the concerned feminist scholar may well find it difficult to explain why some people experience feelings of racial self-hatred while others feel a sense of racial superiority, some people live in poverty while others live in comfort, and some people have to worry about getting pregnant while others do not.

Feminist scholars have begun to note the legislative effect of postmodernism on feminist theorizing. In her essay "Feminism and Postmodernism," Linda Singer points to what she sees as an "impulse" within contemporary feminist discourse "to establish some privileged relationship with postmodern discourse which is intended to have regulative impact on the conduct of feminist theory and practice":

> Both from within and from outside feminist discourse, there re-emerges with regularity these days a cautionary invective with respect to the appropriation of the language concepts and rhetoric —like that of the subject or personal identity—which has been placed in a problematized epistemic suspension by postmodern tactics of deconstruction. While such cautionary considerations are not without merit (and many, at least to my mind, are truly compelling), it is both presumptuous and pre-emptive to assume that such considerations must occupy some privileged position with respect to the development of feminist theory in the range and breadth of its concerns and approaches. (468)

Similarly, in her essay "The Elimination of Experience in Feminist Theory," Linda Alcoff notes that "the rising influence of postmodernism has had a noticeable debilitating effect on [the project of empowering women as knowledge producers], producing a flurry of critical attacks on unproblematized accounts of experience and on identity politics" (4). Such critical attacks have served, in conventional theoretical wisdom, to delegitimize *all* accounts of experience and to undermine *all* forms of identity politics—unproblematized or not.

The problem posed by postmodernism is particularly acute for U.S. feminist scholars and activists of color, for whom "experience" and "identity" continue to be primary organizing principles around which they theorize and mobilize. Even women of color who readily acknowledge the nonessential nature of their political or theoretical commitments persist in referring to themselves as, for instance, "Chicana" or "Black" feminists, and continue to join organizations, such as *Mujeres Activas en Letras y Cambio Social* (MALCS), which are organized around principles of identity. For example, Moraga acknowledges that women of color are not a "'natural' affinity group" even as she works to build a movement around and for people who identify as women of color. She can do this, without contradiction, because her understanding of the identity "women of color" reconceptualizes the notion of "identity" itself. Unlike postmodernist feminists who understand the concept of "identity" as inherently and perniciously "foundational," Moraga understands "identities" as relational and grounded in the historically produced social facts which constitute social locations.

Ironically, Moraga and other women of color are often called upon in postmodernist feminist accounts of identity to delegitimize any theoretical project that attends to the linkages between identity (with its experiential and cognitive components) and social location (the particular nexus of gender, race, class, and sexuality in which a given individual exists in the world). Such projects are derided by postmodernist feminists as theoretically mistaken and dangerously "exclusionary"—particularly in relation to women of color themselves.[1] Accordingly, I devote the first section of this article, "Postmodernist 'Cyborgs' and the Denial of Social Location," to an examination of the theoretical misappropriation of women of color—specifically Chicana activist and theorist Cherríe Moraga—by the influential postmodernist theorists Judith Butler and Donna Haraway. I criticize these two theorists not only because they appropriate Moraga's words without attending to her theoretical insights, but more importantly because they employ her work at key moments in their arguments to legitimate their respective theoretical projects. In the second section, "Toward a Realist Theory of Chicana Identity," I draw upon the work of Satya Mohanty to articulate a "realist" account of Chicana identity that goes beyond essentialism by theorizing the connections between social location, experience, cultural identity, and knowledge.[2] By demonstrating the cognitive component of cultural identity, I underscore the possibility that some identities can be more politically progressive than others *not* because they are "transgressive" or "indeterminate" but because they provide us with a critical perspective from which we can disclose the complicated workings of ideology and oppression. Finally, in "'Theory in the Flesh': Moraga's Realist Feminism," I provide my own realist reading of Moraga, and show—by resituating Moraga's work within the cultural and historical conditions from which it emerged—that her elaboration of a "theory in the flesh" gestures toward a realist theory of identity. A realist reading of Moraga's work presents a strong case for how and why the theoretical insights of women of color are necessary for understanding fundamental aspects of U.S. society.

Postmodernist "Cyborgs" and the Denial of Social Location

In her influential essay "A Manifesto for Cyborgs: Science, Technology and Socialist Feminism in the 1980's," Donna Haraway figures Chicanas as exemplary cyborgs and, as such, prototypical postmodern subjects. Haraway identifies two paradigmatic "groups of texts" that she sees as constructing cyborg identities: "women of color and monstrous selves in feminist science fiction" (216). Although Haraway usually employs the generic term "women of color," she accords Chicanas a privileged position within her framework. According to Haraway, the primary characteristic of the cyborg is that of a creature who transcends, confuses, or destroys boundaries. Chicanas, as the products of the intermixing of Spaniards, Indians, and Africans, cannot claim racial or cultural purity. Their neither/nor racial status, their unclear genealogical relationship to the history of oppression (as descendents of both colonizer and colonized), and their ambiguous national identity (as neither Mexican nor fully "American") give Chicanas their signifying power within the terms of the cyborgian myth. To demonstrate that Haraway does, in fact, figure Chicanas as exemplary cyborgs, I have juxtaposed below a few passages from Haraway's text that describe characteristics first of cyborgs (I), and then of Chicanas/women of color (II). Notice how Haraway's figuration of Chicanas, instead of liberating them from a historically determined discursive position, ironically traps them—as well as their living counterparts in the real world—within a specific *signifying* function:

> I. Cyborg writing must not be about the Fall, the imagination of a once-upon-a-time wholeness before language, before writing, before Man. (217) II. Malinche was the mother here, not Eve before eating the forbidden fruit. Writing affirms Sister Outsider, not the Woman-before-the Fall-into-Writing needed by the phallogocentric Family of Man. (218)
>
> I. A cyborg body is not innocent; it was not born in a garden; it does not seek unitary identity and so generates antagonistic dualisms without end (or until the world ends); it takes irony for granted. (222) II. Cherríe Moraga in *Loving in the War Years* explores the themes of identity when one never possessed the original language, never told the original story, never resided in the harmony of legitimate heterosexuality in the garden of culture, and so cannot base identity on a myth or a fall from innocence and right to natural names, mother's or father's. (217)
>
> I. Writing is preeminently the technology of cyborgs, etched surfaces of the late twentieth century. Cyborg politics is the struggle for language and the struggle against perfect communication, against the one code that translates all meaning perfectly, the central dogma of phallogocentrism. (218) II. Figuratively and literally, language politics pervade the struggles of women of color, and stories about language have a special power in the rich contemporary writing by U.S. women of color. . . . Moraga's writing, her superb literacy, is presented in her poetry as the same kind of violation as Malinche's mastery of the conqueror's language—a violation, an illegitimate production, that allows survival. (217–18)

Haraway claims that "women of color" can be understood as a "cyborg identity, a potent subjectivity synthesized from fusions of outsider identities" (217). She bases her claim, in part, on her appropriation and misreading of the Mexicano/Chicano myth of Malinche—a misreading which allows Haraway to celebrate the symbolic birth of a new "bastard" race and the death of the founding myth of original wholeness:

> For example, retellings of the story of the indigenous woman Malinche, mother of the mestizo "bastard" race of the new world, master of languages, and mistress of Cortés, carry special meaning

> for Chicana constructions of identity. . . . Sister Outsider hints at the possibility of world survival not because of her innocence, but because of her ability to live on the boundaries, to write without the founding myth of original wholeness, . . . Malinche was mother here, not Eve before eating the forbidden fruit. Writing affirms Sister Outsider, not the Woman-before-the-Fall-into-Writing needed by the phallogocentric Family of Man. (217–18)[3]

La Malinche, also referred to as Doña Marina or Malintzín Tenepal, was the Indian woman who served as translator for Hernán Cortés during the decisive period surrounding the fall of the Aztec empire. According to the memoirs of Bernal Díaz del Castillo, who participated in and chronicled the conquest of the Aztec empire, Malintzín was born the daughter of *Caciques* (Aztec nobility) (85). After the death of her father, and while she was still a young girl, her mother and stepfather sold her into captivity, ostensibly to leave the succession to the position of *Cacique* free for her younger half-brother. According to Díaz, she was sold to Indians from Xicalango who then gave or sold her to the Indians of Tabasco (85).

After the battle of Cintla, which took place shortly after Cortés landed at Cozumel, Malintzín was given to Cortés by the Tabascan Indians along with nineteen other women as a part of the spoils of war. From the Tabascans she learned to speak Chontal Maya, and it was her bilingualism that made her invaluable to Cortés. Cortés was able to speak Spanish to the Spaniard Aguilar (who had spent several years as a slave to the Mayan Indians), who then spoke Chontal Maya to Doña Marina who translated into Nahuatl for Moctezuma and his numerous vassals (Díaz del Castillo 86–87). It was in this manner that Cortés effected the communication that was so critical to his conquest of Mexico.

Today, La Malinche lives on as a symbol of enormous cultural significance for Mexicanas and Chicanas. As the mother of Cortés's son, she is figured as the symbolic mother of *mestizaje*, the mixing of Spanish and Indian blood. As the "dark" mother, the "fucked one," the "betrayer of her race," she is the figure against which women of Mexican descent have had to define themselves.[4] As the whore of the virgin/whore dichotomy in a culture that reveres *la Virgen*, she has been despised and reviled.

From the 1970s on, Mexicana and Chicana feminists have addressed the myth of Malinche, and several have attempted to recuperate and revalue her as a figure of empowering or empowered womanhood.[5] Such recuperations are generally problematic, inasmuch as attempts to absolve or empower the historical figure can result in reductive interpretations of what is a very complex situation. Cherríe Moraga's treatment of Malinche is neither naive nor reductive; she confronts the myth and examines its implications for the sexual and social situation of Chicanas today. In her essay "A Long Line of

Vendidas," she looks carefully at "this myth of the inherent unreliability of women, our natural propensity for treachery, which has been carved into the very bone of Mexican/Chicano collective psychology" (*Loving* 101), and addresses the continuing painful effects of the Malinche myth:

> The potential accusation of "traitor" or "vendida" is what hangs above the heads and beats in the hearts of most Chicanas seeking to develop our own autonomous sense of ourselves, particularly through sex and sexuality. Even if a Chicana knew no Mexican history, the concept of betraying one's race through sex and sexual politics is as common as corn. As cultural myths reflect the economics, mores, and social structures of a society, every Chicana suffers from their effects. (*Loving* 103)

Haraway's reading of the Malinche myth ignores the complexity of the situation. She concludes her discussion of Malinche by claiming that, "Stripped of identity, the bastard race teaches about the power of the margins and the importance of a mother like Malinche. Women of color have transformed her from the evil mother of masculinist fear into the originally literate mother who teaches survival" (218–19). With this statement, Haraway conceals the painful legacy of the Malinche myth and overinvests the figure of Malinche with a questionable agency. Moreover, Haraway uncritically affirms a positionality (the margins) and a mode of existence (survival) that real live Chicanas have found to be rather less (instead of more) affirming. I do not mean to suggest that marginality and survival are not, in themselves, important and valuable. Certainly survival is valuable wherever the alternative is extinction. And, as I will argue, the experience and the theorizing of marginalized or oppressed people is important for arriving at a more objective understanding of the world. But I would suggest that neither marginality nor survival are sufficient goals for a feminist project, and that no theoretical account of feminist identity can be based exclusively on such goals.

My point is that Haraway's conflation of cyborgs with women of color raises serious theoretical and political issues because she conceives the social identities of women of color in overly idealized terms. As previously noted, Haraway's conception of a cyborg is that of a creature who transcends or destroys boundaries. It is "the illegitimate offspring of militarism and patriarchal capitalism," "a kind of disassembled and reassembled, postmodern collective and personal self," a being "committed to partiality, irony, intimacy and perversity," who is "not afraid of permanently partial identities and contradictory standpoints," and who is "related [to other cyborgs] not by blood but by *choice*" (193, 205, 192, 196 emphasis added). The porosity and polysemy of the category "cyborg," in effect, leaves no criteria to determine who might *not* be a cyborg. Furthermore, since Haraway sees a lack of any essential criterion for determining who is a woman of color, anyone can be a woman of color. Thus, all cyborgs can be women of color and all women of color can be cyborgs. By sheer force of will (by "choice" as Haraway puts it) and by committing oneself (or refusing to commit oneself) to "permanently partial identities and contradictory standpoints," *anyone* can be either one or the other—or neither.[6]

The key theoretical problem here is Haraway's understanding of identity as an entirely willful construction, as wholly independent of the limiting effects of social location. Lacking an analysis of how the social facts which make up our social locations are causally relevant for the experiences we have, as well as of how those experiences inform our cultural identities, Haraway cannot conceive of a way to ground identities without essentializing them. Although she correctly ascertains that people are not *uniformly* determined by any *one* social fact, she wrongly concludes that social facts (such as gender or race) can be irrelevant to the identities we choose. Haraway's refusal to grant women of color grounded identities has the effect of rendering *all* claims to a woman of color identity equally valid. This theoretical stance allows Haraway to make the political move of assuming the position of the authoritative speaking subject with respect to women of color:

> From the perspective of cyborgs, freed of the need to ground politics in 'our' privileged position of the oppression that incorporates all other dominations, the innocence of the merely violated, the ground of those closer to nature, we can see powerful possibilities. . . . With no available original dream of a common language or original symbiosis promising protection from hostile "masculine" separation, but written into the play of a text that has no finally privileged reading or salvation history, to recognize 'oneself' as fully implicated in the world, frees us of the need to root politics in identification, vanguard parties, purity, and mothering. Stripped of identity, the bastard race teaches about the power of the margins and the importance of a mother like Malinche. Women of color have transformed her from the evil mother of masculinist fear into the originally literate mother who teaches survival. (219)

By freeing herself of the obligation to ground identity in social location, Haraway is able to arrogate the meaning of the term "women of color." With this misappropriation, Haraway authorizes herself to speak for actual women of color, to dismiss our own interpretations of our experiences of oppression, our "need to root politics in identification," and even our identities. Furthermore, she employs several rhetorical strategies designed to undermine "identity" as a concept and "identity politics" as a practice. First, she (incorrectly) implies that players of identity politics necessarily claim the "privileged position of the oppression that incorporates all other dominations"; she then overloads the discussion by linking identity politics to naive forms of essentialism which base themselves in "vanguard parties, purity, and mothering." The fact that most women of color (including Moraga) continue to organize and theorize around their identities as women of color—and that their identities *as* women of color are intimately tied to the social facts (race, gender, etc.) that make up their individual social locations—completely drops from sight in Haraway's representation of their work.

Although far more cursory, Judith Butler's treatment of Moraga's writings is also a highly questionable attempt to enlist women of color for a postmodernist agenda. In her oft-cited work *Gender Trouble*, Butler extracts one sentence from Moraga, buries it in a footnote, and then misreads it in order to justify her own inability to account for the complex interrelations that structure various forms of human identity (see p. 153, n. 24). She reads Moraga's statement that "the danger lies in ranking the oppressions" to mean that we have no way of adjudicating among different kinds of oppressions—that any attempt to causally relate or hierarchize the varieties of oppressions people suffer constitutes an imperializing, colonizing, or totalizing gesture that renders the effort invalid. This misreading of Moraga follows on the heels of Butler's dismissal of Irigaray's notion of phallogocentrism (as globalizing and exclusionary) and clears the way for her to do away with the category of "women" altogether. Thus, although Butler at first appears to have understood the critiques of women (primarily of color) who have been historically precluded from occupying the position of the "subject" of feminism, it becomes clear that their voices have been merely instrumental to her. She writes,

> The opening discussion in this chapter argues that this globalizing gesture [to find universally shared structures of oppression along an axis of sexual difference] has spawned a number of criticisms from women who claim that the category of "women" is normative and exclusionary and is invoked with the unmarked dimensions of class and racial privilege intact. In other words, the insistence upon the coherence and unity of the category of women has effectively refused the multiplicity of cultural, social and political intersections in which the concrete array of 'women' are constructed. (14)

Butler's response to this critique is not to rethink her understanding of the category "women" but rather to throw it out altogether. Underlying her logic are the assumptions that because the varieties of oppressions cannot be "summarily" ranked, they cannot be ranked at all; because epistemological projects have been totalizing and imperializing, they are always and necessarily so; and unless a given category (such as "women") is transhistorical, transcultural, stable, and uncontestable, it is not an analytical and political category at all.

It should be emphasized that the passage in Moraga that Butler cites provides no actual support for Butler's argument. To read Moraga the way Butler reads her is to ignore the italicized statement that immediately follows the caution against ranking oppressions, namely: "*The danger lies in failing to acknowledge the specificity of the oppression,*" as well as to ignore the statement that immediately follows that one: "The danger lies in attempting to deal with oppression purely from a theoretical base" (*Bridge* 52). When Moraga talks about ranking the oppressions in the context from which this sentence is extracted, she is referring to the necessity of theorizing the connections between (and not simply ranking) the different kinds of oppressions people suffer.[7] More specifically, she is referring to the situation in which militant women of color with feminist convictions often find themselves. Militant men of color claim their first loyalty on the basis of race and disparage their involvement with feminism, which is, the men insist, a "white women" thing. Meanwhile, their white feminist sisters claim their first loyalty on the basis of gender, urging women of color to see the way in which they are being exploited by their own fathers, husbands, and brothers.[8] When Moraga writes, "The danger lies in ranking the oppressions," she is warning against the reductive theoretical tendency (whether it be Marxist, feminist, or cultural nationalist) to posit one kind of oppression as primary for all time and in all places. She is not advocating an admission of defeat in the project of trying to figure out how the varieties of oppressions suffered by the woman of color intersect with, or are determined by, each other.

Common to both Haraway's and Butler's accounts of identity is the assumption of a postmodern "subject" of feminism whose identity is unstable, shifting, and contradictory: "she" can claim no grounded tie to any aspect of "her" identit(ies) because "her" anti-imperialist, shifting, and contradictory politics have no cognitive basis in *experience*. Ironically, although both Haraway and Butler lay claim to an anti-imperialist project, their strategies of resistance to oppression lack efficacy in a material world. Their attempts to disrupt gender categories (Butler), or to conjure away identity politics (Haraway), make it difficult to figure out who is "us" and who is "them," who is the "oppressed" and who is the "oppressor," who shares our interests and whose interests are opposed to ours.[9] Distinctions dissolve as all beings (human, plant, animal, and machine) are granted citizenship in the radically fragmented, unstable society of the postmodern world. "Difference" is magically subverted, and we find out that we really are all the same after all!

The key theoretical issue turns on Haraway and Butler's disavowal of the link between identity (with its experiential and cognitive components) and social location (the particular nexus of gender, race, class, and sexuality in which a given individual exists in the world). Haraway and Butler err in the assumption that because there is no *one-to-one* correspondence between social location and identity or knowledge, there is simply *no* connection between social location and identity or knowledge. I agree that in theory boundaries are infinitely permeable and power may be amorphous. The difficulty is that people do not live in an entirely abstract or discursive realm. They live as biologically and temporally limited, as well as socially situated, human beings. Furthermore, while the "postmodern" moment does represent a time of rapid social, political, economic, and discursive shifts, it does not represent a radical break with systems, structures, and meanings of the past. Power is not amorphous because oppression is systematic and structural. A politics of discourse that does not provide for some sort of bodily or concrete action outside the realm of the academic text will forever be inadequate to change the difficult "reality" of our lives. Only by acknowledging the specificity and "simultaneity of oppression," and the fact that some people are more oppressed than others, can we begin to understand the systems and structures that perpetuate oppression in order to place ourselves in a position to contest and change them (Moraga, *Loving* 128).

Until we do so, Cherríe Moraga, together with other women of color, will find herself leaving from Guatemala only to arrive at Guatepeor.[10] She will find herself caught in the dilemma of being reduced to her Chicana lesbian body, or having to deny her social location (for which her body is a compelling metaphor) as the principal place from which she derives her insights. Moraga's dilemma appears as a contradiction to the theorist who recognizes a choice only between essentialist and postmodernist accounts of identity and knowledge. On the one hand, Moraga is articulating a "theory in the flesh," derived from "the physical realities of [women of colors'] lives—[their] skin color, the land or concrete [they] grew up on, [their] sexual longings"; on the other hand, she reminds us that "sex and race do not define a person's politics" (*Loving* 23, 149). How can a theory be derived from the "physical realities of [women of color's] lives" if "sex and race do not define a person's politics"? When we examine this paradox from what I will be calling a "realist" perspective, the contradiction will be dissolved. Theory, knowledge, and understanding can be linked to "our skin color, the land or concrete we grew up on, our sexual longings" without being uniformly determined by them. Rather, those "physical realities of our lives" will profoundly *inform* the contours and the context of both our theories and our knowledge.[11] The effects that the "physical realities of our lives" have on us, then, are what need to be addressed—not dismissed or dispersed—by theorists of social identity.

Toward a Realist Theory of Chicana Identity

In the following section I will draw upon Satya Mohanty's essay "The Epistemic Status of Cultural Identity: On *Beloved* and the Postcolonial Condition," to articulate a realist account of Chicana identity that theorizes the linkages between social location, experience, epistemic privilege, and cultural identity. I must emphasize that this project is not an attempt to rehabilitate an essentialist view of identity. The critiques of essentialism are numerous; the aporias of an essentialist notion of identity have been well documented.[12] The mistake lies in assuming that our options for theorizing identities are inscribed within the postmodernism/essentialism binary—that we are either completely fixed and unitary or unstable and fragmented selves. The advantage of a realist theory of identity is that it allows for an acknowledgement of how the social facts of race, class, gender, and sexuality function in individual lives without *reducing* individuals to those social determinants.

I will begin by clarifying my claims and defining some terms. "Epistemic privilege," as I will use it in this essay, refers to a special advantage with respect to possessing or acquiring knowledge about how fundamental aspects of our society (such as race, class, gender, and sexuality) operate to sustain matrices of power. Although I will claim that oppressed groups may have epistemic privilege, I am not implying that social locations have epistemic or political meanings in a self-evident way. The simple fact of having been born a person of color in the United States or of having suffered the effects of heterosexism or of economic deprivation does not, in and of itself, give someone a better understanding or knowledge of the structure of our society. The key to claiming epistemic privilege for people who have been oppressed in a particular way stems from an acknowledgment that they have experiences—experiences that people who are not oppressed in that same way usually lack—that *can* provide them with information we all need to understand how hierarchies of race, class, gender, and sexuality operate to uphold existing regimes of power in our society. Thus, what is being claimed is not any *a priori* link between social location or identity and knowledge, but a link that is historically variable and mediated through the interpretation of experience.

"Experience," in this essay, refers to the fact of personally observing, encountering, or undergoing a particular event or situation. By this definition, experience is admittedly subjective. Experiences are not wholly external events; they do not just happen. Experiences happen to us, and it is our theoretically mediated interpretation of an event that makes it an "experience." The meanings we give our experiences are inescapably conditioned by the ideologies and "theories" through which we view the world. But what is at stake in my argument is not that experience is theoretically mediated, but rather that experience *in its mediated form* contains a "cognitive component" through which we can gain access to knowledge of the world (Mohanty, "Epistemic Status" 45). It is this contention, that it is "precisely in this *mediated* way that [personal experience] yields knowledge," that signals a theoretical departure from the opposed camps of essentialism and postmodernism (Mohanty, "Epistemic Status" 45).

The first claim of a realist theory of identity is that the different social facts (such as gender, race, class, and sexuality) that mutually constitute an individual's social location are causally relevant for the experiences she will have. Thus, a person who is racially coded as "white" in our society will usually face situations and have experiences that are significantly different from those of a person who is racially coded as "black."[13] Similarly, a person who is racially coded as "black" and who has ample financial resources at her disposal will usually face situations and have experiences that are significantly different from those of a person who is racially coded as "black" and lacks those resources. The examples can proliferate and become increasingly complex, but the basic point is this: the experiences a person is likely to have will be largely determined by her social location in a given society.[14] In order to appreciate the structural causality of the experiences of any given individual, we must take into account the mutual interaction of *all* the different social facts which constitute her social location, and situate them within the particular social, cultural, and historical matrix in which she exists.

The second basic claim of a realist theory of identity is that an individual's experiences will influence, but not entirely determine, the formation of her cultural identity. Thus, while I am suggesting that members of a group may share experiences as a result of their (voluntary or involuntary) membership in that group, I am not suggesting that they all come to the same conclusions about those experiences.[15] Because the theories through which humans interpret their experiences vary from individual to individual, from time to time, and from situation to situation, it follows that different people's interpretations of the same kind of experience will differ. For example, one woman may interpret her jealous husband's monitoring of her interactions with other men as a sign that "he really loves her," while another may interpret it in terms of the social relations of gender domination, in which a man may be socialized to see himself as both responsible for and in control of his wife's behavior. The kinds of identities these women construct for themselves will both condition and be conditioned by the kinds of interpretations they give to the experiences they have. (The first woman may see herself as a treasured wife, while the second sees herself as the victim in a hierarchically organized society in which, by virtue of her gender, she exists in a subordinate position.)

The third claim of a realist theory of identity is that there is a cognitive component to identity which allows for the possibility of error and of accuracy in interpreting experience. It is a feature of theoretically mediated experience that one person's understanding of the same situation may undergo revision over the course of time, thus rendering her subsequent interpretations of that situation more or less accurate. I have as an example my own experience of the fact that the other women in my freshman dorm at Yale treated me differently than they treated each other. My initial interpretation of the situation led me to conclude that they just did not like me—the individual, the particular package of hopes, dreams, habits, and mannerisms that I was. Never having had much trouble making friends, this experience was both troubling and humbling to me. As a "Spanish" girl from New Mexico, neither race nor racism were social realities that I considered as being relevant to me. I might have wondered (but I did not) why I ended up spending my first semester at Yale with the other brown-skinned, Spanish-surnamed woman in my residential college. It was only after I moved to Texas, where prejudice against Mexicans is much more overt, that I realized that regardless of how I saw myself, other people saw me as "Mexican." Reflecting back, I came to understand that while I had not seen the other women in my dorm as being particularly different from me, the reverse was not the case. Simultaneous with that understanding came the suspicion that my claim to a Spanish identity might be both factually and ideologically suspect. A little digging proved my suspicion correct.[16] In Texas, then, I became belatedly and unceremoniously Mexican-American. All this to illustrate the point that identities both condition and are conditioned by the kinds of interpretations people give to the experiences they have. As Mohanty says, "identities are ways of making sense of our experiences." They are "theoretical constructions that enable us to read the world in specific ways" (55).

The fourth claim of a realist theory of identity is that some identities, because they can more adequately account for the social facts constituting an individual's social location, have greater epistemic value than some others that same individual might claim. If, as in the case of my Spanish identity, I am forced to ignore certain salient facts of my social location in order to maintain my self-conception, we can fairly conclude that my identity is epistemically distorted. While my Spanish identity may have a measure of epistemic validity (mine is a Spanish surname; I undoubtedly have some "Spanish blood"), we can consider it less valid than an alternative identity which takes into consideration the ignored social facts (my "Indian blood," my Mexican cultural heritage) together with all the other social facts that are causally relevant for the experiences I might have. Identities have more or less epistemic validity to the extent that they "refer" outward to the world, that they accurately describe and explain the complex interactions between the multiple determinants of an individual's social location.[17]

According to the realist theory of identity, identities are neither self-evident, unchanging, and uncontestable, nor are they absolutely fragmented, contradictory, and unstable. Rather, identities are subject to multiple determinations and to a continual process of verification which takes place over the course of an individual's life through her interaction with the society she lives in. It is in this process of verification that identities can be (and often are) contested, and that they can (and often do) change.

I want to consider now the possibility that my identity as a "Chicana" can grant me a knowledge about the world that is "truer," and more "objective," than an alternative identity I might claim as either a "Mexican-American," a "Hispanic," or an "American" (who happens to be of Mexican descent). When I refer to a Mexican-American, I am referring to a person of Mexican heritage born and/or raised in the United States whose nationality is U.S. American. The term for me is descriptive, rather than political. The term "Hispanic" is generally used to refer to a person of Spanish, Mexican, Puerto Rican, Dominican, Cuban, Chilean, Peruvian, etc. heritage who may or may not have a Spanish-surname, who may or may not speak Spanish, who can be of any racial extraction, and who resides in the U.S. As it is currently deployed, the term is so general as to be virtually useless as a descriptive or analytical tool. Moreover, the term has been shunned by progressive intellectuals for its overt privileging of the "Spanish" part of what, for many of the people it claims to describe, is a racially and culturally mixed heritage. A Chicana, according to the usage of women who identify that way, is a politically aware woman of Mexican heritage who is at least partially descended from the indigenous people of Mesoamerica and who was born and/or raised in the United States. What distinguishes a Chicana from a Mexican-American, a Hispanic, or an American of Mexican descent is her political awareness; her recognition of her disadvantaged position in a hierarchically organized society arranged according to categories of class, race, gender, and sexuality; and her propensity to engage in political struggle aimed at subverting and changing those structures.[18]

The fifth claim of a realist theory of identity is that our ability to understand fundamental aspects of our world will depend on our ability to acknowledge and understand the social, political, economic, and epistemic consequences of our own social location. If we can agree that our *one* social world is, as Mohanty asserts, "constitutively defined by relations of domination" (72), then we can begin to see how my cultural identity as a Chicana, which takes into account an acknowledgment and understanding of those relations, may be more epistemically valid than an alternative identity I might claim as a Mexican-American, a Hispanic, or an American. While a description of myself as a Mexican-American is not technically incorrect, the description implies a structural equivalence with other hyphenated Americans (Italian-Americans, German-Americans, African-Americans, etc.) that erases the differential social, political, and economic relations that obtain for different groups. This erasure is even more marked in the cultural identity of the Hispanic or American (of Mexican descent), whose self-conception often depends upon the idea that she is a member of one more assimilable ethnic group in what is simply a nation of immigrants.[19] Factors of race, gender, and class get obscured in these identities, while a normative heterosexuality is simply presumed. We find that in order to maintain her identity, the Hispanic or American (of Mexican descent) may have to repress or misinterpret her own or others' experiences of oppression. Moreover, she will most likely view her material situation (her "success" or "failure") as entirely a result of her individual merit, and dismiss structural relations of domination as irrelevant to her personal situation. Thus, my claim that social locations have epistemic consequences is not the same as claiming that a particular kind of knowledge inheres in a particular social location. An individual's understanding of herself and the world will be mediated, more or less accurately, through her cultural identity.

The sixth and final claim of a realist theory of identity is that oppositional struggle is fundamental to our ability to understand the world more accurately. Mohanty, drawing upon the work of Sandra Harding and Richard Boyd, explains this Marxian idea in this way:

> In the case of social phenomena like sexism and racism, whose distorted representation benefits the powerful and the established groups and institutions, an attempt at an objective explanation is necessarily continuous with oppositional political struggles. Objective knowledge of such social phenomena is in fact often dependent on the theoretical knowledge that activism creates. For without these alternative constructions and accounts, our capacity to interpret and understand the dominant ideologies and institutions is limited to those created or sanctioned by these very ideologies and institutions. (51–52)

The "alternative constructions and accounts" generated through oppositional struggle provide new ways of looking at our world that always complicate and often challenge dominant conceptions of what is "right," "true," and "beautiful." They call to account the distorted representations of peoples, ideas, and practices whose subjugation is fundamental to the colonial, neo-colonial, imperialist, or capitalist project. Furthermore, because the well-being (and sometimes even survival) of the groups or individuals who engage in oppositional struggle depends on their ability to refute or dismantle dominant ideologies and insitutions, their vision is usually more critical, their efforts more diligent, and their arguments more comprehensive than those of individuals or groups whose well-being is predicated on the maintenance of the status quo. Oppressed groups and individuals have a stake in knowing "*what it would take* to change [our world], on . . . identifying the central relations of power and privilege that sustain it and make the world what it is" (Mohanty, "Epistemic Status" 53). This is why "granting the possibility of epistemological privilege to the oppressed might be more than a sentimental gesture; in many cases in fact it is the only way to push us toward greater social objectivity" (Mohanty, "Epistemic Status" 72). Thus, a realist theory of identity demands oppositional struggle as a necessary (although not sufficient) step toward the achievement of an epistemically privileged position.

"Theory in the Flesh": Cherríe Moraga's Realist Feminism

Yvonne Yarbro-Bejarano, in her essay "Gloria Anzaldúa's *Borderlands/La frontera*: Cultural Studies, 'Difference,' and the Non-Unitary Subject," captures the exasperation and frustration of many Chicana/o academics who have been witness to the way Anzaldúa's work has been used and abused in the service of a postmodern celebration-cum-deconstruction of "difference." Bejarano's concern is that postmodernists have appropriated Anzaldúa's powerful image of the "border" and her theory of "mestiza consciousness" without attending to the social, cultural, and historical conditions that produced Anzaldúa's thought. In the article, Yarbro-Bejarano elaborates what she identifies as "the isolation of this text from its conceptual community and the pitfalls in universalizing the theory of *mestiza* or border consciousness, which the text painstakingly grounds in specific historical and cultural experiences" (7). Taking Yarbro-Bejarano's cue, my goal in this section is two-fold: to resituate Moraga's work within the conceptual community from which it emerges by regrounding it in her specific historical and cultural experiences; and to demonstrate that Moraga's theoretical framework is consistent with a realist theory of identity.

Partly as an outgrowth of ongoing struggles (from 1845) of resistance to American domination, and partly in conjunction with Civil Rights and other left liberation movements taking place during the 60s, the Chicano Movement, as a distinct historical and political phenomenon, was born. Some of the most visible manifestions of the Chicano Movement were the New Mexico-based *La Alianza Federal de Mercedes* led by Reies López Tijerina, the California-based United Farm Worker's movement headed by Cesar Chavez and Dolores Huerta, the university-based Chicano Student Youth Movement, the Colorado-based Crusade for Justice led by Rodolfo "Corky" Gonzales, and, later, the founding of *La Raza Unida* party headed in Colorado by Gonzales, and in South Texas by José Angel Gutiérrez.[20]

Within a larger framework of resistance to Anglo-American hegemony, the groups that formed the Chicano Movement employed distinct strategies and worked toward different goals. La Alianza and the UFW were primarily class- or labor-based movements working toward the economic improvement of the communities they represented. *La Raza Unida* party emphasized electoral politics and working within existing democratic structures and institutions. The Chicano Student Youth Movement focused on Chicanos' lack of access to education and the problems associated with racial and cultural discrimination. Participants in the Youth Movement worked to establish Chicano Studies Programs within existing institutions of higher education and to increase cultural consciousness and pride.

The Chicano Movement, in general, and the Chicano Student Youth Movement, in particular, fostered the development of a cultural nationalist discourse that emphasized the importance of the family in the project of cultural survival.[21] Sociologist Alma García explains:

> Historically, as well as during the 1960s and 1970s, the Chicano family represented a source of cultural and political resistance to the various types of discrimination experienced in American society. At the cultural level, the Chicano movement emphasized the need to safeguard the value of family loyalty. At the political level, the Chicano movement used the family as a strategic organizational tool for protest activities. (219)

The Chicano nationalist emphasis on the importance of family loyalty assigned Chicanas a subordinate and circumscribed role within the movement. They were often relegated to traditional female roles and denied decision-making power. Moreover, although Chicanas were active at every stage and at every level of the Chicano movement, their participation was rarely acknowledged or recorded.

The cultural nationalist emphasis on cultural survival within an Anglo-dominated society further instituted strict controls on the sexual autonomy of Chicanas. Chicanas who dated or married white men were often criticized as *vendidas* and *malinchistas,* responsible for perpetuating the legacy of rape handed down to the Chicano community from the conquest of Mexico. This same standard did not apply to males, whose relations with white women were often seen as rectifying an unjust legacy of emasculation at the hands of the white man. Chicana lesbians were viewed as the greatest threat to the cultural integrity of the Chicano community. By engaging in sexual practices that render the male irrelevant, and by refusing to inhabit the culturally mandated subject position of the good wife and mother, Chicana lesbians create the possibility for a resistant Chicana subjectivity that exists outside the boundaries of culturally inscribed notions of Chicana womanhood.[22]

Chicano cultural nationalism found its most eloquent expression within the Chicano Student Youth Movement, and it is from within that segment of the movement that what is frequently recognized as Chicana Feminism emerged.[23] The Chicana feminist response to the kind of treatment they received from their Chicano brothers was to point out the contradictions inherent in maintaining one form of oppression in the service of abolishing another. Those who were explicit about their feminist convictions found themselves charged with "selling out" to white women's liberation. They were urged by their compañeros to drop their "divisive ideology" and to attend to the "primary" oppression facing all Chicanos—that is, racism. Chicanos often viewed an analysis of sexism within the Chicano movement or community as a threat not only to the movement, but to the culture itself.

Some Chicana feminists, disillusioned with Chicano cultural nationalism, began to work within white women's liberation movements in the 1970s. Long-term coalitions never developed due to the inability of most white women to recognize the class and race biases inherent in the structures of their own organizations. Furthermore, they replicated, in another realm, the same kind of privileging of one kind of oppression over another that had bothered Chicanas in relation to Chicanos. Insisting on the primacy of gender oppression, white feminists disregarded the class- and race-based oppression suffered by the Chicana. This resulted, in the 1980s, in Chicana feminists, together with feminists of other nonwhite racial groups, turning to their own experience as a ground for theorizing their multiple forms of oppression.

Moraga presents an interesting case because she did not participate in the Chicano Movement but has been at the forefront of the Chicana feminist response to both Chicano cultural nationalism and Anglo-American feminism.[24] Her position in the forefront can be explained both by the strength of her writings and by the fact that she was initially published and distributed through white feminist presses. Moraga is an important figure for Chicana feminists in the academy today because she is one of two Chicanas (the other being Gloria Anzaldúa) whose work is more than occasionally taken up outside the field of Chicana/o studies. As such, she is one of the few Chicanas called upon to "represent" Chicanas in women's studies and feminist theory courses throughout the U.S. How she is read, then, is crucial for how we understand the position of the Chicana in U.S. society.

Moraga's Third-World feminist political project takes as its starting point the transformation of the experience of women of color. This transformation can be accomplished, Moraga argues, only when women of color understand how their experiences are shaped by the relations of domination within which they live. Thus, while Moraga does not take the acquisition of knowledge as her goal, she sees the acquisition of knowledge—about women of color and their place in the world—as fundamental to her theoretical project. To that end, Moraga does not advocate turning away from, but turning toward, the bodies of women of color, in order to develop what she calls a "theory in the flesh."

Moraga's theoretical project, which is consonant with her interest in building a movement of/for radical women of color, involves a heartfelt examination and analysis of the sources of her oppression and her pain. Haraway is correct when she says that Moraga never claims the "innocence of the merely violated." What Moraga *does* claim is a knowledge that can be grasped as a result of an interpretation of that violation. In a 1986 interview with Norma Alarcón, Moraga described the contours of her theoretical framework:

> I began to see that, in fact, [*Loving in the War Years*] is very much a love story about my family because they made me the lover I am. And also the belief in political change is similar because it can't be theoretical. It's got to be from your heart. They all seem related to me, and I feel that what happened since *Bridge* came out is that I got closer to my own dilemma and struggle—being both Chicana and lesbian. I really feel that all along that's been the heart of the book. I could see that this book was about trying to make some sense of what is supposed to be a contradiction, but you know it ain't cause it lives in your body. (129)

Condensed in this short passage are five concepts central to Moraga's theoretical approach, all of which I will elaborate below: 1) the family as the primary instrument of socialization ("my family ... made me the lover I am"); 2) the need for theory to be grounded in emotional investment ("political change ... can't be theoretical. It's got to be from your heart"); 3) the link between social location and experience (Moraga represents being Chicana and lesbian in her society as a "dilemma"); 4) the body as a source of knowledge ("you know it ain't cause it lives in your body"); and 5) the centrality of struggle to the formation of her political consciousness. Both in this interview and throughout her writings, Moraga makes clear that it was through her struggles—to deny her *chicanidad* and then to reclaim it; to repress her lesbianism and then to express it; to escape sexism and heterosexism within a Chicano/a cultural context and then to combat racism and classism within an Anglo-American feminist movement—that she comes to understand the necessity for a nonessentialist feminist theory that can explain the political and theoretical salience of social location.

According to Moraga, a "theory in the flesh means one where the physical realities of our lives—our skin color, the land or concrete we grew up on, our sexual longings—all fuse to create a politic born out of necessity" (*Bridge* 23). It attempts to describe "the ways in which Third World women derive a feminist political theory specifically from [their] racial/cultural background and experience" (*Bridge* xxiv). Implicit in these formulations are the realist insights that the different social facts of a woman's existence are relevant for the experiences she will have, and that those experiences will inform her understanding of the world and the development of her politics. Moraga's contribution to the practice she names has been to recognize it and describe it as *theoretically mediated.* Unlike some other feminists of color whose writings seem to imply a self-evident relationship between social location, knowledge, and identity, Moraga explicitly posits the relationship between social location, knowledge, and identity as theoretically mediated through the interpretation of experience in the ways I have outlined.

As we have seen, Moraga's refusal to assume a self-evident or one-to-one correspondence between social location and knowledge opens her work to cooptation by postmodernist feminist critiques of identity. But what postmodernist interpretations of Moraga's writings fail to take into account is her emphasis on bodies and her insistence on the necessity of theorizing from the "flesh and blood experiences of the woman of color" (*Bridge* 23). In her own articulation of a "theory in the flesh," Moraga emphasizes the materiality of the body by conceptualizing "flesh" as the site on or within which the woman of color experiences the painful material effects of living in her particular social location (*Bridge* xviii). Her focus on women of color's vulnerability to pain starkly emphasizes the way they experience themselves as embodied beings. Over the course of their lives, women of color face situations and have experiences that arise as a result of how other people misrecognize them. Others routinely react to women of color with preconceived ideas about the meanings their bodies convey. These misrecognitions can be amusing; often they are painful. Moreover, the way others misrecognize women of color can affect the kind of jobs they will "qualify" for, or where they might be able to live. The material effects these misrecognitions have are why postmodernist theories of identity that do not account for the causal connection between social location and experience have no real liberatory potential for women of color or other multiply oppressed individuals.

Moraga's personal example illustrates that a woman of color's response to her socially disadvantaged position is not uniform and can change over time. Moraga's initial prereflective and visceral response to being Chicana and lesbian was to deny her *chicanidad* and repress her lesbianism. This response represented an attempt on Moraga's part to claim access to the privilege that whiteness and heterosexuality are accorded in U.S. society. In her essay "La Güera," Moraga talks about how the fact of her white skin facilitated her early denial of her Mexican cultural heritage:

> I was educated, and wore it with a keen sense of pride and satisfaction, my head propped up with the knowledge, from my mother, that my life would be easier than hers. I was educated; but more than this, I was "la güera": fair-skinned. Born with the features of my Chicana mother, but the skin of my Anglo father, I had it made. (*Bridge* 28)[25]

As a young girl, Moraga shared her mother's concern that she be in a position to transcend the barriers faced by individuals in U.S. society who are situated as "poor, uneducated, and Chicana" (*Loving* 52). The best way she and her mother could see for Moraga to accomplish this goal was for her to leave behind her Mexican cultural heritage—the presumed "cause" of her poverty and powerlessness. Their unstated goal was for Moraga to become "anglocized," a condition which, they assumed, would give her access to power and privilege. In the conceptual universe within which they were working, Moraga's white skin, her Anglo surname, and her education would be her tickets to the promised land.

Moraga's "anglocization" was at first encouraged by her growing awareness of her lesbian sexuality. The product of a strict Mexican and Catholic upbringing, Moraga concluded at the age of twelve that her strong emotional attachments to women, which she had started to identify as sexual, must have been "impure" and "sinful" (*Loving* 119). Her response to this conclusion was to beat a terrified retreat into the region of religion, thus abandoning the body that was beginning to betray her biological femaleness. In the article she co-authored with Amber Hollibaugh, "What We're Rollin Around in Bed With," Moraga reveals her alarm at the changes her body went through during puberty: "I didn't really think of myself as female, or male. I thought of myself as this hybrid or something. I just kinda thought of myself as this free agent until I got tits. Then I thought, '*oh, oh, some problem has occurred here. . . .*'" (60). Moraga's growing awareness of her own biological femaleness, and the inability to act she associated with that femaleness, caused her to feel "crucially and critically alone and powerless" (*Loving* 120). This awareness, combined with the realization that her sexual feelings for women were inappropriate according to the standards of the society in which she lived, prompted Moraga to disavow her racialized and sexualized body. She writes that "in order to not embody the *chingada*, nor the femalized, and therefore perverse, version of the *chingón*, I became pure spirit—bodiless" (*Loving* 120).[26]

For years, Moraga lived in a state of what she describes as "an absent inarticulate terror" (*Loving* 121). Her feelings for women, which she had tried so hard to suppress, did not fully reawaken until she became sexually active with men. Even then, Moraga could not face her lesbianism. She explains: "The sheer prospect of being a lesbian was too great to bear, fully believing that giving into such desires would find me shot-up with bullets or drugs in a gutter somewhere" (*Loving* 122). She began to be revisited by "feelings of outsiderhood"; she saw herself as "half-animal/half-human, hairy-rumped and cloven-hoofed, como el diablo" (*Loving* 124). It took a series of breakdowns before Moraga could begin the process of learning to live with her sexual desire for women. In that process, she became further alienated from her Chicana/o community. Because Moraga experienced her sexuality as contrary to the social mores of a Chicana/o community, it was that particular community she needed to leave in order to, in the words of Gloria Anzaldúa, "come out as the person [she] really was" (*Loving* 116). Moraga explains, "I became anglocized because I thought it was the only option available to me toward gaining autonomy as a person without being sexually stigmatized.... I instinctively made choices which I thought would allow me greater freedom of movement in the future" (*Loving* 99).

Given the urgency of her need to come to terms with her sexual identity, Moraga became, as if by default, "white." As the light-skinned daughter of a dark-skinned Mexican-origin woman, Moraga had a choice, of sorts, as to which "race" she would identify with. According to the logic of what anthropologist Marvin Harris calls hypo-descent, Moraga is Mexican, and therefore nonwhite (56). The empirical fact that there is no "Mexican" race, that "Mexican" denotes a nationality and not a race, and that some Mexicans are phenotypically "white" seems to have little bearing on the ethnic/racial classification of Mexican-origin people in the U.S. Practically speaking, the "racial" classification into which any given individual is placed in the U.S. today is predicated much more on how she looks, speaks, acts, walks, thinks, and identifies, than on the word or words on her birth certificate. Thus, Moraga can be seen as "white" by those who do not know her well and as a "woman of color" by those who do.

Moraga's identification as "white" was at least partially motivated by two underlying assumptions at work in the conceptual universe from which she emerged. The first assumption is that homosexuality belongs, in an essential way, to white people. Moraga explains that homosexuality is seen by many Chicana/os as "*his* [the white man's] disease with which he sinisterly infects Third-World people, men and women alike" (*Loving* 114). The second assumption, which follows from the first, is that a woman cannot be a Chicana and a lesbian at the same time. These two assumptions, combined with the fact that Moraga was still clinging to the privilege (here figured as "freedom of movement") that the color of her skin might afford her, precluded her from understanding what it meant for her to be a *Chicana* lesbian. As long as Moraga avoided examining how the various social facts that constituted her social location intersected with, and were determined by, each other, she could conceive of her sexuality in isolation from her race. Moraga had not yet acknowledged how her Chicano "family ... made [her] the lover [she is]" (*Loving* 129).

Moraga's eventual coming to terms with her Chicana cultural identity was facilitated by her experience of marginalization within the women's movement.[27] However "white" she might have felt in relation to a Chicana/o community, Moraga felt a sense of cultural dislocation when other women of color were not present in the feminist organizations in which she was active. However accepting of lesbianism the feminist movement tried to be, it did not deal adequately with the the ways in which race and class have shaped women's sexuality.[28] Moraga realized that a feminist movement with an exclusive focus on gender oppression could not provide the home she was looking for (*Loving* 125).

In 1981, partly as a result of the alienation each had suffered within the women's movement, Moraga and Gloria Anzaldúa published *This Bridge Called My Back*. Although the collection was originally conceived as an anthology to be written *by* women of color *to* white women for the purpose of exposing the race and class biases inherent in many feminist organizations and theories, it evolved into "a positive affirmation of the commitment of women of color to [their] *own* feminism" (xxiii). The project was transformative, especially for the women involved in its inception and execution. For Moraga, at least, an examination of the racism, classism, and heterosexism she saw in the society around her entailed an examination of the racism, classism, and homophobia she had internalized from that society. Following Audre Lorde's suggestion, that "each one of us . . . reach down into that deep place of knowledge inside herself and touch that terror and loathing of difference that lives there," Moraga turned her attention to the sources of her own oppression and pain (*Bridge* xvi). It was this self-reflexive examination that allowed Moraga finally to make the connections between the sexual and racial aspects of her cultural identity. By examining her own experience with oppression, Moraga was able to come to an empathetic understanding of the (different yet similar) experience of oppression suffered by her mother (*Bridge* 28–30). Moraga's understanding and empathy thus worked to free her from the internalized racism and classism that had kept her from claiming a Chicana identity.

Moraga's example illustrates the possibility of coming to understand someone else's experience of oppression through empathetic connection—what Moraga, following Emma Goldman, calls "entering into the lives of others" (*Bridge* 27). Her example also illustrates the point that however dependent empathetic understanding is upon personal experience, the simple fact of experiencing oppression is not sufficient for understanding someone else's oppressive situation. Moraga's initial (and largely unexamined) reaction to her own experiences of oppression at first prevented her from empathizing with her mother's plight. It was not until she *reinterpreted* her experiences according to a different and more accurate theoretical framework that Moraga was able to empathize with and understand her mother's position. In other words, "experience is epistemically indispensable but never epistemically sufficient" for arriving at a more objective understanding of a situation (Alcoff 6). How objectively it is understood will depend on how adequately the "theory" explains the intersecting social, economic, and political relations that constitute the subject and object of knowledge. What this suggests is that in order to evaluate how accurately we understand a particular experience, we must first examine our interpretation of that experience. Rather than arguing, as postmodernist feminists do, that the theoretically mediated nature of experience renders it epistemically unreliable, we should address ourselves to the adequacy of the theoretical mediations that inform the different interpretations we give to our knowledge-generating experiences.

When, in her writings, Moraga talks about the need for people to "deal with the primary source of [their] own oppression . . . [and] to emotionally come to terms with what it feels like to be a victim," she is not advocating the kind of narcissistic navel-gazing that equates victimhood with innocence (*Bridge* 30). As Haraway rightly suggests, Moraga does not claim the "privileged position of the oppression that incorporates all other dominations," or the self-righteous "innocence of the merely violated." Central to Moraga's understanding of oppression is that it is a physical, material, psychological, and/or rhetorical manifestation of the intersecting relations of domination that constitute our shared world. To the extent that individuals are differentially situated within those relations, they may be simultaneously constituted as both oppressor *and* oppressed. So, an upper-class white woman can be oppressed by patriarchy at the same time that she oppresses others (such as poor *men* of color) through the privilege afforded to her by her race and class. Moraga would further argue that relinquishing the notion that there is a "privileged position of the oppression that incorporates all other dominations" does not free us of the need to causally relate the intersecting relations of domination that condition our experiences of oppression. And because the exercise of oppression is systematic and relations of domination are structural, Moraga understands that an examination of oppression is simultaneously an examination of fundamental aspects of a world that is hierarchically organized according to categories of class, race, gender, and sexuality. Thus, Moraga's call for women of color to examine their own lives is ultimately a call for women of color to understand the oppressive systems and structures within which they live as part of their larger project to "change the world" (*Bridge* foreword to the Second Edition).

Moraga is aware that what she is asking for will not be easy. She understands that we are often afraid to examine how *we* are implicated in relations of domination, because "*the sources of oppression form not only our radicalism, but also our pain*. Therefore, they are often the places we feel we must protect unexamined at all costs" (*Loving* 134). To do the kind of self-reflexive examination Moraga calls for can mean having to admit "how deeply 'the man's' words have been ingrained in us" (*Bridge* 32). The project of examining our own location within the relations of domination becomes even riskier when we realize that doing so might mean giving up "whatever privileges we have managed to squeeze out of this society by virtue of our gender, race, class or sexuality" (*Bridge* 30). We are afraid to admit that we have benefited from the oppression of others. "[We fear] the immobilization threatened by [our] own incipient guilt." We fear we might have to "change [our lives] once [we] have seen [ourselves] in the bodies of the people [we have] called different. [We fear] the hatred, anger, and vengeance of those [we have] hurt" (*Loving* 56-57).

Moraga's self-interrogation involved acknowledging how she has been guilty of working her own privilege, "ignorantly, at the expense of others" (*Bridge* 34). Moraga *now*, unlike many other white-skinned "Hispanics," has come to understand—through making connections between her experience as a woman in a male world and a lesbian in a heterosexual world—how what functions as the privilege of looking "white" in U.S. society has significantly shaped her experience of the world. The consequences, for Moraga, have been both positive and negative. On the one hand, she credits her light skin and Anglo surname with pushing her into the college prep "A" group in high school and with making her and her siblings "*the* success stories of the family," and, on the other, she has had to "push up against a wall of resistance from [her] own people" in her attempts to claim a Chicana identity (*Loving* 96–97; *Bridge* 33–34).

What should be clear from my analysis of Moraga's work is that her "theory in the flesh" is derived from, although not uniformly determined by, "the physical realities" of her life, her "social location." I have shown that the social facts which make up her particular social location are causally relevant for the experiences she has had, and demonstrated that Moraga's cultural identity both conditions and is conditioned by her interpretations of those experiences. I have also accounted for both the fact, and the way, that Moraga's interpretations of her experiences have changed over time. Moraga's understanding of the world—her knowledge—has been mediated through her cultural identity, which is indissolubly linked, through her experiences, to the various social facts of her particular material existence.

A realist theory of identity thus provides women of color with a non-essentialist way to ground their identities. It gives us a way of knowing and acting from within our own social location or "flesh." Like Moraga, we will no longer have to aspire to a bodiless, genderless, raceless, and sexless existence (an existence that has traditionally been conceptualized in terms of the unmarked but nevertheless privileged heterosexual white male) in order to claim justifiable knowledge of the world around us. A realist theory of identity gives women of color a way to substantiate the fact that we *do* possess knowledge—knowledge important not only for ourselves but for all who wish to more accurately understand the world—and that we possess it partly as a result of the fact that we *are* women of color.

7

Probing "Morality" and State Violence: Feminist Values and Communicative Interaction in Prison Testimonios in India and Argentina

Kavita Panjabi

> Is it surprising that prisons resemble factories, schools, barracks, hospitals, which all resemble prisons?
>
> Michel Foucault

The last five decades of this century have been marked by an increased participation of women in political struggles in India and Latin America. From the Tebhaga movement and the Telangana People's Struggle in the 1940s to the Naxalite movement which started in the 1960s, through the radical movements of the Guatemalan Indians in the 1970s to the Sandinista wars of the 1980s, women have played a prominent role in the liberation of their communities. From these experiences of struggle have emerged important feminist critiques of the hegemonic or authoritarian states in which they battle for survival.

Challenges to the repressive patriarchal functionings of state power have found expression in the testimonial genre. Distinguishing itself from "objective" historiography and marking a move away from the novelistic and the autobiographical genres in its immediate linkages with radical social action,[1] the testimonio has emerged as one of the most important literary sites for the generation of women's collective and oppositional consciousness in Latin America and the Indian subcontinent in the last three decades.[2] Through the political practice of recording eyewitness accounts and the memory of historical struggles, women's testimonios foreground a gendered critique of oppressive state rule.

North American and European feminists of Third-World origins also locate their political agendas firmly in the context of the liberation struggles of their communities. Cheryl Johnson-Odim uses the term "Third World" feminists to refer to both women from "underdeveloped"/overexploited countries and those who are residents of the First World and claims that Third-World women "treat feminism as a fundamentally political movement connected as much to the struggle of their communities for liberation and autonomy as to the work against gender discrimination" (317). I agree with the general thrust of this claim; however, from the standpoint of a woman living in India and working on women's narratives in the Third World, I am pressed to demand greater specificity in theorizations of Third-World feminism, specially with reference to the politics of location.

Seven years of personal experiences of "minority feminism" as a Third-World woman in the United States enable me to appreciate the significance of this particular usage of the term "Third-World feminism," especially in its ability to establish a political difference between minority feminisms and the hegemonic white-bourgeois feminisms of a metropolitan country. From the perspective of a feminist located in the Third World, however, the much-needed establishment of this distinction is achieved at the risk of erasing the other equally important difference between feminisms of color in North America and Europe and women's movements in the geopolitical Third World.

A reading of the testimonial literature of women's struggles in India and Latin America highlights the fact that though there are structural similarities between neocolonial oppression in the Third World and the domestic oppression of various racial and ethnic groups within North American and European nations, there are also critical differences between them on grounds of political economy. Women's movements in the Third World have been compelled to address questions of gender politics not only in tandem with race and class relations but also in the context of the nexus between imperialist powers and the national state.

Amongst other issues, *Hannaman* discusses the effects of residual colonial ideologies in the functioning of the modern Indian postcolonial state, while *The Little School* foregrounds the appropriation of patterns of religious and cultural imperialism for domestic oppression in Argentina. And *Sandino's Daughters*, and the testimonios by Rigoberta Menchú and Domitila Barrios address the role of the *comprador* bourgeoisie, the coalitions between imperialist powers and authoritarian governments, the economic consequences of transfer of capital from the third-world countries to those of the First World, and the exploitation of the labor of women in the Third World by multinational corporations. All these concerns, particular to the lives of women living in the geographical Third World, chart distinctions that need to be taken into account in any rigorous theorization of radical cross-cultural feminisms.

Women's prison testimonios from the Third World occupy a special place in this genre of political struggle because they depict prison life as a focused prismatic index of the functioning of patriarchy and state power, forces that normally control the daily lives of women in a highly diffuse and naturalized fashion. As Massimo Pavarini observes, the prison, as a model for the ideal society, " assumes the dimension of an organized project for the subaltern social world" (149). Rather than being records of historical struggles in the world *outside* in times of political crises, prison testimonios are narrative reconstructions reflecting upon the prison or concentration camp as a microcosmic embodiment of both the hegemonic or authoritarian and the counterhegemonic or antiauthoritarian relations between the state and the individual. Hence, women's prison testimonios perform the critical function of connecting the concentrated experiences of prison life to the everyday oppressions of women. Implicitly issuing a warning against the idealization, and thus distancing, of prison experiences, they instead politicize the everyday in their documentation of these connections.

I will be addressing two narratives here: Jaya Mitra's prison memoir *Hannaman*, a testimony of her experiences of imprisonment for involvement in the revolutionary Naxalite movement in the early 1970s in West Bengal, India; and Alicia Partnoy's *The Little School,* an account of her days in a concentration camp during the "dirty war" of the late 1970s in Argentina.

The Naxalite movement started in Naxalbari, in the northern part of the state of West Bengal, in May 1967. It began as a tribal and peasant revolt against the oppression of the landless peasantry by an unofficial government-landlord collusion. Initially a rural movement demanding widespread land reform, it was led by a peasant-intellectual coalition belonging chiefly to the Communist Party of India (Marxist-Leninist). Soon, it spread to other parts of rural India, especially Andhra Pradesh, and also gained force among youth in the form of urban class struggle in both small towns and in metropolitan centers such as Calcutta. Students joined the movement largely in protest against the massive unemployment rampant in the cities during the economic crisis of the 1960s.

The peasant-student coalition was, however, a fragile one, and, was, in fact, detrimental to the crusade for land reforms, especially when the movement turned toward violence and guerrilla-style insurgency against landowners, industrialists, and representatives of the state, such as the police. This violent turn enabled the government to shift the political focus to questions of "national security," and completely sidestep the originial issues of land reform and employment. In 1971, the "democratic" national government of the Prime Minister Indira Gandhi, in the interests of this "national security," cracked down on the movement, and through severely repressive measures of counterinsurgency, imprisonment, and torture, destroyed the rebellious sections of the population.[3]

While the Naxalite movement started as a peasant movement and then spread to urban areas in the "democratic" nation of India, the "dirty war" in Argentina was perpetrated by a military junta chiefly against workers and urban youth. In 1975, after the death of President Peron, Vice President Isabel Peron took charge and delegated control of the repressive apparatus to the military, which launched a systematic destruction of the workers' and youth movements through kidnapppings and political murder. In March 1976, the military, along with the national oligarchy, and backed by the multinational corporations, launched a coup, came to power, and stayed there until 1983. The junta passed a "Statute for the Process of National Reorganization" *(el Proceso)* that gave it ultimate power to govern. It immediately initiated a reconstruction of the national economy based on an aggressive pursuit of foreign investment and a domestic military war on subversion. This internal war was aimed at shattering the resistance of both the left-wing Peronist youth, who called themselves the Montoneros, and the ERP, the Marxist-Leninist People's Revolutionary Army. From 1976 to 1979, this "dirty war" was marked by mass terror, brutal torture, the imprisonment of over 7,000 youth, students, and workers, and the "disappearances" of almost 30,000 Argentine citizens.[4]

The expertise of the military state in Argentina became evident as it deployed complex and variegated modes of cultural ideologies to legitimize its own rule. As Neil Larsen has shown, the Argentinian junta demarcated the cultural site as the one where its imposed ideologies would need to gain social consensus before it could achieve definitive political victory. In his essay "Sport as Civil Society: The Argentinian Junta Plays Championship Soccer," Larsen demonstrates that the Argentine military state's hosting of the World Cup was a move to appropriate sport for the promotion of its ideologies under the guise of "nationalism." With women, however, the junta used coercion, and manipulated cultural ideologies to strengthen and perpetuate their public authority. Women were forced to retreat to their traditional roles as reproducers and nurturers of future generations. Ximena Bunster-Burotto, in her essay "Surviving Beyond Fear: Women and Torture in Latin America," observes that, for the junta, "Politically committed women who have dared to take control of their own lives by struggling against an oppressive regime *demand* sexual torture" (307).

The power invested in the repressive state apparatuses, the widespread incidence of imprisonment and brutal torture during the Naxalite era, and the "dirty war" mark these two periods as the worst instances of the violation of human rights—especially with regard to the torture of women—in the postcolonial histories of India and Argentina.

Significantly, while both Jaya Mitra and Alicia Partnoy were imprisoned for their participation in these political movements, neither discusses the historical crisis or the central political issues explicitly—these are *not* their foci.

So, why are these testimonios set against this backdrop? What *is* the focus of these narratives? While the texts do not focus on the historical crisis, the moment of crisis brings the sociopolitical conflicts and contradictions of everyday life into sharp focus. This, then, is the relationship between the historical settings and the narratives themselves: the testimonios analytically chart the ways in which the authoritarian crisis of the "dirty war" and the crisis in hegemony marked by the politics of the Naxalite movement unveil the functionings of the patriarchal capitalist state. Focusing on the "microsocial" worlds of women's prison experiences, they enact critiques of the "macrosocial" patriarchal oppressive states, elaborating upon the ways in which women's bodies become one of many sites of state control.

In this study, I focus on the ways the state controls women's bodies, and how this is related to the control of the female psyche. One of the central questions I investigate is the relation between patterns of torture designed specifically for female political prisoners and the more diffuse and "naturalized" forms of female sexual slavery[5] that characterize all patriarchal societies and, in this case, Argentina and India. I have chosen to consider the prison testimonios of a woman in a military state because the patterns of torture are systematic and blatant, hence more accessible to analysis; I hope a comparison of these two narratives will facilitate a better understanding of the less explicit methods of the torture of women in a democratic state. Finally, I wish to explore the responses of the women prisoners to each other and to the torturers; to map their modes of resistance; and to analyze these strategies in an attempt to understand the values that form the basis of an oppositional and collective feminist consciousness.

Interestingly enough, both writers, in discussing the political thrust of their testimonios, assert the need to stress not victimization but resistance and strategies of survival. Mitra emphasizes that she downplayed both the sentiment and the torture, for she wanted to underline "resistance, fearlessness, and the joy of resistance."[6] And Partnoy says, "I don't know how to write about torture. And I don't talk that much about sexual harassment . . . there was a lot going on—I don't describe it [torture] in a way that *adds* something to the reports that already exist on it. The other [thing] is that I wanted to reflect our spirit of survival, and if I went into that [writing about torture], it would be very hard to stress this other point."[7] Narrating the processes of survival is, for both writers, much more than just a question of communicating the spirit of resistance. They both use their experiences as a springboard for probing systems of domination. They juxtapose the physical and psychological torture of women with the discourse of state "morality," revealing it to be a patriarchal construct designed to control women's lives. The central problem for understanding the *systemic* workings of domination from the standpoint of women's experience, is drawing the *connections* between the experiences of the women and the powers exerted upon them, that is, "specifying the relations between the *organization* and *experience* of sexual politics and the concrete historical and political forms of colonialism, imperialism, racism, and capitalism"(Chandra Talpade Mohanty 1991, 14).

In this context, Dorothy Smith introduces the notion of "relations of ruling," a concept that enables a feminist critique of the unquestioned coincidence between patriarchy and ruling:

> "Relations of ruling" is a concept that grasps power, organization, direction and regulation as more pervasively structured than can be expressed in traditional concepts provided by discourses of power. I have come to see a specific interrelation between the dynamic advance of the distinctive forms of organizing and ruling contemporary capitalist society and the patriarchal forms of our contemporary experience. When I write of "ruling" in this context I am identifying a complex of organized practices, including government, law, business and financial management, professional organizations, and educational institutions as well as the discourses in texts that interpenetrate the multiple sites of power. (3)

We can understand how the world of everyday experience is organized by these social relations if we recognize that "it is not just activities and practices as such that give us the social as an object of inquiry but the concerting or coordination of activities or, as Marx and Engels put it [in *The German Ideology*], the forms of cooperation" (Smith 1989, 123). Since the forms of the coordination of activities are the forms through which social relations *organize* the everyday practices of the group locally and historically, Smith's emphasis on inquiry at the ontological level transcends the limitations of a knowledge based only on shared meanings and intersubjecivity. Such an analysis does not limit itself to the description of the immediate appearances of daily life, or the level of "false-consciousness," but attempts to go beneath them to reach a dynamic historical understanding of broader social and class forces. The further significance of this mode of analysis is that it enables us to question the *conflicts* and *contradictions* between concrete experiences of the everyday world and the abstracted social relations which determine them. This makes it possible to locate specific ways in which to challenge and change the "rational" optimal functioning of dominant systems, of the totality, which, as Adorno would say, is, in fact, "the optimum in irrationality" based on the "barbarous suppression" (465) of contradictions.

Finally, since the "rationality" of the system is based on the suppression of the interests of dominated groups, this critique of everyday life becomes an ethical critique. This ethical critique, based on the dialectic between the material and the discursive realms, can facilitate the reintroduction of hitherto suppressed women's reason into the systems of "irrationality."

Bunster-Burotto, exploring the nature of torture in Argentina, asserts that "We can only describe these patterns of state torture, we cannot make them rational" (307). Examining the military ideology underlying the torture of women, for instance, she observes that "one of the essential ideas behind the sexual slavery of a woman in torture is to teach her that she must retreat into the house and fulfill the traditional role of wife and mother" (307). The patriarchal *mother/whore schema,* while global, finds its particular manifestation in Latin America in *marianissimo,* the widespread cult of the Virgin Mother as the simultaneous ideal of womanhood, motherhood, and chastity. Bunster-Burotto's research reveals the irrationality of the modes of torture of women who have dared to violate this stereotype, where the contradictory logic of inversion in the "method of the 'lesson' (forc[es]) a return to the marianissimo ideal [and] simultaneously violates that possibility" (307). Such torture takes various forms: violating the "chastity" of a woman through rape; abusing a woman's nurturing role by raping/torturing her in front of her children, causing irreparable damage to both; and forcing pregnant women into sexual slavery by taking control of their offspring, torturing them into aborting, or appropriating their newborn children. These techniques not only shatter a woman's self-respect, dignity, and physical integrity, they also effect what Bunster-Burotto terms a "cruel double disorientation": first, forcing upon her a stereotype of "ideal womanhood," then making it impossible for her to achieve it.

Such manipulations of diffuse forms of female sexual enslavement are also evident in the modes of bodily torture depicted in *The Little School* and *Hannaman.* However, these prison testimonios enact valuable feminist critiques in their juxtaposition of the inhuman modes of torture with the state's purported reason for torturing, i.e., in the name of "morality" and "justice." In Argentina, the Doctrine of National Security gave "legal sanction" to the "dirty war," which, as the National Commission on the Disappeared asserts, was "perceived as a total, definitive war in defence of a subjective view of nationality" (443). This view was developed in order to safeguard "Western, Christian values," which were being threatened by those labeled "Marxist-Leninist, traitors to the fatherland, materialists and atheists, enemies of Western Christian values" (4–5). Addressing the treatment of the pregnant Graciela, one of the "disappeared" people at the Little School, Partnoy foregrounds one of the ways in which the woman's body becomes the site of political intimidation. In keeping with humane "Christian" values of the state, Graciela is subject to an "exercise program" for her pregnancy. However, her internal monologue discloses this "moral" requirement to be a torture technique, revealing the actual immorality and power strategies of the state:

> But they weren't worried about my belly when they arrested me. The trip from Cutral-CO to Neuquén was pure hell.... They

> knew I was pregnant. It hadn't occurred to me that they could torture me while we were traveling. They did it during the whole trip: the electric prod on my abdomen because they knew about the pregnancy ... One, two, three, four.... Each shock brought that terrible fear of miscarriage ... and that pain, my baby's pain. I think it hurt more because I knew he was being hurt, because they were trying to kill him.... I wonder if this exercise program is one more sham or if they'll let me live until my child is born. And what after that? (Partnoy 1986, 53–54)

In the "dirty war," in which the family was routinely victimized and death had become a political weapon for decimating the "subversives," control over pregnant women's bodies implies much more than the physical and emotional torture of the women themselves. As the text begins to imply, this torture extends to the control of future generations, either by killing them or by controlling their ideology.[8] Thus, women's bodies become sites of physical, mental, and ideological control under the guise of "morality."

Hannaman, too, ruthlessly questions the "morality" and "rationality" of the state. Mitra represents the established views of prisoners, as criminal or insane, through the recurring metaphor of the prisoners as "worms endangering the social health of society" with their crimes. She then proceeds to show how the disease is actually located in the patriarchal functioning of society, the state, and the judiciary, not in the women's actions which are judged to be "criminal." The text reveals how the "rationality of the state, in its treatment of prisoners, focuses on the nature of the crime, not the cause for it."

If morality is a genuine concern, then the crucial question is: what exactly drives the women to madness or crime? In his study of madness and civilization, Foucault points out why the investigation of *causes* proves to be a central threat to the maintenance of the status quo of a society:

> What then is this confrontation beneath the language of reason? ... What realm do we enter which is neither the history of knowledge, nor history itself: which is controlled by neither the teleology of truth nor the rational sequence of causes, since causes have value and meaning only beyond the [reason-madness] division? A realm, no doubt, *where what is in question is the limits rather than the identity of a culture* [emphasis mine]. (Foucault 1965, xi)

Through the description of the concrete realities of women's lives, *Hannaman* delves into the values that motivate their "insane" or "criminal" actions, hence revealing the actual social relations that characterize the women's lives. In most cases, it is either a self-sacrificial love for husbands or sons that leads women to take the crimes of male family members upon themselves or a sense of human dignity that, under impossible circumstances of violence, makes child murder the only way to protect themselves from battery and torture. Confronting the superficial branding of the women by both the state and society with an in-depth probing of causes, *Hannaman* opens up the already broken dialogue, "the already effected separation" between reason and madness, between the criminal act and the lawful act. It thus challenges the limits of mainstream culture, revealing them to be limits demarcated by an oppressive and inhumane patriarchy.

Hannaman enacts a further and crucial critique of the functionings of the state apparatus. It shows, in the treatment of the prisoners, a callous repudiation of the same "morality," for the ostensible breach of which the women were jailed. Women who are sold into prostitution and are forced to practice it illegally, are arrested from time to time to fill up the jail "quotas." The cruel distortion of morality is inherent not only in the fact that it is the women, who have already been coerced into female sexual slavery, who are punished, but also in the favoritism extended to certain women–like Shikha, who is in jail for cheating frauds or Lalmoti, who was imprisoned for trafficking in women–who set up their "undertrial empires" to entice the warders in the prisons (52–53). While some "madwomen" are kept behind bars because they are a danger to society, the prison system itself proves dangerous to women: it drives "mad" inmates to a "natural death" in winter because they are not allowed clothes or blankets for fear that they will hang themselves (137). By stripping women like Shanta in front of their children (23), the prison system doubly tortures them, violating their self-respect and psychologically damaging their children. The warders also deny women their motherhood, driving them to insanity and their newborns to death, by depriving women like Ayata of their children immediately after childbirth. And, in the cases of women serving sentences for having killed their children to save them from incest or starvation, the episodes described in the text foreground exactly how much the prison warders value life. They force Shyamabai to give birth on a broken iron bed in such a manner that the child dies (126), and they shackle a pregnant woman's feet tied twelve inches above the ground so that she is unable to deliver and dies with the child inside her (129).

Both Jaya Mitra and Alicia Partnoy were separated from their infant daughters while in prison. In Partnoy's case, even the whereabouts of her daughter were withheld from her in a further attempt to torture her; in Mitra's context, it was a separation sanctioned by law. *Hannaman* draws attention to the fact that the state *legally* denies women prisoners the right to motherhood; the laws of the colonial Indian state of 1875 were still in force in 1973–the only difference being that, earlier, children above two had had to be sent to "welfare homes" in the absence of their guardians; in

1973, the age limit was raised to six (103). If the mothers in prison are deemed "unfit" to raise children, the text questions the "fitness" of the prescribed welfare homes to do so. And the "example" is set by the Liluah home where female orphans and children of madwomen and prisoners are sent to live in a state of psychological, emotional, and sexual deprivation and complete physical alienation for the rest of their lives, conditions that, for lack of any alternative, force them into intense lesbian relationships which often culminate in murders motivated by jealousy (108).

Hannaman juxtaposes the "moral" discourse of the state that "justifies" its imprisonment of the women with the actual oppression they suffer, emphasizing that the detentions are hardly a matter of safeguarding morality. Hence, it provides grounds for not only a moral but also a social-theoretical critique. It shows how "morality," far from being an *ontological* concern, is a *sociopolitical construct* designed to legitimate patriarchy and perpetuate state control over women's lives.

Implicit in the critiques of the functioning of prisons and concentration camps, in both *Hannaman* and *The Little School,* is the question of feminist values that confront the patriarchal epistemology. Clearly, gender discrimination and oppression are not "natural" qualities of women's lives but ones that result from social constructions of gender. Women's oppositonal consciousness is in fact generated from the ontological conditions of everyday life. And Satya Mohanty, while agreeing that women's experiences are often significant repositories of oppositional language, stresses the importance of the cognitive component of experience that allows us to glean objective knowledge from it. However, he also warns against the possible understandings of experience that are nothing more than socially produced mystification:

> The naturalist-realist account of experience I defend here is neither foundationalist nor skeptical; it argues that experience, properly interpreted, can yield reliable and genuine knowledge, just as it can point up instances and sources of real mystification. Central to this account is the claim that the experience of social subjects has a cognitive component.... All experience ... is socially constructed. But the constructedness does not make it arbitrary or unstable in advance. Experiences are crucial indices of our relationships with our world (which includes our relationships with ourselves), and to stress their cognitive nature is to argue that they can be susceptible to *varying degrees* of socially contructed truth or error, and can serve as sources of objective knowledge or socially produced mystification. (S. Mohanty 1991, 44–45; 50–51)

The crucial task, then, is to distinguish between the mystifications and the objective theorizing, between the potentially destructive and the strategically and ethically beneficial.

One of the outstanding cases Mitra implicitly critiques is that of Budha, a tribal woman from Purulia, who killed her aunt because she believed the aunt was a witch who had destroyed her childbearing capacities (34–35). Mitra comments, "Hence, having killed a witch, she thought that she had only done five others a favor. That is why the thought of trying to run away did not even occur to her" (35). She focuses on the radical incommensurability between the rational ideas of justice and a superstition-based ethic by emphasizing Budha's complete incomprehension at her removal from the dense jungles she had inhabited, and her imprisonment in the dirty concrete structures of the jail. But what is more important is that unlike the sympathetic descriptions of the other women's reasons for commiting "crimes," Mitra, by communicating Budha's belief through the use of "she thought," not only distances Budha's internalization of the socially produced superstitions, which construct women as witches and legitimize witch hunting, from her own beliefs and that of the community of women she locates herself within, but also implies that these superstitious beliefs comprise a subjective world view that is not necessarily right.

Mitra also turns a critical eye toward the role of religion and the internalization of religious ideologies by women in both Islamic and Hindu cultures. Through her conversation with the veiled Shashibibi, she questions the self-image of a religious Muslim woman who uncritically accepts the self-denial and the physical and conceptual restraints imposed by the *purdah* as essential attributes of a good Muslim woman:

> -A woman has to observe modesty and shame, *didi* [elder sister]. . . .
> -But you won't be able to *see* anything from behind such a huge veil [emphasis mine].
> -It's Allah's law *didi*, disaster strikes if one doesn't guard one's honour.
> -And there is no way of being able to *see* to one's satisfaction this large world that Allah created, Shashibibi [emphasis mine]?
> Who has instilled into her head all these laws that denied her even desire? (11–12)

Punning on the word "see," Mitra emphasizes not only Shashibibi's inability to physically see the world from behind the veil but also her inability to understand and comprehend the world, to know what it is all about, to be conscious of the ways it restrains her, denies her, and mystifies her understanding of it by presenting this denial as religious law.

On a more complex note, *Hannaman* extends this denunciation of blind religious faith to a critique of the way in which Hindu ideologies "legitimize" violence and thus create the ground for destructive expressions of deep psychic disturbances. In a moment of frenzy, Jamini, rooting her psychic frustrations in destructive Hindu beliefs, had sacrificed her husband to the goddess Kali and carried his head around the marketplace in a trance.[9] Three days after her appeal had been rejected in the High Court, Jamini grabbed her four-year-old daughter by the legs and began slamming her relentlessly onto the ground for forty minutes. In a distorted voice, she screamed "Here, I'll sacrifice you to Mother Kali," as the warders struggled to find the keys to her cell (16–17). Mitra communicates the horror of such religious ideologies not only through the joint action of the other women who unite to pull Jamini from her daughter but also through Jamini's abjection when she calms down and realizes how her religious frenzy has maimed her daughter.

On yet another level, *Hannaman* enacts a critique of communalism or the political appropriation of religious differences as perpetuated by the media and internalized by civil society. In her description of the other women's treatment of Muslim prisoners of war, Mitra criticizes the women's internalization of the communal[10] role of the media:

> There was a sense of irritation, indifference, even a suppressed hostility in everybody's attitude towards these women. The reason I am bringing this up is because I saw then how much even simple good people are influenced by a communal and bellicose media. (57)

On a parallel note, Partnoy interrogates herself, questioning the role of God and religion in search of beliefs from which she can draw sustenance:

> Sometimes when I'm very scared, I wish I could believe in God: the Christian God, my family's God, any God. . . . The truth is that I would like to believe in any God that protects me and rescues me from her. . . . (62)

Ultimately, she, too, rejects religion on the grounds that it constitutes a ready instrument through which the military seeks legitimation:

> So many priests have blessed the weapons of the military! So many rabbis thank God for the Coup that has saved them from "chaos!" Whenever things like this happen, I'm convinced that God is just a pretext . . . and I instinctively reject pretexts. (63)

Rejecting superstitious and religious ideologies as false beliefs, both Partnoy and Mitra indicate the need for values constructed on independent secular grounds.

Mitra also rejects the notion of a homogeneous women's experience, struggle or perspective as the ground for feminist claims. She introduces the class differential through her representation of the wealthy Niharika Dutta (imprisoned for having driven her daughter-in-law to suicide), who maintained a strict distance from most of the other prisoners, referring to them as "dirty, low-bred people." Mitra sets up a confrontation between Niharika's class values and her own values of justice with the caustic question, "How much does one have to beat a woman to kill her?" (48). *Hannaman* further emphasizes the differences due to hierarchical power relationships between women in dominant and dominated groups through the narration of the visit of a female social worker. Her first question is "Why are they being given paper in prison?" and her next comment, in response to the complaints about the quality of food, is, "You're being given vegetables in prison, isn't that more than enough? . . . You should have been given only black chappatis and water" (124). Juxtaposing such attitudes with those in a report of the Inspector General of Prisons from 1852–55, Mitra situates the female social worker's response within a tradition of regressive prison ideology dating back to the colonial period. Although she is female, the social worker's values are far different from the feminist values of the women prisoners.

Thus, both Mitra and Partnoy, in searching for concepts, notions, belief systems, and ideologies that are a source of strength and security for women, are far removed from any essentialist eulogizing of "women's beliefs" or "women's values." They distinguish social conditions that give rise to false beliefs from those that give rise to less false ones, and they insist on critical and objective analyses of women's lives, perceptions, and experiences. In revealing the fallacies of superstitions and religions—or, at least, the pervasive and divisive ways they have been appropriated by the ruling classes, patriarchy, and the state—these texts reject them as inappropriate grounds for establishing links between people and, especially, for forging communities of resistance based on the oppositional agency of women.

What makes *Hannaman* and *The Little School* extremely significant feminist documents is that they make the move from the critical enterprise of *deconstructing* patriarchal state, religious, colonial, and upper-class ideologies to the pragmatic exigencies of *constructing* an oppositional and collective feminist consciousness. With this politically affirmative step, these narratives of feminist solidarity raise the question of what constitutes a collective consciousness or a collective identity; and they elaborate in the praxis of the prisoners what one of the most fundamental feminist critiques of Marxism has enunciated theoretically. Benhabib and Cornell highlight the disjunction between the "structural model of class" that follows from the primacy of production relations and the "political concept of class" as collective agents of social transformation, and emphasize the importance of women's consciousness, agency, and historical experience:

> [I]s the position of a social group in the production process either necessary or sufficient to define its *collective identity*? Are production relations fundamental in defining *collective consciousness*? When collective actors emerge on the historical scene, is it the memory and consciousness of production alone that moves them to act? What about forms of collective identity and memory rooted in aspects of communal and public life, in legal and public guarantees, or in preindustrial guilds and associations? (3)

In denying the necessity of positioning a social group in the production process or the importance of production relations as at least one of the fundamental factors in defining collective consciousness or collective identity, Benhabib and Cornell's claim to a radical critique of feminist theory becomes rather dubious, and aligns them rather with mainstream versions of bourgeois feminism. However, it is definitely true that neither the positioning of a social group in the production process nor the positioning of production relations are in themselves sufficient for either defining collective identity or consciousness or for conceptualizing what Benhabib and Cornell call a "minimal utopia of social life characterized by nurturant, caring, expressive and non-repressive relations between self and other" (4).

In *The Little School* and *Hannaman*, the women prisoners develop strategies of resistance out of precisely those values that are manipulated to torture them: those of the family, motherhood, and nurturing. Partnoy's text emphasizes that the intersubjective activity of nurturing is crucial for the psychic life of any individual, man or woman. She narrates the soliloquy of her husband, "Ruth's father," in which he alternates an imaginary conversation with their daughter Ruth and a nursery rhyme he used to sing to her with his cries of pain at being tortured:

> Daughter, dear, my tongue hurts and I can't say rib-bit rib-bit; even if I could, you wouldn't hear me. This little poem soothed you when you cried; you went to sleep listening to it . . . I've repeated it for a whole day but I still can't sleep. Rib-bit rib-bit he sings on the roof . . . I won't see you again . . . The electric prods on my genitals . . . Trapped, like the little frog . . . but we hear him all the time. (93)

In representing Ruth's father's need to recall the pleasant memory of soothing his daughter to sleep in order to calm himself, this soliloquy expresses the need to maintain a unifying thread in the fragmentation of daily life, and to ward off the pain and horror of torture. And it emphasizes the critical importance of those memories of nurturing and tenderness in enabling Ruth's father to hold on to a sense of himself. Thus, Partnoy's testimonio extends the acts of nurturing, normally assigned to the sphere of the feminine, to the sphere of all human beings, and represents them as values of nurturing that are crucial to the psychic life of all.[11]

In the *Little School*, where the prisoners are blindfolded, forced to lie down on their beds most of the time, and forbidden to talk to each other, communication, compounded by a complete lack of certainty about what was going to happen next, is a torture that drives the women to devise subversive games for interacting with each other. It is no surprise that the most successful and popular "game" is one based on a communal sharing of food:

> In this climate of overall uncertainty, bread is the only reliable thing. Bread is also a means of communicating, a way of telling the person next to me: "I'm here. I care for you. I want to share the only possession I have." Sometimes it is easy to convey the message. Sometimes it is more difficult; but when hunger hits, the brain becomes sharper. (83–85)

What is noteworthy is that when "the brain becomes sharper," the activities are geared not toward selfish individual survival but toward establishing more ways of communicating with each other. Moreover, sharing food becomes much more than a symbolic gesture or a dramatic metaphor for communication. *Hannaman,* too, is replete with various acts of women sharing their food with other women's children, in acts of extended motherhood. Given the meager rationing, these are gestures critical for the children's survival. In both texts, sharing food becomes a collective strategy for survival, both at the physical and the psychic level. It is a strategy grounded in a mutual caring for each other's lives, and in an ethics of collective survival that forms the basis of their community.

In Partnoy's text, though all the prisoners have a common anti-authoritarian ideological belief, these abstract political beliefs are, in themselves, not enough. As Satya Mohanty asserts, political community cannot be based on a common ideology or "horizontal comradeship" alone—it needs other sources of strength that sustain one through political travails. What he observes of *Beloved* is also true of the communities evoked in *Hannaman* and *The Little School*:

> Central to the novel is a vision of the continuity between experience and identity, a vision only partly articulated in . . . the epigraph's audacious appropriation of God's voice from Hosea, quoted by Paul in Romans, chapter 9: "I will call them my people / which were not my people; / and her beloved / which was not beloved." . . . The community that is sought in *Beloved* involves as its essence a moral and imaginative expansion of oneself, in particular one's capacity to experience. It is only in the context of this expanded capacity that we can understand the trajectory of the moral debate that informs and organizes the narrative. (55)

The "imaginative expansion of oneself" is further reinforced through the sympathetic identification of women both with other women's mothers as their daughters and with other women's children as their mothers. Partnoy says in her introduction, "I was reunited with Vasca and Graciela's mother who told me that even though she does not have any daughters left, she still has me" (18). Mitra's love for Jamini's daughter, Pushpa, fuses with the memory of her own absent daughter, and she takes care of Pushpa when she returns from the hospital as she would have taken care of her own (19). And the women in *Hannaman* all address each other in the familial tropes of *didi* (elder sister), Baroda *ma* (mother), Bimala *bhabi* (brother's wife), Rameja *nani* (maternal grandmother), Shidu *mejho* (middle sister), and Jogmaya *mashi* (mother's sister) (59). Tropes of family become tropes of solidarity, and familial interactions inform the principles of political organization. Memories of "feminine" spaces and the interactive patterns and values of the home forge bonds of solidarity that challenge the order of the prison, the concentration camp, and the state.

The moral trajectory of the political vision of the community of prisoners in each text ultimately goes beyond the political discourses of the anti-authoritarian Argentinian youth and the Indian Naxalites, and cuts its way through to the far more basic and all-pervasive modes of regulating these societies. Smith observes that the exclusion of women from the frame of sociology in the Western world develops with the emergence of the rational type of legitimate authority and administrative practices in the wake of corporate capitalism. Though she refers to Weber in the context of "rationalization" in a footnote, she does not, however, take the next step of addressing Habermas's reformulation of the term in "Technology and Science as 'Ideology.'" Habermas reformulates Weber's concept of "rationalization" and proposes a framework of purposive-rational action and communicative action, starting with the "fundamental distinction between work and interaction":

> By "work" or purposive rational action I understand either instrumental action or rational choice or their conjunction. Instrumental

> action is governed by technical rules based on empirical knowledge.... The conduct of rational choice is governed by strategies based on analytic knowledge.... By "interaction" on the other hand, I understand symbolic interaction. It is governed by consensual norms.... (90–91)

What is crucial in the context of feminist theory is Habermas's foregrounding of the sphere of communicative action, because, as he says, "The validity of social norms is grounded only in the intersubjectivity of the mutual understanding of intentions" (92). It is in the realm of intersubjectivity (which Benhabib and Cornell also emphasize in their critique of the primacy of production implied by orthodox Marxism) and through a recognition of the potential of communicative action that a strategic feminist theory can be constructed.

I see the women prisoners challenging the system of "purposive-rational action" of the state from within the framework of symbolic interaction where they have located themselves. The political vision of the prisoners begins to manifest itself in the implicit critiques of the guards. Mitra's narrative reveals the inevitable and intrinsic fallacies of a system based on "technical rules." As agents of the instrumental action of the state, the warders and jailers become the mere arms of a state machinery, undergoing a mechanization that renders their ethical and collective vision redundant, and that fosters corruption based on individual self-interest. This becomes evident in the description of their greed that drives them to steal not only jail property, such as utensils, and food from the already meager rations sanctioned for the prisoners, but also basic sustenance, such as milk and sugar, from newborn babies, whom they have already callously separated from their mothers. Contrasting such acts of *individual* interest with the *collective solidarity* of the women, Mitra demonstrates how the power equations in the prison are temporarily reversed, with the guards feeling scared of the prisoners behind bars: "The warders pushed the plates to the bars from a great distance. I understand later–fear! If they come near [they think] we could strike them.... We would extend our hands, draw them close and strangle them" (71, 73).

Partnoy depicts the nervousness of the guards when Graciela is about to deliver her baby, using the guard's voice to contrast his fear with Graciela's confidence:

> Problems, problems again. First we run out of wine, and now this fucking child. . . . It's better if I put on my hood right now. Some days ago I went into the kitchen without noticing that she was there. She saw my face. I don't like it at all that she's seen my face. I don't know whether this one will come out alive or not. Afterward, I asked her, " If you run into me once you are released,

> you'll surely shoot me won't you?" "No," she answered, "I'll buy you coffee," and she laughed. I don't believe what these characters say. On top of all this I've got a headache. I guess I had too much wine again. Well! I'd been controlling myself for almost two days, because my boss was coming to visit. (120)

The guard's fear, his fragmented identity, and his violation of the prison rules by drinking on duty all convey his complete lack of belief in the prison system, resulting in a threat to the institution's efficiency. As Partnoy asserts, "I was showing the fragmentation in their personalities because it [their investment in torture] is not built on solid belief. Can it be built on solid belief? Can torture be built on solid belief?"[12]

Both Mitra and Partnoy drive a wedge into the weak points of the theory of "purposive rational action." As Habermas asserts,

> Instrumental action is governed by technical rules based on empirical knowledge. . . . [and] [t]he conduct of rational choice is governed by strategies based on analytic knowledge. . . . But while instrumental action organizes means that are appropriate or inappropriate according to the criteria of an effective control of reality, strategic action depends only on the correct evaluation of possible alternative choices, which results from calculation supplemented by values. (92)

The point is that while the technical rules fail to provide the guards with means of dealing with the women's strategies of resistance, the option of rational choice is also unavailable to them, for it is governed by strategies based on analytic or theoretical knowledge. And, theoretical knowledge of women's lives has been historically denied a place in the realm of objective analysis; their social desires, values, and interests have been consistently suppressed in history. Thus, in the absence of this knowledge, the guards are at a loss for strategies to maintain the efficiency of the system. Moreover, since strategic action depends on calculation supplemented by values, and the prison system and the concentration camp are both based on "values" that the guards obviously have no investment in, they are doubly at a loss for strategies. Emphasizing the women's standpoint and the epistemic privilege they enjoy with respect to their knowledge of their own lives and the worlds they inhabit, these narratives confront the dominant patriarchal capitalist modes of functioning. While the women create a situation in which the oppressors are temporarily at a loss because they have no access to rational choice, the women's "communicative interactions" are governed by consensual norms and are, at the same time, rational, as they are in the interest of their collective survival.

Habermas also claims that "while the validity of technical rules and strategies depends on that of empirically true or analytically correct positions, *the validity of social norms is grounded only in the intersubjectivity of the mutual understanding of intentions*" (emphasis mine), (92). *Hannaman* and *The Little School* show how the "analytically correct positions" for dealing with the women are inaccessible to the repressive state apparatus; on the other hand, the validity of the social norms of the women is grounded in an intersubjectivity which enables the forging of meaningful social relations between themselves and in counteracting the naturalized patriarchal ones imposed upon them by the state. Thus, the women develop modes of personal interaction and draw upon the nurturing, sharing, and caring of the private sphere to forge a "horizontal comradeship" and to develop strategies of collective resistance in the public sphere. From a feminist standpoint, they restore to center stage the value of intersubjectivity, and their "communicative interaction" challenges the "purposive rational action" of a state apparatus that represses the very notion of ethics and egalitarianism as central categories of life.

8

Toward a Genealogy of Black Female Sexuality: The Problematic of Silence

Evelynn M. Hammonds

> To name ourselves rather than be named we must first see ourselves. For some of us this will not be easy. So long unmirrored, we may have forgotten how we look. Nevertheless, we can't theorize in a void; we must have evidence.
>
> Lorraine O'Grady, "Olympia's Maid"[1]

Sexuality has become one of the most visible, contentious and spectacular features of modern life in the United States during this century. Controversies over sexual politics and sexual behavior reveal other tensions in U.S. society, particularly those around changing patterns of work, family organization, disease control, and gender relations. In the wake of Anita Hill's allegations of sexual harassment by Supreme Court nominee Clarence Thomas and the more recent murder charges brought against football star O. J. Simpson, African Americans continue to be used as the terrain upon which contested notions about race, gender, and sexuality are worked out. Yet, while black men have increasingly been the focus of debates about sexuality in the academy and in the media, the specific ways in which black women figure in these discourses has remained largely unanalyzed and untheorized.

In this essay, I will argue that the construction of black women's sexuality, from the nineteenth century to the present, engages three sets of issues. First, there is the way black women's sexuality has been constructed in a binary opposition to that of white women: it is rendered simultaneously invisible, visible (exposed), hypervisible, and pathologized in dominant discourses. Secondly, I will describe how resistance to these dominant discourses has been coded and lived by various groups of black women within black communities at different historical moments. Finally, I will discuss the limitations of these strategies of resistance in disrupting dominant discourses about black women's sexuality and the implications of this for black women with AIDS.

In addressing these questions, I am specifically interested in interrogating the writing of black feminist theorists on black women's sexuality. As sociologist Patricia Hill Collins has noted, while black feminist theorists have written extensively on the impact of such issues as rape, forced sterilization, and homophobia on black women's sexuality, "when it comes to other important issues concerning the sexual politics of Black womanhood, . . . Black feminists have found it almost impossible to say what has happened to Black women."[2] To date, there has been no full-length historical study of African American women's sexuality in the United States. In this essay, I will examine some of the reasons why black feminists have failed to develop a complex, historically specific analysis of black women's sexuality.

Black feminist theorists have almost universally described black women's sexuality, when viewed from the vantage of the dominant discourses, as an absence. In one of the earliest and most compelling discussions of black women's sexuality, literary critic Hortense Spillers wrote, "Black women are the beached whales of the sexual universe, unvoiced, misseen, not doing, awaiting *their* verb."[3] For writer Toni Morrison, black women's sexuality is one of the "unspeakable things unspoken" of the African American experience. Black women's sexuality is often described in metaphors of speechlessness, space, or vision; as a "void" or empty space that is simultaneously ever-visible (exposed) and invisible, where black women's bodies are always already colonized. In addition, this always already colonized black female body has so much sexual potential it has none at all.[4] Historically, black women have reacted to the repressive force of the hegemonic discourses on race and sex that constructed this image with silence, secrecy, and a partially self-chosen invisibility.[5]

Black feminist theorists—historians, literary critics, sociologists, legal scholars, and cultural critics—have drawn upon a specific historical narrative which purportedly describes the factors that have produced and maintained perceptions of black women's sexuality (including their own). Three themes emerge in this history. First, the construction of the black female as the embodiment of sex and the attendant invisibility of black women as the unvoiced, unseen—everything that is not white. Secondly, the resistance of black women both to negative stereotypes of their sexuality and to the material effects of those stereotypes on black women's lives. And, finally, the evolution of a "culture of dissemblance" and a "politics of silence" by black women on the issue of their sexuality.

Colonizing Black Women's Bodies

By all accounts, the history of discussions of black women's sexuality in Western thought begins with the Europeans' first contact with peoples on the African continent. As Sander Gilman argued in his widely cited essay "Black Bodies, White Bodies: Toward an Iconography of Female Sexuality in Late Nineteenth-Century Art, Medicine, and Literature,"[6] the conventions of human diversity that were captured in the iconography of the period linked the image of the prostitute and the black female through the Hottentot female. The Hottentot female most vividly represented in this iconography was Sarah Bartmann, known as the "Hottentot Venus." This southern African black woman was crudely exhibited and objectified by European audiences and scientific experts because of what they regarded as unusual aspects of her physiognomy—her genitalia and buttocks. Gilman argued that Sarah Bartmann, along with other black females brought from southern Africa, became the central image for the black female in Europe through the nineteenth century. The "primitive" genitalia of these women were defined by European commentators as the sign of their "primitive" sexual appetites. Thus, the black female became the antithesis of European sexual mores and beauty and was relegated to the lowest position on the scale of human development. The image of the black female constructed in this period reflected everything the white female was not, or, as art historian Lorraine O'Grady has put it, "White is what woman is [was]; not-white (and the stereotypes not-white gathers in) is what she had better not be."[7] Gilman shows that by the end of the nineteenth century European experts in anthropology, public health, medicine, biology, and psychology had concluded, with ever-increasing "scientific" evidence, that the black female embodied the notion of uncontrolled sexuality.

In addition, as white European elites' anxieties surfaced over the increasing incidence of sexually transmitted diseases, especially syphilis, high rates of these diseases among black women were used to define them further as a source of corruption and disease. It was the association of prostitutes with disease that provided the final link between the black female and the prostitute. Both were bearers of the stigmata of sexual difference and deviance. Gilman concluded that the construction of black female sexuality as inherently immoral and uncontrollable was a product of nineteenth century biological sciences. Ideologically, these sciences reflected Europeans males' fear of difference in the period of colonialism, and their consequent need to control and regulate the sexuality of those rendered "other."

Paula Giddings, following Gilman, pointed out that the negative construction of black women's sexuality as revealed by the Bartmann case also occurred at a time when questions about the entitlement of nonenslaved blacks to citizenship was being debated in the United States. In part, the contradiction presented by slavery was resolved in the U.S. by ascribing certain inherited characteristics to blacks, characteristics that made them unworthy of citizenship; foremost among these was the belief in the unbridled sexuality of black people and specifically that of black women.[8] Thus, racial difference was linked to sexual difference in order to maintain white male supremacy during the period of slavery.

During slavery, the range of ideological uses for the image of the always-already sexual black woman was extraordinarily broad and familiar. This stereotype was used to justify the enslavement, rape, and sexual abuse of black women by white men; the lynching of black men; and, not incidentally, the maintenance of a coherent biological theory of human difference based on fixed racial typologies. Because African American women were defined as property, their social, political, and legal rights barely exceeded those of farm animals–indeed, they were subjected to the same forms of control and abuse as animals. For black feminist scholars, the fact that black women emerged under slavery as speaking subjects at all is worthy of note.[9] And it is the fact that African American women of this period do speak to the fact of their sexual exploitation that counts as their contestation to the dominant discourses of the day. Indeed, as Hazel Carby has described, black women during slavery were faced with having to develop ways to be recognized within the category of woman by whites by asserting a positive value to their sexuality that could stand in both public and private.[10]

The Politics of "Reconstructing Womanhood"[11]

As the discussion of sex roles and sexuality began to shift among whites in the U.S. by the end of the nineteenth century, the binary opposition which characterized black and white female sexuality was perpetuated by both Victorian sexual ideology and state practices of repression. White women were characterized as pure, passionless, and de-sexed, while black women were the epitome of immorality, pathology, impurity, and sex itself. "Respectability" and "sexual control" were set against "promiscuity" in the discourse of middle-class whites, who viewed the lifestyles of black people and the new white immigrants in urban centers as undermining the moral values of the country.[12] Buttressed by the doctrine of the Cult of True Womanhood, this binary opposition seemed to lock black women forever outside the ideology of womanhood so celebrated in the Victorian era. As Beverly Guy Sheftall notes, black women were painfully aware that "they were devalued no matter what their strengths might be, and that the Cult of True Womanhood was not intended to apply to them no matter how intensely they embraced its values."[13]

In the late-nineteenth century, with increasing exploitation and abuse of black women despite the legal end of slavery, U.S. black women reformers recognized the need to develop different strategies to counter negative stereotypes of their sexuality which had been used as justifications for the rape, lynching, and other abuses of black women by whites. More than a straightforward assertion of a normal female sexuality and a claim to the category of protected womanhood was called for in the volatile context of Reconstruction where, in the minds of whites, the political rights of black men were connected to notions of black male sexual agency.[14] Politics, sexuality, and race were already inextricably linked in the U.S., but the problematic established by this link reached new heights of visibility during the period of Reconstruction through the increased lynchings of black men and women by the early decades of the twentieth century.

One of the most cogent analyses by a black woman about the connections between politics and sex in this period was made by Ida B. Wells. Wells understood that the history of the condoned murders of blacks was "a direct consequence of blacks having been granted a political right, the franchise, without being given the means to protect or maintain that right."[15] Wells argued that the cry of "rape" had come to mean any alliance between a "white woman and a colored man," and state and civilian responses were confined entirely to the protection of women who happened to be white.[16] Her analysis of lynching, as Hazel Carby has argued, provided a "detailed dissection of how patriarchal power manipulated sexual ideologies to effect political and economic subordination."[17] On the other hand, educator and activist Anna Julia Cooper emphasized that the interrelated practices of racism and sexism were connected to the consequences of U.S. imperialism. In both instances, these activists argued that African American women had to organize themselves politically to effect their inclusion in the category of protected womanhood. The antilynching movement then became the catalyst for the establishment of the black women's club movement.

Wells is particularly important for my discussion because she demonstrated how the discourses of rape and lynching were categories through which the negative rendering of the sexuality of black people was maintained. Carby, in her discussion of this movement, makes much of the fact that issues surrounding the representation of black female sexuality became the centerpiece of the club movement. These club women strove to break the binary that they had been forced to occupy with white women by asserting that "an injury to one woman is an injury to all women."[18] The primary goal of these women was to retrieve and reconstruct a notion of womanhood that, in the economic and political arena, was being constructed as irredeemably pathologized. Secondarily, they wanted to enlist white women in the destruction of the binary which, they argued, contributed to the oppression of white women as well.

The Politics of Silence

Although some of the strategies used by these black women reformers might have initially been characterized as resistance to dominant and increasingly hegemonic constructions of their sexuality, by the early twentieth century, they had begun to promote a public silence about sexuality which, it could be argued, continues to the present.[19] This "politics of silence," as described by historian Evelyn Brooks Higginbotham, emerged as a political strategy by black women reformers who hoped by their silence and by the promotion of proper Victorian morality to demonstrate the lie of the image of the sexually immoral black woman.[20] Historian Darlene Clark Hine argues that the "culture of dissemblance" which this politics engendered was seen as a way for black women to "protect the sanctity of inner aspects of their lives."[21] She defines this culture as "the behavior and attitudes of Black women that created the appearance of openness and disclosure but actually shielded the truth of their inner lives and selves from their oppressors." "Only with secrecy," Hine argues, "thus achieving a self-imposed invisibility, could ordinary Black women accrue the psychic space and harness the resources needed to hold their own."[22] And by the projection of the image of a "super moral" black woman, they hoped to garner greater respect, justice, and opportunity for all black Americans. Of course, as Higginbotham notes, there were problems with this strategy. First, it did not achieve its goal of ending the negative stereotyping of black women. And second, some middle-class black women engaged in policing the behavior of poor and working-class women and others who deviated from a Victorian norm, in the name of protecting the "race."[23] Black women reformers were responding to the ways in which any black woman could find herself "exposed" and characterized in racist sexual terms no matter what the truth of her individual life; they saw any so-called deviant individual behavior as a threat to the race as a whole. But the most enduring and problematic aspect of this "politics of silence" is that in choosing silence, black women have also lost the ability to articulate any conception of their sexuality.

Yet, this last statement is perhaps too general. Carby notes that during the 1920s, black women in the U.S. risked having all representations of black female sexuality appropriated as primitive and exotic within a largely racist society.[24] She continues, "Racist sexual ideologies proclaimed black women to be rampant sexual beings, and in response black women writers either focused on defending their morality or displaced sexuality onto another terrain."[25] As many black feminist literary and cultural critics have noted, the other terrain on which black women's sexuality was displaced was music, notably the blues. The early blues singers—who were most decidedly not middle class—have been called "pioneers who claimed their sexual subjectivity through their songs and produced a Black women's discourse on Black sexuality."[26] At a moment when middle-class black women's sexuality was "completely underwritten to avoid endorsing sexual stereotypes," the blues women defied and exploited those stereotypes.[27] Yet, ultimately, neither silence nor defiance was able to dethrone negative constructions of black female sexuality. Nor could these strategies allow for the unimpeded expression of self-defined black female sexualities. Such approaches did not allow African American women to gain control over their sexuality.

In previous eras, black women had articulated the ways in which active practices of the state—the definition of black women as property, the sanctioned rape and lynching of black men and women, the denial of the vote—had been supported by a specific ideology about black female sexuality (and black male sexuality). These state practices effaced any notion of differences among and between black women, including those of class, color, and educational and economic privilege; all black women were designated as the same. The assertion of a supermoral black female subject by black women activists did not completely efface such differences nor did it directly address them. For black women reformers of this period, grounded in particular religious traditions, to challenge the negative stereotyping of black women directly meant continuing to reveal the ways in which state power was complicit in the violence against black people. The appropriation of respectability and the denial of sexuality was, therefore, a nobler path to emphasizing that the story of black women's immorality was a lie.[28]

Without more detailed historical studies of black female sexuality in each period, we do not know the extent of this "culture of dissemblance," and many questions remain unanswered.[29] Was it expressed differently in rural and in urban areas; in the north, west, or south? How was it maintained? Where and how was it resisted? How was it shaped by class, color, economic, and educational privilege? And furthermore, how did it change over time? How did something that was initially adopted as a political strategy in a specific historical period become so ingrained in black life as to be recognizable as a culture? Or was it? In the absence of detailed historical studies we can say little about the ways social constructions of sexuality change in tandem with changing social conditions in specific historical moments within black communities.

Persistent Legacies: The Politics of Commodification

This legacy of silence has persisted despite the changing material conditions of African American women. And from even this very incomplete history, we can see that black women's sexuality is ideologically situated between race and gender, where the black female subject is not seen and has no voice. Methodologically, black feminists have found it difficult even to characterize this juncture, this point of erasure where African American women are located. As legal scholar Kimberlé Crenshaw puts it, "Existing within the overlapping margins of race and gender discourse and the empty spaces between, it is a location whose very nature resists telling."[30] And this silence about sexuality is enacted individually and collectively by black women and by black feminist theorists writing about black women. In addition, institutions such as black churches and historically black colleges have also contributed to the maintenance of silence about sexuality.

It should not surprise us that black women are silent about sexuality. The imposed production of silence and the removal of any alternatives to the production of silence, reflect the deployment of power against racialized subjects "wherein those who could speak did not want to and those who did want to speak were prevented from doing so."[31] It is this deployment of power at the level of the social and the individual which has to be historicized. It seems clear that what is needed is a methodology that allows us to contest rather than reproduce the ideological system that has, up to now, defined the terrain of black women's sexuality. Hortense Spillers made this point over a decade ago when she wrote: "Because black American women do not participate, as a category of social and cultural agents, in the legacies of symbolic power, they maintain no allegiances to a strategic formation of texts, or ways of talking about sexual experience, that even remotely resemble the paradigm of symbolic domination, except that such paradigm has been their concrete disaster."[32] To date, largely through the work of black feminist literary critics, we know more about the elision of sexuality by black women than we do about the possible varieties of expression of sexual desire.[33] Thus, what we have is a very narrow view of black women's sexuality. Certainly it is true, as Crenshaw notes, that "in feminist contexts, sexuality represents a central site of the oppression of women; rape and the rape trial are its dominant narrative trope. In antiracist discourse, sexuality is also a central site upon which the repression of blacks has been premised; the lynching narrative is embodied as its trope."[34] Sexuality is also, as Carole Vance defines it, "simultaneously a domain of restriction, repression, and danger as well as a domain of exploration, pleasure, and agency."[35] In the past the restrictive, repressive, and dangerous aspects of black female sexuality have been emphasized by black feminists writers, while pleasure, exploration, and agency have gone underanalyzed.

I want to suggest that contemporary black feminist theorists have not taken up this project in part because of their own status in the academy. Reclaiming the body as well as subjectivity is a process that black feminist theorists in the academy must go through themselves while they are doing the work of producing theory. Black feminist theorists are themselves engaged in a process of fighting to reclaim the body—the maimed, immoral, black female body—which can be and is still being used by others to discredit them as producers of knowledge and as speaking subjects. Legal scholar Patricia J. Williams illuminates my point: "No matter what degree of professional I am, people will greet and dismiss my black femaleness as unreliable, untrustworthy, hostile, angry, powerless, irrational, and probably destitute."[36] When reading student evaluations, she finds comments about her teaching and her body: "I marvel, in a moment of genuine bitterness, that anonymous student evaluations speculating on dimensions of my anatomy are nevertheless counted into the statistical measurement of my teaching proficiency."[37] The hypervisibility of black women academics and the contemporary fascination with what bell hooks calls the "commodification of Otherness."[38] means that black women today find themselves precariously perched in the academy. Ann du Cille notes:

> Mass culture, as hooks argues, produces, promotes, and perpetuates the commodification of Otherness through the exploitation of the black female body. In the 1990s, however, the principal sites of exploitation are not simply the cabaret, the speakeasy, the music video, the glamour magazine; they are also the academy, the publishing industry, the intellectual community.[39]

In tandem with the notion of silence, contemporary black women writers have repeatedly drawn on the notion of the "invisible" to describe aspects of black women's lives in general and sexuality in particular. Audre Lorde writes that "within this country where racial difference creates a constant, if unspoken distortion of vision, Black women have on the one hand always been highly visible, and on the other hand, have been rendered invisible through the depersonalization of racism."[40] The hypervisibility of black women academics means that visibility, too, can be used to control the intellectual issues that black women can and cannot speak about. Already threatened with being sexualized and rendered inauthentic as knowledge producers in the academy by students and colleagues alike, this avoidance of theorizing about sexuality can be read as one contemporary manifestation of their structured silence. I want to stress here that the silence about sexuality on the part of black women academics is no more a "choice" than was the silence practiced by early twentieth-century black women. This production of *silence* instead of *speech* is an effect of the institutions such as the academy which are engaged in the commodification of Otherness.

The "politics of silence" and the "commodification of Otherness" are not simply abstractions. These constructs have material effects on black women's lives. In shifting the site of theorizing about black female sexuality from the literary or legal terrain to that of medicine and the control of disease, we can see some of these effects. In the AIDS epidemic, the experiences and needs of black women have gone unrecognized. I have argued elsewhere that the set of controlling images of black women with AIDS has foregrounded stereotypes of these women that have prevented them from being embraced by the public as people in need of support and care. The AIDS epidemic is being used to "inflect, condense and rearticulate the ideological meanings of race, sexuality, gender, childhood, privacy, morality, and nationalism."[41] Black women with AIDS are largely poor and working-class; many are single mothers; they are constantly represented with regard to their drug use and abuse and uncontrolled sexuality. The supposedly "uncontrolled sexuality" of black women is one of the key features in the representation of black women in the AIDS epidemic.

The position of black women in this epidemic was dire from the beginning and worsens with each passing day. Silence, erasure, and the use of images of immoral sexuality abound in narratives about the experiences of black women with AIDS. Their voices are not heard in discussions of AIDS, while intimate details of their lives are exposed to justify their victimization. In the "war of representation" that is being waged through this epidemic, black women are the victims that are the "other" of the "other," the deviants of the deviants, irrespective of their sexual identities or practices. The representation of black women's sexuality in narratives about AIDS continues to demonstrate the disciplinary practices of the state against black women. The presence of disease is now used to justify denial of welfare benefits, treatment, and some of the basic rights of citizenship, such as privacy for black women and their children. Given the absence of black feminist analyses or a strong movement (such as the one Ida B. Wells led against lynching), the relationship between the treatment of black women in the AIDS epidemic and state practices has not been articulated. While white gay male activists are using the ideological space framed by this epidemic to contest the notion that homosexuality is "abnormal" and to preserve the right to live out their homosexual desires, black women are rendered silent. The gains made by gay activists will do nothing for black women if the stigma continues to be attached to their sexuality. Black feminist critics must work to find ways to contest the historical construction of black female sexualities by illuminating how the dominant view was established and maintained and how it can be disrupted. This work might very well save some black women's lives.

Visibility, in and of itself, is not my only goal, however. Several writers, including bell hooks, have argued that one answer to the silence on the issue of black female sexuality is for black women to see themselves, to mirror themselves. The appeal to the visual and the visible is deployed as an answer to the legacy of silence and repression. Mirroring as a way of negating a legacy of silence needs to be explored in much greater depth than it has been to date by black feminist theorists. An appeal to the visual is not uncomplicated or innocent, however. As theorists, we have to ask how vision is structured and, following that, we have to explore how difference is established, how it operates, and how it constitutes subjects who *see* and *speak* in the world. This we must apply to the ways in which black women are seen and not seen by the dominant society and also how they see themselves in a different landscape. But in overturning the "politics of silence," the goal cannot be merely to be seen. As I have argued, visibility, in and of itself, does not erase a history of silence nor does it challenge the structure of power and domination—symbolic and material—that determines what can and cannot be seen. The goal should be to develop a "politics of articulation" that would build on the interrogation of what makes it possible for black women to speak and act.

As this essay was being written, the current Surgeon General of the United States, Joycelyn Elders, a black woman was removed from her position by President Clinton. The reason given for her ouster was her "outspoken" views on health policies relating to sex education. Elders was the third black woman in as many years, following law professors Anita Hill and Lani Guinier, for whom issues about the visibility, "outspokenness," and sexuality of black women took center stage. Though there are striking differences in the events surrounding these three women, there are equally striking similarities. Hill, Guinier, and Elders were vilified in the public press for speaking out on issues that ran counter to powerful interests of the state: Hill on sexual harassment, Guinier on the rights of minority voters, and Elders on sex education. The response to them was that on these issues—sexual harassment, voting rights, and sex—black women were to be seen and not heard; exposed and victimized but not given serious protection from slander in the expression of their views. The media spectacle surrounding these three women sent a powerful message that the negative representations of black women (especially on issues related to sexuality in the cases of Hill and Elders), produced and maintained by state practices could still be used to justify the silencing of black women. The hypervisibility of these women in the media did not allow their views to challenge the charges put against them. Thus, the question remains: how can black feminists dislodge the negative stereotyping of their sexuality and the attendant denials of citizenship and protection?

Developing a complex analysis of black female sexuality is critical to this project. Black feminist theorizing about black female sexuality has, with a few exceptions (Cheryl Clarke, Jewelle Gomez, Barbara Smith, and Audre Lorde), been focused relentlessly on heterosexuality. The historical narrative that dominates discussions of black female sexuality does not address even the possibility of a black lesbian sexuality or of a lesbian or queer subject. Spillers confirms this point when she notes that "the sexual realities of black American women across the spectrum of sexual preference and widened sexual styles tend to be a missing dialectical feature of the entire discussion."[42] Discussions of black lesbian sexuality have most often focused on differences from or equivalencies with white lesbian sexualities, with "black" added to delimit the fact that black lesbians share a history with other black women. However, this addition tends to obsfucate rather than illuminate the subject position of black lesbians. One obvious example of distortion is that black lesbians do not experience homophobia in the same way as white lesbians do. Here, as with other oppressions, the homophobia experienced by black women is always shaped by racism. What has to be explored and historicized is the specificity of black lesbian experience. I want to understand in what way black lesbians are "outsiders" within black communities. This I think, would force us to examine the construction of the "closet" by black lesbians. Although this is the topic for another essay, I want to suggest here that if we accept the existence of the "politics of silence" as an historical legacy shared by all black women, then certain expressions of black female sexuality will be rendered as dangerous, for individuals and for the collectivity. It follows, then, that the culture of dissemblance makes it acceptable for some heterosexual black women to cast black lesbians as proverbial traitors to the race.[43] And this, in turn, explains why black lesbians—whose "deviant" sexuality is framed within an already existing deviant sexuality—have been wary of embracing the status of "traitor," and the potential loss of community such an embrace engenders.[44]

Of course, while some black lesbians have hidden the truth of their lives, others have developed forms of resistance to the formulation of lesbian as traitor within black communities. Audre Lorde is one obvious example. Lorde's claiming of her black and lesbian difference "forced both her white and Black lesbian friends to contend with her historical agency in the face of [this] larger racial/sexual history that would reinvent her as dead."[45] I would also argue that Lorde's writing, with its focus on the erotic, on passion and desire, suggests that black lesbian sexualities can be read as one expression of the reclamation of the despised black female body. Therefore, the works of Lorde and other black lesbian writers, because they foreground the very aspects of black female sexuality that are submerged—namely, female desire and agency—are critical to our theorizing of black female sexualities. Since silence about sexuality is being produced by black women and black feminist theorists, that silence itself suggests that black women do have some degree of agency. A focus on black lesbian sexualities implies that another discourse—other than silence—can be produced. Black lesbian sexualities are not simply identities. Rather they represent discursive and material terrains where there exists the possibility for the active production of speech, desire, and agency. Black lesbians theorizing sexuality is a site that disrupts silence and imagines a positive affirming sexuality. I am arguing here for a different level of engagement between black heterosexual and black lesbian women as the basis for the development of a black feminist praxis that articulates the ways in which invisibility, otherness, and stigma are produced and re-produced on black women's bodies. And ultimately my hope is that such an engagement will produce black feminist analyses which detail strategies for differently located black women to shape interventions that embody their separate and common interests and perspectives.

9

Post–Third-Worldist Culture: Gender, Nation, and the Cinema

Ella Shohat

At a time when the *grands récits* of the West have been told and retold ad infinitum, when a certain postmodernism (Lyotard) speaks of an "end" to metanarratives, and when Fukayama speaks of an "end of history," we must ask: precisely whose narrative and whose history is being declared at an "end"?[1] Hegemonic Europe may clearly have begun to deplete its strategic repertoire of stories, but Third-World peoples, First-World minoritarian communities, women, and gays and lesbians have only begun to tell, and deconstruct, theirs. For the "Third World," this cinematic counter-telling basically began with the postwar collapse of the European empires and the emergence of independent nation-states. In the face of Eurocentric historicizing, the Third World and its diasporas in the First World have rewritten their own histories, taken control over their own images, spoken in their own voices, reclaiming and reaccentuating colonialism and its ramifications in the present in a vast project of remapping and renaming. Third-World feminists, for their part, have participated in these counternarratives, while insisting that colonialism and national resistance have impinged differently on men and women, and that remapping and renaming is not without its fissures and contradictions.

Although relatively small in number, women directors and producers in the "Third World" already played a role in film production in the first half of this century: Aziza Amir, Assia Daghir, and Fatima Rushdi in Egypt; Carmen Santos and Gilda de Abreu in Brazil; Emilia Saleny in Argentina; and Adela Sequeyro, Matilda Landeta, Candida Beltran Rondon, and Eva Liminano in Mexico. However, their films, even when focusing on female protagonists, were not explicitly feminist in the sense of a declared political project to empower women in the context of both patriarchy and (neo) colonialism. In the postindependence or postrevolution era, women, despite their growing contribution to the diverse aspects of film production, remained less visible than men in the role of film direction. Furthermore, Third-Worldist revolutionary cinemas in places such as China, Cuba, Senegal, and Algeria were not generally shaped by an anticolonial feminist imaginary. As is the case with First-World cinema, women's participation within Third-World cinema has hardly been central, although their growing production over the last decade corresponds to a worldwide burgeoning movement of independent work by women, made possible by new, low-cost technologies of video communication. But quite apart from this relative democratization through technology, postindependence history, with the gradual eclipse of Third-Worldist nationalism and the growth of women's grass roots local organizing, also helps us to understand the emergence of what I call "post–Third-Worldist"[2] feminist film and video.

Here, I am interested in examining recent feminist film and video work within the context of post–Third-Worldist film culture as a simultaneous critique both of Third-Worldist anticolonial nationalism and of First-World Eurocentric feminism. Challenging white feminist film theory and practice that emerged in a major way in the 1970s in First-World metropolises, post–Third-Worldist feminist works have refused a Eurocentric universalizing of "womanhood," and even of "feminism." Eschewing a discourse of universality, such feminisms claim a "location,"[3] arguing for specific forms of resistance in relation to diverse forms of oppression. Aware of white women's advantageous positioning within (neo)colonialist and racist systems, feminist struggles in the Third World (including that in the First World) have not been premised on a facile discourse of global sisterhood, and have often been made within the context of anticolonial and antiracist struggles. But the growing feminist critique of Third-World nationalisms translates those many disappointed hopes for women's empowerment invested in a Third-Worldist national transformation. Navigating between the excommunication as "traitors to the nation" and "betraying the race" by patriarchal nationalism, and the imperial rescue fantasies of clitoridectomized and veiled women proffered by Eurocentric feminism, post–Third-Worldist feminists have not suddenly metamorphosized into "Western" feminists. Feminists of color have, from the outset, been engaged in analysis and activism around the intersection of nation/race/gender. Therefore, while still resisting the ongoing (neo)colonized situation of their "nation" and/or "race," post–Third-Worldist feminist cultural practices also break away from the narrative of the "nation" as a unified entity so as to articulate a contextualized history for women in specific geographies of identity. Such feminist projects, in other words, are often posited in relation to ethnic, racial, regional, and national locations.

Feminist work within national movements and ethnic communities has not formed part of the generally monocultural agenda of Euro-"feminism." In cinema studies, what has been called "feminist film theory" since the

1970s has often suppressed the historical, economic, and cultural contradictions among women. Prestigious feminist film journals have too often ignored the scholarly and cultural feminist work performed in relation to particular Third-Worldist national and racial media contexts; feminist work to empower women within the boundaries of their Third-World communities was dismissed as merely nationalist, not "quite yet" feminist. Universalizing the parameters for feminism and using such ahistorical psychoanalytical categories as "desire," "fetishism," and "castration" led to a discussion of "the female body" and "the female spectator" that was ungrounded in the many different—even opposing—women's experiences, agendas, and political visions. Any dialogue with feminist scholars or filmmakers who insisted on working from and within particular locations was thus inhibited. Is it a coincidence that throughout the 1970s and most of the 1980s, it was Third-World cinema conferences and film programs that first gave prominence to Third-Worldist women filmmakers (for example, the Guadeloupian Sarah Maldoror, the Colombian Marta Rodriguez, the Lebanese Heiny Srour, the Cuban Sara Gomez, the Senegalese Safi Faye, the Indian Prema Karanth, the Sri Lancan Sumitra Peries, the Brazilian Helena Solberg Lad, the Egyptian Atteyat El-Abnoudi, the Tunisian Selma Baccar, the Puerto Rican Ana Maria Garcia) rather than feminist film programs and conferences? A discussion of Ana Maria Garcia's documentary *La Operación*, a film which focuses on U.S.-imposed sterilization policies in Puerto Rico, for example, reveals the historical and theoretical aporias of such concepts as "the female body" when not addressed in terms of race, class, and (neo)colonialism. Whereas a white "female body" might undergo surveillance by the reproductive machine, the dark "female body" is subjected to a *dis-reproductive* apparatus within a hidden, racially coded demographic agenda.

In fact, in the 1970s and most of the 1980s, prestigious feminist film journals paid little attention to the intersection of heterosexism with racism and imperialism; that task was performed by some "Third-World cinema" academics who published in those leftist film and cultural journals that allotted space to Third-World alternative cinema (for example, *Jumpcut*, *Cineaste*, *The Independent*, *Framework*, and *Critical Arts*). Coming in the wake of visible public debates about race and multiculturalism, the task-force on "race" (established in 1988) at the Society for Cinema Studies, along with the increasing substantial representation of the work of women of color in Women Make Movies (a major New York–based distribution outlet for independent work by women film and videomakers), began to have an impact on white feminist film scholars, some of whom gradually came to acknowledge and even address issues of gender in the context of race. Discourses about gender and race still tend *not* to be understood within an anticolonial history, however, while the diverse recent post–Third-Worldist feminist film and video practices tend to be comfortably subsumed as a mere "extension" of a "universal" feminist theory and practice. Applying old paradigms onto new (dark) objects implies, to some extent, "business as usual." Post–Third-Worldist feminist practices now tend to be absorbed into the preoccupations of Eurocentric feminist theories within the homogenizing framework of the shared critique of patriarchal discourse. Examining recent Third-World feminist cultural practices only in relation to theories developed by what has been known as "feminist film theory" reproduces a Eurocentric logic whose narrative beginnings for feminism will inevitably always reside with "Western" cultural pratices and theories seen as straightforwardly pure "feminism," unlike Third-World feminisms, seen as "burdened" by national and ethnic hyphenated identities. Notions of nation and race, along with community-based work are implicitly dismissed as both too "specific" to qualify for the theoretical realm of "feminist film theory" and as too "inclusive" in their concern for nation and race that they presumably "lose sight" of feminism.

Rather than merely "extending" a preexisting First-World feminism, as a certain Euro-"diffusionism"[4] would have it, post–Third-Worldist cultural theories and practices create a more complex space for feminisms open to the specificity of community culture and history. To counter some of the patronizing attitudes toward (post)Third-World feminist filmmakers—the dark women who now also do the "feminist thing"—it is necessary to contextualize feminist work in national/racial discourses locally and globally inscribed within multiple oppressions and resistances. Third-World feminist histories can be understood as feminist if seen in conjunction with the resistance work these women have performed within their communites and nations. Any serious discussion of feminist cinema must therefore engage the complex question of the "national." Third-Worldist films are often produced within the legal codes of the nation-state, often in (hegemonic) national languages, recycling national intertexts (literatures, oral narratives, music), projecting national imaginaries. But if First-World filmmakers have seemed to float "above" petty nationalist concerns, it is because they take for granted the projection of a national power that facilitates the making and the dissemination of their films. The geopolitical positioning of Third-World nation-states continues to imply that their filmmakers cannot assume a substratum of national power.

Here, I am interested in examining the contemporary work of post–Third-Worldist feminist film- and videomakers in light of the ongoing critique of the racialized inequality of the geopolitical distribution of resources and power as a way of looking into the dynamics of rupture and continuity with regard to the antecedent Third-Worldist film culture. These texts, I argue, challenge the masculinist contours of the "nation" in order to continue a feminist decolonization of Third-Worldist historiography, as much as they continue a multicultural decolonization of feminist historiography. My attempt to forge a "beginning" of a post–Third-Worldist narrative for recent film and video work by diverse Third-World, multicultural, diasporic feminists is not intended as an exhaustive survey of the entire spectrum of generic practices. Rather, by highlighting works embedded in the intersection between gender/sexuality and nation/race, this essay attempts to situate such cultural practices. It looks at a moment of historical rupture and continuity, when the macronarrative of women's liberation has long since subsided yet sexism and heterosexism prevail, and in an age when the metanarratives of anticolonial revolution have long since been eclipsed yet (neo)colonialism and racism persist. What, then, are some of the new modes of a multicultural feminist aesthetics of resistance? And in what ways do they simultaneously continue and rupture previous Third-Worldist film culture?

The Eclipse of the Revolutionary Paradigm

Third-Worldist films by women assumed that revolution was crucial for the empowering of women, that the revolution was integral to feminist aspirations. Sarah Maldoror's short film *Monangambe* (Mozambique, 1970) narrates the visit of an Angolan woman to see her husband who has been imprisoned by the Portuguese, while her feature film *Sambizanga* (Mozambique, 1972), based on the struggle of the MPLA in Angola, depicts a woman coming to revolutionary consciousness. Heiny Srour's documentary *Saat al Tahrir* (The Hour of Liberation, Oman, 1973) privileges the role of women fighters as it looks at the revolutionary struggle in Oman, and her *Leila wal dhiab* (Leila and the Wolves, Lebanon, 1984) focuses on the role of women in the Palestine Liberation Movement. Helena Solberg Ladd's *Nicaragua Up From the Ashes* (U.S., 1982) foregrounds the role of women in the Sandanista revolution. Sara Gomez's well-known film *De cierta manera* (One Way or Another, Cuba, 1975), often cited as part of the late 1970s and early 1980s Third-Worldist debates around women's position in revolutionary movements, interweaves documentary and fiction as part of a feminist critique of the Cuban revolution. From a decidedly pro-revolutionary perspective, the film deploys images of building and construction to metaphorize the need for further revolutionary changes. Macho culture is dissected and analyzed within the overlaid cultural histories (African, European, and Cuban), in terms of the need to revolutionize gender relations in the postrevolution era.

Already in the late 1960s and early 1970s, in the wake of the Vietnamese victory over the French, the Cuban revolution, and Algerian independence, Third-Worldist film ideology was crystallized in a wave of militant manifestos—Glauber Rocha's "Aesthetic of Hunger," (1965), Fernando Solanas and Octavio Getino's "Towards a Third Cinema," (1969), and Julio García Espinosa's "For an Imperfect Cinema" (1969)—and in declarations from

Third-World film festivals calling for a tricontinental revolution in politics and an aesthetic and narrative revolution in film form.[5] Within the spirit of a politicized auteurism, Rocha demanded a "hungry" cinema of "sad, ugly films"; Solanas and Getino urged militant guerrilla documentaries; and Espinosa advocated an "imperfect" cinema energized by the "low" forms of popular culture. But the resistant practices of such films are neither homogeneous nor static; they vary over time, from region to region, and, in genre, from epic costume drama to personal small-budget documentary. Their aesthetic strategies range from "progressive realist" to Brechtian deconstructivist to avant-gardist, tropicalist, and resistant postmodern.[6] In their search for an alternative to the dominating style of Hollywood, such films shared a certain preoccupation with First-World feminist independent films which sought alternative images of women. The project of digging into "herstories" involved a search for new cinematic and narrative forms that challenged both the canonical documentaries and mainstream fiction films, subverting the notion of "narrative pleasure" based on the "male gaze." As with Third-Worldist cinema and with First-World independent production, post–Third-Worldist feminist films and videos conduct a struggle on two fronts, at once aesthetic and political, synthesizing revisionist historiography with formal innovation.

The early period of Third-Worldist euphoria has given way to the collapse of Communism, the indefinite postponement of the devoutly wished "tricontinental revolution," the realization that the "wretched of the earth" are not unanimously revolutionary (nor necessarily allies to one another), the appearance of an array of Third-World despots, and the recognition that international geopolitics and the global economic system have forced even the "Second World" to be incorporated into transnational capitalism. Recent years have even witnessed a crisis around the term "Third World" itself; it is now seen as an inconvenient relic of a more militant period. Some have argued that Third-World theory is an open-ended ideological interpellation that papers over class oppression in all three worlds, while limiting socialism to the now nonexistent second world.[7] Three-worlds theory not only flattens heterogeneities, masks contradictions, and elides differences, but also obscures similarities (for example, the common presence of the "Fourth-World," or indigenous, peoples in both "Third-World" and "First-World" countries). Third-World feminist critics such as Nawal El-Saadawi (Egypt), Vina Mazumdar (India), Kumari Jayawardena (Sri Lanka), Fatima Mernissi (Morocco), and Lelia Gonzales (Brazil) have explored these differences and similarities in a feminist light, pointing to the gendered limitations of Third-World nationalism.

But even within the current situation of "dispersed hegemonies" (Arjun Appadurai),[8] the historical thread or inertia of First-World domination remains a powerful presence. Despite the imbrication of "First" and "Third" worlds, the global distribution of power still tends to make the First-World countries cultural "transmitters" and the Third-World countries "receivers." (One byproduct of this situation is that First-World "minorities" have the power to project their cultural productions around the globe). While the Third World is inundated with North American films, TV series, popular music, and news programs, the First World receives precious little of the vast cultural production of the Third World, and what it does receive is usually mediated by multinational corporations.[9] These processes are not entirely negative, of course. The same multinational corporations that disseminate inane blockbusters and canned sitcoms also spread Afro-diasporic music, such as reggae and rap, around the globe. The problem lies not in the exchange but in the unequal terms on which the exchange take place.[10]

At the same time, the media-imperialism thesis, which was dominant in the 1970s, needs drastic retooling. First, it is simplistic to imagine an active First World simply forcing its products on a passive Third World. Second, global mass culture does not so much replace local culture as coexist with it, providing a cultural lingua franca remarked by a "local" accent.[11] Third, there are powerful reverse currents as a number of Third-World countries (Mexico, Brazil, India, Egypt) dominate their own markets and even become cultural exporters.[12] We must distinguish, furthermore, between the ownership and control of the media–an issue of political economy–and the specifically cultural issue of the implications of this domination for the people on the receiving end. The "hypodermic needle" theory is as inadequate for the Third World as it is for the First: everywhere spectators actively engage with texts, and specific communities both incorporate and transform foreign influences.[13] In a world of transnational communications, the central problem becomes one of tension between cultural homogenization and cultural heterogenization, in which hegemonic tendencies, well-documented by Marxist analysts like Mattelart and Schiller, are simultaneously "indigenized" within a complex, disjunctive global cultural economy. At the same time, discernible patterns of domination channel the "fluidities" even of a "multipolar" world; the same hegemony that unifies the world through global networks of circulating goods and information also distributes them according to hierarchical structures of power, even if those hegemonies are now more subtle and dispersed.

Although all cultural practices are on one level products of specific national contexts, Third-World filmmakers (men and women) have been forced to engage in the question of the national precisely because they lack the taken-for-granted power available to First-World nation-states. At the same time, the topos of a unitary nation often camouflages the possible contradictions among different sectors of Third-World society. The nation states of the Americas, of Africa and Asia often "cover" the existence, not only of women, but also of indigenous nations (Fourth World) within them.

Moreover, the exaltation of "the national" provides no criteria for distinguishing exactly what is worth retaining in the "national tradition." A sentimental defense of patriarchal social institutions simply because they are "ours" can hardly be seen as emancipatory. Indeed, some Third-World films criticize exactly such institutions: *Xala* (1990) criticizes polygamy; *Finzan* (1989) and *Fire Eyes* (1993) critique female genital mutilation; films like *Allah Tanto* (1992) focus on the political repression exercised even by a pan-Africanist hero like Sekou Touré; and Sembene's *Guelwaar* (1992) satirizes religious divisions within the Third-World nation. Third, all countries, including Third-World countries, are heterogeneous, at once urban and rural, male and female, religious and secular, native and immigrant. The view of the nation as unitary muffles the "polyphony" of social and ethnic voices within heteroglot cultures. Third-World feminists, especially, have highlighted the ways in which the subject of the Third-World nationalist revolution has been covertly posited as masculine and heterosexual. Fourth, the precise nature of the national "essence" to be recuperated is elusive and chimerical. Some locate it in the precolonial past, or in the country's rural interior (e.g., the African village), or in a prior stage of development (the preindustrial), or in a non-European ethnicity (e.g., the indigenous or African strata in the nation-states of the Americas); and each narrative of origins has had its gender implications. Recent debates have emphasized the ways in which national identity is mediated, textualized, constructed, "imagined," just as the traditions valorized by nationalism are "invented."[14] Any definition of nationality, then, must see nationality as partly discursive in nature, must take class, gender, and sexuality into account, must allow for racial difference and cultural heterogeneity, and must be dynamic, seeing "the nation" as an evolving, imaginary construct rather than an originary essence.

The decline of the Third-Worldist euphoria, which marked feminist films like *One Way or Another*, *The Hour of Liberation,* and *Nicaragua Up From the Ashes*, brought with it a rethinking of political, cultural, and aesthetic possibilities, as the rhetoric of revolution began to be greeted with a certain skepticism. Meanwhile, the socialist-inflected national-liberation struggles of the the 1960s and 1970s were harassed economically and militarily, violently discouraged from becoming revolutionary models for postindependence societies. A combination of IMF pressure, cooptation, and "low-intensity warfare" obliged even socialist regimes to make a sort of peace with transnational capitalism. Some regimes repressed those who wanted to go beyond a purely nationalist bourgeois revolution to restructure class, gender, religion, and ethnic relations. As a result of external pressures and internal self-questioning, the cinema also gave expression to these mutations, with the anticolonial thrust of earlier films gradually giving way to more diversified themes and perspectives. This is not to say that artists and intellectuals became less politicized but that cultural and political critique took new and different forms. Contemporary cultural practices of post–Third-World and multicultural feminists intervene at a precise juncture in the history of the Third World.

Third Worldism Under Feminist Eyes

Largely produced by men, Third-Worldist films were not generally concerned with a feminist critique of nationalist discourse. It would be a mistake to idealize the sexual politics of anticolonial Third-Worldist films like the classic *Battle of Algiers*, for example. On one level, it is true that Algerian women are granted revolutionary agency. In one sequence, three Algerian women fighters are able to pass for Frenchwomen and, consequently, slip through the French checkpoints with bombs in their baskets. The French soldiers treat the Algerians with disciminatory scorn and suspicion but greet the Europeans with amiable "bonjours." The soldiers' sexism leads them to misperceive the three women as French and flirtatious when, in fact, they are Algerian and revolutionary. *The Battle of Algiers* thus underlines the racial and sexual taboos of desire within colonial segregation. As Algerians, the women are the objects of the military as well as the sexual gaze; they are publicly desirable for the soldiers, however, only when they masquerade as French. They use their knowledge of European codes to trick the Europeans, putting their own "looks" and the soldiers' "looking" (and failure to see) to revolutionary purpose. (Masquerade also serves the Algerian male fighters, who veil as Algerian women to better hide their weapons.) Within the psychodynamics of oppression, the colonized knows the mind of the oppressor, while the converse is not true. In *The Battle of Algiers*, the women deploy this cognitive asymmetry to their own advantage, consciously manipulating ethnic, national, and gender stereotypes in the service of their struggle.

On another level, however, the women in the film largely carry out the orders of the male revolutionaries. They certainly appear heroic, but only insofar as they perform their sacrificial service for the "nation." The film does not ultimately address the two-fronted nature of their struggle within a nationalist but still patriarchal revolution.[15] In privileging the nationalist struggle, *Battle of Algiers* elides the gender, class, and religious tensions that fissured the revolutionary process, failing to realize that, as Anne McClintock puts it, "nationalisms are from the outset constituted in gender power" and that "women who are not empowered to organize during the struggle will not be empowered to organize after the struggle."[16] The final shots of a dancing Algerian woman waving the Algerian flag and taunting the French troops, accompanied by a voice-over announcing: "July 2, 1962: Independence. The Algerian Nation is born," has the woman "carry" the allegory of the "birth" of the Algerian nation. But the film does not raise the contradictions that plagued the revolution both before and after victory. The nationalist representation of courage and unity relies on the image of the revolutionary woman precisely because her figure might otherwise evoke a weak link, the fact of a fissured revolution in which unity vis-a-vis the colonizer does not preclude contradictions among the colonized.

Third-Worldist films often favored the generic and gendered space of heroic confrontations, whether set in the streets, the casbah, the mountains, or the jungle. The minimal presence of women corresponded to the place assigned to women both in the anticolonialist revolutions and within Third-Worldist discourse, leaving women's homebound struggles unacknowledged. Women occasionally carried the bombs, as in *Battle of Algiers*, but only in the name of a "Nation." More often, women were made to carry the "burden" of national allegory: the woman dancing with the flag in *Battle of Algiers*, the Argentinian prostitute whose image is underscored by the national anthem in *La Hora de las Hornos* (The Hour of the Furnaces), the mestiza journalist in *Cubagua*, as embodiment of the Venezuelan nation, or scapegoated as personifications of imperialism, for example, the allegorical "whore of Babylon" figure in Rocha's films. Gender contradictions have been subordinated to anticolonial struggle: women were expected to "wait their turn."

A recent Tunisian film, *Samt al Qusur* (The Silence of the Palace, 1994) by Moufida Tlatli, a film editor who had worked on major Tunisian films of the postindependence, "Cinema Jedid" (New Cinema) generation, and who has now directed her first film, exemplifies some of the feminist critiques of the representation of the "nation" in the anticolonial revolutionary films. Rather than privileging direct, violent encounters with the French, which would necessarily have to be set in male-dominated spaces of battle, the film presents 1950s Tunisian women at the height of the national struggle as restricted to the domestic sphere. Yet, it also challenges middle-class assumptions about the domestic sphere as belonging to the isolated wife-mother of a (heterosexual) couple. *The Silence of the Palace* focuses on working-class women, the servants of the rich, pro-French Bey elite, subjugated to hopeless servitude, including at times sexual servitude, but for whom life outside the palace, without the guarantee of shelter and food, would mean the even worse misery of, for example, prostitution. Although they are bound to silence about what they see and know within the palace, the film highlights their survival as a community. As an alternative family, their emotional closeness in crisis and happiness and their supportive involvement in decision-making show their ways of coping with a no-exit situation. They become a nonpatriarchal family within a patriarchal context. Whether through singing as they cook for an exhibitionist banquet, through praying as one of them heals a child who has fallen sick, or through dancing and eating in a joyous moment, the film represents women who did not plant bombs but whose social positioning turns into a critique of failed revolutionary hopes as seen in the postcolonial era. The information about the battles against the besieging French are mediated through the radio and by vendors, who report to the always "besieged" women on what might lead to an all-encompassing national transformation.

Yet, this period of anticolonial struggle is framed as a recollection narrative of a woman singer, a daughter of one of the female servants, illuminating the continuous pressures exerted on women of her class. (With some exceptions, female singers/dancers are still associated in the Middle East with being just a little above the shameful occupation of prostitution.) The gendered and classed oppression that she witnessed as an adolescent in colonized Tunisia led her to believe that things would be different in an independent Tunisia. Such hopes were encouraged by the promises made by the middle-class male intellectual, a tutor for the Bey's family, who suggests that in the new Tunisia not knowing her father's name will not be a barrier for establishing a new life. Their passionate relationship in the heat of revolution, where the "new" is on the verge of being born, is undercut by the framing narrative. Her fatherless servant-history and her low status as a singer haunt her life in the postindependence era; the tutor lives with her but does not marry her, yet gives her the protection she needs as a singer. The film opens on her sad, melancholy face singing a famous Um Kulthum song from the 1960s, "Amal Hayati" (The Hope of My Life). Um Kulthum, an Egyptian, was the leading Arab singer of the twentieth century. Through her unusual musical talents—including her deep knowledge of "fusha" (literary) Arabic—she rose from her small village to become "kawkab al sharq" (the star of the East). Her singing accompanied the Arab world in all its national aspirations and catalyzed a sense of Arab unity that managed to transcend, at least on the cultural level, social tensions and political conflicts. She was closely associated with the charismatic leadership of Gamal Abdul Nasser and his anti-imperial pan-Arab agenda, but the admiration, respect, and love she elicited continued well after her death in 1975. Um Kulthum's transcendental position, however, has not been shared by many female singers or stars in the Arab world.

The protagonist of *The Silence of the Palace* begins her public performance at the invitation of the masters of the palace. This invitation comes partly because of her singing talent but no less because of the sexual advances she begins to experience as soon as one of the masters notices that the child has turned into a young woman. The mother who manages to protect her daughter from sexual harassment is herself raped by one of the masters. On the day of the daughter's first major performance at a party in the palace, the mother dies of excessive bleeding from medical complications caused by aborting the product of the rape. In parallel scenes, the mother shouts from her excruciating pain and the daughter courageously cries out the forbidden Tunisian anthem. The sequence ends with the mother's death and with her daughter leaving the palace for the promising outside world of young Tunisia. In postindependent Tunisia, the film implies, the daughter's situation has somewhat improved. She is no longer a servant but a singer who earns her living, yet needs the protection of her boyfriend against gender-based humiliations. Next to her mother's grave, the daughter articulates, in a voice-over, her awareness of some improvements in the conditions of her life in comparison with that of her mother. The daughter has gone through many abortions, despite her wish to become a mother, in order to keep her relationship with her boyfriend—the revolutionary man who does not transcend class for purposes of marriage. At the end of the film, she confesses at her mother's grave that this time she cannot let this piece of herself go. If, in the opening, the words of Um Kulthum's song relay a desire for the dream not to end—"Khalini, gambak, khalini/ fi hudhni albak, khahlini/ oosibni ahlam bik/ Yaret Zamani ma yesahinish" (Leave me by your side/ in your heart/ and let me dream/ wish time will not wake me up)—the film ends with an awakening to hopes unfulfilled with the birth of the nation. Birth, here, is no longer allegorical as in *The Battle of Algiers*, but concrete, entangled in taboos and obstacles, leaving an open-ended narrative, far from the euphoric closure of the Nation.

The Cinema of Displacement

Third-World nationalist discourse has often assumed an unquestioned national identity, but most contemporary nation-states are "mixed" formations. A country like Brazil, arguably Third World in both racial terms (a *mestizo* majority) and economic ones (given its economically dependent status), is still dominated by a Europeanized elite. The U.S., a "First-World" country, which always had its Native American and African American minorities, is now becoming even more "Third Worldized" by waves of postindependence migrations. Contemporary United States life intertwines First- and Third-World destinies. The song "Are My Hands Clean," by Sweet Honey in the Rock, traces the origins of a blouse on sale at Sears to cotton in El Salvador, oil in Venezuela, refineries in Trinidad, factories in Haiti and South Carolina. Thus, there is no Third World, in Trinh T. Minh-ha's pithy formulation, without its First World, and no First World without its Third. The First-World/Third-World struggle takes place not only *between* nations but also *within* them.

A number of recent diasporic film and video works link issues of postcolonial identity to issues of post–Third-Worldist aesthetics and ideology. The Sankofa production *The Passion of Remembrance* (1986) by Maureen Blackwood and Isaac Julien thematizes post–Third-Worldist discourses and fractured diasporic identity—in this case, Black British identity—by staging a "polylogue" between the 1960s black radical as the (somewhat puritanical) voice of nationalist militancy and the "new," more playful voices of gays and lesbian women, all within a derealized reflexive aesthetic. Film and video works such as Assia Djebar's *Nouba Nisa al Djebel Chenoua* (The Nouba of the Women of Mount Chenoua) (1977), Lourdes Portillo's *After the Earthquake* (1979), Lucia Salinas's *Canto a la Vida* (Song to Life) (1990), Mona Hatoum's *Measures of Distance* (1988), Pratibha Parmar's *Khush* (1991), Trinh T. Minh-ha's *Surname Viet Given Name Nam* (1989) and *Shoot for the Content* (1991), Prajna Paramita Parasher and Den Ellis's *Unbidden Voices* (1989), Lucinda Broadbent *Sex and the Sandinistas* (1991), Mona Smith's *Honored by the Moon* (1990), Indu Krishnan's *Knowing Her Place* (1990), Christine Chang's *Be Good My Children* (1992), Teresa Osa and Hidalgo de la Rivera's *Mujeria* (1992), Marta N. Bautis's *Home is the Struggle* (1991) break away from earlier macronarratives of national liberation, re-envisioning the nation as a heteroglossic multiplicity of trajectories. While remaining anticolonialist, these experimental films call attention to the diversity of experiences within and across nations. Since colonialism had simultaneously aggregated communities fissured by glaring cultural differences and separated communities marked by equally glaring commonalities, these films suggest, many Third-World nation-states were highly artificial and contradictory entities. The films produced in the First World, in particular, raise questions about dislocated identities in a world increasingly marked by the mobility of goods, ideas, and peoples attendant with the "multinationalization" of the global economy.

Third Worldists often fashioned their idea of the nation-state according to the European model, in this sense remaining complicit with a Eurocentric Enlightenment narrative. And the nation-states they built often failed to deliver on their promises. In terms of race, class, gender, and sexuality, in particular, many of them remained, on the whole, ethnocentric, patriarchal, bourgeois, and homophobic. At the same time, a view of Third-World nationalism as the mere echo of European nationalism ignores the international realpolitik that made the end of colonialism coincide with the beginning of the nation-state. The formation of Third-World nation-states often involved a double process of, on the one hand, joining diverse ethnicities and regions that had been separate under colonialism, and, on the other, partitioning regions in a way that forced regional redefinition (Iraq/Kuwait) and a cross-shuffling of populations (Pakistan/India, Israel/Palestine). Furthermore, political geographies and state borders do not always coincide with what Edward Said calls "imaginary geographies," whence the existence of internal emigres, nostalgics, rebels (i.e., groups of people who share the same passport but whose relations to the nation-state are conflicted and ambivalent). In the postcolonial context of a constant flux of peoples, affiliation with the nation-state becomes highly partial and contingent.

While most Third-Worldist films assumed the fundamental coherence of national identity, with the expulsion of the colonial intruder fully completing the process of national becoming, the postnationalist films call attention to the fault lines of gender, class, ethnicity, region, partition, migration, and exile. Many of the films explore the complex identities generated by exile—from one's own geography, from one's own history, from one's own body—within innovative narrative strategies. Fragmented cinematic forms homologize cultural disembodiment. Caren Kaplan's observations about a reconceived "minor" literature as deromanticizing solitude and rewriting "the connections between different parts of the self in order to make a world of possibilities out of the experience of displacement,"[17] are exquisitely appropriate to two autobiographical films by Palestinians in exile, Elia Suleiman's *Homage by Assassination* (1992) and Mona Hatoum's *Measures of Distance. Homage by Assassination* chronicles Suleiman's life in New York during the Persian Gulf War, foregrounding multiple failures of communication: a radio announcer's aborted efforts to reach the filmmaker by phone; the filmmaker's failed attempts to talk to his family in Nazareth (Israel/ Palestine); his impotent look at old family photographs; and despairing answering-machine jokes about the Palestinian situation. The glorious dream of nationhood and return is here reframed as a Palestinian flag on a TV monitor, the land as a map on a wall, and the return (*awda*) as the "return" key on the computer keyboard. At one point, the filmmaker receives a fax from a friend, who narrates her family history as an Arab-Jew, her feelings during the bombing of Iraq and Scud attacks on Israel, and the story of her displacements from Iraq, through Israel/Palestine, and then on to the U.S.[18] The mediums of communication become the imperfect means by which dislocated people struggle to retain their national imaginary, while also fighting for a place in a new national context (the U.S., Britain), in countries whose foreign policies have concretely impacted on their lives. *Homage by Assassination* invokes the diverse spatialities and temporalities that mark the exile experience. A shot of two clocks, in New York and in Nazareth, points to the double time-frame lived by the diasporic subject, a temporal doubleness underlined by an intertitle saying that, due to the Scud attacks, the filmmaker's mother is adjusting her gas mask at that very moment. The friend's letter similarly stresses the fractured space-time of being in the U.S. while identifying with relatives in both Iraq and Israel.

In *Measures of Distance*, the Palestinian video and performance artist Mona Hatoum explores the renewal of friendship between her mother and herself during a brief family reunion in Lebanon in the early 1980s. The film relates the fragmented memories of diverse generations: the mother's tales of the "used-to-be" Palestine, Hatoum's own childhood in Lebanon, the civil war in Lebanon, and the current dispersal of the daughters in the West. (It should be noted that the cinema, from *The Sheik* through *The King and I* to *Out of Africa,* has generally preferred showing Western women travelers in the East rather than Eastern women in the West.) As images of the mother's handwritten Arabic letters to the daughter are superimposed over dissolves of the daughter's color slides of her mother in the shower, we hear an audiotape of their conversations in Arabic, along with excerpts of their letters as translated and read by the filmmaker in English.

The voice-over and script of *Measures of Distance* narrate a paradoxical state of geographical distance and emotional closeness. The textual, visual, and linguistic play between Arabic and English underlines the family's serial dislocations, from Palestine to Lebanon to Britain, where Mona Hatoum has been living since 1975, gradually unfolding the dispersion of Palestinians over very diverse geographies. The foregrounded letters, photographs, and audiotapes call attention to the means by which people in exile negotiate cultural identity. In the mother's voice-over, the repeated phrase "My dear Mona" evokes the diverse "measures of distance" implicit in the film's title. Meanwhile, background dialogue in Arabic, recalling their conversations about sexuality and Palestine during their reunion, recorded in the past but played in the present, parallels shower photos of the mother, also taken in the past but looked at in the present. The multiplication of temporalities continues in Hatoum's reading of a letter in English: to the moments of the letter's sending and its arrival is added the moment of Hatoum's voice-over translation of it for the English-speaking viewer. Each layer of time evokes a distance at once temporal and spatial, historical and geographical; each dialogue is situated, produced, and received in precise historical circumstances.

The linguistic play also marks the distance between mother and daughter, while their separation instantiates the fragmented existence of a nation. When relentless bombing prevents the mother from mailing her letter, the screen fades to black, suggesting an abrupt end to communication. Yet the letter eventually arrives via messenger, while the voice-over narrates the exile's difficulties of maintaining contact with one's culture(s). The negotiation of time and place is here absolutely crucial. The videomaker's voice-over reading her mother's letters in the present interferes with the dialogue recorded in the past in Lebanon. The background conversations in Arabic give a sense of present-tense immediacy, while the more predominant English voice-over speaks of the same conversation in the past tense. The Arabic speaker labors to focus on the Arabic conversation and read the Arabic scripts, while also listening to the English. If the non-Arabic speaking spectator misses some of the film's textual registers, the Arabic-speaking spectator is overwhelmed by competing images and sounds. This strategic refusal to translate Arabic is echoed in Suleiman's *Homage by Assassination* where the director (in person) types out Arab proverbs on a computer screen, without providing any translation. These exiled filmmakers thus cunningly provoke in the spectator the same alienation experienced by a displaced person, reminding us, through inversion, of the asymmetry in social power between exiles and their "host communities." At the same time, they catalyze a sense of community for the minoritarian speech community, a strategy especially suggestive in the case of diasporic filmmakers, who often wind up in the First World precisely because colonial/imperial power has turned them into displaced persons.

Measures of Distance also probes issues of sexuality and the female body in a kind of self-ethnography, its nostalgic rhetoric concerned less with the "public sphere" of national struggle than with the "private sphere" of sexuality, pregnancy, and children. The women's conversations about sexuality leave the father feeling displaced by what he dismisses as "women's nonsense." The daughter's photographs of her nude mother make him profoundly uncomfortable, as if the daughter, as the mother writes, "had trespassed on his possession." To videotape such intimate conversations is not a common practice in Middle Eastern cinema or, for that matter, in any cinema. (Western audiences often ask how Hatoum won her mother's consent to use the nude photographs and how she broached the subject of sexuality.) Paradoxically, the exilic distance from the Middle East authorizes the exposure of intimacy. Displacement and separation make possible a transformative return to the inner sanctum of the home; mother and daughter are together again in the space of the text.

In Western popular culture, the Arab female body, whether in the form of the veiled, barebreasted women who posed for French colonial photographers or the Orientalist harems and belly dancers of Hollywood film, has functioned as a sign of the exotic. But rather than adopt a patriarchal strategy of simply censuring female nudity, Hatoum deploys the diffusely sensuous, almost pointillist images of her mother naked to tell a more complex story with nationalist overtones. She uses diverse strategies to veil the images from voyeuristic scrutiny: already hazy images are concealed by text (fragments of the mother's correspondence, in Arabic script) and are difficult to decipher. The superimposed words in Arabic script serve to "envelop" her nudity. "Barring" the body, the script metaphorizes her inaccessibility, visually undercutting the intimacy verbally expressed in other registers. The fragmented nature of existence in exile is thus underlined by superimposed fragmentations: fragments of letters, dialogue, and the mother's *corps morcelle* (rendered as hands, breasts, and belly). The blurred and fragmented images evoke the dispersed collectivity of the national family itself.[19] Rather than evoke the longing for an ancestral home, *Measures of Distance*, like *Homage by Assassination*, affirms the process of recreating identity in the liminal zone of exile.[20] Video layering makes it possible for Mona Hatoum to capture the fluid, multiple identities of the diasporic subject.

Interrogating the Aesthetic Regime

Exile can also take the form of exile from one's own body. Dominant media have long disseminated the hegemonic white-is-beautiful aesthetic inherited from colonialist discourse, an aesthetic which exiled women of color from their own bodies. Until the late 1960s, the overwhelming majority of Anglo-American fashion journals, films, TV shows, and commercials promoted a canonical notion of beauty within which white women (and, secondarily, white men) were the only legitimate objects of desire. In so doing, the media extended a longstanding philosophical valorization of whiteness. European writing is replete with homages to the ideal of white beauty, implicitly devalorizing the appearance of people of color. For Gobineau, the "white race originally possessed the monopoly of beauty, intelligence and strength."[21] For Buffon, "[Nature] in her most perfect exertions made men white."[22] Fredrich Bluembach called White Europeans "Caucasians" because he believed that the Caucusus mountains were the original home of the most beautiful human species.[23]

Gendered racism left its mark on Enlightenment aesthetics. The measurements and rankings characteristic of the new sciences were wedded to aesthetic value judgments derived from an Apollonian reading of a de-Dionysianized Greece. Thus, Aryanists like Carl Gustav Carus measured the divine in humanity through resemblance to Greek statues. The auratic religion of art, meanwhile, also worshipped at the shrine of whiteness. Clyde Taylor, Cornel West, and bell hooks, among others, have denounced the normative gaze that has systematically devalorized non-European appearance and aesthetics.[24] Where but among Caucasians, the British surgeon Charles White asked rhetorically, does one find "that nobly arched head, containing such a quantity of brain. . . . In what other quarter of the globe shall we find the blush that overspreads the soft features of the beautiful women of Europe."[25] Although White's tumescent descriptions clearly hierarchize male brains over female beauty, they ultimately embrace white women for their genetic membership in the family of (white) Man. In this spirit, countless colonial adventure novels, not to mention films like *Trader Horn* (1930) and *King Kong* (1933), show "natives" in naked adoration of the fetish of white beauty. It is only against the backdrop of this long history of glorification of whiteness and the devalorization of blackness that one can appreciate the emotional force of the counter-expression "Black is Beautiful."

If cinema itself traced its parentage to popular sideshows and fairs, ethnographic cinema and Hollywoodean ethnography were the heirs of a tradition of exhibitions of "real" human objects, a tradition going back to Columbus's importation of "New World" natives to Europe for purposes of scientific study and courtly entertainment. Exhibitions organized the world as a spectacle within an obsessively mimetic aesthetic.[26] Africans and Asians were exhibited as human figures bearing kinship to specific animal species, thus literalizing the colonialist zeugma yoking "native" and "animal," the very fact of exhibition in cages implying that the cages' occupants were less than human. Lapps, Nubians, and Ethiopians were exhibited in Germany in anthropological-zoological exhibits.[27] The conjunction of "Darwinism, Barnumism, [and] pure and simple racism" resulted in the exhibition of Ota Benga, a Pygmy from the Kasai region, alongside the animals in the Bronx Zoo.[28] The 1894 Antwerp World's Fair featured a reconstructed Congolese village with sixteen "authentic" villagers. In many cases, the people exhibited died or fell seriously ill. "Freak shows," too, paraded before the bemused eyes of the West a variety of "exotic" pathologies. A recent video, *The Couple in the Cage: A Gautinaui Odyssey* (1993) by Coco Fusco and Paula Heredia, "writes back" by readdressing the notion of pathology to its scientist "senders." The video is based on a satirical performance by Guillermo Gomez-Peña and Coco Fusco in which they placed themselves in a cage in public squares and museums performing as two newly discovered Gautinaui from an island in the Gulf of Mexico. The video juxtaposes responses of spectators, many of whom took the caged humans to be "real," with archival footage from ethnographic films in a kind of a media jujitsu that returns the colonial gaze.

One of the best-known cases of the exhibition of African woman is that of Saartjie Baartman, the "Hottentot Venus," who was exhibited on the entertainment circuit in England and France.[29] Although her protrusive buttocks constituted the main attraction, the rumored peculiarities of her genitalia also drew crowds, with her racial/sexual "anomaly" constantly being associated with animality.[30] The zoologist and anatomist George Cuvier studied her intimately and presumably dispassionately, and compared her buttocks to those of "female mandrills, baboons . . . which assume at certain epochs of their life a truly monstrous development."[31] After her death at the age of twenty-five, Cuvier received official permission for an even closer look at her private parts, and dissected her to produce a detailed description of her body, inside out.[32] Her genitalia still rest on a shelf in the Musée de l'Homme in Paris alongside the genitalia of "*une negresse*" and "*une peruvienne,*"[33] monuments to a kind of imperial necrophilia. The final placement of the female parts in the patriarchally designated "Museum of Man" provides a crowning irony.

A collage by the artist Renée Green on the subject of the "Hottentot Venus" looks ironically at this specific form of colonizing the black female body. The supposedly oxymoronic naming of the "Hottentot Venus" was aggressive and Eurocentric. The collage turns this same "oxymoron" against its originators. The piece juxtaposes a photograph of a white man looking through a camera; a fragment of a nineteenth-century drawing of the torso of a white woman in a hoop skirt; a fragment of another torso, this time of the nude Hottentot; and finally, an image of the Grand Tetons (the Big Breasts). A text accompanying the collage calls attention to the undercurrents of desire within the scientific enterprise:

> The subinterpreter was married to a charming person, not only a Hottentot in figure, but in that respect a Venus among Hottentots. I was perfectly aghast at her development. I profess to be a scientific man, and was exceeding anxious to obtain accurate measurements of her shape.

The collage evokes a hierarchy of power. The man looking evokes Cuvier, the scientist who measured the historical Hottentot Venus. By fragmenting the African woman's buttocks, Green exaggerates what for the white scientists was already exaggerated. Juxtaposing this image with a fragmented depiction of a white woman whose fashionably hooped skirt also shapes artificially outsized buttocks, she implies that both the African and the European woman have been constructed for masculinist pleasures: one as the acme of coy virginal beauty, adorned with flowers and a delicately held fan; the other, naked, imagined as an exemplum of gross corporality supposedly to be looked at without pleasure, only for the sake of the austere discipline of science. Both drawings easily slide into the image of Nature, the Grand Tetons. The letter "A" appears next to the white woman, "B" next to the Black, and "AB" next to the Grand Tetons, and a punning "C" ("see") next to the white man with camera. The strategic use of European representations of an African woman to underline social ironies about sexuality, gender, and race exploits a boomerang technique; a descendant of Africans literally re-frames the prejudicial images of an earlier African woman as a kind of posthumous accusation.

The hegemony of the Eurocentric gaze, spread not only by First-World media but even at times by Third-World media, explains why *morena* women in Puerto Rico, like Arab-Jewish (Sephardi) women in Israel, paint their hair blond, and why Brazilian TV commercials are more suggestive of Scandinavia than of a black-majority country, and why "Miss Universe" contests can elect blond "queens" even in North African countries, and why Asian women perform cosmetic surgery in order to appear more Western. (I am not questioning the partial "agency" involved in such transformations but highlighting the patterns informing the agency exercised.) Multicultural feminists have criticized the internalized exile of Euro-"wannabees" (who transform themselves through cosmetic surgery or by dying their hair) while at the same time seeking an open, nonessentialist approach to personal aesthetics. The mythical norms of Eurocentric aesthetics come to inhabit the intimacy of self-consciousness, leaving severe psychic wounds. A patriarchal system contrived to generate neurotic self-dissatisfaction in *all* women (whence anorexia, bulimia, and other pathologies of appearance) becomes especially oppressive for women of color by excluding them from the realms of legitimate images of desire.

Set in a Hollywood studio in the 1940s, Julie Dash's *Illusions* (1982) underscores these exclusionary practices by foregrounding a black singer who lends her singing voice to a white Hollywood star. Like Hollywood's classic *Singin' in the Rain*, *Illusions* reflexively focuses on the cinematic technique of postsynchronization, or dubbing. But while the former film exposes the intraethnic appropriation whereby silent movie queen Lina Lamont (Jean Hagen) appropriates the silky dubbed voice of Kathy Selden (Debbie Reynolds), *Illusions* reveals the racial dimension of constructing eroticized images of female stars. The film features two "submerged" black women: Mingon Duprée (Lonette McKee), invisible as an African American studio executive "passing for white," and Esther Jeeter (Rosanne Katon), the invisible singer hired to dub the singing parts for white film star (Lila Grant). Jeeter performs the vocals for a screen role denied her by Hollywood's institutional racism. Black talent and energy are sublimated into a haloed white image. But by reconnecting the black voice with the black image, the film makes the black presence "visible" and therefore "audible," while depicting the operation of the erasure and revealing the film's indebtedness to black performance. But if Gene Kelly can expose the injustice and bring harmony in the world of *Singin' in the Rain*, Lonette McKee–who is far from being a "tragic mulatta" and is portrayed as a woman with agency, struggling to rewrite her community's history–has no such power in *Illusions*, in a studio significantly named the "national studio." *Illusions* references the historical fading in of the African American image into Euro-American entertainment, suggesting that while black sounds were often welcome (for example, on the radio) black images remained taboo, as if their iconic presence would be incendiary after such a long disappearing act.

The existential life of the racialized body has been harsh, subject not only to the indignities of the auction block, to rape, branding, lynching, whipping, stun gunning, and other kinds of physical abuse but also to the kind of cultural erasure enailed in aesthetic stigmatization. Many Third-World and minoritarian feminist film and video projects offer strategies for coping with the psychic violence inflicted by Eurocentric aesthetics, calling attention to the sexualized/racialized body as the site of both brutal oppression and creative resistance. Black creativity turned the body, as a singular form of "cultural capital," into what Stuart Hall calls a "canvas of representation."[34] A number of recent independent films and videos–notably Ayoka Chenzira's *Hairpiece: A Film for Nappy-Headed People* (1985), Ngozi A. Onwurah's *Coffee Coloured Children* (1988), Deborah Gee's *Slaying the Dragon* (1988), Shu Lea Cheang's *Color Schemes* (1989), Pam Tom's *Two Lies* (1989),

Maureen Blackwood's *Perfect Image?* (1990), Helen Lee's *Sally's Beauty Spot* (1990), Camille Billop's *Older Women and Love* (1987), and Kathe Sandler's *A Question of Color* (1993)—meditate on the racialized/sexualized body in order to narrate issues of identity. These semiautobiographical texts link fragmented diasporic identities to larger issues of representation, recovering complex experiences in the face of the hostile condescension of Eurocentric mass culture. *Perfect Image?*, for example, satirizes the mass-mediated ideal of a "perfect image" by focusing on the representation and self-representation of two black British women, one light-skinned and the other dark, lampooning the system that generates self-dissatisfaction in very diverse women, all of whom see themselves as "too" something—too dark, too light, too fat, too tall. Their constant shifting of personae evokes a diversity of women, and thus prevents any essentialist stereotyping along color lines in the Afro-diasporic community.

Pathological syndromes of self-rejection—black skins/white masks—form the psychic fall-out of racial hegemony. Given the construction of dark bodies as ugly and bestial, resistance takes the form of affirming black beauty. The Black Power movement of the 1960s, for example, transformed kinky hair into proud Afro hair. Sandler's *A Question of Color* traces tensions around color-consciousness and internalized racism in the African American community, a process summed up in the popular dictum: "If you're white, you're all right/if you're yellow, you're mellow/if you're brown, stick around/ but if you're black, stay back." (Such tensions formed the subject of Duke Ellington's musical composition "Black, Brown and Beige.") Hegemonic norms of skin color, hair texture, and facial features are expressed even within the community through such euphemisms as "good hair" (i.e., straight hair) and "nice features" (i.e., European-style features), and in inferentially prejudicial locutions like "dark *but* beautiful," or in admonitions not to "look like a Ubangi." The film registers the impact of the "Black is Beautiful" movement, while regarding the present moment as the contradictory site both of the resurgent Afrocentrism of some rap music along with lingering traces of old norms. One interview features a Nigerian cosmetic surgeon who de-Africanizes the appearance of black women, while the film reflects on the valorization of light-skinned black women in rap video and MTV. Sandler also probes intimate relations in order to expose the social pathologies rooted in color hierarchies; the darker-skinned feel devalorized and desexualized, the lighter-skinned—to the extent that their own community assumes they feel superior to it—are obliged to "prove" their blackness. Filtering down from positions of dominance, chromatic hierarchies sow tensions among siblings and friends, all caught by Sandler's exceptionally sensitive direction.

In all these films, internalized models of white beauty become the object of a corrosive critique. Not coincidentally, many of the films pay extraordinary attention to hair as the scene both of humiliation ("bad hair") and of creative self-fashioning, a "popular art form" articulating "aesthetic solutions," in Kobena Mercer's words, to the "problems created by ideologies of race and racism."[35] Already, since the Afro hair style of the late 1960s and 1970s but especially recently, there have been reverse currents linked to the central role of African Americans in mass-mediated culture: whites who thicken their lips and sport dreadlocks, fades, or cornrows. From a multicultural feminist perspective, these cross-cultural transformations (cosmetic surgery, dyeing the hair) on one level are exempla of "internal exile" or "appropriation." But on another level they evoke the possibility of an open, nonessentialist approach to looks and identity. Ayoka Chenzira's ten-minute animated short *Hairpiece: A Film for Nappy-Headed People* addresses hair and its vicissitudes in order to narrate African Americans' history of exile from the body as well as the utopia of empowerment through Afro-consciousness. In a dominant society where beautiful hair is that which "blows in the wind," *Hairpiece* suggests an isomorphism between vital, rebellious hair that refuses to conform to Eurocentric norms and the vital, rebellious people who "wear" the hair. Music by Aretha Franklin, James Brown, and Michael Jackson accompanies a collage of black faces (from Sammy Davis to Angela Davis). Motown tunes underscore a quick-paced visual inventory of relaxers, gels, and curlers, devices painfully familiar to black people, and particularly to black women. The film's voice-over and "happy ending" might seem to imply an essentialist affirmation of "natural African beauty," but as Kobena Mercer points out in another context, "natural hair" is not itself African; it is a syncretic construct.[36] Afro-diasporic hair styles, from the Afro to dreadlocks are not emulations of "real" African styles but rather neologistic projections of diasporic identity. The styles displayed at the film's finale, far from being examples of "politically correct" hair, rather assert a cornucopia of diasporic looks, an empowering expression of a variegated collective body. Satirizing the black internalization of white aesthetic models, the film provokes a comic catharsis for spectators who have experienced the terror and pity of self-colonization.[37]

Ngozi A. Onwurah's lyrical semiautobiographical film *Coffee Coloured Children*, meanwhile, speaks of the black body as hemmed in by racism. The daughter of a white mother and an absent Nigerian father, the film's narrator recalls the pain of growing up in an all-white English neighborhood. The opening sequence immediately demonstrates the kind of racist harassment the family suffered: a neo-Nazi youth defiles their front door with excrement, while the mother, in voice-over, worries about protecting her children from feeling somehow responsible for the violence directed at them. The narrative conveys the traumatic self-hatred provoked by imposed paradigms. In one scene, the daughter doffs a blonde wig and white makeup in front of a mirror, trying to emulate a desired whiteness. If

The Battle of Algiers made the mirror a revolutionary tool, here, it becomes the speculum for a traumatized identity, literally that of a black skin masked with whiteness. The simple act of looking in a mirror is revealed to be multiply specular, as one looks even at oneself through the eyes of many others—one's family, one's peers, one's racial others, as well as the panoptic eyes of the mass media and consumerist culture. The scar inflicted on the victims of this aesthetic hegemony are poignantly suggested in a bath sequence in which the children, using cleaning solutions, frantically try to scrub off a blackness lived as dirt.[38] The narrator's voice-over relating the cleansing ritual is superimposed on a close shot of rapid scrubbing, blurred so as to suggest bleeding, an apt image for colonialism's legacy inscribed on the body of children, a testament to the internalized stigmata of a devastating aesthetic regime.

Rewriting the Exotic Body

While Third-World and First World minoritarian women have experienced diverse histories and sexual regimes, they have also shared a common status as colonial exotics. They have been portrayed as wiggling bodies graced with Tutti Frutti hats, as lascivious dark eyes peering from behind veils, as feathered dark bodies slipping into trance to accelerating rhythms. In contrast to the Orientalist harem imaginary, all-female spaces have been represented very differently in feminist independent cinema, largely directed by Arab women. Documentaries such as Attiat El-Abnoudi's *Ahlam Mumkina* (*Permissible Dreams*) (Egypt, 1989) and Claire Hunt's and Kim Longinotto's *Hidden Faces* (Britain, 1990) examine female agency within a patriarchal context. Both films feature sequences in which Egyptian women speaking together about their lives in the village, recount in ironic terms their dreams and struggles with patriarchy. Through its critical look at the Egyptian feminist Nawal el Saadawi, *Hidden Faces* explores the problems of women working together to create alternative institutions. Elizabeth Fernea's *The Veiled Revolution* (1982) shows Egyptian women redefining not only the meaning of the veil but also the nature of their own sexuality. And Moroccan filmmaker Farida Benlyazid's feature film *Bab Ila Sma Maftouh* (A Door to the Sky) (1988) offers a positive gloss on the notion of an all-female space, counterposing Islamic feminism to Orientalist phantasies.

A Door to the Sky tells the story of a Moroccan woman, Nadia, who returns from Paris to her family home in Fez. That she arrives in Morocco dressed in punk clothing and hair style makes us expect an ironic tale about a Westernized Arab feeling out of place in her homeland. But instead, Nadia rediscovers Morocco and Islam and comes to appreciate the communitarian world of her female relatives, as well as her closeness with her father. She is instructed in the faith by an older woman, Kirana, who has a flexible approach to Islam: "Everyone understands through his own mind and his own era." As Nadia awakens spiritually, she comes to see the oppressive aspects of Western society. At the same time, she sees Arab/Muslim society as a possible space for fulfillment. Within the Islamic tradition of women using their wealth for social charity, she turns part of the family home into a shelter for battered women. The film is not uncritical of the patriarchal abuses of Islam—for example, the laws which count women as "half-persons" and which systematically favor the male in terms of marriage and divorce. The film's aesthetic, however, favors the rhythms of contemplation and spirituality, in slow camera movements that caress the contoured Arabic architecture of courtyards and fountains and soothing inner spaces. Dedicated to a historical muslim woman, Fatima Fihra, the tenth-century founder of one of the world's first universities, *A Door to the Sky* envisions an aesthetic that affirms Islamic culture, while inscribing it with a feminist consciousness, offering an alternative both to the Western imaginary and to an Islamic fundamentalist representation of Muslim women. Whereas contemporary documantaries show all-female gatherings as a space for resistance to patriarchy and fundamentalism, *A Door to the Sky* uses all-female spaces to point to a liberatory project based on unearthing women's history within Islam, a history that includes female spirituality, prophecy, poetry, and intellectual creativity, as well as revolt, material power, and social and political leadership.[39]

Negotiating between past and present is also seen in Tracey Moffat's *Nice Coloured Girls,* which interweaves tales about contemporary urban Australian Aboriginal women and their "captains" (sugar daddies) with tales of Aboriginal women and white men over 200 years before. Moffat interrogates the hackneyed conventions of the "Aboriginal Film," proposing instead the formal experimentalism of *Nice Coloured Girls* itself.[40] And in sharp contrast to the colonial construction of the Aboriginal "female body" seen as a metaphorical extension of an exoticized land, *Nice Coloured Girls* places dynamic, irreverent, resourceful Aboriginal women at the center of the narrative, offering a multitemporal perspective on their "nasty" actions—mild forms of prostitution and conning white Australian men into spending money. By shuttling between present-day Australia and past texts, voices, and images, the film contextualizes their behavior in relation to the asymmetrical exchanges typical of colonial encounters. Two temporally and spatially distinct but conceptually interconnected frames—one associated with images of the sea (or its painterly representation) and set in the past, the other set in a pub in contemporary Australia—contextualize the encounter. In one early pub sequence, an Aboriginal man and woman step behind a frosted glass door to smoke a joint. As their film-noirish silhouettes undulate to the diegetic pub music, a British-accented male voice-over reads excerpts from a historical journal describing an Aboriginal woman's breasts, teeth, and face. The evocation of an earlier historical meeting conditions the viewer's comprehension of latter-day encounters.

Rather than search for an "authentic" Aboriginal culture, *Nice Coloured Girls* constructs a "genealogy" of criminality. While from the vantage point of Eurocentric decorum the Aboriginal women are amoral schemers, the historical context of settler colonialism and its sexualized relations to both land and women switches the ethical and emotional valence. In the pub, the women demonstrate their resilient capacity to survive and to outwit marginalization. Whereas images of the past are set inside a ship or in daylight on shore, images from the present are set in the nighttime city, pointing to the historical "neonization," as it were, of Aboriginal space. The film can thus be seen as a "revenge" narrative in which Aboriginal women trick Euro-Australian men into fantasizing a "fair" exchange of sex and goods, then take their money and run.

Racial and sexual relations from past (the initial encounter between Europeans and Aborigines, in 1788) and present (1987) are interwoven through overlapping images, music, texts, and voice-over. The opening sequence superimposes a text by an early English "explorer" over a dark urban skyscraper, accompanied by the sounds of rowing and of labored rhythmic breathing. While the male voice-over narrates excerpts from journals of the "discovery" of Australia in 1788, subtitles convey the thoughts of present-day Aboriginal women. While the voice-over is in the first-person, the subtitles relay a collective voice. The images reinforce the subtitled version, offering the women's perspective on their trapped "captains," deconstructing the journals not by correcting the historical record but rather through a discursive critique of their racist and masculinist thrust.

The title of *Nice Coloured Girls* is itself ironic, foreshadowing the film's subversion of the "positive" image of "nice" colored girls as the objects of colonial exoticization, and the valorization of the "negative" image of "nastiness." The historical encounters are reconstructed in a minimalist antirealist style, a symbolic evocation rather than a "realistic" depiction. By reflexively foregrounding the artifice of its production through stylized sets, excessive performance style, and ironic subtitles, the film undermines any expectation of sociologically "authentic" or ethnically "positive" representations. Image, sound, and text amplify and contextualize one another, militating against any authoritative history. The constant changes of discursive register—vérité-style hand-held camera, voice-over ethnographic texts, subtitled oral narratives, American soul music of obscure diegetic status—undermine any univocal mode of historical narration. *Nice Coloured Girls* challenges a whole series of discursive, generic, and disciplinary traditions. Looking at official Anglo-Australian discourse through the deconstructive eyes of the Aboriginal women, this densely layered text mocks the prurient "ethnographic" fascination with aboriginal sexuality. Rather than reverse the dichotomy of sexualized Third-World women and virginal European women by proposing an equally virginal image of Aboriginal women, the film rejects the binaristic mode altogether. Finding the kernel of contemporary power relations in the colonial past, *Nice Coloured Girls* shows "nastiness" as a creative response to a specific economic and historical conjuncture.

A discourse which is "purely" feminist or "purely" nationalist, I have tried to argue, cannot apprehend the layered, dissonant identities of diasporic or postindependent feminist subjects. The diasporic and post–Third-Worldist films of the 1980s and 1990s, in this sense, do not so much reject the "nation" as interrogate its repressions and limits, passing nationalist discourse through the grids of class, gender, sexuality, and diasporic identities. While often embedded in the autobiographical, they are not always narrated in the first person, nor are they "merely" personal; rather, the boundaries between the personal and communal, like the generic boundaries between documentary and fiction, the biographic and the ethnographic, are constantly blurred. The diary form, the voice-over, the personal written text, now bear witness to a collective memory of colonial violence and postcolonial displacement. While early Third-Worldist films documented alternative histories through archival footage, interviews, testimonials, and historical reconstructions, generally limiting their attention to the public sphere, the films of the 1980s and 1990s use the camera less as a revolutionary weapon than as a monitor of the gendered and sexualized realms of the personal and the domestic, seen as integral but repressed aspects of national history. They display a certain skepticism toward metanarratives of liberation but do not necessarily abandon the notion that emancipation is worth fighting for. Rather than fleeing from contradiction, they install doubt and crisis at their very core. Rather than a grand anticolonial metanarrative, they favor heteroglossic proliferations of difference within polygeneric narratives, seen not as embodiments of a single truth but rather as energizing political and aesthetic forms of communitarian self-construction.

Since all political struggle in the postmodern era necessarily passes through the simulacral realm of mass culture, the media are absolutely central to any discussion of post–Third-Worldist multicultural and transnational feminist practices. I have tried to link the often ghettoized debates concerning race and identity politics, on the one hand, and nationalism and postcolonial discourse, on the other, as part of an attempt to put in dialogue, as it were, diverse post–Third-Worldist feminist critiques. The global nature of the colonizing process and the global reach of the contemporary media virtually oblige the cultural critic to move beyond the restrictive framework of the nation-state. Within postmodern culture, the media not only set agendas and frame debates but also inflect desire, memory, and fantasy. The contemporary media shape identity; indeed, many argue that they now exist close to the very core of identity production. In a transnational world typified by the global circulation of images and sounds, goods, and peoples, media spectatorship impacts complexly on national identity, communal belonging, and political affiliations. By facilitating a mediated engagement with distant peoples, the media "deterritorialize" the process of imagining communities. And while the media can destroy community and fashion solitude by turning spectators into atomized consumers or self-entertaining monads, they can also fashion community and alternative affiliations. Just as the media can exoticize and disfigure cultures, they have the potential power not only to offer countervailing representations but also to open up parallel spaces for anti-racist feminist transformation. In this historical moment of intense globalization and immense fragmentation, the alternative spectatorship established by the kind of film and video works I have discussed can mobilize desire, memory, and fantasy, where identities are not only the given of where one comes from but also the political identification with where one is trying to go.

Section III

Anatomies of Organizing, Building Feminist Futures

10

Ring Ding in a Tight Corner: Sistren, Collective Democracy, and the Organization of Cultural Production

Honor Ford-Smith

Feminist organizations, certainly in the Caribbean, often seem disturbingly weak. Since the 1970s we have formed groups, raised consciousness, conducted research, given guidelines for national policy, and developed imaginative methodologies for education and organization. Yet, so far, we have not been able to fundamentally affect women's power in the society on as many levels as we would need to if the power relations between the genders were to be significantly challenged. In spite of the existence of a new organized Jamaican women's movement, recent studies show that women's material conditions are getting worse, not better. Not only has the daily scuffle for survival become tougher, but the prevalence of violence in daily life has strengthened women's reliance on male "backative." In the context of the reorganization of international capital and the division of labor and production worldwide, countries like Jamaica have been crippled by a staggering economic decline. The main institutional actor in this process has been the International Monetary Fund. In exchange for loans to governments in foreign currency, the Fund insists on the complete opening of the economy, the whittling away of the nation-state as we know it, and the divestment of state responsibilities into the hands of private enterprise. In Jamaica, the effect has been horrific. The standard of living of the majority of people in the country is way below what it was in the mid-1970s (Levitt 1990). Apart from astronomical inflation, the country has sustained huge cuts in the provisions for social services and education. The brunt of the burden of these policies is borne by women, who have to take up the slack created by these cuts. It is women who, through their labor, replace the services that were once the responsibilities of hospitals, schools, and community centers.

Ironically, all this has happened in a context in which female labor has acquired greater significance and potential than at any other time in this century. During the 1980s, national development strategies targeted female labor as never before. Priority plans for economic development were based on the expansion of free-trade zones, offshore data processing, and tourism. All of these activities rely on female labor, so it is not surprising that female unemployment showed a slight decrease in this period. The traditional male working class was no longer in the forefront of the country's economic plans. Women, moreover, began to talk back in songs which spoke about enjoying male sexual attention without accepting male domination and to celebrate making men pay for sex with women. At the same time, women who participated in a UNESCO study on cultural development stated their willingness to organize with other women around issues of sexual violence, education, and employment, but complained about the failure of women's organizations to speak out, analyze, and act on women's problems. They further criticized women's groups for having pretentious procedures biased in favor of middle-class women (Ford-Smith 1988).

Clearly, then, by the late eighties new feminist organizations operating regionally and nationally faced a critical set of contradictions and challenges. Women's deteriorating material conditions were in contradiction to rising expectations about the job market and their increased mobilization. All this indicated that the time was right for a broad and powerful women's movement, a movement strong enough to intervene and transform national development in women's interests. The stark reality, however, was that the majority of women remained outside of women's organizations and were in the lowest echelons of organizations that were run by men. Understanding the constraints that limit the potential of the women's movement is crucial to deepening our effectiveness.

This account examines the factors that limited the success of one Jamaican women's organization: the Sistren Collective, an organization that worked with women both culturally and politically. I examine the expansion of this organization between 1977 and 1988 and identify some of the major problems it faced. In the context of Jamaica's political and cultural history, I ask two questions: How did the funding policies of international agencies affect the group's development? And, how did the group's internal structure affect its development? In essence, I argue that the dictates of international funding agencies exacerbated internal contradictions in the collective structure around race and class, specifically on issues having to do with service and product delivery, education, decision-making, leadership, power, and authority. As a result, the organization became constrained, both in terms of what it offered the community, its ability to develop clear and effective organizational support, and its ability to satisfy member's needs. I go on to make some suggestions for women's organizations in similar situations, to consider and to propose some of the possible politics and concepts groups might reclaim to avoid some of these problems.

My Location

This study is based on interviews and on an analysis of the papers of the Sistren Collective. An earlier draft of the study was submitted to the collective for comment and I have revised it in light of many of the comments I received. Nevertheless, what I write here is, in the final instance, very much my own responsibility. My reflections are colored by my own position in the group as Artistic Director, a leadership post I held from the founding of the collective until 1989, when I resigned from full-time work in the organization.

I began the process of reflection partly because of my own desire to open up a dialogue with other women on the problems. But I was also motivated by my need to question how what I experienced as a crisis in the work had come about. I wanted to understand how I was implicated in what had taken place. I wanted to deepen my understanding of the problems and potential of working across differences as well as my understanding of how power worked both among us and outside of us.

As the daughter of a light-skinned professional Jamaican woman and an English working-class man whom I hardly knew, my identities make me simultaneously an insider and an outsider in most contexts. I look white and am certainly socially white in the context of a black-majority country, and this makes me a member of a privileged minority. As a young woman in an audience I was addressing once pointed out, I am "not the popular color." I saw my work in the women's movement as a point from which to subvert privileges which I experienced as causing tremendous violence in the country and in each of us, and as a way of making responsible use of skills which the society had given me. Having been raised and educated in Jamaica in the period leading up to independence and in the early postindependence period, I experienced myself as someone called a "Jamaican." I understood that to mean someone whose identity was constituted by the specific history of that society, a history which included internal conflicts and differences.

By 1988, I began to realize dimly how my work was being influenced by other ways of seeing and making meaning. I began to sense in a very immediate way that volunteerism, good intentions, and hard work were not strong enough weapons against the weight of a history of multileveled colonialism. Out of this crisis, it slowly dawned on me that what appears to undermine privilege from one vantage point can be reframed and reread as the reenactment of an old text of privilege or may, in fact, simply consolidate old power relations in new forms. While I framed our actions as insurgent behavior, colonial narratives conditioning the behavior of people who look like me and who work with women who look like the majority of Sistren, and vice versa, regulated our work in the discourses of the missionary, the plantation, and now most recently, the development worker.

One of the subtexts of this account, then, concerns the unraveling of the intricate and thick fabric out of which work for social change is made. An underlying theme in the account is the examination of how work across differences is made. I am trying to get at the meaning of the silences and denials in our work, and I am trying to interrogate what was said and done, in order to reveal the complex interrelationship of layers of power, privilege, and resistances in daily life.

The writing of this study was an extremely painful process for me for several reasons. First, I was writing about problems, and so the emphasis is deliberately negative. I also had to face the things in myself and in the organization that infected me with an overwhelming sense of failure, powerlessness, rage, or guilt. Secondly, I had to grapple with the idea of how useful it would be to make public some of our most knotty conflicts. Part of what made it most difficult was the absence of a language to get across the complexity of the lived crises and often unspoken causes behind the conflicts. I hope that the experience described here will help to stimulate the development of such a language. I also hope that it will spark a debate on funding for women's groups. Perhaps work like this can provoke feminist and antiracist theory to provide a more complete language of organizational process and practice for feminist workplaces. A language is needed that will help to analyze and address the contradiction between the emancipatory goals of groups and their internal practice, between their interest in transforming social relations toward liberatory power relations and the tense, conflicted organizational culture of many women's groups. Organizational development theory, as it currently exists, has been developed largely in the corporate world. It is premised on empiricism and on liberal ideas of the self and the rights of individuals; it is generally devoid of critical content on context or power relations. Little attention has been paid to the task of sorting out what is useful and not useful for addressing problems of practice in a workplace whose concern is intervention for social change. This study, then, aims to provide a focus for some of the critical issues that might confront those wishing to go further in this work.

The History and Impact of Sistren

The Early Years: 1977–1980

In May 1977, twelve women employed in a special government scheme came together voluntarily to present a short play at a workers' cultural festival in celebration of workers' struggles in Jamaica. The Jamaica School of Drama, part of the newly developed complex of schools of the arts at the Cultural Training Centre opened in 1976, was asked to support the workers' festival by supplying the workers with a tutor-director. I was selected from the school's small staff to take on this role. The play was called *Downpression Get a Blow.* After the play was presented, the group decided to stay together. Thus began Sistren, as a part-time voluntary women's drama group.

The Jamaica School of Drama continued to support the group by considering my work with it a part of the school's outreach program and by providing a space in which the group could work. I devised a program of training in acting skills based on the use of personal testimony. Through this method, the problems of women could be shared, the commonalities in their experiences identified and discussed. Through analysis, storytelling and improvisation, we produced a participatory theatrical presentation.

According to early documentation, Sistren's aims were to create theater for and with working-class women, to form a self-reliant cooperative enterprise, and to provide its members with an income. Between 1977 and 1980, the group concentrated on producing one play a year. By 1981, it had presented four major works. One of these plays, *QPH,*[1] won national awards for excellence, and another, *Bellywoman Bangarang,* was honored for its experimental qualities. Two of these plays concentrated on the life stories of women in the group and two others were concerned with women's history. The project was administered with the help of various advisory and action groups who, at different times, met with representatives from Sistren to plan and support its activities. Some training in group administration was provided by the Jamaican Women's Bureau, with which we collaborated until 1981. The cofounders of the organization at this stage were Lorna Burrell-Haslam, Pauline Crawford, Beverley Elliot, Lillian Foster, Lana Finikin, Barbara Gayle, Beverley Hanson, Rebecca Knowles, Vivette Lewis, Jasmine Smith, Cerene Stephenson, and Jerline Todd. Later, these women came to describe themselves as founding members.

Political Context

Sistren was born in a moment of democratic opening—that is, at a moment in history in which there was a possibility for those who are oppressed to intervene in history and transform their society. In our case, this happened in the 1970s when a left-leaning social-democratic government under Michael Manley came to power in Jamaica. State facilities suddenly opened up to grassroots people. Various forms of support were made available to community organizations. New institutional forms were invented. All these things supported needs which had hitherto been invisible or silent.

In 1973, Jamaica became the first Caribbean country to establish a women's bureau, prompted by the United Nations campaign around the situation of women. In 1975, the World Decade of Women was launched. As a result of these initiatives, there was much public discussion in Jamaica about what was then called "women and development." Under the dynamic leadership of Beverley Anderson-Manley, the women's arm of the ruling People's National Party Women's Movement (PNPWM) had mobilized and organized large numbers of women in support of reforms. Collaborative organizational programs with various women's associations were established and the number of women running for posts in local government increased. Minimum-wage legislation aimed at improving the working conditions of domestic servants. A law providing for equal work claimed to make discrimination against women workers illegal. The abolition of bastardy laws meant that women who had children outside of marriage (the majority of the population) would, like their children, no longer be stigmatized. Such widespread mass mobilization of women had not been seen since the 1930s, when there was a major uprising against colonial rule.

The Special Employment Program (SEP), from which the majority of Sistren members came, was created in response to high levels of female unemployment, and the state's commitment to the idea that women should have wage work. The program employed about 10,000 women, who were initially given "temporary" work as street cleaners, with the intention that they would subsequently be trained for something "more productive." Although few women in the program did, in fact, receive further training, the women who made up Sistren were among those who were retrained as teachers' aides and placed in schools. Today, Sistren is the only remaining evidence of the SEP.

The organized women's movement provided the context out of which Sistren grew because it legitimized women's examination of their own struggles. Yet, by its own acknowledgment, that movement was not feminist. At the time, "feminist" was taken to be synonymous with bra-burning white women anxious to kill off the male sex and reduce all political matters to a simple-minded conflict between men and women. This, after all, was what the media were projecting. Any suggestion that men had privileges that women did not have was regarded suspiciously on the left as an attempt to "divide the struggle." Nevertheless, in spite of defensive reassurances that the women's movement was not "anti-man," Sistren provided an organizational space and ideology in which women gained the strength to question their experience. It placed them in situations that made very obvious the contradiction between what was actually happening and the ideal image of women projected in the society.

Sistren's approach, in its early days, differed from that of the organized women's movement in two main ways. First, it paid more attention to the "private" areas of women's lives, to issues such as sexuality and reproductive rights. It brought a more qualitative personal element to the political analysis of the women's movement. It also openly criticized male privileges and did so in a thoroughly Jamaican idiom while serving as a support group around women's personal experiences and struggles. Secondly, and I will discuss this in greater detail below, Sistren emphasized cultural production and the representation of women's experience in the arts and media as an important site of struggle. It linked art and education with politics, offering its work in drama, life history, and other forms as a space to arouse and nurture rebel consciousness.

In the 1970s, political reforms brought the issue of Jamaican culture under serious examination. The way it was defined and the way it functioned were being questioned. The state gave a nod of approval to the importance of what was then called "cultural development" and tried to find ways of giving greater legitimacy to popular creative work. It was as a result of this that the Cultural Training Centre (housing four schools of the arts) was opened. The importance of legitimizing hitherto subordinated popular traditions was emphasized as a means of developing national identity.

In a general sense, then, Sistren was both representative of its time and different from the majority of women's groups in its vision. In its early work, the emphasis on cultural work characterized it as both different from and complementary to other approaches. It is unlikely that a program of this kind would begin today. Then, we had access to state facilities and our project was framed in a particular political context, which included policies directed toward legitimizing the popular.

The Cultural Context and Sistren's Cultural Work

The Caribbean was the base for European colonial expansion in the sixteenth and seventeenth centuries. The islands are among the oldest colonial possessions. Some are still colonies. As one economist has put it, the central contradiction of Caribbean culture is that its activities have been created to satisfy the needs of other societies. This contradiction is very strongly felt in Jamaica where the eradication of the indigenous Taino culture was almost total. There, the violent importation of, first, enslaved Africans and, then, indentured Asians and Africans has meant that cultural legiti-macy belonged, first, to Europeans and, now, to Euro-North Americans. In this sense, Jamaica, like the rest of the Caribbean, differs from many other colonized countries that have maintained more visible signs of precolonial traditions. As a result of this history, in Jamaica, wherever the plantation has been the dominant institution, the history of violence, deep hierarchy, and patronage has resulted in extreme social alienation. The dominant presence of the United States of America—militarily, economically, and through the mass media—means that what is projected as most desirable is only achievable through emigration. Large numbers of people migrate yearly, many of whom are among the country's best educated and most highly skilled citizens.

Attempts to resist this process, to legitimize and make meaning in one's own experience have always existed. They have resulted in the creation of Caribbean religions, languages, oral traditions, and family structures which exist separately and apart from the official systems of meaning that are institutionalized in the society. For example, polygamy and polyandry are against the law; English is the official language; the system of justice is officially administered through courts of law; and Christianity is the official religion. In reality, however, there is an informal, unofficial culture that contradicts many of the official practices. The enforcement of justice between groups, for example, may be administered in religious rituals which have a non-Christian, African base. Many Jamaicans live in long-term relationships with more than one sexual partner and attempts to define the Caribbean family have not yet resulted in any clear consensus.

That which might be labeled "Jamaican," then, is that which has been created in an attempt to meet the needs of, and to give meaning to, the specific experience of those who live on the island, not the needs of dominant forces from outside. Some of the places where creativity has been most evident have been in language, religion, and the popular arts, which have proved more difficult to control than the material resources of the country. We, in so-called Third-World societies, have both inherited and transformed notions of "art" and "culture" transmitted over centuries by European colonizers. In the Western European tradition, centuries of capitalist development have resulted in very specific notions of the artist and of culture. A tension or an animosity between the political and the aesthetic—between the concept of social justice and the concept of beauty and pleasure—has gradually come to be accepted and has been institutionalized in modes of artistic production since the European Enlightenment. Although there are flickering attempts to bridge this opposition, the fundamental dichotomy of the two discourses is an organizing principle under capitalism. By the terms of this arrangement, the artist has come to be thought of as a highly sensitive, innately gifted individual whose work is somehow cordoned off from the economic and political processes that affect the lives of ordinary people.

At the time Sistren was formed, those involved in cultural work were struggling to develop a new relationship between artist and community. The conceptual framework created by Rex Nettleford for training practitioners of the arts at the Cultural Training Centre spoke, for instance, of "cultural agents" rather than artists. This "agent" was to be able to practice at least one of the artistic disciplines and to be able to insert his or her work within a community in order to facilitate that community's representations of itself. In other words, the artist was regarded as a cultural worker, who would serve the community by offering a space and a process for creating representations. The artist was to be a teacher as well as a creator of products—a worker positioned in a continuum with other workers in society. This is a different conception of the artist than that of a gifted individual who exists and produces in a marginal space apparently outside the relations of power, producing lovely commodities within a fairly fixed spectrum for consumption in the world market. The cultural workers' site of intervention is in the production of meaning-making and representation, activities that help to form subjects who desire change.

Times Change: 1980

In 1980, things changed. National elections took place in an atmosphere of undeclared civil war. Against the background of the deaths of at least 1,000 youths, the conservative opposition swept into power. Immediately, national priorities began to be reversed. Across the island, programs that had aimed at building popular power were dismantled. Workers' cooperatives and community enterprise organizations closed down. Nationalized industries were privatized. The monetarist policies of the International Monetary Fund (IMF) dictated local policy. Huge loans flooded the country, so that, by 1988, the tiny island had become one of the most indebted per-capita nations in the world.

Almost overnight, the women's organizations which had been allied to the party in power were unable to command support. Their networks and campaigns disappeared, creating a kind of political vacuum for women. The employment program in which most members of Sistren still worked was threatened because it was seen as partisan and "unproductive." It was not long before the program was discontinued and the women left jobless.

The events of 1980, including the massive defeats of the popular movement, made it clear that in the future any real attention to gender concerns would require the development of an independent women's movement. The party-affiliated movement, while very important, had not developed the power to articulate gender concerns strongly enough to influence party politics consistently. An autonomous women's movement for social change was needed that could function outside of the control of the traditional party political boundaries. By developing guarantees of power outside male-dominated organizations, women would be able to struggle more effectively within them and with them. At the same time, this would mean developing feminist analyses of national problems that would relate the position and condition of women to the problems and political practice of the country and the development strategies being pursued. This way of thinking had many implications for Sistren's work as a theater collective and workers' organization.

Organizing Sister Groups: Expansion of the Workshop Program, 1982

The awareness of the need for a new type of women's organization was based not only on the collapse of the organized women's movement of the 1970s but also on a critique of what had been achieved in that period and in the early 1980s. In creating the play *The Case of Iris Armstrong* (1982), we worked extensively with sugar workers and discussed the limitations of some of the legislation addressing women workers that had been passed in the 1970s. Through the case of a female supervisor in charge of women workers, we demonstrated that work was undervalued whenever women did it. The traditional sexual division of labor resulted in women being paid less and in their labor being consistently devalued in relation to men's. We showed that this situation was tied to the fact that women were primarily regarded as responsible for the care and maintenance of the home, the sick, the aged, the children, and the men. They were expected to do such work for free–*because* they were women. This relationship was then extended into the labor market.

As we began to speak out more on these issues and as we moved across the country doing workshops and plays, more and more women wanted to work with us in the theater or in sister groups. They wanted, as they put it, to "join Sistren."

In 1982, the collective began to organize and serve groups of women using the drama methodology that had been devised with them. Sistren traveled to rural and urban communities to create workshops in which women who worked as vendors and agricultural workers articulated their concerns and worked toward acting on them. This work went beyond the articulation of personal experience to link material uncovered in testimony to information about the society in general and to an analysis of women's position in it. Much of it was facilitated through Joan French's contribution to the critical content of our educational strategy.

By the end of 1984, a number of sister groups had been created. Two of these were in rural areas and two in Kingston. One of these, a group called Friends of Sistren, produced a booklet called *No to Sexual Violence*[2] that was distributed widely. One of the rural groups successfully organized to get water brought into their community. Their membership swelled.

However, at the end of 1985, the majority of the collective voted to discontinue its group-building work with community women, ostensibly because of the intense difficulty of providing organizational support for such work. After 1985, it was decided to offer our services to groups that already existed and that could provide the necessary organizational infrastructure for our work. There was strong feeling and conflict within the group about this decision. At about the same time, the number of plays produced for theater also began to decline. After 1981, instead of producing one new full-length play per year, one play was produced approximately every two or three years.

Sistren's Social Impact

It is difficult to measure Sistren's impact on Jamaican society with any precision. However, we can report some impressions. In 1987, the collective reached approximately 8,000 people through its theater and workshop program. It distributed 3,000 copies of its newsletter three times a year. Not all of this audience was within Jamaica and, based on records kept, it is impossible to determine precisely how much of the readership of the magazine, for instance, comes from overseas. Sistren toured internationally every year, performing to audiences interested in women's theater and Caribbean culture. It offered workshops on drama-in-education locally and abroad, and it also received countless requests to participate in a variety of workshops and seminars on women's issues.

Between 1980 and 1989, the amount of national media coverage Sistren commanded grew steadily. One can assume from this that most Jamaicans have heard of it. At the same time, there are many people, especially among those living in the rural areas, who have never heard of the group's work. Our own straw poll indicates that of those who have heard of it, few know exactly what it does. Some think it is a kind of charity, some a Communist organization, others a feminist group and still others a part-time theater group that is an arm of the Socialist Party. An evaluation carried out by Cheryl Ryman in 1992 showed that Sistren's work in drama is seen as the most important aspect of its approach to work with women.

In particular sectors the impact is stronger. For example, in a 1987 study of Jamaican nongovernmental organizations (NGOs) receiving aid from the Canadian NGO, CUSO, Sistren was cited as one of the few examples of a development agency addressing the concerns of women as a priority. Academics and students, locally and abroad, also make frequent studies of Sistren's work in the theater, and in research. A number of articles on the group's methodology and its origins have been published. A number of post-graduate students have included the work of the group in their theses and at least two have made the group their entire subject. The leaders of most women's organizations, which represent a minority of women in the country, have heard of Sistren, and most of them are familiar with the type of work the group does, although not necessarily in a very specific sense.

Some of these organizations collaborate with Sistren and use the collective as a resource in their projects and programs. Sistren, then, has acted as a catalyst for further organizing on the part of women. In 1989 the research arm of Sistren was associated with a number of networking initiatives with women, among them Free Trade Zone workers, a Media Watch Group, and a Women's Action Committee. Sistren produces an annual celebration of International Women's Day. Sistren also supported the development of the Association of Women's Organizations of Jamaica, which emerged in the late eighties and which functions as an independent women's umbrella organization lobbying for women's interests in the nineties.

In a general sense, the group has offered an alternative image of women, particularly of black working-class women. Through its plays, workshops, and other activities, Sistren has brought to light many of women's hidden experiences; it has shown the strengths and desires of Jamaican working-class women and the importance of this for the future of the society. It has opened a small space within which the forms of resistance created by working-class women are recognized. It has offered a commentary on women's relationship to power in the society and it has tried to create spaces within which critical Caribbean feminist perspectives could be nurtured. It has also encouraged women to organize and to represent their ideas in writing, drama, and other means, although the extent to which it has been able to offer women the concrete means to do this has been limited. In this sense, Sistren has offered an example of an alternative to the glamorized icons presented on television and in the newspapers in Jamaica.

Over the twelve years of its work, the collective has laid the basis for the development of a participatory approach to working with Caribbean women and for a methodology in popular drama and popular education. It has built up an aesthetic which is based on interpretations of the daily realities of Jamaican women combined with popular myths, images, and dramatic poetry. The use of documentary investigations of women's lives, oral tradition, ritual, and popular music have all combined to contribute to the development of Caribbean theater and literature. The collective has created a number of scripts and a book, *Lionheart Gal: Life Stories of Jamaican Women*. Its series of screen-printed pictures has posed alternative visual images of women and gender. Pioneering research has been carried out on women's history, cultural development, and by Imani Tafari-Ama on women and Rastafari. Sistren's magazine, edited by Joan Ross-Frankson, grew in popularity and circulation annually. Both in its method and in its composition, Sistren's approach is original and unusual in the region.

What Sistren Means to Members

According to the majority of the working-class founding members themselves, the principal achievement of Sistren lies not in its impact on the position of women in Jamaican society as a whole but in what the organization has been able to provide for its own members. In the early days, most members of the group regarded our work as an exercise in self-help which would later impact on the society. Jasmine Smith recalls,

> It was my first opportunity to be in the public and to meet other women. From [the time] I leave school, I start having children, then I stay home and work in bars, club, and factories. I didn't have any time to go out, although I had a feeling to leave the yard. I used to be three or four hours early when the group first started, just to leave the yard and meet other people. I didn't know you could go out, sit with other women, and talk your problems in a constructive way. If you live in a tenant yard and you hear people curse each other about their problems, you wouldn't want to talk your own. If anything happen to you, you just want to keep it to yourself.

And, as Lana Finkin remembers,

> Before we did our first play, I had an interest in working around issues of concern to women. I used to work with women in political groups, but that was not enough. We only just meet and sit and talk. We weren't getting anywhere with how to solve the problems, what to do about it. When Sistren came together, I realize that this is something that can speak on behalf of women. There isn't anywhere in our society that working-class women can go and let their voices be heard. When I see Sistren form, I say Sistren can help to make men realize that women can survive on their own.

In interviews conducted for this study, the majority of working-class members said that the greatest achievements of the group have been the international recognition it has won, the provision of a salary to its members, and the purchase of its own organizational base. A smaller number of middle-class resource people and new members, as well as three founding working-class members, felt that the major achievement was what the group meant for Jamaican women. The following quotes represent founders' views of how the work has afftected both their way of thinking about themselves and their skills:

> One time ago you'd look 'pon tings and say 'Cho! Me can't bodder wid how life stay and wid how money stay and how people stay because a jus one of dose tings. Mek it pass by. One time me jus live everyday as it come. But now dat me see dat tings can change and people can change mi jus feel seh, well if dere needs

> to be a change, me jus say someting or do someting den. (*Myrtle Thompson*)
>
> Sistren help to bring about the awareness of women in me definitely, for di first time, even if me go out a street and hear people, whether man or woman, talk tings fi downgrade woman me wouldn't know how to address it. Now me find meself, if me hear anybody say anything to downgrade woman me can address it. It give me courage to deal wid anybody, no care who you may be. (*Becky*)
>
> I've gained a lot of skills, like acting skills. I know how to really move on stage, how to use my voice. I've gained a lot. (*Beverly Elliot*)
>
> Ah get fi find out dat ah am gifted wid drawing and designing. Over di years we build up a silk-screen-printing project. Ah started to mek designs based off a me own life, di lives of women sugar workers, domestic workers, old women, and di teenage maddas. Now di main designer for Sistren prints is me. (*Cerine Stephenson*)

Funding Follies

Funding was a problem for Sistren from the very beginning. This was so both because of the poverty of the country and the poverty of the group. Early on, we had to choose between accepting funding from international agencies and local financing. Below, I shall examine what both options meant for us as well as how they affected our growth.

Local Financing

Between 1977 and 1981, the group was financed largely from local sources, primarily through the generous in-kind contribution of the Jamaica School of Drama, which provided Sistren with office and rehearsal space and with training.[3] The Women's Bureau offered some help in cooperative training and friends of the School of Drama assisted with additional technical support for the theater. Even then, however, one needed a cash budget to pay for correspondence, transport, and subsistence for members, and to mount productions.

It very soon became clear that the amount of time that it took to raise small amounts of money from local businesses was not worth the mental and physical strain involved. Local capital was not interested in giving any significant support to a small women's group that would earn them neither tax deductions nor publicity as champions of the poor.

In 1980, with the withdrawal of state support, we were faced squarely with the option of continuing to depend on the pittance that could be raised locally or shifting our source of support to international agencies. Had we continued to depend on local funding, we would have either faded out altogether, as many groups did at the time, or our program, limited as it then was, would have been seriously affected. Our working-class members were seriously constrained in the amount of time they could offer voluntarily. Self-sacrificing, do-gooding ladies are, with good reason, confined to the upper classes. As the cost of living rose rapidly, even they began to curtail their activities and volunteer work threatened to become a thing of the past.

In effect, then, there was little choice for us. We had to seek international funding if we wanted to continue to work. But, needless to say, the funding process brought with it a whole host of new problems.

International Development Agencies and the Women-and-Development Thrust

All the agencies involved in funding development work are based in the so-called advanced capitalist world. Their policies are often tied to the politics of their governments or to powerful special interest groups in their countries. Aid, to put it somewhat crudely, is related to both the search for markets and the search for international political support. As far as Jamaica is concerned, the agencies with the greatest interest come from Canada, the United States, and, to a lesser extent, Britain. Although the policies of development agencies vary widely, in general, those funding the activities of NGOs involved with women can be said to have three criteria: a) the production of a multiplier effect; b) a direct influence on a grassroots target group; c) the achievement of some kind of measurable "improvement" in a given situation in relation to a particular problem (usually determined by the donor agency).

At its most serious level, the crisis that faced us in 1980–82 was economic. We had to find an income for our members and a space to work. It also meant meeting the above criteria. We had to find a way of filling a need in the society and offering a product or service. This, in itself, had huge implications.

We were not familiar at the time with the subtleties of international development policies. But it seemed that the international women's movement had provided us with a loophole through which we could slip to avoid extinction. Sistren was able to get funding in 1980 because the international women's movement had begun to gain ground and to have an impact on the policies of international aid agencies. By the late seventies a number of agencies were specifically looking for projects which they classified under the heading of "women and development." At that time, many who worked in aid agencies or with women who implemented development projects accepted the idea that "development" was somehow value-free and inherently progressive. It was by and large assumed that women did not participate in the development process. Therefore, work that women were, in fact, doing in their home and on plots of land was not considered part of "developing" the society. Efforts were centered in the 1970s on "integrating women in development" without questioning the assumptions on which the concept of development was based.

Production First: An Experience with "Income Generation"

In 1978, we presented a short series of scenes at a regional workshop for the Women's Bureau suggesting that women organize into producer cooperatives. After the presentation, we were approached by a woman from the Ford Foundation who said that she was sure funding for our work could be found in U.S. Her agency did not fund cultural work, but she would see if she could interest others in our work.

From the beginning of our dialogue, these agencies made it clear that the problem with our work was that it was not "income-generating." Theater, they said, was most interesting but it would not put bread on the table. We argued back about the need to use the arts to educate women about their rights and their position in society. We argued that confidence-building was essential and that there was a huge problem with cultural alienation in the country which could be best redressed through work around culture. Perhaps our work would motivate others to produce. They countered, "Yes, that is all very well and good, but do you expect us to continue putting more and more money into your work? You need to do something that is productive."

"The arts can be productive, and, anyway, that's precisely the problem," we replied. "Isn't women's work always seen as unproductive? Yet, without this so-called unproductive work, no so-called productive work can happen. Besides, why shouldn't we do something we're good at such as drama, participation, and dialogue? We know how to do that."

"Development," came the retort, "means getting your production going. Saving what you make so you can reinvest it. Not spending what you don't have. Choose something sensible that can earn you some money and then you can talk about education and the arts. You need to be self-reliant."

"But the whole region is dependent," we argued. "How do you expect a small group like us to be self-reliant? Do commodity production and education have to be separate? What place do cultural and educational activities have in international assistance?" The arguments went back and forth in this vein.

The whole discussion brought into sharp focus the bias that characterizes much of the thinking on so-called development. It is seen primarily as a process of economic growth through which poor countries are modernized and become absorbed into the market while becoming increasingly reliant on Western science and technology. It has brought about the acceptance of universalized categories of measurement (such as GDP, GNP, per-capita income, and so on) which presuppose Western standards as the ideal and often ignore what is most specific to any given society. In cases where economic growth has occurred, it has brought with it a host of new problems, not the least of which have been extreme inequities in wealth. In many countries, what has been developed are the tastes and desires which lead to national indebtedness and an unequal position in the world market. Development theory has produced a whole discourse which carries its own language, schools, professionals, and institutions. The discourse imprisons those located within it into a tightly regulated perception of reality and a tightly regulated set of relations defined by the international marketplace and foreign aid.

Nadine Gordimer has characterized development workers as the new missionaries. The relationships between many agencies and the projects they support can be compared to work done by the European churches in colonial societies in the nineteenth century. However, the language of development is different. There is no reference to the soul. And the details of how to achieve salvation depend on changing sets of agency priorities that are often applied globally in spite of enormous differences in country conditions. While God reigns supreme in the Christian cosmology, science and economics preside infallibly over the development process. Regulation is implemented in an effort to standarize and measure results in widely differing situations. Issues around the specificity of cultures, the formation of identities, questions of race and language are not part of the development paradigm. Any view that considers the formation of subjects on their own terms is regarded as dangerous, not so much because it threatens large blocs of power (at present, it is rare that such large claims can be made) but because it sets up confrontations with the everyday privileges that, in many cases, justify the labor of the development worker and his or her sense of power.

As far as most development agencies are concerned, the place of theater and the arts is a non-issue. The arts are unproductive frivolities that can be justified only if they can be proven to be "useful" in the crudest forms, as in education. "Development" apparently does not include pleasure, even the pursuit of pleasurable opportunities for reflection or the creation of cultural products that mirror the collective consciousness. "Development," one concludes, is a "scientific" phenomenon opposed, it is implied, to the arts, which are dangerous luxuries threatening to undo all of science's sweet categories and Western social organization.

The debate about income versus education ended with Sistren starting our own screen-printing textile project. Typically, like many young groups with little experience, we did very little research before embarking on our venture. We chose screen-printing in a somewhat arbitrary way. Our costume designer (Beti Campbell) was a trained textile designer. She had taught members of the group screen-printing in the midst of one of our productions. People liked it; it seemed to go with theater, and so we began. Years later, the project continues to fight for its life. Ironically, it has, at times, been supported by earnings from the theater project, which—contrary to predictions—earns more than any of the other areas of Sistren's work. Textiles have never made a profit. It has never been able to afford the cost of enough personnel skilled in marketing and production management. Nor has it been able to afford the time to train its staff in these areas.

The project was born out of pressure from development agencies rather than out of the consideration and commitment of the whole group. It did not have the full support of all Sistren members and, therefore, in practice, it took second place to the theater work. In the early days, production fluctuated widely and was often interrupted. The same table was used for screen-printing as was used for meetings. The same people printed and designed as did theater, and there were disagreements over the division of labor and the prestige and value given to each component of the work. There were no production targets and no clear hours of production. No wonder quality control was inconsistent.

All told, the textile project was unable to develop a profile sufficiently independent of theater. At a national level, in the 1980s, the project functioned in a situation in which small businesses had the highest failure rate of any form of production in the country. The national infrastructure made it far easier for multinational, export-oriented investment to thrive. Locally, lack of credit and unavailability of raw materials are among some of the practical problems which the project still has to overcome. For example, a T-shirt might be available in cotton this week but only in polyester next week. This spells disaster for orders since customers cannot be guaranteed what they want.

Silk-screened products face the same problems that all Caribbean crafts confront. Because of the relatively high cost of imported raw materials and labor, they are more expensive than similar items from other countries which are produced for local consumption. This, coupled with the fact that the cost of living in Jamaica is higher than in many other formerly colonized countries, means that there are no easy solutions to the difficulties of the project. At the same time, because the financial investment in the project has been enormous and because some members of the collective have developed considerable skill in some aspects of the work, the collective has never been able to make the decision to cut its losses and close the project. Neither did it implement proposals that would turn it into a profit-making business.

The advice given to us by development agencies to generate another income-producing area of activity was ill-advised, given the context in which we were operating and the resources available to us. Instead, we should have concentrated our efforts on developing the educational and income-earning potential of the theater. Polarizing education and production in the way that we were encouraged to do was not useful. In fact, any process that aims at releasing human creativity to the fullest involves both education *and* production. We needed to find better ways to make the two work together, not ways of driving them further apart, especially by taking on an extra responsibility we were unprepared to deal with. Involvement in a new area of work forced us to overextend our activities in the following ways: we produced theatre; we were self-managed; we documented our work; we publicized our work; we produced educational workshops for women in the local communities; we did our internal education work; and we now printed and marketed textiles. Our structure, which had been overburdened from the start, creaked, groaned, and expanded again, before it was ready to do so. In the early 1980s, however, we were in no position to argue with any agency. They had the handle and we had the blade.

Intensified Labour

At the start of our relations with funding agencies, we were not a well-known or successful group. We were a small project, just beginning, and we had to prove ourselves. Agencies largely decided which areas of work would be considered part of the "development process," where it was to be done, and with whom. They defined the terms on which they funded groups and we negotiated within them. An early attempt to argue with one of our major funders, the Inter-American Foundation, about what they defined as our "unacceptable political" activities–an anti-apartheid rally–resulted in our discontinuing relations with them. The loss of their grant pushed us dangerously close to total collapse. From this, we learned an important lesson. Dealing with funders is a highly diplomatic art. It involves balancing the power, keeping your fronts covered, and never putting all your eggs in one basket.

Diversifying our funding sources as a young project meant that some agencies who believed we were unknown insisted on funding our work on a project-to-project basis. We were frequently required to present a project document which covered a short-term time frame and which promised to deliver a particular product or outcome. After this period, the agency's responsibility toward us would end. The implications of this were enormous for our work.

For one thing, it meant that the paperwork multiplied. The number of grant applications and the number of appointments with agency representatives all multiplied. The accounting administration dramatically multiplied in an effort to find money for the real needs of the project. Three agencies required us to produce receipts for every penny we spent "in order to give a good example to our donors and to cover for other organizations who are unable to present such a good record." For a small organization with an already overburdened staff and in a country where photocopying costs are astronomical and machines often scarce or far away, this was a deeply oppressive task.

Many agencies funding short-term projects refused to fund administrative overhead costs such as space rental, equipment, and salaries. Money to pay rent, then, had to be squeezed from other areas. The refusal of agencies to take these administrative costs seriously meant that we could hardly pass inspection for adherence to national health and safety laws which any employer is obliged to meet. The poor working conditions that we problematized in our educational work were being reproduced under our very noses.

Accountability to Whom?

Most aid agencies were primarily interested in funding short-term projects that would produce quick and measurable results. But measurable by whom? And by whose standards? Essentially, agencies wanted to know that their funding criteria had been met. The people who were presumably being served had little input in evaluating the achievements of the project; they had even less say in establishing the criteria for evaluation.

Sistren's limited resources made it impossible for us to do more than a very simple on-the-spot evaluation of what had been offered, whether it was a popular education workshop or a play. This minimal assessment allowed us basically to keep up the required level of accounting and reporting to agencies. It was much harder to develop, at the same time, a long-term process of evaluation and accountability to the target group, or even to maintain an awareness of their importance. We were preoccupied with record keeping. Only in this way, we believed, could we maintain our credibility, our chances of getting another grant, and, thus, guarantees of our survival.

Coming at the period in our development when it did, project-to-project funding prevented us from putting into place long-term strategies for the growth and consolidation of the organization. Issues such as staff welfare benefits and incentives were put on the back burner, so that by the end of the 1980s we had to deal with accumulated burnout and exhaustion. While we struggled to meet the criteria set by aid agencies, we also deferred attending to internal organizational problems. Creative workshops for personal development, group recreational activities, and sensitive forms of conflict resolution were luxuries we could hardly consider in the rush to establish one small project after another. There was no time to stop and look at the system in peace, no money for developing procedures for more effective administration. Levels of self-exploitation were extremely high.

All this, coupled with problems in the collective structure, put us firmly on the road to crisis management. The effect of this style of management, together with the pressure imposed by project-to-project funding, was to give more power to certain women within Sistren, namely those who had a variety of skills and who were capable of switching concentration from one task to another. These women acquired various functions within the group and began to monopolize information about different work procedures. Those in the group who found this switching of focus confusing or who did not have the skills to enable them to shift quickly between tasks resented those who did and the power it gave them. And paradoxically, the different skills and capacities to respond to the various demands were essential to the functioning of the group.

The Contradictions of Funding

On the one hand funding agencies claimed that they were setting up self-reliant grassroots structures; but, on the other hand, they required accounting and reporting processes which could only be done by people who had either university-level qualifications or many years of experience. It should come as no surprise that most grassroots women's organizations get no funding at all to boost the specialized skills and procedures required. A rhetorical emphasis was placed on funding grassroots women's work and on building up the productive capacities of women's groups when, in fact, the way that the agencies operated led to exactly the opposite results.

Indeed, to be able to expand and to function efficiently, the organization needed to attract members with a certain level of skill and consciousness, and to provide its grassroots members with the means to acquire such training formally. However, acquiring such skills would mean that they were no longer eligible for "grass-roots" funding. This catch-22 locked them into a structure of eternal dependency.

By 1984, Sistren's funding situation had shifted. The group had become quite well-known. Instead of having to plead for funds, we now had agencies falling over themselves to aid us because we were seen as an example of a successful "women's project." Donor agencies which had been quite rude to us in the early days when we were so desperately in need of money now openly courted us. We had so many visits from so many friendly agencies that it was all we could do to fit them into our schedule. This was especially true in the Northern winter, the preferred time to travel to the sunny Caribbean. Greater aid also meant greater demands on us to deliver, but it did not mean that our staff had any greater access to staff benefits or to more job security than they had had ten years previously.

The personal situation of the working-class members had become more contradictory than ever. On the surface, Sistren had become a great success. But once members stepped outside the organization, they had little chance of getting a better job. Though they had been trained as dramatists and animators, their lack of formal qualifications meant that once they left Sistren, their skills would probably not be recognized. In any case, the society had little demand for cultural workers

On the other hand, Sistren members were no longer seen as being "grass roots" within their communities. They had traveled extensively and been exposed to new and different ideas. In their jobs, they earned salaries that placed them amongst the top one-third in the country, earning more in 1989 than graduate teachers. The theater team were "stars," spoken about on television, radio, and in the newspapers. The irony of this is that they were stars because they were grassroots, but they were no longer grassroots because they were stars. Among members, this contradiction created a deep sense of dependency on the group and, at the same time on the outside, enormous resentment toward it. Each person's identity seemed indelibly bound up with the group. To leave the group would be to become nothing. Yet, the group itself was not secure. Surely one day the aid would dry up. Or we would not be able to negotiate so well. What would happen to us then? Who would we be as individuals without this institution? Would we be anything at all?

This feeling of insecurity was heightened by the local economic and political situation. State support for health, education, and housing had been stripped away by the impact of the IMF on the Jamaican economy. Each woman's ability to earn a relatively high income had become of crucial importance to her survival, let alone her capacity to support a family. Each woman had, therefore, become deeply aware of her responsibility for herself. The need to "have something to show for all these years of work!" expressed itself again and again. In meetings, members frequently expressed the feeling that they had been robbed or exploited by "the group."

This situation increased tension between founding members and new employees. By 1986, the collective had hired approximately seven new employees and had a total (full- and part-time) staff of approximately twenty-one. Inevitably, new employees were skilled in formal ways that the founding members were not, even though the latter may have had more experience. Founding members felt threatened by the income levels that newcomers were able to demand. They felt that expenditure on higher salaries for new employees would undermine their chances for improved job benefits. Newcomers, they thought, might in time become members of the collective. They might "take over," i.e., control power in the organization by commanding a majority vote in the General Meeting. Feeling threatened in this way, founding members bonded together and refused to take disciplinary action against each other, especially where new employees were involved. They also refused to decide on the question of how "membership" in the collective was to be granted and what it meant. The issue of benefits, and who was eligible for them, also became highly contentious.

New employees, on the other hand, wanted to know why Sistren didn't practice what it preached. As far as they were concerned, to be introduced into the organization on a less-than-equal basis was going against the democratic philosophy of collectivism. In their view, the group seemed hypocritical, and inefficient to boot. If they, as employees, could not even become members of the collective, well then, they implied, Sistren was worse than any capitalist business exploiting its employees.

The Contradictions of Collectivity

A big problem which emerged in 1978 was the question of how the group was to be administered. What processes of decision-making could be worked out in relation to artistic policies, funding, welfare, and education? Prior to 1980, the group's structure had been very much that of tutors and students within the context of an extension program of the Jamaica School of Drama. As the work of the group grew, we experimented with structures of decision-making, all of which involved volunteer advisors from outside. Volunteers were brought in to sit on an advisory board and then on an action committee. Some of them made important contributions, but too often they either did the minimum or could not be found when needed. Sistren sent representatives to these groups but this caused conflict among those founders to whom they reported. None of these experiments met the day-to-day administrative needs of the group, nor did they advance the issues of popular culture and gender around which the group worked.

As founding Artistic Director and tutor, I had become central to all the group's activities. By 1981, I was exhausted. It was clear that I had taken on far too many functions. The collective was frequently criticized for being "my" group rather than a genuine collective. It became clear that if the group was to survive into the 1980s and become more democratic, a new structure had to be found. All of us were in agreement about this. The structure which replaced earlier ones was based on the principle of collective decision-making.

The collective structure was intended to be nonhierarchical and self-managing. It was based on the idea that our personal practice within the organization was as important as our active work toward change in the society as a whole. If we were to be a genuine collective, we could not reproduce in our internal structure the inequitable power relations found in the wider society. Instead, we had to develop a broadly democratic structure that emphasized equality among all the members and that gave everyone a chance to participate and influence policy and action. We did not want to reproduce a structure that equated skill with authority or that divided brain from hand. In a sense, the structure that we built aimed to prefigure the kind of ideal society we wanted to create.

It consisted of a central body, "the General Meeting," in which all policy and executive decisions were made. General meetings were weekly or biweekly events. There was a rotating chair. Record keeping was done by the official secretary of the group as these were regarded as important legal documents of the collective. The agenda was devised collectively, each member having a chance to put whatever she wanted on the agenda. Administrative work assigned by the General Meeting was dealt with by teams. There was a finance team, which kept records and raised funds (although anyone could raise funds individually for a special project), a public-relations team, and, at various times, a secretarial team. There was no board, no trustees, no group of people outside of ourselves to whom we were formally accountable (other than, of course, funders). We had no manual of operations, no constitution, no rules, and no job descriptions. We had no formal way of recording General Meeting decisions as a set of precedents, the general principles of which could be applied as part of the collective's practice. We had no system of checks and balances on our operations.

Annually, we held an evaluation. The purpose was to analyze the past year's work and to determine policy for the year to come. Here lay the beginnings of a structure for reporting and assessing the group's impact. Budgeting was done separately, which meant that there was no clear relationship between the annual evaluation, the development of a yearly plan, and the presentation of statements of income and expenditure. As far as earnings went, there was initially a small income differential between full-time people involved in training the Sistren members and founding members. In 1986, this system was abolished in favor of one standard salary.

As a result, there were no salary scales, no clear indications of increments or incentives. There was, however, a commitment to a very high increase of

25 percent per year as concession to the very high levels of national inflation. As early as 1979, the collective offered all full-time members participation in a health plan, and once a year offered a tiny sum of money to a fund for Sistren children. We were never able to clarify the issue of employee benefits because there was always an enormous insecurity about where our budget was going to come from.

Internal Conflicts and Problems

In the 1980s, Sistren was unique among many other feminist organizations in that it brought together middle-class and working-class women to work on a supposedly equal basis. The middle-class women were named resource people by Sistren members. This partnership between different classes is different from middle-class women providing a professional service to working-class women or working-class women working in their own groups "at the base" and then collaborating with middle-class women around specific issues. In many ways, the working relationship between the middle- and working-class women in Sistren was one of the most creative features of the group. It was also one of the most problematic.

Education was a major issue. Though we all had much to learn about the kind of work in which we were involved, the fact is that concentrated among the early group were many of the skills required by the collective to manage its affairs and to deliver a service that would be taken seriously. The educational qualifications of the middle-class people, for instance, were high. All were university educated, most at a post-graduate level. We could type, and some spoke as many as three languages. Two of us had been educated at one of the best schools on the island and had some access to an "old girls" network. All spoke standard English and had traveled widely. Most importantly, our qualifications were recognized in the wider society outside of the collective.

The working-class members, on the other hand, were working to upgrade basic educational skills. Some had finished secondary school, others had not. Some had difficulty reading, and they felt a great deal of stress when their jobs required them to confront their lack of reading skills. As Beverly Elliot put it,

> At that time, whenever I see a script come forward and I know I have to deal with the script, I used to have a lot of migraine headache because I know I just cyaan deal with it. What I totally depend on dat time is me memory. So I always ask one of the Sistren to help me, just read it for me about three times and I try remember. I don't know what really happen why I cyaan spell and read. I have to just blame it on mi young days. My

> mother have eight of us and I was the biggest girl. She didn't get any help from mi fadda for us so she had to go out to work. When di rest a children get to go to school, I don't get to go because I was di biggest one so I had to be dere cooking di food, washing di clothes, and taking care of the house.

It was working-class members who brought to the collective popular cultural knowledge and language which had been made invisible and inferiorized by centuries of colonization. Working-class Sistren, like countless other Jamaican women, could teach the middle class about issues such as orality, the Jamaican language, and the lived reality of black working-class Jamaican culture. In this knowledge and lived experience are buried the contradictory values of Jamaican collective experience. An unstated belief was that naming the insurgent aspect of these values and the forces which give rise to them was central to any liberatory project; within them were contained the seeds of an alternative to the acceptance of oppressive structures.

In the early days of Sistren, this "tradeoff" of the different kinds of skills which middle- and working-class members brought to the group was possible in only a limited way. The way theater was taught to members of Sistren had implications for the validation of popular culture and the development of a sense of self-worth. The process of the drama improvisations taught the language of the theater while, at the same time, allowing people to reveal and reflect on their own experience. But it did not teach people how to theorize about their experience, nor did it teach them how to teach.

When we began to expand and to serve more people outside the organization, the internal educational experiment within Sistren itself received less and less formal attention. The way we came to define "knowledge" shifted. The particular areas in which working-class women had knowledge no longer seemed to count. This problem and the lack of attention to the educational experiment were linked to the pressures we faced in meeting the demands of our funders. They were also linked to our own ambivalence about whether we should give more weight to meeting the internal needs of members or to servicing others.

Very few educational resources exist for working-class women in Jamaica. Those that exist tend to separate the acquisition of skills from the development of critical consciousness. They rarely address, in a thorough way, the difficult issues of power, identity, race, class, and gender. Given the lack of appropriate educational programs that Sistren could draw on, resource people within the group continued to teach members what they could in order to build the organization. Current affairs, feminist theory, Caribbean history, theater skills, accounting, teaching techniques, management, public relations—all these things were being taught in a somewhat haphazard way between rehearsals, workshops, and general meetings.

Failure to Validate New Skills

Unfortunately, no formal recognition was given to the internal education process or to the teaching role of the resource people. This meant that there was no space within Sistren for theorizing the development of the educational methodologies we used. Many, many highly creative non-formal techniques were being implemented, but there was no systematic attempt among the resource people as teachers to analyze pedagogically and methodologically exactly what we were doing. At the same time, the central ingredient of the early work got lost: the focus on working-class women reflecting on "hidden" aspects of working-class culture and communicating those to a broader audience. For example, *Lionheart Gal* teaches a great deal about working-class culture. It is able to do this because members speak for themselves in their own language and are not spoken for. The ability to analyze this culture and the methods of unearthing and reflecting on it would need to have been given very focussed attention if it were to have been nurtured and extended to other groups of women. This work had implications for methodologies of knowledge production across a whole range of disciplines. But the layers of thought and experience being uncovered were never fully theorized. In my view, the problem raised questions of critical pedagogy, cultural production, and the politics of representation. At the same time there was an absence of theoretical tools which could help in the development of decolonized feminist knowledge and a politics/aesthetics around forms of representation. In the context of the Caribbean, this would also have meant developing tools to examine the creolization process—that process of transculturation within which people of Asian, African, Aboriginal, and European backgrounds, clashed, grappled with, adapted to, and transformed each other in the unequal context of colonization.

One of the resource people, Joan French, analyzed the problem in relation to teaching in this way:

> There has never been enough space for the "teaching" lessons to be learnt, partly because objectively that area ha[d] little space within the collective and little hope of getting it (outside of theater in which practice dominates). There was never enough space to question how working-class Sistren's experience with the formal system differed from their experience of being taught by the resource persons or to ask what were the shortcomings of the ways in which

> we taught, or what were the possibilities of new forms of teaching appropriate to the situation of grassroots women. The implications of this are very far-reaching. Things like a sense of self-worth and validation of one's own culture and language while learning another are very important issues.

Linked to the failure to analyze the teaching methodology was the question of how to assess the progress of learners. Learning on the job became an enshrined principle in Sistren but nowhere did learning lead to graduation. Nor was there any clear and systematic way to validate skills and experience learned on the job. This could have led ultimately to the abolition of the distinction between the resource people and other collective members. The lack of formal recognition for gaining skills and experience within the group was compounded by the fact that there was no way of gaining formal recognition in the wider society for what had been taught within Sistren. The consequences of these problems affected both the middle-class resource persons and the working-class members.

The effect of unplanned and inadequately theorized methodologies was that members were overburdened and had to learn too much all at once. Members were expected to learn management, basic English, accounting, acting, teaching skills, and feminist theory. They had to attend dance classes and current-affairs discussions and somewhere, in all of this, actually do the work. In addition, they had to attend interminable meetings and do domestic chores. Joan French commented on the effects of this process:

> In areas where they were actually learning, they were not given one specific area of learning (such as accounting or workshop skills) which could be developed as their skills increased. Rather they were asked to perform equally in all these various fields.

Perhaps this dispersed energy accounts in part for the ambivalence with which working-class members regarded the acquisition of skills which middle-class women had. Some members were reluctant to take on additional responsibilities and wanted things to remain more or less the same. They felt that when they tried they failed and were "put down" by the resource people or teachers. They became afraid to attempt certain things, and doubtful of their own ability to take responsibility. Others wanted the same skills as the resource people and actively agitated to lead struggles within the group to get them. Perhaps if the issue of how to do critical education and cultural production had been addressed more clearly, some of these problems would not have arisen.

The Persistence of Informal Power

The second area of difficulty in the relationship between the working-class and middle-class women related to the issue of the informal power of the resource people (that is, power over other members that was not legitimized in the structure of the group). I need to point out here that it was not only resource people who held informal power within the group. Working-class members also held informal power. However, in the interviews done for this study, it was the power of the resource people that emerged again and again as a problem.

Theoretically, all Sistren members were equal in the General Meeting. Each woman had only one vote and supposedly all had equal power. But, in fact, the power of the resource people was partly guaranteed by their social location outside of Sistren; their skills were more marketable and valued at a higher price. In the 1980s, most of them were lighter-skinned or white in a society where race is deeply associated with class. Within Sistren, that power differential was also assured by the fact that it was the resource people who actually ran the funding and production processes. This was true especially for the first eight or so years of Sistren's development, during which founding members were learning many different skills and producing drama and theatre at the same time. Another difference between the two groups was that they tended to support different political parties. The working-class women supported one party and three out of four resource people were active with another.

The fact that everyone did not have a clear job description amplified the problem. The jobs which did have descriptions changed their boundaries frequently. I held the job of Artistic Director. The meaning of this title was never clearly defined. In practice, I worked out the original concept of the organization, including its image and methodology, and I did some internal training. Until 1986, I presented annual proposals for the program of work and developed the artistic concept behind the theater work. Until 1985, along with Hilary Nicholson, I initiated discussions with many funding agencies. I also directed and wrote scripts. A great deal of this I did without reflecting on the organizational meaning of these tasks and without a sense of their relationship to the institution's development. There was no clear structure of accountability for any of us within this staff-driven organization we had become.

The collective gave no importance to defining job descriptions or to identifying the kinds of decisions which could be made independently of the General Meeting. Without clarity on these issues there was, among the working-class members, a sense that the resource people were using their skills to hold on to power. Hilary Nicholson recalls,

> We started hearing about the executive that sat in the back room, wrote up the agenda, typed it and made sure that things that they wanted to see on the agenda had been passed around before. And we developed the dem [them] and the oonoo [you] syndrome. Members would say, "Dem say oonoo fi organize di workshops on di hill." Translated it means "they say that you must . . ." which somehow leaves "me" out of it.

But the problem went beyond class. No one was clear about her area of work and no one was confident that decision-making was working in practice. Efforts to redress this problem meant that more and more issues were dealt with collectively in general meetings of all forms, varieties, and lengths. No power could be effectively ceded from the General Meeting since any decisions taken outside of this body would be harshly criticized, ignored, or overturned. The effort to democratize the group meant that enormously long hours were spent in meetings. In spite of this, women still spoke as if they were passive recipients of group decisions and claimed to be absolved from responsibility for the consequences of those decisions. The collective process had aimed at achieving the exact opposite, that is, that all members were to participate in and feel responsible for decision-making.

At first, Sistren's claim to be a self-reliant organization was interpreted to mean that everybody could and should do everything. To insist that everyone get involved in the work teams meant going as slow as the slowest person, an extremely costly and ineffective process. This way of working assumed not only that we were equal but that equality meant sameness. The fact that we were not equal and that each person had a different talent or ability became incompatible with the ideal of the system. Gradually, members who were still "not too hot on the reading and writing business" became less and less involved in the administrative work. They found themselves with nothing to do for hours, while others worked overtime. An unequal division of labor sprang up within the collective and began to cause demoralization. On the one hand, there were those who felt they were working harder and taking more responsibility but not being paid extra or receiving sufficient credit. On the other hand, there were those who felt "we all start di same" and that a kind of "elite Sistren" was developing in which some members tried to lord it over others. When a working-class member was given a task that involved organizing other members, another member's response might be, "You cyaan tell me wa fi do. We all start di same." In this way, members sometimes undermined efforts on the part of working-class women to assume leadership.

Race, Middle-Class Women, and the Denial of Power Needs

Perhaps partly as a result of all of these difficulties, working-class members often felt that opinions were being forced on them by middle-class women. During this period, most of the middle-class women were white or light-skinned, and so this power inequity came to be seen as a race issue:

> You have some white-face people, resource people who know how to structure things, but at times they behave like boss, and they would like to turn you inna idiot. Sometimes if you have something to say, you don't really feel to say it because they make you feel like idiot. (*May Thompson*)

> They try to force you to do something you don't want to do or understand. If you don't understand, they make you feel like you are not in their league, you don't understand what they are dealing with. Some resource people have a way of looking down on us Sistren because we are not educated. (*Cerene Stephenson*)

Before 1985, I was often projected as "the leader." The fact that I am apparently white became central to questioning the group's sincerity in projecting the concerns of black working-class women. "How can a black working-class group have a white director, especially if it is a collective?" There were also questions about the power and involvement of other white or light-skinned women in the collective. Cerene Stephenson describes the effect of race on resistance toward the resource people:

> Resource people within di group, I would call dem white-face people dem, dey used to be di people who up-front in everyting, go to meeting, mek decision.... so it becomes a problem weh yuh find dere's a conflict with di working-class and di upper-middle-class people dem. Every time di resource people dem go to a meeting, people would always say, "Where is Sistren? Who is Sistren?" Dey cyaan believe dat dose people is Sistren because deh heard of working-class women and dem no recognize dem as working-class women but as middle class. So dere come a time when each and everybody haffi tek a stand and dat stand is dat since as how we are working-class people and people asking for Sistren, each individual of Sistren have to go there and face up the people and mek decision. We di same one always have a fuss wid dem and say "Dem go out deh and tek decision about dis an no know if people will agree

> to it." Definitely it couldn't work so individual members haffi go out deh and decide fi tek dem own decision.

In the language of organizational development, what Stephenson describes corresponds to what behavioral scientists call the "storming" phase in group development (Laiken 1991). In this phase of development, members struggle against dependency, and conflicts occur around power and decision-making in the organization. The problem in Sistren was that the structure so masked the power relations in the group that any open renegotiation of power was almost impossible. It is difficult to give up power if you deny having it and if you claim to have no power needs. Thus, the organization got stuck, spinning its wheels around the question of power. In its publicity, the group was described as working class. In fact, this publicity and the image Sistren projected had been designed by the middle-class resource people to stress the fact that the group was made up of working-class women whose experience was "living testimony to the meaning of oppression." The middle-class women were members and workers in the organization, too, but we made little effort to analyze our specific situation as women.

We, imposed on ourselves a virtual silence about our own experience of class and of becoming raced and sexed. When we spoke of middle-class women and their actions, it was with such stringent and judgmental criticism that a visitor from another planet might never have suspected that we came from that class. The implied self-hatred was never interrogated. We painted ourselves out of the picture in theory, while we remained at the center of the organization's work struggling to shape things in practice. While the collective had established a method of speaking out about personal experiences of oppression, this was almost always offered to working-class women, while we middle-class women facilitated or coached. Rarely did middle-class women or white women make spontaneous self-disclosures in workshops or forums. Not only did we deny what lay behind our own experiences of race and class but, since we denied it, we had no basis on which to examine the relations between classes and races which we were creating within the organization. And we were attempting and achieving some powerful and positive relations. The silence around our experience of oppression, privilege, and race made it clear that this was something about which we were uncomfortable and something we did not feel free to name. It was as if there was an unwritten rule that we should not interrogate our own lives.

The reasons for all this denial and self-censorship are extremely complex. In my view, part of the problem has to do with the way middle-class women's identity has been constructed in Jamaican colonial history and internalized by women over generations. As many feminist historians have pointed out, in European societies from the late nineteenth century to the mid-twentieth century, the ideal image of women has been that of a maternalistic housewife, a patroness of charity who is either asexual or whose sexual needs could be met by motherhood within the heterosexual family. Ideally, this Lady Bountiful was financially comfortable, which is to say, middle class and white. She was invested with responsibility for passing on morality and social virtues to her children and to society. She was the bearer of the highest cultural values of the society. She did not speak about her own needs and expressions of anger were absolutely taboo. Her domain was the domestic and the private. In public, she became the social worker.

The impact of this image on colonial society was substantial. In a former slave society, in which missionary churches were perceived as important agents of reform for the poor, the importance of these white women in the provision of social services was immense. Their do-gooder image alone fed into the acceptance of cultural dependency, which had already been cultivated through economic institutions like the plantation. Until the end of the 1930s, this image was limited to white expatriate and near-white upper-middle-class women, who, for instance, made up the membership of the Women's Social Service Club, a prominent women's organization formed in 1919. These women achieved high public visibility and wielded considerable power within the domain of social services.

Black and brown women were represented as "uncivilized," "exotic," "laborers," "promiscuous," and "primitive" in colonial discourse. They were forced to struggle against these racist mythologies by fighting for the privileges that went with the feminine ideal: access to education, management of the social services made available to poor black women or jobs in the clerical sector. They fought to gain from the professionalizing of the social services. They struggled to be considered civilizing forces of their race. While this transformed the color of the image, it meant that upwardly mobile women had to distance themselves from poor black women, since it was the latter who had to be "uplifted." Women in the Garvey Movement and the Women's Liberal Club, women such as Amy Bailey and Una Marson, believed that social work was an important duty for educated women. After 1944, the Jamaica Federation of Women brought together women of all classes and sexes around the ideal of voluntary work, marriage, and the notion of separate spheres for men and women. This organization, which at one time incorporated one third of the population in its ranks, spread the domestic ideal so far, so wide and so deep that even today, many women throughout Jamaica still identify women organizing with the activities of making jams and jellies and the crocheting of doilies. Women whose anger with the limitations of the text of Lady Bountiful forces them to step beyond it risk being ridiculed as mad. The madness resonates differently among the races.

Counternarratives and images in the literature through the 1960s have been complicated by representations of black and brown women across class. Peasant and working-class black women have fascinated writers (mainly male ones), who have often romanticized them and depicted them as close to nature, hard-working, humorous, exotic, loyal, and, naturally (if unfortunately), sexually promiscuous. Examples of these stereotypes can be found in the writings of Louise Bennett, Claude McKay, Roger Mais, H. G. DeLisser, and Vic Reid. Middle-class black and brown women, on the other hand, as Rhonda Cobham has pointed out (Cobham 1982), have largely been negatively depicted—as frustrated, artificial, self-seeking temptresses, embodiments of the worst of bourgeois aspirations. For a middle-class woman to be a woman, she has to violate the myth of the "natural" black woman, act in opposition to it.

In the 1930s, Una Marson dramatized this problem in her play *Pocomania,* in which the heroine is caught between a desire to express her African identity, her inability to do this and remain middle class. To become middle class, then, meant acting against one's "nature," and becoming socially white because the cultural symbols of Africa had to be left behind. The heroine Marson evokes is a woman uprooted, paralyzed with loss and marooned in a cultural minefield, unable to act on her own needs and subject to madness as a result. The anger behind her grief and loss is taboo, and inexpressible because middle-class women are not permitted to recognize their own anger, let alone to express it on their own behalf. Marson's heroine loses her voice and collapses. This is the risk to black women who transgress social whiteness and challenge the image of the good woman. Most recently, the work of writers like Jean Binta Breeze and Erna Brodber have suggested alternative narratives, but these women, too, invoke the spirit of madness which must be confronted in the search for a new possibility.

For a white or brown woman to speak against the narrative is to summon up the older, more negative counterimages of collusion in slavery, the violence of interracial sexual contact, and the intergenerational shame associated with those legacies. For white women, to act against the text is to risk being understood in the terms of the other narratives of whiteness that exist in the society. On the one hand, there is the suicidal madwoman in the attic, Charlotte Brontë's creole heiress from Spanish Town, whom Jean Rhys later represented in *Wide Sargasso Sea.* This pathetic figure is unable to speak for herself, out of control, simultaneously derided yet tolerated by callous caregivers. She is anticolonial, but unable to find a role for herself in postslavery society. She ends up dead—having committed suicide. The other popular counterimage is even older and dates back to slavery. It is that of the depraved white woman and is based on the myth of slave owner Annie Palmer, the white witch of Rose Hall. She appropriated African religious practices like obeah and used them to dominate and exploit black people and to sexually tyrannize black and white men. More cruel than the most cruel white master, she, too, ends up dead—murdered by one of her black lovers.

The idea that middle-class women had to act as patrons and "social mothers" if they were to have any interclass relations with working-class women is a narrative that is deeply rooted in the structure of colonial society. But more than this, it has been internalized through education, family, and in forms of representation. It conditions expectations and desires, as well a sense of what is possible for women of different classes and races. It cannot be voluntaristically rewritten by strong-willed individuals simply because they wish to do so. The "good" middle-class woman of both races is she who has no needs, never speaks about herself, and never expresses anger except on another's behalf. She works tirelessly for the welfare of others, and she is passively heterosexual, or if necessary, asexual. She remains at the center, but does so without looking inward to her own needs. She denies her own power needs and stays in control by focusing outward to ward off the confusion that might result from confronting the unexplored self.

This model has been central to the culture of Jamaican women's organizations throughout the twentieth century. No other image has proven as potent or has been as carefully diffused throughout all the social institutions. Caribbean Socialist discourses, with their silence around sexuality, their conflation of race and class, their continued emphasis on notions of unified class identity, on work, and the working class as the class of the future, offer no real alternative to these women. Socialist images of women later supplemented the image by adding a public persona, that of the women worker, but the "nature" of women's identity went largely unchallenged, and women were now expected to be worker, wife, mother *and* do voluntary work for the country. For women to speak about their own needs is to presumably risk being seen as "self-indulgent" in a situation in which oppression is formulated as a fundamentally economic relation and in which solutions to economic instability are equated with psychic well-being.

By not problematizing our own situation, we middle-class women were being "good girls," inadvertently playing into that old colonial image of middle-class femininity. By "facilitating" working-class women's expression of their own oppression and not our own, we were engineering only a partial picture of the situation confronting Jamaican women. Our function was almost voyeuristic: we were collaborating with the economism of Western development models by fetishizing "grass roots" women. None of this is to deny the importance of constructing alternative images of working-class women, of talking back to the dominant classes and to men, and of creating a new vision of society from this standpoint. But our problem was that in silencing ourselves, we were denying our own differences and complexities. We avoided naming our own experience, which might have created a real basis for transforming old class-based dynamics. By keeping our mouths shut, we allowed the construct of the "good woman" to remain intact. We missed an opportunity to envision and formulate new images of women's identity and interclass relations.

The failure to interrogate our own power and position allowed us to use our skills while continuing to deny the issues of power underlying them. At the same time, the working-class members could benefit from the skills of the middle-class women without clarifying the nuts and bolts of the relationship and without learning those skills and risking exercising them. Dependency and patronage implicate both parties.

Yet the resource people contributed much to forming Sistren, to keeping it alive, and to developing its work. We were not only "vessels of authority" or "wielders of power." We also had personal and collective needs for affirmation. In practice, we often deferred to majority working-class decisions. However, these problems were never adequately addressed or resolved. As resource person Joan French put it,

> The structure never honestly recognized the similarities and differences between the resource people. Because we were guilt-ridden about our class power, we made ourselves into nonpersons in theory, but we remained individuals in reality. The failure to deal with that meant tensions developed between resource persons, and these, together with the weight of the individuals' role and their work with Sistren, had an impact on the perceptions and behavior of founding members.... We talked too much about what "grass roots" Sistren "should" do and too little about what we were doing. We needed to examine things like the nature of resource people available, the particularities and limitations of these resource people, regeneration, expansion, and, possibly, eventual abolition of these kinds of resources altogether.

In this failure to fully conceptualize our role, function, and needs, work operated as a proxy for class and color, rather than as a set of skills which could be acquired.

Personality Politics and the Small Group

Personality conflicts also developed and deepened over time. This is probably inevitable in any small, informally differentiated group, particularly where individuals are in close ongoing contact. These conflicts between group and individual were exacerbated by aspects of the group's history.

In Sistren, the early focus on sharing personal experiences of oppression encouraged such expressions in the group. From very early on, close bonds were established between founding members through the drama workshops which emphasized speaking out about personal experiences. Often these workshops got at things that members had long held pent up inside them. This process established the small group as a place where personal difficulties could be reflected upon and reenacted. In a sense, Sistren was like a therapy group, though obviously this was not the intention.

When the group activity of sharing experiences was replaced by decision-making and management, Sistren did not establish another space where the work around personal issues could continue. Suddenly, there was no space for personal problems, everyday crises, or the resolution of conflicts. Members were, of course, free to put whatever they liked on the agenda of the General Meeting. But now no one seemed to want to speak openly about problems with lovers or medical difficulties, especially in between making decisions about policy, tours, or the visits of foreigners. The argumentative style of the General Meeting did not offer a sufficiently judgment-free environment for the full discussion of personal life problems.

Needless to say, the earlier need to discuss such experiences did not just disappear; instead, it became submerged within the management agenda. Meetings often became a place where people unconsciously acted out their personal problems—not by trying to discuss them but by establishing behavioral patterns and conflicts that were repeated again and again. Some of these behavior patterns were related to issues outside the group and some to conflicts between members. Most of these conflicts or patterns were never solved or changed.

Small groups tend to become a substitute for the family, and in this context, individuals tend to reexperience unresolved problems from early childhood. Within Sistren, most of us would have denied that this kind of psychological scenario had anything to do with our organizational patterns. Yet, how else can the repeated patterns around divergent issues be fully explained? The tendency to relive patterns set early in one's life seems to me to be very strong in women's groups, because women's groups often have a commitment to dealing with the personal, giving individuals permission to raise their own unresolved experiences. In particular, it seems inevitable that issues around the mother—generally one's primary caretaker and first intimate relationship—will begin to surface. Unless these are dealt with, they will disrupt group work.

This has many implications for what we call democracy. Issues which surface for debate are often only one aspect of what is really taking place, which might include the dramatization of problems that have plagued a woman all her life. The undifferentiated group structure, such as existed in Sistren, did nothing to establish a working culture in which the demands of production could co-exist with a support structure for resolving self-destructive patterns of behavior.

Language and Rationality in Sistren's "Parliamentary Democracy"

There were other problems specific to the structure and process of the General Meeting. Meetings followed a type of parliamentary procedure in that they relied on argument and debate. They were generally not working meetings where tasks were carried out, although occasionally this happened, too. In the main, however, the meetings were based on discussion. Not surprisingly, Rebecca Knowles dubbed the General Meeting the "Sistren Parliament."

It was assumed that within the meeting, everyone was able to articulate her thoughts in a rational way. In its drama work, Sistren used a methodology that aimed at uniting feeling and action. This approach was based on the understanding that the verbal argument was not always the best educational method for adults who had been excluded from the formal educational system in childhood. We seemed to forget this key principle when we came to work with ourselves.

The greatest problems in making the meeting system work stem from the vast differences in education and language. In the General Meeting language shifted back and forth between Jamaican and English. The resource people, products of colonial education, expressed ideas in English. Working-class women often expressed resistance through body language, sound, and other forms of nonverbal communication. As some members of Sistren point out in *Lionheart Gal,* working-class Jamaican girls are frequently discouraged from questioning or arguing with authority figures, whether these are parents, religious leaders, or school personnel. The belt or the stick is often the reward for enquiry. This means that when questioning does take place, it is often couched in a nonconfrontational, indirect form. There is frequently a tendency to question privately with a friend and then to undermine the positions one has officially agreed to. It is done by signifying disagreement and using personal power to act on the situation. This kind of covert resistance is deeply rooted in Jamaican history. It has been a response to colonial patterns of domination, and extends beyond decision-making processes.

These patterns of culture and communication posed extremely difficult problems for our attempt to build a democratic process. The effectiveness of the system of parliamentary democracy depends on one's ability to construct an argument in language, one's ability to debate and confront. The challenge facing us was how to take the different styles of discourse into consideration, and how to overcome disparity in language and the fear of overt disagreement.

Argument is not equivalent to truth. In our context the conflict between argument and truth caused further problems since it involved women of different classes. Members would sometimes agree to decisions they did not fully understand because they did not want to hold things up or because they could not think of any argument to use in favor of their alternative. This happened even when members were very uncomfortable with the way things were going, and often resulted in a division between discussion and action.

Resistance to the language and power of the resource people was often demonstrated. It usually took the form of silence, pouting, aggressive anger, abuse, tears, or sleeping. Working-class members of Sistren were reluctant to put their ideas into words because that left them open to disagreement. When someone did not understand the English used, they felt humiliated by having to stop the process over and over again to get clarification. Resistance, then, often led to stalemates on issues of great importance.

Collective decisions were uniting positions; the majority ruled. We never discussed the option of operating by consensus rather than by majority rule. Nor did we discuss the possibility of tolerating minority positions within the group on particular issues, though obviously, there was oftentimes a wide variety of opinions. Here, there was a sense that equality signified sameness and rigid agreement, rather than a willingness to tolerate different views and practices within the same organization.

Questions of Discipline, Authority, and Responsibility

The General Meeting was responsible for enforcing discipline in the collective. It failed most of the time. The collective never managed to come up with disciplinary action that could be applied to all without prejudice. This was partly because a majority vote was necessary to enforce discipline and most of the time members balked at the prospect. Some members were afraid of others with particularly dominating personalities. Others wanted to keep the "elite Sistren" from gaining more power, or to attack or condone actions of the resource people. Sometimes, someone wanted to be seen as the power or leader of a team. Thus, the members who had no "posse," or allies to defend them within the collective, were frequently disciplined while others got away with all kinds of things. Added to this, there was no disciplinary code, so each time there was a disciplinary problem, special sanctions had to be invented from scratch. Sometimes consequences varied in intensity and were felt to be unfairly applied. Lorna Burrell comments on the whole problem this way:

> I am not totally against our system, but we need to know more about how the outside deals with problems such as ours. For instance, we, like many other groups, have things like petty thieving. If you have that problem in an outside group and you can't identify the guilty person, everybody else will have to pay the penalty, so they are quick to identify the problem. Sometimes, in our collective, if you have petty thieving going on and you catch a person red-handed, nobody wants to say it is that person because we feel that we begin at one time, so we must be together at all times. Now, I feel this is the height of foolishness and we are supporting slackness. How on earth, then, would you really pull through when you have things like that going on? You are developing hatred. When some people are willing to make decisions for discipline, some are against it. Not only with petty thieving but with everything. When discipline comes about, you have a split and there is no solution.

A number of problems in the collective stemmed from our failure to deal with the question of authority. For example, a decision made by a majority of members in one setting could be overturned by the small group charged with its implementation. This disregard for collective authority affected our ability to do things quickly, especially where a quick response to a specific situation was required. If there were a statement to be made or an action to be taken, a meeting of the entire collective was necessary before approval could be given. The collective could not respond fast enough because of its structure.

The attempts by individual members to exercise authority led to more and more issues being decided in lengthy meetings. The collective refused to accept the authority of one or two people about anything. General meetings would sometimes last as long as eight hours and then spill over into the next day. Sometimes life itself seemed like one long meeting. Some members were not interested in all the details of managing the group but wanted simply to be good actors, teachers, or accountants. Others wanted to specialize in management and administration. This was not possible given the overwhelming amount of time spent in collective decision-making.

The Effects of the Collective Structure

The amount of time required for collective decision-making increased as the group's areas of work expanded. We became so busy debating issues of race, class, political affiliation, finances, and status among ourselves that we had less time to produce. While we were busy feeling the impact of political transformation in our small organization at deeply personal levels, the world continued as it always had. The time we were able to spend addressing issues of education and the transfer of skills diminished. The time we were able to spend clarifying our theater methodology diminished. The time we were able to spend producing new plays, screen-prints, and doing workshops diminished. Between 1984 and 1987, Sistren produced only one major new work, *Muffet Inna All A We*. Magazines and books that were meant to form a documentation center for women piled up and collected dust as no one had time to deal with them. And, we were all tired *all the time.*

In 1984, the collective voted to abandon two years of group-building workshops in urban and rural communities. This had been one of the main areas of work through which the participatory drama methodology around women's issues was being passed on. It was also an area of work through which the collective had systematic contact with the concerns and culture of a broad group of working-class women, and it provided a voice for women who wanted to "join Sistren." This decision to cut off group-building work was taken without consulting the very women with whom we had been working. Still, many women of all classes wanted to have a stake in the group, to become involved in the organization, and to grow as it grew. Sistren decided to continue to serve groups that were already organized. But it did not change the fact that only a very small percentage of women in Jamaica were in *any* organization at all and that an even smaller percentage were in women's organizations. By 1985, Sistren had become one of the most visible women's groups nationally. But the question of its responsibility to its founders, to the women it served and its commitment to different kinds of work remained unresolved.

Conclusion

A major problem in Sistren's internal organization was the way it came to equate democracy with a single notion: collective decision-making. The undifferentiated collective form presents a number of problems. It can be antithetical to productivity and service delivery because it tends to privilege internal practice over external impact. Given the complex networks of power that affect groups and individuals, apparently radical democratic forms of decision-making often mask the perpetuation of central contradictions such as race and class. Where ideological variety or difference exists within a group, these become perceived as obstacles to sameness rather than as opportunities to develop the richness and complexity of the group's work. The undifferentiated collective structure lends itself to the exercise of power by informal leaders whose roles can never be clearly defined, who are not clearly accountable within the group, and who tend to operate covertly.

Real processes of decision-making, then, become masked, and the organization becomes bogged down in a morass of endless meetings, low productivity, a sense of diffused responsibility, and low morale.

I would argue, as others have, that decision-making processes that are entirely collective only work effectively in very small organizations with limited and tightly defined aims and objectives. Given the constraints of Jamaica's political and cultural context and the economic problems facing groups like Sistren, the collective decision-making model may not be the single most effective way to ensure democracy. When an organization grows and takes on varied activities, there is a need to move away from the informal, vaguely defined collective structure. Clearly, a variety of structures need to be created to deal with different objectives. But the model of collective decision-making is sometimes idealistically and dogmatically imposed on situations as varied as campaign activity, production of goods and services, and self-help. In Sistren's history, the phase of intense collectivity was a necessary one. Although I have deliberately stressed its negative features, it unquestionably exposed members to new areas of decision-making and acquainted everyone with the skills of advocacy. By 1988, however, the movement toward some specialization and differentiation also seemed necessary and inevitable, if the problems were to be solved.

What shape can be envisioned for a democratic organization other than the collective? There can be no dogmatic answer to this question. Just as the collective decision-making model works in some situations, but not in others, there can be no one true democratic organizational form that will work effectively in all cultures and in all political and economic contexts. Perhaps, though, there is something to be learned from appropriating and adapting some of the ideas about organizational processes from group psychology and from the practical experiences of businesses, associations, and other organizations, even though ten years ago they were condemned as hierarchical, patriarchal, and bureaucratic. Two concepts that need much fuller discussion within the women's movement are management and leadership, and their relationship to collective forms of governance. In an effort to throw out the charismatic leader, or the emergence of a personality cult, alternative forms of leadership have not really been defined.

Within women's groups, it is especially difficult to grant and accept leadership from other women. Historically, women have been excluded from the allocation of power. Male, white, middle-class privilege has been so founded on hierarchy, division, and specialization that the women's movement has been cautious about reproducing forms that seem to imitate these models. In the Caribbean, it is particularly difficult to come to terms with the issue of leadership in an open way because race, class, and skill are tied together and because resistance to the forms of domination are often covert, informal, and unnamed. However, to avoid the discussion of leadership is no solution. Leadership, as others have argued, always exists, whether it is legitimized or not. Informal leadership can result in far greater authoritarianism than leadership which is formal and accountable. The time has come to get the issue out into the open.

Part of the problem in Sistren was a failure to recognize the need for different kinds of leadership appropriate to different kinds of work and applicable to different moments in the life of the organization. Beyond this, there was a failure to speak openly about women's power needs. The denial of the power and life experience of middle-class women, the failure to recognize and name differences in identities and needs, meant that feminist analysis was only partial. It also meant that there was no way to talk about how to work together across differences, let alone how to negotiate new forms of leadership. The failure to analyze and discuss the position of middle-class women of different identities meant that these women's needs were never explicitly part of the story. When power needs are denied, it is impossible to deal with questions of leadership in ways that lead to creative solutions.

The term "management" is sometimes interpreted as an authoritarian big boot, squeezing the lifeblood out of its underlings. In our setting, "management" carried the connotation of exploiters from "the evil empire" of capitalism. The term certainly does not connote structures that focus the goals of an organization and the needs of those who work in it. Instead, it conjures up images of rigid bureaucracy manipulated by those who occupy top positions in a monolithic hierarchy. In rejecting the worst of capitalism, however, we must not throw out the baby with the bath water. Management and leadership, whether they reside in individuals or in groups of people, need to be controlled. This can be done by defining both what is to be managed and how leaders can be held accountable at different moments in an organization's life. Such structures need to allow for different approaches and greater autonomy within different sections of an organization. Issues of skills transfer and education could then be addressed in a systematic and consistent way. A key concept in thinking about democratic management, then, is accountability, a concept that can be applied differently within an organization and with those it serves.

The second major problem that confronted Sistren was the effect of international funding policies on the organization. International agencies funding development projects have an enormous amount of power. One only has to see the files of any agency involved in "development" to recognize the wealth of information they have accumulated about organizations working for social change. Dispensing funds gives them tremendous power over people's lives all over the world. They are able to shape the lives of the organizations they support, not simply because they fund them, but also because of the processes and regimes of disciplines to which they require the organizations to adhere. The term "partner," currently being used by donor agencies to describe their relationship with recipient organizations, only obscures what remains a very real power relation. This ostensible egalitarian label obscures the way in which the power differential produces and regulates the reality of those who are funded.

The obvious first step toward changing relations here is to use the structures that we have built since the 1970s to begin to raise funds locally to support organizations that serve women. We were not always able to do this, but now we have enough of a history to begin this struggle. All kinds of strategies are possible, including creating a regional foundation, charging for some of the services we offer, and developing partnerships between business and professional women and working-class women in our own countries. Building our own indigenous sources of funding is crucial to the future if we are ever to find our way out of the dependency trap. Surprisingly, little attention has been paid to this among regional women's organizations. Bringing women's groups together to discuss combined strategies for local funding would be a first step.

Organizations like Sistren cannot yet do without foreign funders if they are to continue to offer the same range of services. However, we are at the stage where women's organizations working together—first regionally, then internationally—can use their lobbying power to build alliances. A key factor in such a lobby is the building of relationships with partner groups in host countries and nongovernmental agencies. Such links will strengthen the chances of creating structures that are accountable to the groups at home and abroad. At the moment, very little consultation on funding takes place between women's groups, NGOs, and funders. A first step toward building dialogue would be to establish a forum in which information about the relations of funding and the problems, procedures, and privileges to which they give rise can be discussed. Such a dialogue would strengthen alliances between women's groups and contribute to building joint negotiating power.

One issue that women's groups need to face squarely is the tendency of agencies to prioritize material production over educational and cultural processes, and to see these areas as separate and distinct. In the long run, this separation serves to entrench dependency because it ensures that internal processes of organizational development and transfer of skills are always subsumed under the "more important" processes of production. In fact, culture and economics are inextricably linked. In Sistren's case, it would have been far better to develop the experimental, educational, and cultural work, and to build gradually an economic base from this. Instead, the energies of the group were divided, reproducing the very divisions

Jamaican society has made among creative, educational, and economic work. These separations multiplied the training and administrative needs of the project and ultimately helped to retard the development of Sistren's educational and artistic work.

On the other hand, the importance of building up some form of self-financing in groups like Sistren cannot be ignored. Any single issue or set of issues that are prioritized for funding by agencies can be used against the development of effective organizational processes. International funding agencies often determine priorities, which are then applied in a blanket way. The political and cultural context and the available skills and resources are all areas that need very careful consideration. When local factors are not taken into consideration, choices about program activities can be made with negative consequences for local organizations. This is especially true when organizations are young or when they operate in a conservative context in which there is little capacity for negotiation with more powerful international agencies. When an organization's survival is at stake, meeting the criteria of international agencies will take priority over developing processes of accountability to its constituency. In Sistren's case, the organization did not have the capacity to develop both processes simultaneously. I have shown the negative consequences for Sistren's development of the blanket imposition of "income generation" as a solution to women's problems and have argued that it created many more problems than it solved. Such mistakes cannot be waved away. Their implications mushroom into new difficulties, which are often harder to deal with than the problems they were originally meant to solve. They involve people's lives, hopes, energies, investments, and resources in deep ways. The disillusionment and bitterness they create profoundly affect an organization's potential to have an impact on its community and to build a healthy working culture.

Finally, the emphasis of international agencies on funding "grass-roots" women seems to be contradictory and simplistic. Grass-roots women are not miracle workers, and, like middle-class women, they need to study and understand a situation before they can work effectively in it. The fact that someone is, by birth, "grass-roots" does not necessarily make them more understanding of the causes of poverty, or what will change them. It does not give them a keener sense of justice or of how to deal with others. It does not necessarily make them more effective at their jobs. Funding policies sometimes seem prone to fetishizing grass-roots women, confusing class and sex origins with class and gender consciousness. Agency policies sometimes emphasize the delivery of funding to grass-roots women while ignoring the many complex processes involving gender and class processes that reproduce the very conditions funding is supposed to alleviate. In the end, funding does not always contribute to social transformation. In fact, as was the case with Sistren, funding reproduced the very relationships of dependency and domination between aid agencies and recipients that the group was attempting so desperately to overturn.

The deleterious effects of funding practices which I have mapped in this essay ought not to cloud the possibility of strategic alliance building with certain individuals within agencies. There are staff members in some organizations who are genuinely troubled by the operation of dependency and domination and are interested in reconfiguring questions of accountability. They want to use their organizational leverage to help bring about social change. Yet it is up to us, organizations like Sistren and regional feminist groups, to construct the terms of a genuinely internationalist alliance in order to bring about radical changes in the societies in which we live.

11

Looking at Ourselves: The Women's Movement in Hyderabad

Vasanth Kannabiran and Kalpana Kannabiran

For almost a decade, Stree Shakti Sanghatana, a small, articulate group that set out to politicize women's issues, changed the character of political discourse in Andhra Pradesh. As part of the second-wave feminist movement that emerged throughout India in the 1970s, SSS had a distinctive identity that was rooted in the specific political context from which it emerged.

This essay is not just a history of the group that shaped our consciousness and (re)defined our life course. It is an attempt to theorize our own lived experience, and, in many concrete ways, to link that experience to the historical trajectory of a feminist movement that evolved for over a decade and a half. In other words, while we will map the course of the movement and the tensions therein, we will do this through the prism of our lives, historicizing lived experience in the process.

Locating ourselves in this project as upper-caste, upper-class women, it has been difficult to separate our own need to come to terms with the different crises that arose in SSS—crises of identity, exclusion, and direction—from our own desire to deconstruct our involvement, and in the process distance ourselves from the pain and energy that often accompany organization building. In our experience, they often collided and blurred each other. One of us, a teacher and housewife, carved out her identity and rediscovered lost possibilities through engagement with the group. The other, a student and daughter, was initiated into feminist politics through her mother and SSS. As mother and daughter, we were part of a process of growth that was sometimes smooth, often clotted and confused, the result of both our relationship with each other and our different positionings within the group.

SSS gave us a completely new sense of ourselves. It gave us the strength to make choices we would otherwise have lacked the courage to make without the support of the group. Looking back, we realize that in a very peculiar way, it alienated us from our own contexts. We could no longer relate to our friends and colleagues. SSS had become everything. However, while we were both among the earliest members of the group, and both shared an almost total identification with it, our respective positions differed and shifted with time. One was central to the group by virtue of age and personal friendships; the other was somewhat marginal, with a link that was at once fierce and tenuous, the tenuousness the result of being a daughter.

It is ironic but true that while SSS provided the context for our growth and helped develop our creativity, most of that creativity was expressed outside of the group, even more so after its dissolution. This was the case for both of us and for others in the group as well. SSS was an essential learning ground.

In what follows, we map the tensions, conflicts and struggles within SSS, one of the main organizations of second-wave feminism in India. We also focus on the concerted struggles of the movement as a whole as it confronted several crucial questions. By exploring the contradictions that emerged between political forces that impinged on the movement, as well as those internal to it, we hope to contextualize and historicize the broader political struggles of that time. We believe that the knowledge we have gained can be used tactically today; it can help us to see how feminist discourses and practices, once organized and made coherent, can help guide and prioritize how we think and what we do.

The State and Political Activity in Andhra Pradesh: A Brief Overview

Andhra Pradesh was formed during the linguistic reorganization of states in 1956. Hyderabad, a princely state ruled by the Nizam and part of the British Paramountcy, formed part of the reorganised Andhra, of which the capital was Hyderabad city. In the course of the reorganization, while the Telangana region (which included Hyderabad city) remained part of Andhra, the other two regions, Marathwada and the Kannada-speaking districts, went over to Maharashtra and Karnataka respectively. The state of Hyderabad had a very different history. Hyderabad covered a substantial part of the Deccan Plateau in south India and had a predominantly Hindu population. It consisted of three linguistic regions: the Telugu-speaking Telangana, the Marathi-speaking Marathwada, and three Kannada-speaking districts of Karnataka. Telangana constituted the majority, accounting for 47 percent of the population, while the remaining 12 percent were the Urdu-speaking Muslims. The origin of the state of Hyderabad can be traced to the 1720s, when the Moghul empire disintegrated and the independent state of Hyderabad was set up by Asaf Jah, the Moghul governor in the Deccan. With the consolidation of British colonialism, the Nizam's state, like other princely states, came to be governed by the doctrine of Paramountcy. Roughly a third of the state's total area was organized on the Jagirdari system of land tenure (in which jagirs given to those officers loyal to the Nizam were declared hereditary and included rights over excise, forests, and fisheries, as well as the exercise of police and judicial functions). Of the remaining area, part continued to be ruled by their traditional Hindu rulers in return for a tribute paid annually to the Nizam; another part was gifted away as *inam* in return for some service rendered to the Nizam; and yet another part, the *sarf-e-khas* land, was administered by the Nizam and his family and was meant to meet his personal expenses. The remaining territory was administered directly by the state government on *ryotwari* principles. Prior to land settlement, these lands were administered on behalf of the government by middlemen, who, in the process, acquired vast stretches of land and became big landowners.[1]

However, the Hyderabad state also differed from other Indian princely states in that it retained its original ruling class. This elite had its own interests and aspirations, as well as a limited ability to survive imperial power, in spite of its support for the British cause in India. Simultaneously, imperialism and the international expansion of capitalism managed to integrate parts of the country into the international market. These parts included the cotton-growing areas of Marathwada (which were integrated in the nineteenth century) and the castor- and groundnut-growing sector of the Telangana rural economy (which were internationalized at the turn of the century). Thus, these precapitalist forms of production were turned into producers of commodities. Actively molded by capital, in reality, they existed only in relation to capital despite their precapitalist modes of organization (i.e., forced labor, landlordism, etc). In its search for an independent existence, sections of the ruling class attempted "modernization" in the industrial sector as well. Some of the industries that survived the Paramount power were coal mining, textiles, cement, and tobacco. But problems arose with raising funds for development, as industrial investment was low. The agricultural sector was still the largest part of the economy, and the state was unable to force the landlords, who were its social base, to make productive investments.[2]

Around this time, the Non-Cooperation Movement and the Civil Disobedience Movement rapidly gained ground in the rest of the Indian peninsula. Although activity in Hyderabad was limited, a number of young people who had been instrumental in forming the Andhra Mahasabha in 1930 went over to the coastal districts of Andhra (then part of the Madras Presidency), to participate in the movements there. While the Andhra Mahasabha was originally started to provide an alternative to Muslim cultural hegemony, it soon acquired a strong nationalist character. Meanwhile, a number of Communists joined hands with the Indian National Congress to form the Congress Socialist Party (CSP) within the Congress. Very soon, however, the unwillingness of the Congress to lead a mass struggle against the British prompted CSP members to quit the Congress. Subsequently, the Communist Party of India (CPI) in Kerala was consolidated and the CPI section in Hyderabad was formed. After the outbreak of World War II, the Communist Party was banned in British India, but it nevertheless continued to function under cover in Hyderabad within the Andhra Mahasabha.[3]

In the twenty-five years prior to 1940, a number of women's organizations that provided a public platform for women—especially middle- and upper-class women—had been formed. These groups took up issues related to education, prostitution, abolition of the purdah system, widow remarriage, etc. In the late 1930s, the Andhra Mahila Sangham was formed. Unlike other women's organizations, even the Andhra Mahasabha, the Andhra Mahila Sangham primarily organized peasant women, many of whom joined the Andhra Communist Party, then the strongest unit of the Communist Party of India. Prior to the declaration of Indian independence, the activities of the Communists in Andhra were mainly directed against, on the one hand, oppressive landlords and government officials, and on the other hand, the propaganda of the Ittehadul Mussalmeen, a Muslim fundamentalist organization formed by the politically powerful supporters of the Nizam. By 1946, these struggles had intensified and the Nizam banned both the Communist Party and the Andhra Mahasabha. In 1947, after the declaration of independence, the Nizam refused to join the Indian Union, and deployed the Razakars, the paramilitary wing of the Ittehadul Mussalmeen, to terrorize people. The Indian army was sent in and the Nizam's forces were subdued. But army action against the Communists continued, with the Indian state taking over from the Nizam, until the struggle was called off in 1951.[4] Later, the CPI split, first in 1964, then again, in 1968. The second split prompted the emergence of the Naxalbari Movement, with its radical left politics.

Feudal exploitation of the peasantry was most severe in the Telangana region of the erstwhile Hyderabad state. *Vetti,* or forced labor, and the *bhagela* system bound most of the lowest castes as serfs to the landlords' families. This was especially true for the *malas* and the *madigas* and the aboriginal tribes. People belonging to the service castes were forced to render free service to the families of the landlords as well as visiting state officials. Oppression was by far the most severe in the *jagir* areas, which fell outside civil jurisdiction. A variety of illegal taxes in those areas reduced the actual cultivators to penury and perpetual indebtedness. There was no security of tenure for agricultural tenants, and families of laborers who were unable to repay loans became serfs from generation to generation. Agricultural laborers could work their own lands only after they had worked the landlords' fields, and they were constantly under threat of attack by the landlords' henchmen. Women were systematically exploited by the landlords and their men. It was these oppressive conditions that the Communist Movement fought to change.[5] While they were successful and did actually effect a change in the rural ethos at the time, a look at the context in which the radical movement occurred, especially Andhra Pradesh in the pre-Emergency period, reveals that this systematic feudal exploitation continued well into the postcolonial period, so that radical groups in the seventies and eighties found themselves fighting *vetti*—forced service to landlords' families—and caste oppression.[6]

The Postcolonial Indian State and the Early Feminist Agenda

The postcolonial state was envisioned as an instrument of social transformation, organized to ameliorate the oppressions and disadvantages of underprivileged groups in society. Toward this purpose, the state was to be relatively autonomous, free of dominant or vested interests. Although, as Rajni Kothari argues, this conception of the state is by no means radical, the very fact of its relative autonomy could allow the space for the politically oppressed to foreground social goals in their agenda. There are various dimensions to this question of autonomy, especially in the Indian context.[7] Most importantly, there is the problem of translating political independence into economic self-reliance. However, the national goal of undertaking social transformation at home while pursuing economic self-reliance in global capitalist centers could only be realized by a highly centralized state.[8]

But how far was this possible given the actual nature of the postcolonial Indian state? The state had assumed political power with only minimal disturbance to the existing power and class relations in society. As A. K. Bagchi points out, power was "transferred" and "appropriated" rather than "conquered," "destroyed," or "transformed." So, while the realization of "national goals" was predicated on the vision of an activist state that was also highly centralized, in reality, there was a general consensus among the privileged few that the state would not interfere with the business of money-making and power-wielding within society. This consensus involved a collaboration between the state, Indian big business, foreign capital, and eventually also the rural elite.[9] This consensus was not without its share of internal contradictions and tensions. Some of the more obvious areas of tension centered on definition of the limits of state and central power; demarcation of the private domain of custom, usage, and religion; antagonism between the public and private industrial sectors; and protection of the privileges of the farm lobby. These stresses naturally influenced the implementation of central planning. The achievement of "national goals" required a society and a legal framework that honored equality, national citizenship, and secularization of public life, in place of majority-minority differences and caste oppression.

Given the existing framework, however, this rhetoric of planning was appropriated at the outset by the privileged—the bureaucrats, the political elite, the landlords, the upper castes, and, within the minorities, the privileged few—and quite naturally so, since it was they who had determined the agenda in the first place.[10] Furthermore, while the Indian state was built on principles of Nehruvian secularism, a close look at national communal politics and nationalism in India—both in the colonial and postcolonial periods—reveals serious contradictions between professed ideology and practice.[11] In India, the political practice of the Indian National Congress as well as other major national parties, has been structured along communal and caste lines; hierarchies within the Congress, for example, more often than not replicate hierarchies outside. As a result, the Indian state (which has been dominated by the Congress throughout the postcolonial period), has absorbed the upper-caste-Hindu ethos of the Congress, along with the ideal of secularism. In India, secularism has been defined as a positive respect for all religions, and a separation of religion from the state. However, historically, secular politics has consistently foregrounded the absorption of majoritarian consciousness in state processes, thereby creating a disjunction between the rhetoric and practice. Toward the end of the period covered by this essay, this disjunction, together with a rapidly changing economy, paved the way for the consolidation and strengthening of the Hindu Right, and a complete erosion of secular ideals in the Indian polity.

At yet another level, during the process of modernization, the state had begun to address the problem of "integrating" women into development and production. But in fact, development only further marginalized women, confining them to roles as producers and reproducers by refusing to address the gender division of labor. In addition, the whole process of development systematically depoliticized and made invisible women's subordination, restricting them to home and family. With the penetration of capital, women have been drawn into a monetary system that, while retaining its feudal character, has deprived them of the traditional supports and rights that eased their burden slightly. As a result, the Indian state has been increasingly alienated from the people, both at the center and on the local level. This leaves repression as the only way the state can retain effective control and contain the growing disenchantment among youth and the masses of oppressed people searching for solutions in radical left politics.[12]

The imposition of a state of emergency in 1975, during which fundamental rights were suspended in the interests of state security, immobilized many radical groups. By that point, feminists in India had already begun to address "the woman question," generally within the framework of leftist politics. Andhra Pradesh even witnessed the formation of a women's group, the Progressive Organization for Women (POW), which, though a part of the radical left, struggled to retain a degree of autonomy. The inspiration for POW apparently came from early Marxist feminists like Clara Zetkin and Rosa Luxemburg.[13] After the Emergency, during which much radical political activity was driven underground, there was a gradual disillusionment among certain sections of radical youth. Some of the women who had been part of these groups felt that "the woman question" had not been satisfactorily articulated within left politics. This prompted a situation similar to what women in the West had done earlier: move out of left groups and retain their experiences while establishing their political position independently. This was the political climate in which Stree Shakti Sanghatana was formed.

Stree Shakti Sanghatana

Composition

After the Emergency was lifted in 1977, a group of women came together to form Stree Shakti Sanghatana (SSS). It was their attempt to find meaningful political activity that would connect with and explore their specific experiences as women. There were about fifteen women in the founding group—teachers, doctors, political activists, journalists, researchers, and students. Although SSS was actually located in Hyderabad City, the state capital, it was historically rooted in Telangana, a region known for its economic and cultural marginalization with a tense relation to the rest of the more developed areas of the state.

A large section of the original SSS group had some connection with the left, either through personal involvement or family background. This accounts for the fact that the group's declarations were initially addressed to the radical Marxist-Leninist groups rather than to the established left, like the Communist Party of India (CPI) and the Communist Party of India-Marxist (CPM). Andhra, with its long history of revolutionary movements and armed struggle, also has a strong cultural front with a rich body of literature, songs, poetry, and fiction.[14] The creative energy, the commitment and the force one finds in the Marxist movement is unmatched by other groups. It was therefore only natural that SSS should seek to address this particular section of the left and attempt to provide it with a conceptual focus on women's issues. Still, SSS was quite aware of the danger of being coopted by these groups, and consequently of losing its identity and its efficacy as well. An early joke about SSS was that individual members were Marxist, but the group itself was antileft.

In forming SSS, there was a consensus among the women that (1) the group should consciously reject institutionalization and funding, and (2) it should avoid the practice of providing services to individual women which they felt was basically welfarist and would involve the need to fund-raise and to lobby. These were perceived as activities that would dull its political efficacy. The group decided to concentrate instead on consciousness-raising, and to act as a pressure group, making radical interventions into liberal, welfarist structures. SSS defined itself as an autonomous women's group that would politicize women's issues, drawing a clear distinction between its own character and that of a mass political organization. Characteristically, in this early period, the articulation of women's issues centered upon the state. The women's movement devoted considerable energy to fact-finding missions, investigating export policies of the state (especially vegetable export), atrocities committed by agencies of the state (such as custodial rape or the mismanagement of social welfare hostels), and the rights of women in the unorganized sector (like bidi makers and casual labor in ICRISAT).[15]

As the group's identity grew more distinctive, it consciously attempted to distance itself from the left. By this time, SSS clearly perceived and claimed its connections to Western second-wave feminism and consciously resisted attempts by the Indian Left to coopt and control the women's movement. There were several reasons for this. Western feminism had already established for SSS the points of overlap between Marxism and feminism, as well as the points of divergence. Besides, we, in the Indian Women's Movement, were still in a period when First-World/Third-World differences had not yet begun to be discussed within the women's movement. This was also part of the secular identity of the movement. There was a firm conviction—firm while it lasted—that an internally coherent feminist ideology would transcend all barriers of class, caste, creed, and race. Our basic difference with the Marxists was over the priority they gave to class over gender. In addressing the issues, however, the women's movement assumed the existence of a liberal secular state as uncritically as the left. This acceptance of secularism as a basic value characterized feminist politics for a decade, that is, until identity politics erupted on our consciousness, rocking many cherished assumptions and securities.

Issues and Campaigns

Vegetable Export

The attempts by SSS to distance itself from liberal domains and to maintain its ideological clarity were clearly reflected in the very first issue the group took up—vegetable export. Since locally grown vegetables were being exported to Arab countries, the price of vegetables in India was soaring, out of the reach of Indian housewives. Initially, there was a debate within SSS over whether it should be involved in the issue at all. Was vegetable export really a women's issue? Would work on this campaign only reinforce the stereotype of the "woman as consumer"? Despite these questions, the group did decide to work on the issue and played a fairly important role in organizing various sections of women. While the issue was treated basically as a consumer issue by the other women's organizations participating in the campaign, SSS mobilized vegetable vendors and hawkers and questioned the politics behind the export of foodstuffs. The ability to raise these issues was in no small measure due to some of the members' experience in and with the left. The sharpness with which these issues were articulated seemed to appeal to middle-class and working-class women. Significantly, women participated far more enthusiastically and in far greater numbers in the campaigns against vegetable export than in other campaigns, many of which were strategically far more significant for the women's movement.[16] The strength and durability of mobilization on practical issues (like vegetable exports) was far greater than that on strategic issues (such as rape) which questioned the bases of oppressive structures. And yet, the results of the rape and dowry campaigns by the Indian Women's Movement were far more effective in bringing about concrete changes in the national laws.

Women's Hostels

The next issue that SSS tackled was the mismanagement of social welfare hostels. These hostels were set up by the state to accommodate scheduled caste and scheduled tribe students from rural areas. SSS's involvement began with a survey of living conditions in a few hostels. Here, again, the issue was first seen as a secular one with an accusing finger being pointed at the state. The emphasis and articulation of the issue initially centered on class, and there was no comprehension of the operation of caste or of the state's complicity in caste oppression. However, the energies of the group were soon drawn from social welfare to working-women's hostels, and the subsequent campaign focused on single women. Earlier surveys of conditions in women's hostels, as well as comparative surveys of women's and men's hostels, showed that, invariably, in the name of protection, young women were virtually imprisoned within hostels—and given no space to articulate their grievances.[17]

Residents from working-women's hostels in different parts of the country had begun protesting against mismanagement, the concentration of arbitrary powers in the hands of management, deplorable living conditions, and obsolete rules. In one well-known case, residents of a church-run women's hostel in Panaji, Goa had resisted attempts by the archbishop to replace the hostel with a multistoried commercial complex.

In Hyderabad, SSS worked with residents of two working-women's hostels: the YWCA, a Christian (and, therefore, minority) institution and the Andhra Yuvathi Mandali, a secular hostel managed by recognized, upper-caste, women social workers with connections to the Congress. Both hostels had almost identical problems: insufficient and badly cooked food, artificially created water shortage, unhygienic living conditions, and an inadequate supply of electricity, especially at night. This last problem affected both the work assignments that the residents brought in and the scheduling of meals, which, in turn, disrupted the work routines of the residents.

For SSS, these protests raised two broad issues: first, the question of the rights of single women, and, second, the need for a critique of the historical context in which these hostels were conceived.

The aim of the hostels was to "reform" women and "uplift" them, an aim arising from liberal premises asserted by both Western missionaries and nineteenth- and twentieth-century reformers. The reformers, especially, played an important historic role in the crusade against sati, child marriage, and purdah. Many of these female reformers were also active in the nationalist movement and were instrumental in establishing these institutions for women.

The fact that the hostels have crystallized into structures that are oppressive for women underscores the inability of liberal reform movements to articulate women's issues in a manner that undermines the very basis of patriarchal oppression, and identifies its "root causes." As Susie Tharu and Rama Melkote note,

> Liberalism upholds the idea of individual responsibility and freedom, social justice and compassion for the underprivileged. Therefore its methods of operation are charity and social service aimed at helping the oppressed, but not at treating them as agents. The liberal notion of charity does not permit or tolerate any questioning from those to whom charity or patronage are extended.[18]

At that time, SSS limited itself to seeing the problem of single working women within a framework of feudal, patriarchal hegemonies and class interventions that were secular, leaving little or no room for the role of religion. This narrow view resulted in an unwitting homogenization of the problem of middle-class working women across religion and caste. While it is true that both missionary and reform institutions are based on very similar assumptions, it is not enough to stop there. Looking back, we see that the Andhra Yuvathi Mandali, with its very strong upper-caste-Hindu majority image, and the YWCA, with its Christian minority image, were situated very differently on this issue. Even at the time of the struggle, the support that the Andhra Yuvathi Mandali received from the state and the establishment—and, hence, the real power that rested with them—was far greater than that of the YWCA. Further, considering that the YWCA is a minority institution, the group's struggle should perhaps have been structured differently. Since this institution was directly run by religious churchgoers, the group's protest consisted of marching with placards in a silent procession to the church and squatting on church premises while the Sunday service was on. But while this strategy was politically possible in Hyderabad a decade ago, in retrospect it reveals how SSS held a set of simple assumptions that uncritically absorbed majority-minority differences. With the Andhra Yuvathi Mandali, most of the protest was outside the hostel because it is a voluntary organization, not governed directly by a religious institution or trust. This is precisely where, given the present political context, we need to go back and undertake a critical examination of our own assumptions.

Then, as now, the secular state in India was characterized by a strong Hindu ethos. The Hindu identity permeates the entire institutional apparatus throughout the country, with the exception of minority institutions which in a sense construct their identities both in relation, and in opposition to dominant identities. In the case of institutions like the Andhra Yuvathi Mandali, it is the absence of overt religious affiliation that is most eloquent.[19] With the Andhra Yuvathi Mandali, the protest was a secular protest by which, today, we understand that both the Yuvathi Mandali management and SSS were standing within upper-caste Hinduism, as it were, and fighting the battle. With the YWCA, on the other hand, protest involved the Church, although the issue was one of management. The speed with which Hindu fundamentalist groups demand the closing down of minority institutions for even trivial incidents today forces us to recognize the implications of that protest.

The second issue that this struggle raised was that of the rights of single women. This was one of the earliest articulations of the question of single women in the Indian Women's Movement. At a time when domestic and marital violence occupied a central position on the Indian feminist agenda, even speaking of the rights of single women was a radical departure. One report the group published on this issue stated:

> Only a single, working woman who has tried to find a house for herself can appreciate the problems involved. It is not just a question of what clothes she wears, whether she is good looking, whether she will have visitors or not, what time she will come home, and so on. . . . Most houseowners consider single women a liability, and would rather not rent out accommodation to them. It is amazing how thin the line between "reputable" and "disreputable" is for a single woman attempting to live her own life, outside the "protection" of marriage. Often, especially if her income is

> limited, she has to make do with a hostel. . . . In our society today, the main form of housing for women is marriage. Marriage provides a woman with status, security and shelter. Above all marriage confers on her a certain "virtue." . . . But a single woman has to struggle for shelter and security.[20]

However, the belief that the commonalities of women's oppression would cut across all their identities precluded any kind of investigation into the intersection of caste and community on this issue. In retrospect, the success of one struggle (YWCA) and the utter failure of the other (AYM) were linked to the strength of the enemy. The involvement of the women from both hostels was purely issue-based. Once they had had their say, SSS and its politics became embarrassing for them. For its part, SSS had to reckon with the gap between feminist consciousness and the consciousness of women whose issues were being articulated.[21]

Rape

Rape was an issue on which the group campaigned strongly. After the Mathura case, there was a vigorous campaign calling for changes in the national rape laws. This campaign brought together various women's groups across the country.[22] In fact, it was the first concerted national effort by women's groups, and marked the beginning of networking and joint campaigning on women's issues in India. In other words, it was the beginning of the present phase of the Indian women's movement.

The articulation of the SSS position was clearest in the case of custodial rape. Take the instances of Rameeza Bee, Mathura, Maya Tyagi, or Shakila Bi. In September 1979, less than a year and a half after Rameeza Bee's rape, Shakila died under suspicious circumstances in a government hospital in Hyderabad. She was reported to have died after being gang-raped by the police. Public outrage was high and the town of Bhongir was tense. SSS visited Bhongir soon after the incident and published a report in *The Economic and Political Weekly* and in *Manushi*.[23] What they found was this: Shakila's husband, Henry, had been picked up by the police for pickpocketing; he was charged and detained in police custody for further interrogation. The police brought Shakila to the police station and housed her in a Hindu *dharamshala* in Bhongir. Shakila left the *dharamshala* every evening at 5:00 p.m. and returned the next morning. When she returned on October 9, however, she was in critical condition. She died the following day in a government hospital. Strangely enough, Henry was admitted to another government hospital in an unconscious condition and subsequently died. The police attempted to explain the deaths away as a suicide pact.

It will perhaps be useful to look at the group's response to the incident and the issues they raised:

> Why did Shakila return to the police station every evening for almost three weeks? If she was being molested, what was the threat which made her return every day to the police station? One could speculate that it was the danger to Henry, a fact made all the more poignant if we remember that he was her third husband. The first had deserted her, the second was killed in a cyclone and Henry, who had become a Muslim and married her for love, was in the hands of the police. What could any woman do in a situation like this? She knew no one in Bhongir. A Muslim woman unwanted in a Hindu dharamshala, she was being asked to vacate every day. She had no money. All she had was the hope that Henry would be released. The fact that Shakila did not confide in anyone speaks of her situation as a woman. We are trained not to speak out when we are in trouble, more so if the trouble is sexual. The submissiveness, the strength and the ability to put up with anything is so romanticised in our social mythology that the exploitation inherent in it is never realised.
>
> For those who met Rameeza Bee, the similarity in character traits is striking. The people of Bhongir described Shakila as meek, quiet, pathetic, and innocent-looking. This is what impressed one about Rameeza Bee as well. The very qualities which make the so-called "ideal" woman are the qualities which lay her open to brutal attack.[24]

The issues of custodial rape and atrocities against women by the agencies of the state were raised very clearly and effectively in the group. In part, the political background of the group made it easier to address demands to the state. When the accused was not an official of the state, collective action was not clear and enough to convict him. Looking back now, it seems that the focus was clearer in opposition to the state than in cases of family or organizational violence because the state was perceived as a secular institution that was biased, if at all, only along class lines. The perception of the state as carrying and reinforcing dominant communal and caste identities was not clearly understood or articulated at that point.[25]

Dowry

Gradually, the attention of SSS was diverted from the issue of state violence to that of domestic violence, which had assumed alarming proportions all over the country, especially for middle-class women. However, this did not seem to be a separate phenomenon but in fact linked to the impact of the transformation of the state within the family. With India becoming increasingly subsumed and integrated into the global market, transnational capital and corporate interests began to determine national political and social agendas.

Further, to use Kothari's argument, the agenda of transnational capital decrees a homogeneous global culture as a characteristic of the utopian model of economic development. The main vehicles for this homogeneous global culture are the middle classes, who become the primary targets to set the tone for "social goals."[26] This complete absorption of a consumerist lifestyle by the middle classes had very specific implications for women. For one thing, there was an increase in dowry, an issue that primarily affected middle-class women. A cause for more serious concern, however, was the increase in family violence, which soon came to be vulgarly called "dowry deaths." Indeed, the vast number of cases that were reported to SSS made it difficult for a small group to respond effectively. The sheer repetitiousness of the cases, the kind of perseverance required for investigation, and the difficulty in securing a conviction (or the frustration of finding that the victim's family had reached a financial compromise with the accused) often left the group exhausted and drained.[27]

In retrospect, it appears strange that even with a key issue such as dowry, the question of caste as a factor was never articulated. Although SSS was conscious of the macroperspective in which this issue was situated, its elucidation of the problem was fragmentary and limited. Instead, dowry was perceived as a "reform" with which apolitical middle-class women could easily identify, while keeping the radical politics of SSS at a safe distance. So, the Dowry Death Investigation Committee (DDIC) was formed, with two or three members of SSS offering to work with it. The understanding was that the SSS members would keep a low profile but would work to hold the committee together and to provide ideological coherence. In effect, the creation of a separate forum, with a membership rooted in a completely different context, only meant that as a group SSS had distanced itself from the same middle-class women it initially addressed.

Other Campaigns

SSS investigated the rape of Sattemma, a peasant activist, and filed a public interest case on her behalf; it participated in fact-finding missions to investigate the working and living conditions of *bidi* workers; and it protested police violence against slum dwellers. These actions mostly occurred in response to demands from the left but they were single or sporadic actions that did not require sustained contact or work with working-class women. And so, in spite of all this activity, SSS was not able to address the issues of working-class women in a manner that made it possible for them to move from participating equally in the campaigns into participating equally in the functioning of the group. This was a cause for some anxiety and reflection, but was soon set aside because SSS had clearly defined itself as a pressure group, not a mass organization. Although large numbers of women did not flock to the campaigns, there was a great degree of visibility and considerable public response. The existence of such a pressure group provided courage and hope to women scattered all over the state.

Around this time, SSS also worked on a film on violence in the family, and performed street plays on violence across the city. The popularity of these plays increased the outreach of the group, bringing in a flood of new "cases," although the actual membership of the group did not increase. Not only did middle-class and working-class women stay away from SSS, but women from minority communities did not come to the group in any significant numbers either. This situation was puzzling to the group. The need to reckon with and address multiple identities, however, never reached the point of introspection or self-criticism.

Because of the increasing problem of communal violence in the old city of Hyderabad around 1984, a group called Hyderabad Ekta was formed. This was a loose forum of individuals who wanted to fight the increasing communalization of politics. By then, communal politics was rapidly gaining ground, and it was increasingly important to reckon with the problem. In a situation in which the state's complicity in communalism had been proven beyond a doubt—especially in the case of the post–Indira Gandhi assassination massacres—it was no longer possible for women's groups (or any radical political organization for that matter) to assert their secular nature and to continue fighting for the recognition of "secular" offenses against women.

A few members of SSS began to work with Hyderabad Ekta and attempted to articulate the women's question within anticommunal movements. Although only a few SSS members worked directly with Ekta, the whole group was prepared to provide support during a crisis or major campaign. Significantly, there was no doubt in anyone's mind that the only really radical feminist articulation of issues would come through SSS.

Research

At a time when the intersection between gender and other social divisions became much more stark SSS shifted its focus from campaigns and public activity to research and documentation. It was as if the exclusion of women from certain forms of political organization only served to push SSS into its own brand of exclusionary activity. Ironically, this move was crucial to the growth of SSS and helped it cope with the problems of stagnation, for by this point, its public actions had become repetitive and mechanical and the numerical strength of the group had declined sharply.

The decision to take up two research projects, one on health and another on history, marked a watershed in the growth of SSS. The documentation of women's experiences of health, an attempt to gain control over their lives and bodies, was inspired by *Our Bodies, Our Selves*. The project of recovering women's past history of struggle and action, on the other hand, was more a consolidation of the collective knowledge and skills of SSS members. It provided an opportunity for collective research and gave each member of the group, however marginal her involvement in the actual process, a great sense of identity and achievement. The history project on women's participation in the Telangana Armed Struggle, however, marked a major shift in SSS—from street activity and campaigning to research. It also distinguished itself from Western feminist history, which members of SSS perceived as simultaneously homogenizing and hegemonizing.

The success of these two projects and the creative potential they released encouraged one part of the group to set up a women's studies research center. The goal of the research center was to be as creative as possible and to remain independent of bureaucratic pressures and the political sterility of existing academic institutions. While the logic behind this move was irrefutable and its creative output unquestionable, this move toward institutionalization was, in a sense, ironic.

From the outset, the group had taken a collective position rejecting institutionalization. This was a problem then faced by women's groups all over the country. Many groups had, for instance, turned toward institutionalization in order to provide services for women. Some women's groups in other parts of the country had set up crisis centers to provide legal aid and counselling for women. This balance between institutionalization and activism was much more difficult to maintain with research work, however. Here, SSS had to make a conscious effort to confine itself to research and documentation, and move away from its pioneering activist role. Given the academic background of members of the research group and their institutional experience, the shift, though initially awkward, was ultimately easy to consolidate.

Shifting Perspectives

After rejecting one set of liberal assumptions (favoring institutionalization and the provision of services to women), the group utilized a different set of assumptions to move from action to research. The shift involved a subtle and unconscious privileging of reflective activity over activism, and a gradual separation of the one from the other.

Participation in the women's movement as a part of SSS conferred on each member a certain legitimacy and was the source of her identity—a shared identity. The publication of the history of women's participation in the Telangana Peasant Struggle, although enormously significant, struck at the very core of that identity.[28] While it brought international visibility and recognition to one part of SSS, it also eroded the very notion of the collective. Initially, the problem seemed to be that the time demanded of the members engaged in this project drained energy from the group. But it was evidently much more than a question of time. While a part of the group still believed in the importance of outreach in feminist politics, another part felt that research, reflection, documentation, and a consolidation of feminist learning were most essential. As an extremely close-knit group caught up in collective action, SSS generally refused to acknowledge the existence of internal hierarchies of education, experience, age, and class. Although individuals outside SSS raised these issues, the group dismissed them. Since the collective functioned as a unit, when internal polarities arose, there was no way to articulate what had never been acknowledged or, for that matter, even honestly felt. All that remained was silence, a sense of inadequacy, and impotence. To that extent, part of the group was completely powerless. There was not even the consciousness of a right denied, a possibility of articulating grievance. Instead of building a new direction for the group, individuals became caught up in introspection, self-criticism, and guilt. The hegemony of compartmentalized "knowledge" was complete. The group was sharply divided between activism and research. It no longer seemed possible for everyone to participate and share in every aspect of feminist politics. Paradoxically, this divide coincided with the increased visibility and recognition of certain members of the group.

Despite these differences of self-definition and identity, it was still possible for members to work in areas that interested them—each member working largely on her own—with the shared history of SSS as a source of strength. This meant moving away from active participation in the women's movement and articulating, instead, a feminist politic within academic spheres. While this move was undeniably significant, it left the whole group paralyzed. It was unable to respond to demands for collective action from the women's movement, whether on Muslim women's maintenance or on sex-determination tests.

By this time, there were two distinct trends in the movement that were often in conflict with each other. The recognition of a division between activist and academic work reached a head at the Third National Conference on Women's Studies in India, held at Chandigarh in 1986. Women who were active in mass organizations; who were working with the rural poor; who were working in urban, working-class areas and trade unions; and who, as part of small "autonomous women's groups," were providing shelter and support services to women in need felt a growing anger at being marginalized by women from the academy. These academic feminists had by now controlled a large proportion of the resources allocated to women's studies research. Activists began to feel that women's studies, though it derived its original legitimacy from the women's movement, was now seeking to distance itself from the very politics of that movement. Inevitably, those dubbed as activists came from less privileged, non-English-speaking, rural backgrounds but had a solid base in work at the grass-roots level. Within academia too, there was a clear distinction between research that would benefit the movement (either in terms of accessibility of knowledge or in terms of outreach) and research aimed at academic excellence that was located firmly within the university system (drawing its audience primarily from the West and from the Western-educated Indian intelligentsia). Given the politics of First-World/Third-World relationships, it is not surprising that there was a privileging of university-based academic research and that activists with little formal research training were evaluated against standards set by "professional research."[29]

Our discussion here is relevant for two reasons. First, it puts into focus the relationship between the production of knowledge in the First World and that in the Third World, and stresses the need for a self-conscious Third-World feminism that rejects the privileging of discourses or modes of production of knowledge that do not arise from or are not rooted in Third-World reality. Second, it seems to explain the shift in the politics of SSS that eventually led to the dissolution of the group. Perhaps it would also be useful at this point to locate this argument within the context that facilitated the emergence of radical political activity in the West and in India.

In India, left political activity has, from the outset, been linked to mass movements, drawing large numbers of followers from the peasantry, with a cadre that had little formal education and almost certainly no Western education. This was true for both the early Communist movement and the later Naxalite movement, which, even today, has a very strong presence in rural Andhra. So, while second-wave feminists in Andhra traced their connections to the left, it was the Indian left that served as a point of reference for our early agenda, the Zetkin and Luxemburg ideals notwithstanding. In this context, therefore, the distinction between an activist and an academic is significant.

At the point when some members of SSS felt the need to concentrate on research, the question of the academic/activist divide was raised at the national level. There was a genuine discomfort with this separation among a section of the group which did not see pure research as contradictory to the aims of the larger movement since the framework within which this research was carried out was manifestly feminist. The contradiction for SSS seemed to emerge from the fact that it saw itself basically as an urban activist group that would focus and politicize gender issues. The need for greater clarity on gender issues prompted the shift to research, which, although seen as another activity, gradually drew energy away from mobilizing and campaign work–ostensibly "activist" practice. The discomfort that activist women experienced was also genuine; their political positions were being articulated in a language that was out of their reach and in a manner that precluded their active participation. We can perhaps re-pose the activist/academic split in the following terms: the shift that some feminists, in Hyderabad as elsewhere in India made, was from activism in one context–an activism that was rooted in a Third-World revolutionary praxis–to activism bound to another context–intellectual discourse in the West, which, while radical in its own context, was alien to the majority of feminists in India.[30]

The trend that was discordant with the larger aims of the women's movement in India was the shift into research that was neither backed by outreach nor addressed to as large an audience of women as possible. This was research and feminist theory that assumed that its audience would be men and women with a Western university education, not neoliterate or underprivileged women from rural and urban areas. The privileging of the written word over oral forms, especially where the products of research are concerned, goes completely against feminist politics in the Third World. The balance that service-oriented centers strove to maintain between radical politics and institutional structures seemed inaccessible to those feminists among us who had moved completely into research.

By the end of the decade, however, the reality of communal and caste politics forced us back into a recognition of the indispensability of working actively in a movement. It was no longer possible for feminists to be content with expressing their politics in individual, isolated ways. Academia was no longer the secular institution that we believed it to be some years before. It was becoming imperative for us, as feminists, to reckon with communal and upper-caste politics if we were to resist either being coopted by them or swept out of the way.

The left and radical women's movements have, without doubt, had a considerable impact both in articulating questions of gender, caste, class, and the state, and in mobilizing large numbers of people–especially those from working-class and lower-middle-class backgrounds and the so-called lower castes. We cannot, however, afford today to underestimate, much less ignore, the impact and strength of the new resurgence of communal and caste violence on these sectors.

It has been a cause for anxiety that during communal riots in Ahmedabad and Hyderabad, and in caste riots, women have played an active part, marching and shielding rioters from police. This seems to typify a general trend among upper-caste Hindus. The underside of their participation in communal organizations is the militant assertion by women of their caste identity.[31]

This development is significant for another reason. It raises the question of whether the feminist movement itself has been subsumed within a dominant, upper-caste identity that has become complicit in consolidating majoritarian hegemony by virtue of ignoring differences and excluding *dalit* and minority consciousness. The contradictory deployment of dominant Hindi icons such as Durga and Kali as empowering symbols and images reflects this majoritarian positioning of a radical movement that has adopted these very symbols in recognition of its own alienation from the cultural needs of the people.

Conclusion

As painful as these realizations and questions may be, what is positive is the fact that today the Indian feminist movement perceives very clearly the need to address and work on caste violence and the effects of communalism. It also sees that the movement is linked closely to the struggle of masses of rural and poor urban women across the country. This was articulated in an especially clear way at the National Conference on Women's Movements in India at Calicut in 1990. There, an unprecedented number of rural women from mass political organizations (as well as nongovernmental organizations) and women from urban autonomous women's groups came together to discuss the problems attendant with communalism, religious fundamentalism, and caste.

While there are a variety of groups and a wide range of activity on many fronts, there is a recognition of the need to close ranks against attempts by reactionary and fundamentalist forces to undermine and co-opt the radical politics of the women's movement. On the other hand, minority groups that have been increasingly alienated from the Indian women's-movement political agenda have questioned its urban, upper-class, upper-caste, socialist-feminist orientation. This was expressed clearly at the National Conference on Women's Studies at Jadhavpur in 1991.

Further, as women have sharpened their own political analyses, they have had to grapple with problems other Third-World countries confront: privatization, militarization, and environmental degradation. Our understanding of politics is inevitably global even as we oppose the hegemony of a global feminism. And as the arena shifts from the personal, which was political, to the global, which impinges on the most personal aspects of individual women's lives, there is a risk that these concerns may, by their very (macro) nature, erode and wipe out the micro concerns and micro practices that have been the source of our strength, and on which we have honed our understanding and analyses. The problem now is how to retain the specificity and richness of the movement and still move out to understand the globe. This process, while difficult has been critical, and an ongoing source of tremendous growth. It has been possible to a large extent because of our persistent questioning and clarification of our own assumptions as feminists in the Third World, as well as our questioning of the politics and assumptions of "global" feminism.

12

The Dynamics of WINning: An Analysis of Women in Nigeria (WIN)

Ayesha M. Imam

Introduction

This essay is an assessment of the organization Women in Nigeria (WIN). One Nigerian newspaper distinguished WIN from other organizations in the women's movement for its "radicalism, uncompromising objectives, fearlessness in the face of the dreaded 'feminist' tag, identification with rural and illiterate women and a socialist perspective" (Bryce 1987). Yet Ifi Amadiume argues that all national women's organizations in Nigeria wittingly or unwittingly articulate the interests of Western imperialism and are "irrelevant" for "grass-roots and working-class women." She states that while WIN's posture is radical and politically committed, a "lack of ideological self-definition by WIN has left room for elite opportunism" (Amadiume 1990, 56). Bolanle Awe and Nina Mba of the Women's Research and Documentation Centre at the University of Ibadan provide a different assessment. They point out that "WIN has articulated a powerful socialist/feminist posture on a number of events and issues since 1982." However, they go on to say that while WIN has "represented itself as the voice of the oppressed masses of women, its primary achievement has been the sponsorship of research and teaching about women and the elaboration of a socialist/feminist ideology underpinning its research and other activities" (Awe and Mba 1991, 860). Elsewhere, Awe has also said that "unlike in other post-independence [women's] societies, [WIN] has worked closely at mobilizing women at the grassroots and with other organizations which seek to change the structure of society" (Awe 1988, 10). More than a decade after the first WIN seminar in 1982, it seems crucial to consider WIN's principles and mode of organization, its work and activities, its achievements and failures, its potential, and possible directions for the future.

This essay began as a self-critique of WIN and was circulated within the organization. As WIN grew from a handful of people into a broad, nationally known organization, as WIN began to take on more and more diverse forms of activity, as the economic situation in Nigeria grew more and more grim and the political and ideological climate grew more closed, it seemed necessary to take stock of WIN. Hence, this essay was also one of the two papers commissioned for the "Open Forum on WIN: Yesterday, Today and Tomorrow" at WIN's tenth annual conference in April 1992. For me writing this text was also a way of continuing to contribute to WIN while on study leave in the U.K. The objective was, in part, to document WIN's history, but, at the same time, I wanted to analyze the way WIN had developed and/or changed in response to immediate problems and circumstances, and to consider whether new orientations, activities, and modes of work were required.

Second, it is increasingly being recognized that there is no universal feminism, no abstract feminist theorizing but rather local feminisms that develop in particular contexts, at particular periods, and in particular ways. Hence, at another level, this essay seeks to provide a case history of one set of feminist practices that has developed in one specific historical context–that is, post-oil boom, "structurally adjusting" Nigeria, which has been ruled by military regimes for over twenty of the thirty years since British colonial rule.

Formation and Goals of WIN

WIN was formed after a seminar in 1982. The initiative for the seminar arose from a somewhat acrimonious debate on the nature of women's oppression that took place among social scientists working in Ahmadu Bello University in Zaria. But the seminar quickly grew, through word of mouth alone, to attract participants from all of Nigeria's nineteen states and from many fields of work, including unpaid work. After two days of discussion and argument continuing well into the early hours of each morning, participants concurred that while both men and women are exploited and oppressed in Nigeria, women are also subordinated as a specific group. It was felt therefore that issues relating to both class and gender needed to be tackled, not simply one or the other. During the last session when participatns realized that something concrete had to be done, the idea of WIN was born. The organization was formally constituted in 1983.

The specific experience of women's gender oppression was formulated in WIN's first document thusly: "the founding group believed, and the organization still maintains, that the liberation of women cannot be fully achieved outside the context of the liberation of the oppressed and poor majority of the people in Nigeria." Women needed to organize themselves to fight their oppression, additionally this struggle had to be carried on in alliance with other groups and forces combating all forms of oppression and exploitation. For solidarity work to be successful, however, all participants had to acknowledge that women's subordination was different from, although related to, other forms of oppression in Nigerian society.

The Context in Which WINning Takes Place

Socioeconomic Issues

Since the late 1970s, Nigeria has been plagued by a series of economic crises which the state believes it can solve by using IMF- and World Bank–inspired stabilization and structural adjustment policies (SAP). Nigeria had been insulated from the world recession in the 1970s because of its reliance on oil (now over 90 percent of export earnings and forming 75 percent of the federal state's revenue). Prior to the 1970s, state revenue had relied primarily on agricultural crop exports, following the pattern developed by British colonial rule. Food crop production and marketing, the sector in which most rural women work, had been neglected since the colonial era. However, with the development of the oil-extraction industry, agricultural export crop production was also neglected and productivity declined as returns to farmers (mediated through state marketing boards) fell dramatically relative to other sectors of the economy. The huge earnings from oil were used to finance a massive expansion of commercial, industrial, and construction projects, large-scale agricultural projects, and considerable infrastructural development, as well as an increase in consumer and luxury imports.

The drop in the price of oil on the international market in the early 1980s signalled the end of the construction boom, and around half the import-substitution industries folded, resulting in massive unemployment. At the same time, there was a shortage of consumer goods as well as huge price increases, with a rise in inflation and the beginning of Nigeria's continuing debt-repayment crisis. Stabilization policies which included currency devaluation, import restrictions, cuts in public expenditure, wage freezes and cuts, and retrenchment of public sector employees were started. SAP was formally instituted in 1986. Its policies authorized the lifting of restrictions on currency conversion, making cuts and realignments on import duties, promoting the release of resources to the private sector through changes in prices, tariffs, taxes and interest rates, and through privatization, further cutting public expenditure, and increasing the price of petrol.

The macroeconomic effects of SAP have been mixed. Agricultural export crop production (mostly in cocoa and cotton) increased between 1986 and 1988, but dropped again, in keeping with the fall in the price of cocoa internationally. The rate of growth of manufacturing rose to 7.3 percent in 1990 (from a negative growth rate in the early 1980s), dropping to 6.1 percent in 1991. Manufacturing remains at less than 10 percent of the GDP. Food crop production and producer prices have increased, as the fall in value of the Naira has meant fewer food imports. Nonetheless, most macroeconomic indicators are negative. The rate of growth of GDP fell from 7.9 percent in 1985 to 5.2 percent in 1990, and again to 4.3 percent in 1991. The external debt has almost doubled, from U.S. $18.5 billion in 1984 to over $34 billion in 1990, and both the domestic and the foreign debts' budget-service rations have risen. The value of the Naira against the U.S. dollar fell dramatically from N1.12in 1985 to N20 in 1992. The current rate of exchange now stands at N80 for a U.S. dollar. (EIU Reports) The external debt has almost doubled, from U.S.$18.5 billion in 1984 to over U.S.$34 billion in 1990, and both the have risen. The value of the Naira against the U.S. dollar has fallen from eighty-nine cents in 1985 to five cents in early 1992.

The effects of SAP at the social level, have been almost uniformly negative. There has been a decrease in the general standard of living, with both the lowering of absolute income for many and a general decrease in purchasing power, with even official inflation figures reaching 40 to 50 percent in 1990. In addition, there have been reductions in the already inadequate provision of health, education, and other social services, as well as the introduction of user-charges which include charges for admission to hospitals, prescriptions, levies on parents for uniforms, books for pupils, and so on. The numbers of children, particularly girls, attending school has dropped. Retrenchments in the public sector and industrial plant closings have increased unemployment. Thirty to 40 percent of secondary school leavers are unemployed. Unemployment is estimated at over 5 million workers, in a country where most people do not even register as unemployed since there are no unemployment or social security benefits.

The deepening economic crisis has hit the urban salariat the worst, particularly the low-paid. Many lost their jobs first in the building industry as the construction boom crashed, then in factories or in the public sector. For those still employed, rocketing inflation and the wage freeze dating from 1984, the occasions when wages and/or fringe benefits were paid several months in arrears (and sometimes not at all), has meant increasing poverty. The Nigeria Labour Congress calculated in 1989 that there would need to be an increase of the national minimum wage to N1,490 pcm, to restore it to the level of its 1981 purchasing power. The present national minimum wage is approximately N250 pcm. Although many households depend on a combination of income sources, the increase in unemployment has meant that there is heavy pressure on the informal sector, resulting in increased competition and even lower returns for labor there. There is little appreciation for the ways in which the informal sector depends on the public and formal sectors, providing meals and other services to public-sector employees, for example. A cutback in the public or formal sector often also means a cutback in opportunities in the informal sector. Furthermore, increases in interest rates, licensing charges, and the like, together with the general lack of access to credit, have often meant the closing of medium- and small-scale enterprises.

Even for rural producers—the vast majority of whom are small-scale farmers who rely primarily on household labor—benefiting from higher producer prices needs to be balanced against the need to buy basic commodities. Rural households in Nigeria have not been wholly self-provisioning for years, if ever they were. As with urban households, they need to buy consumer goods (salt, clothes, particular foodstuffs, kerosene for lighting, and soap), as well as make expenditures for agricultural production and marketing (seeds, fertilizers, pesticides, tools, and transportation). For most rural households, the gains of higher crop prices appear to be wiped out by inflation and the general reduction of purchasing power. This entails as well the removal of subsidies on fertilizers, pesticides, and petrol. Thus, for the population of Nigeria as a whole, the average level of food consumption has declined 7 percent, and *Kwashiorkor* has made a comeback. Between 1983 and 1988, the percentage of infants with low birth weight increased 10 percent and the percentage of malnourished under-five-year-olds increased by 14 percent. Furthermore, the level of under-five-year-olds malnourished to the point of permanent stunting increased by 13 percent (Aig-Ojehomon and Akinware, 1989). The health status of Nigerians has also worsened. Due to the lack of adequate health services and control measures Nigeria had not only the second-highest number of cases of cholera in the world in 1991 but also the highest incidence of deaths, with a mortality rate of 13 percent (compared to 1 percent for Latin America).

For those among the rich who have access to large-scale capital, however, the change in interest rates and privatization of public-sector enterprises has meant a large-scale transfer of state resources in their favor. Overall, then, the results of SAP have meant an increasing polarization of the socioeconomic strata, with the rich getting richer and all other groups, including the urban middle class, becoming more immersed in poverty. At the same time, women in all socioeconomic strata, but the rich, have disproportionately borne both the economic and the social costs of SAP.

Relatively few women are formally employed. Most of those who work are employed in the public sector and service industries. As a result, public-sector retrenchment has hit the female labor force particularly hard. The ideology of "man the breadwinner" (largely imported during colonialism) also means that general retrenchment particularly affects unskilled and semi-skilled women before men, despite the fact that in practice virtually all women are expected to make some economic contribution to the household. The increased level of male unemployment also means that men, as well as women, need to seek other means of livelihood, usually in the informal sector, where most women had worked. However, women do not compete in the market on the same terms as men, since they have less access to capital and more constraints on time, etc. So, as the informal sector gets crowded, it becomes even more difficult for women to find gainful employment. Women farmers tend to control only the returns from food crops, even where they also work on cash crops (WIN 1985a), but they have benefited from higher food prices. However, women farmers had always lacked access to agricultural extension services and to fertilizer. As these services are being curtailed, the access of women farmers is becoming even more attenuated.

The cutbacks in the provision of education and the introduction of user-charges have meant lower school attendance for girls even in states where girls are not charged school fees. This situation is most evident in northern Nigeria where suspicion against the education of girls already existed. The high levels of secondary-school-leaver unemployment is likely to further fuel opposition to schooling for boys as well as for girls.

The reduction in health services means that the sick must be cared for (attended to, cleaned up after, cooked and served meals and medicine) within the household, rather than by paid workers in hospitals whether public or, more especially, in nonaffordable expensive private clinics. The division of labor within most households in Nigeria allocates this work to women. Thus, on top of all other tasks they have, women take on the additional work of caring for the sick. Similarly, increases in food prices or the nonavailability of certain foods has meant switching to cheaper foods or unprocessed foods which require longer preparation times. This, too, is allocated to women. Even in the rural areas where food is most often processed from crops, the incidence of the use of energy-saving grinding machines has decreased, for lack of the few kobo (100 kobo=1 Naira) with which to pay for this service, particularly since the costs of grinding have increased with the cost of the petrol needed to power the machines. For the vast majority of women, the extra workload can be measured in increased work hours per day, rather than in minutes.

The issue of food distribution in households is another area in which the consequences of the crisis are exacerbated for some groups because of inegalitarian gender relations. The superior status of men within the household is often symbolized by serving them the best and most nutritious food. It is also the case that men, especially middle-class men, tend to eat meals at home and buy meals outside the home far more often than women. Where food supplies are sufficient, there are no physical consequences for women and children. But in this crisis food is often scarce even in rural areas that produce protein-rich foods. Since the late 1980s and early 1990s, even middle-income professional households have been reducing their intake of meat, fish, oils, rice, beans, and eggs because of the cost. In these situations, children's and women's risk of malnourishment rises (particularly for lactating mothers) even more than that of men, and so does the risk to their health and life.

Hierarchical power relations within households are thrown into stark relief by the crisis. Domestic violence, which is often associated with the increase in poverty and economic hardship, has dramatically increased. In one case in Bauchi, for example, a man did not want his wife to visit her mother after the mother had had another child because he did not have the means to give the customary gift. When she insisted on going, they quarrelled, during which he killed her. Domestic violence includes the increasing violence of adults toward children as well as the results of husbands venting their own frustrations on their wives. In many African cultures, wife-beating ("correction"—*sic*) is seen as a right of husbands. The extreme consequence of this "right" is the increase in the numbers of women killed by their partners (cf., Mama 1990, Wamalwa 1987). The social relations of gender, combined with the class relations that leave some groups more vulnerable to economic crisis than others, have thus placed women in an even more precarious situation than men of the same socioeconomic stratum.

Political and Ideological Issues

During the decade of WIN's existence, Nigeria moved from the civilian Second Republic (1979–83), which followed thirteen years of military rule, to renewed military regimes, first under General Buhari (1983–85), then under General Babangida (1985 to present) and now under General Abacha. It cannot be assumed that civilian regimes are tolerant and democratic while military regimes are necessarily repressive (contrast for instance Sankara's Burkina Faso with Mobutu's Zaire or Banda's Malawi, for cases of the reverse). However, the organizational characteristics of the military tend to promote repression rather than democracy. As rigidly stratified masculinist institutions with centralized authority requiring unquestioning obedience, military regimes achieve power by force. In Nigeria, military regimes have organized coups on the "law and order" ticket (unlike, say, Burkina Faso or Ghana at Rawlings's first coup), and their governance has been concerned with bridling opposition and curbing unrest through the denial of rights to associate freely, speak openly, withdraw labor and so on.

Nonetheless, no power bloc can be confident of remaining in power for long without at least the acquiescence of the ruled. The loss of legitimacy of civilian regimes (the failure of "development" promises, corruption, insecurity, the obvious pillaging of state resources) has often meant that military regimes, and the "discipline" they impose in the political sphere, appear preferable. Moreover, despite the fact that two-thirds of the period since Independence has been under military rule, Nigeria has had a strong tradition of institutions in civil society which make their views known and felt. For instance, Nigeria is generally acknowledged to have one of the freest presses in Africa, and, at the beginning of the 1980s, the trade-union movement as represented by the NLC and its affiliated unions, and the student movements were both strong. Paradoxically, despite the masculinist character of the military and lack of opportunity for women to wield power, it was by fiat of a military decree that women in the northern half of Nigeria became enfranchised in 1976. However, with the consequences of stabilization policies and worsening living conditions, military regimes have increasingly lost popular support. Thus, in order to stay in power and continue to enforce SAP, military regimes have increased their use of suppression and rely less on the use of persuasion. The political terrain became increasingly repressive during the 1980s (Civil Liberties Organization Reports; Ibrahim 1994; Mustapha 1993).

Under the Buhari regime, Decrees 2 and 4 gave the state infinitely renewable powers of detention without charge (i.e., the suspension of habeas corpus) and prohibited the publication of any material likely to embarrass the government,regardless of its truth, making both editors and journalists vulnerable to detention. The Buhari regime also instituted a War Against Indiscipline (WAI). WAI measures included on-the-spot dismissals and "frog-jumping" for people late to work, the knocking-down of marketing stalls and harassment of street-traders, as well as an environmental-sanitation measure that required all individuals to stay at home on specific days to clean their compounds.

The opposition to Buhari led to the Babangida coup which overthrew Buhari by formally espousing a human-rights posture. Two major measures in this gesture were the IMF Debate (on whether or not Nigeria should take an IMF loan) and the Political Bureau-organized debate over Nigeria's future political and socioeconomic structure following a return to civilian rule. On both issues, the Babangida regime called for an open public debate and said that it would be guided by the public consensus. However, in both cases, the regime then ignored the results of the debates, signing a secret agreement with the International Bank for Reconstruction and Development (IBRD) for a loan with virtually the same conditionalities as those of the rejected IMF loan, and instituting a "home-grown" SAP (indistinguishable from IMF-approved SAPs). It simultaneously rejected major sections of the Political Bureau report with its call for multiparty democracy and freedom of association, and state provision of primary health care and primary-level schooling for children.

The reality of the Babangida regime's position on human rights is evident from the following examples. Most of the decrees relating to detention and to press control remain unrepealed and are frequently used. Journalists have been frequently detained or are beaten up by state functionaries and newspapers and magazines have been closed down. Demonstrations against SAP (at least one every year) have been met with firearms, as well as beatings, and, where students were involved, with widespread campus closures. Students' unions, the university teachers union, and doctors' organizations have all been banned, and, if allowed to exist, warned to be "of good behaviour." In 1988, the Nigeria Labour Congress executive committee was dissolved and replaced for several months by a state appointed "administrator." Trade unionists have been questioned by the infelicitously named State Security Service (SSS), prevented from working, and detained. Deportations, sometimes without any pretense of legal documentation, have been used against non-Nigerians who have critized the regime, including foreign-based journalists and individuals married to Nigerians who had lived and worked in Nigeria for years and had residence rights there.

The return to civilian rule proposed at that time was to be undertaken through two political parties whose constitutions were deceptively written by the federal military government. No other parties were permitted. Furthermore, Decree No. 19 (Transition to Civilian Rule) made it a criminal offense (sabotage) to question (among other things) SAP or to suggest alternative economic policies, even when proposing them for after the lifetime of this regime. Under the decree, not only were organizations prevented from holding conferences or seminars on SAP or the state of democracy in Nigeria, but people were harassed, beaten, and/or imprisoned for attempting to organize them. Similarly, following the abortive coup of 1990, individuals were detained for questioning the treatment and mode of trial and punishment of alleged coup-plotters and/or their relatives (for example, protesting the detention of a woman and her children because her husband was wanted for questioning). Since early 1992, there has been an increased campaign of arrest and detention, targeting opponents to that regime, especially those associated with the Campaign for Democracy. Five of the leading members (one of them the lawyer who had filed habeas corpus applications on behalf of the initial detainees) were beaten up in prison and then charged with conspiracy and treason in a village magistrate's court 500 kilometers from Lagos, thus ignoring several Lagos High Court injunctions for their appearance there.

In effect, both the Buhari regime and more especially, the Babangida regime, have used state power to attempt to rule out any public discussion on the causes and nature of the economic crisis, any criticism of economic policies and programs, or any discussion of democratic structures and decision-making other than those they have literally decreed as permissible. Furthermore, both regimes have provided an explanation of the internal causes of the crisis, which served as both a rationale for their own intervention in the body politic and a justification for the form of economic and political programs they have instituted. This explanation hinges on the notion of a failed moral order resulting in indiscipline and corruption, and requiring strict, disciplinary measures to be imposed on Nigeria. Hence, Buhari's WAI, attributed the economic and political crises in Nigeria to the indiscipline on the part of individual Nigerians, particularly women (Dennis 1987).

The failures of the "modernization" and "development" promises of the past few decades, together with the overt corruption and use of patronage under civilian and military rule alike (possibly except under the brief period of the Murtala Mohammed military regime), have led to cynicism and pessimism in Nigeria. An increasingly common reaction to this situation has been an individualistic recourse to forms of religion that stress purity and asceticism, or implicit acceptance of the military government's explanation of the crisis as the failure of morality. There has been a substantial growth in the number of religious groups and in their active membership ("Born Agains," Cherubim and Seraphim, the Celestial Church of Christ, 'Yan Izala, Da'wa, Tijaniyya, Quadiriyya, to name but a few). Religious tension is intensifying as each group tries to win "converts," whether within or across the broad definitions of Christianity and Islam (Kane 1990, Ibrahim 1991). And there have been bloody clashes between Christians and Muslims in Kafanchan in 1987, in Bauchi and in Kano in 1991. This increased attention to identifying with a particular religious community—and the strengthening of the boundaries against those defined as being outside that community—occurs at the same time as an intensifying awareness of membership of, and identification with ethnic community. There has also been an increased number of incidents of interethnic community violence and deaths, between the Tiv and Jukun in Taraba State, the Efik-Ibibio conflict in Akwa Ibom, and the Hausa-Kataf clash in Kaduna, all in early 1992.

The focus on the fighting and bloodshed between people identifying as members of different communities (religious and/or ethnic) serves two purposes. First, it lends credence to the claim of the militarized state to stand over and above groups in society in order to enforce law and order. It is in this context that Babangida had been able to institute a National Guard, answerable only to him. Second, characterizing these conflicts as religious or ethnic helps to obscure the extent to which they reflect deep competition over access to and control of resources in an economic situation in which securing one's livelihood has become precarious. The "ethnic conflict" in Kaduna State, for instance, was sparked by the proposal to relocate a market. Those in Bauchi arose over access to an abattoir, and the violence of the "religious conflict" in Kano was neither indiscriminate nor confined to "religious" symbols like churches and mosques or beer parlors. The targets were businesses and shops rather than homes. There have been previous clashes in Nigeria between members of different religious or ethnic communities, but the incidence and spread of these clashes have increased almost in geometrical progression as the economic crisis and effects of SAP have worsened.

In addition, Babangida's imposition of a two-party system for the proposed return to civil rule gave rise to fears of North/South and/or Christian/Muslim splits. In 1992, the fear of being in the opposition and consequently of being left out of the division of the spoils from (still relatively huge) oil revenue has added impetus to identity politics and religious fundamentalisms. Thus, much of the political-ideological terrain was given over to attempts to mobilize "our" community (whether defined as Muslim, Christian, North, South, Tiv, Jukun . . .) and to decry "theirs." The fact that the boundaries of these "imaginary communities" are not coterminous with existing geography (one may, for example, be from the North and Christian, or, from the South and be Muslim, or from the South and be Christian, Efik or Ibibio) serves to further fragment Nigerians.

The other reaction to the state's foreclosure of political space and the imposition of SAP has been to continue to challenge and resist its very imposition. Students, market women, trade unionists, and others persist in demonstrating against SAP. The Nigerian Bar Association has criticized the regime and reaffirmed its commitment to the rule of law. In 1985, an Association of Democratic Lawyers (ADLA) was formed to defend those detained or otherwise harassed by the state. In 1987, the Civil Liberties Organization (CLO) was started to monitor and publicize human rights violations, publishing reports on prison conditions, election manipulations, and the like. These groups often work in alliance with others that share similar objectives, such as the Committee for Unity and Progress (CUP) and the Campaign for Democracy. WIN has been among those groups engaged in building these alliances.

Why WIN?

WIN is neither the first nor the only existing organization purporting to represent women's interests in Nigeria. Well before colonialism there existed women's age grade associations, as among the Tiv. The Igbo daughters and wives of the village associations had some powers to adjudicate not only among women, but also on some issues between women and men, both individually and at the general village level (Okonjo 1976). They also had the power to enforce their decisions on women and men in the village. During the colonial period, Igbo women's associations protested against colonial taxation in the 1929 Women's War. This effort resulted in the postponement of taxation for some years and the dismantling of parts of the Warrant Chief system. Some voluntary associations, such as the Young Women's Christian Association and the Soroptimists, also date from the colonial period. However, the process of commodification and incorporation into the world economic system, combined with the imposition of British male Victorian chauvinism resulted in the disregard and withering away of precolonial indigenous women's organizations and power.

Since Nigeria's flag independence in 1960, there has been a proliferation of women's groups. In addition to the women's wings of political parties, there were women's organizations like the Nigerian Women's Union and the Federation of Nigerian Women's Societies that attempted to mobilize women and to fight for women's rights during the nationalist struggle for independence from the British (Mba 1982). There has also been craft, trade, and professional associations, service clubs, religious groups, and so on. Many of these have focused on augmenting (or providing) health, education, and social-welfare services to their members and/or local communities (Enabulele 1985). The political parties in civilian regimes continue to have women's wings, the aim of which was primarily to mobilize women's support for their parties. There has also been the National Council of Women's Societies (NCWS), which sees itself (and is recognized by the state) as the "umbrella body for all women's societies."

Thus, it should be clear that the phenomenon of women finding ways of trying to empower themselves and better their conditions, both individually and collectively, is not new in Nigeria. Women have organized in different ways and with different objectives. Their organizing reflects, in part, the general state of the body politic, for the dominance of the military regimes has prompted, for instance, the formation of organizations such as the Association of Army Officers' Wives. Contemporary organizations now find that they have to sort through, as well as draw on, a long, contradictory history of women's organizing in order to shape their own political path.

Nonetheless, a number of combined characteristics make WIN unique and different from other organizations, past and present. First, and most important, WIN is consciously organized around a political ideology, the fundamental principle of which is the necessity of simultaneously transforming the present nature of the social relations of both gender *and* class (including neocolonial relations), which are interrelated. Hence, WIN sees its project as not only empowering women and bringing about changes in women's lives, but also as bringing about changes in men's lives and empowering some groups of men. WIN is open to all who accept its aims and objectives, regardless of gender or nationality.

WIN is autonomous, deciding on its own principles, policies, and practices. WIN branches are never set up by the state (unlike the NCWS, for example, whose Kaduna branch was organized under the auspices of the Ministry of Social Development). Neither is it a "women's wing" of some other male-dominated organization, whether political (like the women's wings of political parties), trade union (like the Nigeria Labour Congress Women's Wing [NLCWW]), or social (like the Inner Wheel of the Rotary Club). Nor is it the national branch of an international organization, like the Soroptimists. Not only is WIN autonomous, but its membership is wholly voluntary. Such independence distinguishes WIN from a NCWS to which many women's groups are affiliated under the mistaken impression that they are either legally obliged to do so or are sometimes coerced into affiliation because they have been refused recognition as a separate organization and with it, the right to hold meetings or even have a bank account.

Unlike the Muslim Sisters' Organization, the Federation of Muslim Women's Associations of Nigeria (FOMWAN), the YWCA, or the many Christian Church Women's Groups, WIN is a secular organization, whose members may be of any religion or have no religious affiliation at all. Likewise, unlike both religious organizations and professional or occupational associations like the Market Women's Associations or the Associations of Women Doctors/Lawyers or development-concerned organizations like the Country Women Association (which is concerned with rural women), WIN is concerned with all women in Nigeria. The basis of WIN's practice and its membership are national. WIN's support and work cover all of Nigeria. There are no regional or ethnic bases of strength, and there are active branches in all parts of the country.

Thus, WIN is the only organization in Nigeria which is organized around promoting all women's interests from a political position aimed at democratically transforming class and gender relations, and which is also autonomous, voluntary, non-religious, nationally based, and, open to all who accept its aims and objectives. WIN is thus unique in its potential to mobilize and inspire women *nationally,* in contrast to most of the "poly-tricks" presently in Nigeria. And because WIN defines women's liberation as an integral focus in the liberation of all women and men, it also has the potential to mobilize men and merge the concern for gender equality into popular democratic struggles.

WIN Activities

Since WIN defines its ultimate objective as the need to transform the system of social and economic relations at its root, while also acknowledging the need for reforms, its canvas for activity is extremely wide. Indeed, WIN can be said to have taken to heart the slogan "Every issue is a women's issue," with the further insistence that "every women's issue is everyone's concern." Consequently, WIN uses a wide range of forms of activity, and works at many different levels: from the individual to the local, from the state to the federal government and beyond, to international networking and collaboration.

In order to raise public awareness about the nature of gender and class relations and on specific issues, WIN organizes numerous seminars, conferences, and workshops (both nationally and locally), participates in radio and television programs and popular theater, and writes and publishes articles in the press. The topics range widely: the economy, sexual harassment, the census, women's reproductive health, the (then proposed) transition to civilian rule, and women's legal rights. Some of these might be more aptly termed "public education" and are part of an activist campaign, as was the case with the mobilization for a water-purification and water-delivery project and education around vesico-vaginal fistulae, which included support for victims as well as a campaign against early and forced marriages. WIN also organizes and takes part in single-issue campaigns, undertaking research on issues affecting women, organizing conferences to discuss and analyze them, and publishing this material. Such issues include access to education, problems affecting rural women, family law, and taxation law and practices.

On the interface between raising social awareness and political mobilization, WIN has been publicly critical of the state's antiwomen and antipeople policies, from Shagari's "Belt-tightening" exercise to the scapegoating of prostitutes and their forced marriage (under threat of imprisonment); the "War Against Indiscipline" ideologies; the imposition of the Structural Adjustment Programme and IMF-type conditionalities; and the imposition of the two-party system and open balloting. WIN has occasionally influenced policy by bringing to public attention some issues affecting women—the removal of school fees for girls in some states, the ideologies behind the "Better Life for Rural Women" program, and the recommendation of the Political Bureau that at least some percentage of legislative offices be occupied by women.

WIN's public interventions are not limited to making representations to government. WIN Lagos was a member of the Committee for Unity and Progress (CUP), which organized the Alternatives to Structural Adjustment Conference. WIN has also participated with other organizations in campaigns for democracy. Similarly, WIN has been part of the struggle for the improvement of the national minimum wage with the CUP, and before that was formed, directly with the NLC and the NLCWW, at the national and at local branch levels. At this level of work, WIN's role is twofold: to ensure that visions, policies, and strategies are constructed in ways that blend gender equality with other forms of social egalitarianism, and to ensure that women's interests and points of view are represented at all levels.

Nonetheless, WIN does not see itself as the sole legitimate representative of women. WIN supports and works with other groups of women with similar objectives or on issues of common concern. For example, in Bendel, Lagos, and Oyo states, the Market Women's Associations have demonstrated against several percentage increases in stall fees and the imposition of education levies on all parents, ostensibly to pay for uniforms, books, and other school equipment. Since the 1950s, both primary and secondary schooling had either been free or required a minimal charge. Unlike the NCWS which argued that the market women had no right to demonstrate without their permission, and should only attempt to influence the government through its own structure, WIN supported the market women's right to take independent action and provided legal aid, media representation, and so on. On a number of occasions, WIN has also taken the initiative to mobilize and coordinate groups to work out and press for particular measures, as in the Political Bureau debates on Nigeria's future in 1986/87 or the national conference in 1991 "Towards National Government Policies for Women," to which all women's organizations were invited to come together "and formulate a package towards definite and clear government policies on women . . . [through] collective representative and democratic input by women themselves."

Much of this political activity could be described as part of a general defense (and extension) of democratic, legal, citizen's rights. In addition, WIN has taken up and fought individual cases of both discrimination against and harassment of women. For instance, following the sexual assault of a woman student by male students, WIN organized with the Association of University Women, a women-only workshop, and fought for the protection of women students and staff from sexual harassment. Similarly, WIN testified before the Abisoye Commission on the sexual harassment and rape of students by the police during the demonstration in Ahmadu Bello University in May 1986; and WIN protected the identities of the women involved. In one case, a village head attempted to force a girl to marry him. WIN provided support and legal representation, and helped her find a scholarship to continue her education after she won the case. Following the horrific case of a thirteen year old girl who died after her husband took an axe to her legs for continuously running away from him, WIN began to press for the prosecution of men who attack and/or murder their wives. Likewise, WIN pressure stopped the denial of medical facilities to married female intermediate and junior staff (e.g., cleaners, cooks, typists). Before WIN's intervention, these women workers (unlike female senior staff and all male staff) had not been allowed to bring their children or husbands for treatment, on the false assumption that the medical facilities of their husbands' jobs would take care of them. Despite the provisions regarding discrimination in the constitution and Nigeria's ratification of the United Nations Convention for the Elimination of Discrimination Against Women, such cases are all too familiar.

As the economic crisis began to bite deeper in the mid-1980s, and, as a result of demands from poor, urban and rural women generated during the political debate workshops, WIN decided that it was necessary to contribute directly to helping women organize and work on satisfying their immediate needs. Following a series of internal mobilization workshops in 1986 and 1987, WIN has been engaging in project work and facilitating the creation of an organizational infrastructure among rural women. In Bauchi, WIN is working with a project to supply water. In Kano, there are five groups facilitated by WIN that are working with a revolving loan scheme to improve their livelihoods. Kaduna WIN's work has been with women who have vesico-vaginal fistulae, providing support, equipment, and funds to enable them to have the necessary corrective surgery. WIN Plateau has started a free legal-aid clinic for women and for low-income people. There are similar projects in Bendel and Cross River, as well.

Finally, WIN has tried to build up a resource and documentation center for materials relating to women's struggles and gender/class issues (See appendix). WIN has also been working on biographies of women who have been active in the struggles for women's rights in Nigeria's history. So far, three have been prepared: Funmilayo Anikulapo-Kuti, who started the National Women's Union in 1946; Gambo Sawaba, who has been active in popular and women's struggles since the early days of the nationalist struggle; and Margaret Ekpo, who, as the first woman head of the Civil Service, was able to institute a good many of the provisions regarding the conditions of women working therein.

The theme of research and its dissemination runs through many WIN activities. As Awe and Mba have pointed out, this has had a significant impact within the academy. But this is merely one useful product as far as WIN is concerned. Research in WIN is oriented to collective teamwork, so that research skills and analysis are shared and demystified as not being the exclusive property of "academics." More to the point, WIN's research activities have clear political ends: to know clearly and concretely how women's and men's lives are structured by the socioeconomic and political conditions in which they live; to speak from a position of strength on the changes required to eradicate oppression and exploitation; to provide hard-to-refute evidence that women's and men's roles and socioeconomic positions are neither natural nor inevitable and are, therefore, amenable to improvement; to be able to represent women's views, to "speak" women's subordination, and thus to dispel the myth that "women are happy with their lot"; and to be able to work with women not only to identify their immediate needs, but also to map a feasible strategy of how to satisfy them in the short-term.

WINning Ways

WIN understands that women are not an undifferentiated category. Indeed, in a multilingual and multireligious state like Nigeria, it would be difficult not to recognize this fact. In aiming to promote the interests of Nigerian women, rather than those of a religious category (Muslim or Christian), a linguistic category (Hausa, Yoruba, Igala, Igbo, Tiv, and so on), or a regionalist category (North, South, East, Middlebelt, minorities), WIN chooses to advocate a gender identity that is national in orientation.

WIN has thus been at the forefront of those criticizing state policies based on "state origin" or "ethnic origin," such as discrimination in the allocation of jobs, scholarships, school places, and the like. WIN points out these inequalities for the many Nigerians who live, work, and pay taxes in states other than their "state of origin," and shows how this discriminates further against women who marry men who are not from the same "state of origin." Such women pay taxes and the like in their husbands' states of origin while not enjoying any of the privileges of being counted in their own state. They are, therefore, discriminated against in both. WIN thus criticizes both the ideology through which wives are considered as appendages of their husbands including ideologies whereby a wife's "domicile" is automatically considered to be that of her husband, as he is the "head," and the divisiveness of such subnationalist identity politics.

The deliberate disavowal of identity based on ethnicity, region, or religion, however, has a price. The tripartite regional structure created by the colonial power allows ruling groups to mobilize identity politics to create power bases which would eventually lead to state power (Ibrahim 1989, 1994; Imam 1994). Obviously, where identity politics is used in securing access to state power, those in control of state power are unlikely to be sympathetic to critics of identity politics like WIN—as WIN has found when applying for registration and the like.

In addition, as religious fundamentalisms of all kinds have gained currency in Nigeria in the last few years, WIN is being increasingly castigated as "a-religious." Such criticism has occurred despite the fact that WIN has been careful not to attack religious sentiments directly, though its denunciation of ethnic chauvinism is uncategorical. Rather, WIN views religious affiliation as a private individual matter, but goes on to argue (as do FOMWAN and some Christian women's groups) for the enforcement of the rights women have in both Islam and Christianity. However, WIN members situate their advocacy within a radical interpretation of women's rights in religion along with a strong critique of men's gender interests in maintaining the status quo. At the same time, WIN maintains that as a secular state with a multireligious population, religious sentiments should not be used to define gender roles and rights in Nigeria (WIN 1985a and n.d.). Furthermore, WIN is at pains to stress that poor women (and men), regardless of religious and ethnic affiliation, are in the same structural situation.

These factors partially explain why there are, nonetheless, deliberate attempts to paint WIN in a negative light and to foster support through publicly expressed approval and endorsement from religious and state leaders, and with donations and other resources for less-threatening women's groups, like the NCWS or FOMWAN. However, forfeiting support given on the basis of linguistic, religious, or regionalist identities is a price WIN is willing to pay. But there are gains, too. As a result of its nationalist orientation, WIN has a very widespread national appeal.

This is not to say that there have not been tensions within WIN relating to religion and region. WIN members include people from practically all Nigeria's linguistic groups (of which there are 250 to 300, depending on which classification is used), and adherents of most religions (including those whose religious practice is merely nominal, as well agnostics and atheists). Despite this, or maybe because of it, WIN's platform on religion and ethnicity was worked out through discussion with little dissension during its formulation, and almost none since. However, the question of who represents and speaks for WIN has been a far more difficult and contentious issue.

WIN has always held that any member of the group (including non-Nigerians) may be mandated to speak on its behalf. The principle here is to move away from identity (*who* is speaking) and emphasize instead *what* is being said. However, it is also the case that all other things being equal, criticisms and recommendations from a person perceived as part of a group will be more favorably received than from someone perceived as an outsider. WIN promotes a national identity, but it works in a context where people often identify themselves with a particular religion, linguistic group, or region first. Hence, there has been conflict in WIN as to whether, as a matter of practical strategy, a WIN representative at a meeting in (for example) Kano must be from Kano. Does this take account of the messenger and the message, or is it simply pandering to regional/religious chauvinist sentiments? WIN's practice has been to stress that its policies are collectively worked out, and to include on public platforms people who will be seen as being from a number of groups (always including that of the area or of the group whose religious or cultural practices are being criticized). Although this may appear to be similar in form to the policy of "Federal Character," its character is quite distinct. The process of constitution is very different in that WIN's platform is strategically, as well as collectively, worked out, instance by instance (rather than as a rigid rule), and takes into account multiple (as opposed to single) criteria. Rather than attempting "representation" of all groups on a numerical basis, WIN's concern is to be sensitive to the environment and avoid being seen as appropriating other people's voices or simply criticizing from the outside.

WIN's adoption of a national identity rests on the assertion that while class and religious/linguistic group differences do exist, women in these groups have, nonetheless, many compatible interests as women and as citizens. However, fundamental to WIN's worldview is a recognition that certain groups and classes of women have interests that are incompatible with those of other groups, and that they gain from the exploitation of those other groups of women (and men). Some members of WIN prioritize class relations over gender relations, and some vice versa, while yet others refuse to prioritize one over the other. But, thus far, these divergences have been far less important than the common agreements: that class exploitation and gender subordination must both be eradicated; that it is necessary to struggle for both simultaneously; and that, in the short-to-medium term, policies favoring all women as a gender category as well as working-class and peasant women and men must be fought for.

This political position has made it impossible for us to affiliate with NCWS (recognized by the state as *the* "umbrella body" for all women's groups), despite the accusation that we thus give credence to the ideology that women are only jealous of each other and that all we do is fight among ourselves. Officials in the Federal Ministry of Social Welfare who administer programs for women, youth, and the disabled have suggested that WIN join NCWS in order both to "reform [WIN] from within" and to gain the kind of legitimacy NCWS has in the eyes of the Nigerian state and, with it, the possibility of greater access to funds, annual government subventions, buildings for offices, tickets and foreign exchange services for traveling abroad, access to the media, and so on. However, the NCWS has supported policies that WIN considers to be antithetical to women's gender interests. For example, the organization mounted successful mobilization for the defeat of the 1981 Abortion Bill. Similarly, NCWS has consistently endorsed policies that are against the interests of the peasantry and working class, as when they called on poor Nigerians to tighten their belts and support the Austerity Programme of 1982–83 and SAP; or when they supported WAI measures that knocked down kiosks and imposed a ban on street trading on which many poor urban women relied for their livelihood. WIN could not affiliate with such an organization without seriously compromising its distinctive worldview.

WIN's attempts to forge an identity for women as a gender group, while recognizing that women in different classes can and do have divergent interests over specific issues, have met with some success. This was most noticeable in the debate over Nigeria's political and socioeconomic structure. By holding workshops throughout Nigeria with thousands of ordinary women in indigenous languages, rather than solely in English, WIN was able to solicit views and perhaps, to influence them. WIN's aim was dual: to raise women's political participation and consciousness by involving them actively in the debate about Nigeria's political and socioeconomic system; and to ensure that the views of women (peasant and working-class women, as well as middle-class and elite women, women of all religious persuasions and denominations, many linguistic groups, and every occupation, whether paid and/or unpaid) be represented to the Political Bureau. The workshops involved many women's and community organizations, and thousands of women (and more than a few men). In this mobilization process, WIN found that across Nigeria, many women could and did identify with this position (WIN n.d.).

In focusing on changing gender relations, WIN argues that men per se are not the enemy (although they are frequently the instruments of oppression), and that it is men's obligation, as well as women's, to struggle to change gender relations so that neither women nor men are subordinated. In other words, WIN holds that the task of building a society in which nonegalitarian gender or class relations are an inherent impossibility (to use Alice Walker's phrase) is everyone's responsibility, not women's alone. Hence, as an organization that explicitly struggles to improve women's conditions, WIN is almost unique in the world in having male members who participate actively in the struggle against gender oppression. WIN sees feminism as a political position which is not tied to the ownership of particular genitalia, and recognizes that some men are good feminists, just as many women are not.

Women and men working together in the struggle has been one of WIN's strengths. It "purges men of their male chauvinism," as one male WINner put it, while at the same time providing support for the struggle against women's oppression, instead of being a drain on women's energies. Having men as active members is one way of dealing with the heavy demands on WIN. It is useful in devising strategies for mobilizing other men to support the principle of gender equality and to understand that women's liberation is a necessary part of the conditions for their own liberation. Men must recognize this as well as women, otherwise social liberation cannot be achieved. WIN provides a forum for working out relationships of equality between women and men in practice. Particularly in a context where, under pressure from religious fundamentalists, some sections of the state are moving towards sex segregation on the grounds that all relations between women and men are inherently sexual and immoral, unless they are married to each other. It is important to demonstrate that there can be camaraderie and solidarity between women and men working for a common cause particularly in a context in which strong foces are aligned against such a political stand.

Obstacles to WINning

Due to WIN's reputation as a radical organization, WIN continually faces the threat of state harassment. The state's reaction to WIN has been diverse. As mentioned above, elements of WIN's critiques and recommendations have sometimes been taken up by federal or state governments. More often, there have been subtle or not-so-subtle attempts to reorient WIN. There have been attempts at co-optation; for instance, the then-President's wife, Maryam Babangida, had asked to meet representatives of WIN and had tried to persuade them to join NCWS and support the government. They were given gifts of cloth and warned against public disclosure of the meeting. Bureaucratic obstacles have been placed in WIN's way. WIN has had problems in being registered; although the application was submitted many years ago and the organization has been the subject of several investigations by the police and security organizations. There are frequent attempts to exclude WIN from public platforms. For instance, unlike other women's organizations, WIN was not invited by the government to the African Development Bank conference on Women in Abuja in 1989, and was represented only because some WINners were known and had been invited as individual researchers by the ADB. And, most ominously, there were threats of incarceration to the WIN delegation to the UN Decade NGO conference, on the grounds that WIN had "denigrated Nigeria's public image abroad" by stating that women were oppressed and exploited in Nigeria.

Harassment does not only come from the state. At times, employers of WINners have threatened them with sanctions, blaming their WIN activities for "poor job performance." Similar amounts of time spent in religious activities or drinking alcohol is apparently no hindrance to performing work duties. While many partners of WINners sympathize, others do not; one WINner was told to leave her WIN ideas outside the door when she came home. Harassment also comes from groups opposed to WIN views. Following the publication of a newspaper article by a WINner on women's rights in Islam, copies of the offending issue were bought in bulk and burned, and the author was threatened with a similar fate.

The most important constraint is a lack of time and energy. Almost all WIN members work full-time, and most are also wives/mothers who do the additional labor of domestic work and childcare. The exigencies of the economic crisis have heightened the demands made on women's time (especially) in coping with everyday living. It is necessary to recognize that questions of lack of time and money are neither trivial nor merely an excuse. Nigeria is a large country and simply attending a meeting can mean spending a day traveling to the venue (over poor roads full of potholes), a day at the meeting (often lasting from early morning until past midnight in order to finish all the business), and a day traveling back. Africa is the continent with the poorest level of infrastructure. Organizing is not a matter of making calls on the telephone, which few people have and for which the charges have been increased by over 1,000 percent in the last few years. Fast or reliable postal communication does not exist. There is little public transport, and its cost, too, has more than quadrupled since 1985. Photocopying is prohibitively expensive, as are typesetting, access to computers, and a host of other facilities even when available at all. In the past few years, even paper has been in short supply and very expensive.

Since WIN insists on its autonomy, it suffers from a chronic shortage of money and facilities: no government subventions, no office, and no full- or part-time organizers. WIN raises money through membership fees, sale of publications, WIN T-shirts and the like, and grants for projects. Of course, this policy means that while there are some activities that funding sources are willing to support, such as academic conferences, agencies are wary of other kinds of activities, especially political mobilization and conscientization. This translates into fewer grants for WIN. Nonetheless, WIN has managed to continue its wide range of activities through two means. First, not only do WIN members give their commitment, time and energy, but they have frequently subsidized WIN activities out of their own pockets, above and beyond the payment of membership fees. Second, the wide national sympathy for WIN's work and worldviews has often meant that facilities such as meeting rooms, printing facilities, accommodation in people's homes for a night or two during a meeting, and typing services have been offered free or have been subsidized by institutions and individuals. With structural adjustment and increasing economic hardship, both of these sources are becoming increasingly constrained.

Issues for a WINning Future

Fourteen years after the first WIN conference, it is time to ask some hard questions. The first is: What has WIN achieved? I think that WIN has accomplished a great deal. Even critics of WIN acknowledge the organization's radical stance and its solid record in promoting women's interests and working-class or peasant interests, defending and pressing for the extension of democratic rights, taking on the state and other establishments when necessary, and working on campaigns, both generally and in individual cases. It has had considerable success in mobilizing women and men to work toward the eradication of discrimination and oppression. It has managed to hold major national conferences every year, and, in connection with this, to publish five books, a report, and a number of pamphlets. Its research has not only influenced academia, but has also been used to promote public awareness on issues of concern to women and sometimes been able to influence government policies. Increasingly, it has begun to facilitate women's organizing on issues they define as immediate. A small organization, with few material resources, operating in an increasingly severe economic and political climate, WIN has a reputation and has achieved certain gains beyond the proportion of its actual numbers.

The next question, and it has to be asked, is: Are WIN and its vision and concerns relevant for the next decade? I believe so. Thus far, WIN remains unique in its potential to mobilize and inspire women and men nationally, keeping the concern for gender equality in popular democratic struggles to change the nature of social relations. For some, a political position aimed at democratically transforming class and gender relations is no longer feasible with the collapse of the Soviet bloc and the so-called "end of ideology." This assumes that the Soviet bloc did, indeed, represent societies in which class exploitation and women's oppression had been, or were in the process of being eradicated. It assumes, too, that liberal democracy, as represented by the U.S., produces conditions in which there is no poverty, no exploitation, no racism, no sexism (a view that is manifestly false and one which WIN has never held). The Soviet Union may no longer exist, but systems of class, imperialist, and gender domination still prevail. And, now, more than ever, they require that a concerted struggle be waged against them.

The third question is: Do WIN's strategies, tactics, and modes of work remain appropriate in the present context. Here, I think that WIN needs to resolve two main issues. The most fundamental concerns the nature of WIN as an organization–is it a mass movement or a pressure and campaigning group? The second and related issue is whether and how WIN can cope with the increasing demands made on its decreasing resources. Before I discuss these two issues, I want to briefly raise a third–that of gender relations, and specifically the role of men within WIN.

Gender Relations in WIN

WIN is an organization for improving women's conditions and (among other things) providing a platform for women to speak. Simultaneously, it is an organization that has both women and men as members, and that believes that men have an equal responsibility to struggle for the end of gender oppression. There has sometimes been a tension between these two considerations. The instances in which this tension has been evident have been rare (i.e., times when most women WINners felt certain concerns were important, and most men WINners did not). I think it is significant that sexual harassment, violence against women, and domestic work have emerged as the major bone of contention within the group. All of these issues relate to entirely different gender experiences which are simulataneously mediated by class.

The crucial point of contention hinges on whether women, as an oppressed category, have the right to define their oppression–and, hence, the issues that are important to be dealt with and fought against–on their own (actual or potential) experience of it. Or, whether this right operates as a form of essentialism in which only the person with direct experience of that situation is believed to have access to that knowledge. I want to suggest that the charge of essentialism conflates two separate issues: the right of the oppressed to define what oppresses them: those who wear the shoe know best where it pinches; and the ways in which knowledge is developed: how to discover why the shoe pinches where and how it does and what to do about it. Oppressed groups have a right and necessity to say what it is they feel in defining their oppression, and which issues need to be dealt with. But felt oppression is not the privileged last word in the analysis of that oppression. Although analysis must draw on and transform experience from the empirical world (otherwise it is merely abstract idealism), a developed consciousness can reflect and analyze experience which is not immediately one's own, and produce knowledge about it admittedly, it is not *experiential* knowledge. Male WINners should stand by and concede positions or become passive supporters of survivors of abuse. Men can be political allies and be truly empathetic by arguing their positions, while recognizing and accepting that women *do* have something significant to say about the nature of their own oppression which must be taken seriously, and which can be neither dismissed nor belittled.

Mass WINning or WINning with the Masses?

Is WIN a mass organization or is it "a protest group, a campaign group, a vigilante group, an awareness group, and no more than that" (Amadiume 1990, 62)? One of the criticisms leveled against WIN is that it consists of middle-class women and men whose life conditions are far removed from the mass of peasant and working-class women for whom it claims to speak. The assessment has some degree of truth. In membership numbers (as a percentage of Nigeria's adult population), WIN is very small. The socioeconomic status of most members is not working-class or peasant. Many WIN members are not only in the tiny minority (less than 20 percent) of those who are literate in English, but also in, or have had, tertiary education. Yet WIN's orientation and policies have consistently focused on the interests of working-class and peasant women and men. And further, WIN is recognized as both pro-women and pro-"the masses." Working-class and peasant women (and, for that matter, men) approach WIN with individual or community problems with the confident expectation that WIN will take up their cases. These men and women do not see themselves as potential members, despite WIN's invitation to membership or its assistance in the successful resolution of problems. If we define "mass" as a numerically large membership or as membership consisting of people who are "grass-roots," it is fair to say that WIN is a mass-oriented organization, but not a mass organization.

WIN's ultimate aim is for the democratic transformation of the social relations of gender and class. To accomplish this goal WIN needs to have both widespread mass support as well as endorsement from mass organizations with access to power. There are too many examples, in Africa and elsewhere, in which small groups or individuals with radical mass orientations (initially, at least) have come to power, only to operate in such a way that the mass base is not empowered and comes to be repressed (as was the case in Ghana under Rawlings's second coming or in Burkina Faso under Campaore). WIN has resisted calls to turn itself into a party, vanguard or otherwise. It has also favored working as part of a broad coalition of mass-oriented, popular, and democratic organizations, rather than seeing itself as the sole "rightly-guided" organization. Both of these positions, I think, are healthy and should be continued.

"Grass-roots" women however, have demanded that WIN work more with them. During the political debate workshops in the mid-1980s, for instance, in many areas, women not only responded with great enthusiasm, but wanted to know why WIN had not come to them before. They demanded that WIN continue working with them. WIN has responded to this demand. The temptation to claim these as WIN branches should be resisted, however, unless all involved see themselves as participating WINners, not as mere recipients of WIN "help." Furthermore, as WIN activities have diversified, the membership of WIN and the beliefs of members have also broadened. For instance, some members appear to focus on short-term actions through project work to improve women's conditions, without much consideration for strategies to transform gender and class relations in the long run. Similarly, other members are not sensitive to the gender-specific oppression of women in, for example, violence against women, and want to prioritize class relations. Crucially, for all WIN branches, sufficient conscientization has to be done so that WIN's aims and objectives, as set out in the constitution, are accepted (see Appendix).

The process of conscientization should not be seen as automatically one-way. WIN's priorities may change in the process. Similarly, the objectives of struggle may diverge from the ways in which WIN has so far defined them. Such changes have happened before. The recommendation that 50 percent of all seats in legislative and executive bodies in Nigeria's government be reserved for women was not originally a WIN position (WIN n.d., 3). It was adopted because so many of the workshops during the political bureau debates recommended it. Groups of Igbo women argued for the recommendation as continuing a tradition of formal political power for women in the precolonial Igbo system. A group of Muslim women wanted it on the grounds that women should not be disbarred from power and decision-making; they felt that if places were not reserved for women, men would neither let them be nominated nor vote for them. Women who were Christian concurred. Yet others argued that simply asking for women to be represented would result in tokenism, but insisting on 50 percent would ensure that women had actual power and could not be ignored. Simultaneously, many aspects of the initial WIN position papers were discussed and adopted by the workshops' participants (WIN 1987).

And yet increasing the mass outreach of WIN, its facilitation of women's groups, the building of sustainable links with other organizations, the initiation of projects, the necessities of mutual conscientization have intensified the demands on WIN's already overstretched resources–in time and energy, in transport costs for meetings between often far-flung groups, of working in many different languages (hard enough to print in one, never mind four or five and more), and raising funds for projects. How can WIN cope with these ever-increasing demands?

WINning Resources and Dealing with the State?

One way of coping with declining resources, of course, would be to decrease the kinds of activity and narrow the focus of work. As I have made clear, WIN has a huge range of activities and foci of struggle. Yet one of WIN's characteristics has been its holistic approach, its recognition of the need for dealing with the immediate as well as the long-term, its concern for personal or individual cases as well as abstract and general campaigns. Which of WIN's modes of work could be discarded as less important?

The issue, then, is one of increasing WIN's resources. Raising money through the sale of WIN products is unlikely at present; when people are cutting back on food expenditure, they are unlikely to be able to buy books, T-shirts, and other such items. Raising membership fees is impossible for the same reason (and WIN already uses a sliding scale dependent on income).The likelihood of continuing to rely on free or subsidized facilities from sympathizers seems bleak. That leaves grants and donations as the only potential sources of funds. WIN is already moving in this direction by applying for grants to support the organization's operations as well as its projects, campaigns, research, meetings, and publishing activities.

WIN has always been aware that accepting funding, especially external funding, poses certain ideological dangers, namely the possible loss of autonomy and accusations of outside control. It has insisted, therefore, that grants be accepted only for those projects WIN has defined. WIN has also been careful to avoid creating "the cult of the personality," and has worked instead to enhance collective responsibility and decision-making by establishing executive committees of nominally equivalent secretaries, rather than hierarchies of presidents, vice-presidents, and so on. The collective chooses those who represent WIN at public events. And no one can voluntarily assume the role ofspokesperson. However, the politics of outside funding tend to reinforce inequalities in access to, and control of, resources given to the organization. How to avoid such dynamics in WIN is a topic that needs very careful consideration.

The hazard of relying on a single major source of funding (however sympathetic) also increases the likelihood of dependence. If WIN must seek funding, it should diversify the sources, even though that would mean a higher administrative workload in application and accounting procedures, and dealing with the notorious difficulties of the Nigerian bureaucracy, a typical catch-22 situation.

Another possible source of funding is the state, which in the past has offered a subvention through the National Women's Commission. The relationship of the state to WIN has varied enormously over the years, ranging from attempts to co-opt the organization or efforts to ignore and marginalize it to threats and harassment or attempts to "borrow" WIN's ideas. Throughout, WIN has been highly critical of the state but has kept its distance although it has continued to communicate its policy recommendations. Clearly, WIN has forced the state to pay more attention to women's politics. Fifteen years ago, the only body concerned with women's issues was the NCWS, which was not taken seriously then even by its own members. Today, there is at least verbal recognition of women's contributions at many levels of the state apparatus,and there are even some state-sponsored programs, such as "Better Life" and the Commission on Women. Now it is being argued that WIN should work both with the state and within it, not just criticize it.

What, in the contemporary context, should be WIN's policy regarding the state? Should WIN accept the N20,000 offered (as an annual subvention)? Are these programs actually improving women's conditions or do they amount to tokenism and "apartheid development" for women? Should WIN examine the programs and make recommendations as to how they could effectively work to improve women's positions, and work with the state to implement these changes? Can WIN work with these programs and still retain autonomy? Can we distinguish between different levels of the state (federal, state, local government) or between different programs (the National Commission, Better Life ...) or even between different states (Kano and Adamawa, for example) and decide that, in some instances, working with the government could open up opportunities for implementing WIN's aims and objectives, while in others they might not? What are the criteria that will enable us to judge whether working with the state will be ultimately useful or whether it will result in the co-optation ofWIN and WINners as passive government supporters?

The issue is not so much whether or not to accept a subvention, but under what conditions and what possible consequences. Working with the state can be useful—WIN accepted a grant from the state in 1986 through the Political Bureau for the workshops on Nigeria's socioeconomic and political future. Nonetheless, it should be remembered that this was for activities that WIN was already undertaking, at a moment in which the sphere of ideological debate was relatively open, and in an area where pressures to conform to the regime's interests were easily perceived and rejected. If accepting a subvention and working with state programs produces conditions that would mean curtailing WIN's autonomy, or inhibit its ability to criticize and work with other organizations for fundamental transformations of social relations in Nigeria, then should WIN continue to keep its distance from the state.

To return to the assessments of WIN quoted earlier, I would argue that Amadiume's assertion of a "lack of ideological self-definition" is not one of WIN's shortcomings. Although WIN has refused to label itself and, perhaps, is not easily categorized, its philosophy is clear to all. WIN's reputation for radicalism, fearlessness, and identification with the interests of women and "the masses" is deserved. It has consistently worked at mobilizing women and has worked with other organizations to change the structure of society, as Bryce, Awe, and Mba state. It is true nonetheless, that though increasing, WIN's mass outreach is still insufficient. WIN is now caught in the cleft of having to decrease its activities or rely on funding from the state—paths that WIN has eschewed in the past. Paradoxically, it is WIN's very success at being recognized as the organization that works at all levels for improving the conditions of *all* Nigerian women that has led to the current situation, in which higher levels of activity are constantly demanded of WIN, despite (or because of) an atmosphere that is increasingly repressive politically and harsh economically.

13

The Public/Private Mirage: Mapping Homes and Undomesticating Violence Work in the South Asian Immigrant Community

Anannya Bhattacharjee

In my work against domestic violence in New York, I have felt increasingly dissatisfied with the fact that much of this work is focused exclusively on the family home. Such a focus is consistent with the understanding that the mainstream battered women's movement in the U.S. has of domestic violence. Domestic violence is mainly understood within the parameters of gender inequality and the patriarchal family home. Such a formulation of domestic violence is directly linked to Western feminist theories of "private" and "public," terms that have been central to the analyses of violence against women (indeed, the general status of women).[1] "Private," in this context, has been understood as the patriarchal family home. Western feminists have established that for the collective condition of women to change, women must project their experiences of oppression in their private lives into the public. "Public," in this analysis, has been generalized as outside-the-family-home.

However, in my experience with immigrants in the South Asian community, I have found that "home," commonly accepted as the primary site of domestic violence, represents multiple concepts for people whose consciousnesses are shaped by migration. An analysis of the entire range of meanings of "home," as experienced by a South Asian immigrant woman, changes conventional notions of "private" and "public." It is my hope that what we learn from such an invesigation will help us redefine the parameters of our understanding of domestic violence work in the U.S.

In the following text, I begin by first examining the term "South Asian," the community within which this study is situated. Proceeding from there, I describe the conventionally understood concepts of public, private, state, and home in Western feminism because these are the concepts with which this essay engages. After this review, I map the multiple "homes," as experienced by South Asian immigrants and South Asian immigrant women. This mapping allows me to demonstrate the need to look at Western feminist theorizations of public, private, and state in new ways. In concluding, I point to possible opportunities for intervention from this perspective.

"South Asian" As Identity and As Community

The term "South Asia" refers most immediately to that area of the world which today contains countries such as Bangladesh, Bhutan, India, Nepal, Pakistan, and Sri Lanka. However, "South Asia" is a term that most people of South Asian origin do not automatically ascribe to themselves. Its specific use as a form of personal identity has mostly evolved recently among people who are working for social change within this community in the U.S. Whereas cultural or mainstream political organizations in the South Asian community in the U.S. define themselves around particular nationalities within South Asia, the progressive groups within this community often identify themselves and organize around the term "South Asia." It is important to examine this term, which has gained such currency among those South Asians who define themselves in terms that are opposed to the mainstream hegemonic (and often nationalist) sentiments.

I am by birth a Hindu and an Indian. I work extensively with the larger South Asian community, and I define myself as South Asian. The label's attraction for South Asians such as myself lies, to a large extent, in its ability to subsume more than one nation. It is thus seen by those skeptical of oppressive conditions of nationhood as something less rigid; it has little institutional authority (such as a flag or an embassy) and less solidified cultural homogeneity. In the competing ethnic realities of the United States, it is also a way to amass numbers.

However, I would like to sound a few cautionary notes here. In the United States, the term "South Asia" has been and still is used to describe a discipline of study within the university and carries Orientalist associations. Regional politics in South Asia also affect the way such an identity is received within the community. Pakistan and Bangladesh have a complicated history, and India has often been described as imperialist vis-à-vis its neighboring countries in South Asia. In this context, the phrase "South Asian," when used in reference to groups of activists composed predominantly of Indians without adequate representation from other South Asian nationalities, can convey overtones of domination and exclusion. Therefore, much as progressive groups would like to organize under an identity that goes beyond oppressive associations of nationhood, some South Asians may actually see their nationality as a positive means for distinction and identification.

I have described the Indian immigrant community in the U.S. at length in an earlier essay, but it is useful to summarize briefly some of those ideas here.[2] In that essay, I argued that the ideological force of the nation plays a dominant role in this immigrant community's construction of its identity. I found this to be consistent with the fact that the community members, who have the resources to construct actively this identity, belong predominantly to the male bourgeoisie, the creator of nations. The bourgeoisie in the South Asian community, upon displacement from the nation of its origin, finds itself represented in the form of an immigrant community in a foreign nation. Where once it had posited itself through a hegemonic process as the universal norm in the nation of its origin, it now perceives itself to be in a position defined by difference and subordination. The immigrant bourgeoisie's desire to overcome this condition and regain its power of self-universalization manifests itself in its projection of itself as the leader of the community, guarding and propagating the essence of national culture. It aligns itself with a nationalist spirit which involves learning Western technology and participating successfully in the U.S. economy while, at the same time, protecting the cultural and spiritual essence of the East. In the essay, I also noted that U.S. institutions describe Asian immigrants as the "model minority," and their encouragement of this community's economic success is based on their satisfaction with a group of people who are perceived to be conciliatory and motivated to succeed according to U.S. standards of success. A competitive relationship between different minorities, who vie with one another for "model" status, is thus set up, at the same time as they are seen to be distinct from the majority. Such a relationship impacts directly on the community's understanding of race relations in the U.S. This, briefly, is the kind of immigrant community in which I situate the discussion here.

In my experience, I have found the South Asian community in the U.S. to be lacking a sharp awareness and understanding of race relations. I find this to be dangerous, particularly when unity among peoples of color has become increasingly necessary in this age of neocolonialism, when covert imperialist policies of First-World countries such as the U.S. are difficult to see. South Asians, it seems, perceive Britain to be more clearly a colonizing power than the U.S. South Asian immigration to Britain (compared to the U.S.) has a longer history and arises directly out of Britain's history of colonization. The South Asian immigrant community in Britain has also been more working-class in character than its U.S. counterpart, although the composition of the community in the U.S. is changing. It is not possible to do an extensive comparison between South Asian immigration to the U.S. and to Britain in this essay, but I would like to note that the comparative histories of political activism in the two South Asian communities demonstrate that South Asians in Britain have a more radical experience and understanding of race relations than those in the U.S.

In response to the U.S. state's racialization of ethnic minorities, the South Asian community resists such categorization of itself. It tries to rescue the Caucasian elements that it imagines itself to possess. In her essay "Racist Response to Racism: The Aryan Myth and South Asians in the United States," Sucheta Mazumdar describes the popularity of the Aryan myth and its use by South Asians to prove that they are white. A representative letter in *India Abroad* (a publication targeting the immigrant East Indian community in the U.S.) illustrates well the community's ahistorical approach to race politics. In this letter, Kaleem Kawaja makes an easy comparison between U.S. immigration history, based on policies that promote the interests of the U.S. capitalist nation-state, and centuries of complex, pre-nation-state Indian history. He says, "From ancient times India welcomed people who came from outside, bringing their religions, their cultures and their practices, and tried to mingle them in the Indian soil. That is how today's rich multicultural Indian society has developed. In that respect there is a parallel with the U.S., where successive waves of immigrants have enriched America." In idealizing immigration from the Third World to the First World, Kawanga erases different histories in a single sweep in order to insist that the U.S. and India are, deep down, one and the same. The writer of the letter does not have to face up to the uncomfortable consequences of racial and ethnic discrimination in the here and now.

On the other hand, Dilip Hiro's description of Asian activism in *Black British, White British* shows at length the radical race politics ascribed to by South Asians in Britain. One example is the United Black Youth League, formed by South Asians who "planned to attract both Asian and West Indian youths, and function as a radical, revolutionary organization" (175). Another example that Hiro provides, illustrating the alliances between Asians and other people of color, is the Southhall Youth movement in 1982, which believed that "its political colour was black, the colour of the oppressed, which represented the social position of the Asian and Afro-Carribean peoples in Britain" (176). Similarly, the goals of the Indian Workers' Association (IWA) formed in 1938, prior to the independence and partition of India and Pakistan, demonstrate an understanding of different forms of oppression. Some of these goals were to "promote co-operation and unity with the trade union and labour movement in Great Britain; fight against all forms of discrimination based on race, colour, creed or sex" (139). These examples illustrate that Asian activism in Britain has a stronger working-class tradition and a commitment to antiracist struggles which allows for greater solidarity with oppressed peoples of color. As Mazumdar notes, in the U.S., "where the urban professional bourgeoisie still are numerically the larger group, it is too early to tell whether segments of the South Asians in the United States will . . . form similar alliances" (53).

This, then, is the South Asian community. I have described the term "South Asian" and the immigrant community at length because its shape and determination form the backdrop to the discussion that follows.

Conventional Mappings

Western feminism has made the separation between the private and public the focus of its debate and struggle, and the volume of Western feminist theorization about these concepts is great and varied. Catharine A. MacKinnon's *Toward a Feminist Theory of the State* is one influential and representative text in this debate on the home, the public, and the private. Since this essay deals with these same concepts, I present my argument as an engagement with MacKinnon's text.

The "private" that MacKinnon examines at length is defined by her as the patriarchal family home. She critically analyzes the privacy doctrine that maintains the separation of the private home from the public on the basis of "individual" (synonymous with "male") freedom in the private space: the "privacy doctrine is most at home at home, the place women experience the most force, in the family" (190–91). She adds that the "the core of privacy doctrine's coverage" is composed of "the very things feminism regards as central to the subjection of women—the very place, the body: the very relations, heterosexual: . . . and the very feelings, intimate" (193). This "private," MacKinnon sees to be opposed to the "public."

The "public" she describes is closely aligned with the liberal state. For example, "public," "government," and "state" are used almost synonymously in her text. She says, for instance,

> the idea of privacy embodies a tension between . . . *public* exposure or *governmental* intrusion . . . and . . . personal self-action. . . . To complain in *public* of inequality within the private contradicts the liberal definition of the private. In the liberal view no act of the *state* contributes to shaping its internal alignments or distributing its internal forces, so no act of the *state* should participate in changing it. (187–90, my italics)

Although she strongly disagrees with the separation of public from private in liberalism, she does not dispute that the public and private spaces *are* different and separate. The state as definitionally public—not private—is the underlying assumption of her argument. She continues to use "state" and "public" interchangeably in her analysis of the problem and in her suggested course of action. The consequences of these assumptions are what I want to analyze in this essay.

MacKinnon understands the power of the state to be "embodied in law, exist[ing] throughout society as male power at the same time as the power of men over women is organized as the power of the state" (170). Law is central to her exposition of state power because "[l]aw, as words in power, writes society in state form and writes the state onto society" (163). Her extensive analysis demonstrates that, contrary to the popular conception of the liberal state "as a neutral arbiter among conflicting interests," the state is a gendered entity (159). Her primary concern is contained in the questions she directs toward the state: "What in gender terms, are the state's norms of accountability, sources of power, real constituency? . . . Is the state constructed upon the subordination of women?" (161).

In light of the fact that definitions of "private" and "public" are critical to feminist theory and that feminist visions of social change involve intervening in these spaces, the importance of thoroughly understanding these spaces and their interactions and intersections cannot be overestimated. In this essay, I focus on South Asian immigrant women's experiences of domestic violence in the U.S. I do not do this so as to introduce yet another missing category into Western feminism's facile embrace of diversity or to include another special case in the feminist encyclopedia. Domestic violence allows me to focus on "home," and in turn map the multiple significations of "home" as experienced by immigrants and as constructed by the U.S. nation-state. This process illuminates the now-you-see-it-now-you-don't, mirage-like quality of spaces understood as public or private.

I choose the example of South Asian immigrant women because the current historical position of the South Asian immigrant woman in the U.S. is useful for the task of challenging conventional definitions of home, private, and public. The South Asian community in the U.S. is a relatively recent immigrant community. Even though its history in the U.S. goes back to the nineteenth century, it has begun to grow significantly only since the mid-twentieth century. In such a community, a South Asian immigrant woman's condition is marked by immigration, which has consequences for the purposes of this discussion. Due to the relatively recent history of immigration, "home" is not yet a solidified concept; it is in flux and still being negotiated. This provides us with an opportunity to see different spaces in formation. Through this discussion, I hope to show that the Western feminist assumptions of home, private, public, and the state are fundamentally questionable. This argument has implications not just for immigrant women but for all women because it calls for a rethinking of the basis of feminist formulations and activism.

Mapping Homes

Home appears to be defined at three different levels for immigrants. One definition is the (conventional) domestic sphere of the heterosexual and patriarchal family.[3] A second definition is as an extended ethnic community separate and distinct from other ethnic communities. The common application of the word "family" by particular communities to themselves is made possible by this definition. The third reference of "home" for many immigrant communities is to their nations of origin, often shaped by nationalist movements and histories of colonialism. These three definitions of "home" have to be examined in the light of migration from ex-colonized Third-World locations, such as South Asia, to the First World.

I want to situate my discussion of domestic violence and "home" in the context of this complex and contradictory history of Third-World immigration to the U.S. Domestic violence, in the heterosexual and patriarchal home, can involve physical, emotional, and sexual abuse. A woman can be denied food, money, adequate clothing, shelter, her right to see a doctor, and all that one may see as part of basic subsistence. She can be forced to live in isolation by her abuser, who can lock her up or instruct her not to answer the phone, thus denying her access to other community members. Isolation is one of the most severe forms of abuse in the home by a man against a woman, contributing to a battered woman's perception that her condition is uncommon and shameful. It is one of the primary ways in which a man makes sure that the woman's voice is never heard and that she remains dependent on him in every way.

Immigration laws are another means by which a man can control his wife in the home. Early U.S. immigration policies allowed only men to petition for their wives to accompany them into the country; women could not do the same. However, immigration activists point out that "[w]hile immigration law has since been changed and policy references are now gender neutral, it is the women who experience continued subjugation and vulnerability under their husbands" (Family Violence Prevention Fund, et al. IV-2). In the South Asian immigrant community, it is common for single men first to come to the U.S. on employment-based visas and later marry a woman from South Asia, or for married men to come here on employment-based visas, accompanied by their wives. In both cases, the woman is dependent on the man's sponsorship in order to obtain her legal immigration status through spouse-based visas. Her dependency on him during this process opens up opportunities for abuse because he knows that without proper status, the woman is, for all practical purposes, nonexistent in the U.S.

Women comprise the majority of applicants for spouse-based visas (FVPF et al. V-18). According to the laws governing spouse-based visas, the woman, when sponsored by her spouse, gets conditional residency status in the U.S. at first. This status becomes permanent only after two years, when she proves to the immigration authorities that she entered into the marriage in "good faith."[4] "Good faith" means that the beneficiary (often a woman) entered into the marriage with the intention of building a family and not for immigration benefits. Thus, a woman's primary motivation, presumably, should be familial commitment to the man she marries, not legal status for herself. She must demonstrate her "good faith" with wedding photographs and invitations, official documents, and oral narratives proving that they have lived together as a "proper" married couple and that they did not marry for immigration benefits. In other words, she has to prove the *nonexistence* of immigration reasons.[5]

This procedure has two implications. One is that the beneficiary is under suspicion of immigration fraud until proven innocent, thus further propagating the image of woman as untrustworthy. This is reminiscent of immigration policies of the late 1800s, which,

> in essence, assumed that all "Oriental" females seeking to immigrate to California were doing so in order to engage in "criminal and demoralizing purposes" [such as prostitution]. This . . . gave the immigration commissioner the right to determine whether the incoming woman was "a person of correct habits and good character." (Sucheta Mazumdar *Making Waves* 3)

The second implication is that the absence of immigration-related motives on the beneficiary's part is enough to establish the "good faith" of the marriage. The motives of the *petitioner* (often a man), though they need not be immigration-related, are not examined. Perhaps he married her to get free domestic help or a free sex partner. Questions regarding such issues are not asked.

Furthermore, it is quite common for a man, on whom the woman is dependent for legal status, to withhold his sponsorship of her even for the conditional (temporary) residency status. In such circumstances, a woman, who perhaps initially came to the U.S. on a different visa following her marriage, with the understanding that her husband would sponsor her once she was here, could easily become undocumented as her short-term legal status expires.

As is well-known, undocumented women are a growing population in the U.S. In order to provide women in these vulnerable positions with some rights and to enable them to regain their legal status, immigrants' rights groups pushed Congress to pass a crucial provision within the Violence Against Women Act that would dramatically help immigrant women.[6] This provision is meant to relieve a woman's dependency on her husband for sponsorship by allowing her to petition for herself, in the event of his refusal and abusive behavior. However, some senators expressed concern about possible misuse of the provision by women who, in "bad faith," may falsely claim to be battered in order to be able to self-petition. Their concern is ironic because other bills which provide far more dangerous opportunities for misuse (often by state agencies themselves) frequently get approved. Misuse of any legislation is always a possibility. But, when it comes to an act that will greatly benefit undocumented immigrant women, exceptions rather than the rule are cited to argue against it.

Yet, very little is said about the "bad faith" of the sponsor, often a male

U.S. resident or citizen, who is refusing to petition. When the husband does not file a petition, he is not held accountable. Such a marriage becomes unstable as the woman is undocumented and subject to deportation, which would, of course, destroy the family. The sanctity of the marriage at that point is not upheld.

At first, the "good faith" argument seems to be based on concern for the immigrants' marriage and family. However, this perception gets dispelled when one realizes that there is no real support for the immigrant woman's right to self-petition and remain legally with her family. What this demonstrates is that the sanctity of the family is selectively respected by the nation-state. Feminists such as MacKinnon see the state, organized around male power and expressed in law, as that which remains conveniently out of private homes. It appears, however, that for immigrant homes, the state can hardly be accused of inaction–if anything, it is actively involved in determining the very existence of the family.

Western feminists also stress the importance of projecting the private into the public so that women can have public recourse. MacKinnon asserts that the public is constituted by laws and judicial process and that ultimately it is possible to remake this space on the basis of feminist jurisprudence. Implicit is the assumption of the existence of available public spaces, to intervene in and transform. In this discussion, the domestic worker, as a worker (often a woman) in a family home, is significant because one sees that the family home can actually be a public space. But its publicness is of no avail to those who are not official members of the public. The condition of the domestic worker overturns a lot of conventional ideas regarding the private and the public.

Domestic workers are primarily poor immigrant women. They may be either undocumented or, in some rare instances, sponsored by their employers for employment visas. In either case, they may face severe abuse from their employers, and their situation is often similar to that of the battered wife. The employer may deny her sponsorship or hold the power to do so over her. She is extremely vulnerable to all forms of abuse, often works around the clock, and may be denied basic subsistence. She, too, can face complete isolation as her employer can control her movements much like a husband controls those of a battered wife.

> The domestic helper is one of the most, if not the most, vulnerable and marginalized among migrant workers. The work is menial and the live-in-arrangement ensures that she is at the beck and call of the employer virtually 24 hours a day. The job demands submission and servility. As a foreigner coming from a poor country, she is in a constant state of powerlessness. (Gina Alunan, *Women on the Move* 53)

This parallel between the domestic worker and the battered wife is particularly relevant to my discussion in this essay because, in the family home, the domestic worker is a worker and the battered woman is a spouse. The former is commonly perceived to be a part of that "public" space, the workplace, and the battered wife is a part of that very "private" space, the home. The "private" home is the domestic worker's workplace (that which is considered "public"): her "public" workplace is her "home" (that which is considered "private"). Her immigration status, which is usually contingent upon an employment-based visa for unskilled workers, makes a private slave of her (almost as does a spouse-based visa), and she is usually isolated from other workers even though her kind of workplace employs many like her (employers disregard or are often ignorant of the fact that labor laws, such as they are, do actually apply to domestic workers). I think her condition illustrates the contradictory, multiple, and shifting definitions of the "private" and the "public," and reveals their construction to be largely imaginary. One sees here the innumerable ways in which what is presumably "public" becomes "private," and what is presumably "private" becomes "public."

In MacKinnon's analysis, a woman's status as a legally recognized member of the public is taken for granted. What remains for feminist jurisprudence is to assert this status better through public (synonymous with state) recourse. However, what remains unexplored is the very ideology of nationhood that forms the basis of the public in a nation-state, that body of people bound together within national boundaries.

By leaving out nationhood, it is possible for MacKinnon to talk about state machinery that is not necessarily tied to a bounded space and people. But bringing nationhood into the discussion immediately introduces the notion of a space to be defended and bounded: in fact a *private* space.

The absence of analysis of the nation-state in U.S. mainstream feminism leads to the uncritical and automatic assumption of a public whose subject, then, is a U.S. citizen. The process of immigration, which has played a singularly significant role in carving out the U.S. nation-state, is erased, and we see a nation that has always been here, from time immemorial. I am reminded of Benedict Anderson's statement about how "nations to which [nation-states] give political expression always loom out of an immemorial past, and, still more important, glide into a limitless future. It is the magic of nationalism to turn chance into destiny" (11–12).

Immigration laws have *privatized* the nation; it is now a bounded space into which only some of the people can walk some of the time. A man's control over his wife or an employer's control over the domestic worker in the home extends to controlling her recognition as a member of what constitutes the public—in this case, being a legal resident of a national community (in itself a private concept). This control is encouraged by the legal structures (such as immigration laws) of a so-called public (but, in a crucial sense, private) space, the U.S. nation. The figure of the undocumented woman, who is an "illegal alien," however, is a reminder of the not-public—that is, private—basis of the nation-state. Family home, then, is not the only unambiguously private space, and public recourse can only be, in the final analysis, a mirage for a feminism that does not recognize the privateness of the national public.

The nation-state's control over its population comes into focus when, as we have seen, the beneficiary is singled out for the "good faith" test, which seems to suggest that in the eyes of the "nation," motives based on immigration are deemed worse than other motives on the part of the petitioner, such as a desire to acquire free labor or mail-order brides. Thus, whereas conditionally admitted individuals (the beneficiaries, who are obviously not part of the "public") must demonstrate their "good faith" in order to be worthy to reside legally on U.S. soil, the petitioners and the "public" need not demonstrate their "good faith" as sponsors committed to abuse-free families. Again, in the case of the domestic worker, her position is defined by U.S. immigration law as an "unskilled" worker. This categorization puts the availability of legal status almost outside her reach; she is low on the priority list for becoming part of the "public" even though her intensely exploited labor contributes significantly to the nation that will not open its actually private space to her.

Nicos Poulantzas points out that in the capitalist state, "everyone is free and equal before the law [based on bourgeois juridical axiom] on condition that he is or becomes a bourgeois. And that, of course, the law at once allows and forbids." (90) In the context of this essay, women of "bad faith" and "unskilled" workers fall outside bourgeois notions of citizenship. Immigration policies of the host country, in their power to define the (non)existence/(il)legality of individuals, can make invisible, for all practical purposes, large sections of the population. As Chandra Mohanty has noted, "Citizenship and immigration laws are fundamentally about defining insiders and outsiders." ("Cartographies" 24).

A second kind of "home" is the ethnic community. South Asian immigrants see their community as an extended "family," separate and distinct from other ethnic communities. The immigrant community sees itself, in all its specific ethnicity, as a private space, within which it must guard its own national heritage against intervention from mainstream U.S. cultural practices. These definitions of national heritage are anchored in ideas of womanhood, as interpreted by the guardians of tradition.[7] However, the very fact that U.S. immigration laws control the composition of the ethnic community indicates the publicness of this space (which is seen as private by the immigrant residing in it). Here, I use the term "publicness" to refer to the crafting of the community through immigration laws that follow the dictates of an appropriate public in the *private* U.S. nation.

In the United States, immigration policy has been "the domestic reflection of United States foreign policy and the expression of industry's needs for labor to produce and compete in domestic and international markets" (FVPF et al. IV-1). Asian immigration began in the nineteenth century with the migration of Chinese laborers, only to be followed by the Chinese Exclusion Act of 1882, a result of labor fights between white Americans and Chinese immigrants. Subsequent Japanese migration then began, again leading to legislation barring Asian immigration for decades after 1917. However, as a result of a labor shortage in the U.S., Filipino immigration was encouraged from 1910 to 1934, after which, Filipinos were also excluded.[8] Legislation such as the National Origins Quota Acts of 1921 and 1924 were passed to "preserve the northern- and western-European character of the population in the United States" (FVPF et al. IV-4). It is not surprising to learn that in keeping with the use of immigration policies to control labor markets, these same policies also served to "deport those who asserted their labor and political rights" (FVPF at al. IV-5).[9] This is the kind of state intervention that Nicos Poulantzas refers to as being sometimes necessary and strategic in a capitalist economy, although such intervention is still dictated by the "*general* coordinates of the reproduction of capital" (181). The state executes such functions, because if they are done directly by capital, they could heighten internal crisis and deepen contradictions, circumstances that would jeopardize capital itself. Thus, immigration laws of the U.S. state, as they set about carving quotas for specified immigrants, fulfill the needs of the free market in the U.S. capitalist economy.

In the Asian community, U.S. immigration laws are mainly employment-based and they encourage professional bourgeois, conservative, and predominantly male immigration, thus leading to a homogenized idea of the community as economically successful.[10] U.S. legislation that punishes undocumented or "illegal aliens" and sets standards for determining the appropriateness of candidates for naturalized citizenship further motivates the "model" immigrant community to dissociate itself from all those that it sees as "undesirable."[11] Those considered to be undesirable could be the undocumented, gays and lesbians, low-income people, and those on public assistance. In this context, a battered woman, who often derives her class and legal status from her husband, may potentially move to an "undesirable" status if she decides to leave her marriage. For a woman from a low-income family, leaving the marital home may plunge her into further obscurity.

At the same time that U.S. laws actively construct immigrant communities, U.S. institutions can *selectively* display "respect" for the privacy of an immigrant's "home" culture, in the sense of an "authentic" culture to be found in its pure form in a distant country of origin. This again demonstrates the confusion surrounding definitions of the "public" and "private." The critical role that conceptions of womanhood play in such "authentic" definitions of cultures and the dangerous implications of such conceptions for a South Asian woman can be seen in the following incidents. In my work on domestic violence, I have done workshops with counselors and teachers of public schools in South Asian neighborhoods in New York, and I have talked extensively to young South Asian women. Guidance counselors in such schools have told me about their experiences regarding young South Asian girls who are taken out of public schools by their fathers to get married early. The father, projecting himself as the protector of his daughter's sexuality, often justifies his decision on the basis of the "home" country's cultural norms. In such cases, the school personnel are hesitant to speak up because, as they have told me, they are fearful of appearing disrespectful of the immigrants' national cultures. Here, the father's judgment of cultural norms is accepted with a certain amount of "good faith" in spite of U.S. laws regarding education and marriage. In this context, school personnel see immigrant national culture as "private," even though U.S. laws carry clear guidelines for education of young people. Thus, as "public" officials working with the "public" (in this case, the young girl), they hesitate to cite U.S. legislation specifically meant for the "public" in the United States that ensures the young immigrant girl's right to education.[12] In this instance, the privacy of an immigrant's national culture is privileged over a young girl's legislated right to education.

Yet, when, as it happened in a real case, a student refuses to stand up during the singing of the American national anthem (since he or she is probably bewildered by this allegiance assumed of him or her), teachers are inclined to worry about the student's inability to conform, to start making phone calls, and to call a meeting with the parents. In this instance, "public" officials in the school find it possible to uphold the public norm of showing respect for the United States anthem, a symbol of the nation-state. But they do not appear anxious about the privateness of the immigrants' allegiance to their home country's national anthem.

Whether the ethnic community is a private or a public place appears to shift and change. In either case, the woman concerned continues to experience marginalization. The ethnic community, as a private space and a second home in which the immigrant community guards its national heritage and cultural values, is oppressive for women, who often serve as the instruments for such safekeeping. In such a community, a battered South Asian woman potentially faces denial of her abusive condition. On the other hand, the battered woman who leaves her abuser faces possible loss of "model" status and risks her standing as an appropriate member of the community, in part because this community occupies a public space policed by U.S. federal laws. Her status often falls outside desirable categories, economically, culturally, and politically. Here again, we see the limitations of Western feminist analysis of public space as a space of recourse and as a zone automatically lying outside an easily and singularly recognized "home."

The nation of origin, the third meaning of "home" for immigrants, is viewed as containing the true principles of their essential national heritage.

These are the principles which the South Asian community seeks to preserve in the foreign country. In such nationalist ideologies of the home countries, "woman" has been an instrument for the founding principles. As Sangari and Vaid point out, "The recovery of tradition throughout the proto-nationalist and nationalist period was always the recovery of the 'traditional' woman—her various shapes continuously readapt the 'eternal' past to the needs of the contingent past." (10) "Woman" has been defined in the crossfire of colonial accounts and Indian male nationalist accounts as each tried to assert its role in protecting "womanhood," a concept that is almost synonymous with the nation itself.

In the South Asian immigrant community, the leaders of the community (predominantly male and wealthy) often invite "cultural/religious experts" from South Asia to come to the U.S. to impart their expertise and to lend authenticity to transplanted cultural activities. In the case of India, these "experts" are mainly of a Hindu, Brahmanical tradition—that is, from the dominant cultural tradition. A consequence of such an essentialized definition of "home" is a homogenization of national culture and, in fact, the provision of immense support for the most vociferous and exclusionary South Asian organizations on issues of "national heritage." Within national histories of South Asia, movements for social change—such as the women's movement or the gay and lesbian movement—are largely unacknowledged.

In the wake of communal violence in South Asia, this is an especially dangerous phenomenon. The parallels one sees among the organizing strategies of Hindu fundamentalist organizations in India and those found among dominant Hindu and Indian cultural organizations and institutions in the U.S. are not accidental. Tanika Sarkar describes the organizing strategies of the RSS (Rashtriya Swayamsevak Sangh, or National Volunteer Corps), an organizaton that has supported attempts by the VHP (Vishwa Hindu Parishad, or World Hindu Council) and the BJP (Bharatiya Janata Party, or Indian People's Party) to create a monolithic Hindu nation.[13] She notes, in particular, the effectiveness of the organizing principles of the RSS, which "calls itself a family." (31) Organizations such as the VHP, which also has counterparts in the United States, see themselves as the keepers of the national culture of a Hindu India. They have been responsible for a resurgence of religious fundamentalist forces and for the politicization of religion both in South Asia and in the immigrant communities in the U.S. In her essay "Compu-Devata: Electronic Bulletin Boards and Political Debates," which deals with fundamentalist discourse in electronic mail (e-mail), S. Sudha objects to the fact that groups in the U.S. (such as student organizations) are sponsored through "financial backing and guidance by VHP members who hold camps and training sessions." The goals of these groups include "re-interpretation of Indian history from a Hindu perspective, and presentation of current events from the viewpoint of the Hindu nationalists." (6) The means "to achieve these goals include study groups and a series of widely publicized VHP-organized conferences." (7) These organizations, because of their self-appointed roles as custodians of the national heritage, have particularly strong appeal in the immigrant communities of the U.S. Their presence is especially ominous as their activities are legitimized under the honorable banner of preserving one's culture for one's children. In the Indian, Hindu portion of the community, one can often see the connections between priests in temples, the leaders of the most wealthy Indian (predominantly Hindu) cultural organizations in the U.S., and the leaders of the Hindu fundamentalist parties in India. These links are well-illustrated by the example of a "respectable" man who is a part of the leadership in a Hindu temple in New York City and conducts marriages and religious festivals for the community. He is also part of the leadership of an umbrella Indian cultural organization in the U.S. that has held benefit dinners to honor leaders of the Hindu fundamentalist party in India. Such a figure highlights the links between the guardians of national culture (as leaders of religious institutions are often seen to be), the financial strength of such guardians (as members of well-funded cultural organizations), and the political leadership (demonstrated by political leaders whom the guardians recognize and honor). What we see here is a clear collusion between money and cultural and political leadership intricately woven into the fabric of the community.

As the above discussion about the multiple "homes" of an immigrant demonstrates, women are in danger of being made invisible in all three "homes" known to them as immigrant women in the United States. Women who are silenced in the heterosexual and patriarchal home are often afraid to leave this home as they face nonrecognition outside it, in the other homes. If they are undocumented (when their spouses refuse to file a petition), they face invisibility in the U.S. with regard to the state, and subsequently, within the immigrant community. At the same time, they also fear rejection and nonrecognition back in their home countries as well as in the extended family of the immigrant community, where a homogeneous and essentialized definition of national culture leads to dismissal or rationalization of abuse against women.

Undomesticating Violence Work

For immigrant women, work against domestic violence has to be seen as global—not only because domestic violence affects women everywhere but also because the parameters of *each* immigrant woman's experience of domestic violence spans the patriarchal home, the community, the host nation, and the nation of origin. Attention to the global parameters of an immigrant woman's experience helps us to contextualize the conventionally accepted spaces of private and public and to show that an unnuanced belief in social change through intervention in public spaces is an illusion; there are no such unambiguous spaces to be labelled "public" or "private." By tracking the private and the public spaces through this essay, I have shown the shifting grounds of both and thus in the process problematized common perceptions of the "public" and the "private."

As shown above, the immigration ideology of the U.S. nation-state controls the composition of immigrant communities within its boundaries. It selectively secures the status of immigrant families and intervenes in their memories as they define their "original" heritage. The immigration policy of a nation-state is more than legal language and dry quota numbers. Behind these surface details lie a whole worldview and a comprehensive approach to global politics. However, mainstream domestic violence organizations often lack a rigorous understanding of the *system* of immigration. Their leadership has primarily consisted of U.S. citizens, for most of whom the system of immigration, *on the surface*, appears not to have immediate relevance. In situations where mainstream organizations do know about immigration laws, they still lack an understanding of the *ideology* of immigration. Mohanty refers to this sort of lack in mainstream feminism in her assertion that

> (white) feminist movements in the West have rarely engaged questions of immigration and nationality . . . analytically these issues are the contemporary metropolitan counterpart of women's struggles against colonial occupation in the geographical third world. In effect, the construction of immigration and nationality laws, and thus of appropriate racialized, gendered citizenship, illustrates the continuity between relationships of colonization and white, masculinist, capitalist state rule ("Cartographies" 23).

Often, the mainstream feminist understanding of immigration, while liberal and well-meaning, is grounded in confused notions about ethnic pluralism and cultural sensitivity. Mainstream domestic violence agencies acknowledge the presence of "minorities" by providing their staffs with multicultural workshops. A new term that is increasingly being used to describe immigrants is "New Americans." The term is seen to compensate for the negative connotations that the word "immigrant" signifies in the current anti-immigrant climate.[14] The term "New Americans" is supposed to evoke images of immigrants going through temporary adjustments in a transitional process, after which they will be like other Americans. Such a view, needless to say, not only homogenizes an entire nation but also leaves out people, such as those that I have described in this essay, for whom legal status is well out of reach.

Immigrant women from the Third World in the United States see difference as more complicated than "temporary" variation in food, clothing, and language. For immigrant women, Cheryl Johnson-Odim's comment in another context is appropriate. She points out that women's progress

> is not just a question of . . . equal opportunity between men and women, but the creation of opportunity itself; not only the position of women in society, but the position of the societies in which Third World women find themselves (320).

Immigrant women working against domestic violence must necessarily traverse all the different spaces of "home." It is not enough to fight the abuse in the family home alone. It is also necessary to fight the violence inherent in the community's use of the figure of the woman to construct its identity, and in its summoning up of essentialized and elitist national culture. It is important to fight the way definitions of the immigrant family, the immigrant community, and immigrants' national heritage conveniently work toward creating a privatized U.S. nation-state based on oppression. Domestic violence work, by its very focus on "home," is radical in that it challenges the foundations of hegemonic and well-entrenched systems. The multiple definitions of home, as set out above, signal the potential challenge for domestic violence work to be carried out through the most rigorous and broad investigation of and intervention in hegemonic social processes. Such an understanding enriches the work against domestic violence and opens up possibilities for building alliances. However, such a status is not usually granted to domestic violence work. Work around domestic violence is often itself *domesticated* as social service.

The battered women's movement's absorption of the full implications of globalizing and undomesticating domestic violence work is constrained in practice by the historical realities of domestic violence work in the U.S. The domestic violence movement in the U.S. aspired to develop on the basis of feminist analysis and "most of the early shelters were begun by feminists or women who were able to work within a feminist framework" (Nicarthy et al. 13). However, as Diane Mitsch Bush observes,

> the original emphasis of the battered women's movement on empowerment of women by shifting responsibility for violence from the woman to the perpetrator and locating his actions in a patriarchal power structure was lost as many shelters and their goals became institutionalized (Bush 587–608).

At this time, the movement has settled relatively comfortably into an institutional and professional pattern that predictably replicates itself across the United States. The subordination of feminist analysis to social service has distanced the battered women's movement from giving attention to the structural or systemic aspects of domestic violence.

However, I question whether it is sufficient for the battered women's movement to align itself simply again along a Western feminist framework, given that such a framework for understanding "home," "private," and "public" leaves certain fundamental assumptions unsatisfactorily analyzed or explored. To return to the example of MacKinnon, she discusses at length the problems with a private ideology that prohibits women from collectively sharing one another's experiences by projecting their private oppression into the public, and thus cuts off their ability to seek state support to end such oppression (193). MacKinnon has argued against the misguided notions of state inaction in the private realm. She finds inaction to be an acceptance by default of the male point of view, and she calls for active feminist jurisprudence among feminists in the United States. She believes that "[t]he law of equality, statutory and constitutional, ... provides a peculiar jurisprudential opportunity, a crack in the wall between law and society"(244). Equality, according to her, will require not state abdication, but state intervention, although according to the terms of feminist jurisprudence (249). But MacKinnon's definition of the state remains reified, primarily legislative, and therefore uncritically "public." She envisions intervention through the eyes of a U.S. citizen who is a (white) woman and definitely part of the public.

Some Western feminists, such as Zillah Eisenstein, have, however, contributed toward establishing the complexity of the situation for people of color. For example, in *Color of Gender,* Eisenstein questions the abstract figure of the individual with universal rights and rethinks democracy by replacing this figure with the concrete body of the pregnant woman of color. Feminists like Aida Hurtado have also pointed out that

> ... white feminist theory has yet to integrate the facts that for women of Color race, class, and gender subordination are experienced simultaneously and that their oppression is not only by members of their own group but by whites of both genders." (839)

Referring back to women's struggles in the nineteenth century in the U.S., Hurtado points out the difference between white suffragists who were married to prominent white men and black women activists who were "at birth *owned* by white men"(841, emphasis in original). She reminds the reader that white abolitionists did not want to give citizenship rights to slaves (839). The analysis here is made with great clarity with regard to race. But, although her point is well-taken, Hurtado's comments remain confined within an unanalyzed nation-state. She indicates the desirability of obtaining citizenship but does not question the exclusionary basis of citizenship itself. However, the figure of the immigrant is a reminder of the oppressive system of exclusion by which some are more citizenlike than others in a private nation that crafts its identity opportunistically according to the needs of its labor market. Citizenship in nation-states is, by definition, a privatized and selective concept; no matter how broadly defined, oppressions remain inscribed in its grain.

Hurtado asserts that white women have focused on making the personal political because they have always had a space that is personal or private. According to her, "Women of Color have not had the benefit of the economic conditions that underlie the public/private distinction." The consciousness of women of color stems from an awareness that the public is *personally* political. Thus, while white women struggle to project private-sphere issues into the public, feminists of color focus instead on public issues. Hurtado describes "Women of Color" as more concerned with public issues such as "affirmative action . . . prison reform . . . voter registration . . . issues that cultivate an awareness of the distinction between public policy and private choice" (850). Hurtado refers to the state as a body that women of color struggle with frequently but, again, her argument lacks a self-conscious and critical analysis of the public/private split and the nation-state.

MacKinnon's exhortation to project the private into the public and Hurtado's emphasis on the public being personal both rely on the underlying assumption that spaces can be identified as private or public in relationship to a nation and a state. As my discussion has shown, there are no such clearly definable spaces. Thus, working for change in commonly perceived public spaces (which feminists like Hurtado and MacKinnon advocate) without examining the national bases of such definitions is ultimately shortsighted and reformist. The oppression that undergirds the so-called public (actually private) space is left intact. As long as that happens, change through the public space can only remain an illusion.

It is useful at this point to consider another conception of state put forth by Poulantzas, while keeping in mind that, for him, class relations remain primary and he pays little attention to other parallel forms of oppression. In *State, Power, Socialism,* Nicos Poulantzas moves away from unambiguously equating the state with repression and ideology because he finds that approach to be too simplistic. Such an approach makes the power of the state appear as only negative, overlooking the positive power of the state in creating and making reality. There is no room, in such a case, for understanding both the repressive and the enabling functions of the state. Instead, he suggests that we look at power relations as being primarily made up of social struggles, and he notes that these relations define the state itself; it cannot be understood as autonomous and separate from them (44-45). He describes the state as the "*material condensation* of a relationship of forces among classes and class fractions" (129). Class contradiction, he notes, is the very stuff of the state.

Like Hurtado and MacKinnon, Poulantzas does not adequately describe the public space. However, his description of the private does acknowledge the active role of the state in selectively creating such spaces. He explains:

> the individual-private is not an intrinsic obstacle to state activity, but a space which the modern State constructs in the process of traversing it. . . . For it is not the "external" space of the modern family which shuts itself off from the State, but rather the State which, at the very time that it sets itself up as the public space, traces and assigns the site of the family through shifting, mobile partitions." (72).

This description of state activity is more attentive to the full complexity of the relationship between private, public, and state than MacKinnon's view of the state as problematically inactive in the private realm because of the dictates of the privacy doctrine.

Instead of a pyramidal structure of state power, Poulantzas sees a network of intersecting powers. Poulantzas's definition of the state has the advantage of discerning state power to be a permeating network of power relations that is not limited only to the conventionally recognized state apparatus. This has immediate significance for resistance because it marks out the opportunities for intervention to be multiple. Thus, the ultimate goal of resistance is not occupying the summit of state power from where state laws can be remade, but rather the overturning of dominance in the network of power relations.

In this essay, I have explored and extended the scope of looking at "home," not to point to larger and better spaces than the family "home," but in order to enable us to think about spaces in a new way. Understanding the historical basis for spaces being declared private or public enables us to seize those opportunities for intervention that fundamentally overturn the opportunistic and oppressive bases of such declarations. Instead of being seduced or hindered by spaces perceived as public or private, we need to be vigilant against their miragelike quality. Only by thoroughly and fundamentally understanding their constructions can we hope to change them.

Organizing Through and Around Home

Organizations working for social change in the South Asian community continually wrestle with questions about their own legitimacy in regard to the multiple "homes" of the immigrant. At the same time, these very same organizations, which challenge the status quo in the multiple "homes," are also in a position to redefine "home." In this position, the organizations need to be self-reflexive about the new definitions they are setting out to establish. They need to ask themselves: who comprises the organizations that create these spaces that are sometimes called "home"; who is excluded from them; and what is the price of maintaining them.

For example, in Sakhi for South Asian Women, the organization with which I have been working, questions about whether Sakhi is located inside or outside the "community" have been important—especially so in the early years of its history.[15] Discussions within the initial group of women in Sakhi would point out that, as individuals, we were not significantly active in mainstream cultural organizations and practices and, as a consequence, Sakhi's position could be easily challenged by mainstream voices in the community. This group was comprised of Indian, Hindu, professional women. But the South Asian women who have contacted Sakhi for information and assistance come from very diverse backgrounds with regard to nationality, religion, class, and educational background. One of our highest priorities and most difficult tasks has been the expansion and diversification of the organization's base and leadership through the inclusion of just the sort of women who approach Sakhi for assistance.

As Sakhi's base began to grow, we actively began to reclaim and assert what has always been true—Sakhi is a community, a "home." However, I feel it is also our responsibility to continually redefine such a home lest it solidify into an oppressive and exclusionary space. Even as Sakhi strives to bring together South Asian women, questions of diversity, political beliefs and decision-making must remain ever open. It is crucial, though difficult, to balance two forces: being united by certain issues, and recognizing that unification is an evolving process and must not become a remaking of oppressive alliances. For example, issues of class or sexual orientation, as introduced into the organization by its expanding composition of women, make it increasingly necessary for women from various class backgrounds or with different sexual orientations to understand the need for different kinds of alliances. It is easy for those who share a certain upbringing and culture to exclude—if not deliberately then unconsciously—those who do not share their backgrounds. In spaces under siege, such as a women's organization or a workers' rights' organization, it is especially tempting to fall into the trap of making alliances that exclude on grounds other than political, as exclusion always makes those within feel safer together. Only through continual self-reflection can one avoid this trap.

My reason for analyzing "home" and uncovering the public/private mirage is so that we, as feminists, can understand and think about these concepts in new and enabling ways. However, even as I show that these definitions need to be fundamentally questioned, we continually succumb to commonly perceived and pernicious notions of home. For example, in my experience of working against domestic violence, we rarely step into the home of the heterosexual, patriarchal family itself. We find ourselves working around the home but never within it. Even in our most radical moments, it is a space we cannot enter, as it is sacred and private. When a woman is at home with her abuser (her spouse), we cannot approach her. Only when she leaves her marital home can we openly approach her. It is that sense of respect for that "sacred" space we call home, and the fear that it inspires, that continues to haunt us in our work.

By demonstrating that spaces hitherto imagined as being opposite to home can display characteristics typical of home and vice versa, this essay takes a step towards rethinking spaces, imagining action in new ways, and committing itself to a thorough investigation of common perceptions of private and public. I would like to conclude by returning to the domestic worker, whose anomalous position makes it possible for us to see spaces in a different way. By including domestic workers as part of the domestic realm, one comes to see the home as a workplace bearing the resonances of publicness rather than privateness. At the same time, we are forced to realize the limitations of public spaces within which a worker, who is undocumented and "unskilled," remains invisible. Interestingly enough, U.S. labor laws do cover undocumented workers; these laws specify only that their subject is a "worker," and say nothing about his or her immigration status. However, for all practical purposes, the undocumented domestic worker remains invisible and fearful, unprotected by other U.S. laws, demonstrating once again the ideological power of citizenship and nationhood regardless of particular pieces of legislation.

Sakhi's attention to domestic workers in the recent past has pushed perspectives on domestic violence and workers' rights in new directions. In domestic violence work, the figure of the abused worker liberates us from conventional mappings and helps us to conceptualize the home as a place not necessarily charged with privacy and familial ties. The isolated position of the domestic worker challenges common assumptions of a laborer surrounded by coworkers and employed in a populated place that one can enter with relative ease.

It is critical for Western feminists to be continually attentive to the ways in which they have taken for granted those spaces they define as "public" and "private." By being uncritical in this regard, most Western feminists circumscribe and domesticate the radical potential of their own work. A rethinking of these constructs would require that feminist theory and practice let go of comfortable and familiar ideas in order to set out in new directions. The "theoretical" component of activism must adhere to a *continual* process of overturning oppressive definitions. At the same time, it must remain watchful for opportunities to make strategic interventions within the "given" definitions themselves.

14

One Finger Does Not Drink Okra Soup: Afro-Surinamese Women and Critical Agency

Gloria Wekker

> This focus, whereby women are seen as a coherent group across contexts, regardless of class or ethnicity, structures the world in ultimately binary, dichotomous terms, where women are always seen in opposition to men, patriarchy is always necessarily male dominance, and the religious, legal, economic, and familial systems are implicitly assumed to be constructed by men.
>
> Chandra Talpade Mohanty,
> "Under Western Eyes:
> Feminist Scholarship and Colonial Discourses"

The *odo,* or proverb, quoted in the title of this essay is used by Creole women in Suriname on particular occasions and expresses a specific, situated worldview.[1] Creole working-class culture, like other cultures in the black diaspora, is an oral culture, replete with proverbs, verbal arts, storytelling, riddles, and songs. *Odo* can be viewed as an Afro-Surinamese example of "black thought pictures," a concept Zora Neale Hurston vividly evoked in her brilliant novel *Their Eyes Were Watching God* (1937).[2] The small vignettes *odo* bring to life, encapsulate orally transmitted wisdom that expresses a particular, subordinated world outlook while also potentially serving as a guideline for action. As the descendants of slaves, working-class Creole women have been the vigilant treasure keepers of the cultural heritage forged in the crucible of this New World, Caribbean society.

Amidst the injustice and cruelty of their daily lives, slaves formulated *odo* as a running commentary on their lived realities. To this day, new *odo* are produced in reaction to everyday occurences that capture people's imagination. This particular proverb has a long history. It is mentioned in a collection of *odo* published in 1835 (Teenstra, II, 1835: 212, nr.17).[3] "Wan finga n' e dring' okro brafu." "One finger does not drink okra soup" reflects the collective insight that one finger is powerless in accomplishing a task, and that cooperation among "fingers" is necessary in any endeavor. The *odo* thus addresses issues of agency and personhood, and though it is not clear whether it was originally coined by a man or a woman, there are strong reasons to believe that it reflects a woman's perspective, a woman's everyday world (Smith, D. 1987). Okra soup, a particularly elaborate and favorite broth considered very nourishing, contains various ingredients: saltmeat, fish, okra, onions, tomatoes, and black pepper. The injunction within the *odo* was an oft-repeated motto during a brief period in the spring of 1991, when a group of Afro-Surinamese working-class women tried to launch a multiethnic women's political party for the general elections in May.[4]

But the *odo* transcends this manifest level. On a deeper level, it is expressive of a particular view of (female) subjectivity in which there is an intricate, delicate, and often shifting interplay between individuality and collectivity, between singularity and plurality, and between "femininity" and "masculinity." At this level, the *odo* suggests that the subject is made up of various "instances," including gods and the spirits of the ancestors, and that all of these need to be acknowledged and held in harmony.

Specific, located conceptions of personhood find expression in local linguistic complexes. These discursive practices construct and confirm local *Weltanschauungen*. Most Western European languages have only one way to refer to the self—with the personal pronouns "I," "je," "ich," or "ik." This suggests a monolithic, static, unique conception of personhood. In contrast, in *Sranan Tongo,* the Surinamese creole, there are a wide variety of ways to make statements about the self. In *Sranan Tongo* it is possible to talk about the self in singular or plural terms, in masculine or feminine forms, and even in third-person constructions, irrespective of one's gender.

Interestingly, this multiplicitous, layered conception of subjectivity exists in concert with an institutionalized range of sexuality that embodies the same interplay of various forms, the same multiplicity. Thus, we find an institution in the Afro-Surinamese working class called the *mati* work, in which Creole men—but also importantly Creole women—engage in sexual relationships with people of the opposite gender and with people of the same gender, either consecutively or simultaneously. I have guesstimated that three out of four Creole working-class women will have engaged in *mati* work at some point during their lifetime (Wekker 1992). In Afro-Surinamese working-class culture, there is virtually no stigma attached to the *mati* work.

In this essay, I want to highlight two ways in which Creole working-class women act as critical agents: one involves the construction of sexualities, the other concerns their organizational activities—specifically, a short-lived women's political party. Both configurations reveal deep-seated notions about female personhood and agency that, I contend, are elaborations of grammatical West African behavioral principles (Mintz and Price 1992). First, I will describe constructions of Creole subjectivity and sexuality as elaborations of West African heritage. My analysis of the *mati* work is based on accounts of the women themselves, who stress the positive, empowering choices they make relating to other women sexually. It is contrary to depictions in hegemonic texts that see the institution mainly from a male perspective. In the second section, I will introduce Suriname and the domestic political economy of women's oppression. Thirdly, I will describe and analyze PVVU (de Politieke Volksvrouwen Unie, or the Political Union of Working-Class Women), a women's political party initiated by Creole women, and its attempts to mobilize women of all classes and ethnicities. In the fourth and final section, I will examine the general lessons of this particular case study, especially in light of the adoption of Structural Adjustment Programs (SAP) that undermine women's capacity to act as the critical agents they have been historically. I see both the *mati* work and women's organizational activities as expressions of a culture of resistance. Women are resisting hegemonic definitions of "normal" social arrangements, i.e., that heterosexuality is "normal" sexuality and that organizations are necessarily male endeavors. Consciousness of the insurgent solutions that black, working-class women have found for perennial problems of living—sexually, politically, and existentially—is particularly urgent at this historical juncture when global homogenizing processes are impinging upon local knowledges with particular intensity.

I define agency here as a crystallization of women's subjectivities in conjunction with the possibility to act. From the nooks and crannies of a bleak landscape where constraining, hegemonic realities systematically disadvantage women, women seek possibilities to enlarge their choices, to enhance their positions. I seek to trace two terrains where working-class women deemed change was both possible and necessary—the areas of sexuality and gender-based organization.

According to black feminist Patricia Hill Collins, in life as in the practice of science:

> Partiality and not universality is the condition of being heard, individuals and groups forwarding knowledge claims without owning their position are deemed less credible than those who do. Dialogue is critical to the success of this epistemological approach. (Hill Collins 1990: 236)

Through my partial, located reading of Creole working-class women's culture, I seek to open a dialogue with others, not in order to arrive at "objective truth," but in order for (black) women to gain empowerment. My own location in this article cannot possibly be elucidated here in full, but includes my having been born in Suriname to a working-class Creole-Amerindian mother and a middle-class Jewish-Creole father. I was raised in the Netherlands and later trained there and in the United States as a sociocultural anthropologist. I have done research in Suriname with Creole working-class women, and am presently based in the Netherlands again. Surely, my interest in sexual and activist constructions of female Creole selves bespeaks issues in my own, situated life (Wekker 1992). As "an outsider within" (Hill Collins 1986), I concur with anthropologist Gananath Obeyesekere's identification of his position while studying "his own people" in Sri Lanka: "I am one with them yet not one of them" (1980: II).

Multiplicitous Subjectivities and Sexualities

Postmodern and feminist discourse in Western academic circles about "the death of the subject" has illuminated the illusory and masculine character of the unitary subject. Yet it has not paid enough attention to the historical and geographical circumscription of the provenance of this subject. While it may be acknowledged that historically the subject has been envisioned as masculine, middle-class and heterosexual (Weedon 1987), the locatedness of the concept in a white world has not been sufficiently taken into account. Thus, we need to realize that the "modern subject" may never have been alive in some Third-World contexts. Anthropologists have, of course, been more aware of and interested in questions of cross-cultural selfhood, yet it is possible to argue that the ways they have gone about pursuing these interests have resulted in accounts heavily fingerprinted with Western assumptions about what it means to be a person (Geertz 1984, Lutz 1988, Kondo 1990, Wekker 1994). The notion of a "true, authentic, coherent, static, inviolable" self that stands in opposition to "society" has bedeviled and reproduced itself in much research. One possible fruitful way to open windows to local conceptions of personhood is to listen carefully to what people have to say about themselves and what terms they use to make these statements. Collecting and studying a contextualized lexicon of the self can provide an understanding of the ways subjectivity is locally conceptualized.

To illuminate this point, I will introduce Renate Druiventak, the Creole woman who took the initative for the PVVU, and describe the way she talks about herself and her activities. Renate is a fifty-four-year-old, gifted, organic intellectual in the spirit in which Gramsci (1971) used the term. According to Gramsci, every social group creates one or more "strata of intellectuals which give it homogeneity and an awareness of its own function not only in the economic, but also in the social and political fields" (1971:5). Academicians are the intellectuals trained to represent the interests of groups in power, while "organic" intellectuals rely on common sense and represent the interests of their own groups. Organic or everyday intellectuals may not be certified as such by the dominant group because their intellectual activity threatens the prevailing social order (Hill Collins 1990: 18).

When I met Renate Druiventak in 1990, she was the leader of a sociocultural group called *Mofina Brasa,* and she was highly dissatisfied with the way traditional political parties disregarded the interests of women. She is fluent in the local creole, *Sranan Tongo.* She also has *odo* and cultural and herbal knowledges at her command, and so figures prominently in the local Creole working-class cultural value system. Her own explanation of her drive to make a difference in the lives of women and children is deeply embedded culturally:

> We, Creoles, have an enormous advantage because we have winti[5] who transmit knowledge to us. Winti come upon you in your dreams, they give you strength and push you in a particular direction. I wasn't consciously thinking of a political party for women, but in my dream Mama Aisa (Mother Goddess of the Earth) came to me and told me to do something for women, to help them cope in these difficult times. Afterwards, I prayed, *mi ben tak' nanga mi 'ik' nanga ni skin* [I talked to my 'I', to 'myself']. Gradually the idea of a women's action group shaped itself and then I asked: how do I go about this? whom do I ask to help me?

Through her explanation of her activities, Renate places herself firmly in the context of the Afro-Surinamese Winti religion, which embodies a specific worldview and conception of subjectivity. She indicates the importance of *winti,* gods or spirits, who transmit knowledge to human beings, and, in particular, she acknowledges her special relationship with Mama Aisa, the Mother Goddess of the Earth. *Winti* are not conceptualized as external, transcendental beings or entities, but as integral parts of the self. Thus, people will say: "Mi ab' Aisa" (I have Aisa), indicating the proprietary intimateness of the relationship. Likewise, when Renate says, "I talked to my 'I,' to 'myself,'" she is indicating that different "instances" of the self need to be consulted. It is clear, then, that long before postmodernism became fashionable in the West, Creoles thought of themselves as fragmented, complex, and multiplicitous.

Coming from West Africa, present-day Ghana, Dahomey, and Congo-Angola, Surinamese slaves carried with them African beliefs centered around an Upper God, a belief in an immortal soul that reincarnates, and an ancestral cult (Wooding 1987, Wekker 1992). These characteristics have been retained in the Creole religious system that came to be known as *Winti.* The word literally means wind and implies that, like the wind, gods and spirits are invisible but can move swiftly and take possession of human beings and natural phenomena like trees and animals. Many Creoles, especially those in the working class, are firmly embedded in the cosmological and ethnopsychological worldview *Winti* provides.

Within this cosmological system, human beings are understood to be partly biological and partly spiritual beings. The biological side of humans, flesh and blood, is supplied by the earthly parents. The spiritual side is made up of three components, two of which are important here: all human beings have a *kra* or *yeye* ("soul") and *dyodyo* (parents in the world of the gods). The *kra* and *dyodyo* together define a person's mind, intellect, consciousness, personality characteristics, and mentality (Wooding 1987). A human being is integrated into the world of the gods by his or her godly parents, who look out for and protect their child throughout life. At birth the *dyodyo* bestow a *kra,* an immortal "soul," with male and female components, upon a human being. Both *kra* and *dyodyo* consist of a male and female being and both of these pairs are conceived of as human beings, with their own personality characteristics. The female (*misi*) and male (*masra*) part of the "soul" are determined by the day of the week on which the person is born. Thus, somebody born on Sunday is "carried" by Kwasi and Kwasiba, and is believed therefore to possess certain traits that make her different from a person born on Wednesday who is carried by Kwaku and Akuba. Likewise, a person, like Renate, who has Aisa as a female godly parent will, regardless of gender, display nurturing and mothering behavior, while somebody who has Leba (Elegba) will be very clean and orderly. *Winti* are recruited from four pantheons: the Earth, the Water, the Sky, and the Forest. Moreover, in addition to being protected by certain *dyodyo,* an individual can temporarily be "possessed" by other gods and spirits of the ancestors. In this state of "trance," the individual is believed to possess the characteristics of that particular god.[6] Thus, all human beings integrate male and female elements within themselves and are conceived as multiplicitous, varied, dynamic, and malleable.

This multiplicitous conceptualization of the person finds expression in the plethora of terms used to refer to "I" in the Surinamese creole, *Sranan Tongo*. Unlike English, in which "I" is a significant repository of personhood, agency, and personal identity (Kondo 1990), and has no synonyms, in *Sranan,* there are infinite possibilities to make statements about self in terms of one specific, male or female instance of the "I." There exists for instance *mi, mi ik, mi ikke, mi kra, mi yeye, mi misi, mi masra, mi misi nanga ni masra, mi dyodyo, mi ma dyodyo, mi pa dyodyo, mi skin, a sma f'mi,* and *den sma f'ni,* or in terms of third-person constructions, one's *winti*. A common statement like "mi Aisa wan' a gowt' linga dati" (My Aisa wants that gold ring) refers to a particular instance of the "I" as the one who has this desire. When Renate explained her drive to found a women's political party, she described it as having been brought to her by Aisa in a dream. Subsequently, she consulted with other instantiations of the "I" in order to profit from their knowledge and to be in harmony with them: "One finger does not drink okra soup." All instances of the "I" have a different "juridisdiction," but they all possess agency. There is also a hierarchy between instantiations of the "I." Some possess more power to act than others. The *kra* or *yeye* is the ultimate gatekeeper, the decisive instance of the "I." Subjectivity, therefore, in an Afro-Surinamese working-class universe, is more profitably conceived of as a kaleidoscopic, ever-moving sequence than as a unique, bounded, static essence.

Whether the slaves who survived the Middle Passage brought an egalitarian gender ethos with them to Suriname will probably remain obscure, but what seems likely is that the system of slavery itself was conducive to such an ethos (cf., Gray White 1985 for the U.S., Wekker 1994). Just as the experience of slavery leveled differences between slave royalty and commoners, it also diminished differences between men and women. The egalitarian ethos of the gender system is most apparent in the fact that every human being has male and female components.[7] In addition, male *winti* (the male parts of the "soul" or of the godly parents) or male characteristics are not valued more than their female counterparts. This means, in effect, that both men and women are seen as full subjects. There is a remarkable parallel here with personhood among African American working-class blacks. Both males and females display emotional expressiveness, "mothering" behavior, and individualism, paired with strong interpersonal connectedness, independent sexual initiative, and a strong sense of self-worth (Lewis 1975, Stack 1986). Different historical configurations constructed these parallel definitions of personhood in Afro-Suriname and Afro-America, but the common cultural heritage—the grammatical West African principles—provided the foundation for this outcome.

Interestingly, the situated conception of subjectivity I have described colludes with a public and varied repertoire of sexual behaviors and styles among the Creole working-class. Thus, there is an institution with its own rules and rituals—the *mati* work—in which Creole women openly engage in sexual relationships with men and with women, either simultaneously or consecutively. "*Mati*" is the creole word for "friend" used by and for males and females. Characteristically, depending on context, the term can have either a neutral meaning, as in "my good friend, my buddy," or a sexual meaning, i.e., "my lover." "*Mati* work" is called *work* by insiders because it involves mutual obligations between two female partners in nurturing, social, sexual, and economic spheres (Wekker 1992). *Mati* distinguish "*mati* work" from just lying down with a woman, which does not involve obligations. *Mati* are women who typically have children, who may be in a variety of relationships with men (e.g., marriage, concubinage, visiting relationships) and who also have sexual relationships with women.[8] The distinctions often made in a Western universe between heterosexual and lesbian women—based on women's sexual "identity" and the supposed underlying psychic economy—do not correspond with realities in this Afro-Surinamese universe where there are more ties than divisions between women who are exclusively involved with men and those who are intimately connected to both men and women. In the Afro-Surinamese construct, these women share the values of a working-class culture that stresses the importance of motherhood, emotional and financial savvy, and a sharp presentation of self. And it is a culture where, importantly, sexual activity is considered healthy and, in itself, more interesting than the gender of the object of one's passion (Wekker 1992).

From quite early on the *mati* work caught the attention of outside observers, surely an indication of the openness and frequency of its practice. The first mention of the institution in hegemonic literature occurs in a 1912 report commissioned by the Dutch colonial government to research the health of the urban, lower-class population. The report mentions that, apart from the health problems afflicting women because of their lack of money and the generally inferior quality of their food intake, the "sexual communion between women ... has ... penetrated deeply into popular mores" (Ambacht 1912: 98). Other hegemonic sources that tried to explain the openness and frequency of the phenomenon among Creole working-class women invariably stressed a "male deficit" perspective, both numerically and psychologically. This argument alleged that the sex ratio was so unfavorable that women simply were unable to find a man, and that in addition, men were psychologically unavailable.

While *mati*'s own accounts do not mince words about how disappointing, untrustworthy, and generally "doglike" men are, they stress the positive choices they make to be intimately connected with other women, citing the companionship, solidarity, and the sharing of childcare and everyday (financial) worries they find in their *mati*. Sexuality, especially with women, is seen as an inherently joyous and healthy part of life. *Mati* work presents a configuration where women unabashedly enjoy sex, take sex seriously, can disengage sex from love, and, strikingly, talk about sex with relish. Sex, both with men and women, is a favorite, yet indirect, topic of conversation among *mati* and they have developed an elaborate linguistic repertoire to discuss the ins and outs of the matter, often in the form of (clipped) *odo,* in-jokes, innuendo, and body language. *Mati* actively exchange sexual knowledge with each other, and girls are often initiated into sex by older women. While sex with women is seen as fun or even as "sport," sexual relations with men are often viewed as transactions, necessary to motherhood, the epitome of womanhood, and a potential source of financial support. Very importantly, women see themselves—and are seen by men—as active sexual subjects (Wekker 1992).

Mati work exists within a rich women's culture. Women celebrate each other with the help of institutions like the birthday party and *lobi singi* (self-composed lovesongs). This women's culture crosscuts deeply with the

Afro-Surinamese *Winti* religion discussed earlier. Engaging in the *mati* work is not conceived of as an innate identity, as is often the case in the Western universe, but rather is seen as engagement in a pleasant activity, instigated by one particular instance of the "I." Thus, female *mati* claim no true, inherent "bisexual" self, but see themselves as carried by a strong male *winti,* Apuku, who cannot bear to see his "child," the woman, engaged in a long-term relationship with a flesh-and-blood male. It is the Apuku who is sexually attracted to women, and thus no innate sexual identity needs to be claimed (Wekker 1992). Because the *mati* work conceptualizes sex with other women as behavior, it represents a different configuration than the genesis of "homosexual identity" under capitalism (D'Emilio 1984, Faderman 1991). Men within the Afro-Surinamese working-class culture often share this vision of the *mati* work and do not object to "their" woman being involved with another woman. Within a middle-class environment, comparable behavior is unthinkable.

I understand the *mati* work within a broad African American, sociocultural, constructionist perspective, that is, I see it as an elaboration of West African principles and ideas about personhood, gender, and sexualities. From this perspective, it becomes possible to see that because of an historically specific set of sociocultural circumstances in Suriname from slavery to the present—demographics, Dutch colonial cultural policies, etc.—the *mati* work found its clearest expression in this part of the black diaspora. But its principles are present in women's cultures in other parts of the diaspora (Wekker 1992), including Jamaica (Silvera 1992), Cariacou and Grenada (Lorde 1982), Curaçao (Marks 1976), St. Vincent (Rubenstein 1987) and the French Caribbean. And although the origin of the *mati* work is often associated with the departure of men to do migrant labor as golddiggers and balata bleeders in the rainforest, near the turn of the last century, there is, from my perspective, no good reason to suppose that *mati* work was not already present in West Africa (Herskovits 1938, Evans-Pritchard 1970, Wekker 1992). Seen from this view, *mati* work sheds a radically different light on the matrifocal family form generally believed to characterize black working-class life in the diaspora. Instead of women passively waiting for the male "hunter" to grant them sexual favors, we find a sizeable group of women who have chosen to be sexually active with each other, and who have chosen to give a certain form to their sexual and family lives.

Mati do not encounter significant stigma within their own, working-class circles. However, they are well aware that other layers of society do not support their "lifestyle." Especially in middle-class circles, where the dominant value pattern projects "feminine," or dependent, behavior for women and stresses that a woman without a male partner is without inherent value, *mati* work is seen as rowdy, unseemly behavior. But through *mati* culture Creole working-class women have succeeded in retaining control of their own sexualities, thus providing an example of an oppressed group that has not accepted the ruling sexual ideology. Certainly in their relations with women, *mati* define themselves as sexually active, full subjects. The common West African cultural heritage needs to be further explored within this acceptance of the completeness of subjectivity, and with all that this entails.

This alternative vision of female subjectivity and sexuality, based on West African principles, also enables a particular form of working-class women's organizing. In fact, some of the Creole working-class organizations have large memberships of *mati,* who support each other in times of sickness and need and who celebrate birthdays together. Predictably, the organizational principles of working-class women's organizations clash with those of the political economy, which privileges men, the heterosexual contract, and hierarchical relationships among people.

Surinamese Women's Locations in the Domestic Political Economy

Suriname's total population numbers about 400,000 people; it is estimated that about 300,000 people have migrated, most intensely in the past two decades, to the Netherlands, the United States, and the Dutch Antilles. Suriname has been termed a plural society (Van Lier 1977), consisting of these seven different main population groups (in order of size): Hindustani, Creoles, Javanese, Maroons, Chinese, Amerindians, and Europeans. The local construction of ethnicity overlooks the reality that many Surinamers are of mixed, intermediary heritage; phenotypical features—skin color, hair texture, the shape of nose and mouth—tend to determine one's location in the ethnic system. Ethnicity has generally proved an overriding element of allegiance among the population, one capitalized upon and manipulated by the male leadership of the ethnically based political parties. There have been attempts in the past to organize the population according to class (de Kom 1934, Hira 1983); among the Creole population gender has traditionally served as a base for uniting women (Coleridge 1958, Pierce 1971, Brana-Shute 1976, 1993).

Surinamese women come in many colors, ethnicities, classes, and sexual practices. The manifold paradoxes that characterize Caribbean women's positions generally (Henri and Wilson 1975, Massiah ed. 1986, Momsen ed. 1993) are also applicable to Afro-Surinamese women. On the one hand, Afro-Surinamese women have a long tradition of economic independence and authority within the household; on the other, they still have secondary status within society at large. They commonly defer to male authority in the public domain, and they often face problems arising from gender discrimination in the labor force and violence from men (Brydon and Chant 1989).

Another inconsistency in Caribbean gender relations applicable, to a certain extent, to Afro-Suriname is a double standard of sexuality (Henri and Wilson 1975). On the basis of my research (Wekker 1992), it is more accurate to say that this double standard is most prevalent within the middle class. But to the extent that working-class people have acculturated to the dominant value structure, they too exhibit features of the double standard. As we saw earlier, practically and ideologically, there remains a marked gender and sexual egalitarianism within a working-class behavioral environment.

There are other inconsistencies and tensions in Caribbean gender relations as well. Men reportedly view women as good, pure, and as "pillars of society"; at the same time they see them as treacherous and manipulative (Henri and Wilson 1975). Massiah (1986) notes that there is a divergence in Caribbean societies between the ways men perceive women and the ways women perceive themselves. Men fairly consistently report that women have no identity apart from their men, while women have relatively autonomous self-definitions. It is not made clear, however, from which populations of women and men these data were gathered. Again, my data make Massiah's findings more precise by pinpointing a class and age dimension. While it is true that working-class women have relatively autonomous self-definitions in comparison with middle-class women, I found that younger working-class women are influenced more by dominant value structures than older women of their class. Discourse in the media, educational materials, the downward economic spiral, and government regulations (all of which promote values that support and depict a nuclear family with a male as head of household) have made younger women more prone to look to men to solve their financial problems. Many older working-class women, on the other hand, tend to rely on all-female networks for emotional, financial, and sexual support (Wekker 1992). Class and gender operate to position men differently in this social matrix. Middle-class men and working-class men who are exposed to dominant value patterns tend to see women's identity as void of a male presence. However, working-class men, who are deeply embedded in Creole culture see women's identity as more complex, more layered, and less dependent on male presence (Wekker 1992).

A further inconsistency is noted in women's attitudes versus their behavior patterns in certain domains. Women express, for example, a lack of confidence in female leadership ability, but at the same time they demonstrate the ability to establish cooperative and supportive networks with each other (Massiah 1986). It has even been argued that Caribbean women are the bearers and perpetuators of inegalitarian, Eurocentric respectability, due to their closer association with the master class during slavery when they had roles as concubines and domestic slaves. Caribbean men, on the other hand, are said to subscribe to the egalitarian value system of reputation, an indigenous counterculture based on the ethos of equality and rooted in personal, as opposed to social, worth (Wilson 1973). However, it has been by now amply demonstrated, from several parts of the Caribbean, that Afro-Caribbean women participate in the main dimensions of reputation, identified by Wilson (Wekker 1992, Besson 1993). Leadership roles in Afro-Surinamese *Winti* religion, spirit possession, prophecy and healing; women's oral skills; motherhood; conferring titles to women in recognition of reputation; and entrepreneurial roles are all ways in which Creole women participate in a reputation system. Afro-Surinamese women have been, and are central to, cultures of resistance rooted in the tradition of slave resistance. These cultures of resistance emerged in response to colonialism and the plantation system and later continued in opposition to hegemonic, middle-class value patterns (Wekker 1992).

But while Creole working-class women have been actively shaping their own realities culturally, they have not been very succesful in altering their political and economic locations. During the past decade, access to foreign currency–U.S. dollars or Dutch guilders–has become vital to one's position in the class structure in Suriname. The Surinamese guilder has charted a dazzling, inflationary course during this time.[9] Access to foreign currency is not gender-blind, but follows clear gender-based patterns. Classes have become multiethnic in the past decades, but women have not kept pace with men of the same ethnic group in gaining access to the upper classes. Except as spouses or concubines, women do not appear in the highest echelon of the class structure, which consists of wholesale international traders, self-employed professionals, politicians, and high military personnel. The middle segment of the class structure is made up of a large miscellaneous group. This group contains the "retired rich," who draw a pension from the Netherlands or the United States; high employees in the bauxite sector and large agricultural and private enterprises; and, finally, some high-salaried civil servants and personnel working for companies that are partly state-owned, partly private enterprise. With teachers and nurses included, the middle class is made up of men and women, with women mainly concentrated in the lower income groups. The majority of people in the highest echelons of this class, such as the "retired rich" and higher industrial personnel, are, almost by definition, men. The working class has traditionally comprised the largest number of people, but today this class has become even more populated as large sectors of the lower middle class move toward the bottom of the class structure. Consisting of the "retired poor," the majority of civil servants and small farmers, informal sector workers, and the unemployed, the working class draws income in Surinamese currency. Here, of course, women of all ethnicities are overrepresented.

Women are estimated to form about 40 percent of the labor force (Tjoa 1990), but it is generally acknowledged that this percentage is not accurate because women are either disproportionately underemployed or they predominate in the informal sector where their work appears to be "hidden."

Women's employment is twice as likely to be unaccounted for as men's. Working in the least professional segments of the informal sectors which function as an extension of "housewifely" duties: baking, catering, hairdressing, washing, ironing, and sewing clothes, they also peddle lottery tickets and, not ironically, they form the backbone of the domestic economy by trading produce in the marketplace. Men, by contrast, are located in the better-paying and more visible segments of the informal sector: driving taxis, doing auto repair, buying and selling foreign currencies, and trafficking in drugs. The government has historically functioned as an economic safety net, contracting and expanding, depending on the fate of the economy. Sixty-seven percent of the female labor force works for the government as cleaners, street sweepers, and lower office personnel, jobs which place them in the lowest salary scales. At the end of the eighties, 80 percent of all working women earned 750 Surinamese guilders a month, which was then already well below the poverty line (Tjoa 1990). These women who head their households singly cannot possibly live on government salaries and are therefore forced into the very sector that is defined as informal, and ultimately believed to be marginal.[9]

Overall we find evidence of a split labor market. In the "heavier" and more profitable sectors of the formal and informal economy, we consistently find men, working under better conditions, for higher salaries; women, on the other hand, work in the "softer" sectors of the economy, for the government, where wages are notoriously low, and where they constitute only 24 percent of workers protected under collectively bargained arrangements. All of this is facilitated by the false, patriarchal premise that women have access to a male head of household and thus need only worry about additional income. This premise damages Creole women disproportionately because they are located at a place where the contradictions between a traditionally heterosexist political economy and their own constructions of subjectivity, with its aspirations for agency and autonomy, are most acutely felt. Moreover, materially, it is among this group that we find more single, female heads of households than in other ethnic groups.

In terms of political empowerment, women have not fared well either. Of the highest political and bureaucratic offices—president, vice-president, fifteen ministers and secretaries of state, numerous government and policy advisorships, and the auditor general's office—none is occupied by a woman. None of the fourteen judges are women. In the National Assembly, the highest representative body, three of the fifty-one members are women. In 1991, for the first time in history, three female directors of ministeries were appointed, two of whom were appointed ad interim. Eighty-three percent of men but only 17 percent of women could be found in the managerial sector of the government in 1992. The ratio between men and women in other important sectors, like higher education, the medical professions, banking, and business consistently show the same patterns (Malmberg-Guicherit 1993). Yet, a survey by the Surinamese Association of Women with an Academic Degree (VVAO) shows that there are 200 women with an academic or equivalent degree in Suriname, and that among younger generations, women outdo men in educational achievements.

We may thus conclude that a political economy of gender inequality is forcefully present in Surinamese society. Women, in general, have not kept pace with men of their ethnic groups in climbing the class structure. Women have difficulty obtaining access to foreign currencies, which secure a better position in the class structure. As elsewhere, male dominance is secured by presenting the sexual division of labor as natural, i.e., that women's place is in the home. Creole working-class women suffer disproportionately from this state of affairs.

PVVU

The proliferation and strength of Creole voluntary organizations, following the end of slavery, has been commented upon in the literature (Pierce 1971, Coleridge 1958, Brana-Shute 1976, 1993). Women's organizations with a religious, social, recreational, economic, educational, or political character, or a combination of these elements, have long been part of the Surinamese landscape. During my field research in 1990 and 1991, there were at least thirty formally registered urban women's organizations. They included working-class rotating-credit and dance associations, the Young Women's Christian Association via upper-middle-class service clubs like the Lionesses and female JC's engaging in charity work, as well as left-wing groups raising consciousness and setting up cooperative employment projects for women.

In the interviews I conducted with older working-class women who recounted their life histories, many commented on the importance women's organizations had played in their lives. Often they had been members of three or four different organizatons at the same time, thus creating an overlapping association of women's networks all over town. Younger women, with their manifold responsibilities, have a much harder time being active members of organizations, but they still try. The organizations often had (and still have) the names of flowers, such as "Switi Roos" (Sweet Rose), "Stanvaste" (Steadfast), and "Faja Lobi" (Fiery Love). Others have names like "Ons Doel" (Our Goal) and "Ons Hoekje" (Our Corner). The members of an organization often have a uniform traditional dress that is worn on special public occasions, such as when the organization celebrates its founding day. Organizations have a formal structure. They are led by elected officers, who have specific duties, and members are expected to contribute fees regularly. The highest officer, externally called "president," is called "mother" by the other women, and she delegates tasks to the other officers. There are also vice presidents, treasurers, secretaries, and general officers. Often there is a designated "mother for the sick" in the organization, who visits a sick member, sees to it that her children are taken care of, accompanies her, if need be, to the hospital, and takes care that she does not have financial problems. The members may engage in a variety of activities together: learning to sew clothes; receiving instruction on cooking nutritional, affordable meals; dancing formal dances (Setdansi); exchanging information about bargains in stores; praying, singing Christian hymns or "cultural" songs; or just watching a rented movie together.[10] Not all members of these working-class organizations are *mati,* but *mati* and non-*mati* share in the same working-class culture to a significant extent. Both value motherhood, autonomy, the ability to take care of business financially and emotionally, and neither orders the world according to hegemonic, hierarchical sexual standards (Wekker 1992).

Interestingly, in olden days, a man was often the ceremonial leader of the club, but he was not allowed to vote and generally did not have real influence. In the past, the fees were used for recreational purposes: going on excursions together or financing the founding day celebration, helping members pay for a big birthday party, and supporting needy individuals. With the economy currently on a downward spiral, the organizations are not capable of keeping up with all their activities, and the recreational trimmings have largely been shorn. However, the cluster of ideas behind the organizations—the deeply felt responsibility to support and take care of one another; to be there in matters of love, life, and death; to nurture and to make positive contributions to each other's lives—finds continuity in the PVVU initiative. After all, "One finger does not drink okra soup."

PVVU was not the first initiative launched by Surinamese women to found their own political party. Once before, in 1949, the Dames Comitee (ladies committee), led by a female dentist, Tine Putscher, participated unsuccessfully in elections (Brana-Shute 1993). Again, in 1973, a new political coalition, the Verenigde Volkspartij/Surinaamse Vrouwen Front (United People's Party/Surinamese Women's Front), tried to gain a seat in parliament. According to Dew, this group was "representing the unlikely alliance of Chinese shopkeepers and militant women's liberationists, men of Chinese and Chinese-Creole ancestry, and women of a variety of origins" (Dew 1978, 169).[11] All in all, 1,225 people gave their vote to this coalition, which wasn't enough to obtain a seat.[12] The PVVU initiative, however, was the first attempt to organize a political party initiated by working-class women.

The women active in PVVU had previously been involved in a grass-roots organization for the poor called *Mofina Brasa.* Renate Druiventak founded this group, inspired by a trip to China in 1983, and by the women she met in communes there. At the end of 1980, in the aftermath of a military coup in

Suriname (inappropriately dubbed afterwards "the Revolution"), the political pendulum swung temporarily toward the nationally disenfranchised. Internationally, Suriname shifted its political position toward socialist or nonaligned Third-World nations (Grenada, Nicaragua, Cuba, Libya, China, and Brazil), ostensibly changing its previous political allegiance to the Netherlands and the United States. In this unique and temporary convergence of political interests after the military coup, it became possible for an individual like Renate Druiventak to travel abroad for the first time in her life and to represent Suriname in China and Libya. With her elementary school education and her twenty-eight years of experience in agriculture, she was hardly the kind of person ordinarily chosen for international diplomatic missions.

Mofina Brasa reflected its goals through its highly symbolic name: the *mofina* (the disenfranchised, the poor) have to *brasa* (embrace each other) in order to develop consciousness and to elevate themselves. When I questioned Renate about the origin of the name, she told me it had been whispered to her by her *winti* in a dream. *Mofina Brasa* specifically targeted youth and women among the poor, and, in keeping with the ethnically segmented nature of Surinamese society, this meant youth and women of the Creole population. Renate felt and still feels very strongly that of all the different population groups in Suriname, Creoles are least aware of their cultural heritage. *Mofina Brasa*'s first activities included educational trips to the hinterland, telling narratives about history, teaching children old Creole songs and plays, and staging plays to raise historical and political consciousness.[13] Courses to sew schoolclothes, which were becoming exceedingly expensive, were set up in several neighborhoods. *Mofina Brasa* also brought together interest groups. For example, women who bake pies, cakes, and cookies for their living were organized in order to facilitate obtaining ingredients like sugar, butter, and eggs. Gradually, Renate sought ways to make the Creole working-class women, who are most often singly responsible for the maintenance of their households, less structurally dependent on expensive store-bought goods. The planting of a vegetable garden became a major mobilizing effort. The idea was that planting a communal vegetable garden would save money and also help provide a more balanced diet for families. Another idea was growing medicinal herbs and plants to create a small, profitable medicine business based on traditional knowledge which would have obviated the need to buy Western-manufactured, imported, often second-rate medicine. The group was not able to secure a plot of land by legal means, however. After many requests and petitions, the women squatted on a piece of land outside the center of the city. So far, the idea has had only limited success, partly because the economy has taken a dramatic downturn, leaving working-class women with even less time to invest in a future garden. But I suspect that this plan has not been entirely successful because with the abolition of slavery, agricultural pursuits have not ignited the imagination of Creole women. Pink-collar jobs are more coveted. Renate's agricultural background is quite atypical, and may have resulted in her overestimating the enthusiasm of other women for such pursuits.

In Suriname, the 1980s were marked by political and economic turmoil. At the end of 1987, following seven years of military rule, the old civilian political parties were returned to power as a result of national and international pressure. A powerful incentive for elections at that time was the projected reinstatement of Dutch development aid, which had been halted in 1982 when the military murdered fifteen of its opponents. For various reasons, the Dutch reneged on their promises of aid, however, and because the other major prop of the domestic economy, bauxite, had been steadily declining on the international market in the 1980s, the civilian government and the population faced a serious economic crisis. The old political parties, once they were back in power—at least nominally—immediately resumed their traditional patronage ties with their ethnic constituencies. The old, corrupt ways of governing, which the military had originally set out to eradicate, again became painfully present. On Christmas Eve of 1990, the military staged a second coup, by telephone. This time, immediate free elections were promised and scheduled for May 1991.

It was in the preparatory phase of these elections that PVVU (Politieke Volks Vrouwen Unie, or Political Union of Working-Class Women) was conceived. For close to a year, I had been meeting regularly with Renate and accompanying her *tap' a veld* (into the field), as she calls her manifold activities with folks in different neighborhoods. We lived in the same working-class neighborhood, just outside the center. In the preceding decade, Renate had been involved with two competing political parties: the NPS (National Partij Suriname), the traditionally Creole political party, and NDP (Nationale Democratische Partij), a party founded to promote "the Revolution," and heavily associated with Creole and military interests. Switching political parties in a Surinamese setting is generally not considered advantageous. In this case, Renate's NDP ties were particularly disadvantageous because, in the eyes of most of the population, NDP was the party responsible for the 1982 murders. Renate's "volatile" party allegiances made her an untrustworthy ally in some women's circles, though others not in others. By and large, this difference in perception mirrored class position, with opposition largely grouped in the middle class, and support located within the working class.

At the beginning of 1991, Renate was active in NPS again, but she was highly dissatisfied with the way the party treated women and women's problems. NPS has traditionally been a party with a large female membership. These women canvass for votes for the male leadership in their neighborhoods during election times; cook elaborate meals, at short notice, for the male politicians; and generally perform all kinds of auxiliary activities from a subordinate position (Brana-Shute, 1976, 1993). Female presence in the party does not translate into commensurate female power, or attention to women's articulated concerns. In this period, Renate told me:

> One hundred members of the party were invited to the vice president's, seventy-five women and twenty-five men. Who do you think did all the talking? Only three of the men. At a certain point I could not stand it anymore, I got up and said what a disgrace this was. There is no place for women at the table, we are only being used. I told all of those *bigiston nengre* (men with big balls) off; they are neglecting women's interests. It is time to do things differently now, male politicians have not accomplished anything. I want to start a women's action group or political party. The group has to be so strong that men will come begging on their knees for us to cooperate with them. Then I will put my demands on the table: at least three or four female ministers in the Cabinet.

During several roundtable discussions at a neighborhood community center, *Mofina Brasa*'s idea for a women's political party started to take shape. Women were concerned about the rising cost of living and the difficulties in finding transportation. Bus fares were on the increase, but because of the unavailability of spare parts, bus service was being severely curtailed. There was also concern about declining education standards. One example mentioned was that teachers had started to sell their pupils sandwiches and drinks at school. Teachers had also begun to charge their students a twenty-five-cent fine every time they came to school late in order to make ends meet. This was seen as another unacceptable way in which teachers boosted their salaries. Frequently lessons were cancelled and children sent home, while the women who cared for them were out working. Classrooms were dirty and not properly maintained. Undernutrition of children and women had just been documented for the first time since the beginning of the century, so women established a school feeding program that could provide milk, possibly a sandwich or a warm meal for all school children. There was concern about clean drinking water and a clean environment because diseases like dysentery and dengue fever were again on the rise. A fair and equitable land-distribution policy was demanded, as were more employment projects for women. And there was concern that increasingly children were seen selling newspapers, candy, and cigarettes on the street. The only discussion of sex that arose during these sessions was a news item, widely reported in the media at the time (and more importantly, through the grapevine), concerning a four-year-old girl who had been sexually molested by her stepfather while her mother was away at work. Women were outraged and deeply disturbed by this "beastly" behavior.[14]

During one of the first meetings of PVVU, an executive board was chosen, consisting of a president, two vice presidents, two secretaries, one recording secretary, two treasurers, and two general officers. I served as recording secretary during several of the initial meetings. The women in attendance came from different parts of town, but all were Creole and working-class. PVVU believed, however, that all women, irrespective of ethnicity or class, should participate. The leadership argued that women of all classes and ethnicities were suffering the consequences of the economic crisis, one caused by and benefiting men. The PVVU women felt that the existing political parties had not shown enough interest in solving their everyday problems and that they, as working-class women and mothers, felt the effects of the receding economy most harshly. Middle-class women in the traditional parties were not inclined to address their problems effectively either because they were too busy "buttering up to the male politicans, or trying to secure a good position for themselves." Even though most middle-class organizations nominally supported the issues raised by PVVU women, the concerns and activities of those middle-class groups had focused more on issues such as abolishing legal strictures against married women; lobbying for more favorable tax laws for married women; securing maternity leave; and having the equality principle for women and men acknowledged at all levels of society and translated into policy formulation and implementation. Although middle-class–led women's organizations had succeeded in starting small-scale cooperatives where working-class women found employment preserving and candying fruit, these initiatives were so small-scale that only a handful of women benefited from them. What was needed, the PVVU women felt, were more and bigger projects, so that more working-class women would benefit. Thus, generally speaking, PVVU juxtaposed a grass-roots platform, involving the most basic elements of daily life, to a neoclassical, liberal feminist platform.

Fissures, stemming from differences of class, ethnicity, political history, and affiliation with existing political parties, are rampant in Suriname's women's organizations. Women have formed numerous organizations that consist mostly of one dominant ethnicity and one dominant class. Not all of these organizations have a political agenda, but of those that do, several are openly tied to, or operating under the umbrella of, traditional, male-dominated political parties. Thus, while the goals of many of the middle-class organizations may not differ very much, the idea of merging them is largely unspeakable. During my interviews with the cadres of different organizations, an attributional bias figured most prominently in their accounts of each other: group X, according to group Y, had acted in an unacceptable way in the past, and this was why cooperation was out of the question. Group Y had a comparable story. And all the organizations subordinated gender issues to other political interests.

There are many factors that contribute to the lack of cohesion and cooperation among different women's organizations. First, people know too much about each other's past political views and affiliations, and this knowledge can effectively bar cooperation or association. Conflict between women in the past centered most acutely around the question of where women stood on the military clashes, especially after the military killed fifteen opponents in December 1982. Organizations and political parties split over this issue, and individuals who had once been close comrades were now torn apart. It took ten years after the military coup for concerted action among various organizations to be undertaken. Not until March 8, 1991, did various organizations come together, for example, to celebrate International Women's Day. They also used the occasion to launch an action demanding that more women be appointed to high positions in the government bureaucracy. Indeed, the general political silence that surrounded the decade of military atrocities deeply affected the women's community.[15]

Second, class differences among women exert a great deal of influence over the kinds of political questions which get articulated. Class itself is a veiled area of discourse among women, yet, consciously or unconsciously, middle-class women's beliefs about who is most worthy of respect and the kind of political alliances that should be formed continue to structure the political agenda. A particular source of class conflict among women involves the reluctance of many middle-class women's organizations to question the "received gender wisdom." Such hesitation is arguably related to the origin of these organizations in, and their ongoing ties with, traditional political parties, which are male-dominated in membership and outlook regardless of political ideology. Women's needs are systematically defined as secondary within these parties, and the need for gender-based organization is, even in the leftist parties, barely acknowledged. For many women, the advantages of these patronage bonds with men, based on ethnicity or on a shared vision of a just society, override possible advantages associated with gender organization. It seems as if working-class women, who have gained precious little from this patronage system, have less to lose in terms of female "respectability" and male approval when they want to enter the political arena. Many middle-class women have difficulty identifying as feminists and function out of a masculinist frame of reference.

I would suggest that what is at stake here in terms of women's organizing has application beyond this particular context. It is a clash of two opposing worldviews: on the one hand, there is a traditional middle-class, heterosexist gender regime which reflects broader processes of uneven, capitalist development shaped in national and international spheres (Nash and Safa 1980, Harrison 1988); on the other hand, there is a working-class conceptualization of full subjectivity which does not privilege men and the heterosexual contract, but is based on precolonial principles in which agency, autonomy, and gender egalitarianism figure prominently. Ever increasing economic and technological globalization, however, has begun to threaten this local subjugated knowledge regime.

All of these circumstances played a part in the demise of PVVU. PVVU's multiethnic and multiclass aspirations, formulated as they were in an agonizing crucible, proved a difficult and, in the end, an insurmountable barrier. In spite of valiant attempts to ban racist discourses and mythologies about different ethnic groups, particularly surrounding the Hindustani population, Creole women repeatedly resorted to using these very mythologies and as a result were constantly being confronted. Furthermore, Renate Druiventak's complicated political history made her an untrustworthy ally in the eyes of many. Several attempts were made to invite middle-class women to join PVVU, but even repeated invitations did not produce the desired result: solidarity, or, at the very least, cooperation. In this universe where middle-class women have learned that it is men who pay the piper, they have also learned that it is political suicide to align oneself with a group of rowdy, unseemly women, with not even a title to their name. The demise of PVVU, then, must ultimately be attributed to the clash of these opposing class regimes where middle-class women in particular have bought into the dominant, male-centered, nonegalitarian one. In that regime women are rewarded for subordinating gender interests to ethnic allegiances.

Paradoxically, instead of appealing to a variety of ethnicities and classes within the Surinamese women's landscape, PVVU turned out to have enormous attraction for the (mostly illegal) Guyanese laborers in Suriname. It was the Hindustani and Afro-Guyanese men and women who overwhelmingly responded to PVVU's call for action. PVVU's eventual decision to focus on the needs of these laborers—who often had been in Suriname for decades without qualifying for citizenship or visas—marked an important first initiative which unfortunately took away from the capacity to build a women's political party.[16] PVVU lacked the time, money, and specific skills needed to build a broader political base, thus losing the support of virtually all sectors of the women's community. In fact, even before the elections, PVVU had already decided to disband. In the end, only three women, nominated by traditional political parties, NPS and VHP, were chosen for the National Assembly's fifty-one seats.[17]

This unprecedented initiative that deserved to be taken much more seriously as a valiant effort to overcome historical fissures between women had run aground. It is highly significant that it was working-class Creole women who took the initiative for creating a multiethnic women's party. Given the political economy of gender oppression, they had the least to gain by perpetuating the prevailing political system in which gender was consistently subordinated to other interests. It was also this group of women who were (and are) most deeply embedded in the cultural system in which women act as full subjects.

Conclusion

Hegemonic Western feminist texts have all too often depicted Third-World women as passive, frozen in history (Mohanty 1992), and as being acted upon, rather than acting individually and collectively to improve their situations. Feminists have not always escaped the imperialist heritage of anthropology, which places the researcher as a subject and those researched as objects. In this article, I have concentrated on two areas in which Creole, working-class women in Suriname have acted to resist dominant structures. Though widely divergent in scope and subject matter, both the construction of sexualities and of women's organizations show that women are active participants in shaping their social realities and that they collectively take part in a culture of resistance. Postmodernism aside, Creole working-class women have always known that they are fragmented, multiple, and in flux. They are aware that the various instances of the "I" need to be held in harmony, just as they know that, in order to make positive change, they need to work collectively.

As this essay shows, it is important not to homogenize Third-World women. Even within one group—urban Creole women—there are many differences between middle-class and working-class women. Working-class women have been in a historically unique position to develop their own culture, which posits itself as a female culture of resistance against many features of middle-class women's culture. Working-class women are aware of middle-class values like monogamy—where one man is preferably both genitor and pater of children—but do not generally strive to emulate these values. They are instead embedded in their own value structure, one that stresses the inherent value women have, no matter the number of partners, male or female, they may have had. It is a value structure that emphasizes motherhood and sexual fulfilment, which bestows full, active subjectivity on both men and women.

The history of the majority of Suriname's middle-class women's organizations places them firmly within an accomodationist position vis-à-vis the male leadership of political parties. Women, in general, are disadvantaged in the political economy, but working-class women really bear the brunt of the deteriorating situation. As I have tried to show, it is no coincidence that the initiative to organize women on the basis of gender, and across class and ethnic divisions, came from a group of Creole, working-class women. One can logically conclude that they have less to lose in a patriarchal system that rewards women who subordinate gender interests to ethnic and class allegiances. But in my reading, it is not only economic imperatives that led working-class women to take this initiative. The psychic economy of female subjectivity, regardless of whether one engages in *mati* work or not, induces working-class women to act individually and collectively in ways that counteract the assault of a hegemonic knowledge regime that privileges men, the heterosexual contract, inequality, and a generally unjust situation. This regime runs counter to working-class women's own subjugated knowledge system. Although the attempt to form PVVU was unsuccessful for a number of reasons, its significance is not to be diminished.

It seems clear that if working-class women are to stave off threats posed by the continuing economic crisis and structural adjustment programs, they will have to heed even more acutely the injunction in the *odo* "One finger does not drink okra soup." Similarly middle-class women's organizations will need to be attentive to this *odo,* and will have to start listening seriously to what working-class women have to say. Consciousness raising around issues of ethnicity, class, gender, and sexuality will be a necessary component of this kind of solidarity politics. Women will need to begin building an autonomous movement, independent from, and not subordinated by, the male leadership of traditional, ethnic-based political parties. Such a movement will not only have to pay attention to the inequalities of law, but also seriously and critically address the impact of worsening political economic conditions on the texture of women's daily lives.

Glossary

mi	I
mi ik	my I
mi ikke	my (little) I
mi kra	my soul
my yeye	my soul
mi misi	my miss / female part of my soul
mi masra	my mister / male part of my soul
mi misi nange mi masra	my miss and mister / female and male parts of my soul
mi dyodyo	my godly parent
mi ma dyodyo	my female godly parent
mi pa dyodyo	my male godly parent
mi skiu	my I (has bodily connotations)
a sma f'mi	that person of mine
den sma f'mi	those people of mine

Notes

Notes to Introduction

1. David Evans, *Sexual Citizenship: The Material Construction of Sexualities* (New York and London: Routledge, 1993).
2. Stuart Hall, "Cultural Studies and Its Theoretical Legacies," in *Cultural Studies*, ed. Lawrence Grossberg et al. (New York and London: Routledge, 1992), pp. 277–294.
3. Examples of this historically based analysis which offer an implicit and explicit critique of liberal feminism are Maria Mies, *Lace Makers of Narsapur: Indian Housewives Produce for the World Market* (London: Zed Press, 1983) and *Patriarchy and Accumulation on a World Scale* (London: Zed Press, 1986); and Vron Ware, *Beyond the Pale: White Women, Racism and History* (London: Verso, 1992).
4. Michael Warner, *Fear of a Queer Planet: Queer Politics and Social Theory* (Minneapolis and London: University of Minnesota Press, 1993); and Cathy Cohen, "Punks, Bulldaggers and Welfare Queens: The Real Radical Potential of Queer Politics," paper presented at a conference entitled "Identity, Space and Power" at the City University of New York, March 1995.
5. Du Bois, W. E. B., *The Souls of Black Folk* (New York: New American Library, 1969).
6. Inderpal Grewal and Caren Kaplan, *Scattered Hegemonies: Postmodernity and Transnational Feminist Practice* (Minneapolis: University of Minnesota Press, 1994); bell hooks, *Outlaw Culture: Resisting Representations* (New York: Routledge, 1994) and *Teaching to Transgress* (New York: Routledge, 1994); Barbara Christian, "The Race for Theory," in *The Nature and Context of Minority Discourse*, ed. Abdul JanMohamed and David Lloyd (New York: Oxford University Press, 1990), pp. 37–49; and Wahneema Lubiano, "Shuckin' Off the African American Native Other: What's 'Po-Mo' Afro-America," *Cultural Critique* vol. 18 (Spring 1991): 149–86.
7. Grewel and Kaplan, ibid.
8. Leslie Roman, "White Is a Color! White Defensiveness, Postmodernism, and Anti-Racist Pedagogy," in *Race, Identity and Representation in Education*, ed. Cameron McCarthy and Warren Crichlow (New York: Routledge, 1993), pp. 71–88.
9. R. Radhakrishnan, "Feminist Historiography," in *The Difference Within: Feminism and Critical Theory*, ed. E. Meese and A. Parker (Amsterdam: J. Benjamins Publishing Co., 1989), pp. 189–203.
10. Robin Morgan, *Sisterhood Is Powerful: An Anthology of Writings from the Women's Liberation Movement* (New York: Random House, 1970) and *Sisterhood Is Global: The International Women's Movement Anthology* (Garden City, NY: Anchor Press/Doubleday, 1984); and Charlotte Bunch, *Passionate Politics: Feminist Theory in Action, Essays, 1968–1986* (New York: St. Martin's Press, 1987).

11. R. W. Connell, *Gender and Power: Society, the Person and Sexual Politics* (Stanford: Stanford University Press, 1987), p. 143.
12. Patricia Williams, *The Alchemy of Race and Rights: Diary of a Law Professor* (Cambridge, MA: Harvard University Press, 1991), p. 54.
13. Evans, *Sexual Citizenship*; Ruthann Robson, *Lesbian (Out)law: Survival under the Rule of Law* (Ithaca: Firebrand, 1992), pp. 247–258; and Kendall Thomas, "Bowers vs. Hardwick: Beyond the Privacy Principle," in *After Identity: A Reader in Law and Culture*, ed. Dan Danielsen and Karen Engle (New York: Routledge, 1995), pp. 277–293.
14. Hamza Alavi, "The State in Post Colonial Society: Pakistan and Bangladesh," *New Left Review*, no. 74 (1972): 59–81. A more contemporary elaboration of this point is made in Henrik Secher Marcussen and Jens Erik Torp, *The Internationalization of Capital: The Prospects for the Third World* (London: Zed Press, 1982).
15. Gita Sahgal and Nira Yuval-Davis, *Refusing Holy Orders: Women and Fundamentalism in Britain* (London: Virago Press, 1992).
16. Amrita Chhachhi, "Forced Identities: The State, Communalism, Fundamentalism and Women in India," in Deniz Kandiyoti, ed., *Women, Islam and the State* (Philadelphia: Temple University Press, 1991), pp. 144–175. See also essays in Valentine M. Moghadam, ed., *Identity Politics and Women: Cultural Reassertions and Feminisms in International Perspective* (Boulder: Westview Press, 1994). Amrita Chhachhi and Renée Pittin, *Multiple Identities, Multiple Strategies: Confronting State, Capital and Patriarchy* (The Hague: Institute of Social Studies, 1991).
17. Thanh-dam Truong, "Foreign Exchange: Prostitution and Tourism in Thailand," in *Sex, Money and Morality* (London: Zed Press, 1990); and Kamala Kempadoo, "Regulating Sexuality: Prostitution in Curaçao," paper delivered at the Caribbean Studies Association Conference, Curaçao, May 1995.
18. Mary G. Dietz, "Context Is All: Feminism and Theories of Citizenship," in Chantal Mouffe (ed.) *Dimensions of Radical Democracy: Pluralism, Citizenship, Community,* New York/ London: Verso, pp. 1–24.
19. Aida Hurtado, "Relating to Privilege: Seduction and Rejection in the Subordination of White Women and Women of Color," *Signs* 14:4 (1989): 833–855; Brenda Joyner, "Fighting Back to Save Women's Lives: The Struggle for Reproductive Freedom," in *From Abortion to Reproductive Freedom: Transforming a Movement*, ed. Marlene Gerber Fried (Boston: South End Press, 1990), pp. 205–211; and Rosalind Pollack Petchesky, *Abortion and Women's Choice: The State, Sexuality and Reproductive Freedom* (Boston: Northeastern University Press, 1985).
20. Sistren with Honor Ford-Smith, *Lionheart Gal: Life Stories of Jamaican Women* (Toronto: Sister Vision Press, 1989).
21. Zillah Eisenstein, *The Color of Gender: Reimaging Democracy* (Berkeley: University of California Press, 1993), p. 171.
22. Frantz Fanon's *Black Skin White Masks* (New York: Grove Press, 1967) and *The Wretched of the Earth* (Harmondsworth: Penguin, 1967); Albert Memmi's *The Colonizer and the Colonized* (Boston: Beacon Press, 1969); and Paulo Freire's *Pedagogy of the Oppressed* (New York: Continuum, 1993) are most instructive here.
23. Cornel West, *Keeping Faith: Philosophy and Race in America* (New York: Routledge, 1993), pp. 107–118; 236–247; *The American Evasion of Philosophy: A Genealogy of Pragmatism* (Madison: University of Wisconsin Press, 1989).
24. Zillah Eisenstein makes a related point when she theorizes democratic rights and equality through the prism of reproductive rights afforded the "pregnant woman of color" (versus a white, masculinist notion of universal rights). This particular location and experience simultaneously provides Eisenstein with the largest, most diverse scope to rethink the concept of universal, individual rights and to retheorize equality in terms of radical pluralism. See Eisenstein, *The Color of Gender.*
25. Ann Ferguson, *Sexual Democracy: Women, Oppression and Revolution* (Boulder: Westview Press, 1991); Nancy Fraser, *Unruly Practices: Power, Discourse and Gender in Contemporary Social Theory* (Minneapolis: University of Minnesota Press, 1989); and Williams, *The Alchemy of Race and Rights.*
26. Iris Marion Young, "Polity and Group Difference: A Critique of the Ideal of Universal Citizenship," in *Feminism and Political Theory*, ed. Cass R. Sunstein (Chicago: University

of Chicago Press, 1990), p. 117. See also essays by Iris Young, *Throwing Like a Girl and Other Essays in Feminist Philosophy and Social Theory* (Bloomington: Indiana University Press, 1990).

27. Janet E. Halley, "The Construction of Sexuality," in *Fear of a Queer Planet: Queer Politics and Social Theory*, ed. Michael Warner (Minneapolis and London: University of Minnesota Press, 1993), pp. 82–102; and Thomas, "Bowers vs. Hardwick."
28. Evans, *Sexual Citizenship*, p. 11.
29. Nancy Fraser and Linda Gordon, "A Genealogy of Dependency: Tracing a Keyword of the U.S. Welfare State," *Signs* 19:2 (Winter 1994): 208–336; and Martha L. Fineman, "Images of Mothers in Poverty Discourses," *Duke Law Journal* 273 (1991): 274–295.
30. Evelina Dagnino, An Alternative World Order and the Meaning of Democracy," in *Global Visions: Beyond the New World Order*, ed. J. Brecher, J. Brown, and J. Cutler (Boston: South End Press, 1993), pp. 239–246.
31. Jean Bethke Elshtain, *Public Man, Private Woman* (Princeton: Princeton University Press, 1981), and "On the Family Crisis," *Democracy* 3:1 (Winter 1993): 138; and Carole Pateman, *The Sexual Contract* (Stanford: Stanford University Press, 1988).
32. Young, "Polity and Group Difference."
33. Chantal Mouffe, "Feminism, Citizenship, and Radical Democratic Politics," in *Feminists Theorize the Political*, ed. J. Butler and J. W. Scott (New York and London: Routledge, 1992), pp. 369–384.
34. Fraser, *Unruly Practices*.
35. Eisenstein, *The Color of Gender*, esp. p. 219.
36. Williams, *The Alchemy of Race and Rights*, pp. 6, 153. See also Nancy Folbre, *Who Pays for the Kids? Gender and the Structures of Constraint* (New York: Routledge, 1994), and essays in the following anthologies: Seyla Benhabib and Drucilla Cornell, eds., *Feminism as Critique* (Minneapolis: University of Minnesota Press, 1987); Carole Pateman and Elizabeth Grosz, eds., *Feminist Challenges: Social and Political Theory* (Boston: Northeastern University Press, 1986); and Kathleen B. Jones and Anna S. Jonasdottir, eds., *The Political Interests of Gender: Developing Theory and Research with a Feminist Face* (London: Sage Publications, 1988).
37. Muto Ichiyo, "For an Alliance of Hope," in *Global Visions: Beyond the New World Order*, ed. J. Brecher, J. Brown, and J. Cutler (Boston: South End Press, 1993), pp. 147–162.
38. Fanon, *The Wretched of the Earth, passim*.

Notes to Chapter 1

Even after a number of new beginnings and revisions, this essay remains work in progress. I have come to the conclusion that this is indicative of both my own level of thinking about these issues as well as the current material and ideological conditions which position Third-World women wage-laborers in contradictory ways. I would like to thank Jacqui Alexander for careful, systematic, and patient feedback on this essay. The essay would not have been possible without Satya Mohanty's pertinent and incisive critique, and his unstinting emotional and intellectual support. My students at Hamilton College and colleagues at various institutions where I have presented sections of this argument are responsible for whatever clarity and lucidity the essay offers—thanks for keeping me on my toes. It is my involvement with the staff and board members of Grassroots Leadership of North Carolina that has sharpened my thinking about the struggles of poor and working people, and about the politics of solidarity and hope it engenders. Finally, it was Lisa Lowe, and then Mary Tong of the Support Committee for Maquiladora Workers, who brought the cross-border organizing of Veronica Vasquez and other workers to my attention. I thank all these organizers for teaching me and for the grassroots organizing work they continue to do in the face of great odds.

1. See Karen Hossfeld, "United States: Why Aren't High-Tech Workers Organised?" in Women Working Worldwide, eds., *Common Interests: Women Organising in Global Electronics* (London: Tavistock), pp. 33–52, esp. pp. 50–51.
2. See "Tijuanans Sue in L.A. after Their Maquiladora Is Closed," by Sandra Dribble, in *The San Diego Union-Tribune,* Friday, December 16, 1994. The Support Committee for Maquiladora Workers promotes cross-border organizing against corporate impunity. This is a San Diego–based volunteer effort of unionists, community activists, and others to

assist workers in building autonomous organizations and facilitating ties between Mexican and U.S. workers. The Committee, which is coordinated by Mary Tong, also sees its task as educating U.S. citizens about the realities of life, work, and efforts for change among maquiladora workers. For more information write the Support Committee at 3909 Centre St., #210, San Diego, CA 92103.

3. See my essay, "Cartographies of Struggle: Third World Women and the Politics of Feminism," in Mohanty, Russo, and Torres, eds. *Third World Women and The Politics of Feminism*, (Bloomington: Indiana University Press, 1991), especially p. 39, where I identified five provisional historical, political, and discursive junctures for understanding Third-World feminist politics: "decolonization and national liberation movements in the third world, the consolidation of white, liberal capitalist patriarchies in Euro-America, the operation of multinational capital within a global economy, . . . anthropology as an example of a discourse of dominance and self-reflexivity, . . . (and) storytelling or autobiography (the practice of writing) as a discourse of oppositional consciousness and agency." This essay represents a continuation of one part of this project: the operation of multinational capital and the location of poor Third-World women workers.
4. See the excellent analysis in Teresa L. Amott and Julie A. Matthaei, *Race, Gender and Work: A Multicultural Economic History of Women in the United States* (Boston: South End Press, 1991), esp. pp. 22–23.
5. See Bagguley, Mark-Lawson, Shapiro, Urry, Walby, and Warde, *Restructuring: Place, Class and Gender* (London: Sage Publications, 1990).
6. Joan Smith has argued, in a similar vein, for the usefulness of a world-systems-theory approach (seeing the various economic and social hierarchies and national divisions around the globe as part of a singular systematic division of labor, with multiple parts, rather than as plural and autonomous national systems) which incorporates the notion of the "household" as integral to understanding the profoundly gendered character of this systemic division of labor. While her analysis is useful in historicizing and analyzing the idea of the household as the constellation of relationships that makes the transfer of wealth possible across age, gender, class, and national lines, the ideologies of masculinity, femininity, and heterosexuality that are internal to the concept of the household are left curiously intact in her analysis—as are differences in understandings of the household in different cultures. In addition, the impact of domesticating ideologies in the sphere of production, in constructions of "women's work" are also not addressed in Smith's analysis. While I find this version of the world-systems approach useful, my own analysis attempts a different series of connections and theorizations. See Joan Smith, "The Creation of the World We Know: The World-Economy and the Re-creation of Gendered Identities," in V. Moghadam, ed., *Identity Politics and Women: Cultural Reassertions in International Perspective* (Boulder: Westview Press, 1994), pp. 27–41
7. The case studies I analyze are: Maria Mies, *The Lacemakers of Narsapur, Indian Housewives Produce for the World Market* (London: Zed Press, 1982); Naomi Katz and David Kemnitzer, "Fast Forward: the Internationalization of the Silicon Valley," in June Nash and M. P. Fernandez-Kelly, *Women, Men, and the International Division of Labor* (Albany: SUNY Press, 1983), pp 273–331; Katz and Kemnitzer, "Women and Work in the Silicon Valley," in Karen Brodkin Sacks, *My Troubles Are Going to Have Trouble with Me: Everyday Trials and Triumphs of Women Workers* (New Brunswick, NJ: Rutgers University Press, 1984), pp 193–208; and Karen J. Hossfeld, "Their Logic Against Them:" Contradictions in Sex, Race, and Class in the Silicon Valley," in Kathryn Ward, ed., *Women Workers and Global Restructuring* (Ithaca: Cornell University Press, 1990), pp. 149–178. I also draw on case studies of Black women workers in the British context in Sallie Westwood and Parminder Bhachu, eds., *Enterprising Women* (New York: Routledge, 1988).
8. See my discussion of "relations of rule" in "Cartographies." There has been an immense amount of excellent feminist scholarship on women and work and women and multinationals in the last decade. In fact, it is this scholarship which makes my argument possible. Without the analytic and political insights and analyses of scholars like Aihwa Ong, Maria Patricia Fernandez-Kelly, Lourdes Beneria and Martha Roldan, Maria Mies, Swasti Mitter, and Sallie Westwood, among others, my attempt to understand and stitch together the lives and struggles of women workers in different geographical spaces would be sharply limited. This essay builds on arguments offered by some of these scholars, while attempt-

ing to move beyond particular cases to an integrated analysis which is not the same as the world-systems model. See especially Nash and Fernandez-Kelly, *Women, Men and the International Division of Labor*; Ward, ed., *Women Workers and Global Restructuring*; *Review of Radical Political Economics*, vol. 23, no. 3–4, (Fall/Winter 1991) special issue on "Women in the International Economy"; Harriet Bradley, *Men's Work, Women's Work* (Minneapolis: University of Minnesota Press, 1989); Lynne Brydon and Sylvia Chant, *Women in the Third World, Gender Issues in Rural and Urban Areas* (New Brunswick, NJ: Rutgers University Press, 1989).

9. See Ella Shohat and Robert Stam, *Unthinking Eurocentrism: Multiculturalism and the Media* (London and New York: Routledge, 1994), esp. pp. 25–27 In a discussion of the analytic and political problems involved in using terms like "Third World," Shohat and Stam draw attention to the adoption of "third world" at the 1955 Bandung Conference of "non-aligned" African and Asian nations, an adoption which was premised on the solidarity of these nations around the anticolonial struggles in Vietnam and Algeria. This is the genealogy of the term that I choose to invoke here.
10. My understanding and appreciation of the links between location, experience, and social identity in political and intellectual matters grows out of numerous discussions with Satya Mohanty. See especially his essay, "Colonial Legacies, Multicultural Futures: Relativism, Objectivity, and the Challenge of Otherness," in *PMLA*, January 1995, pp. 108–117. See also Paula Moya's essay in this collection for further discussion of these issues.
11. Karen Brodkin Sacks, "Introduction," in Karen Brodkin Sacks and D. Remy, eds., *My Troubles Are Going to Have Trouble with Me*, esp. pp. 10–11.
12. Jeremy Brecher, "The Hierarch's New World Order–and Ours," in Jeremy S. Brecher et al., eds., *Global Visions, Beyond the New World Order* (Boston: South End Press, 1993), pp. 3–12.
13. See Maria Mies, *Patriarchy and Accumulation on a World Scale: Women in the International Division of Labor* (London: Zed Press, 1986), pp. 114–15.
14. Richard J. Barnet and John Cavanagh, *Global Dreams: Imperial Corporations and the New World Order* (New York: Simon and Shuster, 1994), esp. pp. 25–41.
15. For examples of cross-national feminist organizing around these issues, see the following texts: Gita Sahgal and Nira Yuval Davis, eds., *Refusing Holy Orders, Women and Fundamentalism in Britain* (London: Virago, 1992); Valentine M. Moghadam, *Identity Politics and Women, Cultural Reassertions and Feminisms in International Perspective* (Boulder: Westview Press, 1994); *Claiming Our Place, Working the Human Rights System to Women's Advantage* (Washington D.C.: Institute for Women, Law and Development, 1993); Sheila Rowbotham and Swasti Mitter, eds., *Dignity and Daily Bread: New Forms of Economic Organizing among Poor Women in the Third World and the First* (New York: Routledge, 1994); and Julie Peters and Andrea Wolper, eds., *Women's Rights, Human Rights: International Feminist Perspectives* (New York: Routledge, 1995).
16. Amott and Matthaei, eds., *Race, Gender and Work*, pp. 316–17.
17. Women Working Worldwide, *Common Interests*, ibid.
18. Aihwa Ong's discussion of the various modes of surveillance of young Malaysian factory women as a way of discursively producing and constructing notions of feminine sexuality is also applicable in this context, where "single" and "married" assume powerful connotations of sexual control. See Aihwa Ong, *Spirits of Resistance and Capitalist Discipline: Factory Women in Malaysia* (Albany: SUNY Press, 1987).
19. Hossfeld, "Their Logic Against Them," p. 149. Hossfeld states that she spoke to workers from at least thirty Third-World nations (including Mexico, Vietnam, the Philippines, Korea, China, Cambodia, Laos, Thailand, Malaysia, Indonesia, India, Pakistan, Iran, Ethiopia, Haiti, Cuba, El Salvador, Nicaragua, Guatemala, Venezuela, as well as southern Europe, especially Portugal and Greece). It may be instructive to pause and reflect on the implications of this level of racial and national diversity on the shop floor in the Silicon Valley. While all these workers are defined as "immigrants," a number of them as recent immigrants, the racial, ethnic, and gender logic of capitalist strategies of recolonization in this situation locate all the workers in similar relationships to the management, as well as to the U.S. state.
20. Assembly lines in the Silicon Valley are often divided along race, ethnic, and gender lines, with workers competing against each other for greater productivity. Individual worker choices, however imaginative or ambitious, do not transform the system. Often they merely

undercut the historically won benefits of the metropolitan working class. Thus, while moonlighting, overtime, and job-hopping are indications of individual modes of resistance, and of an overall strategy of class mobility, it is these very aspects of worker's choices which supports an underground domestic economy which evades or circumvents legal, institutionalized, or contractual arrangements that add to the indirect wages of workers.

21. Hossfeld, "Their Logic Against Them," p. 149: "You're paid less because women are different than men" or "Immigrants need less to get by."
22. Westwood and Bhachu, "Introduction," *Enterprising Women,* p. 5. See also, in the same collection, Annie Phizacklea, "Entrepreneurship, Ethnicity and Gender," pp. 20–33; Parminder Bhachu, "Apni Marzi Kardhi, Home and Work: Sikh Women in Britain," pp. 76–102; Sallie Westwood, "Workers and Wives: Continuities and Discontinuities in the Lives of Gujarati Women," pp. 103–31; and Sasha Josephides, "Honor, Family, and Work: Greek Cypriot Women Before and After Migration," pp. 34–57
23. P. Bhachu, "Apni Marzi Kardhi, Home and Work," p. 85
24. For a thorough discussion of the history and contemporary configurations of homework in the U.S., see Eileen Boris and Cynthia R. Daniels, eds., *Homework, Historical and Contemporary Perspectives on Paid Labor at Home* (Urbana: University of Illinois Press, 1989). See especially the "Introduction," pp. 1–12; M. Patricia Fernandez-Kelly and Anna García, "Hispanic Women and Homework: Women in the Informal Economy of Miami Los Angeles," pp. 165–82; and Sheila Allen, "Locating Homework in an Analysis of the Ideological and Material Constraints on Women's Paid Work," pp. 272–91.
25. Allen, "Locating Homework."
26. See Rowbotham and Mitter, "Introduction," in Rowbotham and Mitter, eds., *Dignity and Daily Bread.*
27. Anna G. Jonasdottir, "On the Concept of Interest, Women's Interests, and the Limitations of Interest Theory," in Kathleen Jones and Anna G. Jonasdottir, eds., *The Political Interests of Gender* (London: Sage Publications, 1988), pp. 33–65, esp. p. 57.
28. Ibid., p. 41.
29. See Women Working Worldwide, eds., *Common Interests.*
30. Ibid., p. 38.
31. Ibid., p. 31.
32. Kumudhini Rosa, "The Conditions and Organisational Activities of Women in Free Trade Zones: Malaysia, Philippines and Sri Lanka, 1970–1990," in Rowbotham and Mitter, eds., *Dignity and Daily Bread*, pp 73–99, esp. p. 86.
33. Swasti Mitter, "On Organising Women in Causalized Work: A Global Overview," in Rowbotham and Mitter, eds., *Dignity and Daily Bread*, pp 14–52, esp. p. 33.
34. Jane Tate, "Homework in West Yorkshire," in Rowbotham and Mitter, eds., *Dignity and Daily Bread*, pp. 193–217, esp. p. 203.
35. Renana Jhabvala, "Self-Employed Women's Association: Organising Women by Struggle and Development," in Rowbotham and Mitter, eds., *Dignity and Daily Bread,* pp. 114–38, esp. p. 116.
36. Ibid., p. 135.

Notes to Chapter 2

This article could not have been completed without the help of Suporn Arriwong, a student of exemplary resourcefulness and a friend of remarkable generosity. Sarinah Terimo, Merilyn Ellorin, and Agnes Tan all lent useful research assistance. Shaan Heng-Devan provided the necessary impetus for the article's completion, and Janadas Devan, in his role as best and most helpful critic, offered a soberingly incisive, essential critique.

1. See, for instance, Marr (1975) on the history of nationalism and feminism in Vietnam; Croll (1978) on the historical record in the People's Republic of China; Vreede-de Stuers (1960) on Indonesian anticolonial history; and individual articles in the excellent collections by Beck and Keddie (1978) and Kandiyoti (1991), documenting women's movements and issues in the Middle East and the Islamic world. More recent scholarship has begun to correct the underemphasis; see, for example, Chatterjee (1989), Halliday (1991), and Katrak (1992). Enloe (1989) offers an instance of an explicit discussion of the contest between feminism and nationalism not only in the Third World but equally in first-world national history (54).

2. As a meaningful narrative, nationalism attains much of its emotive power—and considerable oppositional force in independence struggles—by that specific invocation of imagined (and imaginary) relations between land, language, people, and history. The would-be nation is represented, perhaps, as a cherished 'motherland' to be protected and renewed; an essential 'mother tongue' is recovered and promulgated in the nationalist cause; or a selective configuration of womanhood, or traditional 'mother culture,' is posited, then defended, by those who eventually become the 'founding fathers' of the nation (which is subsequently 'born'). Inevitably, the nationalist invocation of discriminate figures produces a disposition of use, and of power, that is gendered and sexualized—with the feminine being positioned as a crucial foundational term and a resource to be fought over for possession, definition, and control. By way of example, Marr notes that in Vietnam in 1926, the protonationalist author Trinh Dinh Ru urged Vietnamese children to "love our country in the same way as we love our mother," adding, "We are born in Vietnam, making Vietnam our Mother country. Those who keep on referring to France as the Mother Country are really wrong! Only French people can properly call France the Mother Country" (379).
3. In Vietnam, by 1945, Marr observes, "Equal rights for women, and the contributions of women to the new society, served as powerful—perhaps essential—weapons in the post-1945 Resistance War" (371).
4. Partha Chatterjee argues convincingly that modernity can be made "consistent with the nationalist project" also through the institution of a principle of selection that separates the "domain of culture into two spheres": a "material" sphere, or public life, where Westernization may be tolerated, and a "spiritual" sphere, constituted mainly as the private, domestic space inhabited and figured by women, where the encroachments of modernity must be warded off, to preserve a traditional national culture (237–39).
5. On the long and complex history of feminism and nationalism in Indonesia, too tortuous to rehearse here, see Vreede-de Stuers (1960), and Wieringa (1988).
6. Women's groups of other kinds, formed by a tiny minority of English-educated, middle- and upper-middle-class women, also existed in the 1950s. These included a professional association (the Professional Women's Association), a league of voters (the Singapore League of Women Voters), and the Singapore Council of Women (SCW), formed in 1952 by an Iranian woman, Shirin Fozdar. The SCW, under a "committee of fifteen middle-aged wives of wealthy men" (Lim 1984/85, 47) and the dynamic Shirin Fozdar, appealed without success to the British colonial administration and to local political figures for advocacy on issues such as polygamy, concubinage, and marital-status laws (Lim 1984/85, 46–51). None of these groups had the membership base, the mass appeal, or the capacity for mobilization demonstrated by the nationalist and revolutionary women's groups.
7. Ong, Pang Boon. 1979. "Problems of Part Organisation: The Pro-Communist Challenge from Within 1954–57." In *People's Action Party 1954–1979: Petir 25th Anniversary Issue*. Singapore: Central Executive Committee People's Action Party, pp. 44–59. Dennis Bloodworth, a British journalist domiciled in Singapore, chronicles his first encounter with the ranks of Communist women thus: 'When I attended my first anti-colonial rally in Singapore in 1956, the rows of grim, bespectacled female faces beneath dead straight fringes that could have been chopped with shears had me swivelling nervously in my seat to check the exits" (1986, 100). It is, of course, a cliché of Hollywood and Western Orientalist discourse, that Communists and Chinese—unlike the strongly individualized Western hero—are uniformly homogeneous and undifferentiated people, an undiversified "yellow peril," as it were.
8. Chan Choy Siong instituted the Women's League in the PAP. In the 1959 General Elections, the PAP fielded Chan Choy Siong, Ho Puay Choo, Oh Su Chen, Fung Yin Ching, and Sahorah binte Ahmat, all of whom campaigned on women's issues and were successfully elected in their constituencies. All the Chinese women were Chinese-dialect or Mandarin speakers, able to appeal to the public at a grassroots level, and specifically to women in the majority Chinese-speaking population. Kwa Geok Choo, the wife of the man who became Singapore's first Prime Minister, Lee Kuan Yew, was deployed by the party to canvass English-speaking women voters, and made a single speech over Radio Singapore in 1959 on women's issues.
9. By contrast, Article 12 of the Constitution of the Republic of Singapore, in guaranteeing the rights of citizens, no longer makes mention of equality of gender: "There shall be no dis-

crimination against citizens of Singapore on the ground only of religion, race, descent or place of birth in any law or in the appointment of any office or employment under a public authority or in the administration of any law relating to the acquisition, holding or carrying on of any trade, business, profession, vocation or employment." Discrimination in employment on the basis of gender is thus constitutionally legal in Singapore, despite the express declaration of the PAP manifesto of 1959 that "The P.A.P. believes in the principle of equal pay for equal work" (17). A publication of the Singapore Association of Women Lawyers (SAWL) accordingly warns women that "it is not unlawful for a person to refuse to employ you merely on the ground that you are a woman (who may get married, or are already married and have a child or children). It is also not unlawful for a person to refuse to promote you or refuse to send you for training merely on the ground that you are a woman. Because the law is silent, you have no right to equal pay for equal work" (*Legal Status of Singapore Women*, 30). Special provisions in the Constitution also secure citizenship status for the children of male Singapore citizens, when the children are born outside Singapore, but not for the children of female citizens (*Legal Status of Singapore Women*, 20).

10. In contrast to this declaration of 1959, the Prime Minister of Singapore, Goh Chok Tong, was quoted in a 1993 newspaper report as saying that "it is neither possible nor wise to have complete equality of the sexes.... Some differences between the sexes were a product of the society here and would have to be accepted." The report continues: "The Prime Minister argued that minor areas where women were not treated in the same way as men should be expected in a largely patriarchal society.... Mr. Goh said that these differences should not be regarded as 'pockets of discrimination.'" Instead, they were "anthropological asymmetries" or products of the society's traditions. "In other words, these differences have to be accepted" ("Worrying Trends" 1993). Goh's predecessor, Prime Minister Lee Kuan Yew, in 1983, in an exhibition of distress over falling birth rates among highly-educated elites in Singapore, speculated thoughtfully on the possibility of reintroducing polygamy (i.e., polygyny) as a possible solution (see Heng and Devan 1992, 249).
11. One of the six Nominated Members of Parliament—nonconstituency and nonelected MPs who are formally "nominated" by a majority in Parliament to serve as MPs—is, however, a woman. Kanwaljit Soin, a former president of the Association of Women for Action and Research (AWARE) and a dedicated feminist, announced, on acceptance of her nomination, that she would make women her special constituency or electoral "ward." A newspaper columnist observes that from 1970 to 1984 there were no women MPs whatsoever in Parliament, a record that was breached only in 1984, when three women PAP MPs were elected (Henson 1993).
12. For his unauthorized history of Singapore, Dennis Bloodworth successfully interviewed a handful of former Communist women, whom he mentions by name and sobriquet: Linda Chen [Mock Hock], "Sweegor," "Sister Fong," and the "the Red Ballerina" (Goh Lay Kuan).
13. Wazir-jahan Karim, director of the KANITA Project, a women's studies program in Malaysia, considers AWAS a separate organization from PKMM, assigning the impetus for its creation not to "the Executive Committee of the MNP under its [male] president, Dr. Burhanuddin [Helmi]," but to AWAS's core women leaders, Aishah Ghani, Sakinah Junid, and Samsiah Fakeh, with "warm support and encouragement from members of the Malay National Party (PKMM)" [Karim 1983, 722]. Even by this alternative account of its origin, AWAS would seem to have been a strongly nationalist organization, one that saw feminist advocacy in the context of national responsibilities, as its second president, Samsiah Fakeh, made plain: "If the women have sufficient amount of grey matter to see and understand the problems of the country and possess the capacity to realize the significance of their responsibility; if men are born with equal rights; if the world is stepping toward a more stable and sound democratic regime; there is no justifiable excuse for the women being denied their rights in determining internal and external policies when the consequences of such decisions are to be shouldered by both" (Dancz 1987, 86, 87).
14. Karim has argued that the "phenomenal expansion of the political party system in the pre- and immediate post-independence period" in Malaysia co-opted feminist energies and directions after the demise of AWAS, channeling activist women into "formal structures of institutionalized political membership" (Karim 1983, 726) and "government-initiated women's movements like Wanita Umno and KEMAS" (the People's Progress Movement). Here they play "supporting roles in male-dominated organizations and institutions" (729),

but remain essentially "female functionaries" (722, 728). It is "within the women's division of the major political parties that feminist leaders attempt to draw attention to women's issues and rights, though problems relating to sexual discrimination in wages and employment or political under-representation are seldom highlighted or seriously discussed. They generally broach topics of women's welfare, morals and family needs which do not contravene socially acceptable norms and values" (726). The problem of government-sponsored "feminism" and women's groups is discussed below in the context of Singapore.

15. Indeed, much of the Charter extends over what might be called the territory of the sexual: conditions of legal marriage, separation, and divorce; rights and duties of spouses, the welfare of children, and wife and child maintenance; laws pertaining to prostitution, brothels, sexual offenses, intercourse with female minors, etc. Nonsexualized items in the Charter include the right to hold, inherit, and alienate property; to engage in a profession, trade, or social activity; to sue and be sued in one's own name; to enter into contracts on one's own, etc. Interestingly, in the configuration of feminine identity produced by the Charter, a woman has the legal right to retain her personal name and family name after marriage, but the Charter does not protect her right to assign her family name to her children, if she so chooses. The Registration of Births and Deaths Act, Chapter 267, Section 10, awards only fathers the right to transmit their surname to children born in legal marriage. The Charter's provisions do not apply, moreover, to Muslim women in Singapore. Marriage, divorce, and inheritance laws for Muslims fall under the purview of the *shariah* courts.
16. A newspaper report on the 1983 launching of two books commissioned by the PAP's Women's Wing, typically begins, "Singapore women have it good." It continues, "Everything changed after the 1961 Women's Charter. . . . In the wake of the adjustments following that legislation, women have enjoyed equal rights in nearly every area" ("Story of the Singapore Woman," 1993). While the Women's Charter was undeniably a remarkably progressive document for its time, its institution did not prevent the Singapore government itself from enacting inequities against women. Among these are: medical benefits for the children and spouse of male, but not female government employees; a quota for medical training at university level which only admits one woman for every two men; and altered admissions criteria to the National University of Singapore from 1983, when it was discovered that, because of superior academic performance, increased numbers of women were annually being admitted over men to the university.
17. It is worth repeating that all nationalisms seem to require, for their self-description and ideological imperatives, the production and manipulation of feminine identity. Islamic cultural nationalism is no exception: A recent *Newsweek* article ("The Trials of Muslim Europe") on Islamic cultural nationalism in Europe in the 1990s was typically accompanied by a powerfully symbolic photograph of veiled Muslim women in a street march, carrying a banner depicting a veiled woman cradling a peace dove in her hands, and a placard with the blazon, "Le 'Hijab' est notre honneur" prominently displayed. Beck and Keddie (1978, 13) note, in an excellent discussion, that the reproduction of neotraditionalist forms of feminine identity is mitigated where left movements are also active in nationalist struggles, an observation that is more fully developed in Molyneux's (1991) impressive study of legal reforms in socialist Yemen. That the donning of the veil does not, however, automatically signify a retrogressive resubordination of women has of course been argued repeatedly by Third-World feminists. For an instance of the veil's usefulness to Southeast Asian Muslim women—Malay factory workers in Malaysia negotiating complex new economic, sexual, and social identities—see Aihwa Ong (1987, 136 *et passim*).
18. National carriers in Southeast Asia are typically state-owned, state-managed, or government-linked institutions. PT Garuda Indonesia (slated to be privatized in late 1996 or in 1997, according to the Indonesian Transport Minister) is owned and managed by the state; Thai Airways International, Philippine Airlines, and Singapore Airlines are partly privatized, with the government as direct or indirect majority shareholder. Until January 1993, the commander-in-chief of the Thai air force was also chairman of Thai International's board of directors, while the chairman of Singapore Airlines is the current Permanent Secretary of the Ministry of National Development in Singapore.
19. SIA's annual report for 1990–91, for instance, lamenting the slowdown of the global economy, especially in Australia, North America, and the United Kingdom, and the escalation of fuel prices as a result of the Gulf War, recorded the "significantly lower" profit before

tax of $1.16 billion, "down 19.2% from 1989–90" (65). Air traffic to Europe, the Americas, and Australia contributed 64.5 percent of the airline's income in 1990–91(69).

20. Reports in the *Straits Times* have described the molesters as Americans, Germans, British, Australians, Japanese, and Sri Lankans, holding such occupations as businessmen, oil riggers, metal workers, divers, supervisors, etc. The sexual fondling of the flight attendants by male passengers has become so notorious a problem that a *Straits Times* columnist was moved to wonder if it might be "the free flow of liquor" on SIA flights that is responsible for the harrassment (Tan 1993).
21. Troung (1990, 179) quotes typical advertising copy for Thai Airways: "Smooth as silk is a beautifully prepared meal by a delicious hostess"; "Some say it's our beautiful wide-bodied DC-10s that cause so many heads to turn at airports throughout the world. We think our beautiful slim-bodied hostesses have a lot to do with it." A random sampling of print ads in Asian periodicals confirms the directional drift. An Asiana ad (featuring a nude woman wrapped in a transparent cape with the colours of the airline's logo) offers "the charms and softness of our Asiana girls ... happily ironing out all the little wrinkles of business travel, just for you." A Pakistan International ad gushes: "Our air hostesses have an unfair advantage. They begin their training years ahead of others ... in Pakistan, all girls are schooled at home in the art of hospitality." Indeed, not only airlines, but also hotels, vacation resorts, restaurants, etc, in Asia would seem to offer the charms of Asian women in advertising that sells seduction and service simultaneously to the potential consumer. By contrast, advertising for non-Asian airlines may be slightly more diverse in theme. A Qantas print ad features a map of Australia; a Lufthansa ad headlined "We spoil our passengers as much as we spoil our aircraft," depicts a uniformed male flight attendant amusing a little girl, with a glove puppet. Non-Asian airlines, of course, by no means forswear the exploitation of feminine identity and services, as United Airlines' historically infamous "Fly Me" advertising campaign in the U.S. once attested. More recently, Lauda Air of Austria has been castigated by Thai NGOs for an advertisement in the airline's inflight magazine featuring child prostitution in Thailand as a selling point to tempt potential air passengers ("Thai Group Slams Lauda Air Ad" 1992).
22. That Western imperialisms are, in fact, multifarious and resourceful has historically complicated feminist projects and the critique of antifeminist nationalist rhetoric in the Third World. Fatima Mernissi, for instance, cites "the paternalistic defence of Muslim women's lot" by Western colonialists as responsible for alienating nationalist intellectuals "who had previously supported the liberation of Muslim women" (1987, 7). The work of Indian feminists, on the manipulation, by British colonialists, of the traditional Hindu practice of *Sati* or widow-immolation, to support the imperialist project in India and imperialist propaganda, is well-documented.
23. Articles in the Malaysian press have mentioned the revisionary work, for instance, of Amina Wadud-Muhsin, an African-American Koranic scholar formerly with the International Islamic University. While claiming to be an exegetical conservative, Wadud forcefully asserts that "the most sacred postulates" in Islam "are universal and non-sexist," and that it is male bias and "corrupt interpretations" in the exegetical tradition that have been responsible for apparent antifeminism in Islam (Ismail 1990; "A Woman's View"). Hers is a strategy, of course, in line with a time-honored history of similar claims by profeminist male nationalists in the Middle East such as Qasim Amin (see Philipp 1978, Jayawardena 1986, etc). Malaysian feminists—as Norma Mohamed Sharif, a graduate student at the University of Texas at Austin, recently reminded me—might also counter the Islamic nationalist charge that feminism is foreign by pointing out that the exegetical tradition in Islam, grounded in the Middle East and Arabism, is itself foreign to Malaysia. By contrast, Norma observes, *adat,* or customary law governing Malay communal life in Malaysia, is incontestably local in its origins and traditions, and often affords Malay Muslim women more rights than *shariah* law. That is to say, in Malaysia, Malay ethnic nationalism and pride and the historical continuity of Malay identity are at least potentially in conflict with Malay Islamic nationalism, and might constitute fertile ground for feminists who would assert the local origins and rights of feminism.
24. Interestingly, perhaps inevitably, these heroines—particularly when they are figures from contemporary history—are also often nationalist heroines, and figure in themselves and in their historical status the competitive tension of feminism and nationalism. The strategy of

sifting the past for figures, values, and narratives that would serve to provide a legitimizing genealogy for what is essentially a modern movement is, of course, a nationalist strategy as much as a feminist one in the Third World. In the search for an authoritative (and authorizing) orginary past, as in so many other projects, feminism and nationalism find themselves on parallel trajectories.

25. "In the pre-colonial era, indigenous Malay women had a relatively high status, as is generally the case in Southeast Asia. Malay mythology is replete with the legends of queens and matriarchs, particularly in the pre-Islamic era" (Wee 1987, 5).

26. The arrests received worldwide attention from the international human-rights community, from members of the U.S. Congress, and from members of the European Parliament, in part because it was widely believed, both within and outside Singapore, that the government had applied the powers of the Internal Security Act (ISA) against individuals who were critical of the government but who did not constitute a security threat to the state. The ISA, an instrument bequeathed by the British colonial administration to its erstwhile colony, had been periodically invoked by the government to detain individuals linked to the proscribed Malayan Communist Party (MCP). Prior to the 1987 arrests, however, the government had been careful to establish publicly, in each spate of arrests, the precise relation between the persons arrested and the Communist underground in Singapore and Malaysia. Detainees were also typically offered the option of release if they would agree to abjure, in writing, any commitment to violence as a means of political change. By contrast, no mention was made of Communists or the MCP in the 1987 arrests. The government only claimed, confusingly, that the community activists, dramatists, lawyers, student unionists, and feminists they arrested were either "Marxist" conspirators, the dupes of Marxist conspirators, or both simultaneously, and none was offered release in exchange for abjuring the violent overthrow of an elected government. The two founder-members of AWARE arrested were Teresa Lim Li Kok, then treasurer of AWARE, and Tang Fong Har, who escaped rearrest in 1988 by her sojourn in Britain. A number of the other women detainees (this round of political detentions were remarkable also in that more women than men were arrested) were also members of AWARE.

27. "Claire finds the label 'feminist' frightens many people. 'People see feminists as unhappy, ugly, and single. Feminism is a lonely cause. You are always met with disagreement and disfavour. I prefer the term "woman centredness."' AWARE believes that men and women should work in a shared partnership, not see themselves as battle opponents. Feminism is not an anti-man stand." (Saini 1992, 102).

28. While registered societies in Singapore are required to restrict their activity to the nonpolitical, individual women associated with these organizations have sometimes been able to articulate multiple political concerns, especially in their personal capacity. Kanwaljit Soin and Constance Singam, past presidents of AWARE and the Singapore Council of Women's Organizations (SCWO), have written together to the national press on the issue of race; Vivienne Wee, a former Honorary General Secretary of AWARE, has conducted research and analysis on transnational migrant domestic labor in her academic work as an anthropologist; Anamah Tan, president of the SCWO and a lawyer by profession, has written to the press petitioning the government (unfortunately without success) to require standardized legal contracts for the protection of foreign domestic workers in Singapore.

29. The Singapore government is not, of course, unique in thus arrogating to itself the powers of arbitrary definition. A feminist scholar notes, for instance, "Any concern which is now voiced [about the] difficult social and economic situation [of economically-disadvantaged women in Indonesia, and] how this relates to women's subordination, is branded as political" (Wieringa 1988, 85). Nor is AWARE unique, as a feminist group, in its adaptation to the social conditions in which it finds itself. A recent academic study observes that the Thai feminist NGO, Friends of Women, "[i]n past years . . . has tried to get rid of its image as a militant or radical women's group in order to gain general social support. It has tended to take a less active role in controversial issues such as prostitution and instead concentrates on such immediate action as helping rape victims" (Tantiwiramanond and Pandey 1991, 151).

30. Only AWARE has been distinctly identified, in the public mind, as a feminist group. Other organizations that have been active on women's issues include the Singapore Association of Women Lawyers (SAWL), founded in 1974, which offers free legal advocacy services to

women and has directed efforts at educating women on their rights under the law; and the Singapore Council of Women's Organisations (SCWO), founded in 1940, and representing thirty-eight groups and societies, with a total of close to 100,000 members. Because the SCWO is an umbrella body for a diversity of interests, however—member organizations include religious groups, a travel club, business and professional associations, school-alumni groups, government-affilated organizations, and a netball club—much of the SCWO's direction at any point of time is necessarily dependent upon its immediate leadership. In recent years, under presidents Constance Singam and Anamah Tan, the SCWO has had a palpably feminist cast.

31. Unlike his predecessor, former Prime Minister Lee, however, Goh nominally soft-pedals the eugenic equation. Although Goh tartly observed that "[w]omen with no formal schooling produced 2.5 times as many children as those with tertiary qualifications in 1970. The ratio went up to 2.8 in 1940 and 2.9 last year" ("Worrying Trends"), he nonetheless added as a concession, "Do not get me wrong. I am not saying that the less-educated women should have fewer children. It is a question of balance. If the ratio was one to one, or even one to two, it would not be a problem." The newspaper report went on to say that Goh "added that this imbalance was significant as talented people were needed to help create jobs for the less educated."
32. According to one of the two volumes produced by the PAP's Women's Wing, Singapore ranks forty-first among ninety-nine countries in a study on the status of women around the world conducted by the Population Crisis Committee in Washington, D.C. (Wong and Leong 1993, 10). This places Singapore after Hong Kong (thirty-second), Japan (thirty-fourth), and Taiwan (thirty-ninth) in the treatment of female citizens, but, as the editors take the trouble to note, before the other countries of the Association of Southeast Asian Nations (ASEAN), Pakistan and Bangladesh.
33. The Thai groups EMPOWER, Friends of Women (FOW), and the Women's Information Centre (WIC) of the Foundation for Women (FFW), for instance, are small-scale and dynamic, as scholars have noted. EMPOWER's work, in supporting and authorizing the most disenfranchised and alienated of women in Thai society—prostitutes, including children—through drama, education projects, self-help activities, and even a newsletter, is particularly impressive (Tantiwiramanond and Pandey 1991).
34. Since June 1993, a number of fine studies by Deniz Kandiyoti (1994), Rajeswari Mohan (1994), and others have appeared in print, theorizing Third-World feminism along trajectories similar to or divergent from the trajectory I outline above. I have learned much from this recent body of work, and from the lively, interrogative, and very diverse graduate students who participated in my 1995 seminar at the University of Texas on international feminisms.

Works Cited in Chapter 2

"Abusive Bosses Will Be Barred from Hiring Maids: Move to Punish Errant Employers, Says Ministry," *Straits Times* (Singapore), August 7, 1990, p. 3.

Anderson, Benedict. 1983. *Imagined Communities: Reflections on the Origin and Spread of Nationalism.* London: Verso.

AWARE round-up. 1993. *Awareness: A Journal of the Association of Women for Action and Research* (Singapore) 1, no. 1 (May 1993): 38–42.

Beck, Lois, and Nikki Keddie (eds.). 1978. *Women in the Muslim World.* Cambridge, Massachusetts/London: Harvard University Press.

Bloodworth, Dennis. 1986. *The Tiger and the Trojan Horse.* Singapore: Times Books International.

Chatterjee, Partha. 1989. "The Nationalist Resolution of the Women's Question." In Kumkum Sangari and Sudesh Vaid (eds.). *Recasting Women: Essays in Colonial History.* New Delhi: Kali for Women, pp. 233–53.

Croll, Elisabeth. 1978. *Feminism and Socialism in China.* London: Routledge & Kegan Paul.

Dancz, Virginia H. 1987. *Women and Party Politics in Peninsular Malaysia.* Singapore: Oxford University Press.

Enloe, Cynthia. 1989. *Bananas, Beaches, & Bases: Making Feminist Sense of International Politics.* Berkeley/Los Angeles: University of California Press.

"Filipino Senator Calls for Ban on Maids Bound for HK: Rising Abuse and Exploitation, Says Head Senate Labour Panel." *Sunday Times* (Singapore), May 19, 1991, p. 12.

"Govt Likely to Collect $48m in Foreign Worker Levy: About 200,000 Expected to Register by the Middle of Next Year." *Straits Times* (Singapore), December 14, 1991, p. 19.

"Govt Replies to MPs on COE Premiums and Levies Collected." *Straits Times* (Singapore), August 7, 1992, p. 25.

Halliday, Fred. 1991. "Hidden from International Relations: Women and the International Arena." In Rebecca Grant and Kathleen Newland (eds.), *Gender and International Relations.* Bloomington/Indianapolis: Indiana University Press, pp. 158–69.

Heng, Geraldine, and Janadas Devan. 1992. "State Fatherhood: The Politics of Nationalism, Sexuality, and Race in Singapore." In Andrew Parker, Mary Russo, Doris Sommer, Patricia Yaeger (eds.), *Nationalisms and Sexualities,* New York/London: Routledge, pp. 243–64.

Henson, Bertha. 1993. "Double Burden of Home and Career Keeping Women from Politics." *Straits Times* (Singapore), News Extra Section, June 19, 1993, p. 11.

Heyzer, Noeleen. 1986. *Working Women in South-East Asia: Development, Subordination and Emancipation.* Philadelphia: Open University Press, 1986.

Heyzer, Noeleen, and Vivienne Wee. 1992. "Domestic Workers in Transient Overseas Employment: Who Benefits, Who Profits?" Paper presented to the Regional Policy Dialogue on Foreign Domestic Workers: International Migration, Employment and National Politics, Colombo, Sri Lanka, August 10–14, 1992.

Ismail, Rose. "Man, Woman and Erroneous Thoughts." *New Sunday Times,* 20 May 1990.

Jayawardena, Kumari. 1986. *Feminism and Nationalism in the Third World.* London: Zed Books/New Delhi: Kali for Women.

Karim, Wazir-jahan. 1983. "Malay Women's Movements: Leadership and Processes of Change." *International Social Science Journal* 35, no. 4 (1983): 719–31.

Kandiyoti, Deniz (ed.). 1991. *Women, Islam and the State.* London: Macmillan.

——. "Identity and Its Discontents: Women and the Nation." In *Colonial Discourse and Post-Colonial Theory: A Reader.* eds. Patrick Williams and Laura Chrisman. New York: Columbia University Press, 1994, pp. 376–391.

Katrak, Ketu H. 1992. "Indian Nationalism, Gandhian 'Satyagraha,' and Representations of Female Sexuality." In Andrew Parker, Mary Russo, Doris Sommer, and Patricia Yaeger (eds). *Nationalisms and Sexualities.* New York/London: Routledge, pp. 395–406.

Lim, Seow Yoke. 1984/85. "Women in Singapore Politics 1945–1970." Unpublished Academic Exercise, Department of History, National University of Singapore.

"Maid Abuse Very Rare in S'pore, Say Agencies: Fewer than 1% of Maids They Handle Have Reported Ill-Treatment." *Straits Times* (Singapore), February 15, 1991, p. 16.

Marr, David. 1976. "The 1920s Women's Rights Debates in Vietnam." *Journal of Asian Studies* 35, no. 3 (1976): 371–89.

Mernissi, Fatima. 1987. *Beyond the Veil: Male-Female Dynamics in Modern Muslim Society.* Bloomington and Indianapolis: Indiana University Press.

Mohan, Rajeswari. "The Crisis of Femininity and Modernity in the Third World." *Genders,* 19, (1994): 223–56.

Molyneux, Maxine. 1991. "The Law, the State and Socialist Policies with Regard to Women: The Case of the People's Democratic Republic of Yemen 1967–1990." In Deniz Kandiyoti (ed.), *Women, Islam and the State.* London: Macmillan, pp. 237–71.

Ong, Aihwa. 1987: *Spirits of Resistance and Capitalist Discipline.* Albany, State University of New York Press.

Ong, Pang Boon. 1979. "Problems of Party Organisation: The Pro-Communist Challenge from Within 1954–'57." In *People's Action Party 1954–1979: Petir 25th Anniversary Issue.* Singapore: Central Executive Committee People's Action Party, pp. 44–59.

"PAP's Women's Wing Will Inform, Not Lobby: Aline." *Straits Times* (Singapore), July 29, 1992, p. 18.

People's Action Party. 1959. "Women in the New Singapore." In *The Tasks Ahead: P.A.P's Five-year Plan 1959–1964.* Singapore: Petir, Organ of the People's Action Party, pp. 17–19.

Philipp, Thomas. 1978. "Feminism and Nationalist Politics in Egypt." In Lois Beck and Nikki Keddie (eds.), *Women in the Muslim World.* Cambridge, Massachusetts/London: Harvard University Press, pp. 277–94.

Saini, Rohaniah. 1992. "Women for Women." *Her World*, (October 1992): 99–112.
Shahani, Leticia R. 1975. "Liberating the Filipino Woman." *Philippines Quarterly* 7, no. 4 (December 1975): 36–40.
Singapore Airlines Annual Report. 1990–91. Singapore: Singapore National Printers.
Singapore Association of Women Lawyers. 1986. *Legal Status of Singapore Women.* Singapore: Asiapac Books.
"Story of the Singapore Woman." *Straits Times* (Singapore), June 12, 1993, Life! section, p. 2.
Tan, Lian Choo. 1991. "Sex, Generals and Women Wronged in Thailand." *Straits Times* (Singapore), September 27, 1991, p. 34.
Tan, Sai Siong. 1993. "Molesting of S'pore Girls: Time SIA Stopped the Party." *Straits Times* (Singapore), May 8, 1993, p. 35.
Tantiwiramanond, Darunee, and Shashi Ranjan Pandey. 1991. *By Women, For Women: A Study of Women's Organizations in Thailand.* Singapore: Institute of Southeast Asian Studies, Social Issues in Southeast Asia Research, Notes and Discussions Paper No. 72.
"Thai Group Slams Lauda Air Ad: It Encourages Child Sex, Task Force Alleges." *Straits Times* (Singapore), August 11, 1992, p. 17.
"The Trials of Muslim Europe." *Newsweek* (January 27, 1992): 14–15.
Truong, Thanh-Dam. 1990. *Sex, Money and Morality: Prostitution and Tourism in Southeast Asia.* London and New Jersey: Zed Books.
Vargas, Virginia. 1988. "The Feminist Movement in Peru: Inventory and Perspectives." In Saskia Wieringa (ed.), *Women's Struggles and Strategies.* Aldershot: Gower, p. 136–54.
"Veil Viewed as Symbol of Resistance in Gaza Strip." *Straits Times* (Singapore), August 23, 1991, p. 15.
Vreede-de Stuers, Cora. 1960. *The Indonesian Woman: Struggles and Achievements.* The Hague: Mouton.
Wee, Vivienne. "The Ups and Downs of Women's Status in Singapore: A Chronology of Some Landmark Events (1950–1987)." *Commentary: Journal of the National University of Singapore Society.* Vol. 7, nos. 2–3, (December 1987): 5–12.
Wieringa, Saskia. 1988. "Aborted Feminism in Indonesia: A History of Indonesian Socialist Feminism." In Saskia Wieringa (ed.), *Women's Struggles and Strategies.* Aldershot: Gower, pp. 69–89.
"Winning by Persuasion." *Straits Times* (Singapore), September 3, 1993, Life! Section, p. 2.
"A Woman's View." *Straits Times,* 17 August 1992.
"Women's Wing to Study Family Services Idea." *Straits Times* (Singapore), February 27, 1990, p. 25.
Wong, Aline K., and Leong Wai Kum (eds.). 1993. *Singapore Women: Three Decades of Change.* Singapore: Times Academic Press.
"Worrying Trends Threaten Family Life." *Straits Times* (Singapore), June 14, 1993, p. 1.

Notes to Chapter 3

1. The title is inspired by Angela Carter's postholocaust love story *Heroes and Villains,* published by Heinemann in 1969.
2. This essay does not address practices defined as cultural, medical, or cosmetic (for example, clitoridectomy, infibulation, scarification), but focuses on rape and other sexual and physical assaults inflicted on women by men against their will, in both the private and public spheres.
3. The tragedy of Saarjie Baartman's life and the violence done to her even after her death indicate the perverse sexual fascination that an otherwise prudish society had for other races. The colonizers came from a Europe which fetishized Africans in displays and exhibitions, and relegated them to subhuman status (Mama, (1995) *Beyond the Masks: Race, Gender, and Subjectivity,* New York: Routledge.)
4. The Contagious Diseases Acts entitled the authorities to subject women suspected of "immoral" living to regular vaginal examinations and confinement for treatment (by force if necessary). In the colonies, the cost of treating African women identified as prostitutes was deemed prohibitive, so only the colonial forces were offered treatment.

   One cannot help but be reminded of the forced "virginity tests" and vaginal examinations to which Asian and African women were subjected at British ports-of-entry. While "virginity testing" was stopped after public outrage and black feminist campaigns in the early 1980s, vaginal examinations continue to be carried out, particularly on African women. Many African men are subjected to equally intrusive anal examinations. This practice also continues at African ports, enforced by regimes under pressure to counteract the flow of drug trafficking.

5. See Angela Carter's insightful reconstruction of the relationship between Baudelaire and his mistress, Jeanne Duval, in *Black Venus* (Picador, 1985).
6. This particular circular is reported to have been hastily withdrawn because of its "impracticality" (Callaway 1987, 49).
7. These services included catering, beer-brewing, laundry, and sex (White 1990; Naanen 1991).
8. It is a matter of historical record that a significant proportion of the early Western feminists were pro-imperialist (Hooks 1984).
9. Similarly, the practice of purdah increased markedly during the colonial period in Northern Nigeria. (Imam 1991).
10. Colonisers found the fact that African women were "more traditional" a negative trait, while many African men regard it as desirable. Both agree that urban women are "whores" and less "reputable" than the strangely simplified category of "rural women." According to the myth, rural women continue to live contentedly as beasts of burden, never challenging anyone's authority, least of all that of their menfolk.
11. "Kikuyu" here refers exclusively to men.
12. Gambo Sawaba, a leading woman activist, was repeatedly assaulted and harassed for her campaign to change this situation. Women in the North of independent Nigeria were finally allowed to vote in 1976, but regressive forces, continuing to protest during the current transition to civilian rule, have succeeded in their demands for separate arrangements for women voters in 1991.
13. Posters of Palestinian and Eritrean women fighters wearing "Arafat scarves" and the SWAPO poster of a woman with a gun over her shoulder and a baby on her back are found hanging in women's centers all over the West. I have yet to see a poster of a male fighter with a gun and a baby, or one simply carrying a baby, attract the same attention.
14. More recently, I observed the Eritrean celebration of the first anniversary of the end of the war with Ethiopia, referred to by many as the Eritrean Revolution. As many as 30 percent of the EPLF fighters were women, and a great deal has been said and written about the liberation of women on the battlefields. Consequently, I felt it almost sacrilegous that no Eritrean women were in evidence amongst the provisional government dignitaries on the parade ground or at the official reception celebrating the event. The very colorful and skilled cultural displays on that festive occasion were more about remembering the martyred sons and recovering Eritrean "traditional cultures" than about forging new social relations between the genders or sustaining the equality that is reported to have been practiced behind the battlelines.
15. The 1986 edict is almost identical to that issued by the British in colonial Katsina in 1916 (referred to earlier in the text), except that it gave women three months instead of seven days in which to marry.
16. *West Africa* (March 1987). Other examples of religious fraternities perpetrating acts of violence against women in Sudan have been documented by Africa Watch (April 9, 1990).
17. Sources: Accounts of Nairobi residents are given in *Weekly Review*, Aug. 9, 1991. One women's magazine did take the opportunity to observe the extent to which ingrained male violence characterizes Kenyan women's lives. See *Presence* 7, no. 8 (1991).
18. See the Amnesty International 1991 report *Women in the Frontline*, and Africa Watch reports.
19. This rather strangely named legislation was featured in a community theater performance by an African women's group in Amsterdam that same year; it was humorously compared to the South African Immorality Act which made interracial sex illegal!
20. The widespread impact of AIDS on Ugandan society must be one of the reasons for such stringent measures being introduced. It remains to be seen how effectively they will be implemented and whether they will function as a deterrent.
21. Newspaper reports gleaned during October 1992.

Works Cited in Chapter 3

Amadiume, I. 1987. *Male Daughters, Female Husbands: Gender and Sex in an African Society.* London: Zed Press.

Badran, M. 1988. "Dual Liberation: Feminism and Nationalism in Egypt, 1870–1925." *Feminist Issues* 8, no. 1 (1988).

Callaway, H. 1987. *Gender, Culture and Empire: European Women in Colonial Nigeria.* London: Macmillan.

Chelser, P. 1972. *Women and Madness.* New York: Doubleday.

Dobash, R. E. and Dobash, R. 1980. *Violence Against Wives.* London: Open Books.

Edwards, S. 1986. *The Police Responses to Domestic Violence in London.* Polytechnic of Central London.

Enloe, C. 1989. *Bananas, Beaches and Bases: Making Feminist Sense of International Politics.* London: Pandora.

Fanon, F. 1980. *A Dying Colonialism.*London: Writers and Readers.

Gaidzanwa, R. 1991. "Women and Education in Zimbabwe." Paper presented at CODESRIA workshop on "Gender Analysis and African Social Science," Dakar, Sept.16–20, 1991.

Helie-Lucas, M. 1987. "Against Nationalism: The Betrayal of Algerian Women." *Trouble and Strife* 11 (Summer 1987).

hooks, b. 1984. *From Margin to Center.* Boston: South End Press.

Hunt, N. R. 1990. "Domesticity and Colonialism in Belgian Africa: Usumbura's Foyer Social, 1946–1960." *Signs* 15, no. 3 (1990): 447–74.

Imam, A. 1991. "Women Should Neither Be Seen Nor Heard? Identity Politics and Women's Mobilisation in Kano, Northern Nigeria." In Valentin Moghadan, ed. *Identity Politics and Women: Cultural Reassertions and Feminisms in International Perspective* (London: Oxford University Press).

Jacobs, S. and Howard, T. 1987. "Women in Zimbabwe: State Policy and State Action." In *Women, State and Ideology,* ed. H. Afshar. London: Macmillan.

Jayawardena, K. 1986. *Feminism and Nationalism in the Third World.* London: Zed Press.

Kenyatta, J. 1953. *Facing Mount Kenya: The Tribal Life of the Kikuyu.* London: Secker and Warburg.

Mama, A. 1989a. "Violence Against Black Women: Gender, Race and State Responses." *Feminist Review* no. 32 (1989: 30–48.

Mama, A. 1989b. *The Hidden Struggle: Voluntary and Statutory Responses to Violence Against Black Women.* London: Runnymede Trust.

Mba, N. 1982. *Nigerian Women Mobilised: Women's Political Activities in Southern Nigeria 1900–1965.* Berkeley: University of California Press.

McClintock, A. 1991a. "'No Longer in a Future Heaven?': Women and Nationalism in South Africa." *Transition* no. 51 (1991): 104–23.

McClintock, A. 1991b. "The Scandal of the Whorearchy: Prostitution in Colonial Nairobi." *Transition* no. 52 (1991): 92–99.

Mies, M. 1986. *Patriarchy and Accumulation on a World Scale: Women in the International Division of Labour.* London: Zed Press.

Mohammed, P. 1991. "Reflections on the Women's Movement in Trinidad: Calypsoes, Changes and Sexual Violence." *Feminist Review,* no. 38 (1991): 33–47.

Naanen, B. 1991. "'Itinerant Goldmines': Prostitution in the Cross River Basin in Nigeria 1930–1950." *African Studies Review* 34, no. 2 (1991): 57–59.

Okonjo, K. 1976. "The Dual Sex Political System in Operation: Igbo Women and Community Politics in Mid-Western Nigeria." in N. Hafkin and E. Bay. eds. *Women in Africa.* Palo Alto, Calif.: Stanford University Press.

Parpart, J. and Staudt, K. 1989. eds. *Women and the State in Africa.* London: Lynne Rienner Publishers.

Schmidt, E. 1991. "Patriarchy, Capitalism, and the Colonial State in Zimbabwe." *Signs* 16, 4 (Summer 1991): 732–56.

Sharaawi, H. 1986. *Harem Years: The Memoirs of an Egyptian Feminist.* London: Virago.

Stott, R. 1989. "The Dark Continent: Africa as Female Body in Haggard's Adventure Fiction." *Feminist Review,* no. 32 (1989): 69–89.

Tabet, P. 1991. "'I'm the Meat, I'm the Knife': Sexual Service, Migration and Repression in Some African Societies." *Feminist Issues* (Spring 1991): 3–21.

Taylor, J. and Stewart, S. 1991. *Sexual and Domestic Violence: Help, Recovery and Action in Zimbabwe*. Women and Law in Southern Africa, PO Box VA 171, Union Avenue, Harare, Zimbabwe.

Tsikata, E. 1989. "Women's Organisation and the State in Ghana." *Women and History Series*. The Hague: Institute of Social Studies.

Schmidt, E. 1991. "Patriarchy, Capitalism and the Colonial State in Zimbabwe." *Signs* 16, no. 4 (1991): 732–56.

Urdang, S. 1989. *And Still They Dance: Women, War and the Struggle for Change in Mozambique*. New York/London: Monthly Review Press.

Van Allen, J. 1972. "Sitting on a Man: Colonialism and the Lost Political Institutions of Igbo Women." *Canadian Journal of African Studies* 6, no. 2 (1972): 165–82.

Wamalma, B.N. 1989. "Violence Against Wives and the Law in Kenya." in M. A. Mbeo and O. Ooko-Ombaka, eds. *Women and the Law in Kenya,* Nairobi, Public Law Institute.

White, L. 1990. *The Comforts of Home: Women and Prostitution in Colonial Nairobi*. Chicago: University of Chicago Press.

Notes to Chapter 4

This essay would not have been possible had it not been for the women and men in the Bahamas who have been an integral part of movements for social justice. I am profoundly indebted to them and to DAWN for their willingness to be candid under conditions of state repression. I am also grateful to Linda Carty, with whom I did the field work for this essay and with whom there were many late-night conversations to sort through the inevitable residues of research insights. Two in the field are infinitely better than one. I also benefited enormously from the meticulous readings of Marion Bethel, Linda Carty, Jinny Chalmers, Cynthia Enloe, Barbara Herbert, Jerma Jackson, Gary Lemons, Chandra Talpade Mohanty, and Mun Wong, trusting that I have used them wisely. Thanks also to Ana Christie for being a resourceful and patient research spirit, and to Jessica Badonsky for assisting in the job of assembling notes. Mo dúpẹ.

1. Marion Bethel, "And the Trees Still Stand," In Marion Bethel (1994) *Guanahani, Mi Amor Y Otras Poemas,* Cuba: Casa de las Americas, p. 44.
2. The acronym DAWN stands for Developing Alternatives for Women Now. The group was formed in 1986 and from the outset operated as an autonomous women's organization. Beginning with a multifaceted feminist ideology, one of its first tasks was to challenge the state and organized medicine in 1989 on the introduction of Norplant. It has simultaneously politicized questions of women's history, cultural, and artistic production, domestic violence and violence against women, and has also held annual women's fairs.
3. These organizations were formed in the first decade of the twentieth century. They were international organizations with headquarters in London and chapters in the 'British Commonwealth.' Here is a description of the aims of the Imperial Order of Daughters of the Empire: "In May 1902, the first meeting in the Bahamas of the IODE was held. Its aims are loyalty to Queen and Country; service to others, (particularly to Commonwealth servicemen and their survivors); the promotion of education, with an emphasis on history; and the preservation of its records, to assist in the relief of those in poverty or distress." See also Michael Craton (1986) A *History of the Bahamas,* Canada: San Salvador, p. 110.
4. Willis Carey, "Suffragettes Placed Goal Above Threats to Jobs and Careers," *Nassau Guardian*. 25 January 1988; Edda Demons, "Franchise has not solved all Women's Problems," *Nassau Guardian*. 19 November 1987; Sharon Poities, "When Women Won the Vote, Men Began Taking Notice." *Nassau Guardian*. 5 November 1987.
5. Lynda Hart (1994) *Fatal Women: Lesbian Sexuality and the Mark of Aggression*. Princeton: Princeton University Press, p. 7.
6. See for instance, Andrew Parker (1991) *Nationalism and Sexuality*. New York: Routledge; Patricia Williams (1991) *The Alchemy of Race and Rights*. Cambridge: Harvard University Press; Kumkum Sangari and Sudesh Vaid (eds.) (1989) *Recasting Woman: Essays in Indian Colonial History*. New Delhi: Kali for Women; Shabnam Grewal et al (eds.) (1988) *Charting the Journey: Writings by Black and Third World Women*. London: Sheba Feminist Publishers; Cynthia Enloe (1989) *Bananas Beaches and Bases: Making Feminist Sense Of International Politics*. *Berkeley*: University of California Press; Than-dam Truong (1990) *Sex, Money and Morality*. London: Zed Press; Rhoda Reddock (1994) *Women Labor And*

Politics in Trinidad and Tobago, London: Zed Books; Joan French and Michelle Cave, "Sexual Choice as Human Rights: Women Loving Women," paper presented at Critical Perspectives in Human Rights in the Caribbean, Trinidad and Tobago, 26–28 January 1995; "The New Politics of Sex and the State," *Feminist Review* No. 48, Autumn 1994.

7. R.W. Connel, (1987) *Gender and Power,* Stanford: Stanford University Press; Michel Foucault (1979) *Discipline and Punish*. New York: Vintage Books, p. 125.
8. *Ibid*. (Hart) p. 8.
9. M. Jacqui Alexander, "Not Just (Any) *Body* Can Be A Citizen: The Politics of Law, Sexuality and Postcoloniality in Trinidad and Tobago and the Bahamas," *Feminist* Review, No. 48, Autumn 1994, p 5–23.
10. Repression of other kinds also exist. For example, there is a section in the general orders that curtails political activity of public servants. See general orders, "Utterance on Political and Administrative Matters, Statement #932," (1982) Nassau, Bahamas. The injunction reads as follows: "A public officer must in no circumstances become publicly involved in any political controversy, unless he becomes so involved through no fault of his own, for example, in the proper performance of his official duties; and he must have it in mind that publication either orally or in writing of any material, whether of direct political interest or relating to the administration of the Government or of a Department of Government or any matter relating to his official duties or other matters do not affect the public service." See also "An act To Amend the Law Relating to Sexual Offences and to Make Provisions in respect of Related Circumstances Involving Parties To A Marriage." (Date of Assent 29 July 1991) Nassau: Bahamas, Government Printing Office 1991.
11. Craton, p. 112.
12. Jonathan Goldberg, "Sodomy in the New World: Anthropologies Old and New," p. 3–18. in Michael Warner (ed.) (1993) *Fear of A Queer Planet,* Minneapolis: University of Minnesota Press. The move here is an important foundational one. Goldberg draws from a sixteenth century document regarding Balboa's entry into a Panamanian village in which he ordered the killing of about 600 "sodomitic" Indians, and fed another 40 to the dogs. Goldberg argues that the gesture served to establish a link between heterosexual imperial interests and heterosexual 'native' interests, suggesting that 'native' heterosexuals had more in common with imperial heterosexuals than with 'native' homosexuals.
13. *Ibid*. (Warner) p. 15.
14. The recodification of primogeniture here is somewhat paradoxical since from 1982, women's groups have influenced the state to erase primogeniture. A bill, brought before Parliament since that time, now sits on the back burner.
15. David T. Evans (1993) Sexual *Citizenship, The Material Construction of Sexualities*. London: Routledge; Tom Barry, Beth Wood (1984) *The Other Side of Paradise: Foreign Control in the Caribbean,* New York: Grove Press, p. 259; Also, interview with Michael Stevenson, College of the Bahamas, June 1993.
16. *Op. cit* (Hart) p. 5
17. This is one area that has been remarkably undertheorized in the understanding of the American state—the extent to which an advanced capitalist state can be simultaneously nationalist, or even hypernationalist, intervening abroad, while vigorously engaged in the redrawing of its own borders at home. Unfortunately, nationalism has come to be more easily associated with Third World and not advanced capitalist states.

    The specific reference here is to the Californian mobilization in 1995, Proposition 187, against undocumented workers, whom the U.S. North American state defines as "illegal aliens." The effect of this Right wing mobilization would be to deny schooling, health care and a range of social services to both these undocumented workers and their children. Variations of Proposition 187 are being undertaken in different states.
18. Ruthann Robson (1992) *Lesbian (Out)Law: Survival Under the Rule of Law*. Ithaca: Firebrand Press, p. 58.
19. The most significant gesture here is the convergence of Right wing mobilization inside the American state surrounding family values and the deployment of foreign 'aid' in its service. The United States Foreign Relations Committee has, for instance, formulated a policy that links the terms of foreign aid to the outlawing of abortions and increasing sterilization programs, in other words, the further institutionalization of population control at the expense of birth control.

20. Inderpal Grewal and Caren Kaplan (eds.) (1994) *Scattered Hegemonies: Postmodernity and Transnational Feminist Practices,* Minneapolis: University of Minnesota Press.
21. Janet Halley, "The Construction of Heterosexuality," in Warner, *Ibid.,* p. 82–104; see also Kendall Thomas, 'Bowers vs. Hardwick: Beyond the Pleasure Principle," in Dan Danielsen and Karen Engle (eds.) (1995) *After Identity: A Reader in Law and Culture,* New York: Routledge.
22. Edda Dumont, 'Franchise has not Solved All Women's Problems," (Interview with Lady Butler) *Nassau Guardian.* 19 November l987, p. 2.
23. There is both a range and plethora of women's organizations ranging from girl guides and trade union groupings to Business and Professional Women's organizations and feminist groups. A listing compiled by the Women's Desk reveals that there are approximately 67 women's organizations. Women's Affairs Unit, *Directory of Women's Groups,* Nassau, Bahamas: Government Printing Office, 1991.
24. The Women's Desk, established in 1981, was upgraded in 1987 to a Women's Affairs Unit but is still located within the Ministry of Youth, Sports, and Community Development. It has been consistently plagued by a lack of funds. Constraints it faced in 1993 included the following: 1) Inadequate funds for execution of program activities; 2) lack of trained staff in unit; 3) unit unable to meet the demands of the public; 4) no approved national policy (on women) and 5) unclear status. Women's Desk, internal memorandum, 1989. See also, Audrey Roberts, "The Changing Role of Women's Bureaux in the Process of Social Change in the Caribbean," Keynote presentation for the Tenth Anniversary Celebration of the Women's Affairs Unit, 17 June 1991.
25. Interviews with Sandra Dean Patterson, Director of the Women's Crisis Center and Sharon Claire and Camille Barnett, College of the Bahamas, June 1993.
26. *Ibid.* Interviews with Sexual Offences Unit at the Criminal Investigation Division, CID, Bahamas, June 1993.
27. The following provide an indication of the kind of sensationalism generated in the media: "Sixteen-Year-Old School Girl Mother—Teenage mothering is no fun," 22 March 1986, *The Tribune;* "Thirteen-year-old Girls Sexually Molested by a Knife-Wielding Man," July 26, *The Tribune.* "False Cry of Rape Puts Lady Accountant in Jail" (convicted of endeavor to deceive) 18 September 1986, *The Tribune;* "Visitor is Raped at Gunpoint at Paradise Beach," 8 October 1986, *The Tribune.* Also interviews with Alfred Sears and Marion Bethel, Nassau, June 1993.
28. Interviews with Alfred Sears and Marion Bethel, Nassau, June 1993.
29. See here, General Laws, "Personal Rights Arising from Marriage and Proprietary Rights During Marriage" Part 3, Subsection 2 relating to the rights of consortium and the duty of the wife to cohabit with her husband. It states: "it is the duty of the wife to reside and cohabit with her husband." There is no such requirement specified for a husband.
30. "DAWN Galvanizes Resources to Address Issues Arising from Sex Violence Bill," *Nassau Guardian.* 25 November 1989.
31. Interview with Therese Huggins, Member of DAWN, Bahamas, June 1993.
32. The link between domestic sexual violence and state economic violence has been made by CAFRA, the Caribbean Association for Feminist Research and Action and by SISTREN, a women's collaborative theatre group. See, for example, *CAFRA News.* Newsletter of the Caribbean Association for Feminist Research and Action, "Women and Sexuality, Vol. 8. No. 1, 2, January–June 1994. See also, Honor Ford Smith, (1986) Lionheart *Gal: Lifestories of Jamaican Women,* London: The Women's Press.
33. *Ibid.* (Sexual Offences Act).
34. "Women's Crisis Week," *Nassau Guardian.* 29 September 1989.
35. "MPs Passed the Sexual Offences Bill to Provide Greater Protection for Women on the Job," *The Tribune,* 17 May 1991; "Magistrate Supports Move to Educate Public About Incest," 23 June 1986, *Nassau Guardian.*
36. Alicia Mondesire, Leith Dunn, (1994) "Towards Equity in Development: A Report on the Status of Women in 16 Commonwealth Caribbean Countries," prepared for the Fourth World Congress on Women, Georgetown: Guyana, p. 50.
37. *Ibid.*
38. Interview with Marion Bethel, Attorney General's Office, Nassau Bahamas, June 1993. For the question of rethinking issues of coverture in relation to domestic violence in the

United States, see, Isabel Marcus, "Thinking and Teaching about Terrorism in the Home," paper presented at the Feminism and Legal Theory Workshop, Columbia University, 1992.

39. J. G. Miller (1983) *Family Property and Financial Provisions,* London: Sweet and Miller. p. 1–14.
40. *Op. cit.* (Sexual Offences Act) p. 18–19.
41. Family Law Provisions, Miscellaneous Amendments, No. 17 of 1988, p. 851.
42. *Ibid.* (Miller).
43. The Commonwealth of the Bahamas, "Labor Force and Household Income Report, 1989," Nassau, Bahamas: Department of Statistics.
44. *Ibid.*
45. "Salaries and Allowances for Cabinet Ministers," The Bahamas Federation of Labor, 1992.
46. The point is excellently explicated here: Patricia Williams (1991) *The Alchemy of Race and Rights,* Cambridge: Harvard University Press; Patricia Williams, "Attack of the 50-Foot First Lady: The Demonization of Hillary Clinton," *Village Voice,* Vol. XXXVI, p. 35.
47. *Ibid.* (Labor Force and Income).
48. Andrew Stuart, "Women made up 60.5 percent of unemployed in 1989, Party told," 23 October 1989, *Nassau Guardian*; See also *ibid.*, Labor force and Household Income Report," xiv–xv.
49. "Legislation for Women," *Nassau Guardian,* 20 November 1987.
50. Interview with Michael Stevenson, College of the Bahamas, June 1993. Haitians occupy a marginalized status in spite of their work and the fact that they have lived for several generations in the Bahamas. The conflation of the Haitian body with the AIDS infected body has served to further make Haitians the object of state surveillance and repression, and misguided popular disaffection.
51. Interview with Sharon Claire and Camille Barnett.
52. *Ibid.* (Letter to the editor) This gesture of gender parity was first made explicit by women, endorsed by Myrtle Brandt, the principal draftsperson for the Sexual Offences Bill, and then enthusiastically endorsed by the state.
53. Conversation with Mun Wong, City University of New York, 1995.
54. The strictures of these surveillance mechanisms had already become clear to women and women's groups and social service agencies almost immediately after the passage of the bill. Interviews with Ruth Bowe-Darville, Sandra Dean Patterson and ZONTA, June 1993.
55. *Op. cit.* (Sexual Offences Act).
56. All these statements are quotations taken verbatim from parliamentary hearings. At the time of the research in June 1993, four years after the debates, the testimonies, except for the then opposition's statements, had not been transcribed. We, therefore, had access to information which many Bahamians did not have.
57. Letter from Hunster to Colonial Secretary, Trinidad and Tobago, 1804.
58. W. E. B. Du Bois, *The Souls of Black Folk* (1969) New York: Penguin.
59. *Ibid.* (Craton) p. 280–304; Gail Saunders (1985) *Slavery in the Bahamas,* Bahamas: The Nassau Guardian; See also, Ashis Nandy (1983) *The Intimate Enemy,* Oxford: Oxford University Press; (1987) *Traditions, Tyranny and Utopias: Essays on the Politics of Awareness,* Oxford: Oxford University Press.
60. See for instance: Gloria Wekker (1992) "I am Gold Money (I pass Through All Hands, But I do Not Lose My Value): The Construction of Selves, Gender and Sexualities in a Female Working-Class AfroSurinamese Setting," unpublished Ph.D. dissertation, UCLA; Joceline Clemencia, "Women Who Love Women: A Whole Perspective from Kachapera to Open Throats," paper delivered at the Caribbean Studies Association Conference, Curaçao, May 23–26, 1995; Makeda Silvera (1992) "Man Royals and Sodomites: Some thoughts on the Invisibility of Afro-Caribbean Lesbians," *Feminist Studies,* Vol. 18, No. 3; Audre Lorde, (1982) *Zami: A New Spelling of My Name,* New York: The Crossing Press; Dionne Brand, (1988) *Sans Souci,* Toronto: Williams-Wallace.
61. *Op. cit.* (Hart) p. 11.
62. It is the moment of transition from colonial rule to 'independence' symbolized by the new nation flag that is being contested here. The point is that flag independence belies the significant ways in which foreign, imperial interests are still folded into the nation's.

    We first heard of the specter of a band of nationless men from some policemen after an interview at CID. We found the image quite pervasive. It was later corroborated by other interviewees.

63. Interview with Alfred Sears and Marion Bethel, Bahamas, June 1993; See also *Op. cit.* (Craton); Sir Randal Fawkes (1979) *The Faith that Moved the Mountain,* Nassau: The Nassau Guardian; Doris L. Johnson, (1972) *The Quiet Revolution in the Bahamas,* Nassau: Family Islands Press.
64. See for instance, Toni Morrison (1992) *Race-ing Justice, En-gendering Power: Essays on Anita Hill, Clarence Thomas and the Construction of Social Reality,* New York: Pantheon.
65. Marion Bethel, "Where do we Go From Here?" Keynote Presentation, Second National Women's Conference, Nassau, 6 December 1986; Gail Saunders, "Women in the Bahamian Society and Economy in the Late Nineteenth and Early Twentieth Centuries," paper presented at the Twenty-Third Annual Conference of Caribbean Historians, 17–22 March 1991, Dominican Republic; Ministry of Education, Department of Archives, "Aspects of Bahamian History: A Chronological History of Women's Suffrage in the Bahamas, 1952–62," Nassau: Government Printing Office, 1992.
66. Roland Barthes (1957) *Mythologies,* New York: The Noonday Press, p. 109–58.
67. The following has been established as grounds for irretrievable breakdown of a marriage: "being guilty of a homosexual act, sodomy, or having sexual relations with an animal," Sir. Leonard P. Knowles, *Elements of Bahamian Law,* Nassau: Nassau Guardian, p. 41.
68. Evans, *passim.*
69. The state, nonetheless, has to be careful of not entirely usurping the church's own divine mission of salvation. It must therefore legislate against these passions, these sins of the flesh, as a restorative gesture.
70. *Op. cit.* (Evans) p. 111.
71. Mary Louise Pratt (1992) Imperial *Eyes: Travel Writing and Transculturation,* London: Routledge.
72. Throne Speeches, 1967–1992, *Nassau Guardian*; these discussions are conducted in a way that suggests that Bahamians are not in need of an infrastructure.
73. "Rotarians Use Bumper Stickers to Highlight Tourism Campaign," *Nassau Guardian,* 20 August 1991.
74. *Bahamas, Tourist Statistics.* 1990, Nassau: Ministry of Tourism.
75. "Business slump in Freeport caused by rudeness." The *Guardian,* 6 October 1992, p. 36–37.
76. *Op. cit.* (Craton) p. 253.
77. The Bahamas Ministry of Tourism, "The Bahamas: 1991 Guide to Cruising, Fishing, Marinas and Resorts."
78. Ernest Hemingway (1990) *Islands in the Stream,* New York: Charles Scribner's; Jeffrey Meyers (1985) *Hemingway: A Biography,* New York: Harper and Row; Carlos Baker (1969) *Ernest Hemingway: A Life Story.* New York: Charles Scribner's Sons.
79. Toni Morrison (1992) *Playing in the Dark: Whiteness and the Literary Imagination,* Cambridge: Harvard University Press.
80. *Ibid.* Christopher Lehmann-Haupt, "Was Hemingway Gay? There's More to his Story," *New York Times,* 10 November 1994, p. C21.
81. *Ibid.* (Barry) p. 259; Carmen Diana Deere (1990) *In the Shadow of the Sun: Caribbean Development Alternatives and United States Policy,* Boulder: Westview, p. 125.
82. *Op. cit.* (Barry), p. 256.
83. Kobena Mercer, "Black Identity/Queer Identity," paper delivered at the Black Nation/ Queer Nation? Conference, City University of New York, April 1995.
84. Jamaica Kincaid (1988) *A Small Place,* New York: Farrar, Straus and Giroux.
85. *Op. cit.* (Sexual Offences Act) .
86. *Op. cit.* (Evans).
87. There was apparently an opening for gay transvestite cultural expression in the mid- to late 1970s that has since been foreclosed in this period of the commodification and fetishization of culture which cultural workers view as the state's attempt to exploit.
88. bell hooks (1992) *Black Looks: Race and Representation,* Boston: South End Press.
89. Bahamian law conforms to the Westminster model of British governance with a balance among the legislative, judiciary and executive branches and the charge to the legislature to "make laws for the peace, order and good government of the state." Moreover, British

common law has been in full force since 1799, and laws relating to marriage are encoded in the Marriage Act of 1924. It still remains the case that changes made in metropolitan codes may not necessarily be enacted in former colonies. See, Burbin Hall, 'The Legal System of the Bahamas and the Role of the Attorney General, Bahamas: *Bahamian Journal*. Vol. 1. No. l p. 10–13; See also, *Ibid*. (Knowles).

Notes to Chapter 5

1. G. M. Bataille and K. M. Sands, *American Indian Women: Telling Their Lives,* (Lincoln: University of Nebraska Press, 1984). In addition, see Rayna Green, ed., *Native American Women: A Contextual Bibliography,* (Bloomington: Indiana University Press 1983), and her latest book, *Women in American Indian Society* (New York: Chelsea House Publishers 1992).
2. M. A. Jaimes with Theresa Halsey, "American Indian Women: At the Center of Indigenous Resistance in Contemporary North America," in *The State of Native America,* Jaimes, ed., (Boston: South End Press, 1992) pp. 311–44. The term "trickle-down patriarchy" actually came from a review of "Once Upon a Conquest: The Legacy of Five Hundred Years of Survival and Resistance," by Elliot, in *Labyrinth,* (Oct. 1992): 2–3.
3. Ward Churchill, "I Am Indigenist: Notes on the Ideology of the Fourth World," in *Struggle for the Land: Indigenous Resistance to Genocide, Ecocide and Expropriation in Contemporary America,* (ME: Common Courage Press, 1992/93).See also M. A. Jaimes, "Native American Identity and Survival: Indigenism and Environmental Ethics," in *Issues in Native American Culture: Critical Institution* Vol. 2., ed. Peter Lang, 1995.
4. W. Churchill, and Glenn Morris, "Table: Key Indian Laws and Cases," in *The State of Native America,* pp. 13–17.
5. *Ibid. 200–204,* 212. In the historical background, they note the question of individual civil rights in the 1950s, motivated by an effort to record the development of case law pertaining to the articulation of the list of inherent powers (still) possessed by tribes. Such cases involved the power of tribes to tax (or be taxed, a crucial Indian gambling issue today), to lease or consolidate lands, to give rights of way, and other functions (p. 204). In a related issue about "tribal taxation" by the federal or state entities, see M. A. Jaimes, "Gambling Wars: An Assault on American Indian Sovereignty," *New World Times,* (Santa Fe), (August 1992, pp. 17 & 30; and "Our Brother's Keeper," *Turtle Mountain Quarterly* (Winter 1993): 39–42; p. 204 on traditional tribal membership rights for "perfect political freedom."
6. Jaimes w/Halsey, *State,* op. cit., p. 341 (fn# 101); on the Santa Clara Pueblo v. Martinez case (436 U.S.49).
7. *Ibid.* In addition, Ward Churchill and Glenn Morris, in "Table: Key Indian Laws and Cases," op.cit., p. 16, cite the 1978 *Martinez* case; they stated that it also involved habeas corpus interpreted as "relief" in the federal decision.
8. See Jaimes, *State,* op. cit., p. 330–31 on the 1981 Sandra Lovelace (Sappier) case on the Tobique Reserve, in New Brunswick, Canada.
9. Vine Deloria, Jr., "Implications of the 1968 Civil Rights Act in Tribal Autonomy, in *The Indian Historian,* 1977. The (Lakota) Indian scholar wrote, in 1977, "I don't think tribal governments today fully understand what rights they have within the 1968 Indian Civil Rights law. The U.S. government [actually] has two principal concepts of what a tribe is. By the same token I don't think any federal agencies understand what has happened, as far as federal-Indian relationships are concerned; also cited in Jaimes' Dissertation, *op. cit.,* p. 183–5 (fn# 43), where she highlights the case of *U.S. vs. Sandoval (231,* U.S. 31 at 45–47, 1913) as a precedent that was imposed on all American Indian groups as a federal "blanket policy" (fn# 45).
10. Presentation (on tape), "Native American Women in Tribal Leadership," by (former) tribal *chairwoman* Twila Martin Kakehbeh, at Law School Seminar, Cornell University (Ithaca, N.Y.) on Nov. 12, 1991; she also stated, in a keynote presentation at the Great Plains program, "Subaltern Terrain" Conference, the University of Lincoln/Nebraska, on July 12, 1992, that the first barrier she had to overcome in tribal council politics was sexism among the predominantly male members, who expected her to fetch their coffee. Kakehbeh had a productive two year term as the Tribal Chair of the North Dakota Turtle Mountain Band in that state, but she has since lost her second election to her opponent.

11. Deloria and Lytle, *Nations, op. cit.,* 213–14 on *Wounded Knee 1973* siege
12. See Ward Churchill, "Perversions of Justice: Examining the Doctrine of U.S. Rights to Occupancy in North America," in *Struggle for the Land,* pp. 33–83. Churchill quotes Robert Stock's earlier article, "The Settler State and the American Left," *New Studies on the Left,* "Work and Society" special issue, Saxifrage Pubs., Boulder, CO, vol. 154, #3, Winter, (1990–91): 72–78; he also notes that the first time the term "Tribe" was used in a legal context, was in *Lonewolf vs. Hitchcock* (1903), which preempted the use of "Nation."
13. Deloria provides a legal context to this development in "The Application of the U.S. Constitution to American Indians," in *Exiled in the Land of the Free: Democracy, Indian Nations, and the U.S. Constitution,* Oren Lyons and John Mohawk, et al., editors, Clear Light Pubs., Santa Fe, N.M., 1992: 282–315. Deloria stated it thus: "tribes are dependent domestic nations, not the originators of the constitutional social contract or creatures of the national government. The principle announced by the Senate Judiciary Committee in 1870, in finding that Indian nations were excluded from the operation of the (14th) Amendment, was that it would be unfair and unjust to subject them to a rule or law to which they had not consented. Consent, the basis of modern Western social contract theory, can only be found in the Indian treaty relationship with the (U.S.)" (p. 315–15); Deloria is predicating this analysis on his earlier work co-authored with Lytle, *Nations, op. cit.* He does not, however, address the relevant political position some non-treaty (as well as non-ratified) Indian groups hold, (among them the Abenaki of Vermont), that since they never signed a treaty with the U.S. authorities in the first place, they still hold title and sovereignty to their traditional land. The Abenaki of Vermont have asserted their claim to a significant proportion of that particular state. With regards to native American women and their involvement in traditional indigenous governance, the Mohawk and Lyons text, of which Deloria is among other esteemed native male contributors, has a conspicuous absence of native women contributors and marginalizes the importance of the societies of the matrifocal Clan Mothers among the Six Nations in the Iroquois Confederacy.
14. See its judicial developments and legal analysis in Deloria and Lytle, *Nations, op. cit.,* and *American Justice, op. cit.* Regarding the federal authorities handling of Indian affairs, see M. Guerrero's essay, in *State, op. cit.*
15. M. A. Jaimes, on "Federal Indian Identification Policy: *State, op. cit.* in which I refer to this federal process as a form of "statistical genocide." Dr. Susan Lobo is with *Intertribal Friendship House,* in Oakland, CA. She is quoted in John Anner's "To the U.S. Census Bureau, Native Americans are Practically Invisible," *1492–1992; Commemorating 500 Years of Indigenous Resistance: A Community Reader,* Nicolono, Donna, (ed.), Resource Center for Nonviolence, Santa Cruz: CA 1992, 143–46. In addition, refer to Jack Forbe's essay, "Undercounting Native Americans: The 1980 Census and the Manipulation of Racial Identity in the (U.S.)," *Wicazo Sa Review,* vol. VI, no. 1, (Spring 1990): 2–26.
16. Nannette Gross Hanks, "Who's An Indian? The Arts and Crafts Act Is No Help," in *Colors,* (Jan./Feb., 1993):16–19; Walkin-in-stik-man-alone, edited statement titled "Request for an Injunction Against or Revision of (P.L.) 101–644 Indian Arts and Crafts Act of 1990. In addition, W. Churchill's column, "Native America," in *Z/Magazine,* Boston, MA "Nobody's Pet Poodle" on "the case of Jimmie Durham," 1992.
17. Walker, J. R., *Lakota Society,* (Lincoln: Univ. of Nebraska Press, 1982); thanks to Valandra (Lakota) for calling this citation to my attention.
18. Jaimes dissertation, *op. cit.,* chapter 5 on an "American Indian International Perspective" and chapter 6, on "Findings and Recommendations." My current research indicates that clan societies in traditional kinship systems were actually set up to establish taboos that prohibited incestuous practices. In addition, the practice of *exogamy* was encouraged, and even resulted in raiding parties for women and children when there was a survival need to increase its membership. As illustration, I cite Mary Shepardson's "Navajo Ways in Government: A Study in Political Process," in *American Anthropologist Memoir* 96, American Anthropological Association, Vol. 65, #3, Pt. 2, (June 1963): "Navajos, being matrilineal, belong to the clan of their father. Clan exogamy prevents them from marrying into either their mother's or their father's clan. Offending individuals will be punished by illness, insanity, or the birth of deformed children (at one time, however, there was a ceremony to counteract these effects of incest). The exogamic taboo is strong even today.

19. Jack Weatherford, chapter 3, "Women (and a Few Men) who Led the Way," *Native Roots: How the Indians Enriched America,* (New York: Fawcett Columbine, 1991). In addition, Green, *op. cit.;* chapter 3 on "the American Invasion."
20. Relevant to this intermarriage phenomena among Indian peoples in more modern times is the exodus of Indian males from the reservations, generally as draftees or as a result of unemployment. Many of them returned from the world wars suffering from "post traumatic stress syndrome," and had to undergo special ceremonies to heal themselves with the help of their communities. See Tom Holm's work in this area, "Patriots and Paws: State Use of American Indians in the Military and the Process of Nativism in the (U.S.)," chapter XII in Jaimes *State, op. cit.,* p. 345–370. However, Holm did not include in his treatment of this trend, the fact that many of these returnees intermarried non-Indians and drifted to the urban metropolis. This can also be correlated with Indian women on reservations taking over the functions of the communities left behind by the paucity of Indian males during these war years, which were then followed by relocation of many Indian families in the 1940s and the termination of entire tribes in the 1950s.
21. Sandy Gonzales, "Intermarriage and Assimilation: The Beginning or the End?," *Wicazo Sa Review,* vol. 8, no. 2, (Fall 1992): 48–52. Research findings revealed that approximately 50% (*48.0, wife's race; 48.3, husband's race) of American Indian and Alaska Native males and females marry "whites" compared to other non-Indian categories: Black, Asian, Other (Source: 1980 Census of Population on "Marital Characteristics," Table 5:18, p. 49). This percentage is also about 10% higher (46.3, wife's race; 47.6, husband's race) than the number of natives who marry other natives of both genders. However, I don't agree with her conclusion that "interracial" intermarriage inevitably leads to assimilation, since there are many assimilative forces at work without this occurring. Also, there are cases where non-Indian spouses and their offspring have gotten on the trial roles due to this type of intermarriage (i.e., the "Dawes Rolls" of 1887 among Cherokee). Nevertheless, it is evident that the dominant authorities in North American societies hold to restrictive "race" categories which reject "interracial" categories of "mixed-blood' offspring as products of this exogamy. This is poignantly illustrated in the historical fiction of Louise Erdrich, a Turtle Mountain Chippewa meti *(Love Medicine,* 1984, *Tracks,* 1988). There is also the historical literature of Linda Hogan, *Mean Spirit* (1991), where she describes the predicament of Allotment years for "full-blood" Indians who were determined "incompetent" to hold land, and "mixed-blood" Indians who were declared "unqualified" for the allotments. There is also the autobiography *Halfbreed* (1973), by Marie Campbell, a Canadian meti, that highlights the marginalization of "mixed-bloods" both on and off the reservations. I suspect that the reality of "mixed-bloods" among native peoples is not well represented in these "race" categories, since the Census Bureau discourages, if not actually prohibits, any "mixed-blood" categories. Regarding the latter, refer to Jack Ford's essay, *Wicazo Sa Review,* op. cit. In addition, there is Jack Forbe's seminal book, *Black Africans and Native Americans: Color, Race, and Caste in the Evolution of Red-Black Peoples.* A related essay is E.T. Price's "A Geographic Analysis of White Negro-Indian Racial Mixtures in Eastern (U.S.)," in *Association of American Geographers Annals,* vol. 43, (June 1953): 138–55. In addition, Rayna Green, chapter 2 on "traditional roles" in *Women in American Indian Society.* New York: Chelsea Pubs., 1992
22. Ward Churchill, "Genocide: Towards a Functional Definition," in *Alternatives: Social Transformation and Humane Governance,* Buttersworth for the Centre for the Study of Developing Societies and the World Order Models Project, vol. XI, no. 3 (July 1986): 403–30.
23. Regarding Federal Indian policy periods, see M. A. Jaimes's "The Hollow Icon: An American Indian Analysis of the Kennedy Myth and Federal Indian Policy," in *Wicazo SA Review,* vol. VI, no. 1, (Spring 1990): 34–44; also Jaimes's "Federal Indian Identification Policy: A Usurpation of Indigenous Sovereignty in North America," chapter IV, p. 123–38, and Jaimes w/Halsey, "American Indian Women"in *State, op. cit.* also Marianna Guerrero, "American Indian Water Rights: The Blood of Life in Native North America," chapter VII, in *State, op. cit.,* p. 189–216. Quoting LaDuke, among others, she writes on the subordination of native peoples that allows for their economic genocide on the reservations. In addition, Ward Churchill emphasizes this as part of a "Water Plot" between the U.S., Canadian, and Mexican governments, in "The Water Plot: Hydrological Rape in Northern Canada" a plan to divert water tributaries on Indian/Aboriginal lands to other parts of the hemisphere, in *Struggle, op. cit.,* p. 329–74.

24. Elizabeth Martinez, "Defending the Earth 92": A *People's Challenge* to the EPA (U.S. Environmental Protection Agency)" in *Social Justice,* special issue, "Columbus On Trail," vol. 19, no. 2, San Francisco, 1992: 95–105.
25. "Prevalence of HIV and AIDS in American Indians and Alaska Natives," *The Provider,* vol. 17, no. 5, (May 1992): 65–75. The report indicated that in December of 1988, "a panel of AI/AN medical and public health professionals representing national AI/AN organizations met with IHS and CDC (Centers for Disease Control) epidemiologists and agreed that an anonymous survey would provide the best measure of HIV prevalence among AI/AN. During 1989 and 1990, approval was sought from local community health boards or councils for participation in the survey. By June 30, 1991, 58 IHS affiliated facilities were participating in the HIV survey, with over two-thirds of the sites located in rural areas (indicated on figure 3)." Based on the findings in this survey, it was estimated that approximately 2,300 males and 400 females were infected with HIV. Approximately 35 infants were born to AI/AN HIV infected women in 1990, with about 11 of these infants perinatally infected. These are alarming findings that question the survival capacity of native peoples as we enter the twenty first century. This study was conducted with the cooperation of federal IHS and other federal agencies and state authorities, which are known to cover up their malpractices by "whitewashing" their own research studies, as in the case of the sterilization of native women and other women of color in the 1960s and 1970s.
26. *American Indian Anti-Defamation Council* (AIADC) *Newsletter,* July, 1992. This issue included articles on "Hepatitis A Vaccine Testing" as well as "Sexism and Fascism in the Denver Press;" the latter is news coverage on the invisibility of one female defendant among the four Native Americans eventually acquitted in the "Trial of the Columbus Day Four." The AIADC, a Denver-based organization with a directorship and board comprised of native American spokespersons, established to protest the violations of indigenous rights. The council has a strong native women's leadership component. Its mission statement notes: "[we] will actively oppose any human rights or civil rights violation against American Indians. This work will confront anti-Indian racism in the form of sports team mascots, anti-Indian holidays (and celebrations such as parades at the expense of Indian peoples), as in the case of the 1992 Columbus Day (in Denver and other states), and other representations in the public realm that demean and define American Indian people (by way of reviewing films, books, periodicals, and other media, as well as educational curricula). The Council will (also) work in active support of Indian nations (in the third world international arena) moving to break free of the bonds of colonialism, and moving toward ultimate economic and political freedom."
27. WARN News Bulletin, April. *op. cit.*
28. Churchill and Morris, *State, op. cit.*
29. Jaimes w/Halsey, *State, op. cit.,* p. 326 on the *Indian Child Welfare Act of 1978;* this essay also includes other references on the subject of the sterilization of Native women, and other health data with relevant references on pp. 326–27 (fn# 102, 103, 104).
30. P. A. May, "Suicide Youth and Self-Destruction Among American Indian Youth," in American Indian and Alaska Native Mental Health Records, *The Journal of the National Center,* vol. 1 ,no. 1, Denver, CO, June 1987: 52–71.
31. *Women for Racial & Economic Equality (WREE),* "191 Facts About U.S. Women," booklet, New York, N.Y. 1991; statistical data quoted on infant mortality rate among American Indian and Native Alaskan tribes. Earlier data can be found in *Indian Country,* League of Women Voters Educational Fund, Washington D.C., 1976.
32. *Akwesasne Notes,* "Oklahoma: Sterilization of Native Women Charged to I.H.S.," Mohawk Nation, Rooseveltown, N.Y., mid-Winter, 1989: 11–30.
33. Richard Louv, "The Sterilization of American Indian Women," publication unknown, p. 43–57, 100.
34. WARN News Bulletin, "Native American Women," International Treaty Council, N.Y. 1975 and "We Will Remember Group," Porcupine, S. Dakota, 1978; also referenced in Jaimes w/Halsey, *State, op. cit.,* p. 341 (fn# 103).
35. Brad Branan, "Martina Greywind Faces Criminal Charges," *The Circle,* March 1992.
36. Michael Dorris, *The Broken Cord,* (New York: Harper & Row, 1989); this book tells the real life story of a Lakota child who is found to be afflicted with fetal alcohol syndrome after he was adopted by Dorris; it is a relevant case in that he, as the author, is accused of

"blaming the victim" when he takes Indian mothers to task for continuing to drink during pregnancy.

37. Jaimes with Halsey, in *State, op. cit.,* p. 311–19.
38. *Ibid.*
39. M. A. Jaimes, "False Images: Native American Women in Hollywood Cinema," paper presented at "Goodbye Columbus: Media Exploration Since 1492, " symposium, Society for the Humanities, Cornell University, Ithaca, N.Y., April 4, 1992; citing Amerigo Vespucci in his 1504–5 *Mundes Novas.*
40. M. A., Jaimes. "Native American Women and Sacred Traditions." Among the female deities, there is *Corn Daughter* (Hopi); *Changing Woman* (Navajo/Dineh); *First Woman* (Abanaki); *Sky Woman* (Iroquois); *Spider Woman* Navajo/Dineh and Hopi); *Thought Woman* (Laguna); *White Buffalo Calf Woman* (Lakota, Dakota), and in a more secular sphere, the traditional Cherokee had *Beloved Woman of the Nation.*
41. Pierrette Desy, "How Can One Be A Woman? The Paradox of the Berdache," in *Radical Therapy: New Studies on the Left,* vol. 13, no. 3&4, Summer–Fall, 1988: 50–64.
42. Paula Gunn Allen, "Sky Woman and Her Sisters," in *Ms. Magazine,* vol. 3, no. 2, Sept./Oct., 1992: 22–26.
43. Theda Perdue, "Cherokee Women and the Trail of Tears," in *The American Indian: Past and Present,* R .L. Nichols (ed.), 4th ed., McGraw-Hill, Inc., N.Y. 1992: 151–161.
44. M. C. Wright, "Economic Development and Native American Women in the Early (19th) Century," Nicholas, *op. cit.,* p. 99–106.
45. Gunn Allen, *op. cit.,* writes that "squaw" is an Arabic word meaning "sex slave boy," but she doesn't reference her source; article in *Ms. Magazine,* vol. 3, no. 2, Nov., 1992; 22–26. Gunn Allen is an unusual author *in that it is difficult to pin her down.* Even so, I have, on occasion, cited her works, but it has been my concern, in doing so, that she has a strong tendency to pander to Eurocentric feminist ideas. This, therefore, has the effect of confounding her work from an indigenist women's perspective. Her latest inclination in this vein is indicated in a recent interview she did with a feminist separatist journal. See "interview with Paula Gunn Allen," in *Trivia* (no. 16/17, Fall 1990: 50–66), by Jan Caputi.
46. Jaimes w/Halsey, in *State, op. cit.*
47. Even though there seems to be more native women who are becoming involved in Indian politics and running as tribal chairs, it must not be overlooked that they are operating in a very patriarchal and therefore sexist system.
48. Jaimes w/Halsey, in *State, op. cit.*
49. At this time in Canada, native women organizations are protesting their lack of access to the Canadian constitutional process that would amend this document for guarantee of "Aboriginal rights" throughout Canada. There is also the mistrust, expressed by the *Women of the Metis Nation* over the definition of "gender equality" which these women consider a dangerous precedent that pits native women's equality rights against men's collective rights for the Canadian common good. Cited from statements, "Address to Royal Commission on Aboriginal Peoples" and "Action Speaks Louder Than Words: Native Council of Canada Record on Native Women's Rights," in *Native Women Journal* vol. 1, issue 1, Native Women Inc., Aug/Sept., 1992: 6 & 7. There is a forthcoming report, titled "The Best Kept Secret," on the rising family abuse of women and children in native families by a Canadian Aboriginal women's organization as testimony to the Royal Commission of Aboriginal Rights, Sept. 1992; see statement, "S.A.F.E. Community Workshop" by S.A.F.E. Committee, *Native Women Journal, op. cit.,* p. 39.
50. WARN News Bulletin, special edition, Chicago, IL, April 1992; on the *Big Mountain Relocation* case in the "Hopi/Navajo Joint Use Area (JUA) Dispute," there are several documentaries, most notably *Broken Rainbow,* which interview these elder women who are defenders of their land and resistors of genocide; also cited in Jaimes w/Halsey, *State, op. cit.* An Arizona news article (dated 11/16/92), has also indicated that the Hopi Tribe has appealed a land "settlement" that is only a fraction of the 3.5 million acres sought by the Hopi in a dispute over a 1934 law that expanded the Navajo (Dineh) Reservation by 7 million acres.
51. Holly Tibbetts Youngbear, "Without Due Process: The Alienation of Individual Trust Allotments of the White Earth Anishinaabeg," in *American Indian Culture and Research Journal, Special Edition, "The Poetical Geography of Indian Country,"* UCLA publications,

vol. 15, no. 2, 1991; this essay provides a comprehensive analysis of a classic case of "scientific racism" imposed on the White Earth through the Allotment process.

52. Jaimes with Halsey, *State, op. cit.*, p. 328.
53. On Anna Mae Aquash: her biography written after her death by Johanna Brand in *The Life and Death of Anna Mae Aquash* (Toronto, 1978); there is also a documentary, titled "Anna Mae Aquash: Brave Hearted Woman;" both are cited in Jaimes w/Halsey, *State, op. cit.* In addition, see Ward Churchill and Jim Vander Wall, *Agents of Repression: the FBI's Secret Wars Against The Black Panther Party and the American Indian Movement.* See also its sequel, *The COINTELPREO Papers: Documents from the FBI's Secret Wars Against Dissent in the (U.S.)* both published in 1990, (Boston: South End Press). Together they give a comprehensive overview of the historical events centered around the Wounded Knee Siege of 1973, as a U.S. paramilitary operation which targeted the traditional Lakota people in Pine Ridge, South Dakota; for related episodes, also see Jaimes w/ Halsey, *State, op. cit.*
54. George Cornell, "Native Americans and Environmental Thought: Thoreau and the Transcendentalists, *Akwe:kon journal,* vol. 9, no. 3, (Ithaca: Cornell University, Fall of 1992) 4–13. This is a theological premise, from a Native American perspective, in Vine Deloria, Jr.'s *God is Red,* (New York: Delta Books,. 1973) and his later *The Metaphysics of Modern Existence,* (New York: Harper & Row, 1979); in this context, the natural world and other living entities, among the animal, plant, and mineral worlds, mountains, and rivers, have "natural rights" as well. In addition, there is the *Association of American Indian Affairs, bulletin,* Summer, 1988, no. 116, regarding its problems with the *American Indian Religious Freedom Act of 1978.* This bulletin also includes a statement made by Dr. Deward Walker a cultural anthropologist, for the Native American Rights Fund, Boulder, CO on what can be called "sacred geography." Here he lists "Core Features of Native American Religions" for the restoration and preservation of their traditional "sacred sites;" one of these (#9) is "a belief that while all aspects of nature and culture are potentially sacred, there are certain times and geographical locations which together possess great sacredness." In contrast, see the following for a Eurocentric treatment of these matters: Lucian Levy Bruhl, *The "Soul" of the Primitive,* (Chicago:, Regnery Co, Gateway Edition, 1966). In this same vein, the noted anthropologist, Claude Levi Strauss wrote, in *Totemism* (Boston: Beacon Press, 1963), that there are obligatory rules of behavior, such as the prohibitions on eating the totem designated in the kinship traditions of tribes such as the Ojibwe and the Cherokee. There were also other restrictions, such as eating certain animals and their parts by specific ceremonial customs. These totems were thought to prevent disease and to teach lessons from knowledge gained by observing animal behavior.

Notes to Chapter 6

I want to thank Jacqui Alexander and Chandra Talpade Mohanty for pushing me to develop my ideas and giving me the opportunity, in this volume, to express them. Many thanks as well to Linda Alcoff, Bernadette Andrea, Martin Bernal, Junot Díaz, Michael Hames-García, Ben Olguín, and Bill Wilkerson, whose careful readings of the manuscript helped me to think through what are some difficult and politically sensitive issues. I owe a debt of gratitude to Satya Mohanty for his intellectual guidance and scholarly example, and to Tim Young for nourishing me both intellectually and emotionally. Finally, I want to thank my daughters, Halina and Eva Martinez, for their inexhaustible (if not entirely voluntary) patience. It is for their sake I persevere.

1. In their introduction to *Feminists Theorize the Political,* Scott and Butler ask the following questions: "What are the points of convergence between a) poststructualist criticisms of identity and b) recent theory by women of color that critically exposes the unified or coherent subject as a prerogative of white theory?"; "To what extent do the terms used to defend the universal subject encode fears about those cultural minorities excluded in, and by, the construction of that subject; to what extent is the outcry against the 'postmodern' a defense of culturally privileged epistemic positions that leave unexamined the excluded domains of homosexuality, race, and class?"; "What is the significance of the poststructuralist critique of binary logic for the theorization of the subaltern?"; and "How do universal theories of 'patriarchy' or phallogocentrism need to be rethought in order to avoid the consequences of a white-feminist epistemological/cultural imperialism?" My point is that such questions enact an un-self-critical enlistment of the "woman of color," the "sub-

altern," and the "cultural minority" to serve as legitimators of the project entailed in "post-modern" or poststructuralist criticisms of identity.

2. When I use the term "realism" in this essay, I am *not* referring to the literary mode in which the details of the plot or characters are "true to life." I refer, instead, to a philosophical (and in particular, epistemological) position. Broadly speaking, a realist epistemology implies a belief in a "reality" that exists independently of our mental constructions of it. Thus, while our (better or worse) understandings of our world may provide our only access to "reality," our mental constructions of the world do not constitute the totality of what can be considered "real." It ought to be made clear that when the realist says that something is "real," she does not mean to say that it is *not* socially constructed; rather, her point is that is not *only* socially constructed. In the case of identity, for instance, the realist claim is that there is a nonarbitrary limit to the range of identities we can "construct" or "choose" for any person in a given social formation. It is that nonarbitrary limit that forms the boundary between (objective) "reality" and our (subjective) construction—or understanding—of it. For more on the implications of "realism" within the context of literary studies, see Satya Mohanty's "Colonial Legacies, Multicultural Futures: Relativism, Objectivity, and the Challenge of Otherness" esp. pp. 111–15.
3. The name "Sister Outsider" derives from Audre Lorde's book of the same name. Haraway's easy substitution of the name "Sister Outsider" for that of "Malinche," and her conflation of Chicana with Malinche with Sister Outsider signals her inattention to the differences (temporal, historical, and material) that exist between the three distinct categories of identity.
4. See Octavio Paz's influential essay, "The Sons of La Malinche," which, in the process of describing, has served to confirm Malinche's position as the "Mexican Eve."
5. Norma Alarcón, in her two essays "Traddutora, traditora: a paradigmatic figure of Chicana feminism," and "Chicana's Feminist Literature: A Re-Vision Through Malintzin/ or Malintzin: Putting Flesh Back on the Object," provides a useful analysis of some of these attempts, as does Moraga in "A Long Line of Vendidas" in *Loving.* See also Adelaida R. del Castillo, "Malintzin Tenepal: A Preliminary Look into a New Perspective"; Cordelia Candelaria, "La Malinche, Feminist Prototype"; Sylvia Gonzales, "La Chicana: Guadalupe or Malinche"; and Rachel Phillips, "Marina/Malinche: Masks and Shadows."
6. Linda Alcoff has suggested to me that Haraway might not intend to imply that "all cyborgs can be women of color"—that she meant only that "women of color" is one particular *kind* of cyborg identity. If so, we are left with "women of color cyborgs" and "white women cyborgs" (and perhaps other *kinds* of male cyborgs, as well). In that case, of what use is a cyborg identity? Unless a cyborg identity can effectively dismantle "difference" (and the effect "difference" has on our experiences of the world), it is at best innocuous, and at worst quite dangerous. We must acknowledge that a cyborg identity has the potential to become simply another veil to hide behind in order not to have to examine the differences that both constitute and challenge our self-conceptions.
7. See "A Long Line of Vendidas" in *Loving* in which Moraga talks about the necessity of theorizing the "simultaneity of oppression," by which she means taking "race, ethnicity and class into account in determining where women are at sexually," and in which she clearly acknowledges that some people "suffer more" than others (128).
8. For a more developed explanation of this phenomenon, see the section "Who Are My People," in Gloria Anzaldúa's essay "La Prieta" published in *Bridge.* Anzaldúa writes of those who insist on viewing the different parts of her in isolation, "They would chop me up into little fragments and tag each piece with a label." She then goes on to affirm her one-ness, "Only your labels split me" (205). Rather than giving way to fragmentation, she insists upon holding it all together: "The mixture of bloods and affinities, rather than confusing or unbalancing me, has forced me to achieve a kind of equilibrium. . . . I walk the tightrope with ease and grace. I span abysses. . . . I walk the rope—an acrobat in equipoise, expert at the Balancing Act" (209).
9. As long as our world is hierarchically organized along relations of domination, categories such as "us" and "them," or "oppressed" and "oppressor" will retain their explanatory function. This is not because any one group belongs, in an essential way, to a particular category, but rather because the terms describe positions within prevailing social and economic relations.
10. The Spanish-language proverb "Salir de Guatemala para entrar en Guatepeor" plays with the word fragment "mala" in "Guatemala" to suggest the dilemma of a person caught

between a bad (mala) and a worse (peor) situation. The proverb roughly approximates the English-language proverb "To go from the frying pan into the fire."

11. At the risk of stating what should be obvious, this is as true for the white heterosexual politically conservative antifeminist as it is for the radical feminist lesbian of color. And yet, it is primarily women who address gender issues, and primarily people of color who address racial issues (both inside the academy and out). The unspoken assumption is that only women have gender and only people of color are racialized beings. This assumption reflects itself in the work of many male academics who only talk about gender when they are referring to women, and in the work of many white academics who only talk about race when they are referring to people of color. A manifestation of this phenomenon can be found in Judith Butler's book *Bodies that Matter,* where she only theorizes race in the two chapters in which she discusses artistic productions by or about people of color.
12. When I refer to essentialism, I am referring to the notion that individuals or groups have an immutable and discoverable "essence"—a basic, unvariable, and presocial nature. As a theoretical concept, essentialism expresses itself through the tendency to see *one* social fact (class, gender, race, sexuality, etc.) as determinate in the last instance for the cultural identity of the individual or group in question. As a political strategy, essentialism has had both liberatory and reactionary effects. For one poststructuralist critique of essentialism that does not quite escape the postmodernist tendency I am critiquing in this essay, see Diana Fuss's book *Essentially Speaking.*
13. This can happen even if both individuals in the example are born into an African-American community and consider themselves "black." It should be clear that I am not talking about race as a biological category. I am talking about people who, for one reason or another, appear to others as "white" or "black." As I will demonstrate in my discussion of Moraga's work, this is an important distinction for theorizing the link between experience and cultural identity for people with real, but not visible, biological or cultural connections to minority communities.
14. For an illuminating discussion of the way in which the social fact of gender has structured the experiences of at least one woman, and has profoundly informed the formation of her cultural identity, see Mohanty's "Epistemic Status," esp. pp. 46–51.
15. It is not even necessary that they recognize themselves as members of that group. For example, a dark-skinned immigrant from Puerto Rico who refuses identification with African-Americans may nevertheless suffer racist experiences arising from the history of black/white race relations within the U.S. due to mainland U.S. citizens' inability to distinguish between the two distinct cultural groups.
16. For an explanation of the historical origins of the myth that Spanish-surnamed residents of New Mexico are direct descendants of Spanish *conquistadores*, see Roldofo Acuña, *Occupied America*, 55–60; Nancie González, *The Spanish-Americans of New Mexico*, 78–83; and John Chavez, *The Lost Land*, 85–106.
17. Identities can be evaluated, according to Mohanty, "using the same complex epistemological criteria we use to evaluate 'theories.'" He explains: "Since different experiences and identities refer to different aspects of *one* world, one complex causal structure that we call 'social reality,' the realist theory of identity implies that we can evaluate them comparatively by considering how adequately they explain this structure" ("Epistemic Status," 70–71).
18. Historically, the term "Chicano" was a pejorative name applied to lower-class Mexican-Americans. Like the term "Black," it was consciously appropriated and revalued by (primarily) students during the Chicano Movement of the 1960s. According to the *Plan de Santa Barbara* (see note 21) the term specifically implies a politics of resistance to Anglo-American domination.
19. An example of the assimilationist "Hispanic" is Linda Chavez whose book, *Out of the Barrio: Toward a New Politics of Hispanic Assimilation* suggests that Hispanics, like "previous" white ethnic groups, are rapidly assimilating into the mainstream of U.S. culture and society (2). Not only does Chavez play fast and loose with sociological and historical evidence, but her thesis cannot account for the social fact of race. She does not mention race as being causally relevant for the experiences of Hispanics, and she repeatedly refers to "non-Hispanic whites," a grammatical formulation which assumes that all Hispanics are white. She accounts for Puerto Ricans and Dominicans by considering them as "dysfunctional" "exceptions" to the white-Hispanic rule (139–59).
20. For histories of the Chicano Movement, see Rodolfo Acuña, *Occupied America*; Carlos

Muñoz, *Youth, Identity, Power*; Sonia López, "The Role of the Chicana Within the Student Movement"; Alma García, "The Development of Chicana Feminist Discourse, 1970–1980"; and Ramón Gutiérrez, "Community, Patriarchy and Individualism: The Politics of Chicano History and the Dream of Equality."

21. The *Plan de Santa Barbara,* written in the Spring of 1969 at a California statewide conference in Santa Barbara, California, founded MEChA (*Movimiento Estudiantil Chicano de Aztlán*), and is probably the definitive position paper of the Chicano Student Youth Movement. The Plan is published as an appendix in Muñoz, *Youth, Identity, Power,* 191–202.
22. For more information on how both heterosexual and lesbian Chicanas fared within the Chicano movement, see the articles referred to above by López, Gutiérrez, and García, as well as Carla Trujillo, "Chicana Lesbians: Fear and Loathing in the Chicano Community," and Cherríe Moraga, *Loving*, 105–11.
23. This is not to say that Chicanas outside the university were not asserting themselves and coming to consciousness about their disadvantaged positions—just that the most consistently documented and published expressions of Chicana feminism have emerged from within the academy. For documentation of this claim, see the articles referred to above by García, Gutiérrez, López, and Moraga, as well as Beatriz Pesquera and Denise Segura, "There Is No Going Back: Chicanas and Feminism."
24. Moraga explains: "During the late 60s and early 70s, I was not an active part of la causa. I never managed to get myself to walk in the marches in East Los Angeles (I merely watched from the sidelines); I never went to one meeting of MEChA on campus. No soy tonta. I would have been murdered in El Movimiento—light-skinned, unable to speak Spanish well enough to hang; miserably attracted to women and fighting it; and constantly questioning all authority, including men's. I felt I did not belong there. Maybe I had really come to believe that 'Chicanos' were 'different,' not 'like us,' as my mother would say. But I fully knew that there was a part of me that was a part of that movement, but it seemed that part would have to go unexpressed until the time I could be a Chicano and the woman I had to be, too" (*Loving* 113).
25. The fact of Moraga's "whiteness" is central to an accurate mapping of her social location and crucial to an understanding of the formation of her cultural identity. The fact that her "whiteness" has been systematically overlooked by postmodernist readings of Moraga's work is symptomatic of the failure of postmodernist theories of identity to take account of the complex interactions among the multiple determinants of human identity.
26. The Spanish verb *chingar* is stronger than the English verb "to fuck." A highly gendered word, it carries within it connotations of the English verb "to rape." Thus, *chingón* refers to the (active) male rapist/fucker and *chingada* refers to the (passive) female who is raped/fucked.
27. Although I use the term "women's movement" in the singular, I am aware that the various feminisms are diverse and multidimensional. If I am vague, it is because Moraga does not specify which feminist group(s) she involved herself with. Throughout most of her writings, Moraga equates the "women's movement" or "feminism" with an unspecified and predominantly middle-class white women's movement. She does, at one point, specifically critique "radical feminism" (*Loving* 125–30).
28. See Amber Hollibaugh and Cherríe Moraga, "What We're Rollin Around in Bed With." In this conversation, Moraga and Hollibaugh address the failure of feminist theory and rhetoric to deal adequately with women's lived experiences of sexuality. They accuse the feminist movement of desexualizing women's sexuality by confusing sexuality with sexual oppression. They suggest that the refusal to acknowledge butch/femme roles in lesbian relationships, and the failure to understand how those sexual identities influence and condition sexual behavior, have led to 1) a delegitimization of sexual desire; and 2) bad theory. They contend that a woman's sexual identity, which is necessarily influenced by her race and class background, can tell us something fundamental about the way she constitutes herself/is constituted as a woman.

Works Cited in Chapter 6

Acuña, Rodolfo. 1988. *Occupied America: A History of Chicanos.* Third ed. New York: HarperCollins.

Alarcón, Norma. 1983. "Chicana's Feminist Literature: A Re-vision Through Malintzin/or

Malintzin: Putting Flesh Back on the Object." In *This Bridge Called My Back: Writings By Radical Women of Color.* Gloria Anzaldúa and Cherríe Moraga, eds., Second ed. New York: Kitchen Table/Women of Color Press. 182–90.

——. 1986. "Interview with Cherríe Moraga." *Third Woman* 3, no. 1–2: 127–34.

——. 1989. "Traddutora, traditora: a paradigmatic figure of Chicana feminism," *Cultural Critique* 13 (Fall): 57–87.

Alcoff, Linda. 1995. "The Elimination of Experience in Feminist Theory." Paper presented at the Women's Studies Symposium, Cornell University, Feb. 3.

Butler, Judith. 1990. *Gender Trouble.* New York: Routledge.

——. 1993. *Bodies That Matter: On the Discursive Limits of "Sex".* New York: Routledge.

—— and Joan Scott, eds. 1992. *Feminists Theorize the Political.* New York: Routledge.

Candelaria, Cordelia. 1980. "La Malinche, Feminist Prototype." *Frontiers: A Journal of Women's Studies* 5, no. 2: 1–6.

Chávez, John R. 1984. *The Lost Land: The Chicano Image of the Southwest.* Albuquerque: University of New Mexico Press.

Chavez, Linda. 1991. *Out of the Barrio: Toward a New Politics of Hispanic Assimilation.* New York: Basic Books.

Del Castillo, Adelaida R. 1977. "Malintzin Tenepal: A Preliminary Look Into a New Perspective." In *Essays on La Mujer,* Rosaura Sanchez and Rosa Martinez Cruz, eds., Los Angeles: Chicano Studies Publications, UCLA. 124–49.

Díaz del Castillo, Bernal. 1963. *The Conquest of New Spain.* Trans. J. M. Cohen. Aylesbury, England: Penguin.

Fuss, Diana. 1989. *Essentially Speaking: Feminism, Nature & Difference.* New York: Routledge.

García, Alma M. 1989. "The Development of Chicana Feminist Discourse, 1970–1980." *Gender & Society* 3.2: 217–38.

Gonzales, Sylvia. 1980. "La Chicana: Guadalupe or Malinche." In *Comparative Perspectives on Third World Women, The Impact of Race, Sex, and Class,* ed. Beverly Lindsay. New York: Praeger.

González, Nancie L. 1967. *The Spanish-Americans of New Mexico: A Heritage of Pride.* Albuquerque: University of New Mexico Press.

Gutiérrez, Ramón A. 1993. "Community, Patriarchy and Individualism: The Politics of Chicano History and the Dream of Equality." *American Quarterly* 45, no. 1: 44–72.

Haraway, Donna. 1990. "A Manifesto for Cyborgs: Science, Technology, and Socialist Feminism in the 1980s." In *Feminism/Postmodernism,* ed. Linda J. Nicholson. New York: Routledge, 190–233.

Harris, Marvin. 1964. *Patterns of Race in the Americas.* New York: Norton.

Hollibaugh, Amber, and Cherríe Moraga. 1981. "What We're Rollin Around in Bed With: Sexual Silences in Feminism, A Conversation Toward Ending Them." *Heresies* 12 (Spring): 58–62.

López, Sonia. 1977. "The Role of the Chicana Within the Student Movement." In *Essays on La Mujer,* eds. R. Sanchez and R. Martinez Cruz. Los Angeles: University of California Press.

Lorde, Audre. 1984. *Sister Outsider.* Freedom, CA: The Crossing Press.

Mohanty, Satya P. 1993. "The Epistemic Status of Cultural Identity: On *Beloved* and the Postcolonial Condition." *Cultural Critique* 24 (Spring): 41–80.

——. 1995. "Colonial Legacies, Multicultural Futures: Relativism, Objectivity, and the Challenge of Otherness," *PMLA* 110, no. 1:108–18.

Moraga, Cherríe. 1983. *Loving in the War Years: Lo que nunca pasó por sus labios.* Boston: South End Press.

—— and Gloria Anzaldúa, eds. 1983. *This Bridge Called My Back: Writings by Radical Women of Color.* New York: Kitchen Table/Women of Color Press.

Muñoz, Carlos, Jr. 1989. *Youth, Identity, Power: The Chicano Movement.* London: Verso.

Paz, Octavio. 1985. "The Sons of La Malinche." *The Labyrinth of Solitude.* Trans. Lysander Kemp. New York: Grove Press.

Pesquera, Beatriz M., and Denise M. Segura. 1993. "There Is No Going Back: Chicanas and Feminism." In *Chicana Critical Issues,* eds. Norma Alarcón et al. Berkeley: Third Woman Press.

Phillips, Rachel. 1983. "Marina/Malinche: Masks and Shadows." In *Women in Hispanic Literature,* ed. Beth Miller. Berkeley: University of California Press.

Singer, Linda. 1992. "Feminism and Postmodernism." In *Feminists Theorize the Political*, eds. Judith Butler and Joan Scott. New York: Routledge.

Trujillo, Carla. 1991. "Chicana Lesbians: Fear and Loathing in the Chicano Community." *Chicana Lesbians: The Girls Our Mothers Warned Us About*, ed. Carla Trujillo. Berkeley: Third Woman Press.

Yarbro-Bejarano, Yvonne. 1994. "Gloria Anzaldúa's *Borderlands/La frontera*: Cultural Studies, 'Difference,' and the Non-Unitary Subject." *Cultural Critique*, no. 28 (Fall): 5–28.

Notes to Chapter 7

I would like to express my deep gratitude to Alicia Partnoy, Jaya Mitra, Ipshita Chanda, Asoke Sen, Sibaji Bandyopadhyay, and Debra Castillo for their extreme generosity in sharing their experiences, analyses, and comments with me; and especially to Satya Mohanty, without whose constant intellectual and moral support and invaluable discussions of the issues addressed here this paper would never have been written. Many thanks also to Jacqui Alexander and Chandra Mohanty for their incisive editorial comments that have conceptually enriched my work.

1. See my essay "The Social Function and Generic Location of Women's Testimonial Writing in India and Latin America," *Jadavpur Journal of Comparative Literature* (Calcutta) 30 (1993).
2. In Latin America, with the publication of large numbers of testimonios and their legitimation as a literary genre by Cuba's cultural center, the Casa de las Americas, in 1970, the testimonio has come to stay. *Sandino's Daughters* from Nicaragua, *I, Rigoberta Menchú*, based in Guatemala, and *Let Me Speak! Testimony of Domitila, a Woman of the Bolivian Mines*, are just some of the pioneering women's testimonial literature from Latin America. In the Indian subcontinent, however, the testimonio is still in the nascent stage and has yet to gain recognition as a distinct genre. However, the presence of important testimonios narrating women's experiences of political struggle in the last two and a half decades testifies to the growing significance of this genre in the subcontinent, too. *We Were Making History: Women and the Telangana Uprising* is a collection of testimonies of women who participated in the Telangana People's Struggle of the 1940s in the state of Hyderabad; Jaya Mitra's and Meenakshi Sen's prison testimonios, titled *Hannaman* and *Jailer Bhetor Jail* respectively, were both written in the context of the Naxalite movement in West Bengal; and Akhtar Baluch's "Sister, are you still here?" is the diary of a Sindhi woman prisoner, arrested for having protested against the detention of Sindhi nationalist and peasant leaders in Pakistan in 1970, during the interim regime of General Yahya Khan.
3. See Sumanta Banerjee, *India's Simmering Revolution: The Naxalite Uprising* (London: Zed Books, 1984); Marcus Franda, *Radical Politics in West Bengal* (Cambridge, Mass.: M.I.T. Press, 1971); and Rabindra Ray, *The Naxalites and Their Ideology* (New Delhi: Oxford University Press, 1988) for detailed accounts of the movement. For reports on the imprisonment and torture of Naxalite activists, see Amnesty International, *Report on Torture* (New York: Farrar, Strauss and Giroux, 1973), pp. 149–50; and *CPI's Defence of Naxalite Prisoners* (New Delhi: Communist Party Publications, 1978).
4. For comprehensive accounts of the "dirty war," see William Smith, *Authoritarianism and the Crisis of the Argentine Political Economy* (Palo Alto, Calif.: Stanford University Press, 1989), and Ronald Dworkin, "Introduction" in *Never Again: Report of the Commission on the Disappeared* (New York: Faber and Faber, 1986), originally published as *Nunca Más* (Buenos Aires: Editorial Universitaria, 1984).
5. I borrow this term from Kathleen Barry, who asserts that "Female sexual slavery is present in ALL situations where women or girls cannot change the immediate conditions of their existence; where regardless of how they got into those conditions they cannot get out; and where they are subject to sexual violence and exploitation." Kathleen Barry, *Female Sexual Slavery*, p. 40, quoted in Ximena Bunster-Burotto, "Surviving Beyond Fear: Women and Torture in Latin America," in June Nash and Helen Safa, eds., *Women and Change in Latin America: New Directions in Sex and Class* (Boston: Greenwood Press, 1985), p. 298.
6. Jaya Mitra, in an unpublished interview with Ipshita Chanda, held in Calcutta on December 12th, 1992.
7. Alicia Partnoy, in an unpublished interview with the author, Washington, D.C., December 18, 1991.

8. This is an imperative that is being reiterated in the present day, with plans for the "Serbification" of the children of Bosnian women at official Serbian rape camps.
9. The goddess Kali is both creator and nurturer, the iconic embodiment of mother-love and feminine energy, or *shakti*. She is usually depicted in the latter form, as the *shakti* that manifests itself as Kali to annihilate demonic male power; in this guise, she is often presented as cruel, horrific, and violent.
10. I use the word "communal" here in the sense of "communalism," referring to a political attitude and praxis based on religious differentiation, privileging followers of one religion against those of another. In fact, this critique of communalism is even more relevant today, when the whole Indian subcontinent is being rent by a communal strife between sections of the Hindu and Muslim populations. The rise of communalism is a matter of grave concern, especially for women; c.f. Sangari (1991) and Sunder Rajan and Pathak (1989) for excellent analyses of how this situation has resulted in increased patriarchal control over women's lives in the name of religion.
11. In fact, pointing to the stereotypical notions of nurturing and expressions of tenderness as "feminine" activities, Partnoy states, in a bemused fashion, that "the tenderness in the father-daughter relationship led many people (who did not read the text closely) to mistake it for a mother-daughter relationship." Partnoy, interview with the author, December 18, 1991, Washington, D.C.
12. Partnoy, interview with the author, December 18, 1991, Washington, D.C.

Works Cited in Chapter 7

Adorno, Theodor. 1978. "Sociology of Knowledge and its Consciousness." In Andrew Arato and Eike Gebhardt, eds. *The Essential Frankfurt School Reader*. New York: Urizen Books, 452–65.

Amnesty International. 1973. *Report on Torture*. New York: Farrar, Strauss and Giroux.

Baluch, Akhtar. 1977. "'Sister, are you still here?' The Diary of a Sindhi Woman Prisoner." *Race and Class* 18, no. 3: 219–45.

Banerjee, Sumanta, ed. 1984. *India's Simmering Revolution: The Naxalite Uprising*. London: Zed Books.

Barrios de Chungara, Domitila, with Moema Viezzer. 1978. *Let Me Speak! Testimony of Domitila, A Woman of the Bolivian Mines*. Trans. Victoria Ortiz. New York: Monthly Review Press.

Barry, Kathleen. 1979. *Female Sexual Slavery*. New York: Avon Books.

Benhabib, Seyla, and Drucilla Cornell. 1987. *Feminism as Critique: On the Politics of Gender*. Minneapolis: University of Minnesota Press.

Bunster-Burotto, Ximena. 1985. "Surviving Beyond Fear: Women and Torture in Latin America." In June Nash and Helen Safa, eds. *Women and Change in Latin America: New Directions in Sex and Class*. Westport: Greenwood Press, 297–324.

Communist Party of India. 1978. *CPI's Defence of Naxalite Prisoners*. New Delhi: Communist Party Publications.

Dworkin, Ronald. 1986. *Never Again: Report of the Commission on the Disappeared*. New York: Faber and Faber (Trans. of Nunca Más. Buenos Aires: Editorial Universitaria, 1984).

Foucault, Michel. 1965. *Discipline and Punish: The Birth of the Prison*. New York, Pantheon Books.

Franda, Marcus 1971. *Radical Politics in West Bengal*. Cambridge, Mass.: MIT Press.

Habermas, Jürgen. 1970. "Technology and Science as 'Ideology.'" *Toward a Rational Society: Student Protest, Science, and Politics*. Trans. Jeremy J. Shapiro. Boston: Beacon Press, 81–122.

Johnson-Odim, Cheryl. 1991. "Common Themes, Different Contexts." In Chandra Talpade Mohanty, Ann Russo, and Lourdes Torres, eds. *Third World Women and the Politics of Feminism*. Bloomington: Indiana University Press, 314–29.

Larsen, Neil. 1983. "Sport as Civil Society: The Argentinean Junta Plays Championship Soccer." In Neil Larsen, ed. *The Discourse of Power: Culture, Hegemony and the Authoritarian State*. Minneapolis: Institute for the Study of Ideologies and Literature, 113–28.

Masiello, Francine. 1987. "La Argentina durante el Proceso: Las multiples resistencias de la cultura." In Daniel Balderston et. al., eds. *Ficción y politica: La narrativa argentina durante el proceso militar,* Minneapolis: Institute for the Study of Ideologies and Literature.

Melossi, Dario, and Massimo Pavarini. 1981. *The Prison and the Factory: Origins of the Penitentiary System*. Trans. Evans Glynis Cousin, Totowa, N. J.: Barnes and Noble.
Menchú, Rigoberta. 1984. *I, Rigoberta Menchú: An Indian Woman in Guatemala*. ed. Elizabeth Burgos-Debray. Trans. Ann Wright. London: Verso.
Mohanty, Chandra Talpade, Ann Russo, and Lourdes Torres, eds. 1991. *Third World Women and the Politics of Feminism*. Bloomington: Indiana University Press.
Mohanty, Satya P. 1993. "The Epistemic Status of Cultural Identity: On *Beloved* and the Postcolonial Condition." *Cultural Critique* 24, 41–80.
Partnoy, Alicia. 1986. *The Little School: Tales of Disappearance and Survival in Argentina*. Pittsburgh: Cleis Press.
Randall. Margaret. 1981. *Sandino's Daughters: Testimonies of Nicaraguan Women in Struggle*. ed. Lyna Yanz. Toronto: New Star Books.
Ray, Rabindra. 1988. *The Naxalites and their Ideology*. New Delhi: Oxford University Press.
Sangari, Kumkum. 1991. "Institutions, Beliefs, Ideologies: Widow Immolation in Contemporary Rajasthan." *Economic and Political Weekly* (April 27, 1991): WS2–WS18.
Sen, Minakshi. 1993. *Jailer Bhetor Jail: Pagolbari Parba*. Calcutta: Spandan.
Sengupta, Promode. 1983. *Naxalbari and Indian Revolution*. Calcutta: Research India Publications.
Smith, Dorothy E. 1987. *The Everyday World as Problematic: A Feminist Sociology*. Boston: Northeastern University Press.
Smith, William. 1989. *Authoritarianism and the Crisis of the Argentine Political Economy*. Stanford: Stanford University Press.
Stree Shakti Sanghatana. 1989. *We Were Making History: Women and the Telangana Uprising*. London: Zed Press.
Sunder Rajan, Rajeswari and Zakia Pathak. 1989. "Shahbano." *Signs: Journal of Women in Culture and Society* 14, no. 3 (Spring 1989): 558–82.

Notes to Chapter 8

1. Lorraine O'Grady, "Olympia's Maid: Reclaiming Black Female Subjectivity," *Afterimage* (Summer, 1992): 14.
2. Patricia Hill Collins, *Black Feminist Thought: Knowledge, Consciousness and the Politics of Empowerment* (Boston: Unwin Hyman, 1990), p. 164.
3. Hortense Spillers, "Interstices: A Small Drama of Words," in Carole S. Vance, ed., *Pleasure and Danger*, pp. 73–100.
4. Ibid.
5. Darlene Clark Hine, "Rape and the Inner Lives of Black Women in the Middle West: Preliminary Thoughts on the Culture of Dissemblance," *Signs* 14, no. 4 (1989): 915–20.
6. Sander L. Gilman, "Black Bodies, White Bodies: Toward an Iconography of Female Sexuality in Late Nineteenth Century Art, Medicine, and Literature," *Critical Inquiry* 12, no. 1 (Autumn 1985): 204–42.
7. O'Grady, "Olympia's Maid."
8. Paula Giddings, "The Last Taboo," in Toni Morrison, ed., *Race-ing Justice, En-gendering Power: Essays on Anita Hill, Clarence Thomas and the Construction of Social Reality* (New York: Pantheon Books, 1992), p. 445.
9. See the studies of Harriet Jacobs and Linda Brent.
10. Hazel Carby, *Reconstructing Womanhood: The Emergence of the Black Female Novelist* (New York: Oxford University Press, 1987), pp. 40–61.
11. This heading is taken from the title of Carby's book cited above.
12. Giddings, "The Last Taboo."
13. Beverly Guy-Sheftall, *Daughters of Sorrow: Attitudes Toward Black Women, 1880–1920* Black Women in United States History, vol. 11 (Brooklyn: Carlson Publishing, 1990), p. 90.
14. Martha Hodes, "The Sexualization of Reconstruction Politics: White Women and Black Men in the South after the Civil War," in John C. Fout and Maura S. Tantillo, eds., *American Sexual Politics: Sex Gender and Race since the Civil War* (Chicago: The University of Chicago Press, 1993), pp. 60–61.
15. Carby, *Reconstructing Womanhood,* p. 113.
16. Ibid.
17. Ibid., p. 114.
18. Ibid., p. 118.

19. See Evelyn Brooks Higginbotham, "African-American Women's History and the Metalanguage of Race," *Signs* 17, no. 2 (1992): 251–74; Elsa Barkley Brown, "Negotiating and Transforming the Public Sphere: African American Political Life in the Transition From Slavery to Freedom," *Public Culture* 7, no. 1 (Fall 1994): 107–46; as well as Hine, Giddings, and Carby.
20. Higginbotham, "African American Women's History," p. 262.
21. Hine, "Rape and the Inner Lives," p. 915.
22. Ibid.
23. See Carby, "Policing the Black Woman's Body." Elsa Barkley Brown argues that the desexualization of black women was not just a middle-class phenomenon imposed on working-class women. Though many working-class women resisted Victorian attitudes toward womanhood and developed their own notions of sexuality and respectability, some, also from their own experiences, embraced a desexualized image. Brown, "Negotiating and Transforming the Public Sphere," p. 144.
24. Hazel Carby, *Reconstructing Womanhood,* p. 174.
25. Ibid.
26. Ann DuCille, "Blues Notes on Black Sexuality: Sex and the Texts of Jessie Fauset and Nella Larsen," *Journal of the History of Sexuality* 3, no. 3 (1993): 419. See also Hazel Carby, "'It Just Be's Dat Way Sometime': The Sexual Politics of Black Women's Blues," in Ellen DuBois and Vicki Ruiz, eds., *Unequal Sisters: A Multicultural Reader in U.S. Women's History* (New York: Routledge, 1990).
27. Here, I am paraphrasing Ducille, "Blues Notes," p. 443.
28. Evelyn Brooks Higginbotham, *Righteous Discontent: The Women's Movement in the Black Baptist Church, 1880–1920* (Cambridge, Mass.: Harvard University Press, 1993).
29. The historical narrative discussed here is very incomplete. To date, there are no detailed historical studies of black women's sexuality.
30. Kimberle Crenshaw, "Whose Story Is It Anyway?: Feminist and Antiracist Appropriations of Anita Hill," in Morrison, ed., *Race-ing Justice, En-gendering Power*, p. 403.
31. Abdul JanMohamed, "Sexuality on/of the Racial Border: Foucault, Wright, and the Articulation of Racialized Sexuality," in Domna Stanton, ed., *Discourses of Sexuality: From Aristotle to AIDS* (Ann Arbor: University of Michigan Press, 1992), p. 105.
32. Spillers, "Interstices," p. 80.
33. See analyses of novels by Nella Larsen and Jessie Fauset by Carby, McDowell, and others.
34. Crenshaw, "Whose Story Is It Anyway?" p. 405.
35. Carole S. Vance, "Pleasure and Danger: Towards a Politics of Sexuality," in Carole S. Vance (ed.) *Pleasure and Danger: Exploring Female Sexuality,* London: Pandora Press, 1989.
36. Patricia J. Williams, *The Alchemy of Race and Rights* (Cambridge: Harvard University Press, 1991), p. 95.
37. Ibid.
38. bell hooks, *Black Looks: Race, and Representation* (Boston: South End Press, 1992), p. 21.
39. Ann du Cille, "The Occult of True Black Womanhood: Critical Demeanor and Black Feminist Studies," *Signs* 19, no. 3 (1994): 591–629.
40. Karla Scott, as quoted in Teresa De Lauretis, "The Practice of Love: Lesbian Sexuality and Perverse Desire" (Bloomington: Indiana University Press, 1994), p. 36.
41. Simon Watney, *Policing Desire: Pornography, AIDS and the Media* (Minneapolis: University of Minnesota Press, 1989), p. ix.
42. Spillers, *Ibid.,* "Interstices."
43. In a group discussion of two novels written by black women, Jill Nelson's *Volunteer Slavery* and Audre Lorde's *Zami,* a black woman remarked that while she thought Lorde's book was better written than Nelson's, she was disturbed that Lorde spoke so much about sex, and "aired all of her dirty linen in public." She held to this view even after it was pointed out to her that Nelson's book also included descriptions of her sexual encounters.
44. I am reminded of my mother's response when I "came out" to her. She asked me why, given that I was already black and had a nontraditional profession for a woman, I would want to take on one more thing to make my life difficult. My mother's point, which is echoed by many black women, is that in announcing my homosexuality, I was choosing to alienate myself from the black community.
45. See Scott, quoted in Teresa DeLauretis, *The Practice of Love: Lesbian Sexuality and Perverse Desire* (Bloomington: Indiana University Press, 1994), p. 36.

Notes to Chapter 9

I would like to thank Robert Stam for generously allowing me to use some shared material from our coauthored book *Unthinking Eurocentrism* (New York: Routledge, 1994). I am also grateful to the editors of this volume, Chandra Talpade Mohanty and Jacqui Alexander, for their useful suggestions and insightful comments, and for their truly dialogical spirit.

1. Lyotard, despite his skepticism about "metanarratives," supported the Persian Gulf War in a collective manifesto published in *Liberation*, thus endorsing George Bush's metanarrative of a "New World Order."
2. I am proposing here the term "post–Third-Worldist" to point to a move beyond the ideology of Third Worldism. Whereas the term "postcolonial" implies a movement beyond anticolonial nationalist ideology and a movement beyond a specific point of colonial history, post–Third-Worldism conveys a movement "beyond" a specific ideology—Third-Worldist nationalism. A post–Third-Worldist perspective assumes the fundamental validity of the anticolonial movement, but also interrogates the fissures that rend the Third-World nation. See Ella Shohat, "Notes on the Post-Colonial," *Social Text*, nos. 31–32 (Spring 1992).
3. For more on the concept of "location," see, for example, Chandra Talpade Mohanty, "Feminist Encounters: Locating the Politics of Experience," *Copyright* 1 (Fall 1987); Michele Wallace, "The Politics of Location: Cinema/Theory/Literature/Ethnicity/Sexuality/Me," *Framework* no. 36 (1989); Lata Mani, "Multiple Mediations: Feminist Scholarship in the Age of Multinational Reception," *Inscriptions* 5 (1989); and Inderpal Grewal, "Autobiographic Subjects and Diasporic Locations: *Meatless Days* and *Borderlands*" and Caren Kaplan, "The Politics of Location as Transnational Feminist Practice," in Inderpal Grewal and Caren Kaplan, *Scattered Hegemonies: Postmodernity and Transnational Feminist Practice* (Minneapolis: University of Minnesota Press, 1994).
4. See J. M. Blaut, *The Colonizer's Model of the World: Geographical Diffusionism and Eurocentric History* (New York and London: Guilford Press, 1993).
5. The various film festivals—in Havana, Cuba (dedicated to New Latin American cinema), in Carthage, Tunisia (for Arab and African Cinemas), in Ougadoogoo, Burkino Faso (for African and Afro-diasporic cinemas)—gave further expression to these movements.
6. In relation to cinema, the term "Third World" has been empowering in that it calls attention to the collectively vast cinematic productions of Asia, Africa, and Latin America, as well as the minoritarian cinema in the First World. While some, such as Roy Armes (1987), define "Third-World cinema" broadly as the ensemble of films produced by Third-World countries (including films produced before the very idea of the "Third World" was current), others, such as Paul Willemen (1989), prefer to speak of "Third cinema" as an ideological project (i.e., as a body of films adhering to a certain political and aesthetic program, whether or not they are produced by Third-World peoples themselves). As long as they are not taken as "essential" entities but as collective projects to be forged, both "Third-World cinema" and "Third cinema" retain important tactical and polemical uses for a politically inflected cultural practice. In purely classificatory terms, we might envision overlapping circles of denotation: 1) a core circle of "Third-Worldist" films produced by and for Third-World people (no matter where those people happen to be) and adhering to the principles of "third cinema"; 2) a wider circle of the cinematic productions of Third-World peoples (retroactively defined as such), whether or not the films adhere to the principles of third cinema and irrespective of the period of their making; 3) another circle consisting of films made by First- or Second-World people in support of Third-World peoples and adhering to the principles of third cinema; and 4) a final circle, somewhat anomalous in status, at once "inside" and "outside," comprising recent diasporic hybrid films (for example, those of Mona Hatoum or Hanif Kureishi), which both build on and interrogate the conventions of "third cinema." See Shohat/Stam, *Unthinking Eurocentrism*.
7. See Aijaz Ahmad, "Jameson's Rhetoric of Otherness and the National Allegory," *Social Text* no. 17 (Fall 1987): 3–25; Julianne Burton, "Marginal Cinemas," *Screen* 26, nos. 3–4 (May–August 1985).
8. See Arjun Appadurai, "Disjuncture and Difference in the Global Cultural Economy," *Public Culture* 2, no. 2 (1990). A similar concept, "scattered hegemonies," is advanced by Inderpal Grewal and Caren Kaplan, who offer a feminist critique of global-local relations in their introduction to *Scattered Hegemonies*.

9. In the cinema, this hegemonizing process intensified shortly after World War I, when U.S. film distribution companies (and, secondarily, European companies) began to dominate Third-World markets, and was further accelerated after World War II, with the growth of transnational media corporations. The continuing economic dependency of Third-World cinemas makes them vulnerable to neocolonial pressures. When dependent countries try to strengthen their own film industries by setting up trade barriers to foreign films, for example, First-World countries can threaten retaliation in some other economic area such as the pricing or purchase of raw materials. Hollywood films, furthermore, often cover their costs in the domestic market and can, therefore, be profitably "dumped" on Third-World markets at very low prices.
10. Although direct colonial rule has largely come to an end, much of the world remains entangled in neocolonial globalization. Partially as a result of colonialism, the contemporary global scene is now dominated by a coterie of powerful nation-states, consisting basically of Western Europe, the U.S., and Japan. This domination is economic ("the Group of Seven," the IMF, the World Bank, GATT), political (the five veto-holding members of the UN Security Council), military (the new "unipolar" NATO), and techno-informational-cultural (Hollywood, UPI, Reuters, France Presse, CNN). Neocolonial domination is enforced through deteriorating terms of trade and the "austerity programs" by which the World Bank and the IMF, often with the self-serving complicity of Third-World elites, impose rules that First-World countries would themselves never tolerate.
11. For a similar argument, see Grewal and Kaplan's introduction to *Scattered Hegemonies*.
12. The Indian TV version of the *Mahabharata* won a 90 percent domestic viewer share during a three-year run, and Brazil's Rede Globo now exports its *telenovelas* to more than eighty countries around the world.
13. For Appadurai, the global cultural situation is now more interactive; the U.S. is no longer the puppeteer of a world system of images, but only one mode of a complex transnational construction of "imaginary landscapes." In this new conjuncture, he argues, the invention of tradition, ethnicity, and other identity markers becomes "slippery, as the search for certainties is regularly frustrated by the fluidities of transnational communication." See Appadurai, "Disjuncture and Difference in the Global Cultural Economy."
14. See Benedict Anderson, *Imagined Communities: Reflexions on the Origins and Spread of Nationalism* (London: Verso, 1983); and E. J. Hobsbawm and Terence Ranger, eds., *The Invention of Tradition* (Cambridge: Cambridge University Press, 1983).
15. Pontecorvo returned to Algiers in 1991 to make *Gillo Pontecorvo Returns to Algiers*, a film about the evolution of Algeria during the twenty-five years that have elapsed since *Battle of Algiers* was filmed, and focusing on such topics as Islamic fundamentalism, the subordinate status of women, the veil, and so forth.
16. Anne McClintock, "No Longer in a Future Heaven: Women and Nationalism in South Africa," *Transition*, no. 51 (1991): 120.
17. Caren Kaplan, "Deterritorializations: The Rewriting of Home and Exile in Western Feminist Discourse," *Cultural Critique*, no. 6 (Spring 1987): 198.
18. The friend in question is Ella Habiba Shohat.
19. Or as the letters put it: "This bloody war takes my daughters to the four corners of the world." This reference to the dispersion of the family, as metonym and metaphor for the displacement of a people, is particularly ironic given that Zionist disourse itself has often imaged its own national character through the notion of "the ingathering of exiles from the four corners of the globe."
20. In this sense, *Measures of Distance* goes against the tendency criticized by Hamid Naficy which turns nostalgia into a ritualized denial of history. See "The Poetics and Practice of Iranian Nostalgia in Exile," *Diaspora*, no. 3 (1992).
21. Quoted in Brian V. Street, *The Savage in Literature* (London: Routledge and Kegan Paul, 1975), p. 99.
22. Georges-Louis Leclerc de Buffon, *The History of Man and Quadrupeds*, trans. William Smellie (London: T. Cadell and W. Davies, 1812), p. 422.
23. George Mosse, *Toward the Final Solution: A History of European Racism* (London: Dent, 1978), p. 44.
24. See Cornel West, *Prophesy Deliverance: An Afro-American Revolutionary Christianity* (Philadelphia: Westminster, 1982); Clyde Taylor, "Black Cinema in the Post-Aesthetic

Era," in Jim Pines and Paul Willemen, eds. *Questions of Third Cinema* (London: BFI, 1989); and bell hooks, *Black Looks: Race and Representation* (Boston: South End Press, 1992).

25. Charles White, *Account of the Regular Gradation in Man*, quoted in Stephen Jay Gould, *The Mismeasure of Man* (New York: W.W. Norton, 1981), p. 42.
26. Egyptians at an orientalist exposition were amazed to discover that the Egyptian pastries on sale were authentic. See Tim Mitchell, *Colonizing Egypt* (Berkeley: University of California Press, 1991), p. 10.
27. See Jon Pietersie, *White on Black: Images of Africa and Blacks in Western Popular Culture* (New Haven: Yale University Press, 1992). On the colonial safari as a kind of traveling minisociety, see Donna Haraway, "Teddy Bear Patriarchy: Taxidermy in the Garden Of Eden, New York City, 1908–1936," *Social Text,* no. 11 (Winter 1984–85).
28. See Phillips Verner Bradford and Harvey Blume, *Ota Benga: The Pygmy in the Zoo* (New York: St. Martins, 1992).
29. The real name of the "Hottentot Venus" remains unknown since it was never referred to by those who "studied" her.
30. For further discussion on science and the racial/sexual body, see Sander Gilman, "Black Bodies, White Bodies: Toward an Iconography of Female Sexuality in Late Nineteenth-Century Art, Medicine, and Literature," *Critical Inquiry* 12, no. 1 (Autumn 1985); and, in conjuction with early cinema, see Fatimah Tobing Rony, "Those Who Squat and Those Who Sit: The Iconography of Race in the 1895 Films of Felix-Louis Regnault," *Camera Obscura,* no. 28 (1992), a special issue on "Imaging Technologies, Inscribing Science," edited by Paula A. Treichler and Lisa Cartwright.
31. "Flower and Murie on the Dissection of a Bushwoman," *Anthropological Review* 5 (July 1867): 268.
32. Richard Altick, *The Shows of London* (Cambridge and London: Harvard University Press, 1978), p. 272.
33. Stephen Jay Gould, *The Flamingo's Smile* (New York: W.W. Norton & Co., 1985), p. 292. On a recent visit to the Musée de l'Homme, I found no traces of the Hottentot Venus; neither the official catalogue, nor officials themselves, acknowledged her existence.
34. Stuart Hall, "What Is This 'Black' in Black Popular Culture?" in Gina Dent, ed. *Black Popular Culture* (Seattle: Bay Press, 1992), p. 27.
35. Kobena Mercer, "Black Hair/Style Politics," *New Formations,* no. 3 (Winter 1987).
36. Ibid.
37. Not surprisingly, the film has been screened in museums and churches, and even for social workers and hair stylists, as a provocative contemplation of the intersection of fashion, politics, and identity.
38. This association is especially ironic given the colonial legacy of slavery and servitude in which black men (janitors) and women (maids) were obliged to clean up the "mess" created by white Europeans.
39. See Fatima Mernissi, *The Forgotton Queens of Islam,* trans. Mary Jo Lakeland (Minneapolis: University of Minnesota Press, 1993).
40. The juxtaposition of ethnographic diaries/writings and aboriginal images in *Nice Coloured Girls*' is hardly coincidental, since the first photographic and cinematographic representations of Aboriginies reflected the culture-bound ethnography of white settlers. (Walter Baldwin Spencer's 1901 footage of the Arrente tribe performing a kangaroo dance and rain ceremony marks the historical beginning of ethnographic filmmaking about the Aboriginies.) See Karl C. Heider, *Ethnographic Film* (Austin: University of Texas Press, 1976), p.19.

Notes to Chapter 10

This article is extracted from a monograph originally published in English and Spanish in 1989 by the Women's Program of the International Council for Adult Education in Toronto. I would like to acknowledge the support and editorial assistance of the members and staff of the Sistren Collective, the Bunting Institute, Radcliffe College; Jacqui Alexander, Yvonne Bobb Smith, Joan French, Ketu Katrak, Linzi Manicom, Sherene Razack, Judy Soares, Saabine Preuss, Lynda Yanz, Kate Young, and many, many others.

1. *QPH* was first presented at the Barn Theatre in Kingston in 1981. It was devised from collective creation, directed and written by Hertencer Lindsey. *Bellywoman Bangarang, Bandoolu Version,* and *Domestic* were likewise created and directed and written by me.

Nana Yah was directed and written by Jean Small.

2. *No to Sexual Violence* edited by Joan French. A revised version was re-issued in 1989.
3. The Jamaica School of Drama was, at that time, under the directorship of Dennis Scott, teacher, playwright, dancer, and director, who died in 1991. Scott's eclectic approach stressed the importance of drama as a strategy for collective and self development and encouraged the development of a specifically regional aesthetic language.

Works Cited in Chapter 10

Antrobus, Peggy. 1987. "Gender Implications of the Debt Crisis in the Commonwealth Caribbean: The Case of Jamaica." Unpublished paper, presented at the First Conference of Caribbean Economists, Kingston, Jamaica.

Bennett, Louise. 1982. *Selected Poems*, ed. Mervyn Morris. Kingston, Jamaica: Sangster's Book Stores.

Boyce Davis, C. and E. Savory Fido. 1990. *Out of the Kumbla: Caribbean Women and Literature*. Trenton, New Jersey: Africa World Press, Inc.

Breeze, J. B. 1988. *Riddym Ravings and Other Poems,* ed. Mervyn Morris. London: Race Today Publications.

Brodber, E. 1980. *Jane and Louisa Will Soon Come Home*. London: New Beacon Books.

——. 1988. *Myal*. London: New Beacon Books.

Brontë, C. 1983. *Jane Eyre*. New York: Penguin Books. (Originally published in 1847.)

Chevannes, Barry. 1987. "Community Development Research Project." Unpublished research document for the Association of Development Agencies, Jamaica.

Cobham-Sander, C. Rhonda. 1982. "The Creative Writer and West Indian Society: Jamaica 1900–1950." Unpublished Ph.D. diss., University of St. Andrews.

Davies, O., and P. Anderson. 1987. "The Impact of the Recession and Adjustment Policies on Poor Urban Women." Unpublished paper commissioned by UNICEF.

Dawes, Neville. 1977. "Cultural Policy in Jamaica." Unpublished paper presented at UNESCO meeting.

de Lisser, H.G. 1972. *Jane's Career*. Kingston, Jamaica: Sangster's Book Stores. (Originally published 1949.)

——. 1982. *The White Witch of Rosehall*. London and Basingstoke: Macmillan Education. (Originally published 1929 by Ernest Benn Ltd.)

Dunn, Leith. 1987. "Report on Women in Industry: A Participatory Research Project on Garment Workers in Jamaica." Unpublished paper for CUSO-Jamaica/JTURDC Research Project, Kingston.

Ford-Smith, Honor. 1988. "Jamaican Women and Cultural Development: A Pilot Project." Unpublished research document prepared for UNESCO.

French, Joan. 1987. *The CBI (Caribbean Basin Initiative) and Jamaica: Objectives and Impact*. Washington, D.C.: Development Gap.

French, Joan, and Honor Ford-Smith. 1986. "Women, Work and Organization in Jamaica, 1900–1944." Unpublished research paper for Institute of Social Studies, The Hague.

Friends of Sistren (ed. Joan French). 1984. *No To Sexual Violence*. Jamaica: Sistren.

Hall, C. 1992. *White, Male, and Middle Class: Explorations in Feminism and History*. New York: Routledge.

Henry, Maxine. 1987. "Women's Participation in the Social and Political Process in Jamaica in the 1970's." Unpublished paper presented at the Conference on Women's Studies, University of the West Indies.

Laiken, Marilyn. 1991. *The Anatomy of High Performing Teams: A Leader's Handbook*. Toronto: OISE Press.

Landry, Charles, et al. 1985. *What a Way to Run a Railroad: An Analysis of Radical Failure*. London: Comedia Publishing Group.

Levitt, Kari Polyani. 1990. *The Origins and Consequences of Jamaica's Debt Crisis*. Mona, Jamaica: Consortium Graduate School of Social Sciences.

Marson, Una. 1937. *Pocomania*. Unpublished manuscript, Archives, National Library of Jamaica.

Mies, Maria. 1986. *Toward a Methodology of Women's Studies*. The Hague: Institute of Social Studies.

Nettleford, Rex M. 1985. *Dance Jamaica: Cultural Definition and Artistic Discovery: The National Dance Theatre Company of Jamaica, 1962–1983*. New York: Grove Press.

Rhys, Jean. 1966. *Wide Sargasso Sea*. London: Andre Deutsch.

Rogers, Barbara. 1980. *The Domestication of Women: Discrimination in Developing Societies.* London: Tavistock Publications.
Sen, Gita, and Karen Grown. 1985. *Development Crisis and Alternative Visions: Third World Women's Perspectives.* New Delhi: DAWN.
Sistren, with Honor Ford-Smith. 1986. *Lionheart Gal: Life Stories of Jamaican Women.* London: The Women's Press.
Stromquist, Nelly. 1986. "Empowering Women Through Education: Lessons from International Cooperation." Unpublished paper presented at the International Council for Adult Education seminar in Kungalv, Sweden.
Sturdy, Carole. 1987. "Questioning the Sphinx: An Experience of Working in a Women's Organization." In *Living with the Sphinx: Papers from the Women's Therapy Centre*, ed. Sheila Ernst and Marie Maguire. London: The Women's Press.
Vassell, Lynnette. 1987. "CUSO's Mandate on Women: Problems and Prospects in Jamaica." Unpublished report for CUSO-Jamaica, Kingston.
Witter, M. 1987. "Culture and Economy." Unpublished paper presented to Organization of American States Caricult Seminar.

Government Documents
Bureau of Women's Affairs. 1987. Ministry of Social Security and Consumer Affairs, Government of Jamaica. "Income Generating and Skill Training Projects." June.
——. "An Overview of the Work of the Bureau of Women's Affairs: The National Machinery."
——. National Advisory Council on Women's Affairs. "Terms of Reference."

Notes to Chapter 11

1. Stree Shakti Sanghatana, *"We Were Making History...": Life Stories of Women in the Telangana Peoples' Struggle* (London: Zed Books Ltd., 1989), pp. 1–3.
2. Barry Pavier, *The Telangana Movement: 1944–51* (New Delhi: Vikas, 1981), pp. 18–62.
3. Ibid., pp. 78–82.
4. Stree Shakti Sanghatana, *We Were Making History*, 7–18.
5. Ibid., p. 5.
6. K. Balagopal, *Probings in the Political Economy of Agrarian Classes and Conflicts* (Hyderabad: Perspectives, 1988).
7. Rajni Kothari, "State and Statelessness in Our Time," *Economic and Political Weekly,* 26, nos. 11–12 (1991): 553–58.
8. Ibid. While these were characteristics of the "positive state," the very conception of the postcolonial state was built on European/Western conceptions of the nation-state that, paradoxically, undergird nationalist and anticolonial struggles all over the Third World.
9. This is nowhere more evident than in Andhra, where, immediately after independence, the Indian army was sent in to suppress a peasant uprising and put the landlords at ease. After over two decades of planning, radical movements are still fighting against absentee landlordism and feudal social oppression that is perpetuated with the active connivance of the agencies of the state. Apart from the police and army enforcing "order" on behalf of the landlords and upper castes, the state also vests control over development subsidies and other benefits in the hands of the landlords. To quote Balagopal, "All in all, this class of rural rich is the dominant pole of the peculiar semi-feudal relations spawned by imperialist capital impinging on traditional social relations, intent on commoditising the product without revolutionising the production relations." Balagopal, *Probings,* pp. 45–46.
10. A. K. Bagchi, "From Fractured Compromise to Democratic Consensus: Planning and Political Economy in Post Colonial India," *Economic and Political Weekly* 26, nos. 11–12 (1991), pp. 611–28.
11. Kalpana Kannabiran, "Rape and the Construction of Communal Identity," unpublished paper presented at the South Asian Feminist Workshop, Colombo, 1992.
12. The growing naxalite movement in West Bengal and Andhra and the student movements in Bihar and Gujarat inspired by Jayaprakash Narayan were expressions of this discontent.
13. In fact, the leaders of this group were called the Zetkin and Luxemburg of Andhra.
14. Significantly, the group documented women's experience in the armed struggle. See Stree Shakti Sanghatana, *We Were Making History.*

15. ICRISAT stands for International Crop Research Institute for the Semi-Arid Tropics. For reports of the group's activities, see Vasanth Kannabiran, "Report from SSS, A Women's Organization in Hyderabad, Andhra Pradesh, India," *Feminist Studies* 112, no. 3 (Fall 1986): 601–12; and Vasanth Kannabiran and Veena Shatrugna, "The Relocation of Political Practice," *Lokayan Bulletin* 4, no. 6 (1986): 23–43.
16. We could probably look at this discussion in terms of the distinction Maxine Molyneux makes between practical and strategic gender needs, although we would like to stress the fact that these are not mutually exclusive categories. See Maxine Molyneux, "Mobilization without Emancipation? Women's Interests, the State and Revolution in Nicaragua," *Feminist Studies* 11, no. 2 (Summer 1985): 227–54.
17. *Manushi* (January 1979): 36–40.
18. Susie Tharu and Rama Melkote, "Living Outside the Protection of Marriage: Patriarchal Relations in Working Women's Hostel," *Manushi* no. 9 (1981): 33.
19. As with the women's question, the minority question, or the dalit question, it is the silences and absences that speak the most.
20. Ibid., p. 32.
21. Sheila Rowbotham, "What Do Women Want? Woman-Centred Values and the World As It Is," *Feminist Review* no. 20 (summer 1985).
22. For a review of the debate generated by the Mathura case, see Nandita Gandhi and Nandita Shah, *The Issues at Stake: Theory and Practice in the Contemporary Women's Movement in India* (New Delhi: Kali for Women, 1992).
23. Vasanth Kannabiran, "Death in Police Custody," *Economic and Political Weekly* 14 (1979): 1829–31; and report in *Manushi* (December 1979–January 1980): 30–32.
24. *Manushi* (December 1979–January 1980): 31.
25. For instance, one case that came to the attention of the group was the "suicide" of the wife of a revolutionary writer. Sensing the discomfort in the revolutionary writer's group, SSS decided not to take up the issue but to leave it to be handled as an internal issue. While this was a serious decision for SSS, it was also indicative of who the group perceived as its allies at that point in its history.
26. Kothari, "State and Statelessness in Our Time."
27. Dealing with individual cases on a sustained basis acutely raises the problem of the lack of institutions built on feminist principles. No matter how supportive welfarist institutions may seem, to work with them on a continuing basis would inevitably affect the group's public stands on issues and force it to compromise on feminist principles.
28. Stree Shakti Sanghatana, *We Were Making History.*
29. Ashok Rudra, "In a Theoretical Vacuum," *Economic and Political Weekly* 24, no. 17 (April 29, 1989): 917–18. There is, of course, the danger of dubious research, but that is a danger with any kind of research, and activists were needlessly singled out for this accusation.
30. One can perhaps extend this argument, linking it to transnational networks, the hierarchization of knowledge, and the appropriation of political activism in First-World/Third-World relationships.
31. In the recent massacre of dalits by upper-caste Reddi landlords in Tsundur in Andhra Pradesh, Reddi women, for the first time, played an active, public role in defending their men. Their defense was a collective public declaration that they (and there were 300 of them) had been raped by the dalits in that village. Reddis are a landowning peasant caste who are economically and politically dominant in the Telangana region and parts of other regions in the state. Reports of this incident appeared in the *Economic and Political Weekly.* See M. Shatrugna, "Road to Raktakshetram: Report from Chunduru," *Economic and Political Weekly* 26, no. 34 (August 24, 1991): 1967–69; and "Upper Caste Violence: Study of Chunduru Carnage," *Economic and Political Weekly* 26, no. 36 (September 7, 1991): 2079–84. For an analysis of caste violence and its implications for women, see Vasanth Kannabiran and Kalpana Kannabiran, "Caste and Gender: Understanding Dynamics of Power and Violence," *Economic and Political Weekly* 26, no. 37 (September 14, 1991): 2130–33.

Works Cited in Chapter 12

Aig-Ojehomon, M. W., and M. A. Akinware. 1989. "Child Malnutrition in Nigeria: Causes and Solutions." Paper presented at the World Economics Day Seminar, organized by the Federal Ministry of Education, March 20.

Amadiume, Ifi. 1990. "Contemporary Women's Organizations, Contradictions and Irrelevance in the Struggle for Grassroots Participatory Democracy in Nigeria." Paper presented at the Workshop on Social Movements, Social Transformation and the Struggle for Democracy in Nigeria, CODESRIA, Tunis, May 21–23.

Awe, Bolanle. 1988. "Nigerian Women's Visions and Movements: An Overview." Paper presented at the Africa Regional Meeting of Food, Energy and Debt Crises in Relation to Women, Development of Alternatives with Women for a New Era (DAWN), Ibadan, September 27–29.

Awe, Bolanle, and Nina Mba. 1991. "Women's Research and Documentation Centre (Nigeria)." *Signs* (Summer): 859–64.

Bryce, Jane. 1987. "Liberation, Feminism and Nigeria." *The Guardian Sunday* (1 February).

Civil Liberties Organization (Nigeria) Reports.

Dennis, Carolyne. 1987. "Women and the State in Nigeria: the Case of the Federal Military Government 1984–85." In Haleh Afshar (ed.) *Women, State and Ideology*. London: Macmillan, pp. 13–27.

Economist Intelligence Unit (EIU). *Country Profiles* and *Country Reports* 1982–1992.

Enabulele, Arlene Bene. 1985. "The Role of Women's Associations in Nigeria's Development: Social Welfare Perspective." In *Women in Nigeria Today*. London: Zed Books, 187–94.

Ibrahim, Jibrin. 1993. "Transition to Civil Rule: Sapping Democracy." In Adebayo Olukoshi, (ed.) *The Politics of Structural Adjustment in Nigeria*. Portsmouth, N.H.: J. Currey.

——. 1991. "Religion and Political Turbulence in Nigeria." *Journal of Modern African Studies* . 29: 115–36.

——. 1989. "The State, Accumulation, and Democratic Forces in Nigeria." Seminar Paper to C.E.A.N., Université de Bordeaux I.

Imam, Ayesha M. 1994. "Politics, Islam and Women in Kano, Northern Nigeria." In *Identity Politics and Women: Cultural Reassertions and Feminisms in International Perspective,* ed. Valentine Moghadam. Boulder: Westview Press, 123–44.

——. 1986a. "Women's Liberation: Myth or Reality." Paper presented at the Muslim Sisters' Organization Conference, Kano, 1985. In *Women's Struggles and Strategies: Third World Perspectives*. Rome: ISIS, pp. 68–73. Also in *The Muslim Woman in the Fourteenth Hijab.* FOMWAN, 1989.

——. 1986b. "Ideological Manipulation, Political Repression and African Women." *AAWORD in Nairobi*. AAWORD Occasional Paper 3, pp. 18–24.

Isamah, Austin. 1990. "Organized Labour Under the Military Regimes in Nigeria." *Africa Development* 15: 81–94.

Kabir, Zainab. 1989. "Women's Liberation: Myth or Reality." Paper presented at the Muslim Sisters' Organization Conference, Kano, 1985. In *The Muslim Woman in the Fourteenth Hijab*. FOMWAN, 1989.

Kane, Ousmane. 1990. "Les mouvements religieux et le champ politique au Nigeria septentrional: le cas du reformisme musulman a Kano." *Islam et societies au sud du Sahara,* no. 4 (November): 7–24.

Kano State Committee on Women Affairs. 1987. *Report of the Kano State on Women Affairs* Kano: Government Printer.

Mahdi, Hauwa. 1985 (reprint 1989). "The Position of Women in Islam." *Women and the Family in Nigeria*. Dakar: CODESRIA, pp. 59–64.

Mama, Amina. 1990. "The Impact of Violence and Coercion on Women's Health." Paper presented at the Conference on Women and Health, Women in Nigeria, Lagos, April 9–12.

Mba, Nina. 1982. *Nigerian Women Mobilized: Women's Political Activity in Southern Nigeria, 1900–1965*. Berkeley: University of California at Berkeley Institute of International Studies.

Mustapha, Abdulrauf. 1993. "Ever-Decreasing Circles: Democratic Rights in Nigeria." In *Dead-End to Nigerian Development: An Investigation of the Economic and Political Crisis in Nigeria,* ed. Okwudiba Nnoli. Dakar: CODESRIA, 79–96.

Okonjo, Kamene. 1976. "The Dual Sex Political System: Igbo Women and Community Politics in Mid-Western Nigeria." In *Women in Africa: Studies in Social and Economic Change,* ed. Nancy Hafkin and Edna G. Bay. Stanford: Stanford University Press.

Osaghae, Eghosa E. 1989. "The Character of the State, Legitimacy Crisis and Social Mobilization in Africa: An Explanation of Form and Character." *Africa Development* 14: 27–47.
Shettima, Kole Ahmed. 1995. "Engendering Nigeria's Third Republic." *African Studies Review* 38, no. 3, pp. 61–98.
Tahzib, Farhang. 1985 (reprint 1989). "Social Factors in the Aetiology of Vesico-Vaginal Fistulae." In *Women and the Family in Nigeria*. Dakar: CODESRIA, pp. 75–80.
Wamalwa, B. N. 1987. "Violence against Wives and the Law in Kenya." Paper presented at the Regional Meeting of Africa and the Middle East on Law and Shelter by the International Federation of Women Lawyers, Nairobi.
WIN (Women in Nigeria). 1985a. *The WIN Document: The Conditions of Women in Nigeria and Policy Recommendations to 2,000 AD*. Zaria: WIN.
——. 1985b. *Women in Nigeria Today*. London: Zed Books.
——. 1985c (reprint 1989). *Women and the Family in Nigeria*. Dakar: CODESRIA.
——. 1987. *What Women Want for Nigeria's Political and Socio-Economic System: Report to the Political Bureau*. Unpublished mimeograph.
——. n.d. *WIN Pamphlet on Women in Politics*.
——. 1992a. *Women and Education: Proceedings of the Third Annual Women in Nigeria Conference*. Zaria: WIN.
——. 1992b. *Child Abuse in Nigeria: Proceedings of the Seventh Annual Women in Nigeria Conference*. Zaria: WIN.

Appendix

A. WIN National Conferences and Workshops*

Women in Nigeria (1982)
Women and the Family (1983)
Women and Education (1984)
Women in the Rural Areas (1985)
Conscientisation and Mobilization (1986)
What Women Want for Nigeria's Political and Socio-Economic System (1987)
Child Abuse (1988)
Women and the Transition to Democracy (1989)
Women and Health (1990)
Women and the National Census (1990)
Women and the Economy (1991)
Violence Against Women (1992)
* In addition to conferences and activities organized nationally, WIN's state branches have also organized numerous seminars, workshops, campaigns, and projects.

Extract from the WIN Constitution

Preamble

The organization Women in Nigeria (WIN) holds that:
a) The majority of women, like the majority of men, suffer from the exploitative and oppressive character of Nigerian society;
b) Women suffer additional forms of exploitation and oppression;
c) Women, therefore, suffer double oppression and exploitation as members of subordinate classes and as women.

Aims and Objectives

WIN engages in research, policy making, dissemination of information, and action aimed at improving the conditions of women. In pursuance of the above, the organization acts:
a) To promote the study of the conditions of women in Nigeria, with the aim of combating discriminatory and sexist practices in the family, in the workplace, and in the wider society;
b) To defend the rights of women under the Nigerian constitution and the United Nations Human Rights Conventions;
c) To provide nonsexist alternatives to government and institutional policies;

d) To fight against the harassment and sexual abuse of females in the family and elsewhere;
e) To promote an equitable distribution of domestic work in the family;
f) To provide a forum for women to express themselves;
g) To ensure for women equal access to equal education;
h) To combat sexist stereotypes in literature, the media, and educational materials;
i) To provide the means of educating women on relevant issues;
j) To form links and work with other organizations to fight for social justice.

Notes to Chapter 13

I am grateful to S. Shankar for his patient reading and valuable discussions and Yumna Siddiqui for her thoughtful comments. I would also like to thank Carla Petievich and Jael Silliman for their comments and Margaret Abraham for her assistance on certain citations.

1. Aida Hurtado, in her reference to Western feminism, claims that "[a]cademic production requires time and financial resources. . . . Not surprisingly, therefore, most contemporary published feminist theory in the United States has been written by white, educated women" (838). I would like the reader to keep this in mind as I make references to Western feminist theory. I realize that Western feminism has many strands and is not monolithic; however, there is a dominant mainstream feminism, and this is what I refer to in this essay. I also do not mean to say that the criticisms I make of Western feminisms cannot be made of feminisms elsewhere.
2 For a longer discussion, see Bhattacharjee, "The Habit of Ex-nomination: Nation, Woman and the Indian Immigrant Bourgeoisie."
3. I choose to discuss the *heterosexual* family because immigration law defines the family as such and also because that is the conventional perception of the home in which violence occurs. We need to remember that, in reality, domestic violence can take place in other relationships as well, such as those of lesbians or gays. I would also like to note that the family home I will be discussing in this essay is based on marriage specifically, because immigration laws, as we will see, are heavily invested in marital relationships.
4. If the man is a U.S. citizen, he can sponsor the woman for conditional residency, which she can get within a short period. After that, she can come to reside with him in the U.S. and, after two years, he can sponsor her for permanent status. If the man is a permanent resident (that is, not a citizen), she is not eligible for conditional residency but only for permanent residency after two years or more. In the meantime, she can either stay in South Asia for the waiting period or come to the U.S. on a different temporary visa and wait until she is called for permanent residency. In the first case, the man often tries to abandon the marriage, and in the second case, her temporary visa makes her immigration status precarious during the waiting period.
5. These laws also apply to men whose legal status is sponsored by women. However, these cases are fewer and, even when they exist, instances of a woman using her power to abuse a man are rarer.
6. The Violence Against Women Act was passed in Congress subsequently, primarily because it was included in the Crime Bill, thus pitting women against people of color. It is not possible to describe, in this essay, the act or the debates around it, as it contains numerous provisions. I have focused on the provisions that significantly help immigrant women and that were heavily contested. It is fair to say that although there have been senators who are against it, there are some who have responded favorably to the arguments presented by the lobbying groups.
7. For a longer discussion, see Bhattacharjee, "The Habit of Ex-nomination."
8. A similar tale of opportunistic "open door" periods alternating with periods of exclusion and mass deportations characterized the history of Mexican immigration.
9. U.S. immigration history is well-documented in "The Evolution of U.S. Immigration Policy," in Family Violence Prevention Fund, et al., *Domestic Violence in Immigrant and Refugee Communities: Asserting the Rights of Battered Women*; and in "General Introduction: A Woman-Centered Perspective on Asian American History," in *Making Waves: An Anthology of Writings By and About Asian American Women*.
10. The Center for Immigrants Rights documented in March 1991 that the number of employment-based visas have "increased from 54,000 to 140,000 with new categories instituted for: 1) 'priority workers,' including individuals with 'extraordinary ability, out-

standing professors and researchers and . . . executives and managers'; 2) professionals holding advanced degrees or aliens of exceptional ability in the sciences, arts or business; 3) professionals with Bachelors degrees, skilled workers and other workers."

11. The likely candidates for residency or citizenship with the U.S. can be seen in the details of the Immigration Reform and Control Act of 1986 and U.S. criteria for testing the eligibility of naturalization candidates. Both are favorable toward heterosexual men with an established trail of the "proper" documents in the U.S.
12. In one workshop, a white male counselor remarked that he wished he could take his daughter out of school just like the South Asian father did because of his anxiety about the sexually open environment in the U.S. Here, the counselor saw his daughter as being part of a public that had certain rights defined by the state which he could not interfere with, whereas the South Asian young woman was supposedly part of a space *outside* that public.
13. See Sarkar, 'Women's Agency within Authoritarian Communalism: The Rashtrasevika Samiti and Ramjanmabhoomi."
14. A detailed documentation of the current anti-immigrant climate in the U.S. is beyond the scope of this essay. I am referring to the general political mood towards stopping or drastically reducing immigration, and legislative efforts or recommendations for regressive policies towards immigrants in the U.S.
15. Sakhi for South Asian Women was founded in 1989 by women of South Asian origin in New York City. It addresses issues of violence against women in the South Asian community through individual advocacy and community outreach and organizing. Sakhi is committed to the view that only through empowerment can women ultimately resist violence in their lives. Sakhi also believes that community education is integral to its work because it is only through the raising of awareness that fundamental change can occur.

Works Cited in Chapter 13

Alunan, Gina. 1993. "Abuses Against Asian Migrant Women: A Human Rights Issue." *Women on the Move: Proceedings of the Workshop on Human Rights Abuses Against Immigrant and Refugee Women.* Vienna: Family Violence Prevention Fund.

Benedict, Anderson, *Imagined Communities: Reflections on the Origin and Spread of Nationalism*. London: Verso, 1983.

Bhattacharjee, Anannya. 1992. "The Habit of Ex-nomination: Nation, Woman and the Indian Immigrant Bourgeoisie." *Public Culture.* Vol 5, no. 1 (Fall 1992: 19–44).

Bush, Diane Mitsch. 1992. "Women's Movements and State Policy Reform Aimed at Domestic Violence Against Women: A Comparison of the Consequences of Movement Mobilization in the U.S. and India." *Gender and Society* 6: 587–608.

Center for Immigrants Rights. 1991. "'Give Me Your Professionals, Your Experts, Your Investors': The Immigration Act of 1990."

Eisenstein, Zillah R. 1994. *The Color of Gender.* Berkeley: University of California Press.

Family Violence Prevention Fund, Coalition for Immigration Rights and Services, Immigrant Women's Task Force, and National Immigration Project of the National Lawyer's Guild, Inc. 1991. *Domestic Violence in Immigrant and Refugee Communities: Asserting the Rights of Battered Women.*

Hiro, Dilip. 1991. *Black British, White British*. London: Grafton Books.

Hurtado, Aida. 1989. "Relating to Privilege: Seduction and Rejection in the Subordination of White Women and Women of Color." *Signs: Journal of Women in Culture and Society* 14: 833–55.

Johnson-Odim, Cheryl. 1991. "Common Themes, Different Contexts: Third World Women and Feminism." In *Third World Women and the Politics of Feminism*, eds. Chandra Talpade Mohanty, Ann Russo, and Lourdes Torres. Bloomington: Indiana University Press.

Kawaja, Kaleem. 1993. "Brotherhood Needed." *India Abroad*. (November). Letter to the editor.

MacKinnon, Catharine. 1989. *Toward A Feminist Theory of the State.* Cambridge, Mass.: Harvard University Press.

Mazumdar, Sucheta. 1989a. "General Introduction: A Woman-Centered Perspective on Asian American History." In *Making Waves: An Anthology of Writings By and About Asian American Women,* ed. Asian Women United of California. Boston: Beacon Press.

——. 1989b. "Racist Responses to Racism: The Aryan Myth and South Asians in the United States." *South Asia Bulletin* 9, no. 1.

Mohanty, Chandra Talpade. "Feminist Politics: What's Home Got To Do With It?" In *Feminist Studies/Critical Studies,* ed. Teresa de Lauretis. Bloomington: Indiana University Press, 1986.

——. 1991. "Cartographies of Struggle: Third World Women and the Politics of Feminism." In *Third World Women and the Politics of Feminism,* eds. Chandra Talpade Mohanty, Ann Russo, and Lourdes Torres. Bloomington: Indiana University Press.

NiCarthy, Ginny, Karen Merriam, and Sandra Coffman. 1984. *Talking it Out: A Guide to Groups for Abused Women.* Seattle: The Seal Press.

Poulantzas, Nicos. 1980. *State, Power, Socialism.* London: Verso.

Sangari, Kumkum, and Sangari Vaid. 1989. "Recasting Women: An Introduction." In *Recasting Women: Essays in Colonial History.* New Delhi: Kali for Women.

Sarkar, Tanika. 1993. "Women's Agency within Authoritarian Communalism: The Rashtrasevika Samiti and Ramjanmabhoomi." In *Hindus and Others,* ed. Gyanendra Pandey. New Delhi: Viking.

Sudha, S. 1993. "Compu-Devata: Elecronic Bulletin Boards and Political Debates." *South Asian Magazine For Action and Reflection.* no. 2 (Summer): 4–10.

Notes to Chapter 14

Even though I am often not in agreement with the strategies of Suriname's (middle-class) women's organizations, I deeply admire their perseverance in the face of most difficult circumstances. I want to thank the leadership and the individual members who took their time to tell me the history and the activities of the various organizations.

1. In this essay, I will speak alternatively of Creole and Afro-Surinamese women. The first is the local term, applied to the mainly urban descendants of slaves, who form about 40 percent of the entire population. As a group, they distinguish themselves–culturally, linguistically, socially, and psychologically–from other blacks, i.e., Maroons, the descendants of runaway slaves who formed viable communities in the interior of the country from the seventeenth century on.
2. Describing Janie's feelings on the gatherings of the Eatonville folks, Hurston writes: "When the people sat around on the porch and passed around the pictures of their thoughts for the others to look at and see, it was nice" (1937: 81).
3. Slavery ended in Suriname in 1863.
4. This article is based on anthropological fieldwork in Paramaribo, the capitol of Suriname, during 1990 until August 1991. The fieldwork was made possible by grants from Inter American Foundation (Washington, D.C.) and the Institute of American Cultures (UCLA). See my dissertation, Wekker, 1992.
5. The word "Winti" is used in three ways: it refers to 1) the Afro-Surinamese religion (*Winti*); 2) the Gods and spirits of ancesors, who, when they are honored, help human beings (*winti*); and 3) the state of being "possessed" by a god or spirit (*winti*) (Wekker 1992).
6. Terms like "trance" or "dissociation," as it is also sometimes called, are really inappropriate. They reflect a medical discourse and they, moreover, strengthen the illusory belief in a unitary subject. I understand "being possessed" as the temporary foregrounding of a particular, unconscious part of the multiple self (Wekker 1992).
7. Another feature of egalitarianism, which is beyond the scope of this article to explore, is that, as in African cosmological systems (Mbiti 1969), there is an intense unity between the living and the dead. There is no opposition between these worlds; one is an extension of the other.
8. I expressly avoid terms like "heterosexuality," "homosexuality," and "bisexuality," due to their situated, Western baggage.
9. At the end of 1995, one Dutch guilder (=nf) was worth 250 Surinamese guilders (=sf); one U.S. $ was approximately 460 sf. At the beginning of my research period, 1990, the corresponding figures were 1 nf = 10 sf and 1 U.S. $ = 20 sf.
10. On one occasion when I was present at an organization, we watched "A Mother's Story," about Mary Thomas, the mother of Isiah Thomas of the Detroit Pistons basketball team.
11. Dew does not spell out what he means by "militant women's liberationists." I would be put in a quandary if I had to qualify any Surinamese women's group, past or present, as "militant." Bestowing of adjectives does not occur from a vacuum, but points to the locatedness of any description.

12. From interview with F. Cederboom, National Women's Council, Jan. 30, 1991.
13. Paramaribo, the capital of Suriname located on the Northern coastline, houses two-thirds of the nation's population and is the hub of cultural, economic, and political activity. In the surrounding districts, there are Javanese and Hindustani, who work in agriculture. Further away, in the hinterland, are Maroons and Amerindians, the original population.
14. Since then, in 1992, a group called "Stop gewweld tegen Vrouwen" (Stop the Violence against Women) was formed, which calls for systematic investigaton of sexual violence against women and children, a first in Surinamese history.
15. There are two exceptional organizations which call for an investigation of the violation of human rights in the 1980s: Moi Wana and Organisatie voor Gerechtigheid en Vrede (Organization for Justice and Peace). Both of these organizations are led by women, Ineke de Miranda and Ilse Labadie. The founder of Moi Wana is Stanley Rensch, a Maroon, and it is no coincidence that all these courageous individuals are outside the conventional corridors of power.
16. Nowadays, VHP stands for Vooruitstrevende Hervormings Partij (Progressive Reform Party), but it used to be called Verenigde Hindustaanse Partij (United Hindustani Party). The original membership has not changed much, however. During the 1991 elections, for the first time in history, a woman was nominated by VHP and chosen for the Assembly by preferential votes.
17. See Petition to the President of the Republic of Suriname on the position of Guyanese immigrants, April 15, 1991.

Works Cited in Chapter 14

Ambacht. 1912. *Het Ambacht in Suriname.* Rapport van de Commissie benoemd bij Goeverne-mentsresolutie van 13 januarie 1910, no. 13. Paramaribo

Besson, Jean. 1993. "Reputation and Respectability Reconsidered: A new Perspective on Afro-Caribbean Peasant Women." In *Women and Change in the Caribbean: A Pan-Caribbean Perspective,* ed. J. Momsen. Bloomington: Indiana University Press.

Brana-Shute Rosemary. 1976. "Women, Clubs, and Politics: The Case of a Lower Class Neighbourhood in Paramaribo, Suriname." *Urban Anthropology* 5, no. 2.

——. 1993. "Neighbourhood Networks and National Politics among Working-class Afro-Surinamese Women." In *Women and Change in the Caribbean: A Pan-Caribbean Perspective,* ed. J. Momsen. Bloomington: Indiana University Press.

Brydon, L., and S. Chant. 1989. *Women in the Third World: Gender Issues in Rural and Urban Areas.* Aldershot: Elgar.

Coleridge, P. 1958. "Vrouwenleven in Paramaribo." In *Suriname in Stroomlijnen.* Amsterdam: Wereld-Bibliotheek.

D'Emilio, John. 1984. "Capitalism and Gay Identity." In *Powers of Desire: The Politics of Sexuality,* eds. A. Snitow, C. Stansell, and S. Thompson. London:Virago.

Dew, Edward. 1978. *The Difficult Flowering of Suriname: Ethnicity and Politics in a Plural Society.* The Hague: Martinus Nijhoff.

Evans-Pritchard, Edward. 1970. "Sexual Inversion Among the Azande." *American Anthropologist,* 72 no. 6, pp. 1429–47.

Faderman, Lillian. 1991. *Odd Girls and Twilight Lovers: A History of Lesbian Life in Twentieth Century America.* New York: Columbia University Press.

Geertz, Clifford. 1984. "'From the Native's Point of View': On the Nature of Anthropological Understanding." In *Culture Theory: Essays on Mind, Self and Emotion* (eds.) R. Shweder and R. Levine. Cambridge: Cambridge University Press.

Gramsci, Antonio. 1971. *Selections from the Prison Notebooks.* London: Lawrence and Wishhart.

Gray White, Deborah. 1985. *Ar'n't I a Woman? Female Slaves in the Plantation South.* New York/London: W.W. Norton.

Harrison, Faye. 1988. "Women in Jamaica's Informal Economy: Insights from a Kingston Slum." *Nieuwe West-Indische Gids* 62, nos. 3–4.

Henry, Frances, and Pamela Wilson. 1975. "The Status of Women in Caribbean Societies: An Overview of their Social, Economic and Sexual Roles." *Social and Economic Studies* 24.

Herskovits, Melville. 1938. *Dahomey: An Ancient West African Kingdom,* vols. I and II. Evanston: Northwestern University Press.

Hill Collins, Patricia. 1986. "The Social Construction of Black Feminist Thought: An Essay in the Sociology of Knowledge." *Signs: Journal of Women in Culture and Society* 14, no. 4.

——. 1990. *Black Feminist Thought: Knowledge, Consciousness and the Politics of Empowerment.* London: HarperCollins Academic.
Hira, Sandew. 1983. "Class Formation and Class Struggle in Suriname." In *Crisis in the Caribbean* (eds). F. Ambursley and R. Cohen. London: Heinemann.
Hurston, Zora Neale. 1937. *Their Eyes Were Watching God.* Chicago: University of Illinois Press.
de Kom, Anton. 1934. *Wij Slaven van Suriname.* Amsterdam: Contact.
Kondo, Dorinne. 1990. *Crafting Selves: Power, Gender and Discourses of Identity in a Japanese Workplace.* Chicago: University of Chicago Press.
Lewis, Diane. 1975. "The Black Family: Socialization and Sex Roles." *Phylon.* Vol. 36, no. 3.
van Lier, Rudolf. 1977. *Samenleving in een grensgebied. Een sociaal-historische Studie van Suriname.* Amsterdam: Emmering.
Lorde, Audre. 1983. *Zami: A New Spelling of my Name.* New York: The Crossing Press.
Lutz, Catherine. 1988. *Unnatural Emotions: Everyday Sentiments on a Micronesian Atoll and Their Challenges to Western Theory.* Chicago: University of Chicago Press.
Malmberg-Guicherit, Henna. 1993. "DePositie van het Vrouwelijk Hoger Kader, Den Sabiuma fu Sranan." In *Congresbundel "Vrouwen, Ontwikkeling en Leiderschap."* Paramaribo: V.V.A.O.
Marks, Arnaud. 1976. *Male and Female in the Afro-Curaçaoan Household.* The Hague: KITLV, nr. 77.
Massiah, Jocelyn, ed. 1986. "Women in the Caribbean. Parts 1 and 2." *Social and Economic Studies* 35, nos. 1 and 2.
Mbiti, John 1969. *African Religions and Philosophy.* London: Heinemann.
Mintz, Sidney, and Richard Price. 1992. *The Birth of African-American Culture: An Anthropological Perspective.* Boston: Beacon Press.
Mohanty, Chandra Talpade. 1991. "Under Western Eyes: Feminist Scholarship and Colonial Discourses." In *Third World Women and the Politics of Feminism* (eds.) C. T. Mohanty, A. Russo, and L. Torres. Bloomington: Indiana University Press.
Momsen, Janet (ed.) 1993. *Women and Change in the Caribbean: A Pan-Caribbean Perspective.* Bloomington: Indiana University Press.
Nash, June, and Helen Safa (eds.). 1980. *Sex and Class in Latin America: Women's Perspectives on Politics, Economics and the Family in the Third World.* South Hadley: Bergin and Garvey Publishers.
Obeyesekere, Gananath. 1980. *Medusa's Hair: An Essay on Personal Symbols and Religious Experience.* Chicago/London: University of Chicago Press.
Pierce, Benjamin. 1971. "Kinship and Residence among the Urban Nengre of Suriname: A Reevaluation of Concepts and Theories of the Afro-American Family." Unpublished Ph.D. dissertation, Tulane University.
Rubenstein, H. 1987. *Coping with Poverty: Adaptive Strategies in a Caribbean Village.* Boulder/London: Westview Press.
Silvera, Makeda. 1992. "Man Royals and Sodomites: Some Thoughts on the Invisibility of Afro-Caribbean Lesbians." *Feminist Studies* 18, no. 3.
Smith, Dorothy. 1987. *The Everyday World as Problematic: A Feminist Sociology.* Boston: Northeastern University Press.
Stack, Carol. 1986. "The Culure of Gender: Women and Men of Color." *Signs: Journal of Women in Culture and Society* 11, no. 2.
Teenstra, M. 1835. *De Landbouw in de Kolonie Suriname, voorafgegaan door eene Geschied-en Natuurkundige Beschouwing dier Kolonie.* Groningen: Eekhoorn.
Tjoa, Twie. 1990. *Vrouw Zijn in Suriname.* Inleiding in het Kader van de Vierde Lustrumviering van de Vereniging van Medici in Suriname, Ms.
Weedon, Chris. 1987. *Feminist Practice and Poststructuralist Theory.* Oxford and Cambridge: Blackwell.
Wekker Gloria. 1992. "I Am Gold Money (I Pass Through All Hands, but I Do Not Lose My Value): The Construction of Selves, Gender and Sexualities in a Female, Working-Class, Afro-Surinamese Setting." Unpublished Ph.D. dissertation, UCLA.
——. 1994. "'Eindelijk Kom ik tot Mijzelf': Subjectiviteit in een Westers en een Afro-Surinaams Universum." In *Hulpverlening bij Surinamers, Antillianen en Molukkers,* ed. J. Hoogsteder. Utrecht: Landelijke Federatie van Surinaamse Welzijnsinstellingen.
Wilson, Peter. 1969. "Reputation and Respectability: A Suggestion for Caribbean Ethnology." *Man,* n.s. 4, no. 1.
Wooding, Charles. 1972. *Winti: Een Afro-Amerikaanse Godsdienst.* Meppel: Krips Repro (1987).

Contributors

M. Jacqui Alexander teaches in the programs in Gender Studies and Feminist Theory and Cultural Studies at the New School for Social Research in New York. Her courses are grounded in feminist critiques of imperialism, colonization, and heterosexuality. She has been actively involved in feminist movements in the Caribbean as well as in feminist and lesbian and gay movements in the United States of North America. She is a coeditor of *The Third Wave*, forthcoming from Kitchen Table/Women of Color Press.

Anannya Bhattacharjee is currently the Executive Director of the Committee Against Anti-Asian Violence in New York City. She is a founding member and the former Program Coordinator of *Sakhi* for South Asian Women, an organization with which she continues volunteer work. She also cofounded a semi-annual publication called *Samar* (South Asian Magazine for Action and Reflection) and is a member of the editoral collective. Her essay "The Habit of Ex-nomination: Nation, Woman and the Indian Immigrant Bourgeoisie" appeared in *Public Culture* (Fall 1992).

Honor Ford-Smith was (founding) Artistic Director of the Sistren Theatre Collective, a Jamaican feminist organization known for its work in drama and popular education. Presently she is studying in the doctoral program at the Ontario Institute for Studies in Education in Toronto, Canada.

Marie Anna Jaimes Guerrero is a (BIA certified) Juaneño (California Mission Band) from the San Capistrano Southern California area, an (unenrolled) Yaqui/Opata born and raised in Arizona, with ancestry in Mexico (Sonora and Durango), on the maternal side of her descendency and family heritage. Her most recent distinctions include a summer fellowship at the Newberry Library (Chicago) to research her next book, *Kinship, Identity, and Native Womanism*. Jaimes Guerrero is a member of the Indigenous Women's Network, a grass-roots organization with a bioregional grass-roots agenda and an inter-American and international human rights focus. She is Visiting Professor in the School of Justice Studies at Arizona State University. Jaimes Guerrero has edited several books, including *The State of Native America* (South End Press, 1992), and a collection of essays on contemporary Indian cultural issues and political agendas.

Evelynn M. Hammonds is Assistant Professor of the History of Science at the Massachusetts Institute of Technology. Her current projects include a historical study of African-American women and sexuality, and a study of the changing conceptions of race and gender in medicine, biology, and anthropology.

Geraldine Heng teaches medieval and women's studies in the Department of English at the University of Texas, Austin. She taught at the National University of Singapore's Department of English from September 1989 to January 1994, and has been a member of AWARE, the Association of Women for Action and Research (Singapore), since September 1989. She was a counseling advocate, and a funding committee member, of the Tompkins County (New York) Task Force for Battered Women from 1983 to 1985.

Ayesha Mei-Tje Imam is a lecturer in the Department of Sociology, Ahmadu Bello University, Zaria, Nigeria. She has coedited a number of books and published several articles. Her research interests have focused on ideology, mass media, women's work, and gender analysis. She is presently working on women's seclusion in northern Nigeria, as well as cooperating in an international research project on women under Muslim law, and coediting a publication on gender analysis of Africa. She is also active in women's and democratic struggles.

Kalpana Kannabiran is a feminist sociologist and activist from Hyderabad, India. She has been involved in feminist politics, and has written on questions of caste, communalism, identity, and gender.

Vasanth Kannabiran is a feminist poet and activist living in Hyderabad, India. Once a teacher of English Literature, she is currently involved in feminist politics and movements against communalism and caste chauvinism. She is also part of the civil liberties movement in India.

Amina Mama is a Nigeria-based researcher with a doctorate in organizational psychology from the University of London. She has been a postgraduate teacher of psychology and Women and Development Studies at various international institutions, including the Institute of Social Studies in The Hague. She is currently visiting lecturer at the University of Bradford. Her 1989 book, *The Hidden Struggle,* was the first major study of the abuse of black women in Europe. Her work on race, gender, and postcolonial subjectivity, *Beyond the Masks,* was published by Routledge in 1995.

Chandra Talpade Mohanty teaches feminist and antiracist studies at Hamilton College in Clinton, N.Y. She is also a member of the core faculty at the Union Institute in Cincinnati, and the editor of a book series titled "Gender, Culture and Global Politics" for Garland Publishing. She works with two grassroots organizations: Grassroots Leadership of North Carolina, USA, and Awareness of Orissa, India. She is coeditor of *Third World Women and the Politics of Feminism*, (Indiana University Press, 1991), and is currently working on questions of feminist theory, pedagogy, and democratic culture.

Paula M. L. Moya completed her Ph.D in English from Cornell University. In Fall 1996, she begins at Stanford University as Assistant Professor of English. Her work focuses on feminism, cultural theory, and U.S. Latina/o literature.

Kavita Panjabi is a lecturer (assistant professor) in Comparative Literature at Jadavpur University, Calcutta, India, and also an active member of the School of Women's Studies there. She graduated from Smith College, did her M.A. at Jadavpur University, and received her Ph.D. in Comparative Literature from Cornell University. The special focus of her research in contemporary Indian and Latin American literature has been women's political narratives of the Naxalite movement in West Bengal and the Dirty War in Argentina.

Ella Habiba Shohat is Associate Professor of Women's Studies and Cultural Studies at the City University of New York–Graduate Center and the coordinator of the Cinema Studies program at CUNY–College of Staten Island. A coeditor of the journal *Social Text,* she has also lectured and published widely on issues related to postcolonial and gender discourses, Middle Eastern culture and politics, and multiculturalism. When published in Hebrew, her *Israeli Cinema: East/West and the Politics of Representation* (University of Texas Press, 1989) generated a major national polemic in Israel. She has been active over the years in various Arab-Jewish (Sephardi) organizations, including the NGO World Organization of Jews from Islamic Countries for "The Question of Palestine." Her book (with Robert Stam) *Unthinking Eurocentrism: Multiculturalism and the Media* was published by Routledge in 1994. She is currently editing a collection of essays on multicultural feminism to be published by MIT Press.

Gloria Wekker, born in Paramaribo, Suriname, completed her Ph.D. in cultural anthropology at the University of California at Los Angeles in 1991. Her research interests include constructions of subjectivity and sexuality in the black diaspora. She currently works at the Women's Studies Department in the Humanities at the University of Utrecht, the Netherlands, as the coordinator of "Women, the Environment and Sustainable Development."

Index